e17/10

Ireland and Irish America

Ireland and Irish America
Culture, Class, and Transatlantic Migration

Kerby A. Miller

Field Day Files 3

Series Editors: Seamus Deane and Breandán Mac Suibhne

Field Day
Dublin, 2008

ISBN 978-0-946755-39-4

Published by Field Day in association with the Keough-Naughton Institute for Irish Studies at the University of Notre Dame

Field Day
Newman House
86 St. Stephen's Green
Dublin 2
Ireland

Set in 10.5pt/13.5pt Quadraat
Designed and typeset by Red Dog Design Consultants
Printed on Arctic Gloss and Munken Lynx

For Cara —
darling daughter —
who deserves a book of her own.

And in tribute
to the Whiteboys,
the Steelboys,
and others who strove with gods
against their world's destruction.

Contents

Acknowledgements

The research, initial writing, and revisions of the essays in this book have incurred many debts, over many years, that I am very glad to acknowledge. Perhaps the most important are to Arnold Schrier, who kindly gave me access to his pioneering discoveries of Irish immigrants' letters; to David N. Doyle, Ireland's premier scholar of the Irish in North America, who has generously shared with me his vast knowledge of that subject; and to Bruce D. Boling, whose reflections on Irish culture and language, and whose eloquent translations from Irish, have informed and adorned my work. Scarcely less valuable have been the aid and advice provided by Kenneth M. Stampp, who inadvertently turned my doctoral research in Irish directions, and by a host of other friends and colleagues, including: the late Thomas B. Alexander, Malcolm Campbell, Marion Casey, the late Dennis Clark, the late Patrick J. Dowling, David Emmons, David Fitzpatrick, Peter Gilmore, the late E. R. R. Green, Patrick Griffin, Patricia Kelleher, Carla King, Ted Koditschek, Joe Lee, Dale Light, Peggy Lynch-Brennan, Steve and Beth Ruffin MacIntyre, Breandán Mac Suibhne, Tim Meagher, Michael Montgomery, Gerry Moran, Cormac Ó Gráda, Trevor Parkhill, Linda Reeder, Bob Scally, the late William V. Shannon, Peter Toner, Vic Walsh, Kevin Whelan, and David Wilson. Special thanks must go to: Jim Donnelly and David W. Miller, who have provided advice and support since the early 1970s; to Liam Kennedy, my long-time friend and collaborator on many scholarly projects; and to my former colleague, Michael Thorn, who taught me how to think critically about Irish history and everything else. Of course, none of these individuals is in any way responsible for the accuracy or the interpretations of the material in these chapters. Indeed, on many issues, some of these historians and I have profound disagreements; yet, in the rancorous worlds of Irish and Irish diasporan scholarship, it is gratifying that we have shared our discoveries and opinions with mutual respect and (I hope) mutual enrichment.

I also wish to thank Seamus Deane and Breandán Mac Suibhne, for inviting me to publish my essays with Field Day. I am grateful as well to the editors of many academic journals and book publishers, detailed in the first citation to each chapter, for granting Field Day permission to republish my essays, as revised, in this volume. A heartfelt thanks also to the hundreds of people, on both sides of the ocean, who over the past thirty-five years have patiently guided my quests for Irish immigrants' letters, memoirs, and similar documents in their libraries and archives, or who kindly granted me access to the privately held manuscripts written by or to their own immigrant ancestors; some of these donors, too, are mentioned in the citations to the chapters in this work.

In addition, I gratefully acknowledge the support of many institutions and funding agencies that have made my scholarship possible, including: the Research Council of the University of Missouri-Columbia, the Weldon Spring Foundation and the Research Board of the University of Missouri system, the National Endowment for the Humanities, the Harry Frank Guggenheim Foundation, the Irish American Cultural Institute, the Cushwa Center for the Study of American Catholicism at the University of Notre Dame, the American Council of Learned Societies, the American Philosophical Society, the Huntington Library, the Ford Foundation, the Mabelle McLeod Lewis Memorial Foundation, the American Irish Foundation, the University of California at Berkeley, and the Institute of Irish Studies at the Queen's University of Belfast.

For their unfailing assistance and patience, my sincere thanks as well to the current and former members of the staffs of the Missouri State Historical Society and of the University of Missouri's History Department and Ellis Library — especially of the latter's inter-library borrowing service. I am grateful also to Hilary Bell and Ciarán Deane, both in Ireland, who respectively copy-edited the text and worked on the page-proofs of this book manuscript, and to Autumn Dolan, of the University of Missouri's history graduate programme, who created the index.

Finally, I can never express sufficient gratitude to my beautiful wife Patricia and to our three wonderful children — Eoghan, Michael, and Cara — for all the years of love and support.

Introduction

For more than thirty-five years, I have studied the histories of modern Ireland, of Irish emigration, and of the Irish in America. I am often asked, Why? — particularly since neither my own ethno-religious background nor even my graduate training in history holds any clues to explain my scholarship's trajectory. One response seems obvious. Between the early 1600s and the early 1900s, Irish emigration comprised one of the largest global movements of men and women in modern times, one that had profound effects on the histories, societies, and political cultures of Ireland and the United States alike. A second, broader answer is that the importance of past Irish migrations is further magnified in view of the enormous contemporary rural-to-urban migrations from and within the so-called 'developing world'. Like Irish migrations in previous centuries, those today are driven and shaped by the march of imperial capitalism, by its socio-economic, cultural, and political systems, processes, and consequences. Put starkly, from Elizabethan Munster to 'Black '47', to Fallujah and post-Katrina New Orleans, 'accumulation by dispossession' is the iron thread that weaves Ireland's past and the global present into a seamless and often bloody tapestry.[1] The accumulated, accelerating result is that we now inhabit a 'planet of slums' and of refugees from imperial-capitalist 're-structurings'[2] — a world ravaged by armed and unfettered greed and corruption, poised on the edge of ecological catastrophe. Thus, a final response is that to me resistance to those systems, processes, and consequences, to their tyrannies and inequities, seems both necessary and desirable. And, however inadequately or transiently, in both the distant and recent pasts the Irish — sometimes Protestants as well as Catholics — were often in the forefront of such resistance, at home and

---

1   David Harvey, *Spaces of Global Capitalism* (London, 2006), 43; also see his *The New Imperialism* (Oxford, 2003), esp. ch. 4.
2   Mike Davis, *Planet of Slums* (New York, 2006).

abroad. Arguably, their country's history had left many of them with little to lose. More important, it had prepared them to recognize all too clearly, as one Irish Protestant put it, that 'the rich always betray the poor',[3] and, in the words of a Catholic contemporary, that 'society' was in essence 'a combination of those who *have* against those who *have not*'.[4] Indeed, as Elizabeth Gurley Flynn once posited, an Irish or an Irish-immigrant heritage should always have been excellent preparation for militant radicalism, for '[w]hen one understood British imperialism, it was an open window to all imperialism'.[5]

Of course, human limitations, the cultural and psychological effects of colonialism, and the exigencies of emigration ensured that many Irish 'understood' but darkly, and others not at all. In recent years, moreover, most writers about Irish history and migration have sought to keep that 'window' of insight and empathy tightly closed — or to deny its very existence — cloaking such subjects in the allegedly neutral 'inevitabilities' of 'progress', 'market forces', or 'legitimate national interests' and 'security'. My own writings, by contrast, are attuned to the essentially political contexts that shaped Irish (and other) mass migrations: to the structures and consequences — and to the horrors and humiliations — of old and new forms of imperial power; and also to the 'accommodations' that most ordinary people were obliged or 'encouraged' to make within those structures. My work is likewise sensitive to the conflicting class and cultural forces, structurally conditioned but arising from within Irish and Irish-American societies, that sometimes prompted but also circumscribed the forms and outcomes of Irish resistance — in the process often warping Flynn's 'window' into a mirror of narcissistic or even paralysing illusions.

When I began my research, I turned for evidence of Irish emigrants' experiences and attitudes to their personal letters, memoirs, and similar documents — initially to collections in Irish and North American archives, then to those still in private hands. Among these I found rich and largely untapped information on the causes, methods, and tangible results of Irish migration, and, equally important, on the perceptions of the emigrants, and their Irish correspondents, regarding their homeland, departures, and lives overseas. Both the continuities and the discrepancies between the attitudes expressed by the emigrants, and the Irish and Irish-American 'public' interpretations of emigration, led me to examine more closely the social, cultural, and political systems that had generated such oft-contradictory views. Likewise, the similarities and differences among the accounts written by Irish emigrants of varying regional, social, religious, and cultural backgrounds, prompted still deeper investigations into Irish and

3 Henry Joy McCracken (1767–98), leader of the United Irishmen at the battle of Antrim, executed thereafter; see Mary McNeill's *The Life and Times of Mary Ann McCracken, 1770–1866: A Belfast Panorama* (Dublin, 1960); and A. T. Q. Stewart, *The Summer Soldiers: The 1798 Rebellion in Antrim and Down* (Belfast, 1995), quotation on p. 239.

4 Theobald McKenna (d. 1808), cited in David N. Doyle, *Ireland, Irishmen and Revolutionary America, 1760–1820* (Dublin, 1981), 168. McKenna was an aristocratic conservative, not a revolutionary like McCracken; nevertheless, what Doyle calls his 'Hobbesian view' would have resonated in his lifetime among Catholic Whiteboys and Defenders, and, later, among Fenians.

5 Elizabeth Gurley Flynn, *The Rebel Girl: An Autobiography, My First Life*, rev. edn. (New York, 1973), 35.

Irish-American societies. That research uncovered demographic and other data that often qualified or contradicted both scholarly and popular interpretations of Irish and Irish migration history.

The result is a body of work that focuses, in different but complementary ways, on mass migration as the key factor in shaping — and understanding — the histories of modern Ireland and, of course, of Irish America. The essays in this book address both, because mass migration made them inextricable. Likewise, they deal with Irish Protestants as well as Catholics, because Ireland's conquest and colonization — executed, justified, and often resisted in religious as well as secular frameworks and language — determined that their histories and identities would unfold in dialectical (and oft-malign) relationships, in Ireland and America alike.

This book is divided into three parts, followed by an epilogue. The five chapters in Part I focus primarily on Catholic Ireland: on how its culture's 'traditional' emphases were hammered by conquest and poverty, and later shaped by the needs of its own secular and religious spokesmen, into ideological programmes and imagery that promoted Irish aversion to British rule and to mass migration — yet that also ensured the hegemony of an Irish Catholic 'establishment' whose wealth depended on both British capitalism and mass migration. The essays in Part II likewise explore the interplay of culture and class, on both sides of the Atlantic, but principally among Irish Presbyterians and Anglicans. At least implicitly, these chapters challenge the conventional 'two traditions' (Protestant versus Catholic) paradigm of Irish and Irish diasporan history, which has underpinned Ireland's partition and bifurcated the study of the Irish in the US into separate 'Irish-American' (Catholic) and 'Scotch-Irish' (Protestant) camps.[6] Instead, I contend that Irish Protestant identities were forged, not only in the Protestant-Catholic (colonist-native) dialectic, but by the power relationships *within* Protestant Irish societies in Ireland and in the US. Finally, the chapters in Part III focus primarily on Irish America (Catholic, as conventionally defined). Paralleling those in Part I, they explore how class and culture, and gender as well, shaped Irish-American society and its political culture, in symbiotic relationships with those both in Ireland and in Protestant Anglo-America.

All chapters are based heavily on Irish emigrants' transatlantic letters and memoirs: my principal 'windows' into the lives and attitudes of the emigrants and their correspondents in Ireland. The essays were produced initially and (with one exception) published between 1980 and 2006: three in 1980–89; seven in 1990–99; and six (including the Epilogue)

---

6 For further discussion of this paradigm and its political implications, see the Epilogue of this volume; and also Kerby A. Miller, 'Ulster Presbyterians and the "Two Traditions" in Ireland and America', in Terry Brotherstone, Anna Clark, and Kevin Whelan, eds., *These Fissured Isles: Varieties of British and Irish Identities* (Edinburgh, 2005), 260–77; and reprinted in J. J. Lee and Marion R. Casey, eds., *Making the Irish American: History and Heritage of the Irish in the United States* (New York, 2006), 255–70. And for a broad critique of this and other paradigms dominant in recent Irish and Irish migration historiography, see: Kerby A. Miller, 'Re-Imagining Irish Revisionism', in Andrew Higgins Wyndham, ed., *Re-Imagining Ireland* (Charlottesville, Va., 2006), 223–43.

in 2000–06. Because of that lengthy time span, and their complementary subject matter, all chapters required at least minimal revisions to create a collection that would be coherent and (hopefully) without undue repetitions. Otherwise, however, these essays remain substantially the same as originally written.

I   Culture, Class, and Emigration in Irish Society

1 Emigrants and Exiles:
Irish Cultures and Irish Emigration to North America

From the early 1700s through the 1920s, at least 7 million people emigrated from Ireland to North America.[1] Arguably, if there are any patterns in modern Irish history, a cultural analysis of this vast flow may help to reveal them. For although the Irish question is usually defined in Anglo/Irish terms of conflict, it has even more universal import as the painful 'adjustment' of Irish society, culture, and identity — both personal and national — to the demands of the modern industrializing world. Emigration afforded one such response; Irish nationalism another; and Irish-American nationalism linked the two. Scholars such as Robert Kennedy, Cormac Ó Gráda, and others have studied emigration in terms of Ireland's economic and social transformations, but it may also

---

1 The evolution of this chapter is somewhat unusual. It was originally written in 1977–78, as a paper delivered at a Dublin seminar, and solicited for publication by David Harkness, then editor of *Irish Historical Studies* as well as professor of Irish history at the Queen's University of Belfast. However, when I returned to America and began teaching at the University of Missouri, and discovered I had no time to make the necessary changes for *Irish Historical Studies*, Dr. David N. Doyle of University College, Dublin, kindly offered to revise it for me, melding what I had written (originally in a format too long for publication) with his own insights and research. The resultant article also drew heavily on the expertise in linguistics and the Irish language previously provided by Dr. Bruce D. Boling (then at the University of Wyoming, now professor emeritus at the University of New Mexico), which had been incorporated in the original paper and, earlier still, in my doctoral dissertation (University of California, Berkeley, 1976). Hence, the article's subsequent publication, as formally and deservedly designated as authored 'with' Boling and Doyle, in *Irish Historical Studies*, 22, 86 (September 1980), 97–125. My dissertation and this article were, in a sense, the prototypes for my first book, *Emigrants and Exiles: Ireland and the Irish Exodus to North America* (New York, 1985); and readers may wish to examine that work's Introduction and ch. 3, especially, for elaborations of this chapter's major themes. I wish to thank the current editors of *Irish Historical Studies* for permission to republish the article in this volume, with revisions, and of course Boling and Doyle for their invaluable assistance then and subsequently. Of course, neither Boling nor Doyle is responsible for the changes I have made in the present version.

be studied culturally as a revealing cross-section of Ireland's attendant cultural and even psychological changes and tensions. Indeed, it provides some of the only large-scale aggregate of sources for such a study — the value of which has been shown for Norway, the most emigration-prone European society next to Ireland, and one also nationally resurgent by 1900.[2]

Of course, culture is one of many variables. It is not timeless, absolute, homogeneous, or 'essential' to any society or ethno-religious or national group. Its emphases (often conflicting) and development (often contradictory) are contingent on a host of temporal and environmental factors, perhaps chief among them the dominant modes of production and the consequent social structures that prevail within each group, as well as the power relationships that govern the group and its relationship with others. In the Irish case this ultimately means that its cultures must be viewed in the contexts of Anglo-American capitalism, British imperialism, and Irish colonialism, and of their effects on the structures of Irish Catholic and Protestant societies, and the power relationships both within and between them. In the case of Irish America, its cultural expressions and social forms must be analysed not only in the contexts of Irish social and cultural legacies but also in terms of the effects of American socio-economic structures and relationships that were dominated by native-Protestant hierarchies. These social — and ultimately political — issues are crucial and will be discussed further in other chapters. Here, however, the principal focus is on Irish cultures themselves and how they affected Irish emigration and Irish America.

This attempt to analyse Irish emigration culturally focuses on three questions. First, how did the Irish in general perceive and interpret emigration from Ireland, and what determined their more individual views of it? Second, was there a group of dominant ideas that constituted a discernible 'worldview' that predisposed them to such attitudes towards migration? Third, to what extent did their outlook shape their actual experiences of emigration and life in America, colouring or even constraining their objective situation?

Of course, during the centuries of emigration, the conditions of Irish and Irish-American life were neither static nor homogeneous. Nevertheless, a study of over 6,000

2 Statistical analyses of the migration are contained in: David N. Doyle, *Ireland, Irishmen and Revolutionary America, 1760–1820* (Dublin, 1980), 51–76; William Forbes Adams, *Ireland and Irish Emigration to the New World, from 1815 to the Famine* (New Haven, Conn., 1932); Robert E. Kennedy, *The Irish: Emigration, Marriage and Fertility* (London, 1973); Kerby A. Miller, 'Emigrants and Exiles: Ireland and Irish Emigration to North America' (PhD diss., University of California, Berkeley, 1976), 367–85 (and as subsequently published in 1985); David Fitzpatrick, 'Irish Emigration in the Later Nineteenth Century', *Irish Historical Studies*, 22, 86 (September 1980), 126–43; Oliver MacDonagh, 'Irish Famine Emigration to the U.S.', *Perspectives in American History*, 10 (1976), 357–446; Cormac Ó Gráda, 'A Note on Nineteenth Century Irish Emigration Statistics', *Population Studies*, 29 (1975), 143–49; and in studies listed in these works. On Norway, see Sigmund Skard, *The United States in Norwegian History* (Westport, Conn., 1976). For a critical overview, see Cormac Ó Gráda, 'Irish Emigration to the United States in the Nineteenth Century', in David N. Doyle and Owen Dudley Edwards, eds., *America and Ireland, 1776–1976* (Westport, Conn., 1980), 93–103.

Irish emigrants' letters, plus a wide range of other sources, in both English and Irish, has generated three broad conclusions. First, collectively and often individually, the Irish — and particularly Irish Catholics — regarded emigration as involuntary exile, although their specific cultural background and social position, among other factors, determined their degrees of consistency and intensity in expressing that outlook. Second, that perspective reflected a distinctively 'Irish' worldview that had evolved for centuries — and continued to evolve during the era of mass migration — through a series of interactions among historical experience, culture, class, and even gender. Finally, both the exile motif and its underlying determinants led Irish emigrants — again, especially collectively but often personally — to interpret American experiences and/or to adapt to American society in ways that were contradictory: in some ways alienating and perhaps even 'dysfunctional' in terms of certain individuals' 'successful adjustment' overseas; but in other ways both personally expedient and conducive to the survival overseas of a collective 'Irish' identity and to the eventual, if incomplete, success of Irish-American nationalism.[3]

Members of earlier generations of US immigration historians often argued that the Irish saw themselves as unhappy exiles in the New World. However, such scholars did not sufficiently prove or explain that phenomenon. Moreover, until recently few scholars — especially in America — provided more than a cursory treatment of the migrants' cultural backgrounds, and even fewer utilized evidence that demonstrated how the 'ordinary' Irish themselves regarded their emigrations.[4] These deficiencies were linked, for if the Irish in North America did see themselves as exiles, that self-image might derive as much, if not more, from their Irish cultural backgrounds as from their American experience. Only evidence of the emigrants' personal opinions might reveal whether the exile image was merely rhetorical or whether it might afford insights into the very character of Irish emigration and of Irish and Irish-American societies. Based on explorations of the exile metaphor's cultural origins and of its personal expression by many emigrants, this essay posits that the exile motif is of real scholarly significance, both for what it can reveal and for what it sometimes obscured.

---

3 For a more expansive treatment of the issues raised here, more examples from Irish emigrants' writings, and more numerous citations, see Miller, *Emigrants and Exiles*.
4 Arnold Schrier used emigrants' letters (and oral reminiscences) in his *Ireland and the American Emigration, 1850–1900* (Minneapolis, Minn., 1958), as did E. R. R. Green, 'Ulster Emigrants' Letters', in Green, ed., *Essays in Scotch-Irish History* (London, 1969), 87–103. I wish to thank both Schrier and Green, the latter now deceased, for allowing me access to their collections of emigrants' letters.

Florence Gibson was one of many early US historians who claimed that the Irish in North America regarded themselves as homesick exiles. 'Many Irish-Americans had moved to the United States physically,' she wrote, 'but spiritually and emotionally they were back home in Ireland.' Edith Abbott and Carl Wittke, who possessed considerable knowledge of other immigrant groups, concurred and argued that Irishmen's and -women's unique attachments to their homeland inhibited their adjustment to American life and concentrated much of their attention upon dreams and schemes to free Ireland. As Thomas N. Brown concluded, the Irish in America charged their loneliness and unhappiness 'upon the conscience of England'.[5]

It would be much easier to dismiss the image of the self-pitying, Anglophobic Irish 'exile' as a cliché if the emigrants themselves and their spokesmen had not employed it so frequently. Irish and Irish-American newspapers and orators commonly characterized those who left Ireland as 'exiles', compelled to emigrate, either directly or indirectly, by what they called 'English tyranny' and/or 'landlord oppression'. Nationalists, politicians, and clerical leaders continually 'reminded' their audiences that the Irish were being 'driven out of Erin', like the 'children of Israel'.[6] Thus, Irish emigration was 'not natural but artificial', claimed Clan na Gael leader Alexander Sullivan of Chicago, 'since the poverty of Ireland is produced by English law, and not by the law of nature'; in short, he concluded, Irish emigration was 'not a social necessity, but a political oppression'.[7] In addition, the pervasive note of the emigrants' ballads and poems, whether commercial or folk compositions, was one of sorrowing and enforced exile.

Much more important is the evidence of the Irish emigrants' own letters and memoirs that frequently they regarded their situation as one of unhappy exile. This feeling was usually rooted in an acute homesickness. For example, a Catholic from County Limerick admitted that, in America, although materially comfortable, 'in spite of all I can never forget home … . At night when I lay in bed my mind wanders off across the Continent and over the Atlantic to the hills of Cratloe.'[8] Sometimes the note is more insistent, poignant, and alienated: 'i wish i ner came to new york,' lamented a woman from County Monaghan; 'it is a hell upon erth … i cannot get no rest thinking of home'.[9] Indeed, the burden of homesickness could drain ambition as well as emotion, as several migrants

---

5 Florence E. Gibson, *The Attitudes of the New York Irish towards State and National Affairs, 1848–1892* (New York, 1951), 26; Edith Abbott, ed., *Historical Aspects of the Immigration Problem: Select Documents* (Chicago, 1926), 413, 438; Thomas N. Brown, 'The Origins and Character of Irish-American Nationalism', *Review of Politics*, 18 (July 1956), 329.

6 e.g., Jeremiah O'Donovan, *A Brief Account of the Author's Interview with His Countrymen* (Pittsburgh, 1864), 151.

7 O'Sullivan's speech, 1883 (HO 45/9635/A29278, in the Public Record Office, Kew, London; hereafter PRO).

8 Maurice H. Woulfe, Fort D. A. Russell, Wyoming Terr., to Michael Woulfe, Tralee, County Kerry, 26 January 1870 (Woulfe family letters, courtesy of Dr. Kevin Danaher, Dublin; also in microfilm p3887 in the National Library of Ireland, Dublin; hereafter NLI).

9 Alice McDonald, New York City, to Brigid McDonnell, Clonnagore, Drumully, County Monaghan, 3 February 1868 (courtesy of Fr. Theo McMahon, Monaghan).

understood.[10] Thus, Michael MacGowan, an Irish-speaker from County Donegal, lamented that many of his friends and relatives in Chicago saw 'their lives slipping away ... while their hearts were away at home'; they 'were sad enough', he wrote, and 'would have preferred to live [in Ireland] on one meal a day than to have owned the whole of Chicago'.[11]

Some emigrants overtly politicized their personal sentiments and specifically blamed their exile upon the British government or the British-enforced landlord system, which they regarded as the master-causes of all outward migration. For example, as soon as he landed in New York in early 1848, Thomas Reilly, a craftsman from Dublin, declared himself an 'exile' and joined an Irish-American militia company which was, he claimed, preparing to invade and liberate Ireland from British rule.[12] Although most Irish emigrants only gave sympathy or cash, not blood, to Ireland's 'sacred cause', Reilly's sentiments were not uncommon. Other emigrants long-retained similar emotions: decades after the Great Famine of 1845–52, ordinary 'family letters' written by Lewis Doyle in Minnesota, Patrick O'Callaghan from Philadelphia, and Michael Flanagan in California, among others, as well as by hardened Fenians like John Cronin in Massachusetts, blamed England for Irish emigration and vowed vengeance on 'the Vile Saxon oppressor'.[13] As late as the 1970s an elderly (and prosperous) Irish emigrant in San Francisco could declare, 'We didn't want to leave Ireland, but we *had* to' because of the effects of centuries of British misrule.[14]

Of course, not all Irish emigrants regarded themselves as exiles, or as victims of British oppression, or even as acutely homesick. But large numbers of them certainly did so, if not always consistently, and their letters suggest why the image offered so pervasive and unifying a sentiment to the politics of Irish-American nationalism.

Yet the standard, nationalist explanation for the Irish emigrants' self-image is inadequate and somewhat misleading. Until the 1940s, many Irish historians (and most Irish-American historians for several decades thereafter) accepted the rhetoric of such true exiles as John Mitchel, who proclaimed that his people's homesickness and Anglophobia were but natural since the Irish were in North America 'only because of

---

10 e.g., Rev. John O'Hanlon, *Irish Emigrant's Guide to the United States* (1851), ed. Edward J. Maguire (New York, 1976), 9–14, 232–33.
11 Michael MacGowan, *The Hard Road to Klondike*, trans. Valentine Iremonger (London, 1962), 136.
12 Thomas Reilly, Albany, NY, to John M. Kelly, Dublin, 24 April 1848 (Ms. 10,511, NLI); also see Chapter 3 in this volume, for quotations from Reilly's letter.
13 Lewis Doyle, Kilkenny, Minn., to John Doyle, Pollerton, County Carlow, 27 January 1880 (courtesy of Seamus Murphy, Pollerton Little, Carlow); Patrick O'Callaghan, Fort Snelling, Minn., to Maggie O'Callaghan, Fallagh, Kilmachomas, County Waterford, 17 August 1883 (courtesy of Eugene O'Callaghan and Mary Flynn, Fallagh); Michael Flanagan, Napa, Calif., to John Flanagan, Tubbertoby, Clogherhead, County Louth, 14 April 1877 (courtesy of Peter and Mary Flanagan, Tubbertoby); and John Conin, Waverly, Mass., to Jeremiah O'Donovan Rossa, New York City, 16 July 1876 (John Devoy Papers, Ms. 18,001, NLI). For full quotations from these and similar letters, see Chapter 3 in this volume.
14 Taped conversation with Patrick J. Dowling and Michael Carroll (San Francisco, 1977).

insufferable political tyranny which has made their native land uninhabitable to them'.[15] Unlike Mitchel, however, the vast majority of the Irish who crossed the Atlantic were not political exiles in a literal sense. To be sure, large numbers were farmers, craftsmen, and rural labourers who left Ireland under severe duress, particularly during the Great Famine and in other subsistence crises, as in 1816–17, the mid-1820s, and 1879–82. Sometimes, too, they emigrated after suffering eviction from their homes, and some scholars estimate that at least a half-million, perhaps closer to a million, Irishmen and -women were evicted in the Great Famine alone.[16] Nevertheless, the great majority — even among the Famine emigrants — were those normally (if perhaps too complacently) described as 'voluntary emigrants' who responded 'rationally' to adverse economic conditions at home by transferring their ambitions, savings, skills, and labour to more remunerative markets overseas. The most common reason why young Irishmen and -women emigrated was to escape poverty and unemployment. Equally important, especially in the post-Famine period, was that Irish farmers' adoption of impartible inheritance and restricted marriage consigned most of their non-inheriting sons and non-dowered daughters to the emigrant ships. Moreover, a very large but undetermined proportion of the emigrants who had been evicted from their holdings had not been displaced directly by members of an 'alien landlord class', as nationalists commonly charged, but rather — as subtenants, cottiers, and labourers — by profit-minded commercial farmers who also were tenants and usually of the same religion as those they evicted.[17]

Of course, it is arguable that Ireland represented a classic case of 'uneven development' caused by the operations of a capitalist system imposed on Ireland by British imperial policies, past and present. In that sense, Irish nationalists — especially radical ones such as Michael Davitt and James Connolly — were quite justified in perceiving emigration in systemic and political terms, as a collective imposition rather than as individual 'opportunity'. However, if most Irish emigrants were correct in rejecting a 'liberal' interpretation of their departures, why were they more prescient in that regard than, say, Italians, Swedes, or Greeks, who emigrated for reasons (both broad and particular) similar to those that impelled Irish departures, yet who did not perceive or advertise themselves as exiles? Indeed, it is remarkable that, despite the exile motif, so few Irish emigrants actually returned to Ireland, especially compared with the sizeable return

15 Gibson, *Attitudes of the New York Irish*, 98. For a synopsis of John Mitchel's career, see Chapter 12, note 26.
16 For a recent high-end estimate, see Tim P. O'Neill, 'Famine Evictions', in Carla King, ed., *Famine, Land and Culture in Ireland* (Dublin, 2000), 29–70.
17 See Chapter 4 in this volume. A cottier was a 'bound labourer', who worked year-round for a particular tenant farmer in return for a small patch of land (usually two acres or less) on which to build a cabin, raise potatoes, and, if fortunate, to graze a cow. By contrast, a landless labourer sold his labour (usually to multiple employers), and used his wages to rent potato-ground, on the 'open market'. At least marginally, therefore, a landless labourer was engaged in a cash economy, and hence was proletarianized, whereas a cottier's arrangement with his 'master' (that is, with a farmer who was at once his immediate landlord and his employer) was based principally on barter.

migrations of southern and eastern Europeans, who went back to live under regimes that in most respects were at least as oppressive as British rule over Ireland.[18]

Despite the prevalence and persistence of the exile image, relatively few emigrants were directly compelled by actual force or imminent starvation to leave Ireland. This was true during the century prior to the Famine (when at least 1.5 million departed) and especially during the post-Famine era, roughly 1856–1929, when at least 4 and perhaps 5 million emigrated — most of them to North America.[19] Even during the Famine period itself (1845–55), although many of the roughly 2.1 million emigrants in that decade fled out of sheer panic, fear of death, or as a result of eviction — and although, as nationalists charged, some were helpless paupers 'shovelled' overseas by landlords and public officials — for many others, long-accustomed to contemplating migration, the crisis was simply the final determinant in their decisions. In short, and like most of their peers from elsewhere in Europe, Irish families and individual Irishmen and -women generally emigrated more or less 'voluntarily' and in order, they hoped, to better themselves. At least in theory, many could have remained in Ireland, even granted the pressures against this — the decline of farm subdivision; the mechanization of farm labourers' tasks; and, most important, the relative absence of local urban-industrial opportunities (save in northeast Ulster's trenchantly sectarian economy).

And yet, the image of the Irish emigrant-as-exile prevailed and persisted. Why? If it did not reflect the immediate realities of the personal experiences of millions of 'ordinary' emigrants, why was it employed so frequently by their spokesmen, and why did it evoke such an instinctive, emotional response among so many? What cultural traditions, social functions, or psychological needs did the image reflect or fulfil?

The exile image was not just a rhetorical device employed by Irish and Irish-American nationalists. Nor was it merely an American creation, like the St. Patrick's Day parades, simply a product of Irish estrangement or self-assertion in the New World. All emigrants in America expressed some degree of alienation, but the Irish image of themselves as exiles sprang from sources even more profound than the poverty and prejudice they endured abroad. Indeed, as David N. Doyle has shown, by the end of the nineteenth century most of the American Irish (including the emigrants' US-born children) had achieved relatively decent levels of socio-economic status and political influence. Hence it is difficult to explain, on the basis of American conditions alone, why the exile image persisted, why Irish-American nationalists could continue to evoke it so successfully, and why, as Doyle himself notes, for all its achievements the

---

18 Schrier, *Ireland and the American Emigration*, 129–43; George R. Gilkey, 'The United States and Italy: Migration and Repatriation', *Journal of Developing Areas*, 2 (1967), 23–35; Theodore Saloutos, *They Remember America: The Story of the Repatriated Greek-Americans* (Berkeley, Calif., 1966); L. G. Tedebrand, 'Remigration from America to Sweden', in Harold Rublom and Hans Norman, eds., *From Sweden to America: A History of the Migration* (Uppsala, 1976), 201–27.

19 The uncertainty as to total Irish emigration, 1856–1929, reflects the lack of reliable data for emigrants who went to Great Britain.

Irish-American Catholic community in 1900 was still characterized by a 'self-indulgent communal morbidity'.[20]

Of course, in the middle decades of the nineteenth century Irish-American poverty had been intense and widespread, and even in 1900 many newcomers, especially from the West of Ireland, faced pressure and privation. Furthermore, there is no doubt that such poverty-stricken emigrants were often most pathetically homesick and alienated.[21] What is anomalous is that throughout the century, prosperous (as well as poor) Irish Americans often expressed the same basic sentiments of exile. 'However much my mind is enraptured with this free Country,' wrote John Reilly from Baltimore, 'my heart still lingers in dear native Erin and I long to be again treading her green fields ...'[22] Thus, there seems no reason inherent in the material conditions of Irish-American life that automatically translated a homesickness perhaps common to all emigrants into a depressed or angry image of themselves as involuntary exiles, victims of British misgovernment. After all, the great majority of Irish emigrants — again, like their counterparts from elsewhere — had made economically 'rational' choices in response to structural changes in Irish society: choices that generally bettered their material circumstances, as recent scholarship indicates.

Indeed, Thomas N. Brown has argued that Irish-American nationalism was not a product of dire poverty overseas, but rather a means by which upwardly mobile emigrants and their American-born children achieved status and acceptance in the New World: a point of view held by contemporary observers such as Monsignor Michael Buckley of Cork after wide travels in America in 1870–71.[23] However, Irish-American nationalism was a problematic path to assimilation in a United States whose socio-economic and political élites were generally Anglophile (as well as determinedly Protestant); indeed, it is arguable that the Irish sentiments that sustained emigrant Anglophobia overseas likely exacerbated rather than resolved some of the emigrants' most fundamental problems of adjustment and identity. Thus, it makes at least equal sense to search for the cultural roots of Irish-American nationalism in Ireland itself; and insofar as Famine and post-Famine emigration was heavily derived from west Munster, south and west Ulster, and Connacht, it drew upon those regions of Ireland most increasingly and intensely

20 David N. Doyle, Irish-Americans, Native Rights, and National Empires: The Structure, Divisions and Attitudes of the Catholic Minority in the Decade of Expansion, 1890–1901 (New York, 1976), 36–90, 187–88, 226, 303, 334.

21 David N. Doyle, 'Inimircigh Nua agus Meiriceá Tionsclaíoch, 1870–1910', in Stiofán Ó hAnnracháin, ed., Go Meiriceá Siar (Baile Átha Cliath, 1979), 159–87; for examples, see below in this chapter.

22 John Reilly, Baltimore, Md., to Edward Reilly, Ballinagh, County Cavan, February 1841 (from the collection of Professor Arnold Schrier, University of Cincinnati; cited hereafter as Schrier collection; copy in Ms. 8347, NLI).

23 Thomas N. Brown, Irish-American Nationalism, 1870–1890 (Philadelphia, 1966), 18–24; Kate Buckley, ed., Diary of a Tour in America by Rev. M. B. Buckley, of Cork, Ireland: A Special Missionary in North America and Canada in 1870 and 1871 (Dublin, 1889), 165, 257–61.

nationalistic.[24] In short, the way of handling the strains of capitalist transformation via nationalistic self-assertion seems to have been rooted in similar tensions in both Ireland and Irish America, and transatlantically reinforced from Famine times onward by letters and communal rhetoric.

This interpretation is strengthened if we accept that difficulties encountered in America, although they might prompt, nurture, or sharpen expressions of the exile motif, were insufficient to cause its form, shape, and full intensity, given that, by 1900, it had long outlived significant improvements in Irish-American circumstances. Hence, this chapter posits that the subculture of exile was rooted less in the realities of Irish-American life than in the history and culture of Ireland's more distant pasts.

The exile image was much older than the Great Famine. Although it reached its apogee as Irish nationalists denounced the attendant great migrations, rural folk tradition suggests that Irish peasants at least initially regarded the Famine not as the climactic evidence of British tyranny but rather as 'the will' or 'the wrath' of God, and that they viewed the vast Famine migration as unique. Not exile, but escape, was how many of those who left then regarded their going.[25] Thus, for Famine emigrants such as John Burke, who left County Westmeath in 'Black '47', time and distance — and sustained exposure to Irish-American nationalist rhetoric — were required before they could interpret individual experience in terms of the communal story of 'exile' caused by British malevolence.[26]

Yet long before the Famine, Catholic Ireland had had bitter experience of political exile or banishment as a result of unsuccessful resistance to English rule — an experience expressed in both Gaelic poetry and nationalist literature in English. It fed on crucial events such as the 'Flight of the Earls' (1607), the Cromwellian transportations (1650s), and the departure of thousands of 'Wild Geese' after Sarsfield's surrender at Limerick

---

24 David Fitzpatrick, 'The Geography of Irish Nationalism', Past and Present, 78 (1978), 113–44, esp. maps 1–3; cf. with maps of emigration in Fitzpatrick's 'Irish Emigration in the Later Nineteenth Century', and in Doyle, 'Inimircigh Nua', 346–47.

25 Roger J. McHugh, 'The Famine in Irish Oral Tradition', in R. D. Edwards and T. D. Williams, eds., The Great Famine: Studies in Irish History, 1845–52 (New York, 1957), 395; Miller, Emigrants and Exiles, 300–12. Although in some quarters the terms peasant[s] and peasantry may have pejorative connotations, none is implied by my usages in this chapter or subsequently. Rather, I employ the terms to signify Irish country folk in what I define (in Chapter 2 of this work) as the 'subsistence' or 'semi-subsistence' sectors of Irish rural society: smallholders, cottiers, landless labourers, servants, and the poorer craftsmen who produced or laboured principally for their families' subsistence — i.e., for food, shelter, clothing, and other minimal necessities — rather than for profit or capital accumulation. In some contexts below, the term also connotes Irish-speaking and its associated customs and folkways.

26 John Burke, 'Reminiscences', c. 1891 (Ms. in New-York Historical Society, New York City).

(1691): all provided occasions for poetic laments, often composed by Catholic exiles in Europe, for *'Ár gcuraidhe tréana leirscrios uainn tar sáil'* — 'Our mighty heroes swept from us beyond the sea'.[27] However, the exile motif antedated the English Protestant conquest that began in the 1530s under Henry VIII, and it even preceded the Norman invasions of 1167–71. From earliest times, the very act of leaving Ireland, for *any* reason, was perceived sorrowfully in Gaelic culture. In the sixth and seventh centuries, for example, early missionaries such as St. Columcille described themselves as mournful 'exiles for Christ'. Such ideas persisted into modern times, in non-political as well as political contexts.[28]

The specific words used by Irish-speakers to describe emigration expose the sources of this thought pattern. Words, like all linguistic phenomena, are social facts and do not exist apart from the particular culture that uses them as a means of communication. It has been argued by B. L. Whorf and others that careful examination of words, both etymologically and in their relationship with other words in the same semantic system, can reveal much about the social structure and social thought of a given society. Although it must be conceded that these techniques and their related assumptions remain contested, the subject of this study suggests their usefulness.[29]

Significantly, the Irish language had no equivalent for the English word 'emigrant', with its voluntary and emotionally neutral connotations. Rather, the Irish word primarily used to describe one who left Ireland has been *deoraí*, the literal meaning of which is 'exile'. In Old Irish the form *deoraid* was a legal term referring to one who was without property, and, given the intimate relationships among property, family, and social bonds (particularly the tangible ties between lords and clients) under the Brehon laws which regulated pre-conquest Gaelic society, the word also implied one without kinfolk or social 'place', and one who was therefore an outsider, a stranger, even an 'outlaw'. In addition, Irish poets employed two other words to describe a person who left Ireland: *díthreabhach*, which meant one who was homeless; and *díbeartach*, meaning one who suffered banishment. Thus, the Irish language, when combined with the poets' interpretation of post-conquest Irish history, provided both patterns and heroic models to predispose the 'native Irish' to regard all those who left Ireland as unwilling and tragic political exiles. Indeed, the seventeenth-century poets used even stronger terms linking expatriation with coercion: *priosail*, meaning 'impressed' or 'conscripted', for example.[30]

27 Daniel Corkery, *The Hidden Ireland: A Study of Gaelic Munster in the Eighteenth Century* (1925; repr. Dublin, 1967), 119.
28 Miller, *Emigrants and Exiles*, 103–05.
29 Benjamin Lee Whorf, *Language, Thought, and Reality: Selected Writings* (Cambridge, Mass., 1956); and for initial critiques of Whorf's hypotheses, see the essays in Dell H. Hymes, ed., *Language in Culture and Society: A Reader in Linguistics and Anthropology* (New York, 1964), 115–63; Harry Hoijer, *Language in Culture* (Chicago, 1954); and Paul Henle, ed., *Language, Thought, and Culture* (Ann Arbor, Mich., 1958).
30 The neutral *eisimirceach* is a recent coinage. For the older terms, see M. E. Byrne and M. Joynt, *Contributions to a Dictionary of the Irish Language: Degra-Dodelbtha Dhuainaire* 1 (Dublin, 1971), 31; and it is notable that the terms for 'journeying', *aistrech* and *aistriugad*, also carried the connotations of 'restless' and 'unsteady': see *Contributions*, vol. A., fasc. 1, by A. O'Sullivan and E. Quinn (Dublin, 1964), 250.

In addition, the acute yearning of many Irish abroad for their birthplace probably had its roots in an unusually intimate attachment between Irish-speakers and their native surroundings: topographical, social, and cultural. This is evident in several overlapping categories of Irish poetry both popular and still produced in the period 1750–1850: the poetry in praise of place (*dánta faoin dúlraidh*), patriotic verse (*dánta tír ghradh*), and exile poetry. It is also evident in more recent and famous autobiographies of Irish-speakers, as on the Blasket Islands, for example. The same sources, and the related *aislingí* — the 'vision' poetry of the late 1600s and 1700s — also evince a strong and resentful ethno-religious exclusiveness: an 'us-versus-them' of Catholic *Gaeil* versus Protestant *Sasanaigh* (literally, 'Saxons' — that is, English and/or Protestants), which intensified from the late sixteenth century on as political and cultural disruptions were experienced inseparably from economic despoliation and religious persecution.[31] Modern Irish nationalism later corroborated and focused those resentments and attachments, which survived into the age of mass migration in a tendency to blame Protestant superiors and British misgovernment for all the ills afflicting Irish society, even the most impersonal or ostensibly 'apolitical'. Throughout the country, but most especially in western areas, the Irish regretted remarkably late the downfall of a dead Gaelic order in which they fancied their ancestors had lived content. One expression was that of Kilkenny diarist Humphrey O'Sullivan, for whom the decline of the Irish language was only one of 'a thousand million other meannesses and wants from which we have been suffering since the day on which the Saxons got a grip on our beloved country — poor, tortured Ireland'. Another was the Mayo poet Anthony Raftery's 'Dialogue with an Old Bush'; another, the work of Clare poet Mícheál Óg Ó Longáin; another, the fiercer songs of Armagh men Peadar Ó Doirnín and Art Mac Cumhaigh — to take examples from each of the country's Irish-speaking sectors.[32]

Yet neither the force of the terms *deoraí* and *díbeartach*, nor the passion of localism in Gaelic culture, nor even the strength of — or the historical justifications for — the anti-*Sasanach* tradition, fully explains the persistence of the image of exile or its prevalence among nineteenth-century Irish emigrants, the great majority of whom were predominately or exclusively English-speaking. Rather, the resentment of all

31 Key texts include: Cecile O'Rahilly, *Five Seventeenth Century Political Poems* (Dublin, 1952); J. C. MacErlean, ed., *Duanaire Dháibhidh Uí Brudaair*, 3 vols. (London, 1910–17); and Pádraig Ó Duinnin, ed., *Eoghan Rua Ó Súilleabháin* (Baile Átha Cliath, 1932).
32 Michael McGrath, ed., *The Diary of Humphrey O'Sullivan*, 4 vols. (Dublin, 1937), vol. 1, 119; Douglas Hyde, *Poems Ascribed to Raftery* (Dublin, 1903), 285–321; and on another Mayo poet, see: Nicholas Williams, *Riocard Bairéad: Amhráin* (Baile Átha Cliath, 1978). In 1980 Ó Longáin's work was still unpublished, but now see Rónán Ó Donnachadha, ed., *Mícheál Óg Ó Longáin, File* (Baile Átha Cliath, 1994). For south Ulster, see Tomás Ó Fiaich, ed., *Art Mac Cumhaigh: Dánta* (Baile Átha Cliath, 1973); Breandán Ó Buachalla, ed., *Peadar Ó Doirnín: Amhráin* (Baile Átha Cliath, 1969). For the fullest mapping of the survival of the Irish language, enabling collation with the migration maps cited above in n. 24, see Comisiún na Gaeltachta, *Number and Percentage of Irish Speakers in Each District Electoral Division, 1911*, map no. 1 (Dublin, 1926): small percentages allow rough reconstruction of language decline by approximate age-cohort, and show much wider residual use than Brian Ó Cuív, ed., *A View of the Irish Language* (Dublin, 1969), 138–39.

discontinuities, of all forms of exploitation, and their interpretation in a context of conquest and injustice, found renewed expression in a broader cultural matrix in which modern emigration was interpreted as forced exile — as the final, culminating oppression. Both tradition and outcome merged in sources as separate as Donnchadh Ruadh Mac Conmara's *Bán Chnuic Éireann Óighe* (c. 1780; extant since), and the forceful novel *Deoraidheacht* (1910) by Pádraic Ó Conaire, who linked exile and displacement with Anglicization and demoralization.[33] In popular songs such as 'An Díbeartach Ó Éireann' and 'An Díbirteach', collected in Connacht in the early twentieth century, the tradition was less precisely diffused, yet so pervasively as to shape the emergent broadside balladry of emigration in English from c. 1800 onwards. Indeed, it is not possible to maintain an artificial distinction between the supposed authenticity of Gaelic materials and a synthetic strain sometimes attributed to their English replacements: the direct lineage is too intimate.[34]

Thus, patterns of culture persisted, despite the demise or contraction of the Irish language, to produce a native Irish worldview in which the old exile motif had continuing validity. Perhaps all that survives here is an archaic mode of conceiving expatriation, later politicized and refashioned by Irish writers in an English shaped by nineteenth-century romanticism and Victorian sentimentalism. However, the materials themselves suggest much more: a series of basic cultural distinctions that may be 'characterized' as between a 'traditional' native-Irish Catholic culture and 'modern' (that is, capitalist, bourgeois) British, American, and Irish Protestant cultures.

Of course, the danger in this kind of analysis is that Irish, British, and American Protestants frequently employed such characterizations for deeply invidious purposes: to 'explain' Irish Catholics' poverty in terms of their alleged 'moral' deficiencies, and to justify conquest, prejudice (both informal and institutional), and Protestant social and political ascendancy in Ireland and overseas. Ever since the early Middle Ages, English (and, ironically, Roman Church) apologists had characterized the Gaelic Irish as 'savage' and 'barbaric', and long before the nineteenth century the Anglo-American press and stage had created in 'Teague' and in 'Paddy' (and 'Biddy') a figure whose pathetic, comic, or malevolent qualities made him (or her) the supposed antithesis of the 'respectable' and 'civilized' (hence, Protestant) English or American man (or woman).[35]

Despite such abuse, if employed sensitively, cultural distinctions consonant with recent scholarly findings are useful to the degree they aid explanation of the exile

33 Risteárd Ó Foghludha, ed., *Donnchadh Ruadh Mac Conmara, 1715–1810* (Baile Átha Cliath, 1933), 31–32; Pádraic Ó Conaire, *Deoraidheacht* (Baile Átha Cliath, 1910).
34 Eileen Costello, *Traditional Folk Songs from Galway and Mayo* (London, 1919, and Dublin, 1923), 248–49; Séamus Clandillon and Margaret Hannigan, eds., *Songs of the Irish Gaels* (London, 1927), 15–16; Richard L. Wright, ed., *Irish Emigrant Ballads and Songs* (Bowling Green, Ohio, 1975), 107–428.
35 L. M. Cullen, *Life in Ireland* (London, 1968), 27; Dale T. Knobel's 1976 doctoral dissertation, since published as *Paddy and the Republic: Ethnicity and Nationality in Antebellum America* (Middletown, Conn., 1986); L. P. Curtis, Jr., *Anglo-Saxons and Celts: A Study of Anti-Irish Prejudices in Victorian England* (Bridgeport, Conn., 1968), 53, and *Apes and Angels: the Irishman in Victorian Caricature* (Newton Abbot, 1971).

motif's cultural location as well as of various anomalies in Irish and Irish-American societies. Emphasis on residual, as against Anglicizing, elements in Irish culture have been used lately to illuminate Irish life in Philadelphia, in California, in New York, and in the Americanizing generations.[36] George Templeton Strong, a mid-Victorian New Yorker, commented in his diary that the poor Irish immigrants in his city, many of them Irish-speakers, were 'almost as remote from us in temperament and constitution as the Chinese'.[37] Strong's statement of course reflected patrician disdain, provoked when he witnessed poor Irishwomen keening on the street over the broken, rag-clothed body of an Irish labourer, crushed to death in a work accident. However, his statement reflected the real distance between traditional rural Irish and bourgeois Protestant American attitudes and customs. Although many Americans, and some Irish and British Protestants, were notably more sympathetic, they usually believed that any 'understanding' of most, if not all, Irish Catholics required considerable effort and forbearance.[38]

The argument here is that different cultural emphases as to 'proper' attitudes and behaviour exist and are important. For historical reasons, in some societies, in certain periods, some values are more dominant than in others. In the eighteenth and early nineteenth centuries, when Irish mass migration began, but continuing and even strengthening thereafter for reasons explained below, there *were* significant differences between the worldview that predominated in Irish Catholic society and those that prevailed among its Protestant Irish, English, and American critics. In the broadest terms, an array of sources suggest that, during the age of mass migration, many Catholic Irish were more communal, dependent, fatalistic, and prone to accept conditions passively than were most of the Protestants they encountered in either Ireland or America. Put another way, the former were less individualistic, independent, optimistic, and given to initiative than were those Protestants. In short, they displayed what social scientists often call 'pre-modern' or pre-capitalist values: they were more sensitive to the weight of tradition than to innovative or 'progressive' possibilities for the future. Indeed, their perspectives often appeared so pre-modern that to 'manly', bourgeois observers from modern business cultures, they often seemed 'irresponsible', even 'feckless', 'adolescent', or 'feminine'. To 'improving' Protestants, from Arthur Young, an English

36 Patrick J. Blessing, 'West among Strangers: Irish Migration to California, 1850–1880' (PhD diss., University of California, Los Angeles, 1977); Michael A. Gordon, 'Studies in Irish and Irish-American Thought and Behavior in Gilded Age New York City' (PhD diss., University of Rochester, 1977); Dale B. Light, 'Class, Ethnicity, and the Urban Ecology in a Nineteenth-Century City: Philadelphia's Irish, 1840–1890 (PhD diss., University of Pennsylvania, 1979); and John Duffy Ibson's 1979 doctoral dissertation, since published as *Will the World Break Your Heart? Dimensions and Consequences of Irish-American Assimilation* (New York, 1990).

37 Allan Nevins and M. H. Thomas, eds., *The Diary of George Templeton Strong*, 4 vols. (New York, 1952), vol. 1, 348.

38 e.g., Yankee convert Orestes Brownson: 'I love the Irish for their attachment to the faith and for many amiable and noble qualities, but they are deficient in good sense, sound judgement, and manly character' (Orestes Brownson Papers, undated Ms. I–3-d, University of Notre Dame Archives).

visitor, in the 1770s to Horace Plunkett in the early 1900s — and even to sympathetic but commercially minded priests such as John O'Hanlon and John Ireland — many Irish Catholics appeared to avoid or obscure personal initiative and individual responsibility, even as to livelihood. Such broad evidence suggests that more was involved here than what Victorians misread as widespread Irish character-failure. Rather, most Irish Catholics did come from a socio-cultural framework in which the concept of individuality was less sharply defined and hence less important than in contemporary Protestant/bourgeois frameworks.[39]

In abstract terms, both Irish Catholic and Anglo-American Protestant worldviews made a clear distinction between *stasis* (or patience) and *action*, with all the attendant features of that paradigm: communalism versus individualism; authority versus freedom; custom versus innovation; non-responsibility versus responsibility. The greater Irish emphases on the first of these polarities stemmed from the pre-eminence they gave to stasis, as against the Anglo-American Protestant emphasis on action, with Irish Protestants tending more towards the latter outlook (except when individual freedom, innovation, etcetera, threatened pan-Protestant privilege or solidarity against Catholics).

Of course, the distinction is a conceptual one not necessarily carried over into behaviour. It describes an ideal ordering of things: the ideal does not constrain behaviour absolutely, but rather guides or, alternatively, 'explains' it. Indeed, traditional conceptualizations of new endeavours become most necessary in periods of rapid and destabilizing socio-economic change, as in Ireland from 1770 onwards, to restore the psychic equilibrium between inherited attitudes and current activity. To members of the society concerned, the resultant 'compromise' may be fairly satisfying, but to less sensitive outsiders, it might appear neither 'rational' nor even 'honest'. Indeed, theorists of 'cultural lag' (the phenomenon described here) would hold that such adjustments can modify socio-economic change itself, by restricting the uses made of new 'opportunities', and can also affect the psychological readjustments of the people involved, sometimes very considerably. Contemporary scholarship in the behavioural sciences has applied these ideas to more recent Irish development. Some discern widespread 'social sickness' when the rapidly changing society is one, like the Irish, which assigns a less significant value to change or 'progress' than do the 'modern' societies which it seeks to

---

39 Sympathetic admissions of such 'inadequacies' include: Thomas D'Arcy McGee, *History of the Irish Settlers in North America* (Boston, 1855), 194–235; Rev. Stephen Byrne, *Irish Emigration to the United States* (New York, 1873), 12, 27, 35, 41, and 52; O'Hanlon, *Irish Emigrant's Guide*, 217–35; James Cardinal Gibbons, 'Irish Immigration to the United States', *Irish Ecclesiastical Record*, 4th ser., 1 (1897), 97–109; also see J. H. Moynihan, *Archbishop John Ireland* (New York, 1953), 26–30. The term 'Protestant/bourgeois' does not of course imply that all Irish, British, or American Protestants in the nineteenth century were 'middle class' in status or even *mentalité*. However, thanks largely to the processes of cultural hegemony (discussed in subsequent chapters), the dominant Protestant worldview in those societies privileged capitalist (i.e., 'modern') norms, such as individualism, competition, progress, etcetera, and usually linked those qualities to Protestantism (and their absence to Catholicism, especially as practiced by its Irish adherents).

emulate. The resultant stress may generate structures of thought, or ideologies, having 'the character of answers, cures, excuses or even remorse'.[40]

Such 'explanatory' thought-structures can function on both conscious and unconscious levels. Whether 'dysfunctional' or not in the long term, their Irish versions certainly assisted 'modernization': first, they provided a defence for a society faced with profound and potentially disruptive change; second, they moderated the tensions between older pressures towards conformity and the thrust to forms of 'modern', individualistic behaviour demanded and (at least in theory) rewarded by the capitalist marketplace. By accounting for their often innovative actions in pre-individualist categories, many Catholic Irish squared their traditional outlook with the practice of a new and broader 'freedom'-of-action. The very anonymity of those categories disguised the growing element of personal calculation: 'the boys have in mind that we all ...', as it would be expressed in the peer group. Some social pressures, emanating from government, landlords, or secret agrarian societies, had behind them the sanction of force, real or implied. Others, such as the Church, nationalist movements, political factions, and neighbourhood groups, could threaten isolation, ostracism or ridicule, the Church adding dire spiritual penalties. Indeed, in many respects, Catholic Ireland's own socio-economic hierarchies — ranging from head tenants, merchant-creditors, and employers to subtenants, farm labourers, and debtors, generally—were more immediate and often as repressive as those imposed by the 'Protestant Ascendancy'. Perhaps the most basic pressures, however, were familial, emphasizing 'duty' and enforced by outward shame or personal guilt.[41] Through all these mechanisms, common allegiance to the prescribed adjustments to change was sustained. Of course, individuals experienced these pressures very differently, according to their social positions and personal situations: some more, some less, which may partly explain their variant responses to emigration as 'exile' or as 'escape' or 'opportunity', as well as their various reactions to life in America. But large numbers were sufficiently influenced by the common attitudes to maintain this chapter's central thesis — that a generally prevalent worldview helped determine a discernibly 'national' response to emigration as exile.

---

40 Claude Lévi-Strauss, *Structural Anthropology*, 2 vols., trans. Claire Jacobson and Brooke Grundfest (New York, 1963), vol. 1, 241.
41 Conrad Arensberg and Solon T. Kimball, *Family and Community in Ireland* (Cambridge, Mass., 1940); Damien Hannan and L. Katsiaouni, *Traditional Families: From Culturally Prescribed to Negotiated Roles in Irish Farm Families* (Dublin, 1977); Damien Hannan, *Displacement and Development: Class, Kinship, and Social Change in Irish Rural Communities* (Dublin, 1979); and A. J. Humphreys, 'The Family in Ireland', in M. F. Nimkhoff, ed., *Comparative Family Systems* (Boston, 1965), 232–58, are the chief works on the family in rural Ireland. Apart from work on marriage patterns, little has been done to explore this theme historically, except Kevin O'Neill's 1979 doctoral dissertation, since published as *Family and Farm in Pre-Famine Ireland: The Parish of Killashandra* (Madison, Wisc., 1984); Albert G. Mitchell, 'Irish Family Patterns in Nineteenth-Century Ireland and Lowell, Massachusetts' (PhD diss., Boston University, 1976); and Margaret E. Conners, 'Their Own Kind: Family and Community in Albany, 1850–1915' (PhD diss., Harvard University, 1975).

Of course, an outlook oriented towards stasis was not unique to Ireland. It was similar to those held by other pre-capitalist societies, especially by the dependent majority in old rural communities. Anthropologist Louis Dumont's observation is pertinent: 'As opposed to modern society', he writes, 'traditional societies, which know nothing of equality and liberty as values, which know nothing, in short, of the individual, have a basically collective idea of man.'[42] It may be that a society such as Ireland's never could provide much space for an idea of individuality: although law and religion may have introduced the concept, conquest and colonization conspired to erode it. Yet, neither were conquest and colonization unique to Ireland, and perhaps contemporary accounts reflect no more than a resultant culture of poverty and quasi-serfdom. Many Irish themselves believed this to be so. In 1839 Daniel O'Connell characterized his followers as 'crawling slaves', and in 1848 a Wexford priest ascribed the riotous behaviour of recently arrived Irishmen in America 'to the state of serfdom, vassalage, and ignorance in which ... they have been kept down by law and unprincipled rulers. ... [O]ur people still have, and will, for a long time, have many of the vices of slaves.'[43] Country folk themselves complained that 'Our feet, wearied night & day by exorbitant labour for impoverished Masters, now tremble with feebleness whilst treading the paths of uncompensated toil: Our heads, long bent beneath a Slavish yoke, require Support & encouragement towards their being raised to a natural Consistency.'[44] Indeed, despite brief periods of relative prosperity for graziers and larger tenants, especially between 1770 and the end of the Napoleonic Wars, Irish countrymen from the late sixteenth to the mid-nineteenth century generally experienced both poverty and the need for submission. Arguably, the cumulative effects of this on Irish Catholic outlook or 'character' often rendered them, as they said, 'patient and resigned to their humble condition in life'.[45] The impact is traceable, for instance, in the changes that took place in Gaelic poetry during the seventeenth and eighteenth centuries. In the earlier period, poets prophesied that the Gaels themselves would expel the foreign 'upstarts' by their own efforts. By the later period, after 1690 or so, the poets despaired of victory except through the intercession of heaven or of foreign armies, reflecting a more realistic conception of British might, continental circumstances, and their own powerlessness.[46]

42 Louis Dumont, Homo Hierarchus: The Caste System and Its Implications (London, 1972), 42.
43 Seán O'Faolain, King of the Beggars: A Life of Daniel O'Connell, the Irish Liberator, in a Study of the Rise of Modern Irish Democracy (New York, 1938), 12; Fr. William Purcell, Wexford, to Bishop John Purcell, Cincinnati, 10 December 1848 (Bishop Purcell Papers, Ms. II–4-k, University of Notre Dame Archives).
44 Tighe MacMahon, Six Mile Bridge, County Clare, petition to the Colonial Office, London, [1825] (CO 384/11, PRO).
45 James Martyn, et al., Coonagh and Oneybeg baronies, County Limerick, to the Colonial Office, London, [1825] (CO 384/11, PRO).
46 See the sources cited above in nos. 31 and 32. For evidence of transmission into English-speaking culture, see Enrí Ó Muirgheasa, Céad de Cheoltaibh Uladh (Baile Átha Cliath, 1915), 175–341 (provenances and notes of Ulster tradition, in English); Georges-Denis Zimmermann, Irish Political Street Ballads and Rebel Songs, 1780–1900 (Geneva, 1966), passim; Gréagóir Ó Dúill, 'Ballads and the Law, 1830–1832', Ulster Folklife, 19 (1973), 38–40.

Yet, although material circumstances and political experiences no doubt confirmed cultural emphases on communalism, fatalism, and passivity, the roots of those outlooks lay deeper still: in the secular, religious, and even linguistic aspects of Gaelic culture — and in the culture of the 'Old English in Ireland' (that is, those of Norman descent), insofar as it had been assimilated to 'Irish' norms by the late seventeenth century. What follows here is only the most skeletal analysis of these roots.

First, the *secular*: Irish society was ideally hierarchical, aristocratic, familial, and traditional — each feature diminishing the importance of the individual in relation to society as a whole. Despite some social mobility, pre-conquest Gaelic society was status-bound, with status dependent upon family and inherited property. The system of clientage enabled short-term acquisition of cattle or land, but early modern attitudes and practices regarding such dependants appear to have become increasingly arbitrary and autocratic. Although evidence such as the anonymous seventeenth-century poem *Páirliment Chloinne Tomáis* suggests that conquest actually offered those of lower status greater economic security, while debasing the condition of those of higher rank, such literary sources also demonstrate the harsh strictures levied on those who attempted to rise above ascribed status. In general, it is probable that sustained amelioration was rare and was more than counterbalanced by rising population, rents and other costs, and by most tenants' own practices of partible inheritance and, under the old partnership-leasing and rundale systems, co-tillage and periodic land redistribution. Most tenants relied heavily on the *meitheal* — co-operative seasonal farm work, involving reciprocal exchanges of labour and farm animals among kin and neighbours — whereas the rural poor were dependent on patronage or neighbourly charity for sheer survival. Hence, despite Ireland's overall commercialization from 1750, for most rural Catholics economic circumstances challenged but also reaffirmed their traditional patterns of interdependence: their practical reliance on family and community, for example, but also on the values that sustained those patterns by circumscribing individual ambitions or by mitigating their communally destructive consequences. Thus, ambition was both thwarted materially and stigmatized culturally. The system both denied advancement and supported, cushioned, and 'explained' the failure to rise. Ideally, the individual's duties did not include *self*-betterment, rather the opposite: profit-seeking or innovation often brought scorn, ridicule, even physical hindrance, from diverse sources such as the secret agrarian societies.

Also in the secular realm, the pre-eminence of the family in Gaelic culture likewise diminished the individual's importance. In Brehon law an Irishman without a family was legally and socially a non-entity; hence the great importance which kin groups placed on genealogy, in both pre-modern and modern times. Moreover, the traditional family was authoritarian and patriarchal: sons waiting for inheritance and women in general had limited public personalities; child-rearing practices stigmatized 'boldness', and 'shame' imposed and guilt internalized were primary control mechanisms. In addition, larger social structures, such as the Gaelic *tuatha* (roughly, tribes), the Church, the whole people, the secret societies, and the nation-to-be, were all conceived as extensions or analogues of the family. Thus, the native Irish were 'children of the Gael', and the Blasket Islanders 'children of the one mother'. The maternal characterization of social units was archaic, but the persistent imagery must have heightened pressures for conformity within the community.[47] Likewise, traditional attitudes also buttressed dependent behaviour and curtailed personal innovation. The weight of custom was tremendous always. Brehon law was regarded as ideally immutable and comprehensive. Gaelic poets scorned originality where it involved deviation from received types of composition. In everyday life, proverbs fitted events to a pre-existing scheme. Typically, these received aphorisms stressed continuity and curbed individuality; many specifically counselled passivity: 'Holy and blessed is he who is patient'; 'What is fated for me is hard to shun'; 'Good fortune is better than rising early' — to cite but a few employed in the late nineteenth century by Donegal Irish-speakers.[48]

With regard to the *religious* aspects of Irish society, they reinforced the temporal side of life and sacralized its emphasis on tradition and communalism. In contrast to, say, Florentine Catholicism, with its considerable individualism, late medieval and early modern Irish Catholicism may have been shaped in these respects by the surrounding culture. Nevertheless, there were some basic affinities between intrinsic features of Catholicism and these aspects of the culture: for example, the Church, too, was a normative community and analogous to the authoritative family. In certain areas, individuality was inappropriate: the Church authoritatively required uniformity of belief and restricted personal interpretation of central doctrines. Even in the realm of behaviour, Irish Catholicism provided a framework which — while it intensified responsibility to obey what emigrant Thomas Garry called 'the laws of Church' — limited the scope of individuality.[49] In the nineteenth and early twentieth centuries, contemporaries often charged that Irish Churchmen greatly overemphasized these constraints. Certainly, Irish Catholicism promoted a worldview that subordinated what sociologist Will Herberg called the 'active virtues' of enterprise, initiative, and action to the exigencies of the community of charity: the interlocking Church-and-society of local people. Bruce Biever, SJ, and Richard Rose delineated the marked results of such emphases on Irish attitudes in the mid-1900s, by contrast with migrants affected by American standards.[50]

---

47 Robin Fox, The Tory Islanders: A People of the Celtic Fringe (Cambridge, 1978), 31–81, 99–126, 136–37, 157n; Limerick Rural Survey, Interim Reports, 3: Social Structure (Tipperary, 1961), portrays familial dominance within social structures (rather than family-in-itself), as in the sources cited above in n. 41.

48 Enrí Ua Muirgheasa, ed., Seanfhocla Uladh (Baile Átha Cliath, 1907), 58, 68, 78. Also see An Seabhac (pseud. Pádraig Ó Siochfhradha), ed., Seanfhocail na Muimhneach (Baile Átha Cliath, 1926), passim.

49 Thomas Garry, Peekskill, NY, to his wife, County Sligo, 8 March 1848, in the Third Report from the Select Committee on Colonization from Ireland, HL 1849 (86), Minutes of Evidence, Appendix X, in the Irish University Press series of the British Parliamentary Papers (hereafter BPP [IUP ser.]): Emigration, Vol. 5 (Shannon, 1968), 129.

50 Will Herberg, Protestant, Catholic, Jew: An Essay in American Religious Sociology (Garden City, NY, 1960), 149; 'Religious Motivation in Economics' (Ireland) and 'Church Influence in Economics' (Irish-born

Of course, before the Great Famine the Irish Church lacked the means fully to order, much less homogenize, Irish Catholicism.[51] Yet the peasantry's pre-modern Catholicism also emphasized passivity and fatalism by stressing customary elements of religion and by retaining pre-Christian predictive beliefs such as those designed to ensure bountiful crops and healthy livestock. Widespread belief in the fairies — 'religious' in that it concerned the supernatural — likewise reinforced the inhibitions of Gaelic society: fairies had to be propitiated by rigid adherence to set forms. Thus, through both orthodox and customary rites, the Irish sought to perpetuate their universe, not to change it.[52]

Indeed, the religious and secular sanctions against explicit individualism so intertwined in Gaelic rural society that the effects of the two can scarcely be separated. The result was an outlook sharply different — ideally and often practically — from that of Irish Protestants. Jack White has written: 'Deep in the fabric of all Protestants there is a belief in the importance of the Reformation as one of the great liberations of human history. They believe in it as a bursting of the bars, as a triumph of the spirit of the individual over the dead hand of the institution.'[53] In Irish practice, of course, pressures for Protestant settler solidarity against the colonized Catholic majority constrained — in some areas, stultified — the individualist logic of such convictions. In the United States, however, they had full play: Alexis de Tocqueville coined the term 'individualism' in his long

in America), in Bruce F. Biever, *Religion, Culture, and Values: Native Irish and American Irish Catholicism* (New York, 1976), 383–93, 673–88; Richard Rose, *Governing without Consensus: An Irish Perspective* (Boston, 1971), 285; and for nineteenth-century expression, see Pádraig Ó hEalaí, 'Moral Values in Irish Religious Tales', in *Béaloídeas: The Journal of the Folklore of Ireland Society*, 42–43 (1973–74), 176–212; and T. P. O'Neill, 'The Catholic Church and the Relief of the Poor', in *Archivium Hibernicum*, 31 (1973), 132–45. Such problems greatly exercised the new Irish-American middle class before Max Weber: e.g. Fr. John Hanc, 'The Prosperity of Ulster Compared with the Rest of Ireland', *Donohoe's Magazine* (Boston), 48 (1902), 453–56, or Thomas Shanahan, 'Catholicism and Civilization', *Catholic University Bulletin*, 4 (1898), 467–80, the latter conceding that differential development interacted with greater unworldliness, areligious political economies with spiritual motivations, a mature anticipation of Kurt Samuelsson, *Religion and Economic Action*, ed. D. C. Coleman (New York, 1961).

51 David W. Miller, 'Catholic Religious Practice in Pre-Famine Ireland', *Journal of Social History*, 8 (1975), 81–98; S. J. Connolly, 'Catholicism and Social Discipline in Pre-Famine Ireland', *Bulletin of the Irish Committee of Historical Sciences: Thesis Abstracts*, 1 (1976), 30–36, since published in full as *Priests and People in Pre-Famine Ireland, 1780–1845* (Dublin, 1982).

52 E. Estyn Evans, 'Peasant Beliefs in Nineteenth-Century Ireland', in Daniel J. Casey and Robert E. Rhodes, eds., *Views of the Irish Peasantry, 1800–1916* (Hamden, Conn., 1977), 37–56.

53 Jack White, *Minority Report: The Protestant Community in the Irish Republic* (Dublin, 1975), 62. For critical mid-twentieth-century studies both establishing yet modifying salient Catholic/Protestant differences, see (Ireland) Rose, *Governing without Consensus*, 247–356; (United States) Gerhard E. Lenski, *The Religious Factor: A Sociological Study of Religion's Impact on Politics, Economics, and Family Life* (Garden City, NY, 1961); (south Germany) Günter Golde, *Catholics and Protestants: Agricultural Modernization in Two German Villages* (New York, 1975). Such studies have not yet been convincingly related to more imprecise studies of western business development, e.g., S. N. Eisenstadt, ed., *The Protestant Ethic and Modernization: A Comparative View* (New York, 1968), but see David W. Miller, 'Presbyterians and "Modernisation" in Ulster', *Past and Present*, 80 (1978), 66–90.

analysis of the effects of both Protestantism and equality on the American character.[54] The results were alien to Irish Catholics' more traditional patterns of faith and religious expression. For example, Arthur Quin, a poor emigrant from County Tyrone, saw things very differently than did his Protestant neighbours in upstate New York, lately 'burned over' by revivalism, sect formation, and interdenominational rivalry. 'There is a great change for the better since we came here,' he wrote home in 1873; 'it will be our neglect if we dont attend our duty   there was only one priest [here] before but now there is two and the[y] have mass every Sunday and the[y] *make* the people attend there duty well ...' Quin's wording betrays an outlook worlds removed from the region's special dedication to personal inspiration, associated with leaders Charles G. Finney, Joseph Smith, and John Humphrey Noyes.[55] Unquestionably, the Irish tended to link their faith's prescribed obligations to a degree of impersonal behavior that astonished outsiders. Even the papal emissary, Archbishop Gaetano Bedini, wrote in 1853 that Irish immigrants 'see in their priests not a simple minister of religion; but their father, their magistrate, their judge, their king, their "papa", their idol'. As historians Oscar Handlin, Jay Dolan, and James Roohan observed, the travails of labouring life in industrial America often helped perpetuate such attitudes among Irish emigrants.[56]

Finally, the linguistic aspects of Gaelic culture also made their mark. It is arguable that the semantic structure of the Irish language itself reflected and reinforced an Irish worldview which emphasized the virtues of patience and dependence. As noted above, it is debatable whether words and grammars available to speakers pre-determine their experienced world. But none deny that languages vary widely in the way they 'cut up' or classify experience, in apparently arbitrary ways. Languages are not pre-determined by the structures of the 'facts' with which they must deal. The relationships are not closed and given. Languages and the cultures related to them in turn variously influence the received world, and hence the outlook, of their speakers. The categories of a language

54 Alexis de Tocqueville, *Democracy in America*, ed. J. P. Mayer, trans. George Lawrence (Garden City, NY, 1969), 46–47, 288, 293, 528–30; Michael Chevalier, *Society, Manners, and Politics in the United States: Letters on North America* (1838), ed. John W. Ward (Garden City, NY, 1961), 273, 355–56. Also see Philip Greven, *The Protestant Temperament: Patterns of Child-Rearing, Religious Experience, and the Self in Early America* (New York, 1977), which roots it in the colonial family, but contrast Alan Macfarlane, *The Origins of English Individualism: The Family, Property, and Social Transition* (Oxford, 1978).

55 Arthur Quin, Barrytown, NY, to his siblings, Stewartstown, County Tyrone, 22 September 1873 (D.1819/4, in Public Record Office of Northern Ireland, Belfast; hereafter PRONI), emphasis added. On upstate New York, see Paul E. Johnson, *A Shopkeeper's Millennium: Society and Revivals in Rochester, New York, 1815–1837* (New York, 1978), and Whitney R. Cross, *The Burned-Over District: The Social and Intellectual History of Enthusiastic Religion in Western New York, 1800–1850* (Ithaca, NY, 1950). Rev. Michael O'Riordan, *Catholicity and Progress in Ireland* (London, 1906), 64, is a trenchant statement of the bounds of individuality, as expressed by an Irish priest of that era.

56 Bedini's observation in John Tracy Ellis, ed., *The Catholic Priest in the United States: Historical Investigations* (Collegeville, Minn., 1971), 307; Oscar Handlin, *Boston's Immigrants: A Study in Acculturation*, 2nd edn. (New York, 1972), 125–35; Jay P. Dolan, *The Immigrant Church: New York's Irish and German Catholics, 1815–1865* (Baltimore, Md., 1975), 115–20; James E. Roohan, *American Catholics and the Social Question, 1865–1900* (New York, 1976), 12–25, 103–18, 247–63.

such as Irish may represent one mode (related to others) whereby society 'explains' its
values to itself and constitutes its culture. Language thus plays a corroborative rather than
a leading role in the formation of a worldview, and a culture can be seen as a structure of
conceptual systems, including language, each of which, using its own peculiar terms,
reinforces the others.[57]

In each of its systems traditional Gaelic culture draws a careful distinction between
what may be called 'patience' and 'action'. Indeed, the opposition between these
categories may be regarded as a central element of the Irish worldview. Simply stated,
the one category ('action') views the participant in a given event as an 'initiator', the other
category ('patience') as an 'experiencer'. The initiator is viewed as exercising control,
while the experiencer is regarded as passive: one either causes an event to happen, or
an event happens to one. According to the Irish worldview, certain phenomena are
marked as appropriate for active participation, while others are marked as appropriate
for patient participation; in other words, areas of responsibility and non-responsibility
are clearly delimited.

The Irish language belongs to a large group of languages that give explicit formal
expression to the patience–action opposition.[58] Such languages are known as 'stative-
active' as opposed to 'nominitive' languages such as English, in which the underlying
semantic opposition is blurred. The difference between the two types of language can be
illustrated by comparing equivalent sentences:

English	Irish	
1. I met [i.e., chanced upon] him	Do casadh orm é	Patience
		vs.
2. I struck him	Do bhuaileas é	Action

In the first pair of sentences, there is, semantically, no initiator: the (chance) meeting
'happens' to both participants. In the second pair, there are both an initiator and an
experiencer. The Irish sentences reflect this distinction directly, but their English
counterparts obscure it by merging them into a single form, 'I': 'I' both designates an
experiencer in the first sentence, and an initiator in the second.

Even within the category of patience, Irish is capable of drawing formal distinctions
between greater and lesser control on the part of the participant. For example:

57 Claude Lévi-Strauss, 'Introduction ...', in Marcel Mauss, Sociologie et Anthropologie (Paris, 1966); Clifford
   Geertz, 'Ritual and Social Change', in his The Interpretation of Cultures: Selected Essays (New York, 1973), 144–
   45, together with the works cited in n. 29 above.
58 The following interpretation of Irish as a stative-active language was first set out by Bruce D. Boling,
   initially in 'Irish Language and Culture' (Berkeley, Calif., 1976), a paper later delivered at the Kentucky
   Foreign Language Conference (Lexington, April 1978).

English	Irish	
1. I hate	Tá fuath *agam*	Control
		vs.
2. I am blond-haired	Tá ceann fionn *orm*	Non-control

In the first sentence, the experience of hate is an emotion which is in some degree subject to the control of the experiencer, while still remaining a 'non-action'. In the second, the experience of 'blond-hairedness' is, in the natural course of events, imposed on the experiencer and lies outside his or her control.

Thus, in English the formal opposition between initiator and experiencer (in the first person, for example) is expressed formally by 'I' versus 'me' (or, as the case may be, by 'I' versus 'for me', 'I' versus 'to me', etcetera). Whenever a formal merger of such underlying semantic opposition takes place in English and other typically nominitive languages, it is always in favour of the initiator (the 'I'-form). Under such circumstances, the experiencer is inevitably coloured with a tinge of agency, since the general meaning of the 'I'-form is 'initiator'. In other words, the English language is weighted towards action: its speakers will 'see' a greater range of phenomena in terms of action than will speakers of a stative-active language such as Irish.

Speakers of Irish thus employ a language that classifies a far broader range of phenomena into an area in which action and self-assertion are inappropriate. In this respect, the Irish language provides a close analogue to — and therefore a reinforcer of — the other constituent systems of Irish culture. Although these linguistic oppositions are subtle, they are no more subtle or any less psychologically real than the stative-active oppositions that characterize law, religion, and mythology.[59]

Finally, with regard to this chapter's central thesis, it is very significant that the most common way for an Irish-speaker to describe his emigration to America was *dob éigean dom imeacht go Meiriceá*: 'I had to go to America'; literally, 'going to America was a necessity for me'. Irish-speakers thus chose a patient over an active way of expressing their emigration. In fact, this sentence belongs to a type known in Irish grammar as 'impersonal', which downgrades active participation and presents inexorable fact. The message of the sentence is entirely consistent with the use of the word *deoraí* (exile) to designate 'emigrant', as one subject to imposed pressures. In short, *dob éigean dom imeacht go Meiriceá* meant that emigration was fate or compulsion more than choice. It was a natural, if perhaps unhistorical, step for a traditionalist people to inflate and politicize it by reference to the involuntary exile of past heroes, such as O'Neill and O'Donnell in 1607, and Sarsfield and the Wild Geese in 1691 and thereafter.

Thus, Gaelic culture may be viewed as three interlocking subsystems (secular, religious, and linguistic) supporting a worldview that valued conservatism, collective

---

59 See Edward Sapir, 'The Psychological Reality of Phonemes', in David G. Mendelbaum, ed., *Selected Writings of Edward Sapir in Language, Culture, and Personality* (Berkeley, Calif., 1963), 46–60.

behaviour, and dependence, and which limited personal responsibility in broad areas. As most conditions of Irish Catholic life steadily and, in some periods, dramatically worsened from Tudor times onwards, it is likely these archaic constraints took on a new reality in explanation of successive defeats, poverty and proscription, and the need for collective endurance. But from the late eighteenth century onwards, a wave of commercial transactions, improved communications, and population growth began to challenge their relevance. Contemporary descriptions of Ireland, such as William Shaw Mason's *Statistical Account, or Parochial Survey of Ireland* (1814–19), reflected a society whose different regions and classes were in rapid (albeit markedly uneven) transition to modern, market-oriented ways of thinking and behaving, as current scholarship confirms. Older formulae no longer so much constrained as provided psychological continuity during this phase; traditional nostrums were still relevant to continuing hardships and heightened anxieties, even as individual behaviour objectively changed.

The widespread persistence of such traits was the staple of much comment upon Ireland throughout the period from the 1770s to the 1920s. If many of these observations were made by outsiders such as Arthur Young, the Halls, Asenath Nicholson, Johann G. Kohl, and others, individual Irishmen also often made them: the Galway merchant, for example, who in 1827 remarked on Irish country people's unwillingness to emigrate because of their (to him) inexplicable attachment to 'the place where they are bred'; and the Catholic bishop of Kilkenny, who, in 1835, admitted that, although Irish Catholics had 'all the virtues dear to God', they 'basically lack[ed] the civil virtues' of the English.[60] More than a half-century after the Famine, other Irishmen, such as Fr. William Burke, Horace Plunkett, and the anonymous author of *My Countrymen*, made similar observations, while nineteenth-century broadside ballads in English showed the same 'obsession with failure, and an apparent acceptance of misfortune', which those writers detected and which had been a staple of eighteenth-century Gaelic poetry. Like Fr. Burke, Plunkett, who had spent years in the United States, decried among most Irish Catholics what he called their 'lack of moral courage, initiative, independence, and self-reliance', and their habit of ascribing Ireland's problems solely to British malevolence. Aspects of the old worldview persisted even more recently, as a west Corkman implied when he acknowledged that country people still preferred anonymity of action over the assumption or attribution of individual responsibility.[61]

Recent Irish historians, searching eagerly for a 'modernizing' Ireland, have perhaps insufficiently attended to these survivals. Yet, dramatically, much of the social

---

60 For the Galway merchant's testimony, see *Third Report of the Select Committee on Emigration from the United Kingdom*, HC 1826–27, in BPP [IUP ser.]: *Emigration, Vol. 2* (Shannon, 1968), 274, 277; the bishop is quoted by Alexis de Tocqueville, in his *Journeys to England and Ireland* (London, 1963), 141.

61 R. F. Smith, *Ireland's Renaissance* (Dublin, 1903); Fr. William P. Burke, *Irish Priests in the Penal Times, 1660–1760* (Waterford, 1914), 207–08; Horace Plunkett, *Ireland in the New Century* (London, 1904), viii; An Irishman (pseud.), *My Countrymen* (Edinburgh, 1929), 46–47, 86–97; Zimmermann, *Irish Political Street Ballads*, 11; interview with Dennis Wholley (Berkeley, Calif., 1977).

organisms and task orientations of the past which underlay such traits and outlooks lasted well into the twentieth century to permit scholars such as E. Estyn Evans and Robin Fox to reconstruct a great deal from such survivals. The sheer body of surviving folklore materials is itself crucial: 2.7 million pages in the archives of the Irish Folklore Commission may be problematic for the historians' uses, but the transmission of such a vast body of oral culture, largely archaic, is itself a historical fact of the first magnitude. Indeed, it is precisely from the regions in which such survivals and oral materials were most abundant before the Second World War that emigration was disproportionately concentrated.[62]

However, the outlooks that ensured the transmission of these things survived, not as impermeable bulwarks against change, but as modulators of change, both in such areas and even in earlier commercialized and Anglicized districts such as east Cork. First, and despite its Dublin and bourgeois origins, the growing southern and westward tilt of the new Irish nationalist ideology suggests that it early appropriated and became a carrier of such traditions, especially of those elements of localism, traditionalism, the perception of most discontinuity as enforced, and the coupling of such 'fate' with the effects of British rule. Unsurprisingly, the new nationalist balladry carried over the 'exile' image.[63] Second, the drastic reorientation of family, marriage, and farm to the full pressures of the market economy left behind, however altered, the principal outlook and its chief constraint (by American standards): the subordination of the individual.[64] Third, although the process remains controversial, Catholic Churchmen likewise anticipated and sought to shape the effects of modernization — as through their control over Catholic education (primary initially, secondary later), for example — to ensure the Church became a nexus of continuity and a centre of criticism of too sweeping change: thus, its espousal of rural smallholdings, as the principal bulwarks of Catholic morality and 'national' identity, and its sacralization of the new family relationships. Hence, the Church's expanded authority helped perpetuate traditional patterns of outlook and behaviour, even as it aided the hierarchy's campaign to modernize devotional practices.[65] Arguably, also, even the modern, 'devotional revolution' Church of Cardinal Paul Cullen was affected by its overwhelmingly rural environment. Of course, the *ideology* of modern

---

62 Bo Almquist, 'The Irish Folklore Commission', *Béaloídeas*, 45–47 (1977–79), 6–26; Seán O'Sullivan, *Folktales of Ireland* (Chicago, 1966), xxxiii–iv, xxxvi–vii.

63 Wright, *Irish Emigrant Ballads*, 29–105; Gearóid Ó Tuathaigh, 'Gaelic Ireland: Popular Politics and Daniel O'Connell', *Journal of the Galway Archaeological and Historical Society*, 74 (1974–75), 21–34; and for transmission of related language patterns, P. L. Henry, *An Anglo-Irish Dialect of North Roscommon* (Dublin, 1955); also see Fitzpatrick, 'Geography of Irish Nationalism'.

64 In this regard, the incapacity of the American Irish and urban Irish authors of the essays in John A. O'Brien, ed., *The Vanishing Irish: The Enigma of the Modern World* (New York, 1953), to perceive this pattern is itself most revealing.

65 Emmet Larkin, *Historical Dimensions of Irish Catholicism* (New York, 1976); K. H. Connell, 'Catholicism and Marriage in the Century after the Famine', in his *Irish Peasant Society: Four Historical Essays* (Oxford, 1968), 113–61.

Catholicism had emerged in Ireland by the mid-nineteenth century (historians debate its prevalence before the Famine), but it seems to have been an urban phenomenon, with 'foreign' (Roman and English) cultural roots, and in the Irish countryside cultural continuity, rather than dramatic change, seems predominant.[66] Likewise, although some Irish Churchmen *overseas*, such as Bishop John Ireland, often quite consciously expressed the need for a new, more personalized, faith, many others, more fearful of immigrant 'leakage' (that is, apostasy) in America, strove to reinforce traditional, communal outlooks — to insulate their Irish flocks against 'selfish materialism' (what they called 'Anglo-Saxonism'), as well as against nativist scorn.[67]

All these trends receive continuing study, but it seems reasonably certain that together nationalism, family change, and the Catholic Church did transmit, while transmuting, vibrant portions of the old traditionalism, especially as they formed would-be emigrants. They fostered common attitudes so effectively that, unionism apart, and despite residual differences of language and culture, no regional political movements developed in Ireland before 1922 that sharply divided traditional from non-traditional areas, as happened in Spain, Germany, and Italy.[68] Consequently, most Irish Catholic emigrants carried similar characteristics abroad, and hence were usually not distinguished by Americans as to regional traits (as were Italians), despite their own parochial factionalisms. Even after the Famine, as before, and whether from areas such as east Cork, where heavy change had been leavened by the modulating forces of Church, family, and nationalist culture, or from less affected western areas, most Irish emigrants brought to the United States a distinctive attitudinal pattern marked by localism, familism, and a relatively

66 The nature and prevalence of pre-Famine Catholicism are debated between Larkin, David W. Miller, and S. J. Connolly, on the one hand (see above, n. 51 and 65), and Patrick J. Corish on the other; see Corish, 'The Shaping of a Religious Culture', in his *The Catholic Community in the Seventeenth and Eighteenth Centuries* (Dublin, 1981), 82–114. Eugene Hynes, 'The Great Hunger and Irish Catholicism', *Societas*, 8 (1978), 135–56, also offers a theoretical critique of Larkin and Miller. Kevin Whelan, then of Carysfort College, Blackrock, County Dublin (now director of the University of Notre Dame's Dublin-based Irish Studies programme), kindly showed us his provisional findings from mapping church/people and priest/people ratios for the 1830s and 1840s and 1910–14.

On overseas influences, see: Doyle, *Irish Americans, Native Rights, and National Empires*, 186–202; Lynn H. Lees, *Exiles of Erin: Irish Migrants in Victorian London* (Ithaca, NY, 1979), 164–212; Sheridan Gilley, 'Supernaturalised Culture: Catholic Attitudes and Latin Lands, 1840–1860', *Studies in Church History*, 11 (1975), 309–23; M. Peter Carthy, *English Influences on Early American Catholicism* (Washington, DC, 1959). Neither Dolan nor Handlin (see n. 56 above) distinguish between the Irish social sources and English cultural ones of this ideology, and confuse both with the traditional religious beliefs these forces enclosed.

67 e.g., Byrne, *Irish Emigration to the United States*, 33–37; O'Hanlon, *Irish Emigrant's Guide*, 59–62; Buckley, *Diary of a Tour*, 144, 169–70; Robert D. Cross, *The Emergence of Liberal Catholicism in America* (Cambridge, Mass., 1958), 162–81; also see Miller, *Emigrants and Exiles*, 526–33.

68 That is, notwithstanding a westward tilt to nationalist, anti-Treaty, and early Fianna Fáil support: see Erhard Rumpf and A. C. Hepburn, *Nationalism and Socialism in Twentieth-Century Ireland* (Liverpool, 1977), 38–68.

non-individualist psychology. And this was so even when they proved fully capable of adjusting to the challenges of commercial or industrial America.

Nevertheless, there were minorities of Catholic emigrants — from urban, educated, and/or exceptionally business-industrial backgrounds — who carried points of view that were more attuned to life in the United States. They had been doing so since the late 1700s, and they may have constituted a disproportionately large minority of the emigrant stream in the pre-Famine era, when a combination of economic depression and structural changes 'squeezed' much of the commercial and industrial 'middling' classes out of Ireland.[69] Indeed, most Irish Catholics who in the United States became nationally noteworthy during the 1800s were drawn from this relatively small caste, from prelates through publishers and writers to business tycoons.[70] During the same century, many — perhaps most — Irish Protestants, Presbyterian or Anglican, also carried attitudes more attuned to capitalist endeavours, which perhaps helped to underscore their separation in America from the Catholic majority. It is symptomatic that William McGuffey, schoolmaster *par excellence* to America's businesslike Victorian consensus, was an offspring of the late eighteenth-century Ulster Protestant emigration, whereas Irish Catholic parents were known to discourage Catholic schools from hiring teachers direct from Ireland, since they were unaccustomed to the demands of American life.[71]

Sampling the detailed evidence of such different attitudes in thousands of emigrant letters and memoirs illuminates the arguments made above. First, with regard to the

69 See Chapter 2 in this volume; also, Miller, *Emigrants and Exiles*, 169–279.

70 e.g., see: Samuel J. Miller, 'Peter Richard Kenrick', *Records of the American Catholic Historical Society*, 84 (1973), 3–4; Stephen Birmingham, *Real Lace: America's Irish Rich* (New York, 1973), 75–77, 138; Clifford Lewis and John D. Kernan, eds., *Devereux of the Leap, County Wexford, Ireland, and of Utica, New York: Nicholas Devereux, 1791–1855* (St. Bonaventure, NY, 1974); Alice C. Cochran, *The Descendants of John Mullanphy* (New York, 1976), 12–16; Earl F. Niehaus, *The Irish in New Orleans, 1800–1860* (Baton Rouge, La., 1965), 10–11, 40–41; Katherine E. Conway, *Charles Francis Donnelly: A Memoir* (New York, 1909), 5–10; James Jeffrey Roche, *Life of John Boyle O'Reilly* (Boston, 1891), 1–7; and *Dictionary of American Biography* (New York, 1960 edn.), vol. 7, pt. 1, 18, 131, 189, 318, 352, 608, 612–13; vol. 7, pt. 2, 52–53; and vol. 8, pt. 2, 262–64, 283–84, for material on the Sadliers, John Murphy, E. Bailey O'Callaghan, Fitz-James O'Brien, and John Boyle O'Reilly (writers, publishers), on Patrick Moriarty, OSA, James and Michael O'Connor, J. B. Purcell, Edward G. Ryan and Patrick Ryan (Churchmen), and on Henry O'Reilly and St. Clair Mulholland (businessman and general). The pattern is dramatic enough to warrant further study.

71 John H. Westerhoff, *McGuffey and His Readers: Piety, Morality, and Education in 19th-Century America* (Nashville, 1978), ch. 1; Howard R. Weisz, *Irish-American and Italian-American Educational Views and Activities: A Comparison* (New York, 1976), 33–34. On Irish Protestant attitudes on socio-economic issues in the early and mid-nineteenth century, see below, Chapters 2 (generally), 8 and 10 (Ulster Presbyterians) and 11 (southern Anglicans).

Protestant Irish, both Anglican and Dissenting, northern and southern. The insistence with which most of them emphasized the motive of *personal* economic betterment as the cause both of disenchantment with Ireland and of assessing America, sets them apart. Familial and localist loyalties are far from absent, but they are relatively quite subordinate. As John King wrote from Pittsburgh to County Antrim in 1832, 'In Ireland, unless a young man has Capital, or Connections able to assist him, and I may add *willing* to do so, he may toil all his life and never find an independent feeling occupy his breast', whereas in America, 'if a man is industrious, and saving[,] he will Eventually Succeed'. Nathaniel Corrothers from Fermanagh wrote from Upper Canada (now Ontario) to Lisbellaw in 1853 that he and his fellows hoped to better 'their condishon by Coming to america far beyont what it was posible for them to have done had the[y] stoped in Ireland'. Southern Irish Protestants wrote likewise: William Radcliff wrote from Adelaide, also in Upper Canada, to his brother in Dublin in 1832 that he quelled his homesickness by looking at his rent-free land, 'and I ask myself, if I were back again, how could I command such certain *independence*'. William Lyster, an Anglican minister from County Wexford, moved his family to Michigan in the 1830s, since 'our own & posterity's attainment of a useful & comfortable, perhaps affluent independence ... is to be found in perfection in America'. For Quaker emigrant Samuel Fogarty from Limerick, 'gaining an independence' meant the chance to improve 'my mind, manners, and conduct' among strangers. Revealingly, in their assessment of America for prospective migrants, not desire for family reconstitution or fraternal obligation, but the advice of one individual to another was the hallmark of their letters. In times of recession, drawbacks to personal advancement were strongly emphasized: not atypical was the letter a textile weaver in upstate New York wrote to his father in County Antrim, enjoining the latter, 'dont Give anyone Letters of recommendation to me ... [L]et them push their fortune as I have done.' Such emigrants might at times appear to confess a poignant homesickness, but usually it was tightly controlled by calculated self-interest.[72]

There were Anglicized Catholics from the market towns, from better-off farm families, and generally from Leinster who regarded emigration in not dissimilar ways. To the

72 John King, Pittsburgh, to Robert Nevin, Carnduff, Dervock, County Antrim, 1 September 1832 (King Family Papers, Illinois State Historical Society, Springfield). Nathaniel Carrothers, Westminster, Upper Canada, to William Carrothers, Farnagh, Lisbellaw, County Fermanagh, 5 December 1853 (Schrier collection); Upper Canada was officially known as Canada West after 1840, but the earlier name continued in popular usage; the province became Ontario with Canadian Confederation in 1867. William Radcliff, Adelaide, Upper Canada, to Arthur Radcliff, Dublin, December 1832, in Thomas William McGrath, *Authentic Letters from Upper Canada* (Dublin, 1833; repr. Toronto, 1953), 110; William N. Lyster, [Cleveland, Ohio?], to Armstrong Lyster, Sion Hill, County Wexford, 4 July 1839 (W. N. Lyster Papers, Michigan Historical Collections, University of Michigan, Ann Arbor); Samuel N. Fogarty, New York City, to Joseph Fogarty, Limerick, 4 March 1839 (Schrier collection); John McBride, Watertown, NY, to James McBride, Derriaghy, County Antrim, 9 January 1820 and 24 February 1822 (T.2613, PRONI). For homesickness, see William N. Lyster, Eyry Forest, Springville, Mich., to his father, Sion Hill, County Wexford, July–September 1841 (W. N. Lyster Papers); and Samuel Buchanan, Maysville, Ala., to Augusta Buchanan, Dublin, n.d. [1870s] (Box PC 431, NLI; also in Schrier collection).

well-educated, like Robert Elliott, Michael McDermott, and Richard O'Gorman, America meant a chance to pursue their professions with greater reward and less hindrance (from prejudice or established competition) than at home.[73] To William Lalor, son of a wealthy grazier from Queen's County, 'independence' meant an escape from parental authority. Gerald Griffin, a prosperous tenant in County Limerick, tried to arrange to settle some of his twelve children with a nephew in Pennsylvania, a task found more urgent by his widow Annie in 1826; for them, too, America meant 'independence' for those ambitious but unestablished in Ireland.[74]

However, the majority of Catholics derived from a culture that meant that even a fortunate emigration and a secure calculation often proved an inadequate basis for personal happiness. Unfortunately, letters in Irish from Irish-speaking emigrants are lacking, with one major exception, that of poet Pádraig Cúndún, and a few strays. Nonetheless, these and other forms of evidence suggest the great difficulty those of Gaelic culture often had in adjusting to individualized, or even family, migration. Moreover, many of the English-language letters evincing similar disorientation are by emigrants from zones of recent socio-cultural and linguistic transition, areas in which old familial and traditionalist forms of personality were deeply rooted: such as mid- and south Ulster, south Waterford, south Kilkenny, Carlow, and east Connacht. Before 1860 many migrants from such areas, and from Munster generally, were almost wholly traditionalist in outlook and thereafter largely so. From the 1870s, as these areas became more Anglicized and emigration more prosaic, the tide of emigration began to flow heavily from more western areas still, and arguably young emigrants from west Connacht, west Munster, and Donegal faced even more poignant dilemmas, given the greater rationalization and (as returned emigrants often decried) ruthless competitiveness of industrial America. Certainly, few Irish-speaking migrants appear to have adjusted as successfully to factory America after 1870 as Cúndún did to farm America in the 1830s.[75]

73 Michael McDermott, 'Recollections and Memories by Michl McDermott, Civil Engineer and Surveyor [of] Chicago', c. 1884 (Ms. 2–15–1000, Library of Congress); 'Memoir of the Late Honorable Richard Robert Elliott', Michigan Historical and Pioneer Collections, 37 (1909), 644; Helen F. Mulvey, ed., 'New York City in 1859: A Letter to William Smith O'Brien [from Richard O'Gorman, New York City]', New York History, 34 (1943), 85–90; on O'Gorman, see this volume, Chapter 12.

74 William Lalor, Lima, Ind., to Patrick Lalor, Tinakill, Abbeyleix, Queen's County, 12 May 1834 (Ms. 8567, NLI). Gerald Griffin, Corgrigg, County Limerick, to James Griffin, Silverlake, Susquehanna Co., Pa., 24 November 1825 and 29 January 1826; Annie Griffin, Corgrigg, to same, 4 August 1826 (Lewis Neale Whittle Papers, Georgia State Archives, Atlanta); these were kin of novelist Gerald Griffin, whose own father emigrated: see Ethel Mannin, Two Studies in Integrity: Gerald Griffin and the Rev. Francis Mahony ('Father Prout') (London, 1954), 76–78, 97. On the varying connotations of 'independence' in pre-Famine Ireland, see Chapter 2 below.

75 David N. Doyle, 'Unestablished Irishmen: New Immigrants and Industrial America, 1870–1910', in Dirk Hoerder, ed., American Labor and Immigration History, 1877–1920s: Recent European Research (Urbana, Ill., 1983), 193–220. And see Chapter 14 in this volume.

Prior to the Famine, both Irish and foreign observers often remarked on what they regarded as the peasantry's 'irrational' aversion to transatlantic migration. As one Catholic immigrant from mid-Tyrone put it in 1818, describing his reluctant countrymen, 'if the[y] would only bild A New End to thire house the[y] Could not find from thire heart to lave it'. Or as Cúndún wrote, 'the poor senseless Irishman [will] stay behind forever until he's broken, and then he won't have anything' — that is, no capital left to emigrate or recommence life in America. In the highly coloured, semi-messianic mentality that pervaded these areas in the era of Wildgoose Lodge, O'Connell, and the tithe troubles, not rational planning but a sense of doom (and this before the Famine) was an impelling factor in migration: as Edward Toner warned his fellows in 1819, 'there is a Disolation Aproching to … Ireland. … [T]hire time is nerely At an End.'[76]

For many poor Catholics who did emigrate, then and later, adjustment was often difficult and sometimes quite painful. James Mitchell from Ahascragh, County Galway, memorialized his leave-taking in a special account, noting of his last days at home: 'every object that met my gaze filled me with sorrow'. Although Cúndún upbraided himself in retrospect for the reluctance with which he had left east Cork around 1826, given his later success as a farmer near Utica, New York, he was at bottom unhappy with America, which he described poetically as a land of back-breaking toil, peopled by 'a malicious host' who were 'treacherous, lying, vicious, [and] lewd', and infested by 'Wild animals growling defiance, and poisonous snakes slithering in venom'. Cúndún even attributed his declining literary skills to the 'depressing and harassing nature of the frightful, restless life I have here, which has made a chaos of my mind'; even 'if I owned America,' he concluded, 'there's no place I know of under the sun I'd rather die than in Ireland'.[77] 'Every one who comes here,' wrote T. W. Magrath from Erindale, Upper Canada, in 1832, 'feels at the outset the difficulties … [and] laments the loneliness of his situation, and experiences a sinking of the heart, and a longing after potatoes and buttermilk at home.' Anastasia Dowling wrote from Buffalo home to Sleaty, County Carlow, in 1870 most simply: 'I feel very lonesome here [because] the ways of this place is so different from

---

76 Edward Toner, Unity Township, Westmoreland Co., Pa., to Peter Toner, Knockavaddy, c. Pomeroy, County Tyrone, 21 January 1819 (Ms. 2300, NLI); full text of Toner's letter in Kerby A. Miller, Arnold Schrier, Bruce D. Boling and David Noel Doyle, *Irish Immigrants in the Land of Canaan: Letters and Memoirs from Colonial and Revolutionary America, 1675–1815* (New York, 2003), 228–33. Pádraig Cúndún, Deerfield, Utica, NY, to Partolán Suipéal, Cluain Aird, County Cork, 17 December 1834, in Risteárd Ó Foghludha, ed., *Pádraig Phiarais Cúndún, 1777–1856* (Baile Átha Cliath, 1932), 24–30 (trans. Bruce D. Boling). Wildgoose Lodge, at Corcreagh, County Louth, was in 1816 the site of an infamous 'agrarian outrage' that became emblematic of the violence that often convulsed pre-Famine Ireland — and of the government's capacity for equally savage repression; on this incident, see Raymond Murray, *The Burning of Wildgoose Lodge* (Armagh, 2005).

77 James J. Mitchell, 'A Journal Kept by Jas J Mitchell, Commenced on Leaving Ahascragh, Co. Galway, Ireland, For the United States of America, March 16, 1853' (Ms. in New-York Historical Society, New York City); Pádraig Cúndún, poem [1834], and letter to Partolán Suipéal, 17 December 1834, in Ó Foghludha, *Pádraig Phiarais Cúndún*, 30, 40–44 (trans. Bruce D. Boling).

home.'[78] For some, the change was dramatic: 'Dear Aunt,' wrote another emigrant to his kinsmen in County Sligo, 'this country is not what I thought it was. ... I am sorry now I ever came.' 'In the new country,' lamented Maurice Woulfe from County Limerick, 'a man's mind changes a good deal'; 'A man cant depend on any friend ... however near in Kin'; and the cities were 'the most wicked places[s] I ever saw for Cursing Blasphemy and other immoral habits'. Little wonder that to him 'Every stone gap and field in Cratloe and its surroundings are as clear in my mind as when I left home', although admittedly in America he had 'everything that would tend to make life comfortable'. Bartholomew Colgan, who like Woulfe went to America's Far West in the 1860s, likewise '[i]n all my travels ... never seen the place that I would say hear is a place that I would like to live and contently die'.[79]

Less direct but also persuasive evidence of such attitudes are the migration ballads of this period. As Georges-Denis Zimmerman and Colm Ó Lochlainn have argued, the broadside ballads were the principal artefact and expression of a culture retaining Gaelic attitudes, albeit transferring them into semi-Anglicized rural culture. Unoriginal, often poorly rhymed and mawkishly sentimental, yet their great numbers and immense popularity show that they accurately reflected at least the conventional Irish emotions about emigration. That they flourished on both sides of the Atlantic, and proved so consonant with personal letters, suggests that those ballads of the 'Poor Pat Must Emigrate' type constitute both a category of evidence and yet also themselves a fact of cultural history: they helped to fix popular preconceptions about migration and thereby to slow down the transition from a communal mentality, damaged by the demands of personal self-advancement in a harsh new world, to a more individualist one in which such motivations were 'natural' or at least acceptable. A careful recent work establishes the provenance of most of these ballads in the 1830s to 1870s, a period (spanning the Famine) when change throughout Ireland was especially profound and traumatic.[80]

Insofar as migration before the 1870s came from a transitional Ireland to a still fluid America, the newcomers' objective experiences, often ones of at least incremental

78 T. W. Magrath, Erindale, Upper Canada [Ontario], to Rev. Thomas Radcliff, Dublin, January 1832, in Magrath, *Authentic Letters*, 64; Anastasia Dowling, Buffalo, NY, to Thomas and Mrs. Dunny, Sleaty, County Carlow, 20 January 1870 (Schrier collection).

79 Charles Mullen, Brooklyn, NY, to his uncle and aunt, [County Sligo?], 28 December 1883 (T.1866/9, PRONI). Maurice H. Woulfe, Washington, DC, to his uncle, Cratloe, County Limerick, 25 September 1863 and 19 November 1863; same, Fort Sedgwick, Colorado Terr., to same, 12 May 1867; and same, 26 January 1870 (Woulfe family letters; see n. 8 above). Bartholomew Colgan, Carson City, Nevada Terr., to Thomas Dunny, Sleaty, County Carlow, 13 June 1862 (Schrier collection). For similar sentiments, see: George Crosby, Boston Navy Yard, Mass., to Bridget Crosby, Aggardbeg, Croughwell, County Galway, 28 March 1848 (Ms. 3549, NLI); and Annie Heggarty, Ottumwa, Iowa, to Michael and Mrs. McFadden, Kilcar, County Donegal, 19 July 1884 (Schrier collection).

80 Zimmermann, *Irish Political Street Ballads*, and Colm Ó Lochlainn, *Irish Street Ballads*, 2nd edn. (Dublin, 1963), argue this transmission thesis in their introductions; for emigrant balladry provenance, see Wright, *Irish Emigrant Ballads*, 107–14, 205–06, 331–38, 429–33, 485–90, and 697–712; a less scholarly collection is James N. Healy, *Old Irish Street Ballads, 4: No Place Like Home* (Cork, 1969).

improvement, usually if gradually eased the burden of their subjective preconceptions. Many migrants' letters show themselves aware of their own changing circumstances and attitudes, although for many — like Cúndún and Woulfe — the transformation would never be complete. However, for emigrants from the more immediately Gaelic and post-Gaelic western districts, coming in such large numbers from the late 1870s on, actual experience of America, far more industrialized than earlier, was often the counterpart in economic reality of the socio-cultural disorientation they suffered with peculiar force. Damian Hannan and others have shown how skilfully West-of-Ireland society fended off the full implications of an 'open market' farm economy, by creating instead a buffer-culture that minimized dependence on outside cash networks, protected the family farm through selective migration, and preserved a measure of social cohesion (and even early marriage) from the 1870s into the early 1900s.[81] Yet the region's relative success in resisting the competitive and individualizing realities of the rest of Ireland meant that its emigrants were cast directly into a society where their parents' constructive engagement was impossible — and their residual values all the more poignant in their contradictions with American norms. This was the case although many of the migrants could scarcely leave fast enough the material deprivation of these regions, so much of which was classified as formally impoverished by the Congested Districts Board.[82]

From the late 1870s through the 1920s, so many emigrants left the western counties, from west Cork north through Connacht to Donegal, it is likely that at least half of them were Irish-speakers or the children of Irish-speakers (a proportion perhaps equalled only during the Great Famine). The results for Irish America were profound, although often highly localized and otherwise 'hidden' by the overall ethnic community's stratification and by its social and numerical dominance, respectively, by the successful and, after 1880, by the American-born.[83] The evidence of western emigrants' responses are few but compelling. In 1902 an unknown Irish-speaker from County Clare wrote to a friend in Boston from his home (perhaps a Massachusetts mill town?) that he was 'depressed by this rotten, lonely, starving place. Muck and shit and dung all around and poverty and piety vying with one another (Pluide is cac is aoileach ar go h-aon taobh diom, is bochtanacht is cráibheacht a crádh le an ceile)'. Likewise, Séamus Ó Muircheartaigh wrote of his experiences, 'Alas, when I landed / I made for the city without delay; / But I never saw gold on the street corners / Alas, I was a poor aimless person cast adrift (Foraoir, bhios im stroille bocht caithe ar an bhfan)'. Seán Ruiséal, also from west Kerry, lamented similarly that through all his journeys in America, he 'never saw a place like the village / I left at the break of day'. Michael MacGowan from west Donegal described his fellow Irish-speakers in Chicago as spending 'two-thirds of the day nostalgically recalling to themselves the

---

81 See Chapter 5 in this volume.

82 S. H. Cousens, 'Regional Variation in Population Changes in Ireland, 1861–1881', *Economic History Review*, 17 (1964–65), 301–21; Hannan, *Displacement and Development*, 27–67; Miller, *Emigrants and Exiles*, tables 2–10, pp. 570–80.

83 Miller, *Emigrants and Exiles*, 297, 349–53, and the tables cited in n. 82 above.

places where they first saw the light'. Cathy Greene, from the recently Anglicized Callan area of County Kilkenny, wrote from Brooklyn in 1884 of her loneliness: 'I am heart sick fretting. I cannot sleep the night ... I feel as if I'm dead to the world.' Acute homesickness both fed upon and could feed alienation from America. In 1897 James McFadden wrote home from Iowa to Kilcar in Donegal that life in the United States was 'the same as in Ireland': 'every year something new Comes up to make the rich man richer and the poor man poorer'; while Eoin Ua Cathail wrote from Michigan in 1902 that work was heavy and pay small, and 'if you knew this country, it would be better for you to stay where there is neither cold nor heat'.[84] Unsurprisingly, Martin Waters and Liam Ó Dochartaigh have separately discovered the origins of the Philo-Celtic and the Gaelic Leagues in the United States among disenchanted emigrants of this period. Likewise, Sam Bass Warner established that recent Irish emigrants concentrated in more compact neighbourhoods in the early twentieth century than did their predecessors in the mid-nineteenth. Thus there were concrete reactions against the new America as well as complaining letters.[85]

Just as ballads underscored the preconceptions of migration among English-speakers, so the rituals of the 'American wake' burned the emotional sundering of the parting into those who left Gaelic and post-Gaelic areas. In the West of Ireland these remained 'harrowing affairs'. Arguably, these stereotyped events, exhaustively described in the folklore collections, were almost purposely designed both to formalize otherwise unendurable emotion and also to impress a deep and lasting sense of grief, obligation, and even guilt upon the departing emigrants. They constituted a final, intensive exposure to the values of the culture and ensured that remittances and pre-paid passages sent from America would be linked with indelible filial memory. They also carried strong connotations of inexorable fate, as too did the written memoirs of Blasket Islanders and others about migration, thus helping both to vindicate neighbourly pressures on 'idle' youths to go abroad and to assuage any misgiving children might feel at leaving aged parents. Otherwise, the traumas of the American wakes were too great, as in the keen

84 Seághan ar Fán [pseud.], n.p., to Michael?, 25 December 1902 (original in possession of Dr. Kenneth Nilsen, then in Cambridge, Mass., now at St. Francis Xavier University, Antigonish, Nova Scotia); Séamus Ó Muircheartaigh's and Seán Ruiséal's poems (both probably written in — or from experiences in — Butte, Montana, c. 1900), in Seán Ó Dubhda, OS, ed., Duanaire Duibhneach (Baile Átha Cliath, 1933), 130–33 (trans. Bruce D. Boling); MacGowan, Hard Road to Klondike, 138; Cathy Greene, Brooklyn, NY, to her mother, Ballylarkin, Callan, County Kilkenny, 1 August 1884 (Greene/Norris Family Papers, Archives Department, University College, Dublin); in her letter Greene wrote 'hearth' instead of 'heart'. James McFadden, Battle Creek, Iowa, to Michael McFadden, Kilcar, County Donegal, 17 October 1897 (Schrier collection); Eoin Ua Cathail, Pentwater, Mich., to editor, An Claidheamh Soluis, 4 (26 April 1902), 124–25 (trans. Bruce D. Boling).
85 Martin Waters, 'Peasants and Emigrants: The Social Origins of the Gaelic League', in Casey and Rhodes, Views of the Irish Peasantry, 150–77; Liam Ó Dochartaigh, 'Nótaí ar Ghluaiseacht na Gaeilge i Meiriceá, 1872–1891', Breandán Ó Buachalla, 'An Gaodhal i Meiriceá', and Breandán Ó Conaire, 'Pádraig Ó Beirn: Fear a d'Fhill', all in Ó hAnnracháin, Go Meiriceá Siar, 65–90, 38–56, and 111–24; Sam Bass Warner and Colin Burke, 'Cultural Change and the Ghetto', Journal of Contemporary History, 4 (1969), 173–87; and MacGowan, Hard Road to Klondike, 75–76, 121–22, for later clustering.

recorded by Fr. Patrick Dinneen of a west Kerry mother about to lose a beloved child: 'Alas, my destruction ... / Will you leave me alone behind you / With death calling me every day of my life?' Yet these occasions re-impressed political and religious messages as well: the songs sung at the American wakes often reiterated that emigration was ultimately caused by British misgovernment, landlord tyranny, and even religious persecution — and this a century after the Penal Laws had been repealed — thus also relieving responsibilities, obscuring personal volition and material calculation.[86]

These emotions were all far removed from any realistic preparation for life in industrial America. These later migrants, usually destined for unskilled and non-unionized labour, rarely or minimally benefited from Irish America's overall gains in the years following the American Civil War of 1861–65; and their emphasis upon passivity and fate may have tended to cause them to adopt a certain fatalism in the face of the manipulations wreaked on them by an expanding but highly unstable economy — and by a society where, as returned emigrants complained, 'it was a case of "every man for himself"', and where those who faltered 'got it in the neck'.[87] Theirs may have been a realistic view, but it may also have diminished the range of their possible responses. In 1849 John Griffin in County Clare (where the Famine's latter years were worse than those preceding) had worried that intending emigrants from his neighbourhood, the great majority of them Irish-speakers, 'cannot be made to understand that their own hands must build their fortune ... [T]he great misfortune with our countrymen is that they are willing to depend on any one but themselves, and want in sup[e]rlative degree the virtue of *Self reliance*.'[88] Griffin was unusually well-educated, from an affluent, Anglicized family of Limerick graziers, and himself a Protestant convert yet also sympathetic to Young Ireland; his observation was typically bourgeois, but, like those cited earlier, it reflected the gap between cultures as well as classes. And, by the 1880s, the 'virtue of Self reliance' might well have been only partly helpful, and that to a minority of newcomers.

Of course, at all times there were those who were definitely glad to leave Ireland and therefore predisposed to enjoy or at least acquiesce in the different life offered in America. As marriage patterns in Ireland changed towards low rates and late ages, especially in the East and South, young women often went readily. Even for those with decent prospects at home, the dowry system and the prospects of drudgery in their own families or in hired service prompted many to seek 'love and liberty' in America, as Mary

86 Keen in Pádraig Ua Duinnin, *Muinntear Chiarraidhe roimh an Drochsaoghal* (Baile Átha Cliath, 1905), 55–56 (trans. by Bruce D. Boling). On the American wakes, generally, see: Mss. 1407–1411, Archives, Department of Irish Folklore, University College, Dublin (hereafter DIF/UCD); Mary Carbery, *The Farm by Lough Gur* (1937; repr. Cork, 1973), 44; Schrier, *Ireland and the American Emigration*, 84–94; and Miller, *Emigrants and Exiles*, 556–68.
87 Miller, *Emigrants and Exiles*, 509.
88 John Griffin, Kilkee, County Clare, to Mary Griffin, Columbus, Ga., 22 June 1849 (Lewis Neale Whittle Papers, Georgia State Archives, Atlanta).

Brown from County Wexford put it.[89] Likewise, and concurring with findings about the growth of en masse migration among farm labourers after 1860, as relations between rural classes became monetarized and estranged, many labourers were glad to be gone: 'sooner than I would work for a farmer in Ireland, I would cut off my good right hand,' wrote J. F. Costello in 1883, a bitterness corroborated in the journal of Clan na Gael member Timothy Cashman, an Irish-speaking farm labourer from east Cork, and by Monsignor Buckley, who was at first surprised by it but eventually recognized its inevitable logic. And there were also those who fled absolute destitution, both during the Famine years and also under the aegis of various removal schemes, such as James Hack Tuke's for Arranmore, Belmullet, and Connemara in the 1880s. Yet even in these cases initial relief did not always ensure successful adjustment, economic or cultural, as Bishop Ireland complained (often unfairly) of assisted Irish-speakers who settled in Minnesota and whose alleged 'fecklessness' embarrassed him and other members of Irish Catholic Minnesota's nascent bourgeoisie.[90] Likewise, 'love and liberty' often proved elusive for young Irishwomen who were ill-prepared for the demands of Victorian domesticity, and much evidence suggests that non-inheriting sons expelled from 'comfortable' farms often had great psychological difficulties in adjusting to the loss of status and the harsh, unaccustomed work regimen experienced in America. In response, emigrants from both groups often expressed acute homesickness and disillusionment in their letters, falling back on traditional categories to 'explain' thwarted ambitions in terms of involuntary exile.[91]

In conclusion, these patterns can be linked to the history of Irish-American nationalism. Studies of the actual supporters of nationalist movements suggest that such support, particularly for radical groups, was drawn disproportionately from newer (and poorer) immigrants, and more especially, and unsurprisingly, among those from the Southwest and West of Ireland: the heartland of radical nationalism at home and the source of an

89 Mary Brown, New York City, to Mary Brown, Tomhaggard, County Wexford, 11 March 1858 and quoted in
   20 January 1859 (Schrier collection; originals in Ms. 1408, DIF/UCD); Connell, *Irish Peasant Society*, 113–61,
   but contrast Edward E. McKenna, 'Age, Region, and Marriage in Post-Famine Ireland', in *Economic History
   Review*, 31 (1978), 238–56; and particularly Lynn H. Lees and John Modell, 'The Irishman Urbanized: A
   Comparative Perspective on the Famine Migration', *Journal of Urban History*, 3, 4 (August 1977), 391–408,
   for comparative evidence of higher marriage rates among the Irish in Philadelphia and London than in
   Ireland. Also see Chapter 13 in this volume.
90 J. F. Costello, White River Valley, Washington Terr., to his parents, Croagh, County Limerick, 11 January
   1883 (Schrier collection); Timothy Cashman, Memoirs (courtesy of Timothy D. Cashman, San Francisco,
   and Patrick J. Clancy, Youghal, County Cork); Buckley, *Diary of a Tour*, 170, 241; assisted emigrants' letters
   (early 1880s) in James Hack Tuke, *Reports and Papers Relating to the Proceedings of the Committee of 'Mr. Tuke's
   Fund' for Assisting Emigration from Ireland during ... 1882, 1883, and 1884* (Dublin, 1883), 150–62, 223–28 (copy
   in NLI). On Bishop Ireland and his relationships with the assisted colonists from Connacht, see: James P.
   Shannon, *Catholic Colonization on the Western Frontier* (New Haven, Conn., 1957), and, more critically, Bridget
   Connelly, *Forgetting Ireland: Uncovering a Family's Secret History* (St. Paul, Minn., 2003).
91 Miller, *Emigrants and Exiles*, 512–18; on Irish female emigrants in America and on post-Famine emigrants,
   generally, see Chapters 13 and 14, respectively, in this volume.

alienating mentality among those who settled in America.[92] Marginal and under severe pressure in Ireland (as also, for different reasons, were Catholics in Ulster and in urban Ireland's lower working-class neighborhoods), the western Irish were likewise under similar pressures in industrial America. Irish-American nationalist rhetoric exploited, explained, justified, politicized, and even ennobled the sentiments imported — and the disorientation suffered — by those whose outlooks had been nurtured in a context of *dúchas* (familiarity of place and face), pained by emigration, and sharpened amid the hardships of mine, factory, or warehouse. A pre-capitalist and fatalistic view of all reality focused upon England as the master-key to displacement, to failed expectations, and to social subordination in America. Irish-American nationalists, whose own project generally required the obscuring of intragroup conflicts in Ireland and America alike, sought in turn to 'remind' the emigrants of their 'duty' to Ireland: one often couched in familial terms. Mothers' tears, fathers' graves, siblings' sufferings, emigrants' alleged ingratitude, landlords' oppressions, broken homes, and British tyranny were such orators' stock-in-trade. Freeing Ireland, declared one writer, 'is a debt we owe to nature and nature's God, and until it is discharged, all who call themselves Irishmen ... cannot be at peace'.[93] For the miners of Woods' Run and Scranton, for the mill workers of Pittsburgh, the car men of Chicago, or the teamsters of Boston, such rhetoric acted as a catalyst on anxieties rooted in their youthful departures from Mayo, Clare, or Cork. Working against time, for all youthful emotional commitments dwindle unless fed in the stream of changing circumstance, it was perhaps fortunate that Irish-American nationalist leaders could mobilize such widespread loyalty before the decline of emigration and the ageing of emigrants cut away their sources of support. 'Mother Ireland' never again had so many 'exiled children' abroad to give credibility to her cause as in 1890, and in 1916–21 their numbers and their memories were still potent. Not merely exiles like John Devoy and Joseph McGarrity, or returnees like Batt O'Connor and Thomas Clarke, but domestic rebel leaders like James Connolly and Patrick Pearse were deeply influenced by the collective emotion here described.[94]

And these reactions were not unique to the Irish diaspora. Indeed, there are significant parallels between the estrangement from American capitalist modernity — from its

92 e.g., see W. J. Bennett, 'Iron Workers in Woods Run and Johnstown: The Union Era, 1865–1895' (PhD diss., University of Pittsburgh, 1977); and Victor A. Walsh, 'Across "The Big Wather": Irish Community Life in Pittsburgh and Allegheny City, 1850–1885 (PhD diss., University of Pittsburgh, 1983).

93 Hibernicus, *Address to the Irish and Their Descendants in the United States and the British Provinces, October 1848* (Columbia, SC, 1848), 12, 20. On the nationalism of recent Irish-speaking migrants, see Miller, *Emigrants and Exiles*, 552–55.

94 John Devoy, *Recollections of an Irish Rebel* (New York, 1929), *passim*; Marie Veronica Tarpey, *The Role of Joseph McGarrity in the Struggle for Irish Independence* (New York, 1976), 19–64; Batt O'Connor, *With Michael Collins in the Fight for Irish Independence* (London, 1929), 14–16; Louis N. LeRoux, *Tom Clarke and the Irish Freedom Movement* (Dublin, 1936), 17–25, 55–73; Carl Reeve and Ann Barton Reeve, *James Connolly and the United States: The Road to the 1916 Irish Rebellion* (Atlantic Highlands, NJ, 1978), *passim*; Ruth Dudley Edwards, *Patrick Pearse: The Triumph of Failure* (London, 1977), 184–97.

harshly competitive, materialist, and individualized aspects — expressed by several thousand forgotten Irish letter-writers and the deepest criticisms of American life made by foreign commentators and by indigenous intellectuals throughout the nineteenth and early twentieth centuries. This might suggest that while the immigrant Irish were sometimes at odds with the new urban-industrial society — perhaps even 'inadequate' to it, from a business or Rotary club perspective — conversely that society was often inadequate to those with deeper and more traditional notions of humanity, as Oliver Wendell Holmes recognized in his close friendship with west Cork's leading fictional historian of his people, Canon Patrick A. Sheehan.[95] Although one authority has suggested that the exile identity runs deeply within the character of all Americans, nonetheless, and despite their shared commitment to idealism, Holmes as the co-founder of legal realism, of the social-functional approach to jurisprudence, could not really understand the Cork priest's cultural and religious perspectives — nor, one suspects, those of the ordinary Irish in his own Boston. For Sheehan and his parishioners, at home and abroad, Catholicism (like Irish nationalism) both confirmed and transcended the sense of exile, as in the version of the Salve Regina favoured in the south Ulster oral tradition: 'Is Orsta a sgairteamuid ...': 'It is on you we cry, poor exiled descendants of Eve ... and when our banishment in this life is finished, show to us the blessed fruit of thy womb, Jesus.'[96]

Thus, scholars such as Robert Burchell are very wide of the mark in their neo-Manchester School assertions that Irish contentment abroad was simply a function of material status, with culture (including Catholicism) merely a differentiating or communalizing element, in a general urban experience, that gathered the Irish into a superficially distinct ethno-religious community.[97] Instead, it is argued here, there was a certain 'Irishness' — a fusion of traditional culture with the explicit exigencies of family, Church, and nationalism — that prevented such a precise and easy accommodation, instead qualifying or delaying eventual resolution. Was that traditional outlook, expressed in the exile motif and reified by both Irish and American experience, in any way 'disabling' for the emigrants, personally or collectively? Some of their own letters and memoirs suggested so, as did the strictures of middle-class observers, American Protestants and Irish-American Catholics alike. However, the question assumes that the American form of hyper-capitalism, in both its domestic and imperial aspects, is the norm that should shape culture and personality, and therefore all deviations are ideally as well as practically 'marginal' or 'dysfunctional'. On the one hand, it is possible that some aspects of a traditional Irish worldview — patience, fatalism, 'clannishness' — allowed many emigrants to acquiesce in, and adapt too easily

95 David H. Burton, 'The Friendship of Justice Holmes and Canon Sheehan', Harvard Library Bulletin, 25 (1977), 155–69.
96 Robin Winks, 'The American as Exile', in Doyle and Edwards, America and Ireland, 1776–1976, 43–56; Tomás S. Mac Cionnaith, coll., An Paidirín Páirteach agus Urnaighte eile in gCanamhain Bhreifne (An Cabhán, 1921), 8.
97 R. A. Burchell, The San Francisco Irish, 1848–1880 (Berkeley, Calif., 1979), 15, 52–53, 155–78.

to, American capitalism's structural inequities and personal injustices. Yet it is also arguable that the Irish outlook, especially as it was hardened by American experience and formalized (however expediently) by many Irish-American institutions, perpetuated and heightened an 'outsider's' critical perspective in ways that often found expression in labour radicalism, in the urban liberalism described by historian John Buenker, and in the forms of Catholic social action and Irish-American nationalism that challenged the social hierarchies as well as the foreign-policy preferences of American Protestant élites.[98] Irish 'alienation', in other words, implied a moral (and potentially political) point of view that could be perfectly 'rational' and justifiable. And to the degree that the traditional Irish worldview and the exile motif fostered such perspectives, they not only helped ensure the survival of a distinctive, albeit conflicted, communal identity in the United States, but they also promoted the achievement of at least partial independence for Ireland — no mean accomplishment for impoverished 'exiles' whose nationalist efforts generally faced native-American disapproval as well as the might of the globe's most powerful empire.[99]

98 John D. Buenker, *Urban Liberalism and Progressive Reform* (New York, 1973).
99 In this volume, native-born American Protestants are often designated as 'native Americans' (or, as in this instance, 'native-American'). Unfortunately, therefore, to avoid possible confusion it has been necessary to designate the 'original' inhabitants of the US by the old and inaccurate term 'Indians', rather than as 'Native Americans'. Only in Chapter 15 is the term 'Native American' occasionally employed, as in the 'Native American civil rights movement' of the late twentieth century, as a synonym for 'Indians'.

2 Emigration and Society in Pre-Famine Ireland

Mass transatlantic migration from Ireland long preceded the Great Famine.[1] During the 1600s at least 25,000 Irish Catholics were transported, often involuntarily, to North America, principally to the Caribbean and the Chesapeake region. In the 1680s Irish Quakers and other Protestant Dissenters began migrating to the mainland colonies, and in the 1710s large-scale Presbyterian emigration — first to New England, later to Pennsylvania and the Carolinas — became a permanent feature of Ulster society. During the 1700s also there were smaller but significant migrations of Irish Catholics and Anglicans overseas, both from Ulster (where they were largely 'hidden' in the Presbyterian exodus) and from southern Ireland. In addition, there were seasonal migrations of some 3,000 to 5,000 Catholics per year from Waterford to Newfoundland, where a minority settled or moved on to the mainland. Finally, departures soared after the Napoleonic Wars ended in 1814–15, and during the three decades between Waterloo and the Famine's eve at least 800,000 and perhaps 1 million Irish crossed the Atlantic.[2]

In all, between about 1750 and 1844 — that is, during the century preceding the Great Famine — as many as 1.5 million men and women left Ireland for North America. During the 1700s most emigrants were Protestants, and about two-thirds were Presbyterians

1   This chapter is a revised version of a paper delivered at the American Historical Association's national conference, held in New York City in late December 1979. An expanded version of the evidence and arguments presented here can be found in my *Emigrants and Exiles: Ireland and the Irish Exodus to North America* (New York, 1985), esp. chs. 5–6. I would like to thank Professor Liam Kennedy, of the Queen's University of Belfast, as well as the panelists and audience members at the conference, for their comments on the original paper.
2   Miller, *Emigrants and Exiles*, ch. 4; on early Irish emigration, generally, see Kerby A. Miller, *et al.*, *Irish Immigrants in the Land of Canaan: Letters and Memoirs from Colonial and Revolutionary America, 1675–1815* (New York, 2003). In addition, between a quarter- and a half-million Irish migrated to Britain in the pre-Famine decades.

from Ulster. This Protestant preponderance seems surprising, given that Catholics comprised about three-fourths of Ireland's inhabitants, suffered severe poverty and legal proscription in their homeland, and yet had access to the same transatlantic trade in indentured servants that prior to c. 1800 enabled even the poorest Protestants to reach the New World. After the American Revolution, Catholic departures and southern Irish emigration, generally, steadily increased, but Presbyterians and other Protestants remained a majority of the emigrants until the early 1830s. From that point, Catholic emigrants increasingly outnumbered Protestants, yet the annual rates of Catholic emigration still remained below those of Ulster Presbyterians. Moreover, the poorest and most densely populated Catholic districts in the West of Ireland still witnessed relatively few departures; most emigrants, Catholics as well as Protestants, continued to depart from Ulster or from the most commercialized districts of Leinster, Munster, and east Connacht.

Pioneering works by scholars such as R. J. Dickson, William Forbes Adams, and S. H. Cousins have revealed these patterns, as well as the socio-economic and demographic changes in Ireland that encouraged or impelled the migrations.[3] However, historians still lack a full understanding of how Irish country people responded to those changes, and of how overseas migration related to their overall responses.

Until fairly recently, historians commonly viewed pre-Famine Irish rural society and its Catholic inhabitants through the eyes of contemporary witnesses such as Gustave de Beaumont and Johann G. Kohl, and through the writings of early twentieth-century Irish scholars such as Daniel Corkery and George O'Brien.[4] In general, these writers portrayed pre-Famine Irish Catholic society as almost uniformly destitute and Catholic country people as a largely undifferentiated mass of impoverished peasants. Often in these works, moreover, the Catholic peasantry appeared united as well in stubborn opposition to any 'modern' economic 'improvements' that landlords, commercial farmers, or British officials tried to encourage or foist upon them. The most dramatic forms of resistance were the violent activities of the Whiteboys and other secret agrarian societies, whose opposition to enclosures, farm consolidations, evictions, high rents, low wages, tithes, taxes, and other demands convulsed much of Ireland in the late eighteenth and early nineteenth centuries.

Contemporary British and Irish Protestant observers commonly attributed Whiteboy actions and other examples of peasants' recalcitrance to their 'ignorance', 'fecklessness',

3 R. J. Dickson, *Ulster Emigration to Colonial America, 1718–1785* (Belfast, 1966); William Forbes Adams, *Ireland and Irish Emigration to the New World, from 1815 to the Famine* (New Haven, Conn., 1932); S. H. Cousins, 'The Regional Variations in Emigration from Ireland between 1821 and 1841', *Transactions and Papers of the Institute of British Geographers*, 37 (December 1965), 15–30.

4 Gustave de Beaumont, *Ireland, Social, Political and Religious* (London, 1839); J. G. Kohl, *Travels in Ireland* (London, 1844); Daniel Corkery, *The Hidden Ireland: A Study of Gaelic Munster in the Eighteenth Century* (1925; repr. Dublin, 1967); and George O'Brien, *The Economic History of Ireland from the Union to the Famine* (London, 1921). For another example, see historian Constantia Maxwell's *Country and Town in Ireland under the Georges* (London, 1940).

and even 'savagery'. By contrast, middle-class Catholics usually contended that peasant resistance to authority, albeit deplorable from bourgeois and clerical perspectives, stemmed from the Catholic masses' inevitably desperate responses to their dire poverty and continued sufferings at the hands of a landlord system and a Protestant Ascendancy imposed by past conquests and confiscations. Such sympathetic images of pre-Famine Irish society — as economically destitute because politically oppressed — often accompanied a traditional Irish perception of Catholic emigration as 'exile'. According to that interpretation, Irish emigration was at bottom involuntary, for, despite their hardships, Irish Catholics rarely left Ireland from secular ambitions for personal gain. Instead, communal loyalties, religious faith, and cultural ties bound them to a beloved if impoverished homeland, and so they were literally driven out of Ireland by a combination of impositions, rooted in the English conquest, that, for the most part, they bravely resisted until the catastrophe of the Great Famine overwhelmed them.

Ironically, this view of Irish Catholics, as laudably averse to emigration, was a mirror image of the invidious comparisons that British and Irish Protestants often made between themselves and Ireland's Catholics. Irish Protestants, especially in Ulster, usually were characterized as more energetic, industrious, innovative, thrifty, and individualistic — more capitalist-minded, in other words — than their Catholic countrymen. Some observers attributed these distinctions to the relatively congenial, less exploitive relationship with their landlords that Protestant tenants purportedly enjoyed, particularly in the North of Ireland. Much more common, however, was the claim that Protestants' alleged cultural and moral superiority was a 'natural' result of their religion and British origins. Such traits allegedly made intelligible, for instance, the prevalence of domestic manufacturing in 'Protestant Ulster'. More important, they supposedly 'explained' Irish — and especially Ulster — Protestants' greater and more 'rational' willingness to emigrate in pursuit of economic advantage. Thus, albeit from quite different perspectives, both Catholic and Protestant observers pointed to cultural, religious, and broadly 'political' factors as 'explaining' the chronological lag between Irish Protestant and Catholic migrations that prevailed until nearly the very eve of the Famine.[5]

In the 1960s and 1970s, however, Irish economic and social historians set forth a new, 'revisionist' interpretation of pre-Famine Irish society. The new paradigm was radically different from the old, and it had important implications for understanding pre-Famine emigration.[6] First, the new research illuminated crucial socio-economic and regional distinctions among Irish rural dwellers in both the Protestant and Catholic communities. Significant differences — often overlooked by contemporary observers and earlier scholars — now appeared among strong and middling farmers,

5   See Chapter 1 in this volume on Catholic and nationalist understandings of emigration as 'exile' and on Protestant views of Irish Catholic religion, culture, and 'character'.
6   A key text is Louis M. Cullen, *An Economic History of Ireland since 1660* (London, 1972), but also see his edited volume, *The Formation of the Irish Economy* (Cork, 1969), and chs. 4–6 in his *Life in Ireland* (London, 1968).

smallholders, cottiers, and labourers — all varying as well among the island's different regions and even from estate to estate. Second, scholars now argued that by the late eighteenth century, if not earlier, a large majority of Irish rural dwellers were thoroughly enmeshed in a rapidly developing market economy. Far from producing only for subsistence or even for local exchange, most Irish country people were engaged in the production of grain, beef, butter, pork, yarn, and/or cloth for wider markets in Ireland, Britain, and overseas. Moreover, revisionist historians contended that by the late 1700s there were no significant differences between Irish Protestants' and Catholics' degrees of involvement in the marketplace. In Ulster, north Leinster, north Connacht, and even parts of Munster, for example, Catholic smallholders and cottiers were as deeply (if not usually as profitably) involved in cottage textile manufactures as their Protestant peers. Finally, new research demonstrated that the Irish economy was far from uniformly stagnant or depressed during the century preceding the Famine. Instead, as a result of increasing British and overseas demands for Irish farm products and textiles, Ireland experienced dramatic economic expansion. This was especially true before 1814, when prices for Irish products began to fall significantly below their wartime levels, but the processes of commercialization persisted and even accelerated after that date — as shown by fairly steady increases in most Irish exports and imports, and by the continued spread of banking facilities, rural shops, and the use of cash instead of barter. Both the pre-1814 prosperity and the subsequent fall in prices encouraged landlords and tenants alike to rationalize the management of their concerns in the interests of greater economy, efficiency, and productivity.

Thus, the revised portrait of pre-Famine rural Ireland shows a society experiencing what many economists and social scientists then called 'modernization'. In Ireland, as elsewhere, this process involved the spread of commerce and industry; rising national levels of production, income, and consumption; increased population; growing socio-economic differentiation; increasing urbanization and improved facilities for transportation and communication; rising levels of education and literacy; and an increasing rationalization of public, religious, and private administrative systems. Also, it is argued that pre-Famine Ireland's modernization resulted in a rapid erosion of the parochial loyalties, the deferential social and political relationships, and the customary folk beliefs and practices that were antithetical to the growth of a market system geared to considerations of profit and mobility instead of traditional concerns for subsistence and stability.

The new interpretation of pre-Famine Ireland is certainly more complex than the one it superseded. In general, its outlines can be verified by the macro-statistics that L. M. Cullen and other historians cited — concerning Irish imports and exports, for example. On the local level, detailed contemporary descriptions, such as those in Mason's *Statistical Account* (compiled in the 1810s), illuminate a society whose different regions and classes were in various stages of transition between traditional and 'modern' ways of thinking and behaving: fairs and markets were proliferating; former co-tenants of subsistence holdings, once farmed under the traditional rundale system, were becoming profit-oriented tenants of compact farms — or falling into the ranks of cottiers and landless labourers; rural habits of clothing and diet were changing radically; illiterate Irish-speakers were urging education in English upon their children; and so forth.[7]

Yet despite its general accuracy, the new interpretation of pre-Famine Ireland has perhaps been accepted too hastily and uncritically, for it entails several assumptions that deserve closer scrutiny. Most broadly, it must be recognized that 'modernization' is a somewhat euphemistic term for the effects of capitalist relationships that, in Ireland's case, were imposed by imperial policies on a semi-peripheral, largely agrarian, highly stratified, and deeply inequitable society, which in turn was dominated by a largely 'alien' (and often absentee) élite that was itself planted and maintained in power by the social and political results of conquest, confiscation, and colonization. In those circumstances, as in much of the so-called 'developing world' today, Ireland's 'modernization' would almost inevitably produce extremely mixed, profoundly destabilizing, and highly contentious results.

Rather problematic, therefore, is the revisionist argument that 'modernization' brought significant benefits to Irish rural society as a whole: that before 1814 it diffused economic well-being throughout the rural population, and that, even after the Napoleonic Wars, its blessings continued to be felt by a substantial segment of Irish country people. Equally problematic is the related contention that the great majority of Irish rural dwellers were not only affected by the expansion of a market economy but that they participated in the process eagerly and primarily because of a 'modern' desire to maximize profits and future investments. Indeed, the revisionist thesis replaces the old image of a tradition-bound subsistence peasant with a 'neo-liberal' model of the Irish countryman as incipient capitalist, with the same 'progressive' values and acquisitive goals as his landlord or a Belfast linen merchant. In the context of this new model, therefore, any visible economic differences between Catholic and Protestant country people can be explained solely by the former's relative lack of capital or opportunity, rather than by any religious, cultural, or political criteria.

Of course, the revisionist paradigm has important implications for interpreting the nature of pre-Famine emigration. No longer unhappy 'exiles', compelled to leave Ireland by oppressive forces beyond their control, pre-Famine emigrants now appear as 'rational', decisive agents, operating in a transnational 'free labour' market, who maximized their opportunities by emigrating from an island where land and provisions were scarce and dear, and labour was abundant and cheap, to a continent where that ratio was fortuitously reversed. Indeed, the new thesis implies that the typical pre-Famine emigrant was a frustrated would-be entrepreneur, leaving home because his rising

7 William Shaw Mason, *A Statistical Account, or Parochial Survey of Ireland*, 3 vols. (Dublin, 1814–19). On the distinctions between cottiers and landless labourers, see Chapter 1, n. 17. In the rural textile-producing districts, as in Ulster, cottiers often 'paid' farmer-employers, for their cottages and garden plots, by weaving cloth rather than by farm labour; hence, the term 'cottier-weavers' (as on p. 50 and *passim*).

economic expectations were thwarted by inadequate opportunities to satisfy new desires for upward mobility. It also implies that, because modern motives and frustrations allegedly transcended social and cultural-religious boundaries, any variations in emigration rates among different groups of Irish country people were due solely or primarily to lack of means rather than desire. Thus, the revisionist view discountenances allegations of popular reluctance to emigrate for cultural or (especially) for political reasons.

Support for this interpretation of pre-Famine emigration can be found among contemporary British parliamentary reports on Ireland and also among the thousands of petitions for assisted emigration, penned by both Catholics and Protestants, which flooded the British Colonial Office in London between 1817 and the early 1840s. Both categories of evidence testified to a widespread desire to emigrate in the decades following the Napoleonic Wars.[8] Nevertheless, the revisionist portrait has been greatly overdrawn. An overly sanguine interpretation of much evidence has generated a distorted view of the conditions endured by most of pre-Famine Ireland's inhabitants and of their responses to those conditions. And this in turn has fostered at least a partial misunderstanding of the character of most pre-Famine emigration.

It is questionable, for example, whether the expansion of a market economy brought more benefits than hardships to Irish country people as a whole — even *before* the catastrophic decline in the prices of farm products and textiles that commenced at the war's end. Most obviously, the rewards of Irish 'development' were grossly mal-distributed because the actual or effective ownership of Irish land — the most important means of market production *and* subsistence — was concentrated in the hands of a very small proportion of the rural population.[9] Actual landowners (about one-third of whom were absentees) accounted for less than 1 per cent of Irish families and (together with their salaried agents and a small number of affluent 'middlemen' and head tenants) constituted what a development economist would call rural Ireland's 'modernizing élite': it was principally their desire for greater income and hence their imposition of higher rents that directly pushed their tenants (and, indirectly, their subtenants) into an increasing dependence on market production and prices. Often proprietors

8 The petitions to the British Colonial Office, principally from Ireland, 1817–44, are bound in the first 77 volumes of CO 384, located in PRO).

9 Although landed proprietors numbered less than 1 per cent of Ireland's inhabitants, if one includes middlemen with long (sometimes perpetuity) leases, and strong farmers who rented at least 30 acres and normally enjoyed fairly long and relatively secure leases, the proportion of owners and 'effective owners' can rise to about 8 per cent of the rural population. That estimate may be overgenerous, however, because between 1814 and 1844 many and, in the worst years, most strong farmers were distressed and insecure, while landlords were pushing the once favoured middleman class towards extinction. Thus, the proportion of those who enjoyed a significant degree of real control over their own fortunes likely constituted only 3 to 5 per cent of Ireland's rural inhabitants. On the rural social structure of pre-Famine Ireland, see James S. Donnelly, Jr., *Landlord and Society in Nineteenth-Century Ireland* (Dublin, 1973), 5; Miller, *Emigrants and Exiles*, 48–54; and on the plight of middlemen, see below, Chapter 9 in this volume.

accomplished this goal by improving estate management and by rationalizing tenant holdings according to 'English practice' — a process that usually entailed the eviction or at least the social degradation (to the ranks of cottiers or landless labourers) of those tenants and subtenants deemed economically 'superfluous'. Of course, landlords often offered positive inducements in the forms of bounties, prizes, and even temporary rent reductions, or, as Eric Almquist has shown, by the creation of local fairs and markets, and by the distribution of looms and spinning wheels.[10] More often, however, landlords relied on coercion, obliging their lessees (and, indirectly, their sub-lessees) to produce marketable surpluses through higher rents, large fines for lease renewal, competitive bidding for holdings, and shorter leases or tenancies-at-will, with yearly rent levels geared to market prices. Thus, it was the landlords (and a small, favoured minority of head tenants with long leases) who absorbed the lion's share of modernization's economic benefits.

This is not to say that ordinary smallholders, cottiers, and even labourers experienced no ameliorative effects from this process, at least before 1814. Contemporary accounts, especially by English visitors, were replete with delighted remarks on the 'improvement' in rural lifestyles since the mid-eighteenth century, particularly with regard to increased consumption of imported clothes and 'luxury goods' such as sugar, tea, and tobacco. However, as estate agent William Greig testified in 1821, after an exhaustive survey of the Gosford properties in County Armagh, such observations were often superficial. 'In Ireland,' he wrote, 'although much improvement has in several respects taken place, with some increase of industry and a prodigious rise in the value of the land, improvements in the systems of agriculture among the mere occupying tenants ... are almost too inconsiderable to be traced.' Moreover, he concluded, 'Their comforts and opulence have not augmented in any considerable degree. On the contrary, it is most certain that in a great proportion of instances they are much lessened, even *before* the late calamitous events [that is, the post-war price collapse]; the increase of rents having been often made up from increased privations and from excessive cropping, and other expedients [such as subletting] which have only served to entail and produce future loss and inconvenience.'[11]

Initially, before the pressures of rising rents, costs, and population began to erode precarious gains, the ordinary inhabitants of an Irish estate might reap financial benefits from increased involvement in national and international markets. In the long term, however, it is arguable that market dependence placed many of them in an increasingly untenable position even before the post-war depression began. One result of the commercialization of Irish rural society was a sharpening of social or class differences and the creation or at least the widening of the gap between those who were able to

10 Eric Almquist, 'Mayo and Beyond: Land, Domestic Industry, and Rural Transformation in the Irish West' (PhD diss., Boston University, 1977), 20–75.
11 William Greig, *General Report on the Gosford Estates in County Armagh, 1821* (Belfast, 1976), 89 (emphasis added).

live 'comfortably' and those who were reduced to a state of relative and even absolute deprivation. Among leaseholders, for instance, tenants with long leases signed *before* the late eighteenth-century (and especially the wartime) inflations of rents and land values were able to accumulate considerable capital. By contrast, tenants obliged to renew their leases during the boom usually did so at sharply increased rent levels and thus experienced significant reductions in profit margins and living standards even before 1814 — and often found themselves unable to pay inflated rents after that date. Although 'distressed' tenants often endeavoured to continue earlier consumption patterns, to maintain claims to social equality with more fortunate neighbours, Greig and others testified that they usually did so at the expense of a reduced quantity or quality of diet: a result of their increased devotion of acreage and energy to market production rather than family subsistence.[12] Indeed, major reasons for the prevalence of tenant subletting in pre-Famine Ireland — whether to relatives or to cottiers and labourers — were to offset shrinking incomes and/or to secure cheap labour in the face of rising costs. Among the cottiers and labourers themselves, the rising value of land and other expenses, coupled with stagnant or declining wages and frequent unemployment, further pauperized those who had little access to capital and whose numbers were continually increased both by natural growth and by the social descent of 'broken farmers' and their children. Likewise, some observers believed that the increased use of tobacco, tea, and whiskey among the pre-Famine poor was less a benign symptom of rural Ireland's commercialization than an indication that so-called 'luxuries' often served as cheap food-substitutes for the milk, butter, eggs, and pork which increasingly had to be taken to market.[13]

Thus, the actual dynamics of pre-Famine Irish society at least qualify the modernization thesis, particularly the rather dogmatic notion that an expanding market economy 'naturally' or inevitably diffused prosperity in the countryside, even before 1814. After that date, the pernicious effects of the Irish economy's dependence on export price levels, and its post-Union vulnerability to British industrial competition, would seem self-evident, but negative consequences of dependence were already obvious: in the textile, dairying, and grazing districts of Munster, for instance, as well as among the smallholders and cottier-weavers of mid-Ulster; both regions, significantly, were major epicentres of social unrest. Between the period 1814–15 and the Famine, contemporaries (both sympathetic and prejudiced) chronicled the dire condition of most of rural Ireland so consistently that it would seem superfluous to remark upon it further. However, the tendency of some revisionist historians to concentrate attention on the profit-making

---

12 Thus, in 1834 English visitor H. D. Inglis reported that, 'with few exceptions', Irish tenants 'cannot pay the rents which are exacted unless by limiting their diet and their comforts within the bounds prescribed by the absolute necessities of nature; and that notwithstanding their privations, a large proportion are in arrears'; H. D. Inglis, *Ireland in 1834: A Journey throughout Ireland, during the Spring, Summer, and Autumn of 1834*, 2 vols. (London, 1835), vol. 2, 295; also see vol. 1, 100.

13 e.g., Mason, *Statistical Account, or Parochial Survey*, vol. 2 (1816), 16.

and still relatively comfortable tenant classes has partly obscured the magnitude of Ireland's rural crisis after Waterloo.

In his *Economic History of Ireland*, for example, Cullen argued that falling prices after 1814 were largely offset by greatly increased production; thus, after initial dislocations and readjustments, 'the farming community fared well'.[14] However, Cullen conflated the welfare of the entire 'farming community' — which elsewhere he defined as comprising all those who rented more than merely four acres — with the relative prosperity of the very small minority of tenants — graziers and 'strong farmers' — who held thirty acres or more and engaged principally or exclusively in commercial farming. In truth, the great majority of 'farmers', as Cullen himself defined them, were struggling smallholders, with fifteen or fewer acres, whose families suffered great hardships in the pre-Famine decades. Many, if not most, were either subtenants or lacked the security of written leases or both. If subtenants, they paid much higher per-acre rents than did the large commercial farmers, and, without written leases, they were much more likely to face eviction. Moreover, in 1841 some two-thirds of *all* of Ireland's country people comprised what should be termed the 'subsistence' or at best the 'semi-subsistence' sectors of rural and village society: that is, those whom Cullen himself described as 'labourers, smallholders with less than five acres, and the less prosperous [sic] artisans'.[15]

Because Irish land-access and land-use were controlled by a tiny, affluent minority, most of the expansion of agricultural productivity that occurred after 1814 took place at the expense of rural Ireland's most vulnerable inhabitants: those in the subsistence or semi-subsistence sectors. Parliamentary commission reports indicate that in the pre-Famine decades very large numbers suffered eviction at the instigation of either landlords or 'improving' commercial farmers. And although many relocated on new holdings, others remained what contemporaries called 'broken farmers': often marginalized both socially (as cottiers or labourers) and geographically — to the borders of large farms, to the verges of roads (where they begged from travellers), to

14 Cullen, *Economic History of Ireland*, 109 and *passim* (esp. ch. 5).
15 Cullen, *Economic History of Ireland*, 110–11. In 1841 Ireland's 128,000 strong-farmer families comprised only 15 per cent of all those who, by any stretch of the imagination, could be termed 'farmers' — i.e., of those who held more than two acres. Moreover, strong farmers constituted merely 7.6 per cent of all rural families, some 900,000 of which were those of cottiers and landless labourers; see Miller, *Emigrants and Exiles*, 48–54; and also Joseph Lee, *The Modernisation of Irish Society, 1848–1918* (Dublin, 1973), 2. As for those Cullen calls 'less prosperous artisans', most contemporaries remarked on the wretched condition of weavers and other artisans (female spinners, in particular) who, despite excessive work and self-privation, could not compete with cheap factory goods made in Belfast or Britain.
      In 1834 H. D. Inglis provided a perceptive answer to the question, 'Is Ireland an improving country?' 'The reply,' he wrote, 'ought to depend altogether on the meaning we affix to the word improvement. If by improvement, be meant expanding tillage, and improved modes of husbandry, — more commercial importance, evinced in larger exports, — better roads, — better modes of communication, — increase of buildings, — then Ireland is a highly improving county; but ... I have found nothing to warrant the belief, that any improvement has taken place in the condition of the people.' Rather, he concluded, 'a visible deterioration has taken place in the condition of the labouring classes and of the small farmers' — that is, in the condition of the great majority of the rural population; Inglis, *Ireland in 1834*, vol. 1, 79–81.

wretched 'cabin suburbs' on the outskirts of towns, or to 'waste lands' with rocky, mountainous, or boggy soils. The precise number of pre-Famine evictees is unknown, but one source alleged that 150,000 ejectments occurred in 1839–43 alone; at merely five persons per family, these would account for 750,000 Irish men, women, and children — and during a period when both distress and evictions were reputedly less prevalent than in earlier decades.[16]

Also problematic is the contention (at least implicit in the modernization paradigm) that Irish country people generally, even enthusiastically, embraced a modern, market-oriented value-system. Ironically, some of the evidence often cited to support that contention does not promote a very complacent view of pre-Famine rural society. For example, Mason's *Statistical Account* contains numerous descriptions of parishes where involvement in the market economy produced widespread social and cultural disorganization. Thus, whereas the Anglican clergyman who described the parish of Maghera, in County Derry, praised its inhabitants as 'opulent' because of the influence of the market towns of Maghera and Magherafelt, he also lamented that 'the same love of money, which urges the honest part of our community to these great exertions on lawful industry, stimulates many of a contrary character to the most nefarious practices', such as robbery, petty thieving, gambling, swindling, and murder. Due to rising land values and population, the gap between the comfortable and the poor was increasing sharply; even in 1814 the latter could no longer afford milk, which, the minister believed, resulted in the prevalence of disease, quack doctors, and healing potions among them. In the mountainous parts of the parish, the rundale system was degenerating into endless disputes and litigation, and in the lowlands smallholders and cottier-weavers were falling deeply into debt to village usurers and being reduced to the status of landless day-labourers. Thus, although a drive for money seemed ubiquitous in highly commercialized parishes such as Maghera and St. Peter's, Athlone, in County Roscommon, its benefits to many appeared dubious, and its causes seemed as rooted in imposed necessity as in desires for accumulation.[17]

Even among those who did benefit from wartime price increases, much evidence casts doubt on the notion that greater involvement in the marketplace quickly transformed

16 Miller, *Emigrants and Exiles*, 213.

17 Mason, *Statistical Account, or Parochial Survey*, vol. 1 (1814), 577–612, for Maghera parish; vol. 3 (1819), 49–108, for St. Peter's, Athlone. The latter account contains an interesting example of market values transforming traditional customs. Among the country people of St. Peter's parish, Athlone, it had long been customary to hold Sunday evening dances known as 'cakes', so-called because the prize of a large cake had traditionally been awarded to the best female dancer. By the time the local clergyman's description was written, however, the cake had come to be purchased, by the young man with the most money, to give to his sweetheart. According to the author, young people frequently stole money from their parents or employers so they could attend these dances and bid for the prize; but this merely mirrored their parents' general behaviour, he claimed, for among them 'lying were no sin, and fraud no crime' (105–09). For an account of this local custom in the late 1600s, see: Sir Henry Piers, 'A Chorographical Description of the County of Westmeath [1682]', in Charles Vallancey, ed., *Collectanea de Rebus Hibernicus*, 2 vols. (Dublin, 1770), vol. 1, 108–20.

subsistence-oriented countrymen into incipient capitalists. During his tour through Ireland in the late 1770s, for example, Young complained frequently that, in the absence of landlords' express coercion, neither higher prices nor higher rents induced most tenant farmers to modernize farming methods or improve their housing or farm buildings. Likewise, neither Young nor Edward Wakefield, another English visitor in the 1810s, found much evidence of bourgeois-capitalist norms among the smallholders and weavers in east Ulster's 'linen triangle' — one of the most 'Protestant' and allegedly most 'industrious' and 'progressive' rural districts in Ireland. Instead, they complained, the area's inhabitants seemed inveterately 'idle', working only in response to 'present necessity' rather than for long-term 'improvement'.[18] In other parts of Ireland, tenants and cottiers used the 'extra' cash they earned from market sales in distinctly pre-modern ways: hoarding their money instead of investing it, as Young and other observers decried; or expending it lavishly in traditional forms of 'conspicuous waste', such as wedding feasts and funeral entertainments.[19] Even the oft-praised popular enthusiasms for stylish imported clothes and for education can be interpreted at least partly in traditional status terms.

In short, it is questionable whether the Irish peasantry's increasing involvement in market-oriented *activities* was automatically accompanied by a widespread conversion to a market-oriented *value-system*. Instead, it is arguable that many country people in pre-Famine Ireland were actually engaged in a sustained effort to *avoid* the full implications of a 'free market' in land and labour — partly because they had good reason to fear the potentially adverse effects of total dependence on an impersonal price system, and partly because such dependence violated an older, pre-market worldview that poverty and uncertainty continued to validate. As J. E. Bicheno, a British economist, lamented in 1830, Ireland remained 'a country not yet emerged from the ancient territorial [that is, feudal] relations, and upon which the commercial principle has been grafted with very imperfect success'.[20] Thus, much evidence indicates that, although most rural dwellers in pre-Famine Ireland were engaged in market-oriented activities, many of them — out of need or expedience — were simply utilizing 'modern' means to achieve the traditional goals of what historian E. P. Thompson called, in the context of contemporary English society, a 'moral economy'.[21]

---

18 Arthur W. Hutton, ed., *Arthur Young's Tour in Ireland (1776–1779)*, 2 vols. (Dublin, 1892), vol. 1, 120–32; Edward Wakefield, *An Account of Ireland, Statistical and Political*, 2 vols. (London, 1812), vol. 2, 739–40, 778–80.

19 Hutton, *Arthur Young's Tour*, vol. 1, 79, 87, 120, 213, and *passim*; Wakefield, *Account of Ireland*, vol. 2, 764; T. Crofton Croker, *Researches in the South of Ireland* (London, 1824), 166–67; and similar observations cited in Miller, *Emigrants and Exiles*, 108, 114, 157. Also see the remarkably detailed description of Kilmactige parish, County Sligo, in Mason, *Statistical Account, or Parochial Survey*, vol. 2 (1816), 349–88.

20 J. E. Bicheno, *Ireland and Its Economy* (London, 1830), cited in Miller, *Emigrants and Exiles*, 237.

21 E. P. Thompson, 'The Moral Economy of the English Crowd in the Eighteenth Century', *Past and Present*, 50 (February 1971), 76–136. The term 'moral economy' does not necessarily designate a *pre-capitalist* worldview — much less one that is fixed or unambiguous; rather, it suggests a set of values designed

A variety of contemporary evidence and secondary studies — especially recent research on the Whiteboys and other secret agrarian societies[22] — suggests that an 'Irish moral economy' consisted of at least four complementary beliefs. Perhaps the most basic notion was that the first priority for the use of Irish land should be the provision of familial and communal subsistence rather than individual profit. This did not imply that the Irish countryman's worldview was egalitarian, although a superficial analysis of the archaic but still extant rundale system might give that impression. Rather, a second conviction was in the propriety of a 'traditional' social hierarchy, as long as relationships between the higher and lower ranks were based on a sense of mutual obligation rather than on profit-maximization, and as long as members of the same class did not take undue advantage of market conditions to raise themselves out of their ascribed status, particularly by exploiting their peers or dependants. Third was the belief that all families in the community deserved, not equal access to the means of production, but sufficient access to maintain the degrees of subsistence or comfort which they were traditionally deemed to deserve. Hence, the interrelated demands of the secret agrarian societies that both rents and food prices be lowered, and that wages and employment opportunities be adjusted according to the criterion of need rather than by supply and demand. A final notion was that familial access to land and/or employment should be sufficient to provide for more than one generation, to ensure that most if not all children could secure subsistence within a reasonable proximity to their parents' homes and — as country people often said — to their ancestors' graves.

All aspects of this traditional worldview were summed up in the Irish countryman's frequently expressed desire to achieve or retain an 'independence' — that is, sufficient security to maintain each family's ascribed status and to avoid the proletarianizing and pauperizing consequences of total dependence on price and wage systems determined by remote, impersonal forces and on a land market controlled by a fortunate and powerful few. For most farmers, 'independence' usually meant 'comfortable self-sufficiency':

to restrict or regulate early capitalist processes and outcomes, for the benefit or protection of the general community, and its purportedly 'traditional' standards inevitably shift (usually towards greater accommodation with marketplace norms) with the development of capitalism and its effects on social structure, political culture, and popular well-being and consciousness. On the eve of the American Revolution, for example, Philadelphia's craftsmen and labourers still demanded a traditionally regulated marketplace, with 'just prices' imposed by law and élite paternalism, whereas their peers in Boston now demanded a 'free market', unrestricted by what they denounced, in the name of 'traditional liberties', as 'aristocratic' influence and 'artificial monopolies'; see Gary B. Nash, *The Urban Crucible: Social Change, Political Consciousness, and the Origins of the American Revolution* (Cambridge, Mass., 1979).

22 James S. Donnelly, Jr., 'The Whiteboy Movement, 1761–5', *Irish Historical Studies*, 21, 81 (1978), 20–54; and 'The Rightboy Movement', *Studia Hibernica*, 17, 88 (1977–78), 120–202. Thanks also to Jim Donnelly for granting me access to his then unpublished research, later appearing as: 'Hearts of Oak, Hearts of Steel', *Studia Hibernica*, 21 (1981), 7–73; and 'Irish Agrarian Rebellion: The Whiteboys of 1769–76', *Proceedings of the Royal Irish Academy*, 83C, 12 (1983), 293–331. Also see George Cornewall Lewis, *Local Disturbances in Ireland* (1836; repr. Cork, 1977); and Michael Beames, *Peasants and Power: The Whiteboy Movements and their Control in Pre-Famine Ireland* (Sussex, 1983).

enough land to maintain themselves and their children above the 'Ebb of Poverty', free from burdens of 'Rents Tyths and Taxes' so oppressive that tenants were 'eternally apprehensive' of being evicted and 'throwen on the woulrd'. For weavers and other artisans, 'independence' meant relief from wage-labour's 'Slavish yoke' — and from the danger of being forced to go 'Begging on the Road'. For cottiers and landless labourers, as well as for most craftsmen, the goal was simply a potato-garden, perhaps a cow, and, as one workman begged, a 'place to Stop that I can call my Own'.[23]

By the late nineteenth century, of course, the capitalist marketplace had largely triumphed over an older moral economy, thus reflecting a society that the Great Famine had radically transformed. However, some revisionist scholars have argued that early nineteenth-century Irish society was already so 'modernized' that the Famine was relatively unimportant: major economic, social, and cultural changes were already so far advanced, they contend, that the Famine merely expedited 'natural', inevitable, and (at least by implication) beneficial trends.[24] By contrast, this chapter posits that in crucial respects pre-Famine Irish society remained far from 'modern', and that the advance of the capitalist marketplace was neither easy nor painless. Rather, much evidence suggests that the latter was stoutly resisted, because the market system's uneven expansion, and its grossly unequal distribution of rewards, threatened to deny 'independence' to a large majority of Irish country people and reduce them to a condition of abject dependence — to what Irish farmers called 'slavery' (*sclábhaíocht* in Irish) — that is, to a situation where traditional aspirations for sufficient land (or, for artisans, decent incomes) to ensure minimal comfort and family integrity were virtually impossible to achieve.[25]

Viewing most pre-Famine Irish country people as more inspired by the values of a moral — versus a market — economy generates an interpretation of pre-Famine emigration sharply at odds with the revisionist paradigm. For if Irish country people had generally accepted and internalized market values, as the modernization thesis

23 The quoted phrases and similar sentiments appear in the following petitions to the British Colonial Office, preserved in the PRO: John McCudden, Randalstown, County Antrim, 1 November 1819 (CO 384/5); Michael Heaton, Cloghan, King's County, 26 March 1822 (CO 384/8); T. Brady, King's County, 21 March 1823, and Hugh Rock, Multyfarnham, County Westmeath, 30 November 1823 (CO 384/9); Timothy O'Connell, Cahirconlish, County Limerick, 29 January 1824, John H. Montgomery, Dungannon, County Tyrone, 18 January 1824, and John Quinlivan, Cork, 11 September 1824 (CO 384/10); Tighe McMahon, *et al.*, Six Mile Bridge, County Clare, n.d. [1825] (CO 384/11); Thomas Fitzpatrick, Nenagh, County Tipperary, 2 June 1831; and John Tovil, Kinnary, County Tyrone, 16 April 1842 (CO 384/69). See also the old resentments and anxieties recalled in the letters of east Cork emigrant Pádraig Cúndún, 1830s to 1850s, in Risteard Ó Foghludha, *Pádraig Phiarais Cúndún* (Baile Átha Cliath, 1932), 24–30, 85, and *passim* (trans. Bruce D. Boling).

   As discussed below in this chapter, for commercially minded emigrants, 'independence' meant opportunity for upward mobility rather than mere self-sufficiency; see Miller, *Emigrants and Exiles*, 202–03. For unmarried and non-dowered young women, especially in post-Famine Ireland, the goal was what the County Wexford emigrant Mary Brown called 'love and liberty'; see Chapter 13 in this volume.

24 Lee, *Modernisation of Irish Society*; Cullen, *Economic History of Ireland*, 131–39.

25 The word 'slavery' appears frequently in the petitions sent to the Colonial Office; e.g., T. Brady, 21 March 1823 (CO 384/9, PRO).

implies, the volume of pre-Famine emigration should have been considerably greater than it was. As one scholar has remarked, 'when the social condition of pre-famine Ireland is considered, it is the *paucity* and not the magnitude of the emigration which is astonishing'.[26] Thus, despite unprecedented numbers of departures in 1815–44, Ireland's population continued to mount, from 6.2 million in 1821 to c. 8.5 million on the Famine's eve. Indeed, it is arguable that the convictions central to an Irish moral economy generally relegated emigration to a last resort when all other strategies for maintaining 'independence' at home had failed. Hence, despite the numerous petitions begging for assistance to emigrate, there was still considerable resistance to that economically 'rational' alternative to pauperization in Ireland.

A remarkable testament to that resistance is contained in an 1814 description of the parish of Dungiven, County Derry, across the Sperrin Mountains from the parish of Maghera described earlier. According to the local Anglican clergyman, Dungiven's inhabitants were sharply divided into two groups. The first consisted of comfortable Presbyterian farmers in the lowlands, whose full acceptance of market values was indicated not only by heavy involvement in linen manufacture but also by the universal practice of impartible inheritance. Their non-inheriting sons they either educated for business or trades, or else (and more often) they sent them to America — thus maximizing profits at the expense of social continuity and familial (that is, intergenerational) cohesion, and this despite the fact that transatlantic communications were then so uncertain — and voyage conditions reputedly so dangerous — that the likelihood that parents would ever hear from their emigrant children (much less see them again) was at best quite problematic. The second group in Dungiven consisted of Irish-speaking Catholics who lived in the parish's poorer, mountainous townlands, and who continued to believe in what the clergyman called 'the equal and inalienable right of all the children to the inheritance of their father's property' — an 'opinion' which 'is interwoven in such a manner in the very constitutions of their minds, that it seems next to impossible to eradicate it'. Despite the pressures of rising rents and population, which were reducing their holdings to less than five acres per family, Dungiven's Catholics not only refused to emulate their Protestant neighbours by practising impartible inheritance, but they also disdained both linen weaving and permanent emigration. Instead, they employed a unique combination of modern and traditional economic means to retain a relative degree of 'independence' from the potentially disruptive effects of commercialization. Based on large loans secured from 'country banks', Dungiven Catholics speculated in cattle, which they purchased at local fairs and then took to the annual livestock market at Carlisle, in northern England. With the 'surplus' income earned at Carlisle, they were able to pay rents, purchase necessary provisions, display 'extravagance at fairs, wakes,

---

26 Oliver MacDonagh, 'Irish Famine Emigration to the United States', *Perspectives in American History*, 10 (1976), 393, 407 (emphasis added).

and merry-makings', and maintain a degree of social cohesion and cultural integrity that even their Anglican critic grudgingly admired.[27]

Of course, such strategies could not be prolonged indefinitely, especially after 1814, and by 1834 the Ordnance Survey reports show a considerable amount of permanent emigration from Dungiven's upland districts.[28] The point, however, is that many of the 'modern' economic activities in which pre-Famine Irishmen were engaged should not necessarily be seen as indications that they embraced capitalist values, but rather as their expedient attempts to adopt novel means in order to realize traditional ends. Likewise, the seasonal migrations of Mayo and Donegal smallholders to Britain, and of Waterford and south Wexford cottiers to Newfoundland, should be viewed in this light. So should also many other alternatives to emigration, including subletting and subdivision, wasteland colonization, illicit whiskey distillation, and, perhaps especially, peasant involvement in the secret agrarian societies: the activities of which were invariably centred in those districts where the pressures attendant on commercialization were most novel and hence most strongly felt. All these and other strategies served to prevent or at least postpone the ultimate consequences of total exposure to a system of unlimited competition for land and employment.[29]

Nevertheless, in the context of this interpretation, how to explain the substantial pre-Famine emigrations that did occur? First, there is no doubt that the revisionist or neo-liberal model is applicable to many pre-Famine emigrants. Increasing numbers left Ireland for North America because — as townsmen or as members of strong-farmer families — long-standing involvement in commercial agriculture, trade, or industry had caused them to redefine 'independence' in terms of capitalist and acquisitive-individualist goals. Like John Bell, a young medical student who left County Monaghan in 1811, many were prompted less by the sting of necessity than by what he called 'the whisperings of ambition'.[30] Arguably, such views were more widespread among Irish Protestants than among Catholics, in large part because of the former's longer engagement, and on more favourable terms, in commercial activities — perhaps corroborating cultural

27 Mason, *Statistical Account, or Parochial Survey*, vol. 1 (1814), 234–341.

28 Ordnance Survey Papers, Box 39, II (Dungiven), 23, in the Royal Irish Academy, Dublin (hereafter RIA); now published in Angélique Day and Patrick McWilliams, eds., *Ordnance Survey Memoirs of Ireland, Vol. 15: Parishes of Co. Londonderry IV, 1824, 1833–5; Roe Valley Upper: Dungiven* (Belfast, 1992).

29 Other patterns of pre-Famine behaviour may also be relevant. For example, despite the bourgeois mentalité of the Catholic townsmen, priests, and strong farmers who led the pre-Famine crusades for emancipation, repeal, and total abstinence, much evidence suggests that the common people regarded these 'modern' movements in very traditional terms: as prefacing a return to an idealized, pastoral, and pre-conquest millennium; see Miller, *Emigrants and Exiles*, 241, 248.

30 John Bell, Philadelphia, Pa., to Anne Jane Bell, New Charleville, Tenn., 12 July 1834 (Bell Family Papers, Manuscripts Section, Acc. No. 1200, Tennessee State Library and Archives, Nashville). Similarly, an ambitious tenant in County Wicklow admitted that, although he was 'pretty comfortable at home', he wanted to emigrate '"because," he said, "I can never be better as I am"', whereas in America, as another emigrant declared, opportunities for 'making money' were abundant; see Miller, *Emigrants and Exiles*, 173, 201, 205–06.

characteristics that were more conducive, or at least less resistant, to such practices. Frustrated at home, Irishmen who embraced bourgeois norms generally disdained the desperate strategies described above. Instead, they calculated on emigration to a country where they might realize 'modern' aspirations for profitable investments and upward mobility.

Nevertheless, most pre-Famine emigrants' letters and petitions suggest that a large proportion, even a substantial majority (including many Protestant smallholders and weavers), went abroad primarily because, after long struggles, they despaired of achieving traditional goals of 'independence' as even minimal security in Ireland itself, and so finally, reluctantly, and sometimes bitterly, they projected those ideals across the ocean.[31] And 'despaired' is not too strong a term: as noted in Chapter 1, after 1814 pre-Famine Ireland — wracked by epidemics of typhus (1817) and cholera (1832), as well as by poverty and by social and sectarian conflicts, all in the context of a burgeoning population — was rife with millennial prophecies of impending disaster or violent upheaval; either vision boding catastrophe for poor Catholics, or Protestants, or both. Indeed, many letters and petitions written by ordinary Irishmen and -women in 1815–44 reflect a widespread pessimism, a conviction that their homeland was doomed. Thus, Ulster Catholic Edward Toner predicted Ireland's 'Disolation'; another farmer declared, 'The cuntery is done'; and yet a third lamented that 'the miserable world seems to be tottering to its centre'. In these circumstances, it was no wonder that many Irishmen viewed emigration not as a 'rational' choice but — in a millennial framework — as 'a Joyful deliverance' from inevitable disaster, and that they envisioned the United States itself not 'realistically' but as the total antithesis of a rural Ireland that seemed poised on the edge of destruction.[32]

Despite such forebodings, however, contemporary observers continued to remark, often with astonishment, on the apparent reluctance of poor Catholics to go abroad, especially from parishes (the majority still) where most adults spoke the Irish language, principally or solely.[33] More important, although emigration among rural Catholics did increase markedly during the pre-Famine decades, their motives and decisions — like those of many poor Protestants — remained at least as responsive to traditional, communal, and familial aspirations as to modern, individualistic calculations. Like the earliest migrations of Ulster Presbyterian congregations in the 1710s and 1720s,

---

31 As one observer of east Leinster's tenants and cottiers testified in 1836, 'Many who have hitherto forborne to emigrate would now accept the offer of a free passage, notwithstanding their great affection for the land of their birth, from their increasing misery and hopelessness of improvement in their condition by any other means'; Miller, *Emigrants and Exiles*, 238.

    On the pre-Famine countryman's compensatory vision of America, see Kerby A. Miller and Bruce D. Boling, 'Golden Streets, Bitter Tears: The Irish Image of America during the Era of Mass Migration', *Journal of American Ethnic History*, 10, 1–2 (1990–91), 16–35; much of the information in that essay is included in Chapter 5 in the present volume.

32 Miller, *Emigrants and Exiles*, 205; Miller and Boling, 'Golden Streets, Bitter Tears'; and Chapter 5 below.

33 Miller, *Emigrants and Exiles*, 227, 235–37.

for example, the emigrations of extended families of south Leinster Catholics in the 1810s and 1820s represented attempts to re-establish traditional communities in the American wilderness. Certainly, the latter were exceptional: few Catholics possessed the economic resources enjoyed by the Murphys and other clans whose patriarchs built self-sufficient colonies in Mexican Texas and California.[34] If read closely, however, thousands of the would-be emigrants' petitions to the Colonial Office, between 1817 and 1844, can be interpreted in a similar vein. Of course, the petitioners expressed ardent desires for official assistance to emigrate. Yet despite their destitution and desperation, most petitioners' aim was not to obtain passage money for single individuals, as would become the norm of post-Famine migration. Rather, their goal was to secure sufficient aid to enable *all* family members (and often neighbours also) to emigrate and settle together on grants of free land in British North America, thus enabling them to obtain what could no longer be achieved in Ireland: 'independence' as comfortable self-sufficiency, and for their children and other kinfolk as well as for themselves. Without those anticipated 'encouragements' — which many claimed as the government's paternalistic obligation to them — it was clear that most petitioners still regarded *individual* emigration as an undesirable alternative to life, however meagre, at home.[35]

As for those Irishmen and -women who did go to America, many of their personal letters also indicate that the paramount motive was to avert or escape 'dependence' and find security overseas — to avoid what both Catholic smallholders and Presbyterian weavers, such as John McBride from County Antrim, described as the 'slavish' effects of proletarianization.[36] Indeed, pre-Famine emigrants' letters often reflected a markedly pre-entrepreneurial and pastoral vision of America: as a 'land of promise flowing with milk and honey', where 'the millions of uncultivated acres' could give 'independence' to all, and where any emigrant could own sufficient land to 'dwell in your home and sit under your own fig tree, and no one to make you afraid'.[37] As the Corkman Pádraig Cúndún testified, when he left Ireland in the mid-1820s he was 'cast down, but what

34 On early eighteenth-century Ulster migrations by Presbyterian congregations led by clergymen, see Chapter 6 in this volume; and for an example of early clan migration from County Wexford, see the Murphy Family Papers in the Bancroft Library, University of California, Berkeley, as well as the recent book by Graham Davis, *Land! Irish Pioneers in Mexican and Revolutionary Texas* (College Station, Tex., 2002).

35 Miller, *Emigrants and Exiles*, 239.

36 e.g., see John McBride, Watertown, NY, to James McBride, Derriaghy, County Antrim, 9 January 1820 (T. 2613, PRONI).

37 Margaret Wright, Aughintober, County Tyrone, to Alexander McNish, Salem, NY, 27 May 1808 (McNish Papers, Cornell University Archives, Ithaca, NY); David Robinson, Lexington, Ky., to Mary Robinson, Londonderry city, 4 May 1817 (D. 2013/1, PRONI); and James Christie, Clyman, Wisc., to Elizabeth Christie, Hartford, Conn., 3 February 1847 (Christie Family Letters, Minnesota Historical Society, St. Paul). Wright's and Robinson's letters are now published (the former with commentary) in Miller, *et al.*, *Irish Immigrants in the Land of Canaan*, 45–50 and 681–83.

For similar sentiments and phrases, also see: Neal Campbell, Youngstown, Ohio, to John Campbell, Coalisland, County Tyrone, 30 October 1819, and Edward and Mary Toner, Unity township, Westmoreland Co., Pa., 21 January 1819 (Ms. 2300, NLI; the latter also published in Miller, *et al.*, *Irish Immigrants in the Land of Canaan*, 224–35); James Reford, Bloomfield, NJ, to Mrs. Joseph Reford, Antrim, County Antrim, 15 May

could I do? I had seen strong and mighty men clothed in rags at work for their masters on rented land, often without [even] their fill of shrivelled potatoes to eat. I told myself that I would die before I put up with that, and I decided to come here.' Now, eight years later, he wrote, 'I ... own outright a fine farm of land; no one can demand rent of me. My family and I can eat our fill of bread and meat, butter and milk, any day we like throughout the year, and thus I think it is better to be as we are than to have stayed in Ireland without land, without independence, without food, without clothing.'[38]

The emigrants whose writings are cited above became farmers or at least, as in the case of the weaver McBride, owners of substantial garden plots in the New World. We still know too little about the patterns of early nineteenth-century Irish-American settlement to challenge, authoritatively, the old belief that pre-Famine emigrants, especially Catholics, commonly became urbanized in the United States, as did their Famine and post-Famine successors. Recent research on the Irish in Ontario and the Maritimes indicates that most pre-Famine emigrants who landed in British North America and *remained there* did become farmers; however, early and mid-nineteenth-century Canada was much less urbanized and industrialized than the American republic, and, perhaps partly for that reason, most pre-Famine Irish (especially Catholics but also most Presbyterians) who landed in Canada quickly re-migrated, in search of employment, to the United States.[39] Yet, what we know about the pre-Famine emigrants' generous remittances to their families in Ireland, coupled with local studies (such as Stephen Thernstrom's of mid-nineteenth-century Newburyport, Massachusetts), suggests that a traditional Irish worldview that valued security and family cohesion above personal advancement was still at work in America.[40] More certainly, letters by pre-Famine emigrants like Cúndún and McBride demonstrate that many Irishmen accepted great initial hardship as canal workers or factory hands to achieve their ultimate goal of 'independence' as farmers in the United States. Protestant and Catholic Irishmen such as James Christie, James McCleer, and Edward Hanlon laboured for years in urban-industrial occupations until they could afford to purchase homesteads in the Midwest. As Christie explained to his wife, 'I have always told you that it was for the sake of our children that I would take upon me the Toils of a Settlers life, and if God spares them, how much easier Will it Be

1844 (T. 3026/B4, PRONI), and Henry Hutcheson, Detroit, Mich., to Alexander Hutcheson, Tanderagee, County Armagh, 30 September 1845 (from Mrs. A. Hutcheson, Mountnorris, County Armagh).

38 Pádraig Cúndún, Deerfield, NY, to Partolán Suipéal, Cluain Aird, Clonpriest parish, County Cork, 17 December 1834, in Ó Foghludha, *Pádraig Phiarais Cúndún*, 24–30 (trans. by Bruce D. Boling); despite his material success, however, Cúndún was unhappy in an American society he described as harsh and immoral; see Chapter 1 in this volume.

39 John J. Mannion, *Irish Settlements in Eastern Canada: A Study of Cultural Transfer and Adaptation* (Toronto, 1974); and, appearing after this paper's initial composition, Donald H. Akenson, 'Ontario: Whatever Happened to the Irish?', in Akenson, ed., *Canadian Papers in Rural History*, vol. 3 (Gananoque, Ont., 1982), 204–56; and Cecil J. Houston and William J. Smyth, *Irish Emigration and Canadian Settlement: Patterns, Links, and Letters* (Toronto, 1990).

40 On pre-Famine remittances, see Miller, *Emigrants and Exiles*, 271. Stephen Thernstrom, *Poverty and Progress: Social Mobility in a Nineteenth Century City* (Cambridge, Mass., 1964).

for me to die, knowing that they Will be independent. We will each of us have 40 acres of good land, and my 40 will be still there when I am gone — not as if Working in a Mill where when you die, it is likely you may leave a legacy of Debt to your Children, and the same Eternal Round of Slavery which has been your own Lot.'[41]

Strikingly, this interpretation of pre-Famine Irish emigration resembles much less the revisionist view than it does the traditional, nationalist interpretation of emigration as unwilling exile. For the argument here is that most early Irish migration to the New World was part of a general pattern of rural and artisanal resistance to a model of economic 'development' that (however ratified by bourgeois middlemen) was ultimately imposed on most Irish people by an élite and — for many Presbyterians as well as Catholics — an 'alien' class. Moreover, it was a model enjoined by British law and ultimately enforced by landlords, employers, and British officials, who, while perhaps not totally indifferent to the fate of their social inferiors, regarded the latter's attempts to impede 'progress' — by urban trade unions as well as by secret agrarian societies — merely as examples of their ignorance and barbarism. Indeed, whether among Presbyterian Steelboys in rural Ulster in the early 1770s, or religiously 'mixed' trade-union members in early nineteenth-century Belfast and Dublin, or Catholic Whiteboys throughout southern Ireland during the entire pre-Famine era, there were obvious relationships between the efforts of these 'illegal combinations' to halt detrimental 'progress' and the surges of emigration from the affected districts that inevitably followed their failures to do so. Equally illuminating were contemporary claims that poor Catholics postponed emigration when they anticipated that political changes (Catholic Emancipation in the late 1820s, repeal of the Act of Union in the early 1840s) would restore a pastoral Gaelic commonwealth in which, they fancied, their ancestors had lived content. At the very least, failed resistance and political disappointments confirmed old notions that emigration was at bottom involuntary exile.[42]

41 James Christie, 3 February 1847; Robert E. Stack, 'The McCleers and the Birneys — Irish Immigrant Families — into Michigan and the California Gold Fields, 1820–1893' (PhD diss., St. Louis University, 1972). James McCleer's Michigan farm contained mostly poor land, but as his son explained in 1843, to his mother in Connecticut, 'We are All agreed in Keeping and staying on this place if Possible for we all think that it is Beter to have a home than to trust to a factory Eaven if times were Beter ...' (129). Edward Hanlon [O'Hanlon] letters, 1843–71 (D. 885, PRONI); Hanlon, a Catholic like McCleer, was a craftsman from Ballymote, County Down, who emigrated c. 1840 and laboured for twenty years in Pittsburgh and on canal works until he purchased a farm in Nebraska. In 1836 another Catholic from Ulster expressed at least some of their motivations: 'I am ... fully convinced,' he wrote, 'that the family that has a good comfortable way of living together or near each other at home ... in Ireland have more real heartfelt enjoyment in that home than they ever can have by coming to this country *unless* they can ... establish them[selves] on a farm'; F. D., Philadelphia, Pa., to 'Uncle Daniel', Maghera parish, County Derry, 9 July 1836 (Ordnance Survey Papers, Box 44, RIA); now published in Day and McWilliams, eds., *Ordnance Survey Memoirs of Ireland, Vol. 18: Parishes of Co. Londonderry V, 1830, 1833, 1836–7; Maghera and Tamlaght O'Crilly* (Belfast, 1993), 19–20 (emphasis added).
42 e.g., Miller, *Emigrants and Exiles*, 225–27, 240–52. On trade-union activities — and their suppression — in early nineteenth-century Belfast, see Chapter 8 in this volume.

As suggested above, although notions of a moral economy were shared to a degree by Protestant and Catholic Irish country dwellers and craftsmen, the differences between them help explain the time lag between their respective migrations to the New World. Because of their prolonged involvement, beginning in the early 1700s, with linen manufacturing, cash exchange, and trans-local trade, Irish Protestants (especially Ulster Presbyterians) comprised the first large sector of Irish rural society to experience the fluctuations and ultimately adverse effects of a 'global' market system. Even before 1814, rent and population increases, coupled with social differentiation based on widely varying access to land and capital, had detrimental effects on the North's Protestant smallholders and cottier-weavers. After that date, price and wage declines, the mechanization of spinning, and the consolidation of weaving (under capitalist control) around Belfast effectively de-industrialized much of rural Ulster (as of southern Ireland), sharply reduced rural incomes, and produced pauperization or proletarianization among many once 'independent' craftsmen. As one Ulsterman lamented in 1840, 'men cannot live for what they get for weaving now'.[43] In addition, their early and sustained immersion in marketplace activities (especially in urbanized east Ulster) no doubt had the effect of converting more Protestants than Catholics to capitalism's implicit values, as Dungiven's clergyman observed among that parish's Presbyterian inhabitants. Also, as suggested in Chapter 1, Protestants generally lacked the cultural resources, the harsh historical experiences, and hence the political perspectives that persuaded most Irish Catholics to harden, communalize, and systematize personal resentments against detrimental change — into emigration as exile, for example. Put another way, ordinary Irish Protestants — conditioned by a colonial or settler mentality that reflected communal privilege and demanded minority solidarity — were highly susceptible to the cultural and ideological influence of Protestant authorities: landlords and bourgeois figures such as merchants, manufacturers, and clergy.[44]

Of course, in the late 1700s and early 1800s many Ulster Presbyterians (relative 'outsiders' in an Anglican-dominated society) did express socio-economic and political grievances against landlords and officialdom. However, massive emigration itself decimated the ranks of those Presbyterians inclined to generalize and politicize their resentments. Likewise, after 1814 Protestant evangelicalism, with its emphasis on personal salvation, corroborated and sacralized capitalism's emphasis on individual

---

43 Quotation in P. E. Razzel, 'Population Growth and Economic Change in Eighteenth- and Early Nineteenth-Century England and Ireland', in E. L. Jones and G. E. Mingay, eds., *Land, Labour and Population in the Industrial Revolution: Essays Presented to J. D. Chambers* (London, 1967), 278.

44 For example, in 1825, when members of a select parliamentary committee asked Irish witnesses why 'the Catholic peasant was more attached to the country than the Protestant', John Rochefort of County Carlow replied that the Catholic considered 'himself and his religion indigenous to the land — that he is one of the original inhabitants' — whereas he regarded Protestants as mere 'usurpers' who had 'deprived … the Catholics … of their inheritance' and belonged 'to another country'; John Rochefort, [1825] (newspaper clipping from the *Cork Constitution*, 7 May 1825, in CO 384/13, PRO). On Irish Protestant political economy and culture, see Chapters 8–10 in this volume.

responsibility. In addition, both evangelicalism and fear of Catholic resurgence increasingly channelled Protestant anxieties into religious and political movements led by a 'modernizing élite' whose spokesmen commonly deflected lower-class Protestants' resentments onto the latter's putative Catholic competitors. Thus, even if half-'modernized' Protestants accepted a market ethic of 'free' competition within their own community, usually they refused to recognize its applicability across sectarian lines. As David Miller has argued, many Protestants' first response to their landlords' violation of the 'moral' principle of Protestant immunity from Catholic competition was the Orange Order, with its formal claims on élite paternalism in return for loyalty and deference.[45] Ultimately, however, the response was emigration, as even the Orange Order quickly became a vehicle facilitating overseas migration.[46]

   A more thorough (albeit never total) victory of market values over traditional norms was not achieved until after the Great Famine. Contrary to the revisionist view, that catastrophe was immensely important, in part because it destroyed or demoralized most of those who had opposed (physically or culturally) the capitalist restructuring of Irish rural society and its 'rational' concomitants: farm consolidation, wholesale eviction and proletarianization, the adoption by remaining farmers of impartible inheritance and restricted marriage, and the mass emigration of 'free' individuals. Yet even before the Famine, many Catholics, responding to market pressures, had begun to emulate their 'betters' by 'modernizing' family relationships in ways that consigned most of their children to life overseas. This chapter concludes with the embittered remarks of one victim of that process, the emigrant William Lalor: 'I must say,' he wrote to his affluent grazier father in Queen's County in 1843, 'that your opinions and mine as regards the treatment of Children differ very widely ... What I mean is keeping your property until you have no one to leave it to but old Men perhaps old Bachelors who never can enjoy any thing — I say it is almost unnatural.'[47] Fortunately, Lalor later attained his own 'independence' on a Wisconsin farm, although his resentment never abated. However, what is important about his statement is its reminder that, not only were old Patrick Lalor's actions still regarded as violations of tradition — even in the rich grasslands of

45 David W. Miller, personal communication; but see his *Queen's Rebels: Ulster Loyalism in Historical Perspective* (Dublin, 1978), 55–64; and, on evangelicalism, his 'Presbyterianism and "Modernisation" in Ulster', *Past and Present*, 80 (1978), 66–90. On Ulster Presbyterian emigration and political culture, especially in the pre-Famine period, see Chapters 7–8 in this volume.
46 e.g., the testimony of a Protestant farmer in County Down in the mid-1830s: 'until lately the Roman Catholics got no leases of land, but the Protestants had good ones; and when their leases were falling in now the landlords were raising the rent on them as well as on the Roman Catholics, so that now they were no better off than the Roman Catholics, and may-be some of them did not like that, and went away'; in Appendix F to the *First Report of the Commissioners for Inquiring in the Condition of the Poorest Classes in Ireland*, in the *British Parliamentary Papers* (hereafter BPP), HC 1836 (38), xxxiii, 142; however, see Chapter 8 in this volume. On the Orange Order and emigration to Canada, see: Cecil Houston and William J. Smyth, 'The Orange Order and the Expansion of the Frontier in Ontario, 1830–1900', *Journal of Historical Geography*, 4, 3 (1978), 251–64.
47 William Lalor, Lima, Ind., to Patrick Lalor, Tinakill, Queen's County, 12 May 1843 (Ms. 8567, NLI).

mid-Leinster and as late as 1843 — but that one of the greatest tragedies of post-Famine Ireland was that his 'opinions' would then no longer be viewed as 'unnatural' — but as perfectly 'normal' and commonplace.

3 'Revenge for Skibbereen':
Irish Emigration and the Meaning of the Great Famine

In the late nineteenth and early twentieth centuries, Irish observers as disparate as the nationalist politician John Francis Maguire and the unionist historian W. E. H. Lecky agreed that it was primarily the experiences and memories of the Great Famine which engendered 'the savage hatred of England that animates great bodies of Irishmen on either side of the Atlantic' — especially among the Irish in the United States — inspiring their repeated efforts to destroy the Irish landlord system and free Ireland from British rule.[1] Those efforts, such as the Fenian movement of 1858–71 — itself largely the product of Irish America's urban neighbourhoods, worksites, and army camps — often seemed animated as much by Irish immigrants' hatred for England as by their love of Ireland. Thus, thirty years after the Famine, Michael Flanagan, an Irish farmer in California's Napa Valley, recalled 'the rich ... Devils ... who drove the [Irish] population into the Poorhouse or across the Atlantic' and dreamed that the Irish in America might pay them 'a just reward for their oppression'.[2] Likewise in the 1880s, Patrick O'Callaghan, a soldier in Minnesota, prayed for the 'day of retribution', and another immigrant, John Cronin, vowed that the Irish 'exiles' in America eagerly awaited an opportunity 'to go back [to Ireland] with a double undying vengeance to hurl the Vile Saxon oppressor from

1   Based on my *Emigrants and Exiles: Ireland and the Irish Exodus to North America* (New York, 1985), and presented in the early 1990s as an academic conference and seminar paper, this chapter is a slightly revised version of an essay, with the same title, that later was published in Arthur Gribben, ed., *The Great Famine and the Irish Diaspora in America* (Amherst, Mass., 1999), 180–95. My thanks to the University of Massachusetts Press for permission to republish it, with minor changes, in this volume.

    W. E. H. Lecky, quoted in Miller, *Emigrants and Exiles*, 305. As in the original essay, to conserve space only direct quotations are cited. For full citations, see the endnotes to chapter 7 of *Emigrants and Exiles*.

2   Michael Flanagan, Napa, Calif., to John Flanagan, Tubbertoby, Clogherhead, County Louth, 14 April 1877 (courtesy of Peter and Mary Flanagan, Tubbertoby).

the Shores of Erin'.[3] Indeed, the Fenian movement was inspired by just such a desire to transport thousands of Irish Americans, ex-soldiers from the American Civil War, back to Ireland so that they could reverse the Famine's consequences and re-establish their families on Irish soil. And it was the Fenian movement that inspired the Irish-American ballad, one line of which provides the title of this chapter: 'Oh father dear', the song prophesied,

> ... the day will come when vengeance loud will call,
> And we will rise with Erin's boys to rally one and all.
> I'll be the man to lead the van beneath our flag of green,
> And loud and high will raise the cry, 'Revenge for Skibbereen!'[4]

Skibbereen in west County Cork was a town where the local scenes of Famine suffering gained special notoriety from their published description by Nicholas Cummins, an absentee landlord, who in 1846 discovered to his horror that the cabins on his estate were inhabited by 'famished and ghastly skeletons'.[5] However, conditions were at least equally awful in other districts, such as west Connacht and the north midlands where, a year later, another visitor 'saw sights that will never wholly leave the eyes that beheld them, cowering wretches almost naked in the savage weather, prowling in turnip fields, and endeavouring to grub up roots ... little children ... their limbs fleshless, ... their faces bloated yet wrinkled and of a pale greenish hue, ... who would never, it was too plain, grow up to be men and women'.[6] Such personal accounts give terrible meaning to the dry statistical consequences of the Great Famine: between 1.1 and 1.5 million persons dead of starvation or famine-related diseases between 1845 and 1851; at least 500,000, and perhaps closer to 1 million, people evicted from their homes by landlords and strong farmers; some 3 million people (about 40 per cent of the Irish population) on some form of official relief; over 1 million people crammed into poorhouses designed to hold only a small fraction of that number; and, between 1845 and 1855, over 2.1 million Irish (about one-fourth of the island's pre-Famine population) emigrants overseas, nearly 1.9 million of them to North America, of whom perhaps as many as 40,000 died aboard the 'coffin ships' or in Canadian and American quarantine hospitals.

However, it may be that even these appalling statistics cannot fully explain the 'savage hatred' for England which the Famine engendered among the Irish, especially in the New World, and at least one Irish Catholic politician later wondered why what he called

3 Patrick O'Callaghan, Fort Snelling, Minn., to Maggie O'Callaghan, Fallagh, Kilmacthomas, County Waterford, 17 August 1883 (courtesy of Eugene O'Callaghan and Mary Flynn, Fallagh); John Cronin, Waverly, [Mass.?], to Jeremiah O'Donovan Rossa, New York City, 16 July 1876 (John Devoy Papers, Ms. 18,001, NLI).
4 Richard L. Wright, Irish Emigrant Ballads and Songs (Bowling Green, Ohio, 1975), 54.
5 Miller, Emigrants and Exiles, 284–85; James S. Donnelly, Jr., The Land and the People of Nineteenth-Century Cork: The Rural Economy and the Land Question (London, 1975), 85–86.
6 Seumas MacManus, The Story of the Irish Race: A Popular History of Ireland (New York, 1944), 607.

'the noble generosity of the English people appears to be forgotten in a frenzy of reproach against the English government'.[7] Indeed, one modern scholar, Roger McHugh, who analysed Irish folklore of the Great Famine, concluded that most Irish country people interpreted that catastrophe as an 'act of God' rather than in nationalist terms.[8] Contemporary Irish Catholic clergymen also viewed the Famine as a divine rather than a political phenomenon, as 'a calamity with which God wishes to purify ... the Irish people', as Archbishop (later Cardinal) Cullen put it, and which would 'scatter ... the blessing of the catholic religion over distant lands', in the words of his rival, Archbishop John MacHale.[9] Likewise, visitors to Ireland during the Famine, such as American missionary Asenath Nicholson, noted that the starving poor did not curse the government for their suffering but instead thanked God that the 'kind English' sent them food.[10] '[W]ere it not for the English government that sent all that American Corn,' testified one grateful farmer, 'there would not be 100 persons alive.'[11] Fatalism and patience, the traditional characteristics of the Irish peasantry, seemed to be their most common responses to the Great Famine: 'they have made no battle for their lives,' observed one Quaker relief worker in County Mayo; 'They have presented no resistance to the progress of pinching destitution, except an extraordinary amount of patient endurance.'[12] Other observers noted that most Famine emigrants left Ireland eagerly, expressing 'nothing but joy at their escape, as if from a doomed land', 'instead of the sorrow usual on leaving their native country'.[13] Indeed, once in America at least a few emigrants wrote grateful letters to former landlords and estate agents whose financial and other assistance had enabled them to leave what one called 'the Gulf of Miserary oppression Degradetion and Ruin'. 'I am [now] Employed in the rail road line earning 5s. a day,' wrote Michael Byrne in Vermont to 'your Honour' in Galway; 'And instead of being chained with poverty in Boughill I am crowned with glory.'[14]

---

7 A. M. Sullivan, *New Ireland: Political Sketches and Personal Reminiscences of Thirty Years of Irish Public Life*, 15th edn. (London, n.d. [orig. 1877]), 58.

8 Roger J. McHugh, 'The Famine in Irish Oral Tradition', in R. D. Edwards and T. W. Williams, eds., *The Great Famine: Studies in Irish History, 1845–52* (New York, 1957), 391–436.

9 Peadar Mac Suibhne, *Paul Cullen and His Contemporaries, with Their Letters from 1820–1902*, 5 vols. (Naas, 1961–77), vol. 2, 23; Oliver MacDonagh, 'The Irish Catholic Clergy and Emigration during the Great Famine', *Irish Historical Studies*, 5, 20 (September 1947), 293.

10 Asenath Nicholson, *Lights and Shades of Ireland* (London, 1850), 8–9.

11 John Nowlan, Newtownbarry, County Wexford, to Patrick Nowlan, Digby Co., Nova Scotia, 30 September 1847 (Nowlan Mss., MC24 I127, Public Archives of Canada, Ottawa).

12 Richard D. Webb, 'Narrative of a Tour through Erris in 1848' (Ms. in the Library of the Society of Friends, Friends' House, London).

13 William S. Balch, *Ireland as I Saw It: The Character, Condition, and Prospects of the People* (New York, 1850), 136–37, 201–02.

14 Margaret McCarthy, New York City, to Alexander McCarthy, Kingwilliamstown, Kanturk, County Cork, 22 September 1850; and Michael Byrne, Middlebury, Vt., to Golding Bird, Galway city, 13 September 1848, in Elish Ellis, ed., 'Letters from the Quit Rent Office, The Four Courts, Dublin', *Analecta Hibernica*, 22 (1960), 390–94.

What, then, were the sources and causes of the subsequent desire for 'revenge for Skibbereen' that purportedly animated large numbers of Irishmen and -women on both sides of the Atlantic? First of all, despite certain continuities between the pre-Famine and Famine emigrations, there were significant differences between those who left Ireland in 1845–55 and their predecessors. In general, the Famine emigrants were much poorer, less skilled, and more in need of charity to finance their departures than the pre-Famine emigrants. Some 50,000 were 'assisted emigrants', whose voyage costs were paid by their landlords or local officials, and in the Famine's latter years, especially, the great majority of the emigrants could pay for their passages only with money sent by relatives in America. Also, an unusually large proportion of the Famine emigration was composed of families, many of whose members, the very young and the very old, ordinarily did not emigrate and who were often helpless encumbrances in the New World. In addition, the Famine exodus was overwhelmingly Catholic and as many as a third of the emigrants were Irish-speakers, Gaelic peasants from far western counties which had sent relatively few emigrants to America prior to 1845. Finally, and perhaps most important, the motives governing most Famine emigrants were qualitatively different from those which had inspired earlier departures. In the pre-Famine decades ambitious or frustrated emigrants sought what they called 'independence', economic advancement or at least 'comfortable self-sufficiency', in a land fabled for opportunity and abundance. During the Famine, however, most emigrants aspired merely to survive, and desperate panic and despair fairly screamed from their letters, petitions, and songs. '[P]ity our hard case,' wrote Mary Rush of County Sligo to her father in Canada; 'For God's sake take us out of poverty, and don't let us die with the hunger.'[15]

Second, it is important to note that such panic and despair reflected not only Ireland's food crisis but also the fact that the social and cultural bonds that had held pre-Famine rural society together, despite its dire poverty, were fast dissolving under the Famine's impact. Not only was British government relief inadequate in amount and punitive in its effects, and not only did many Protestant landlords seize the opportunity of their tenants' helplessness by clearing them from their estates, but many Catholics proved equally heartless towards their neighbours and dependants. Indeed, it is likely that a large proportion of evicted farmers and labourers were sub-lessees, dispossessed not by Protestant landowners but by Catholic head tenants, graziers and strong farmers, who sought thereby both to rationalize their holdings and to avoid paying local taxes (the poor rates) for the maintenance of their former subtenants. There were other indices of social breakdown as well. Petty rural jealousies, endemic before the Famine, now had

---

15 Michael and Mary Rush, Ardnaglass, County Sligo, to Thomas Barrett, St. Columban, Deux-Montagnes Co., Canada East [Quebec], 6 September 1846, in 'Further Papers Relative to Emigration to the British Provinces in North America [June 1847]', in the BBP, 1847, [824] xxix, 70–77. On the Rush/Barrett families, see Chapter 12 in this volume. The exceptionally large numbers who left Ireland in winter, as in 1846–47, when voyage conditions were most hazardous and job opportunities on arrival were very scarce, also attests to the desperate or 'panic' nature of much Famine emigration.

fatal consequences. Even 'the bonds of domestic affection were loosening under the pressure of want,' testified one relief worker; and reports were common of husbands deserting wives, of grown children turning their parents out on the roads, and of fathers and mothers withholding food from starving offspring.[16] Even the peasants' ancient customs surrounding death, communal attendance at wakes and funerals, fell into disuse as the island degenerated into a vast charnel house. In short, Famine Ireland was in a state of social and moral collapse. '[G]azing hopelessly into infinite darkness and despair ... , stalking by with a fierce but vacant scowl,' the famine-stricken Irish, reported one observer, 'realized that all this ought not to be, but knew not whom to blame.'[17]

Third, it must also be remembered that there was an ancient tradition, woven into the social, religious, and linguistic fabric of Irish Catholic society, which viewed all Irish Catholic emigration negatively, as involuntary and sorrowful exile; and in addition there was a more recent tradition that attributed all of the tragic dislocations in Irish Catholic history, including emigration as exile, to the tyranny of the British government and of the Sasanaigh, particularly the Protestant landlord class imposed by past conquests and confiscations.[18] In this regard, it is important to note that these beliefs were held most strongly, commonly expressed in songs and folklore, among precisely those sectors of the Irish Catholic population — the peasantry and especially the Irish-speaking peasantry—that comprised such an unusually large proportion of the Famine emigrants. In addition, for many Irish country people the events of 1845–55 (estate clearances and 'assisted' emigration by landlords, parsimonious government relief measures, and mass emigrations by many who, in ordinary circumstances, might not have left Ireland) logically served to corroborate these ancient traditions of emigration as forced banishment caused by English and Protestant oppression. Furthermore, for decades prior to the Famine, Daniel O'Connell and other nationalist leaders had striven with much success to politicize these ancient resentments in order to mobilize the Catholic masses in their crusades for Catholic Emancipation and repeal of the Act of Union.

Nevertheless, modern nationalism's impact on pre-Famine Ireland had been partial and uneven, especially in the western counties that witnessed so much suffering and emigration after 1845. Also, the early Famine years were so devastating and demoralizing that abstract nationalist slogans may have had little clear relevance to people threatened with immediate starvation. Moreover, at first the crisis seemed to obscure Ireland's usual sectarian and political divisions. When the 'kind English' sent food which some local Catholic relief committees misappropriated; when some Protestant landlords publicly condemned Catholic strong farmers for turning their labourers and servants out on the roads to starve; when Catholic priests denounced as 'wicked' proselytizers

16 *Transactions of the Central Relief Committee of the Society of Friends during the Famine in Ireland in 1846 and 1847* (Dublin, 1852), 254; William Bennett, *Narrative of a Recent Journey of Six Weeks in Ireland* (London, 1847), 130.
17 MacManus, *Story of the Irish Race*, 607.
18 See Miller, *Emigrants and Exiles*, esp. ch. 3.

the Protestant missionaries who gave soup to starving peasants; and when, in the face of such widespread misery, Archbishop Cullen could declare that Ireland's greatest problem was 'the schools system'[19] — then the strict distinctions which nationalist politicians tried to draw between the people's 'champions' and 'enemies' sometimes became dangerously blurred.

Thus, although the Famine and its emigrations did inspire some peasant anger and resistance early on, such emotions were at first imperfectly assimilated to the sharp, ideal dichotomies of modern Irish Catholic nationalism. Of course, the wholesale clearances of grieving paupers, carried out under British laws and often enforced by British troops, inevitably linked the government to the cruelest actions of the Irish landlord class. However, subtler psychological processes were also at work to politicize the Irish response to the Great Famine. As one historian has noted, the disintegrations of personal relationships and the social dislocations (including panic migration) that occurred after 1845 reflected not just a failure of the potato crop but 'a failure of morale as well'.[20] Frightened and demoralized, often able to save themselves only at the expense of neighbours and kinsmen, desperate country folk frequently displayed what one observer called 'the most unscrupulous ... knavery, cunning & falsehood'.[21] During and after the Famine, it was natural that those who survived the crisis — or emerged with more land than they had held before, thanks to their neighbours' deaths or evictions — might feel tremendous popular resentment or personal shame for such extensive violations of communal mores and that they would seek 'explanations' for what had occurred which would project blame and resentment upon 'outsiders'. It was also natural that the Irish, faced with the failures of traditional beliefs and customs to avert the catastrophe, would turn more attentively to Catholic clerics and nationalist politicians who offered for the crisis an embracing 'explanation' which obviated personal guilt, obscured intracommunal conflicts, and generalized the people's individual grievances into a powerful political and cultural weapon against the traditional antagonist. As a result, Catholic Ireland and Irish America emerged from the Famine's terrible crucible more vehemently and unanimously opposed to Protestant England and its Irish representatives than ever before.

However, this is looking ahead, for in the Famine's early years most Irish Catholic politicians and clergy made only muted or confused responses to the crisis: partly because they were paralysed by its enormity and its apparently natural or divine origins; partly because they hoped that conciliatory words and actions might ensure adequate relief from the government; and partly because they were distracted by the bitter conflicts between Daniel O'Connell and the Young Ireland faction of the Repeal Movement. Moreover, some nationalist spokesmen, including both the O'Connellite landlord

19 Mac Suibhne, *Paul Cullen and His Contemporaries*, vol. 3, 98–101.
20 Oliver MacDonagh, 'Irish Emigration to the United States of America and the British Colonies during the Famine', in Edwards and Williams, eds., *The Great Famine*, 329.
21 Webb, 'Narrative of a Tour through Erris in 1848'.

Sir Thomas Wyse and the Young Ireland leader William Smith O'Brien, initially advocated massive, government-assisted emigration as the best solution to the people's distress. Nevertheless, by 1847–48 Catholic clerics and nationalists of all persuasions had begun to question, then attack British actions towards Ireland, and to stigmatize Famine emigration as forced exile. For example, during this period Dublin's leading Catholic newspaper, the *Freeman's Journal*, moved from acquiescence in emigration to adamant hostility. Young Irelanders, such as the Protestant firebrand John Mitchel, were most violent in attributing Famine deaths and departures to British malevolence. In editorials and orations Mitchel and his peers raged at Irishmen so supine as to regard the Famine as 'a visitation of Providence' instead of 'a visitation of English landlordism' — which was, in Mitchel's words, 'as great a curse to Ireland as if it was the archfiend himself had the government of the country'. And by the early 1850s Catholic political and clerical opinion was virtually unanimous in blaming the British government for Irish suffering and in denouncing emigration as 'a devilish plot' by Ireland's 'hereditary oppressors' to 'exterminate' the Irish people or 'exile' them overseas.[22]

In the light of Catholic Ireland's past sufferings at British and Protestant hands, such criticism was logical and was at least partly justified by contemporary events, particularly when the London *Times*, the mouthpiece of the British establishment, described the Famine as 'a great blessing', exulted in Irish evictions and emigration, and gleefully predicted that, 'In a few years more, a Celtic Irishman will be as rare in Connemara as is the Red Indian on the shores of Manhattan.' No wonder that dedicated nationalists such as Mitchel were filled with 'a sacred wrath' against England and that ordinary Irishmen and Irish Americans — who first learned of such callous statements through nationalist channels — soon became equally convinced that their sufferings were intentional, their emigration exile.[23] However, as Mitchel and his radical Young Ireland compatriot James Fintan Lalor realized, only far-reaching *social* as well as political revolution, involving the destruction of landlordism itself, could eradicate the root causes of Irish rural distress, yet most middle-class Catholic nationalists — wealthy farmers and townsmen — were too conservative to countenance a peasant assault on Irish capitalism. There were still too many landless labourers in Ireland for the Irish bourgeoisie to dare echo Lalor's cry, 'The Land for the People!', since a social upheaval from below would threaten the property of the Catholic middle classes as well as of the Protestant landlords.

Consequently, the gathering nationalist/clerical outcry against England and emigration may have had sources other than genuine rage, and it may be significant that public criticisms of government policy and emigration became ubiquitous only in the Famine's latter years — *after* the decimation of the lower classes — when once-comfortable tenants began to flee en masse from crushing taxation and when the continued flood

---

22 Robert Kee, *The Green Flag: The Turbulent History of the Irish Nationalist Movement* (New York, 1972), 243–55; Malcolm Brown, *The Politics of Irish Literature: From Thomas Davis to W. B. Yeats* (Seattle, 1973), 105.
23 Brown, *Politics of Irish Literature*, 105; Sullivan, *New Ireland*, 118–19, 136.

tide overseas began seriously to threaten Catholic strong farmers, shopkeepers, and clergymen with a loss of cheap labour, valuable customers, and devout parishioners. Thus, Mitchel, Lalor, and a few dedicated revolutionaries aside, the primary function of nationalist and Church leaders' attacks on British misgovernment and emigration was not to inspire violence, or even to halt the exodus, but to articulate popular outrage in ways that would reunite the remnants of the fractured Catholic 'nation' behind bourgeois leadership and reconsolidate Catholic opinion against 'English tyranny' to better realize the pragmatic and essentially conservative middle-class and clerical goals — the legalization of tenant-right (chiefly, to protect head tenants against eviction) and Church control over Catholic education — that dominated the Irish political agenda in the 1850s.

It was ironic, then, that it was Young Ireland's futile but symbolically crucial revolt in 1848 against British rule — a revolt vehemently opposed both by Catholic clerics and by nearly all Catholic politicians — that ensured the future credibility of the nationalist interpretation of the Famine and of Irish emigration. As revolution, Young Ireland's effort was a sad farce, but as Irish revolutionary theatre it was a grand, if hopeless, gesture, which enshrined its defeated leaders in the pantheon of Irish martyrs to the centuries-old struggle against the Sasanaigh. Furthermore, the Young Ireland leaders' subsequent personal experiences gave them special authority to interpret all Irish emigration as political exile, for many of them avoided arrest and fled directly to America, while others, including John Mitchel himself, escaped in the early 1850s from the British penal colony in Van Diemen's Land (now Tasmania) and went to the United States. There they received heroes' welcomes and, along with the earlier refugees, engaged in Irish-American journalism and politics, agitated and plotted for Irish freedom, and dramatically personified their own contention that emigration was forced banishment.

Even before the Famine's end, it may be that Young Ireland's rhetoric influenced the interpretations of contemporary events by some Irish emigrants, such as the young Dublin artisan Thomas Reilly, who sailed in early 1848 to New York praying that 'the atlantic ocean be never so deep as the hell which shall belch down the oppressors of my race'.[24] Young Ireland's successful politicization of Famine sufferings may also be evident in the occasional accounts of evicted farmers swearing vengeance on the British government and on their landlords as they embarked for America. Such stories may have been apocryphal, but they conformed to nationalist models of experience and emotion that gained increasing credibility and currency after the 1848 rebellion. Moreover, the Young Irelanders' influence on Irish and Irish-American political culture long outlived the crisis that precipitated their revolt. Their bitter interpretations of Famine, evictions, and emigration — enshrined in innumerable speeches, poems, songs, sermons, and a few minor masterpieces such as Mitchel's Jail Journal — provided much of the nationalist catechism for later generations on both sides of the ocean. Thus, subsequent emigrants,

24 Thomas Reilly, Saratoga, NY, to John M. Kelly, Dublin, 19 July 1848 (Ms. 10,511, NLI).

who never experienced either the horrors or the ambiguities of the Great Famine, learned from childhood 'how Erin's children [were] butchered, starved, and ground by the iron heel of the robber Saxon, till worn and broken, the decimated remnant fled their homes and country, to find peace and a grave in a foreign land'.[25]

Young Ireland's greatest influence may have been on the Irish in America, particularly on the Famine emigrants and their children. Thanks to the efforts of the United Irishmen in the 1790s, of O'Connell from the 1820s, and of Young Ireland since the early 1840s, it is arguable that by the Famine's eve ordinary Irish Catholics, even the illiterate majority, may have been the most politically conscious populace in western Europe. Yet, although townsmen such as Thomas Reilly, as well as other literate emigrants, were politicized before their departures, it is arguable that many of those who left home during the Famine needed the perspectives of time and distance before they could translate their intensely personal, localized sufferings into broad, nationalist terms. Once in the New World, however, the Famine emigrants proved especially receptive to nationalist interpretations of their experiences.

One reason, as suggested earlier, was that so many of those who departed during the crisis were poor country folk, often Irish-speakers, who shared a communal culture that had always discouraged emigration and viewed it as forced banishment: reflections of a deeply conservative worldview that devalued individual initiative and responsibility for innovative actions, such as emigration, and which their helplessness in the face of blight, disease, and ruthless evictions had too clearly corroborated. Of course, these peasants had escaped death by emigrating, but unlike most pre-Famine emigrants, the Famine refugees had not made informed, calculated decisions to seek 'independence' overseas. Rather, they had fled in panicked desperation, compelled by fear and by forces perhaps beyond their understanding and certainly beyond their powers of resistance. Thus, Irishmen who initially had viewed the Famine as God's chastisement for their sins, who felt guilty for their demoralized and antisocial behaviour during the crisis, and who emigrated because customary sanctions temporarily crumbled in the face of death — all these had cultural and psychological needs for the examples and exhortations of the Young Ireland leaders, who ceaselessly (and justifiably) blamed England, the perennial enemy, for forcing the Irish to abandon their homes and to endure the shame and 'degradation into which hunger and want will reduce human nature'.[26]

In short, the Young Ireland exiles both validated and modernized traditional perceptions and resentments by 'explaining' that the Famine emigrants, like themselves, were in truth 'exiles' who had been 'driven out of Erin' by political tyranny. Moreover, the Irish-American nationalists offered a redemptive solution as well as an explanation for Irish suffering, for if the Famine emigrants rose above self-pity, renewed communal fealty, and united behind nationalist leadership, then they might expunge their shame,

25 Miller, Emigrants and Exiles, 311.
26 Jeremiah O'Donovan Rossa, Rossa's Recollections (Mariner's Harbor, NY, 1899), 110.

win freedom for Ireland, and take bloody vengeance on those deemed responsible for the Famine graves and the coffin ships: they might, in other words, win 'Revenge for Skibbereen'.

Finally, it is arguable that the Famine immigrants in America would have been much less receptive to such rhetoric, and the fires of late nineteenth-century Irish-American nationalism might have burned much less intensely, if those immigrants' overall experiences in the United States had been less impoverished and embittering. To be sure, many Famine immigrants, especially those who succeeded in establishing themselves on American farms, achieved at least modest prosperity. However, after an initial period of rambling about, searching for employment, most lived and died in American cities, mining camps, and public works sites, where the great majority — semi-skilled and unskilled labourers and servants — seldom rose far from the bottom of American white society. Despite regional variations, nearly all studies of the Irish in mid-century America exhibit depressing similarities. Whether in large eastern seaports like Boston and New York, in small industrial centres like Lawrence and Poughkeepsie, in midwestern cities like South Bend and Milwaukee, even in frontier towns like Denver and Sacramento: in all these, Irish immigrants were disproportionately concentrated in the lowest-paid, least-skilled, and most dangerous and insecure employment. With few exceptions, they also displayed the highest rates of transience, residential density and segregation, inadequate housing and sanitation, commitments to prisons and charity institutions, and excess mortality. 'It is a well established fact,' reported one Irish American, 'that the average length of life of the emigrant after landing here is six years; and many believe it is much less': probably an exaggeration, but one that reflected the Famine immigrants' alarming mortality from disease, exposure, occupational accidents, and sheer overwork — as well as the effects of the privations they had endured in Ireland before departing or in their voyages to America. In addition, from Protestant Yankees the Irish encountered a pervasive religious and ethnic prejudice that assumed nationwide political dimensions in the nativist Know-Nothing movement of the 1850s and which often resulted in brutal exploitation by bigoted employers and co-workers. As one outraged immigrant declared, the life of an Irish labourer in mid-century America was often 'despicable, humiliating, [and] slavish', for there 'was no love for him — no protection of life — [he] can be shot down, run through, kicked, cuffed, spat on — and no redress, but a response of served the damn son of an Irish b[itch] right, damn him'.[27]

27 Patrick Kieran Walsh, Cleveland, Ohio, n.d., in Cork Examiner, 11 June 1860; and Michael J. Adams, Sweet Springs, Va., 26 June 1860, in Cork Examiner, 10 August 1860 (both from the Schrier collection). In 1854–56 a new 'American party' represented native-Protestants' anti-Catholic, anti-immigrant, and especially anti-Irish Catholic fears and prejudices; the party was popularly known as the 'Know-Nothings' because many of its adherents, members as well of secret and sometimes violent local nativist and anti-Catholic societies, were sworn to secrecy and, if questioned about the latter, were supposed to reply that they 'knew nothing'. In the mid-1850s the party assumed or shared power in many state and municipal governments, principally in northern states such as Massachusetts and Pennsylvania, where large numbers of Famine Irish had settled; in the 1856 presidential election, however, the Know Nothing party

Thus, Thomas Doyle, a British spy in the United States, was only partly right when, in the late 1850s, he reported to London that it was the Famine immigrants' old memories of the 'horrifying cruelties of the Crowbar Brigade' (that is, of mass evictions) that inspired their loyalty to the nascent Fenian movement and their desire to 'wreak vengeance on the persecutors of their race and creed'.[28] Perhaps equally important were the Famine immigrants' harsh experiences in the United States, for they often engendered bitter disillusion and profound homesickness among those who once fondly imagined they had escaped from poverty and Protestant prejudice. For example, working-class immigrants such as Daniel Rowntree soon had their fill of the so-called 'promised land'. 'I have suffered more than I thought I could endure,' Rowntree wrote, 'in a strange Country far from a friend, necessitated to go on public works from four oClock of a Summer Morning until Eight at Night enduring the hardships of a burning Sun, [and] then by Sickness losing what I dearly earned.'[29] 'We dont like this country very well,' wrote another recently arrived Irish labourer, and 'I think as soon as possible we will come home to old Ireland.'[30] Indeed, according to many observers, poverty and prejudice encouraged many Famine immigrants at least to entertain the unrealistic dream of actually returning to Ireland. 'So hopelessly irksome do our people find their condition in this country,' wrote one Irish-American journalist, 'that ... hundreds of thousands ... would ask no greater boon from Heaven ... than an opportunity to Stake their lives to regain a foothold on their native soil.'[31] Thus, another immigrant, the aforementioned Thomas Reilly, confessed that he was merely 'a Slave in the land of liberty' and announced his intention of joining an Irish-American militia company 'preparing ... to invade Ireland'. 'Perhaps, I will return with the green flag flying above me,' he wrote; 'I care not if it becomes my shroud. I have no regard for life while I am in exile.'[32]

Impoverished Irish labourers and domestic servants who dreamed such dreams and resented poverty and mistreatment in America may have been especially susceptible to the appeals of Irish-American nationalists who characterized emigration as sorrowful exile, blamed it — and the immigrants' sad condition — on British and landlord oppression, and promised that, by working and sacrificing to liberate Ireland, they could redeem their sufferings and at least enjoy a vicarious realization of their longings.

performed worse than many had anticipated, and thereafter most of its leaders and members melded into the new Republican party.

28 Subinspector Thomas Doyle, Report no. 40, 26 August 1859 (Fenian Movement Reports, carton 62, formerly in the Irish State Paper Office, now in the National Archives of Ireland, Dublin). Also see Summary, Doyle Reports (Sir Thomas A. Larcom Papers, Ms. 7697, 4–6, in NLI).

29 Daniel Rowntree, Washington, DC., to Laurence Rowntree, Dublin, 23 March 1852 (Schrier collection).

30 Lewis Reford, Newburgh, NY, to Frances Reford, Antrim town, 15 July 1849 (T. 3028/B5, PRONI). Also see the letter by the 'Broken hearted and destitu[t]e' Anne Brown, Paint Rock, Iowa, to Fr. Clement Reville, Wexford, County Wexford, 18 November 1852 (courtesy of Fr. Bartholomew Eagan, Franciscan Library, Killiney, County Dublin): 'to tell our tales of sorrow since we came to America I dont Know where to begin'.

31 Patrick Kieran Walsh, Cleveland, Ohio, in Cork Examiner, 11 June 1860.

32 Thomas Reilly, Albany, NY, to John M. Kelly, Dublin, 24 April 1848 (Ms. 10,511, NLI).

However, even relatively affluent Irish immigrants were also responsive to — and often employed — nationalist rhetoric: in part because as businessmen, Democratic party politicians, and Catholic clergy, they found appeals to Irish nationalism useful in mobilizing their Irish customers, employees, constituents, and parishioners for practical *American* purposes; but also in part because even economically successful Irish Americans often endured insecurity and prejudice in the United States. Thus, William Lalor, who had become a comfortable farmer in Wisconsin, never forgot or forgave the 'Yankee tricks' that native-born Americans had played upon him during his first, difficult years in the United States, and even in late middle age he was prone to indulge the hope of returning to Ireland in the ranks of the 'Fenian army'.[33]

However, many Irish Americans who supported the nationalist cause, especially the upwardly mobile, were less concerned to free Ireland from British rule than to free themselves from nativist scorn and proscription: for only if Ireland were independent and prosperous, editorialized one New York Irish newspaper in the 1850s, would her 'exiled children [be] honored or respected'; only then, declared another Irish-American journalist, could they meet native Americans 'without being inflamed with feelings of ... shame' for their heritage.[34] Likewise, for Famine immigrants such as Patrick Ford, who came to America as a child and, as he later wrote, had 'brought nothing with me from Ireland ... to make me what I am', as well as for Irish Americans born in the United States, Irish-American nationalism could help resolve questions of personal identity as well as the immigrants' problematic status in American society. Hence, Ford, who in the late nineteenth century became Irish America's most influential journalist, readily concluded that 'it was necessary for everyone of Irish blood to do all in his power' to elevate the Irish in America by liberating the Irish in Ireland.[35] In short, Irish-American nationalism — and its recurrent theme of emigration as exile caused by British oppression — could appeal to those who aspired to full assimilation in American society, even if especially to the impoverished masses of Famine immigrants for whom such a goal was usually unattainable.

Thus, in terms of mass involvement and its avowed goal to transport thousands of disaffected, armed immigrants back to Ireland, the Fenian movement of the 1860s was unique in the history of Irish-American nationalism, for later generations of Irish Americans were less alienated than the Famine immigrants, more successful economically, and integrated into political, religious, and social institutions, which promoted security and contentment. Nevertheless, the Famine exodus and its

33 William Lalor, Lima, Ind., to Patrick Lalor, Tinakill, Queen's County, 12 May 1843; and from same, Dunn township, Wisc., to Richard Lalor, same address, 4 July 1867 and 10 February 1868 (Ms. 8567, NLI).

34 New York *Irish News*, 17 April 1858; New York *Phoenix*, undated clipping in Subinspector Thomas Doyle, Report no. 47, 28 October 1859 (Fenian Movement, Reports, as in n. 28 above).

35 Thomas N. Brown, *Irish-American Nationalism, 1870–1890* (Philadelphia, 1966), 21–22; and Joseph P. Rodechko, *Patrick Ford and His Search for America: A Case Study of Irish-American Journalism, 1870–1913* (New York, 1976), 56.

nationalist fervour left an indelible mark on Irish and Irish-American societies alike, influencing future developments on both sides of the Atlantic. In Ireland, beginning with the Fenians, all future Irish nationalist movements were heavily dependent on Irish-American approval and funds. On the American side, nationalist interpretations of the Great Famine enshrined a now permanent model for Irish emigration, to which all immigrants, present and future, usually conformed, at least publicly. For example, the shoemaker John Burke, who left his native Westmeath in 1847, did so not on compulsion but from 'disgust' at Ireland's inadequate economic opportunities. Yet despite the relative prosperity Burke achieved in America, forty years after his departure, when he finished his memoirs, he accommodated his life story to communal traditions and nationalist rhetoric, and asserted that he, too, was an 'exile' whose emigration had been caused by the Famine and by British oppression.[36] In addition, the Famine immigrants and their nationalist spokesmen passed down a legacy of lasting bitterness and unfulfilled dreams to their American-born offspring. 'Keep bright in your mind the story of Ireland,' demanded one ex-Fenian of his young son, 'and should God send the opportunity during your life [to] aid by voice or means the great struggle which is but postponed, then I charge you in your manhood to act as becometh your race.'[37]

'Revenge for Skibbereen' — for 'the tears your mothers shed' — was a terrible burden for American-born innocents to bear. However, for their immigrant parents neither time nor success had dulled recollections of the years 'when gaunt hunger and death stalked abroad',[38] and when thousands of evicted peasants had perished on the roads or sailed in disease-ridden coffin ships to a not-so-promised land. Thus, thirty years after such events had caused his own emigration, Lewis Doyle, an Irish farmer in Minnesota, still remembered and hated 'the cursed government' of Ireland, and in a letter home he asked his cousin, 'Why dont you in the name of God Just shake the dust from your feet & leave your curse upon the system that Exiled ... all good honest and faithful Irishmen from their native land?'[39]

36 John Burke, 'Reminiscences', c. 1891 (Ms. in New-York Historical Society, New York City).
37 J. P. Carbery, book inscription (25 June 1870), in Colton Storm, ed., Catalogue of the Everett D. Graff Collection of Western Americana (Chicago, 1968), 388.
38 M. McAuley, letter in Fermanagh Reporter, 5 April 1878 (from the collection of the late Professor E. R. R. Green, Queen's University, Belfast, since deposited in PRONI; hereafter the Green collection).
39 Lewis Doyle, Kilkenny, Minn., to John Doyle, Pollerton, County Carlow, 17 January 1880 (courtesy of Seamus Murphy, Pollerton Little, Carlow); published in abridged form in T. Kelly, ed., 'Letters from America (II)', Carloviana: Journal of the Old Carlow Society, 1, 2 (January 1948), 87.

4 Emigration as Exile:
Cultural Hegemony in Post-Famine Ireland

In post-Famine Ireland emigration was the predominant fact of life: between 1856 and 1929 perhaps as many as 5 million people left the island, some 4 million of them for the United States. As a result, Ireland's population steadily declined, from 5.8 million in 1861 (already down from c. 8.5 million on the Famine's eve) to less than 4.3 million by 1926.[1]

In post-Famine Ireland, as before, the interpretation of emigration that enjoyed greatest legitimacy, at least in Irish Catholic society, was that of emigration as exile, as involuntary expatriation obliged by forces beyond individual choice or control, sometimes by fate or destiny, but usually by the operations or consequences of what Irish nationalists commonly called 'British misrule' or 'landlord tyranny'. As argued in Chapter 1, however, on individual levels this interpretation was in most cases not literally credible. Certainly, British imperialism and landlordism influenced — indeed, distorted — Ireland's economic development. And the exile label was quite appropriate for Irish political rebels, for transported felons, and arguably even for evicted tenants, as in the early 1860s and especially during the Land War of 1879–82. Nevertheless, the great majority of emigrants left post-Famine Ireland for essentially mundane reasons similar or identical to those that produced mass migration from other European countries: the decline of cottage industries, crop failures, falling agricultural prices, the exigencies of impartible inheritance and the dowry system, and the increasing redundancy of petty

1 This chapter is a slightly revised and expanded version of an essay, with the same title, published in Rudolph J. Vecoli and Suzanne M. Sinke, eds., *A Century of European Migrations, 1830–1930* (Urbana, Ill., 1991), 339–63. My thanks to the University of Illinois Press for permission to republish the essay in this volume. Emigration figures in Kerby A. Miller, *Emigrants and Exiles: Ireland and the Irish Exodus to North America* (New York, 1985), 346 and *passim*.

farmers and agricultural labourers brought about by the consolidation of holdings, the conversion of tillage to pasture, and the introduction of labour-saving farm machinery. In short, the processes of modern agrarian and industrial capitalism were primarily responsible for an Irish emigration that was, in general, more or less as 'voluntary' as contemporary mass movements to America from Germany, Sicily, or Poland. Moreover, many of the most compelling and immediate causes of Irish emigration were generated within the Irish Catholic community, especially during the post-Famine era when most departures occurred, and it is problematic how much suffering and emigration among the rural lower classes (labourers, smallholders, farmers' non-inheriting children) were really more attributable to profit-maximization among Catholic commercial farmers and rural parents, generally, than to the machinations of Protestant landlords or British officials.[2]

Nor is this to say that Irish emigrants invariably characterized themselves as unwilling exiles — as in their personal letters and memoirs — although some certainly did so. Among those who remained in Ireland or who had not yet emigrated there were alternative conceptualizations of emigration — as opportunity or even escape — that contradicted the unhappy, compulsory connotations of exile. However, popular interpretations of complex social realities are often inconsistent or contradictory, and although the Irish at home and abroad individually employed the exile motif sporadically and situationally, they expressed it collectively with great regularity in their songs, poems, speeches, sermons, and newspapers. Moreover, the fact that it was utilized so often and so successfully in the appeals of Irish and Irish-American nationalists and clerics indicates that the hearts and purses of ordinary Irish people on both sides of the Atlantic were almost instinctively open to the imagery of political banishment.[3]

2   For a fuller exposition of many points in this chapter and for more complete citations, see Miller, *Emigrants and Exiles*, esp. 427–92 on post-Famine emigration, and, on the interpretation of emigration as exile, 102–30; and also Chapter 1 of this volume. On the causes of Irish emigration during the pre-Famine, Famine, and post-Famine periods, respectively, see: William Forbes Adams, *Ireland and Irish Emigration to the New World, from 1815 to the Famine* (New Haven, Conn., 1932); Oliver MacDonagh, 'The Irish Famine Emigration to the United States', *Perspectives in American History*, 10 (1976), 357–448; and Arnold Schrier, *Ireland and the American Emigration, 1850–1900* (Minneapolis, Minn., 1958); as well as chs. 6–8 of Miller, *Emigrants and Exiles*.

3   On varying popular interpretations of Irish emigration and of America, see Kerby A. Miller and Bruce D. Boling, 'Golden Streets, Bitter Tears: The Irish Image of America during the Era of Mass Migration', *Journal of American Ethnic History*, 10 (1990–91), 16–35, as well as Chapter 5 in this volume. On Irish-American nationalists, see especially Thomas N. Brown, *Irish-American Nationalism, 1870–1890* (Philadelphia, 1966), and William L. Joyce, *Editors and Ethnicity: A History of the Irish-American Press, 1848–1883* (New York, 1976).

A useful framework for understanding the prevalence of the notion that emigration was exile is provided by Antonio Gramsci's theory of cultural hegemony, as elaborated by Raymond Williams.[4] According to Gramsci, every individual has a 'spontaneous philosophy', embodied in language, religion, conventional wisdom, and empirical knowledge, that usually contains profound discrepancies between inherited or externally received notions and those implicit in everyday actions, experiences, and social position. This 'contradictory consciousness', often producing political passivity or paralysis, is the result of the processes of 'cultural hegemony' by which a ruling class disseminates its values; it does this through a variety of institutional means and through pervasive cultural expressions that reflect the society's economic 'base' or governing social processes — for example, industrial capitalism. Although the ruling class could exercise authority through 'political' coercion, in a capitalist society it more commonly creates a hegemony ('intellectual and moral leadership') through the agencies of 'civil' society's 'ideological superstructure', such as law, religion, selective historical tradition, formal education, the structures of work and family life, political parties, trade unions, and other ostensibly 'voluntary' organizations and media. Of course, the 'political' and 'civil' realms are analytically rather than actually distinct. Gramsci defined the nature of power in contemporary society as 'hegemony armoured by coercion'; however, the function of hegemony is to produce among the masses a *spontaneous* consent to what another scholar calls 'the values, norms, perceptions, beliefs, sentiments, and prejudices that support and define the existing distribution of goods, the institutions that decide how this distribution occurs, and the permissible range of disagreement about those processes'. In other words, what Raymond Williams has termed the 'dominant' culture so saturates a given society that its norms and values seem to be 'commonsensical' — organized, experienced, and ratified through popular participation in the processes that generate them.[5]

Williams also points out that the dominant or hegemonic culture is neither static nor monolithic. It reflects the dynamism, fluidity, and diversity of society's governing processes, institutions, and classes (which can themselves exhibit contradictory consciousness), and furthermore, it also interacts with potential 'counter-hegemonies' — that is, with 'alternative' or 'oppositional' cultures that reflect 'deviant' practices, experiences, and norms. Williams defines these other cultures as either 'residual' or 'emergent'. Residual values are holdovers from previously dominant social formations (for example, feudal or pre-industrial), whereas emergent cultures express new meanings

---

4   Unless otherwise cited, the material in this and the two following paragraphs are derived from Antonio Gramsci, *The Modern Prince and Other Writings* (New York, 1957); Quentin Hoare and Geoffrey Nowell Smith, eds., *Selections from the Prison Notebooks of Antonio Gramsci* (New York, 1971); and Raymond Williams, 'Base and Superstructure in Marxist Cultural Theory', *New Left Review*, 82 (November–December, 1983), 3–16.

5   Joseph V. Femia, *Gramsci's Political Thought: Hegemony, Consciousness, and the Revolutionary Process* (Oxford, 1981), 28; T. J. Jackson Lears, 'The Concept of Cultural Hegemony: Problems and Possibilities', *American Historical Review*, 90 (June 1985), 569.

rooted in actual, contemporary experiences and reflect the embryonic self-consciousness of new classes (such as the proletariat) and social realities and practices not yet recognized by the dominant culture. The dominant culture usually incorporates certain aspects of the residual and emergent alternatives, thereby reducing their potential opposition; thus, the process of cultural hegemony is 'open at both ends'.[6]

According to Gramsci, it is primarily society's intellectuals who perform the historical task or function of articulating the hegemonic culture and incorporating or reconciling its potential oppositions. In Gramsci's view, every ruling class, as it advances to power, creates its own 'organic' intellectuals. Hence, the needs of the capitalist entrepreneur give rise to the engineer, the scientist, the economist, the journalist, and others who 'explain' and express those needs or 'hegemonic imperatives' in contemporary and 'materialistic' ways. Yet, before a class can exercise hegemony over its rivals and subordinates, it must confront and assimilate what Gramsci calls the 'traditional' intellectuals — for example, ecclesiastics and lawyers — that is, the organic intellectuals of previously dominant social formations, whose 'residual' wisdom, adapted to contemporary conditions, can invest the new hegemonic culture with an apparently timeless and even 'spiritual' authority in the consciousness of the subordinate classes. Although Gramsci's distinction between organic and traditional intellectuals is somewhat artificial and vague, the point is that, together, they articulate the ideology of the ruling classes in ways that not only incorporate elements of residual and emergent culture, but in the process also facilitate the creation of ideological blocs or transcendent political alliances (for example, between the bourgeoisie and, say, the Church, skilled trade unions, or farmers, versus the industrial proletariat), which themselves disseminate the dominant culture and generate popular consent.

Before examining how cultural hegemony theory can illuminate the origins and functions of the Irish perception of emigration as exile, it is necessary to describe briefly some salient features of post-Famine Irish Catholic society. First, that society remained overwhelmingly rural. As late as 1911, two-thirds of Ireland's population still lived on farms or in villages and towns containing fewer than 2,000 inhabitants. More than two-thirds of Irish farms enclosed fewer than 30 acres, and nearly half contained less than 15 acres. These were family farms on the 'peasant model', characterized by 'a subsistence economy, where production for the market [was] not the dominating

---

6   Lears, 'Concept of Cultural Hegemony', 571–73.

purpose of production'. In addition, about one-third of those employed in agriculture were landless labourers and farm servants.[7]

However, despite Catholic Ireland's relative 'backwardness', from the late eighteenth century it was a society in rapid transition to agrarian capitalism. As described in Chapter 2, British demands for Irish foodstuffs generated greater profits from market production and greater financial pressures by landlords through higher rents and estate rationalization, to which tenants and subtenants responded by producing more grain and, especially, livestock for British consumption. Well before the Great Famine, contemporaries noted the emergence of a prosperous Catholic bourgeoisie, based on a partnership between urban businessmen and professionals, on the one hand, and large commercial or strong farmers — especially rich graziers and speculators — on the other. Simultaneously, Catholic Ireland's commercial growth stimulated a comparable increase in the wealth, infrastructure, and influence of the Irish Catholic Church, largely financed and staffed by the donations and the offspring of the Catholic middle classes.[8]

Ironically, the tragedy of the Great Famine enabled the Catholic bourgeoisie and the Church to consolidate their socio-economic position and moral authority. The deaths and departures of c. 3 million people during the Famine and its immediate aftermath (1845–55) ravaged the subsistence sector of Irish society (smallholders, cottiers, and landless labourers), broke the hitherto-fierce resistance of the Whiteboys and other peasant-based secret agrarian societies to the commercialization and consolidation of agriculture, and enabled the middle classes to gain greater influence over a relatively more affluent, literate, and shrunken populace. During the post-Famine period, the ranks of small farmers and, especially, cottiers and farm labourers continued to shrink, largely through emigration, as industrial and rural employment steadily declined and as middling and small farmers abandoned the once common custom of partible inheritance in favour of impartible inheritance, which designated most farmers' children as future emigrants. Religious strictures increasingly reinforced bourgeois norms, as Catholic Church leaders such as Cardinal Cullen promulgated a devotional revolution, which conformed Catholic country folk, formerly lax in religious observance or fidelity to clerical authority, to Roman prescriptions of belief and practice.[9]

7 Miller, Emigrants and Exiles, 380–83, 430; Damian F. Hannan, 'Peasant Models and the Understanding of Social and Cultural Change in Rural Ireland', in P. J. Drudy, ed., Irish Studies 2: Ireland — Land, Politics and People (Cambridge, 1982), 142–44, 146. When this essay was written, the standard general work on Irish economic development was Louis M. Cullen, An Economic History of Ireland since 1660 (London, 1972). In this chapter I have excluded consideration of the Protestant-dominated and heavily urbanized and industrialized counties of northeastern Ireland, which formed the core of Northern Ireland when it was created in 1921; however, see the chapters in Part II of this volume.

8 Cullen, Economic History of Ireland, 50–133; also see Cullen's The Emergence of Modern Ireland, 1600–1900 (London, 1981). On the Irish Catholic Church before the Famine, see S. J. Connolly, Priests and People in Pre-Famine Ireland, 1780–1845 (Dublin, 1982).

9 On post-Famine Irish economy and society, see Cullen, Economic History of Ireland, 134–70; and Joseph Lee, The Modernisation of Irish Society, 1848–1918 (Dublin, 1973). On the causes of post-Famine emigration, see Miller, Emigrants and Exiles, 353–426. On the secret agrarian societies, see Samuel Clark and James S.

Finally, it is important to remember that, before the War of Independence of 1919–21 and the subsequent creation of the semi-independent Irish Free State, Catholic Ireland was not a nation-state. Legally, since 1800 Ireland had been an integral part of the United Kingdom, but historically and economically it was a British colony, established by conquest and maintained ultimately by force. England's conquest had imposed on Ireland a Protestant Ascendancy, led by a handful of landlords who owned 90 per cent of Irish soil. Although Catholics constituted roughly three-fourths of Ireland's inhabitants (81 per cent in 1831, 74 per cent in 1911), until 1829 they were subject to a variety of politically and economically disabling Penal Laws, and until 1869 the Protestant Church of Ireland was the legally established religion. Even after those dates, the Ascendancy remained disproportionately powerful until the Land War and the subsequent rise of the Home Rule movement obliged the British government to dismantle Irish landlordism and democratize Irish politics. However, the Irish economy was so thoroughly integrated to British capitalism that even the achievement of independence for southern Ireland in 1921 was, in economic terms at least, merely nominal.[10]

With respect to the theory of cultural hegemony, the position of the Catholic bourgeoisie was greatly complicated by Ireland's colonial status. Looking at the United Kingdom as a whole, the Irish middle class could be seen as merely a regional component of a ruling British bourgeoisie instead of a dominant or potentially dominant class in its own right. In that view, what might be called the Catholic bourgeoisie's hegemonic imperatives with respect to its subordinate classes (the small farmers and the rural and urban proletariat) would be virtually identical to the imperatives of the British governing classes. From an all-UK perspective, the dominant Irish Catholic subculture could be classed as a regional variant of the dominant British culture, especially with respect to values that ratified and reinforced capitalist institutions and processes, such as private property, 'free market' competition, and individual acquisitiveness, as well as in regard to certain notions of style or taste emanating from the British metropolis. Indeed, in some respects Catholic Ireland's dominant culture was extremely emulative or, as critics charged, 'West British'.

However, the unequal development of southern Ireland's agrarian economy in its dependent relationship to English industrial and finance capitalism, coupled with Catholic resentments against Irish political inferiority at Westminster and the Protestant Ascendancy at home, inspired much of the Catholic middle class to seek regional

Donnelly, Jr., eds., *Irish Peasants: Violence and Political Unrest, 1780–1914* (Madison, Wisc., 1983). On the Irish Catholic Church after the Famine, see Emmet Larkin, 'The Devotional Revolution in Ireland, 1850–75', *American Historical Review*, 77 (June 1972), 625–52.

10 When this essay was initially written, the best one-volume studies of modern Irish political history were Tom Garvin, *The Evolution of Irish Nationalist Politics* (Dublin, 1981); E. Strauss, *Irish Nationalism and British Democracy* (London, 1951); and (for the post-Famine period) F. S. L. Lyons, *Ireland since the Famine* (London, 1971). The Catholic proportion of Ireland's population in 1831 is calculated from the parish data in the *First Report of the Commission of Public Instruction, Ireland*, in BPP, HC 1835, xxxiii; for 1861–1911 see W. E. Vaughan and A. J. Fitzpatrick, eds., *Irish Historical Statistics, 1821–1971* (Dublin, 1978), 49.

self-government or even total independence as a means of becoming a 'national' rather than a colonial ruling class. To achieve 'national' authority, however, the Catholic bourgeoisie had to supplant British/Protestant hegemony over Irish civil society before it could challenge British political dominion. In Gramsci's terms, it first had to generate an emergent, nationalist counter-hegemony in order to achieve autonomy from its British/Protestant opponents *and* in order to secure support from allies — primarily within Irish Catholic society but also among the Irish emigrants abroad. The success or failure of those external and internal 'projects' of the Catholic middle class were inextricably related. The attainment of political independence from Britain was contingent on the achievement of internal hegemony and the mobilization of the Irish and the Irish emigrant masses behind the nationalists' programme, despite the fact that that programme entailed the creation of an Irish bourgeois state governed by the same capitalist processes and classes that were directly responsible for most lower-class Catholics' social marginalization, immiseration, and emigration. Conversely, as long as Ireland remained a political colony, the Catholic middle class lacked the authority to order Irish society and incorporate its values throughout the ideological and institutional superstructure.[11]

In such circumstances, the processes through which the Catholic middle class 'made itself' were necessarily complex and subtle. That class began to emerge as a self-conscious entity in the relatively prosperous late eighteenth century, led by urban merchants and professionals whose ideas and ambitions, shaped by the capitalist 'spirit of improvement', were distinct from those of the old Catholic gentry and the peasantry alike. Initially, in the 1770s and 1780s, the Catholic middle class desired only the creation of economic and political conditions that would promote their interests within the British constitution: repeal of the Penal Laws, equal economic opportunities, and equal political rights for propertied Catholics. After 1789 and inspired by the success of the French Revolution, some middle-class Catholics joined with like-minded Protestants in the Society of United Irishmen, whose rebellion in the name of an independent, non-sectarian Irish republic was crushed in 1798. However, most members of the Catholic middle class abhorred the radical egalitarianism and anti-clericalism of French republicanism; hence, they welcomed both the defeat of the United Irishmen and the subsequent Act of Union in 1800, especially because the latter seemed to presage the granting of full Catholic rights by the British government. Unfortunately, between 1800 and 1829 the parliament at Westminster frustrated Catholic hopes. Moreover, the effects of the post-Napoleonic War depression not only gave added urgency to Catholics' desire for economic and political equality, but also convinced many that only repeal of the Act of Union and the creation of a new, popularly elected (hence, Catholic-dominated)

---

11 On the development of Irish nationalism, see Garvin, *Evolution of Irish Nationalist Politics*; and Strauss, *Irish Nationalism and British Democracy*; as well as Michael Hechter, *Internal Colonialism: The Celtic Fringe in British National Development, 1536–1966* (Berkeley, Calif., 1975); and D. George Boyce, *Nationalism in Ireland* (Baltimore, Md., 1982).

Irish legislature would enable them to protect and promote their interests. During the pre-Famine period (1815–44) what Gramsci would call the organic intellectuals of the Catholic bourgeoisie, especially lawyers like Daniel O'Connell, borrowed the theories of Adam Smith, William Godwin, and other British political economists to justify their class's economic and political aspirations as well as their successive political campaigns for Catholic Emancipation, the abolition of tithes to the Church of Ireland, and repeal of the Act of Union.[12]

However, the political notions shared by most rural Catholics differed greatly from the liberal ideals and programmes of their putative leaders. Usually illiterate and often Irish-speakers, Catholic artisans, smallholders, and, especially, cottiers and labourers were intensely parochial, their sense of Irish identity bound to specific localities or to tribal traditions and hatreds rather than to bourgeois concepts of political economy and nationalism. For leaders, Irish-speaking peasants and members of the Whiteboys, Rockites, and other secret agrarian societies generally preferred men of their own class (or even paternalistic landlords) rather than middle-class townsmen and wealthy cattle-graziers, whom they regarded as half-Anglicized snobs, who eulogized capitalist 'progress' and ignored its consequences for the exploited masses. When such men thought in political terms, they oscillated between visions of a pastoral Gaelic commonwealth and the radical, half-assimilated ideals of the French Revolution and the United Irishmen. Thus, to mobilize and control these potential but dangerous allies, the Catholic middle class had to broaden its ideological appeal. The fragmented and transitional nature of Catholic society, and the precarious social position of the middle class itself, demanded that the nationalist counter-hegemony incorporate a range of values and symbols that in more 'advanced' capitalist societies would be characterized as residual or pre-modern. It did so in at least three major ways.

First, early in the nineteenth century, under the leadership of Daniel O'Connell, the middle class formed a nationalist alliance with the Irish Catholic Church. It thus assimilated the Church's traditional intellectuals, who gave a 'spiritual' substance and legitimacy to the political goals of the middle class, and gained access to Catholic society's most elaborate and pervasive institutional infrastructure — including new temperance societies and confraternities, as well as an increasingly comprehensive network of parish churches and schools. In return, the Church and its clergy assumed a 'patriotic' stature in popular opinion, and also gained influence over the course and content of Catholic nationalism — plus the implicit promise of predominant influence (over education and social policy, for example) in any future Irish government. Because the Catholic clergy's ideal Irish society was organic and authoritarian, guided by religion instead of the marketplace or popular opinion, the alliance between middle-class nationalists and the

---

12 Garvin, Evolution of Irish Nationalist Politics, 14–52; and Marianne Elliott, Partners in Revolution: The United Irishmen and France (New Haven, Conn., 1982). On O'Connell, see Fergus O'Ferrall, Daniel O'Connell (Dublin, 1981).

Church created a contradictory ideological synthesis that some historians have termed 'Catholic liberalism'.[13]

Second, the Catholic bourgeoisie mobilized the land hunger of the lower classes in the nationalist crusade. This was a delicate and complicated process because middle-class graziers and other strong farmers, although sharing the peasants' resentments against landlordism, high rents, and evictions, held sharply divergent attitudes towards agrarian capitalism and the sanctity of private property. Hence, it was no wonder that middle-class Catholic nationalists were unwilling to raise the rallying cry — 'The Land for the People!' — until after the Great Famine, mass emigration, and the Catholic Church's devotional revolution had reduced and tamed the rural lower classes. Driven by peasant land hunger and led hesitantly by bourgeois nationalists and clerics, the Land War of 1879–82 initiated legal changes, which, by 1920, had virtually abolished landlordism and enabled Irish tenants to become farm-owners. However, although the successful agitation against landlordism provided an enormous stimulus to the penultimate phase of middle-class nationalism, the Home Rule movement, the creation of a so-called peasant proprietorship only ratified the inequitable distribution of Irish soil among the Catholic population. Many land-poor smallholders, landless labourers, and farmers' non-inheriting sons remained bitterly frustrated, but the Catholic bourgeoisie vehemently rejected more radical schemes for the redistribution or the nationalization of Irish land, as proposed by the peasant-born leader of the Land War, Michael Davitt, or by the Dublin socialist James Connolly.[14]

In a sense, the Catholic middle class's alliances with the Church and the peasants' desire for land only incorporated within the nationalist bloc the class and cultural tensions caused by rapid commercialization and social differentiation. And so, third, the Catholic middle class had to resolve or obscure those tensions by broadening its hegemonic culture further to incorporate other notions that were embedded in traditional Irish Catholic culture.

13 On Irish peasant *mentalité*, see the essays by Paul E. W. Roberts and James S. Donnelly, Jr., in Clark and Donnelly, eds., *Irish Peasants*, 64–139; and Miller, *Emigrants and Exiles*, 60–130. On O'Connell, the Church, and 'Catholic liberalism', see Fergus O'Ferrall, *Catholic Emancipation: Daniel O'Connell and the Birth of Irish Democracy* (Dublin, 1985).

14 On post-Famine Irish politics, see Garvin, *Evolution of Irish Nationalist Politics*, 53–134; also, Paul Bew, *Land and the National Question, 1858–82* (Dublin, 1979); and David Seth Jones, 'Agrarian Capitalism and Rural Social Development in Ireland' (PhD thesis, Queen's University of Belfast, 1977), since published as *Graziers, Land Reform, and Political Conflict in Ireland* (Washington, DC, 1995). On Davitt and Connolly, see Theodore W. Moody, *Davitt and Irish Revolution, 1846–1882* (Oxford, 1982); and C. Desmond Greaves, *The Life and Times of James Connolly* (New York, 1961).

The popular belief that all Irish emigration was involuntary exile, tantamount to political banishment, was an integral and residual element of the Irish Catholic worldview — or, in Gramsci's terms, spontaneous philosophy — the pervasive cultural system (outlined in Chapter 1) that devalued 'modern' norms such as individual action, ambition, and innovation. Because that belief contradicted or obscured emigration's actual, immediate causes, which were rooted in the dynamics and inequalities of Irish rural capitalism, it epitomized the contradictory popular consciousness produced, or at least deepened, by the process of cultural hegemony.[15]

On one level, both the interpretation of emigration as exile and the pre-capitalist value system that supported that interpretation remained part of the popular consciousness in post-Famine Ireland because of the structural contradictions and psychological tensions that characterized a society in swift but uneven transition. Although contemporaries sometimes decried the rationalization or 'Anglicization' of rural values that accompanied agrarian-capitalist development, and complained that some culturally deracinated Irish youths no longer viewed emigration sorrowfully, the expatriate imagery and many aspects of its corroboratory worldview still seemed applicable to certain social realities that were 'explainable' in pre-modern terms. As a result of the uneven impact of commercialization, many traditional institutions, task orientations, and even linguistic patterns (in Hiberno-English as well as the vanishing Irish language) lasted well into the twentieth century. Moreover, not only did the influence of externally imposed authorities (Protestant landlords, British officials) long remain potent, but within Catholic Ireland the disappearance of secret agrarian societies, increased clerical authority (most especially in education), the marginalization of farm labourers and of farmers' non-inheriting children, and the enmeshing of smallholders in webs of debt also may have reduced, rather than widened, the scope of responsible choice most rural dwellers enjoyed. Thus, some aspects of Irish 'development' may not have promoted more individualistic or independent outlooks; instead, it is likely they enjoined a continued or even increased dependence on and deference to familial obligations, patron–client ties, and communal authorities in order to ensure survival and status.[16]

---

15 See Chapter 1 in this volume, as well as Miller, Emigrants and Exiles, 103–21.
16 For example, it was symptomatic that few post-Famine emigrants financed the transatlantic passage from their own earnings or capital, as had been more common earlier. Rather, most were dependent on the initiative and largesse of relatives at home or, most often, abroad: a situation which probably encouraged the retention of passive attitudes among emigrants who, as they commonly expressed it, simply 'had to go' to America because the (allegedly unsolicited and unexpected) arrival in Ireland of their passage tickets from relations overseas supposedly gave them no choice in the matter.

   For complaints of emigrant 'disloyalty', see George R. C. Keep, 'Some Irish Opinions on Population and Emigration, 1851–1901', Irish Ecclesiastical Record, 5th ser., 84 (1954), 377–86. Both Garvin, Evolution of Irish Nationalist Politics, and David Fitzpatrick, Politics and Irish Life, 1913–1921 (Dublin, 1977), stress continuities between pre- and post-Famine Irish political culture, in contrast to Lee, Modernisation of Irish Society; see also Chapter 1, this volume, and Miller, Emigrants and Exiles, 427–35.

However, although mitigated, socio-economic and cultural changes in post-Famine Ireland were great, even traumatic, especially in the western districts that produced a disproportionately large share of Irish emigrants from the mid-1850s (and especially from the late 1870s) through the 1920s. But those very innovations, so pregnant with social disruption and demoralization, encouraged greater popular reliance on residual outlooks and 'explanations' which could relieve the tensions consequent on rapid transition — producing in the process a deeply contradictory consciousness with respect to new social realities. In order to ensure social and psychological equilibrium, especially among subordinate social groups, changes had to be interpreted in customary, comforting ways. Thus, whereas in practice most post-Famine Irish responded 'rationally' to new economic exigencies or 'opportunities' (for example, by adopting impartible inheritance or by emigrating), they often fell back on traditional cultural categories ('it was a necessity …') to justify, exculpate, or obscure causation and accountability — sometimes, as in the case of emigration, projecting responsibility for change on uncontrollable and/or 'alien' forces. Hence, they could square traditional values and customary, communal sanctions with the actual practice of new, 'freer' actions implicit in agrarian capitalism, cloaking the rising tide of individual calculation in the assumed anonymity of explanatory strategies which assuaged psychological and social tensions.[17]

Arguably, such compromises between tradition and innovation may have been psychological necessities. However, it was Catholic Ireland's middle classes that largely determined the precise forms of such ideological adjustments — such as the fiction that all contemporary emigration was basically political exile, forced directly by British or landlord oppression. They did so by generating a new, dominant culture, which incorporated such residual outlooks in a symbiotic relationship with the socio-cultural and psychological predispositions and needs of the subordinate classes. Certainly, the archaic *deoraí* tradition remained vibrant in the Irish-speaking western counties. However, its formalized expression throughout the commercialized, English-speaking Ireland of the post-Famine era served as an instrument of cultural hegemony for the social classes that had emerged pre-eminent from the wreckage of pre-Famine society and which found it essential to explain their social position in traditional terms which could inhibit resentment from subordinates and potential allies who felt disadvantaged by the socio-economic and cultural discontinuities caused by the Famine and by the inequities of capitalist development, generally.

In the post-Famine period the hegemonic culture of the Catholic bourgeoisie was incorporated primarily through three media: the Catholic Church, which dominated Catholic education as well as religious life; Irish nationalist movements, which shaped popular political consciousness; and, most intimately, the strong-farmer *type* of rural

---

17 On social and cultural tensions in post-Famine Ireland, especially in the western counties, see Miller, *Emigrants and Exiles*, 469–92; also see Chapter 5 in this volume.

family (what anthropologists call the 'stem family'), characterized by impartible inheritance, the dowry system, postponed or averted marriage for offspring, and (circumstances permitting) capital accumulation.[18] All three institutions reflected the recent embourgeoisement of Catholic society — adopted by or imposed on smallholders and labourers from models of 'proper' religious, political, and socio-economic behaviour enjoined by middle-class townspeople, clerics, and farmers. To a degree, all three upset or challenged traditional peasant practices and outlooks — sometimes to people's obvious disadvantage, as in the case of farmers' disinherited children — yet all demanded absolute conformity and proscribed deviations as familial ingratitude, religious apostasy, or even national treason.

The success of the Catholic bourgeoisie's complementary projects (cultural hegemony and political domination) depended on the articulation of its values through these and other media in order to contain intracommunal conflicts, mobilize the masses, and win regional self-government or Irish independence. Consequently, the Catholic bourgeoisie's hegemonic culture had to incorporate the residual imagery of emigration as exile because the bourgeoisie itself shared major responsibility for mass lower-class emigration: generally, through the processes of agrarian capitalism; particularly, through the operations of the stem family; and finally, some critics charged, because of the Catholic Church's stifling impact on social life and personal expression. The remainder of this chapter focuses on political and clerical ideals concerning emigration, but, with regard to the rural family, the notion of emigration forced by fate or British oppression, rather than economic calculation, was vital in mitigating potentially explosive conflicts between parents and offspring and between inheriting and non-inheriting children.[19] However, just as the intrafamilial tensions and resolutions respecting emigration were much more complex than that brief statement suggests, so also did the Catholic bourgeoisie's political and clerical spokesmen have to balance middle-class interests and peasant and proletarian sensibilities. In the process, they often produced messages, which, in their inconsistency, both mirrored and exacerbated the contradictory popular consciousness.

Given capitalism's impact on Irish society, it was predictable that a few Catholic leaders regarded emigration 'rationally', openly acknowledging that many people's 'irredeemable poverty' or laudable ambition made at least some emigration 'absolutely

---

18 The classic study of the Irish rural family is Conrad M. Arensberg and Solon T. Kimball, *Family and Community in Ireland*, 2nd edn. (Cambridge, Mass., 1968).
19 On emigration and the Irish family, see Chapter 5 in this volume.

necessary' or even 'natural' and praiseworthy. For example, many priests viewed their parishioners' departures with resignation or even approval. However, both the hegemonic imperatives of the Catholic bourgeoisie and the traditions and prejudices of the masses determined that emigration had to be interpreted communally and symbolically, in political and religious contexts. On one hand, Catholic spokesmen often eulogized the accomplishments of the 'Irish Race' overseas, and clergy were especially prone to describe the exodus as 'divine destiny' and the emigrants as 'holy missionaries' for the Catholic faith. On the other hand, negative characterizations of emigration predominated, and after the Great Famine most clerics and nationalists united in condemning it. For Ireland as a whole emigration was described as tragic because it deprived the country of its young men and women, its 'bone and sinew', and so threatened ultimate depopulation. Likewise, critics charged that emigration was tragic and potentially dangerous for the emigrants themselves. Catholic clerics, in particular, espoused this argument: at mid-century they emphasized primarily the hazards of the voyage and the poverty and physical dangers that awaited poor emigrants in the New World, but later they broadened their attack and stigmatized the United States itself as a vicious, materialistic, 'godless' society, which corrupted the emigrants' morals and destroyed their faith. According to such priests as Peter O'Leary, Joseph Guinan, and Patrick Sheehan, America was an 'unnatural land', where innocent Irish youths would be 'dragged down to shame and crime', and they urged their listeners 'to save their souls in Holy Ireland rather than … hazard them for this world's goods among American heretics'.[20]

Although agreeing that emigration was lamentable, nationalists and clergymen were inconsistent in assigning blame for its prevalence. Some charged that the emigrants themselves were culpable, either because they were too naïve to resist the blandishments of ticket brokers, relatives overseas, and 'returned Yanks', or, more harshly, because they were 'coward[s]', 'sordid churl[s]', and 'lucre-loving wretch[es]', as the nationalist poet and agitator Fanny Parnell charged in 1880, or 'traitor[s] to the Irish State' and 'deserters who have left their posts', as Patrick Pearse, the leader of the 1916 Easter rebellion, later claimed. Nevertheless, it was much more common to blame emigration on landlordism and British oppression and to characterize the emigrants as sorrowing, vengeful 'exiles'. According to priests such as Guinan and Thomas Burke,

---

20 One Churchman's favourable views on emigration are in Walter McDonald's *Reminiscences of a Maynooth Professor* (London, 1925), 221–23; also see Oliver MacDonagh, 'Irish Emigration to the United States of America and the British Colonies during the Famine', in R. Dudley Edwards and T. Desmond Williams, eds., *The Great Famine: Studies in Irish History* (New York, 1957), 300–01; Thomas N. Burke, *Lectures on Faith and Fatherland* (London, n.d.), 212–13; and M. O'Connor, 'The Destiny of the Irish Race', *Irish Ecclesiastical Record*, 1 (November 1864), 70. For negative views on emigration, see Keep, 'Some Irish Opinions', 377–81; Rev. John O'Hanlon, *Irish Emigrants' Guide for the United States* (Boston, 1851), 10–13; Peadar Ó Laoghaire, *Sgothbhualadh* (Baile Átha Cliath, 1907), 107–9 (trans. Bruce D. Boling); Rev. Joseph Guinan, *Scenes and Sketches of an Irish Parish* (Dublin, 1906), 43–45, 118–19; and Rev. Patrick Sheehan, 'The Effect of Emigration on the Irish Church', *Irish Ecclesiastical Record*, 3rd series, 3 (1882), 602–15.

the emigrants were victims of religious and political persecution, while the Irish abroad were purportedly consumed with a passionate 'love for Ireland' and an ardent desire to 'breathe once more the peat-scented air of their native valleys'. Likewise, nearly all nationalist politicians characterized the exodus as a 'reluctant emigration', which would cease only when Ireland was self-governing or independent and thus able to provide employment and prosperity for her citizens at home. 'Ireland has resources to feed five times her population,' Pearse asserted; hence, 'a free Ireland would not, and could not, have hunger in her fertile vales and squalor in her cities'.[21]

Such contradictory attributions of blame for emigration reflected the Catholic bourgeoisie's tortuous efforts to reconcile traditional social ideals and their own hegemonic imperatives with new social realities that violated those ideals and yet, paradoxically, both sustained and threatened their authority over the Catholic masses. Save in the context of wholesale emigration by the dispossessed and disinherited, bourgeois ascendancy over rural Ireland could not have been achieved without immeasurably greater tension and conflict within Catholic society. Many Catholic spokesmen were conscious of the fact that only the massive, lower-class exodus had created the relatively commercialized Ireland that had been a precondition for the success of disciplined nationalist movements and of the Church's devotional revolution. Lower-class emigration had enabled the comparatively conflict-free expansion and consolidation of many strong farmers' and graziers' holdings, and those affluent groups and their shopkeeper allies were vital support sources for institutionalized piety and patriotism. Similarly, emigration stabilized the family farm, helped preclude overt social and generational strife over land, and prevented the subdivision, pauperization, and subterranean agrarian violence that had characterized the pre-Famine decades. In addition, Catholic leaders understood that emigration brought specific material benefits to key strata of the bourgeoisie. For instance, publicans and shopkeepers — proverbially vociferous nationalists — profited from the sale of passage tickets, while much of the £1 million in annual remittances from the Irish in America found its way to the retailers' coffers and the priests' collection boxes. More crucially, clerics and constitutional nationalists relied heavily on Irish Americans' loyalty and contributions to finance church-building and political agitation; ultimately the more radical nationalists needed Irish-American support for successful insurrection at home. Thus, Catholic spokesmen had good reason to praise the emigrants and rationalize the exodus as the 'Divine Mission of the Irish Race'.[22]

21 Ó Laoghaire, Sgothbhualadh; Guinan, Scenes and Sketches; Burke, Lectures on Faith and Fatherland, 228–31; R. F. Foster, Charles Stewart Parnell: The Man and His Family (Atlantic Highlands, NJ, 1979), 323–25; Patrick O'Farrell, 'Emigrant Attitudes and Behaviour as a Source for Irish History', Historical Studies X (Dublin, 1976), 114–16; A. M. Sullivan, 'Why Send More Irish out of Ireland?' Nineteenth Century, 14 (July 1883), 131–44; Ruth Dudley Edwards, Patrick Pearse: The Triumph of Failure (London, 1977), 78–79, 183.

22 One Irish haute bourgeois nationalist who argued for the 'salutary' effects of the Famine and agrarian capitalism on Irish society and culture was A. M. Sullivan, in his New Ireland: Political Sketches and Personal

However, Irish nationalists had to denounce emigration, for emigration, and popular opposition to it and its causes, threatened to undermine the dual projects of the Catholic bourgeoisie. Symbolically as well as in reality, emigration connoted depopulation, and throughout the nineteenth century, when British economists and journalists frequently urged the wholesale removal of Ireland's 'superfluous' inhabitants, the issue of Irish population was charged with politics and emotion. In that context — as well as the older ones of the Cromwellian transportations and the Wild Geese — both the Famine clearances and more recent evictions of Irish tenants, as during the Land War, made the equation of emigration with banishment and even planned 'extermination' seem perfectly logical if, from an 'objective' perspective, ahistorical. Also, in practical terms, emigration endangered nationalists' hopes for Ireland's future and their efforts to oppose British authority and Anglicizing influences. For example, the nationalists' proposed rejuvenation of Ireland's economy appeared threatened by the drain of potential entrepreneurs, workers, and consumers. More immediately, many leaders feared that mass departures were undermining Catholic Ireland's religious and political bulwarks by either eroding Church membership or providing a safety valve for discontent that otherwise could be mobilized against British rule. Thus, in 1920 during the War of Independence, the minister of defence for the Dáil, the republicans' alternative parliament, issued a manifesto warning that the British administration was attempting to stimulate more emigration and thereby weaken the nationalist struggle: 'The young men of Ireland must stand fast', he demanded, for '[t]o leave their country at this supreme crisis would be nothing less than base desertion in the face of the enemy'. Catholic leaders were also apprehensive lest emigration deprive them of political and religious influence over the emigrants, especially those who left home for 'selfish', materialistic reasons. Lay nationalists feared the emigrants 'were casting off all allegiance to the motherland', while Churchmen were concerned about the dangers of apostasy or 'spiritual ruin' overseas.[23]

Hence, their self-assumed roles as Ireland's champions obliged the Catholic bourgeoisie's spokesmen to denounce emigration. As Bishop George Butler of Limerick put it in 1864 in a letter to fellow Churchmen, 'The depopulation of our Country is progressing at an awful pace and *we must not appear to be taking it too easy.*' Such opposition was usually sincere, and many of post-Famine Ireland's most prominent men had spent time abroad, witnessed emigrant poverty, and returned home determined to oppose the exodus. Nevertheless, Bishop Butler's private remark, made in response to the rumblings of lower-class discontent, revealed the profound difficulties faced

Reminiscences, 2 vols. (London, 1877). On post-Famine remittances and donations, see Schrier, *Ireland and the American Immigration*, 103–28, 167–68; and Miller, *Emigrants and Exiles*, 458–59.

23 For British comments on Irish population and emigration, see R. D. Collison Black, *Economic Thought and the Irish Question* (London, 1960). For typical Irish responses, see Schrier, *Ireland and the American Immigration*, 45–65; Sullivan, 'Why Send More Irish out of Ireland?', 131–44; Sheehan, 'Effect of Emigration', 613; Guinan, *Scenes and Sketches*, 54–55; and O'Farrell, 'Emigrant Attitudes and Behaviour', 115, 128–29.

by the Catholic bourgeoisie. Middle-class nationalists had to address emigration and its socio-economic causes because those issues, rather than political abstractions, were the ones that most concerned the disadvantaged elements of Irish society whose mass support the nationalists wanted and needed. Grass-roots pressures thus forced nationalists to link the political goals of the bourgeoisie to the practical grievances and aspirations of the masses — specifically, to promises of fundamental socio-economic changes that would obviate the need for mass migration.[24]

Nationalists were successful in forging that link. Historical research indicates that among nationalism's fiercest partisans were members of precisely those groups most threatened by economic displacement and the necessity of emigration. However, the social issues that mobilized small farmers, landless labourers, farmers' non-inheriting sons, and urban workers were potentially dangerous. If thwarted in their aspirations by their political leaders' concessions to British authority, or by the reactionary influence of indigenous bourgeois interests, lower-class nationalists might disrupt Catholic unity, assault middle-class 'patriots', or switch allegiance to schismatic or 'purist' varieties of extreme nationalism opposed by dominant sectors of the bourgeoisie, as during the Fenian movement in the 1860s, the rise of Sinn Féin in 1916–19, and the Civil War in 1922–23. Thus, while mass emigration among the subordinate classes would weaken nationalist movements, their continued presence in Ireland threatened to disrupt or divert them. The dilemma was stated clearly during the War of Independence, when the Dáil's defence minister urged Ireland's sons to 'stand fast', while its minister of agriculture warned that, if they did, in their land hunger they would 'swarm ... onto the land' belonging to Catholic graziers and strong farmers, thus alienating key segments of the bourgeoisie from the national struggle.[25]

The source of their dilemma was that most Catholic leaders had little or no inclination to take the radical measures necessary to restructure Irish economic and social relationships in ways that might have halted emigration. Indeed, they had risen to the top of an Irish Catholic society whose very shape and stability depended to a large degree on emigration's continuance, and the success of their complementary projects, their very affluence and authority, derived ultimately from socio-economic systems, institutions, and inequities that might not survive if emigration ceased. Consequently, with very few exceptions such as Michael Davitt, no post-Famine politicians advocated or implemented measures sufficient to stop emigration once they had achieved national

24 Bishop Butler quotation, courtesy of Professor Emmet Larkin, University of Chicago; since published in Larkin's The Consolidation of the Roman Catholic Church in Ireland, 1860–1870 (Dublin, 1987), 279 (emphasis added). For evidence of lower-class political consciousness, see Bernard Becker, Disturbed Ireland (London, 1882); and Guardian of the Poor, The Irish Peasant: A Sociological Study (London, 1892), 14.

25 On post-Famine nationalism and its adherents, see Garvin, Evolution of Irish Nationalist Politics, 53–134; R. V. Comerford, The Fenians in Context: Irish Politics and Society, 1848–82 (Dublin, 1985); Bew, Land and the National Question; Fitzpatrick, Politics and Irish Life; and E. Rumpf and A. C. Hepburn, Nationalism and Socialism in Twentieth-Century Ireland (New York, 1977). Quotation from David Fitzpatrick, 'Class, Family, and Rural Unrest in Nineteenth-Century Ireland', in Drudy, Irish Studies 2, 48–49.

prominence. For example, in the face of grazier opposition, Charles Stewart Parnell, leader of the Home Rule movement in the 1880s, retreated from his suggestion that western peasants might colonize the rich north Leinster grasslands; and in the 1920s the political successors of Arthur Griffith, founder of Sinn Féin, eschewed the protective tariffs he had urged to create industrial employment. Likewise, the publicans, traders, and strong farmers who led nationalist movements at the parish level were staunchly opposed to the peasants' dream of land redistribution, to Davitt's scheme of land nationalization, to James Connolly's and James Larkin's socialism — indeed, even to tariffs and co-operative enterprises — in short, to any fundamental changes in a social system that had institutionalized lower-class emigration.[26]

Caught between their poor followers' demands that they support radical measures to halt emigration and their own aversion to such steps, bourgeois nationalists and Churchmen had to formulate broad, ideological 'explanations' of emigration, in residual and even 'spiritual' terms, which would ignore or obscure post-Famine Ireland's real social processes and conflicts. As a result, their interpretations of emigration were integrally related to their idealization of a mythical 'holy Ireland' that could be defended against external assault and internal schism, thus ensuring the success of the bourgeoisie's twin projects. The 'holy Ireland' ideal had emerged by the early nineteenth century, but after the Famine it became more elaborate and pervasive and assumed a profoundly anti-modernist thrust. After 1850 the growing influence of the Catholic Church on Irish society, the papacy's own crusade against modernism, and the sentimentalism pervading much Victorian culture all reinforced and romanticized Irish opposition to the allegedly 'British' or 'Anglo-Saxon' influences transforming Catholic society. In response, middle-class Catholics conceptualized a fortress Hibernia, an ideal and purportedly 'traditional' Irish society antithetical to their negative images of England (and of America) and to the modern and purportedly 'alien' tendencies within Ireland itself. According to Catholic leaders, especially Churchmen, Irish Catholics were morally superior to English and other Protestants because of their relative indifference to material success and other false gods of urban-industrial societies. Because of such unworldliness, allegedly the

26 On Parnell, see F. S. L. Lyons, 'The Economic Ideas of Parnell', *Historical Studies II* (London, 1959), 67–73; and Paul Bew, *C. S. Parnell* (Dublin, 1980), 49. On Griffith and his successors, see Richard P. Davis, *Arthur Griffith and Non-Violent Sinn Féin* (Dublin, 1974), 127–44; and Terence Brown, *Ireland: A Social and Cultural History, 1922–1979* (London, 1981), 15–16. On local élites, see especially Liam Kennedy, 'The Early Response of the Irish Catholic Clergy to the Co-operative Movement', *Irish Historical Studies*, 21 (March 1978), 55–74, and 'Farmers, Traders, and Agricultural Politics in Pre-Independence Ireland', in Clark and Donnelly, *Irish Peasants*, 339–73.

Irish were profoundly conservative, content to live simple lives at home under clerical guidance and in harmony with family, neighbours, and natural environment. The ideal society for such folk was static, organic, and paternalistic: a divinely ordered, hierarchical community devoid of internal conflicts, insulated by faith and patriotism from potential 'contamination'. To ensure such stability and continuity, 'holy Ireland' needed to remain overwhelmingly agricultural, allegedly pre-capitalist, and based on the parish church and the peasant family — the devout and patriarchal microcosm of the larger, corporate society. Lay and clerical nationalists played variations on these themes,[27] but all save a few radicals such as Davitt and Connolly conceptualized an ideally unchanging social order that, in theory, could support all Ireland's people in frugal comfort at home. Sometimes their rhetoric implied that this model society was still in the process of creation, at other times it indicated that it was already in being. In either case its perceived enemies — British oppression, landlordism, Protestantism, secularism, and socialism — were legion, and so 'holy Ireland' needed constant, vigorous defence. Consequently, the Church made assiduous efforts to shape Catholic minds by controlling education; it supported Irish self-government as a means to insulate the faithful from pernicious British laws and Anglicizing influences; and, despite the bishops' usual concern for property rights, it espoused agrarian reforms designed to root the 'peasantry' in the soil and so secure 'holy Ireland's' social and moral foundation.[28]

Within this conceptual framework, nationalists and clerics could both oppose emigration and condemn the emigrants themselves. Although the notion of a divinely ordered Irish society could reinforce Churchmen's sometime boast that its pious emigrants were furthering God's work overseas, the more prevalent imagery of 'holy Ireland' struggling for birth or survival against the forces of evil implied that mass departures constituted an intolerable weakening of its ranks. In addition, the very ideal of 'holy Ireland' made emigration seem highly inappropriate, if not treacherous. If, as many Catholic spokesmen claimed by the 1890s, the ideal Irish society was already in being, then continued emigration indicated that subtle, subversive forces were at work internally. Because Catholic leaders had, they claimed, already created most or all of the conditions and institutions that purportedly obviated emigration's continued necessity, then by the logic of their vision any departures that still occurred implied the emigrants' self-willed or self-deluded repudiation of the organic nation-as-family and their violation

27 For example, nationalists regarded the Home Rule movement or, later, Sinn Féin as co-guardians with the Church of the people's traditions, and Parnell hoped that a 'patriotic' landlord class might play a guiding role. Likewise, urban-oriented nationalists such as Arthur Griffith envisioned a partnership between agriculture and indigenous industry, while Irish-Ireland enthusiasts demanded that the idealized peasant-citizen should be Irish-speaking as well as pious. Nevertheless, basic similarities of vision outweighed these and other differences.
28 In general, see Patrick O'Farrell, *Ireland's English Question: Anglo-Irish Relations, 1534–1970* (New York, 1971), 189–241; and Tom Garvin, 'Priests and Patriots: Irish Separatism and Fear of the Modern, 1890–1914', *Irish Historical Studies*, 25 (May 1986), 67–81. For more complete citations, see Miller, *Emigrants and Exiles*, 636, nos. 137–38.

of the sacralized peasant ethos on which the nation was supposedly based. After all, even if America did still offer superior material advantages (which many Catholic spokesmen were no longer willing to admit), Irish Catholics by definition were allegedly too selfless and unworldly to succumb to such lures. Hence, the emigrants must be either 'fools' or 'traitors', and devout nationalists such as Pearse stigmatized them as both.[29]

Of course, the ideology of 'holy Ireland' selectively and imperfectly reflected only some residual aspects of post-Famine society's complex realities, and in the sense that it ignored, obscured, or denied the real and often ruthless workings of Irish capitalism, the concept was at best an appealing illusion, at worst a pious fraud. Not only did those who propagated the concept fail to use their influence to make reality match the dream of an organic society capable of sustaining all its people, but even conceptually the notion of 'holy Ireland' was grievously flawed with respect to emigration. To a degree, it was merely a rhetorical cloak, woven of medieval dogmas and Victorian pieties, masking a petty bourgeois society whose vaunted stability and sacralized family farm both mandated and depended on constant emigration. The concept not only ignored Irish Protestants, but also failed to make concessions to the need for Irish cities and industries as outlets for the countryside's 'surplus' population: Ireland must remain rural, Churchmen demanded, for urbanization and industrialization connoted secularism, social fragmentation, and the 'black devil of Socialism'. In light of such anomalies, Catholic spokesmen's demands that emigrants not desert 'the holy peace of home' for the fleshpots of America smacked of wilful blindness, if not overt hypocrisy.[30]

However, the hegemonic imperatives of the Catholic bourgeoisie—and the sensibilities of the masses — demanded that the 'holy Ireland' concept be further elaborated with respect to emigration. For if the real social processes that were 'explained' or masked by the dominant culture were in fact the primary causes of mass migration, then how could 'holy Ireland's' champions explain the continuing waves of departures without admitting their own culpability or ineffectiveness, or without exposing the concept's inadequacies — and, in either case, without thereby alienating the lower classes and the emigrants from the society left behind? Of course, nationalists and clerics could redouble their denunciations of the emigrants as fools and traitors, but such epithets violated realities too obviously and threatened to embitter the emigrants towards 'holy Ireland' and its guardians. Or, they could resort to the old religious rationalization 'that God in his inscrutable wisdom ... had intended and used the Irish race to carry Catholicism to the ends of the earth', but, as one proletarian critic shrewdly perceived, 'The Irishman who accepts this teaching cannot any longer lay the misfortunes of his country upon the shoulders of the British government.' Thus, in order to secure the twin projects of the Catholic bourgeoisie, the capstone of the dominant culture had to remain the

29 Edwards, Patrick Pearse, 78–79.
30 O'Farrell, Ireland's English Question, 170–71; J. A. MacMahon, 'The Catholic Clergy and the Social Question in Ireland', Studies, 70 (1981), 263–86; Emmet Larkin, 'Socialism and Catholicism in Ireland', Church History, 30 (1964), 462–83; Guinan, Scenes and Sketches, 43.

oldest and most residual 'explanation' of all — that all emigration was 'exile' forced by British oppression.[31]

This interpretation of emigration as exile implied no criticism of 'holy Ireland' or its spokesmen. It postponed embarrassing socio-economic questions until after self-government or independence was won, and in the meantime, it deflected the emigrants' 'fierce rage and fury' against the 'British misgovernment' which alone purportedly obliged emigration from an island allegedly 'capable of supporting twice its present population'. Nor did that interpretation imply criticism of the emigrants themselves, for in the terms of the dominant culture they were merely 'victims' whose assiduously cultivated love for their homeland and hatred for England would inspire their unceasing devotion and donations to 'holy Ireland's' staunch defenders: the Irish and Irish-American nationalists and clerics who promised that emigration would cease only when 'holy Ireland' was free at last from British rule.[32]

To be sure, socialist James Connolly and others voiced dissent from both the dominant Catholic culture and its facile 'explanations' of emigration, and many emigrants themselves were too ambitious, realistic, or alienated to conceptualize their departures in prescribed ways. Nevertheless, the flood of remittances and donations from America indicates that many, if not most, Catholic Irish emigrants adhered to the dominant culture and remained emotionally or at least publicly loyal to the society that had expelled them. In part, this was because the concept of emigration as exile was both deeply rooted in Irish tradition and constantly reinforced by contemporary conflicts with Protestant landlords, Orangemen, and British officials, thus easily corroborating 'official' Catholic-nationalist rhetoric. However, since the proximate causes of most post-Famine emigration stemmed from the dynamics and structures of Catholic society itself, it is doubtful whether the archaic notion of emigration as exile would have remained credible had the notion and the 'holy Ireland' imagery not been seemingly natural and logical expressions of a still extant, traditional worldview that condemned innovation and individualism while externalizing responsibility for unsettling change. Not only did 'holy Ireland' seem to be at least a partly valid metaphor for a society still locally centred on family farm and parish church, but more crucially, it was a systematic expression of what a people in rapid social and cultural transition desperately wanted and needed to believe was still entirely true about their society and themselves. Emigration as exile's ultimate appeal thus lay in its symbolic resolution of the discrepancies between the reality of social fragmentation and exploitation and the ideal of an organic, harmonious, self-sustaining community. If England could yet be blamed for emigration's causes, for the inability of 'holy Ireland' to support all her children, then both the emigrants and those who in fact profited by their departures could be absolved of culpability, while the consequent resentments against England

31 Greaves, *Life and Times of James Connolly*, 52.
32 Guinan, *Scenes and Sketches*, 46.

could reinforce the outlooks and allegiances that held Catholic Ireland together in the face of the disintegrative and potentially demoralizing or alienating effects of commercialization and Anglicization.[33]

Thus, the residual culture of the Catholic masses, their needs for continuity and reassurance, and the hegemonic imperatives of the Catholic bourgeoisie and its nationalist and clerical spokesmen all converged to create a hegemonic culture and a contradictory popular consciousness that controlled and obscured the discontinuities and conflicts within Irish Catholic society. Consequently, in 1887, when a traveller in Tipperary, a county ravaged prior to the Famine by fierce conflicts between peasants and graziers, asked a farm labourer whether he and his exploited fellow workers now subscribed to the bourgeois-defined and bourgeois-led nationalist movement, the man replied that, although the labourers 'hate the farmers, ... *they love Ireland, and they all stand together for the counthry*'. And, mystified by an imagery that reflected peasant traditions yet both mitigated and externalized their resentments, such men usually blamed England when they emigrated in search of the dignity and decent wages denied them by the 'patriotic' graziers and shopkeepers of 'holy Ireland'.[34]

33 On Connolly, see Owen Dudley Edwards and Bernard Ransom, eds., *James Connolly: Selected Political Writings* (New York, 1974), 363–64.
34 William Henry Hurlbert, *Ireland under Coercion*, 2nd edn., 2 vols. (Edinburgh, 1888), vol. 2, 257 (emphasis added).

5 Paddy's Paradox:
Emigration to America in Irish Imagination and Rhetoric

'Paddy's Paradox' — or 'Kathleen's Conundrum', since roughly half of Ireland's post-Famine emigrants were women — signifies the striking contradictions between the 'realities' of Irish migration overseas and the popular perceptions of that phenomenon.[1] It denotes also the equally remarkable contrasts between Irish popular images of the United States, the emigrants' principal destination. Both discrepancies were arguably most marked in the post-Famine period, 1856–1929, when the largest Irish migration occurred. They were particularly evident among Irish-speakers in Ireland's western counties, but, even more important, they reflected basic tensions within Irish farm families throughout the island.[2]

   As argued in previous chapters, it was the dynamics of agrarian and industrial capitalism that generated mass emigration from post-Famine Ireland, as from other 'peripheral' or semi-colonial regions of Europe (Sicily, Galicia, Slovakia, Lithuania, et cetera). Irish landlordism and other effects of British imperialism definitely exacerbated the usual results of capitalist 'development', but the immediate causes for emigration

---

1   The original version of this chapter was published, with the present title, in Dirk Hoerder and Horst Rössler, eds., *Distant Magnets: Expectations and Realities in the Immigrant Experience, 1840–1930* (New York, 1993), 264–93. I wish to thank Holmes and Meier Publishers for permission to republish the essay, with revisions, in this volume. Although arranged and presented differently, the data and analyses herein were based on my research for *Emigrants and Exiles: Ireland and the Irish Exodus to North America* (New York, 1985), esp. chs. 3 and 8 (sections 2–3). To economize, therefore, many of the following citations refer to that work. This revision also includes, particularly in the notes, material in Kerby A. Miller and Bruce D. Boling, 'Golden Streets, Bitter Tears: The Irish Image of America during the Era of Mass Migration', *Journal of American Ethnic History*, 10, 1–2 (1990–91), 16–35.
2   As noted in Chapter 4, between 1856 and 1929 about 5 million Irish emigrated (c. 4 million of them to the US), considerably more than had emigrated in the two preceding centuries. See Miller, *Emigrants and Exiles*, 137, 169, 193–201, 291–93, and 346–53.

among the Irish lower classes (labourers, smallholders, farmers' non-inheriting sons and non-dowered daughters) stemmed from the profit-maximization strategies pursued by Catholic graziers, strong farmers, and rural parents, generally.[3] Likewise, although many Famine-era emigrants (1845–55) had indeed suffered severe deprivation and much discrimination in the United States, by the early twentieth century — and despite frequent economic depressions — Irish Americans (that is, the immigrants and their US-born children) had amassed considerable property, approached 'occupational parity' with native-born Protestant Americans, and acquired considerable influence in the Democratic party, the Catholic Church, and organized labour.[4]

Yet, as we have seen, collectively and often individually, the Irish in the post-Famine period did not always respond 'rationally' to the effects of capitalism — including mass emigration — on Irish society. Nor, as will be elaborated in this chapter, did they always view the United States itself 'realistically' — as a land where hard work, good luck, and the aid of an increasingly 'established' Irish-American community, were likely to achieve for them, if not riches, at least better employment and more economic security than were available in Ireland.

Of course, many men and women in post-Famine Ireland did view emigration in positive, instrumental terms. Moreover, the letters the emigrants sent back to Ireland certainly provided those at home with a wealth of objective information concerning American conditions and opportunities. Also, the fact that relatively few post-Famine emigrants ever returned to Ireland (perhaps 10 per cent) suggests that most found relative material comfort and contentment in the New World.[5] Nevertheless, Irish perceptions of the United States and of emigration remained extremely contradictory and, in a sense, 'irrational'. Especially in the far West of Ireland, country folk commonly held two, diametrically opposed images of America, neither of which comported closely with what most scholars describe as the objective realities of the Irish-American experience. In rural Ireland, particularly in the West, the United States was seen either as a land of incredible and easily attainable wealth — as 'sort of a halfway stage to heaven'[6] —

3 Miller, Emigrants and Exiles, 361–412.
4 See David N. Doyle, Irish Americans, Native Rights, and National Empires: The Structure, Divisions and Attitudes of the Catholic Minority in the Decade of Expansion, 1890–1901 (New York, 1976), 48–49, 59–63; Miller, Emigrants and Exiles, 492–534 passim.
5 On returned migrants, see Marjolein 't Hart, '"Heading for Paddy's Green Shamrock Shore": The Returned Emigrants in Nineteenth-Century Ireland', Irish Economic and Social History, 10 (1983), 96–97; and John Bodnar, The Transplanted: A History of Immigrants in Urban America (Bloomington, Ind., 1987), 53–54.
6 Quotation from North American Review, 52 (1837), 202. Likewise, in 1808 a woman in County Tyrone wrote that, for her and her fellow Presbyterians, the United States was 'the land of freedom and of liberty and is accounted like the land of promise flowing with milk and honey ... to those labouring under Egyptian bondage'. Some thirty years later a poor farmer in County Longford begged for an assisted passage to what he called 'the land that flows with milk and hon[e]y — the land of work and peace'. During the post-Famine period, the classic expressions of America as 'half-way stage to heaven' came from western Irish-speakers, such as Maurice O'Sullivan (quoted later in this chapter), Peig Sayers, and Tomás Ó Crohan, a west Kerryman who reported that his countrymen believed that all emigrants 'were on the

or else as an awful, forbidding place, where many, if not most, Irish emigrants pined and starved their way to early graves. Likewise, the Irish at home often interpreted emigration itself in terms of communal compulsion or of personal obligation and sacrifice. As noted in previous chapters, the oldest and most popular interpretation was that emigration was involuntary 'exile', compelled by extraneous forces such as fate, destiny, and, most commonly, by British oppression or landlord tyranny. That interpretation was not literally applicable to most post-Famine emigrants, despite the mass evictions that occurred in the early 1860s and in 1879–82, yet it remained current even in the 1920s, after the creation of the Irish Free State. Emigration as exile remained a persistent theme in the appeals of Irish and Irish-American nationalists and clerics — and so successfully that, even in their personal letters and memoirs, some ordinary emigrants characterized themselves or the exodus, generally, in terms of sorrowing or vengeful exile.[7]

How, then, to account for Paddy's Paradox? — for the disparity between, on one hand, the apparent realities of post-Famine emigration and of the Irish-American experience, 1860s–1920s, and, on the other, the popular perceptions of those phenomena? Likewise, how to account for the profound contradictions between some of the popular perceptions themselves — for instance, between the fabulously favourable and the fantastically negative images of the United States?

Throughout the nineteenth century, many Irishmen claimed that at least some 'false' images or perceptions were disseminated by Irish emigrants' letters and remittances from America or by 'returned Yanks' — that is, by the relatively few emigrants who returned to Ireland for visits or to settle. Allegedly, this was particularly true of the notion that America was a veritable paradise. Thus, in 1836 one emigrant warned that 'nine-tenths of the letters sent home to Ireland contain exaggerated statements',[8] which deluded naïve, would-be migrants such as the poor Kerrywoman who, after arriving in New York much later in the century, lamented bitterly that 'she was like many other fools [in Ireland] who were led to believe they would pick up money in the streets of America'.[9]

---

pig's back since they were on the other side' of the ocean; Miller and Boling, 'Golden Streets, Bitter Tears', 17–18.

7   Miller, *Emigrants and Exiles*, 270–79, 334–44, 535–68.

8   William Simpson, Peterborough, Upper Canada [Ontario], to Major Charles O'Hara, Collooney, County Sligo, 6 June 1836 (Ms.20,340, NLI); G. R. C. Keep, 'Some Irish Opinions on Population and Emigration, 1851–1901', *Irish Ecclesiastical Record* 85, 6 (1955), 385–86. Likewise, in 1848 Henry Johnson, an emigrant from County Antrim, warned his wife 'to beware of the most of American letters you may hear as they either greatly overrate the matter or through ignorance put a false face upon the nature of things altogether'; Miller and Boling, 'Golden Streets, Bitter Tears', 21.

9   Reports of deluded Irish emigrants were common, especially in the early nineteenth century: e.g., in 1818 Thomas Addis Emmet, an exiled United Irish leader in New York, lamented that most Irish immigrants were 'grievously disappointed, because they [had] set out [from Ireland] with false notions'. Two decades later, the leaders of Boston's Irish Charitable Society charged that Irish peasants pictured the United States as 'a paradise ... the very El Dorado of Spanish romance'; and in 1849 the officers of the New York Irish Emigrant Society cautioned their countrymen at home 'against entertaining any fantastic idea, such as that magnificence, ease, and health' were 'universally enjoyed' in the New World. Miller and Boling, 'Golden Streets, Bitter Tears', 17.

Similarly, many contemporaries believed that Irish-American remittances (averaging £1 million annually after mid-century) 'raised a furor' for emigration among impoverished peasants, who responded to such unheard-of wealth by crying 'Hurrah for Amerikey!' as they stampeded to the nearest embarkation ports.[10] Also, it was commonly believed that returned Yanks, sporting stylish clothes and proverbial gold watches, 'always g[a]ve a grand account of themselves' and of the land where they had amassed their reputed fortunes.[11]

Certainly, prior to 1819 (the year of the first major US financial panic) the letters sent home by Irish emigrants (most of them Ulster Presbyterians) often described the New World as an arcadian 'promised land'.[12] Likewise, some later letters written by refugees from the Great Famine and from the rural crisis of 1879–82 glowingly contrasted American bounty with Irish poverty.[13] Nevertheless, it is very doubtful whether emigrants' letters, returned Yanks' boastings, or even Irish-American remittances and pre-paid passage tickets were primarily responsible for propagating the paradisiacal image of the United States.[14] Research in thousands of Irish emigrants' letters and in the folklore collections at University College, Dublin, indicates instead that the great majority of such letters and returned emigrants imparted objective and carefully balanced information concerning the United States and its comparative advantages and disadvantages for potential migrants. This was particularly so in the post-Famine period, when Irishmen and -women in America generally provided very cautious and even derogatory information about the United States, especially during the economic depressions that occurred so frequently between the American Civil War and First World War. Moreover, the emigrants often made conscious attempts to shatter the naïve illusions and expectations that, they believed, prevailed in rural Ireland, warning their correspondents that the remittances sent home were usually the products of great effort, hardship, and sacrifice by the donors themselves.[15] Thus, in 1853 an Irishwoman in New York City wrote of a friend back in County Donegal, remembering that the latter

10 *Cork Examiner*, 20 April 1859.

11 *Kilkenny Journal*, 25 September 1901. On 'returned Yanks' generally, see Arnold Schrier, *Ireland and the American Emigration, 1850–1900*, reprint edn. (New York, 1970), 129–43, 152.

12 Thus, in 1770 one Ulsterman described the American countryside as full of 'wild Roses [and] Grape Vines', and a few years later another emigrant boasted from Virginia that 'we have here everything of Arcadia but its flocks and fountains'; the American Revolution added a political gloss to this vision, among Protestant Dissenters as well as Catholics. Miller and Boling, 'Golden Streets, Bitter Tears', 21.

13 This was especially true of emigrants who received official or charitable assistance to leave Ireland during those crises: thus, Famine refugee Michael Byrne wrote that in America he was 'crowned with glory', and in 1884 one of the emigrants assisted by philanthropist James Hack Tuke described the United States as 'Heaven' compared with the 'Devil's den' of poverty in west Connacht; Miller and Boling, 'Golden Streets, Bitter Tears', 22.

14 e.g., Miller, *Emigrants and Exiles*, 160–61, 203, 312–313, 472, 507.

15 e.g., Miller, *Emigrants and Exiles*, 357–59, 506–20.

'used to think money was got on the streets here, but if ever she arrives in this country she will find it quite different, as there is nothing got here by idleness'.[16]

Nor is it likely that Irish emigrants' letters played a major role in propagating the other 'irrational' perceptions of America or of emigration. With respect to the fantastically negative image of the United States, for example, although many migrants admonished their relatives not to leave home during American economic crises, and although not a few Irish Americans were thoroughly estranged from their adopted country,[17] most emigrants (as noted above) balanced warnings of specific, avoidable dangers with broadly favourable information concerning America's generally superior economic advantages. Likewise, although emigrants' letters (usually written to ageing parents) were normally couched in dutiful, familial terms, most missives could not support the notion that migration had resulted from personal sacrifice. Indeed, many writers made clear that personal ambition (if not alienation from certain aspects of Irish society) had inspired their departures, sometimes in the face of parental or communal disapproval. Finally, although many letter-writers expressed homesickness, and although some clearly regretted leaving Ireland and longed to return, only a minority (albeit perhaps a significant one) openly described themselves as 'exiles' or specifically blamed their own departures on British or landlord oppression. Instead, most migrants tempered homesickness with reason, as was the case, for instance, with J. F. Costello, a farm labourer from County Limerick. Now a ranch-hand in the Pacific Northwest, Costello admitted that he considered Ireland to be 'the dearest spot in the world', but he rationalized that 'home sickness is something that's natural': 'I often get a relapse of it,' he acknowledged, 'but somehow there seems to be no cure only to stand it. ... [W]hen you cannot have what you like, you must learn to like what you have', and, after all, he concluded, 'I still think I am in as good a country as there is in the world today for a poor man.'[18]

It would seem, then, that the Irish at home made highly selective use of the information conveyed by the 'American letters' and by returned Yanks, for only such usage — ignoring contradictory or objective evidence — could corroborate the images and perceptions that persisted in post-Famine Ireland regardless of such evidence. Thus, with respect to the popular illusion that America was an earthly paradise, one emigrant despaired that his Irish correspondents did not want to read letters that 'never contained anything of the marvellous ... and [were] not at all calculated to make people believe that riches

16 Jane Fleming, New York City, to Mrs. McVitty, c. Bundoran, County Donegal, 3 May 1853 (D.1047/1, PRONI). Similarly, in 1853 Joseph Hewitt, an emigrant from County Armagh, promised that in his own letters he would 'try and give a true character of America ... for it is very little true accounts of it ever go back to Ireland'; Miller and Boling, 'Golden Streets, Bitter Tears', 21 and also 25 for similar warnings.
17 e.g., see Risteard Ó Foghludha, ed., Pádraig Phiarais Cúndún (Baile Átha Cliath, 1932), 40–44 and passim (trans. Bruce D. Boling).
18 J. F. Costello, White River Valley, Washington Terr., to his parents, Coagh, County Limerick, 11 January 1883 (from the Schrier collection).

grow like grass' in the United States.[19] Similarly, the notion that all Irish emigration was tantamount to political banishment flourished in speeches, sermons, and popular music and literature regardless of a wealth of mundane and contrary evidence. One can only conclude that, for the most part, the Irish in America were not deluding the Irish in Ireland; rather, the Irish in Ireland were deluding themselves.

These perceptions of emigration and of America were grounded in the most archaic aspects of Irish popular culture. As noted in Chapter 1, Irish missionaries to sixth- and seventh-century Europe had described themselves as 'exiles', enduring 'white martyrdom' for Christ's sake; and Gaelic poets, both before and after the English Protestant conquests, applied *deoraí* (exile) and similar terms to anyone who left Ireland, especially to Catholic Ireland's expatriated heroes.[20] Similarly, the compensatory notion that the New World was a 'promised land' or an earthly paradise might be traced to biblical prophecies and millennial visions, as expressed by the spokesmen of a defeated people — 'Like the Children of Israel,' one poet cried — or to embellished stories of Golconda, the fabulous riches of the Spanish Indies, as told in the sixteenth century by, say, Iberian merchants in Connacht or Elizabethan soldiers in Munster.[21] Likewise, the contradictory but equally fantastic negative image of the New World may be rooted in ancient voyage tales or other traditions that associated travelling westward with death or banishment. Such legends later gained apparent corroboration by stories of the harsh treatment and high mortality endured by Irish indentured servants and prisoners transported to the American colonies in the 1600s and 1700s, as well as by the earliest travel accounts penned by Irish poets, such as Donnchadh Ruadh Mac Conmara, who in the mid-eighteenth century returned home to County Waterford to describe the New World as a howling wilderness.[22] Also, to discourage emigration the Irish and, after the Act of Union in 1800, the British government tried to reinforce such sentiments,

19 Brian Garahan, Orange County, NY, to the Rev. Edward Anthony Garahan, Ballinegar, French Park, County Roscommon, 19 December 1817 (Ms. 9.1:098, O'Conor Don Papers, Clonalis House, Castlerea, County Roscommon); thanks to Dr. Marion Casey, of the Irish Studies programme at New York University, for her transcription of this letter.

20 Seán de Fréine, *The Great Silence: The Study of a Relationship between Language and Nationality* (Dublin, 1965), 25; Miller, *Emigrants and Exiles*, 105; and see Chapter 1 in this volume.

21 T. F. O'Rahilly, ed., *Measgra Dánta: Miscellaneous Irish Poems*, 2 vols. (Cork, 1927), vol. 2, 146 (trans. Bruce D. Boling); Miller, *Emigrants and Exiles*, 485.

22 Miller, *Emigrants and Exiles*, 142–49, 557–58. For another, equally negative poetic description of eighteenth-century America, also in the Irish language but from Ulster, see Kerby A. Miller, *et al.*, *Irish Immigrants in the Land of Canaan: Letters and Memoirs from Colonial and Revolutionary America, 1675–1815* (New York, 2003), 53–55.

circulating reports in the late 1810s, for example, that North America was 'a vast snowy desert'.[23]

Whatever their ultimate origins, these images — especially the negative ones — were common in the Irish countryside, particularly during the earliest years of Catholic migration and, generally, among impoverished country folk whose parochialism was so great that they could barely conceive of life beyond their native parishes.[24] In the post-Famine era, these perceptions of America and of overseas migration, generally, persisted most widely among the most culturally traditional and least literate Irish-speaking communities along the west Atlantic coast. In these districts, deoraí remained the only term for 'emigrant', and — in contrast to eastern Ireland, where their Anglicized countrymen, long accustomed to transatlantic migration, usually assessed America more 'rationally' — western Irishmen commonly still believed that the United States was either a 'land of gold' or, conversely, a 'land of sweat' and 'snakes'. Perhaps one reason these images endured despite contradictory evidence was that, for pre- or semi-literate Irish-speakers, steeped in archaic legends, there was no sharp distinction between what their more 'modernized', urbanized countrymen called 'mythology' and the 'real world'; thus, for Irish-speaking peasants, the unseen, 'rationally' unprovable world of the fairies was just as authentic as the physical objects they could see and touch. Furthermore, the users of Irish — a language elaborate in vocabulary and nuance — seemed to delight in extravagant superlatives and fantastic analogies. Hence, for such people emigration could appear as either a descent into hell or an ascent to heaven, and America could become more than just a barely imaginable place — it could become a 'wonder'. And so the stories told around western Irish hearths about An tOileán Úr (literally,

---

23 William Forbes Adams, *Ireland and the Irish Emigration to the New World, from 1815 to the Famine* (New Haven, Conn., 1932), 125. As noted in the preceding chapter, during the nineteenth century, particularly after the Famine, many Catholic clergymen and nationalist spokesmen also opposed and tried to discourage emigration rhetorically, often by disseminating 'horror stories' about Irish-American conditions in sermons, newspapers, guidebooks, and other publications; however, as the US correspondent for the *London Daily News* stated in 1864, nothing that appeared in print was effective in encouraging or discouraging Irish emigration, because 'Cork or Galway peasant[s]' learned about the United States mainly or only from the letters their relatives sent from overseas, and they were 'not in the least likely to trust' other sources of information; Miller and Boling, 'Golden Streets, Bitter Tears', 19–20. Of course, this begs the question whether such letters were primarily responsible for either the fantastically positive or the fabulously negative images of America that prevailed in the Irish countryside; the argument in this chapter is that they were not.

24 Thus, in 1823 Peter Robinson found that before he could interest the destitute cottiers of north Cork in assisted emigration to free Canadian homesteads, he first had to dissipate their 'apprehensions concerning wild beasts and the dangers of being lost in the woods'; a few years earlier a returned emigrant discovered that impoverished country folk in County Carlow would not consider going to America, in part because they believed its inhabitants were 'Black' savages; Miller and Boling, 'Golden Streets, Bitter Tears', 26–27; Miller, *Emigrants and Exiles*, 235.

The New Island: America) took on the same fabulous dimensions as the ancient tales of Tír na nÓg and other mythical lands across the western ocean.[25]

However, in 1901 only 14 per cent of Ireland's people still spoke Irish, and by then even the inhabitants of the western coasts had experienced at least several decades of mass migration, its mundane causes, and its practical and — given their intense poverty at home — relatively beneficial consequences.[26] How and why, then, did these archaic and objectively anachronistic perceptions still prevail and even flourish (as in the case of emigration as exile), not only in the western counties, but throughout a Catholic Irish society that was now overwhelmingly literate, English-speaking, and virtually inundated by letters and other information from or about America? These notions must have had deep cultural roots — and must have performed crucial functions in post-Famine Ireland — or they would not have survived so pervasively.

As argued in previous chapters, traditional perceptions of emigration and of the New World were more than literary affectations or quaint fragments of folklore. Rather, they were expressions of a still extant cultural system that discouraged 'individualism' and novel actions such as emigration. This belief-system pervaded traditional Gaelic society, and although conquests and confiscations had destroyed the classes that once dominated that society, certain aspects of post-conquest life still validated many elements of that system, particularly among poor, Irish-speaking Catholics.[27] In the context of this pre-capitalist worldview, with its overriding emphases on communal obligations and the authority of tradition, it was perfectly 'natural' that the New World, so alien to received wisdom, would be conceptualized in customary, magical, and Manichaean terms. Likewise, it was logical that emigration itself would be perceived as an act of self-sacrifice or even exile, especially since, as noted in Chapter 1, an Irish-speaker usually described his or her emigration as *dob éigean dom imeacht go Meiriceá* — 'I had to go to America' — which in turn was consistent with the designation of *deoraí* for 'emigrant' and the cultural impacts of rebellion, defeat, and banishment.[28]

Despite post-Famine Ireland's 'modernization' and Anglicization, such notions and the traditional worldview that supported them survived well into the early 1900s. One reason was that substantial continuities remained in a society where change was profound but uneven. For example, although by 1911 graziers, speculators, and other members of the rural bourgeoisie had engrossed some 60 per cent of all Irish *farmland*, over two-thirds of all *farm families* occupied holdings valued at less than £15, practised a semi-subsistence economy characterized primarily by 'use values rather than exchange values', and directed family activities less for profit (of which at least half such farms

25 Miller, *Emigrants and Exiles*, 477–78. Ms. 1408, 148, 188, 319–28 and *passim*; Ms. 1409, 240–43; Ms. 1410, 132; and Ms. 1411, 338–39, 356 (DIF/UCD).
26 Statistics re Irish-speaking and literacy, 1851–1901, tabulated in Donald H. Akenson, *The Irish Education Experiment: The National System of Education in the Nineteenth Century* (London, 1970), 379–80.
27 Miller, *Emigrants and Exiles*, 107–30.
28 Miller, *Emigrants and Exiles*, 121.

were incapable) than for the perpetuation of the family holding itself.[29] Post-Famine rural society also remained hierarchical and deferential, for while landlord and British authority waned and, in the Free State after 1921, disappeared, the hegemony of local Catholic élites, lay and religious, became omnipresent, especially among the rural poor, thus ensuring that at least some aspects of 'modernization' did not promote self-assertion but instead increased popular dependence on parochial authority figures and the institutions they controlled.[30]

Moreover, to the extent that some social and cultural changes were real, rapid, and often painful — threatening social disruption and even widespread demoralization — they, too, encouraged popular reliance on traditional 'explanations' that maintained, however superficially, a sense of continuity with an idealized yet broken past. Of course, most rural Irishmen and -women responded 'rationally' to post-Famine Ireland's new economic exigencies and 'opportunities' — particularly by adopting impartible inheritance and mass migration. Indeed, contemporaries often charged that capitalist values had so 'Anglicized' young emigrants that they no longer lamented their departures. Yet commonly Irish people still fell back on old cultural categories to obscure causation and accountability. In the case of emigration, this meant projecting responsibility on uncontrollable or 'alien' forces. It also meant conceptualizing America, the emigrants' usual destination, in terms of traditional images — whether fabulously favourable or fantastically awful — that seemingly compelled certain responses regardless of personal desire or volition. Hence, the old images and their corroboratory worldview remained applicable: they assimilated traditional values and customary sanctions to novel practices — mandated or 'encouraged' by Ireland's peripheral location in the transatlantic market system — and thereby enabled emigrants and others to adopt explanatory strategies that deflected personal responsibility, obscured social conflicts, and relieved psychological tensions.[31]

Nowhere in post-Famine Ireland were such strategies more necessary or prevalent than in the island's own periphery: in the western counties, from west Munster north to Connacht and County Donegal, where in the late 1800s change came so swiftly that it threatened to cause social and cultural collapse. Prior to 1878, the West was still dominated by petty farmers — many of them Irish-speakers — who depended heavily

29 Miller, *Emigrants and Exiles*, 380–83, 429–30. Also, see Moritz Bonn, *Modern Ireland and Her Agrarian Problem* (Dublin, 1906), 48–50.
30 Miller, *Emigrants and Exiles*, 121–24, 412–13, 428–35.
31 Miller, *Emigrants and Exiles*, 121–24, 428–35.

on potatoes for subsistence, who practised partible inheritance and often various forms of co-tillage, and who still exhibited a marked cultural insularity and a comparatively strong aversion to permanent emigration — 'cling[ing] to their inhospitable mountains as a woman clings to a deformed or idiot child', as one critic remarked. However, in the late 1870s and early 1880s, a combination of potato-crop failures, collapsing farm prices, widespread evictions, and other factors destroyed the fragile economic props of the West's semi-traditional society and unleashed a flood tide of desperate emigrants from the region. Although the immediate crisis subsided by 1882, it institutionalized permanently high rates of western migration, because those who survived the depressed 1880s and 1890s did so largely through increased dependence on commercial agriculture, primarily grazing, and on village traders, shopkeepers, and usurers. In turn, this commercialization entailed the abandonment of communal farming patterns and farm subdivision, and the adoption of consolidated farmsteads and, most important, impartible inheritance.[32] Consequently, in western as in eastern Ireland (where these patterns had long prevailed), social relationships became more instrumental and migration became a societal and familial imperative: 'One son will stay at home and keep on the farm', as a west Kerryman declared, 'and the others will go away because they must go'.[33] Simultaneously, rapid Anglicization accompanied commercialization, eroding western peasants' cultural ties to their homeland and thereby facilitating departures mandated by structural changes. Moreover, emigration itself promoted cultural discontinuities that in turn encouraged more departures, for letters and gifts from relatives overseas invited obvious comparisons between American bounty and western Irish poverty, inspiring intense dissatisfaction with customary and now purportedly 'inferior' lifestyles at home.[34]

In great measure, commercialization and Anglicization had profound and logically predictable effects on the ways western peasants viewed emigration. Thus, visitors to western hearths reported that adolescents in west Kerry 'talked of nothing else' but emigration, that their peers in west Connacht were 'delighted when their passage arrived', and that westerners who were too old to emigrate bitterly envied the good fortune of the departed.[35] However, while traditional western society and culture seemed 'like a sea on ebb', many customary features remained despite, or even because of, the contradictory effects of rapid change.[36] In turn, these residual relationships and outlooks continued to generate or reinforce traditional interpretations of emigration.

32 Miller, Emigrants and Exiles, 397–402, 469–73.
33 John M. Synge, The Aran Islands and Other Writings, ed. Robert Tracy (New York, 1962), 218.
34 Miller, Emigrants and Exiles, 424–26, 472–73.
35 Pádraig Ua Duinnín, Muinntear Chiarraidhe Roimh an Drochsaoghal (Baile Átha Cliath, 1905), 54–61 (trans. Bruce D. Boling); Synge, Aran Islands, 291; Ms. 1407, 45–46, and Ms. 1409, 4–5, 11–32 (DIF/UCD).
36 Robin Flower, The Western Island, or the Great Blasket (New York, 1945), 18.

For example, although increased dependence on grazing, retail, and credit networks entailed the ultimate destruction of peasant agriculture, in the short run such involvement shored up the semi-subsistence family farms that still dominated the western landscape. Likewise, government policies designed to relieve the West's distress gave family farmers time to adjust to market conditions in ways designed to realize traditional 'peasant' goals. Many of these adjustments, particularly impartible inheritance and obligatory emigration for the disinherited and the non-dowered, were radical innovations in western contexts, but the goals themselves were decidedly conservative: generational continuity, relative self-sufficiency, and security on the family holding. Thus, emigration, like the earlier (and still continuing) seasonal migration, served highly conservative functions in western Ireland, because the departures and remittances of 'superfluous' youngsters precluded felt necessities for even greater changes among those who remained at home. Similarly, despite Anglicization, in many districts cultural and linguistic continuities remained remarkably strong, and while some visitors to the West lamented what they perceived as the region's social fragmentation and cultural decline, other observers complained of the seemingly intransigent conservatism of its inhabitants — 'held down by the weight of old custom and prejudices'. Consequently, although western Ireland *as a whole* exhibited the island's highest emigration rates after 1880, popular aversion and resistance to emigration remained equally marked. This was especially true in isolated districts along the coast (where the population actually increased in some decades), but, throughout the West, farmers' sons who *inherited* land were much more likely to stay at home and marry than were their counterparts elsewhere in Ireland, despite the fact that the holdings that westerners inherited were generally much smaller and poorer than those in the eastern counties. Moreover, even among non-inheriting children *preferences* to remain at home seemed unusually strong, for on the average western farm families supported much larger numbers of dependent relatives — postponing or avoiding emigration — than did eastern families. Finally, the western Irish who did emigrate appear to have had much higher rates of return than their eastern peers, and in many western communities *all* the emigrants' eventual returns seem to have been commonly, if erroneously, anticipated.[37]

In part, cultural conservatism alone — the continued strength in western districts of the Irish language and its associated folklore — can help explain the persistence of old images, rooted in Gaelic culture, concerning emigration and America. Thus, the belief that emigration was exile and the notions that the United States was either 'the Land of the Snakes' or a place where 'gold and silver [lay] out on the ditches, and nothing to do but to gather it', as one west Kerryman fantasized, could persist among country folk who only understood that the New World was the antithesis, positive or negative, of western

---

37 Miller, *Emigrants and Exiles*, 473–76; Congested Districts Board, Inspectors' Confidential ['Baseline'] Reports, 1891–95 (Trinity College, Dublin), 106–07, 459, 500.

Ireland.[38] However, considering the flood of objective information about emigration that reached the West after 1880, these archaic perceptions could not have survived and flourished had they not performed crucial social and psychological functions — had they not relieved, as well as reflected, the contradictions and tensions of western Irish society, especially with regard to emigration.

In the late nineteenth and early twentieth centuries, western Ireland was an almost schizophrenic society, where strikingly novel social processes and outlooks co-existed with others that remained obdurately conservative. In turn, these inconsistencies inspired widespread demoralization, alienation, and insecurity: change was too rapid, exposure to radically different and purportedly superior lifestyles too sudden, and the discrepancies between tradition and innovation, ideals and realities, were too profound to be assimilated easily or explained 'rationally'. Thus, for example, a growing sense that western Ireland was doomed, coupled with traditional prophetic visions, could strengthen the belief that America, and particularly its cities — the sources of most of the remittances that now poured into the West — were what the Donegal novelist Séamus Ó Grianna called caisleáin óir (castles of gold); in turn, this image of a paradise overseas helped overcome traditional resistance to and fear of emigration and so encouraged or facilitated the mass departures of the disinherited, which the new social order demanded. Conversely, the equally popular and traditional negative image of the New World not only reflected the fact that many western Irish, poor and unskilled for the most part, experienced great hardship and homesickness overseas, but, more important, its discouraging effects may have helped prevent the total depopulation of a region whose inhabitants evinced growing contempt for their native parishes and folkways.[39]

In another sense, however, these mythical notions were so irreconcilable that they only further exposed and exacerbated the demoralizing contradictions of western society. For while the lure of the caisleáin óir threatened the West with demographic and cultural deracination, the fears inspired or intensified by the opposing image threatened to discourage the wholesale migration necessary to secure the region's relative stability. In the last analysis, the conflicts between those perceptions, like the tensions they reflected, could only be 'resolved' (or ignored) by the maintenance of the archaic fiction that emigration was exile, a departure for which the emigrant was not responsible, and thus attributable neither to the emigrants themselves nor to the new dynamics of western Irish society. Only that 'explanation' could mitigate popular enthusiasm for the 'land of gold', reconcile popular fears of the 'land of sweat', and so assimilate mass migration to the traditional categories of western thought. Hence, emigration was sanctioned, but as the 'fated' result of uncontrollable forces rather than as the consequence either of individual ambitions or of non-traditional and inequitable social arrangements.

38 Maurice O'Sullivan, Twenty Years A-Growing (New York, 1933), 239.
39 Miller, Emigrants and Exiles, 478–79; 'Máire' [Séamus Ó Grianna], Caisleáin Óir (Dundalk, 1924); trans. Bruce D. Boling.

Instead, according to accepted wisdom, the emigrants just 'had to go', for it was 'the way of the world'. Such fatalism was customary and comforting — both to the emigrants and to those left behind — for the exile motif absolved community members of responsibility for actions that violated every inherited notion of community, and it helped those who feared leaving home to endure stoically a supposedly pre-determined present and an uncertain future that they were unable or unwilling to conceptualize realistically. Moreover, since in the Irish-speaking West the image of involuntary expatriation was inextricably linked to a centuries-old folklore of protest against the hated Sasanaigh, the fervent nationalist agitation that characterized much of the region from 1879 to 1923 could draw on, politicize, and thus reinforce the archaic belief that emigration was ultimately caused by British oppression. In turn, that perception further externalized causation and obscured socio-economic conflicts within western Irish society itself.[40]

Yet as argued in Chapter 4, whereas such compromises between innovation and tradition may have been psychological necessities, and although these images may have been rooted in legends and folklore, the force and precision of such ideological adjustments were largely determined by Catholic Ireland's governing classes and institutions. In the post-Famine period, especially, the Catholic bourgeoisie, in alliance with the Church, generated a dominant Catholic nationalist culture that assimilated the peasantry's traditional values and aspirations to the middle class's hegemonic imperatives — that is, to its need for authority over the Catholic lower classes in order to mitigate social conflict and mobilize the latter's grievances against British rule. Moreover, because of conflicting middle- and lower-class interests with regard to emigration and its proximate causes, the Catholic bourgeoisie's construction of cultural hegemony required appropriation of the residual belief that all Irish emigration was political exile and its elaboration in the context of an idealized 'holy Ireland' (organic, patriarchal, and pre-capitalist) from which emigration would be unknown if not for British misrule and Anglicization's corrosive effects. In this ideological system, emigration could only be forced exile — or the product of personal selfishness tantamount to betrayal of 'holy Ireland' itself.[41]

Middle-class cultural hegemony was exercised not only through the Catholic Church and Irish nationalism. On the most intimate and pervasive level, it was mediated

40 Miller, Emigrants and Exiles, 478–81.
41 On cultural hegemony theory and its application to Irish society, see Chapter 4 in this volume and, for relevant citations, nos. 4–5. See the same chapter for a more detailed discussion of the 'holy Ireland' myth, and also Miller, Emigrants and Exiles, 435–69. A prime example of emigration interpreted in the 'holy Ireland' context is Rev. Joseph Guinan, Scenes and Sketches in an Irish Parish; or, Priest and People in Doon (Dublin, 1906), 43.

through the strong-farmer *type* of rural Irish family — the stem family. Although 'holy Ireland' was illusory, its cultural force lay not only in its incorporation 'from above' — via religious and political media — but in its reinforcement of traditional rural beliefs. Ironically, just as the idealized peasant family (unchanging, corporate, and paternalistic) was the purported microcosm of 'holy Ireland', so post-Famine Ireland's *real* farm families — in the Anglicized East as well as in the Gaelic West — required and helped generate such notions and images to 'explain' their members' emigration in traditional, non-responsible terms. Thus, because Irish family dynamics reproduced the larger processes of Irish agrarian capitalism, the rural stem family's own needs coincided with the hegemonic imperatives of the Irish Catholic bourgeoisie.[42]

Despite the commercialization of post-Famine society, a persistent lack of scope for individual enterprise in Ireland confirmed the farm family's position as the dominant socio-economic and cultural unit. Family bonds still took precedence over other associational ties, and religious teachings sacralized patriarchy, authoritarian parent-child relationships, and the co-operative ethos mandated by the exigencies of small-farm agriculture. Most farmers depended heavily on children's unpaid labour and their willingness to support parents in old age. In general, all children, and especially females, were trained to be dutiful, submissive, and self-effacing — to subordinate individual motives and desires to customary notions of family welfare and status: 'boldness' in children, in sons as well as daughters, was thus stigmatized as 'sinful' and countered with shame and guilt. Although relationships between fathers and children were often distant and domineering, emotional bonds between mothers and sons were proverbially close, at times smothering, as frustrated farmers' wives — often trapped by the dowry system in loveless marriages to men much older than themselves — lavished compensatory affection on male offspring.[43]

The family's importance, its close-knit relationships and socialization patterns, produced highly ambivalent attitudes towards emigration among parents and offspring alike. On the one hand, emigration threatened family integrity, physically sundered ties to birthplace and kin, and violated customary notions of proper behaviour. 'The Irish are distinguished for love of their kindred', wrote the American consul at Londonderry in 1883, 'and that love has hitherto acted as a check to the obvious motives that induce them to leave their homes'. Consequently, parents — especially mothers — often reacted to their children's impending emigration with opposition or desperate grief, and expressed fears that the latter's departure would condemn them to a comfortless old age and a lonely death. Sometimes parental protests prevented, or at least postponed, their children's emigration, and although in most instances ambition or financial imperatives overcame parental objections, most emigrants felt genuine sorrow at leaving childhood homes

---

42 Miller, *Emigrants and Exiles*, 465–69, 481. As noted in Chapter 4, the Irish stem family was characterized by impartible inheritance, the dowry system, postponed or averted marriage, and emigration for most non-inheriting and non-dowered offspring.

43 Miller, *Emigrants and Exiles*, 54–60, 115, 481–82.

and kinsmen. Moreover, many letters and memoirs indicate that parents and emigrants alike frequently mourned their separation for many years, often until death.[44]

On the other hand, there is no doubt that many emigrants were eager to leave home, both to fulfil ambitions and to escape parental repression. It is equally certain that many, perhaps most, parents either explicitly or implicitly urged their children's departure as a vital necessity to preserve social stability and improve the material welfare of those who remained at home. Given the dearth of non-farm employment, farmers' near-universal adoption of impartible inheritance made emigration mandatory for the great majority of sons and daughters who would receive neither land nor dowries and whose continued presence threatened to create intrafamilial and social strife. In addition, most parents wanted money from the children sent abroad, both to finance further emigration and to bolster Ireland's small-farm economy. Money from America not only purchased most passage tickets but also was used by farmers to pay rents and shop bills, to enlarge acreage and livestock herds, and to improve farmhouses and living standards, generally.[45] For example, in 1907 a witness before a parliamentary commission testified that rural savings accounts were 'largely earned abroad', and one year later a French traveller noted that, 'throughout the West of Ireland', 'the landlord's rents are often merely a tax levied on the filial piety of child emigrants'.[46]

Thus, 'holy Ireland's' basic social unit, the family farm, both mandated emigration and fed vampirelike upon the meagre resources its victims earned abroad—a contradiction that outraged James Connolly, who urged, 'Those who prate glibly about the "sacredness of the home" and the "sanctity of the family circle" would do well to consider what home in Ireland to-day is sacred from the influence of the greedy mercenary spirit ... ; what family circle is unbroken by the emigration of its most gentle and loving ones?'[47] Indeed, emigration at once reflected and reinforced an increasing instrumentalism in family relationships that defied traditional norms and prescribed emotions. For instance, although family bonds were probably closest in the one- and two-room cabins of western Ireland, even there economic considerations predominated. Thus, when Paddy Gallagher's family in west Donegal received an offer from a cousin in Philadelphia to pay his sisters' fares to America, his parents at first wept loudly at the prospect of 'breaking up ... the family'. However, a neighbour, hearing the commotion, consoled them: 'You may thank God', he admonished, 'that the door is going to be opened for your children going to America. Look at our children that sent us twenty pounds at Christmas. Thank God, we were able to pay our debts and raise our heads'.[48] In these

44 Miller, Emigrants and Exiles, 482–83; quotation from Arthur Livermore, Londonderry, 31 July 1883 (US Consular Reports, Ireland, microfilm T-368, National Archives, Washington, DC).
45 Miller, Emigrants and Exiles, 483.
46 Royal Commission on Congestion in Ireland, in BPP — House of Commons, Reports, vol. 5 (3630), 1907, 466; L. Paul-Dubois, Contemporary Ireland (Dublin, 1908), 305.
47 James Connolly, Labour in Ireland (Dublin, n.d.), 226.
48 Patrick Gallagher, Paddy the Cope: An Autobiography (New York, 1942), 62–63.

circumstances, even the most devoted parents usually became reconciled to their children's emigration.

Yet Irish parents' pragmatic if not calculating attitudes towards their sons' and daughters' departures had potential dangers that threatened the very interests that emigration was designed to promote. Impartible inheritance, the fathers' arbitrary selection of male heirs and dowered daughters, postponed marriage even for ostensibly fortunate children, emigration or social sterility for the rest: all exacerbated the intergenerational tensions normally expected in periods of rapid social and cultural change. Moreover, for various reasons, some farmers' children did not want to emigrate: in part because of their extreme youth, inexperience, and attachment to relatives and familiar scenes; in part because of child-rearing practices that encouraged dependence and portrayed the outside world as 'dangerous and hostile'. Thus, whereas the old notion of America as 'the Land of the Snakes' could serve the interests of those few parents who wanted to *prevent* their children's emigration, the fears of the New World which that image reflected and reinforced could make the offspring of other farm families reluctant to obey social imperatives and parental injunctions that mandated their departures. The point is that, whether emigrants left home eagerly or reluctantly, *if* they perceived and resented the explicit or implicit compulsion that parents and neighbours had exerted upon them, then they might refuse to render either the emotional or the financial homage that parents and society demanded.[49]

Those dangers were real — at least a few popular ballads blamed emigration on the capricious decisions of 'cruel parents'; and the fact that a typical emigrant such as Annie Lough felt obliged to assure her mother, in a letter from Connecticut, that 'you need not ever be afraid ... we will ever say you were the cause of sending us away', indicated parents' awareness of their children's potential resentment.[50] Indeed, although contemporary eulogists and Irish countrymen themselves claimed that nearly all emigrants dutifully remitted money home, other testimony suggests that a large number rarely or never did so. Thus, one elderly informant from County Mayo admitted that although 'there were many requests for financial assistance from home, ... it can be truthfully said, that not even half these importunate letters were answered, much less complied with'.[51] Of course, failure to write and send remittances could stem from many causes, including illiteracy, poverty, and consequent shame intensified by the emigrants' awareness that 'american letters is no use in ireland without money in them'.[52] Nevertheless, many 'neglected' parents could justly blame themselves for their sons' and daughters' alleged

---

49 Miller, *Emigrants and Exiles*, 484.
50 Robert L. Wright, ed., *Irish Emigrant Ballads and Songs* (Bowling Green, Ohio, 1975), 12–13; Annie Lough, Winsted, Conn., to her mother, Meelick, Queen's County, 29 October 1891 (courtesy of Edward Dunne and Mrs. Kate Tynan, Portlaoise, County Laois, and Canice and Eilish O'Mahony, Dundalk, County Louth).
51 Ms. 1410, 129 (DIF/UCD).
52 A. B. McMillan, Pittsburgh, Pa., to Eliza Crossen, Newtownards, County Down, 4 May 1895 (D. 1195/5/41, PRONI); James Kells, Grant County, Ky., to Thomas Kells, Grange, Oneilland, County Armagh, 18 November 1883 (M. 7075, National Archives of Ireland); Ms. 1407, 281 (DIF/UCD).

'ingratitude': for at worst they had compelled their children's emigration, at best they had helped rationalize family relationships. In the first case they often engendered lasting resentments, while in the latter they undermined the traditional and emotional bases of their own authority and implicitly encouraged their children to demonstrate similar pragmatism.

In these circumstances, it was necessary for Irish parents — indeed, for rural society as a whole — to generate perceptions of emigration that would obscure causation and responsibility, that would encourage or at least sanction emigration, yet, at the same time, neither inspire their children's indignation nor allow them to feel so self-motivated or ambitious that they would forswear or forget their filial obligations. The discrepancies between customary expectations and mass migration — and the consequent fear, grief, and bitterness — were most blatant in western districts, where agrarian capitalism, impartible inheritance, and large-scale emigration were relatively recent innovations. However, emigration itself quickly generated its own corroborating folkways — one of the most important of which was the already described belief that the New World was an earthly paradise, whereas by contrast Ireland was 'a Purgatory, where the Irish must suffer in patience before going to America'.[53] In general, the fabulous image of the United States reflected Irish countrymen's diminishing faith in their own society: their attempt to compensate for Irish poverty and insecurity by projecting archaic legends and traditional aspirations for comfortable self-sufficiency onto a barely comprehended urban-industrial society. Since, after 1840, the great majority of Irish emigrants no longer settled on American farms, the peasants' old Arcadian vision was translated into an equally mythical urban setting, where, in the words of one ballad, 'The houses were all jasper / And the streets were paved in gold ...'[54]

The fact that this vision survived the impact of mass public education, much information to the contrary, and the Irish countryman's proverbial scepticism indicates that belief in the *caisleáin óir* served practical functions vital to the families that composed rural society. For example, in many parts of Ireland interfamilial relationships were characterized by a jealous and secretive competitiveness. Emigration played a role in this rivalry, because in order to maintain its own petty status each family that sent children to America carefully guarded the news that came home and always pretended that its offspring were doing well. Many families burned their children's letters as soon as they read them, and the receipt of an 'empty American letter' (that is, one that contained no remittances) was rarely admitted. Thus, given endemic rural jealousy, every family's pretence that its own children were prospering overseas naturally encouraged the common notion that America was so rich that *anyone* could prosper there: in every household, the feeling was that, 'if such lazy, shiftless creatures as the neighbour's children could afford to send

---

53 Miller, *Emigrants and Exiles*, 485; Paul-Dubois, *Contemporary Ireland*, 359.
54 Miller, *Emigrants and Exiles*, 485–86; C. Mac Mathúna, 'Song of the Exile', *Irish Times* (Dublin), 16 December 1976.

home £10 every month, then America must truly be a land where gold can be picked up off the streets'. Furthermore, since all young emigrants would be expected at least to equal this spurious standard of achievement, it was only natural that parents would ignore letters that described America realistically or that pleaded poverty as an excuse for not sending remittances. 'They might not have bothered sending their pictures', exclaimed the angry father of emigrants from County Roscommon, 'for we know well what they look like. The pictures I would like to see are a few of Abraham Lincoln's'.[55]

However, the most important function of America's alluring mythical image was in assuaging the bitterness of departure for potentially reluctant young emigrants. Given the abundance of contradictory information, Irish child-rearing practices must have been crucial in transmitting that image from generation to generation. Parents who knew that their own decisions concerning inheritances would inevitably consign most of their children to the United States could try to forestall any resentment by holding the fabulous vision of the New World before their youthful imaginations. As a French visitor to Ireland remarked, 'Children are brought up with the idea of probably becoming emigrants' — 'trained to regard life "in the country" as a transitory matter, merely a period of waiting until the time shall come for them to begin life "over there"'.[56] Indeed, even Canon Michael O'Riordan, one of the staunchest defenders of 'holy Ireland', admitted parental culpability when he wrote, 'Children learn from their childhood that their destiny is America; and as they grow up, the thought is set before them as a thing to hope for.'[57] Thus, whereas traditional proverbs — vital instruments of socialization — formerly enjoined loyalty to birthplace, new aphorisms suited to new social realities stigmatized Irish life as hopelessly impoverished, and condemned stay-at-homes as lazy or weak. Given such an upbringing, reinforced by Irish youngsters' own perceptions of Ireland's real inadequacies and America's real attractions, it was no wonder that travellers in the Irish countryside reported that 'the lads of fourteen and fifteen are all growing up with the determination to bid adieu for ever to their native land'.[58]

The vision of the caisleán óir must have struck a responsive chord in many Irish youths. Among those who feared or resented the 'necessity' to leave home, the prospect of a promised land, with 'gold and silver out on the ditches', surely made that imperative much easier to fulfil. Moreover, the image was also useful for would-be emigrants who faced parental opposition to their departures, for if the United States was the paradise it was reputed to be, then they would be fools not to go there — and, once abroad, they could send back enough of that proverbial gold to stem their parents' tears. However, before the emigrants left Ireland, the lure of America had to be carefully balanced by parental and communal sanctions against individualism and materialism. Otherwise,

55 Miller, *Emigrants and Exiles*, 486–87; Ms. 1407, 36–37, and Ms. 1409, 297 (DIF/UCD).
56 Miller, *Emigrants and Exiles*, 487; Paul-Dubois, *Contemporary Ireland*, 359.
57 Rev. Michael O'Riordan, *Catholicity and Progress in Ireland* (London, 1906), 292.
58 See Miller, *Emigrants and Exiles*, 487; Ms. 1407, 45–46 (DIF/UCD); Henry Coulter, *The West of Ireland* (London, 1862), 287–88.

there was the danger that emigrants who eagerly rejected Ireland for the land of gold might also reject Irish associations (familial, especially, but also religious and political) in their lust for wealth and excitement. In 1978 the anthropologist Robin Fox noted the consequent paradox still extant on Ireland's remote Tory Island: although a child who did not emigrate was 'lazy', one who did was 'disloyal'.[59] In other words, although Irish parents encouraged emigration, they demanded that departures take place not from hedonistic ambition but only out of familial obligations to relatives at home or already abroad. Thus, on the one hand, parents criticized emigrating children as 'selfish', 'ungrateful', and 'disloyal' for 'abandoning' them, and yet, on the other hand, made clear that emigration for the family's sake was a duty that children could not ignore or avoid. Eager emigrants, enraptured by their vision of the *caisleán óir*, were cautioned that 'it's not wealth and riches that make a person satisfied', constantly reminded of the lonely misery their 'deserted' parents would endure, yet also admonished to depart in order to relieve pressure at home and to remit money: 'Confound you', neighbours would say, 'what's the use of spending your life here — would it not be better for you to go to America and earn something for your father and mother?' Such conflicting messages placed would-be emigrants in an extremely difficult position: it was 'shameful' to emigrate, but also 'shameful' to remain at home. However, while 'selfish' emigration threatened family welfare and psychic peace — and violated both traditional norms and the 'holy Ireland' ideal — emigration undertaken in a proper, 'dutiful' spirit promised to mitigate all conflicts and resolve all contradictions. In short, sufficient expressions of sorrow (often truly felt) and, most important, steady and ample remittances (often willingly sent) constituted the 'price' that many emigrants paid to relieve the tensions between desire and duty.[60]

Clerical and nationalist strictures against 'selfish' emigration and materialism in general served to reinforce parental injunctions — persuading, for example, the emigrant Thomas Garry not to 'delay in Relieving [his family in Ireland] as it is a duty Encumbered on me by the laws of Church'.[61] Again, however, traditional child-rearing practices were probably crucial insofar as they stigmatized 'boldness', enjoined conformity to authority and communal opinion, and inspired the felt need to avoid personal responsibility. Moreover, the very process of chain-migration both reflected and corroborated such tendencies. One's ability to emigrate usually depended on family ties stretching across the Atlantic in the forms of letters and remittances, and the fact that most post-Famine migrants at least initially joined relatives overseas made departures seem much less acts

59 Miller, *Emigrants and Exiles*, 487–88; Robin Fox, *The Tory Islanders: A People of the Celtic Fringe* (Cambridge, 1978), 29.
60 Miller, *Emigrants and Exiles*, 488–89; Micheál Ó Gaoithín, *Beatha Peig Sayers* (Baile Átha Cliath, 1970), 89–90 (trans. Bruce D. Boling); Ms. 1409, pp. 45–46, 60 (DIF/UCD); Hugh Brody, *Inishkillane: Change and Decline in the West of Ireland* (London, 1973), 165–66.
61 Thomas Garry, Peekskill, NY, to his wife, County Sligo, 8 March 1848, in the *Third Report from the Select Committee on Colonization from Ireland*, HL 1849 (86), Minutes of Evidence, Appendix X, in BPP [IUP ser.]: *Emigration*, vol. 5 (Shannon, 1968), 129.

of *self*-assertion than of conformity to established custom — much less as disruptions of all family bonds than as a process of reunion whose continuance depended on the new emigrant's persistent loyalty.[62] In addition, if youthful socialization was not sufficient to instill grief and guilt, highly ritualized leave-taking ceremonies — American wakes — seemed almost purposely designed to obscure emigration's mundane causes, wring the last drops of sorrow and self-recrimination from the intending emigrant, and impress upon him or her a sense of eternal obligation to those left at home. And, once the migrants were overseas, parents and other relatives often deluged them with letters, either piteously entreating or imperiously demanding that their children or siblings remit some of that reputedly plentiful gold to their personal 'mother Irelands'.[63]

Finally, the key notion that resolved both familial tensions and the contradictions between America's opposing images was the perception that emigration was exile — an enforced process for which neither parents nor their children were ultimately responsible. Even if departure was desirable because of the supposedly enormous gulf between Irish poverty and American prosperity, even if it was obligatory to preserve the stem family and the smooth functioning of Irish agrarian capitalism, in the last analysis the emigrants simply 'had to go' because past oppression and contemporary misgovernment by England had ruined Ireland and, as one priest put it, made emigration an 'artificial' necessity.[64] In a sense, this politicization of emigration was natural, given historical and literary traditions — corroborated and formalized by pervasive nationalist agitation — that 'explained' all discontinuities and offered such an appealing, externalizing resolution of the conflicts and inequities within Irish Catholic society. Thus, as a nationalist politician testified before parliament in 1908, although rural parents' real attitude towards emigration was 'the more children in America the better', those children themselves obligingly 'attribute[d] their being in exile to landlordism and the support given it in the past by the [British] Government'.[65] Such a perception helped to ensure that the departed remained emotionally tied to a beloved and beleaguered 'holy Ireland' whose families and farms, parish churches and patriotic cause, fully deserved the self-perceived exile's eternal devotion and dollars. And through such fidelity, as one popular ballad put it, Ireland's 'banished children' would fulfil their duty and 'prove their worth wheresoever they roam / True to their country, their God, and their home'.[66]

Of course, some migrants refused to conform to the prescribed perceptions of emigration as political exile, for whether they left home bitterly or joyfully they clearly recognized the gross discrepancies between the harsh realities and the 'idolatrous self-image' of 'holy Ireland' — the actual, immediate sources of socio-economic or

---

62 e.g., see O'Sullivan, *Twenty Years A-Growing*, 240–41.
63 Miller, *Emigrants and Exiles*, 489–90, 556–68.
64 Miller, *Emigrants and Exiles*, 490; O'Riordan, *Catholicity and Progress*, 292.
65 Royal Commission on Congestion in Ireland, in *BPP — House of Commons, Reports*, vol. 7 (3748), 1908, 811.
66 Schrier, *Ireland and American Emigration*, 100.

personal repression that made life at home untenable or unbearable.[67] For instance, Irish farm labourers and women, generally, seemed the most consciously self-motivated migrants: realistic about America's material advantages and openly eager to escape from exploitive situations. However, most post-Famine emigrants were neither alienated nor self-assertive enough to defy openly or consistently communal demands that they de-emphasize individual motivation and conceptualize emigration in dutiful or compulsory terms — especially when such attitudes and perceptions had been internalized from birth and reinforced by every institution shaping rural life. For the emigrants themselves, as well as for their parents, the interpretations of emigration as obligation or as exile were both customary and expedient. Fortunately for eager emigrants, the process of chain-migration enabled independent volition to be 'explained' as passive acquiescence. As a result, it was common for post-Famine emigrants to make the highly dubious claim that they never had the slightest notion of leaving Ireland until the purportedly unexpected arrival of supposedly unsolicited passage tickets from America confronted them with an inescapable 'duty' or 'fate'. Thus, while Irish clerics and nationalists might denounce emigrants as 'traitors' to 'holy Ireland' and its 'sacred cause', the very process of emigration enabled young Irishmen and -women to circumvent such injunctions in terms that seemingly validated traditional, dependent outlooks. For example, when interviewed decades later, an elderly man in County Westmeath mistakenly 'remembered' that in the early 1880s, during the Land War, '*except* when pre-paid sailing tickets came, emigration was over, [for] all were wanted at home to carry on the fight' against Protestant landlords and 'English tyranny'; however, he added, 'when pre-paid sailing tickets came', eager young emigrants could then argue that they simply '*had* to go', while nationalists, priests, and parents could claim that such excused and supposedly exceptional departures implied no renunciation of communal loyalties.[68]

In conclusion, it is vital to remember that Paddy's Paradox or Kathleen's Conundrum was internalized, and so the conflicts that emigrants found most difficult and painful to resolve were often those in their own minds. In his short story significantly entitled 'Going into Exile', the Irish novelist Liam O'Flaherty convincingly and movingly portrays a girl's contradictory emotions on the night before her departure for America: at one moment she was filled with 'thoughts of love and of foreign men and of clothes and of houses where there were more than three rooms and where people ate meat every day', yet in the next instant 'she was stricken with horror at the thought of leaving her mother and at the selfishness of her thoughts ... that made her hate herself as a cruel, heartless,

67 Miller, *Emigrants and Exiles*, 490–91; Joseph J. Lee, 'Women and the Church since the Famine', in Margaret MacCurtain and Donncha Ó Corráin, eds., *Women in Irish Society: The Historical Dimension* (Dublin, 1978), 43.
68 Miller, *Emigrants and Exiles*, 490–92; Ms. 1408, 130 (DIF/UCD), emphasis added.

lazy, selfish wretch'.[69] Even the obligatory grief and promises expressed at the American wakes did not fully erase or alleviate such tensions between desire and duty. For instance, in a letter from New York the emigrant Anne Flood oscillated between self-assertion and self-destruction as her internalized conflicts threatened her psychic well-being. She began her letter boldly, telling her mother — who wanted her to return to County Meath — that she was 'happy and contented ... and never enjoyed better health' in her life. 'I never once thought of coming home', she admitted, and 'you know when I was home I often wished myself in this Country and now to return I think would be quite a folly'. However, she faltered, 'I would say more on this subject but I feel so nerv[ou]s I do not know from what effect', and so terminated the letter rather abruptly, in handwriting the increasing unsteadiness of which showed the effects of growing strain.[70]

In fact, few recently arrived emigrants dared be as 'bold' as Anne Flood, and whether sincerely or calculatingly it was thus much easier — and, perhaps, kinder to all concerned — to obscure motivation by claiming or implying that migration was either fated and unwilling exile or informed solely by filial piety and self-sacrifice. '[F]or God's sake and for ours', begged one harassed emigrant of his parents at home, 'endeavour to shake off your sorrow and do not leave us to accuse ourselves of bringing down your grey hairs with sorrow to the grave, by leaving you when we should have staid by you. Our intentions were good and still continue so, and, if God prosper our endeavours, we will soon be able to assist you and cheer you'.[71] As that plaintive plea indicates, although its practical resolutions financially sustained 'holy Ireland's' family farms and nationalist movements, in personal, psychological terms Paddy's Paradox could be a painful and an oppressive burden.

69 Liam O'Flaherty, 'Going into Exile', in Vivian Mercier and David H. Greene, eds., *1000 Years of Irish Prose* (New York, 1952), 369–78.

70 Anne Flood, New York City, to her mother, Creevagh, County Meath, 5 February 1853 (courtesy of Pádraig Ó Droighneain, Navan, County Meath).

71 F. D., Sandyhill, [Pa.?], to his parents and siblings, Maghera parish, County Londonderry, 12 August 1835 (Ordnance Survey Papers, Box 44, RIA); now published (as transcribed here) in Angélique Day and Patrick McWilliams, eds., *Ordnance Survey Memoirs of Ireland, Vol. 18: Parishes of Co. Londonderry V, 1830, 1833, 1836–7; Maghera and Tamlaght O'Crilly* (Belfast, 1993), 21.

II   Irish Protestants in Ireland and America

6   'Scotch-Irish' Ethnicity in Early America: Its Regional and Political Origins

Since the early 1700s Ulster Presbyterians' ethnic identity—its nomenclature, definition, and social and political implications — have been sharply contested issues in America as well as in Ireland.[1] Between 1650 and 1776 merely 10 per cent of Ulster emigrants settled in New England, yet their leaders and descendants contributed disproportionately to these controversies. Of the early combatants, few were as important as the Rev. James McGregor and his followers, who in 1719 settled what became the township of Londonderry, New Hampshire.

   James McGregor was born in 1677 near Magilligan Point in the parish of Tamlaghtard in northwest County Londonderry. According to tradition, McGregor received part of his education in Europe, but he graduated from the University of Glasgow and had returned to Ulster by 1701, when he was ordained as Presbyterian minister of Aghadowey parish, on the banks of the lower Bann River, in northeast County Derry. In 1704 the Synod of Ulster 'severely admonished' McGregor for intemperance, but marriage in 1706 may have settled him, and in 1710 the Synod commissioned him to preach in Ulster Irish

1   In 2001–02 this essay was solicited for publication in William Kelly and John R. Young, eds., *Ulster and Scotland, 1600–2000: History, Language and Identity* (Dublin, 2004), where it was titled 'The New England and Federalist Origins of "Scotch-Irish" Ethnicity'. This was an early and shorter version of what became ch. 49 in Kerby A. Miller, *et al., Irish Immigrants in the Land of Canaan: Letters and Memoirs from Colonial and Revolutionary America, 1675–1815* (New York, 2003). I wish to thank Four Courts Press for permission to republish the essay in this volume, with minor revisions. As in the initial publication, to conserve space the number of citations has been limited largely to direct quotations, but see *Irish Immigrants in the Land of Canaan*, ch. 49, and in the Sources section of that book.

(then virtually interchangeable with Scots Gaelic) to additional congregations in Derry, Antrim, and Tyrone.[2]

McGregor was still pastor of Aghadowey in 1717 when he and several other clergymen in the Bann Valley determined to transport themselves and their flocks to New England, as encouraged by Samuel Shute, royal governor of Massachusetts. Thus, in early 1718, at the nearby port of Coleraine, McGregor delivered a farewell sermon, charging that he and his people were fleeing Ireland 'to avoid oppression and cruel bondage, to shun persecution and designed ruin, to withdraw from the communion of idolaters and to have an opportunity of worshipping God according to the dictates of conscience and the rules of His inspired Word'.[3]

It is notable that McGregor complained of harassment not from Ulster's despoiled Catholics, but from magistrates and clergy of the Church of Ireland 'by law established', and his sermon set the tone for subsequent interpretations of Ulster Presbyterian emigration as a communal exodus from 'Egyptian bondage'. Anglican critics dismissed McGregor's and other ministers' claims of religious and political persecution as mere pretences, arguing that their real reasons for emigration were economic. Historians generally agree, citing the sharp rent increases and severe distress that afflicted Ulster in the 1717–20 period. Indeed, by 1718 McGregor's own salary from his congregation was three years in arrears. Yet his sermon was not entirely disingenuous. Although by 1717–18 the times of severe persecution under Queen Anne (1702–14) had ended, Presbyterians remained bitterly aggrieved by the Irish results of a so-called Glorious Revolution that had returned to power an Anglican establishment that questioned their loyalty to the Crown, belittled their sacrifices at the siege of Derry (1688–89), and in 1704 imposed a Sacramental Test Act that excluded Presbyterians from all civil and military offices. Indeed, some Anglicans contended that Ulster's Presbyterians were 'a more knavish, wicked, thievish race than even the natural Irish of the other three provinces'.[4] Thus, it was not illogical for McGregor to interpret his flock's departure in political and religious terms, and his sermon was designed in part as a warning to officials in Dublin and London that northern Ireland might lose its Presbyterian garrison to emigration if the Test Act was not repealed. In fact, the Act was suspended in 1719, a year after

2 In 1710 the Synod reaffirmed its late seventeenth-century initiatives to convert Irish Catholics to Presbyterianism, by printing the Bible, the Westminster Confession, and the Catechisms in Irish, and by appointing McGregor and other clergymen to preach in the Irish language. In 1720 Synod records claimed that 27 of its 130 ministers could preach in Irish, but the crusade soon faltered, in part because of the severe economic distress and high rates of Presbyterian emigration that characterized Ulster in the 1720s.

   To avoid repetition, in this chapter, 'Londonderry' and 'Derry' are employed interchangeably to designate both the Ulster city and county, and the former's siege in 1688–89; however, 'Londonderry' is the sole name applied to the New Hampshire settlement after it was re-named (from Nutfield) in 1723.

3 R. J. Dickson, *Ulster Emigration to Colonial America, 1718–1725* (London, 1966), 26.

4 David Hayton, 'Anglo-Irish Attitudes: Changing Perceptions of National Identity among the Protestant Ascendancy in Ireland, ca. 1690–1750', in J. Yulton and L. E. Brown, eds., *Studies in Eighteenth-Century Culture*, 17 (1987), 152.

McGregor's company arrived at Boston, but Presbyterians remained aggrieved by tithes and other disabilities.

McGregor may also have calculated his words to appeal to the sympathies of New England's Congregationalists, to their own memories of past persecutions at Anglican hands. If so, he must have been disappointed, for the approximately 800–1,000 Ulster immigrants who landed at Boston in summer 1718 met a hostile reception from New Englanders, who feared that ships from Ireland brought only disease, paupers, and 'papists'. However, in late October McGregor successfully petitioned Governor Shute for a grant of land on the frontier of Maine, Massachusetts' northeastern province, and although McGregor himself first settled near Boston, his brother-in-law James McKeen and about 300 immigrants went north and spent an uncomfortable winter at Casco Bay. In spring 1719 McKeen's family and about twenty others abandoned Maine and sailed south to the Merrimac and up the river to Haverhill, Massachusetts, where they disembarked and travelled overland twenty miles northwest to an unsettled tract called Nutfield for its abundance of chestnut, butternut, and walnut trees. On 12 April McGregor joined them, preached a memorable sermon describing their new home as 'a great rock in a weary land' (Isaiah 32:2), and agreed to be pastor and effective leader of the first major Ulster Presbyterian settlement in the New World.

Unfortunately, Nutfield was an area disputed by the governments of Massachusetts and New Hampshire, and although Shute was royal governor of both provinces, rival groups of proprietors and speculators, backed by their respective legislatures in Boston and Portsmouth, jealously contested ownership of the upper Merrimac Valley. Furthermore, Shute and Massachusetts legislators were angry that the Ulstermen had left Maine, and so in June 1719, when McGregor and McKeen petitioned Boston for a land grant on the Merrimac, they were refused on the grounds that Nutfield belonged to Haverhill's proprietors. Consequently, in October Nutfield's settlers sent a similar petition to New Hampshire's legislature. New Hampshire's lieutenant governor, John Wentworth, although Shute's nominal subordinate, was much more sympathetic to the Nutfield colonists, perhaps because of his own family's Irish connections, but certainly because western settlements would increase New Hampshire's trade and population, create a barrier against Indian incursions, and strengthen his colony's claims to the upper Merrimac Valley.

While their petition to Portsmouth was pending, McGregor and McKeen fortified their claim to Nutfield by purchasing from Colonel John Wheelright of Wells, Maine, an old deed to the area that Wheelright's grandfather had purportedly bought from the Indians in 1629. Despite this move, however, during the winter of 1719–20 Nutfield's settlers were harassed, legally and physically, by rival claimants from Haverhill and Boston, who alleged that the Ulstermen were not only illegal squatters but also 'poor Irish', 'not wholesome inhabitants', and, most damning of all, Roman Catholics. To refute those charges, and to assert his people's claims to their settlement, that winter McGregor wrote a petition, titled 'The Humble Apology of the People of Nutfield', to Governor Shute in Boston. 'We were Surprised to hear our Selves termed *Irish People*', McGregor protested, 'when we So frequently ventured our all for the British Crown and Liberties against the Irish papists & gave all tests of our Loyalty w[hich] the Government of Ireland Required ... .' Moreover, McGregor argued, his people's legal right to Nutfield was superior to that of Haverhill's proprietors, for the former was based on Colonel Wheelright's 'Indian ... Deed being of Ninety Years Standing', whereas the Haverford claim was merely 'twenty Years Old'.[5]

McGregor's petition may have had its intended effect, for in April 1720 Governor Shute authorized Nutfield's inhabitants to choose their own officials. Furthermore, in June 1722 New Hampshire's government gave the settlers full incorporation, with a grant of land ten miles square, for a 'town',[6] whose inhabitants, a year later, officially renamed Londonderry. Meanwhile, the settlement had grown rapidly — to 360 inhabitants by April 1721 — as Ulster immigrants converged on the upper Merrimac Valley, attracted by the free lands, Presbyterian worship, and refuge from Puritan prejudice that Nutfield/ Londonderry offered. However, Londonderry's conflicts with Haverhill and Boston were just beginning, as the settlement now became the focal point of an intense political struggle between Massachusetts and New Hampshire. The result was a boundary war, spearheaded by the Haverhill proprietors, that assumed a variety of forms: innumerable petitions, arrests and trials for trespassing, seizures of property for non-payment of taxes, destruction of crops and farm buildings, physical assaults and mob violence. On 5 March 1729, McGregor died in the midst of the strife, but in a town meeting held on 15 December of that year, Londonderry's inhabitants voted to send James McKeen, town moderator, and John McMurphy to Portsmouth, to petition the New Hampshire government concerning 'our Grivances with respect to Law Shuits that arises from our neighbouring town (viz) Heverhill'. The petition itself, probably written by McMurphy as town clerk, was in turn forwarded by Lieutenant Governor Wentworth to London, as part of his own strategy to persuade the Crown to recognize New Hampshire's title to the disputed area. Unlike the settlers' first petition, which had focused primarily on legal issues, McMurphy dwelt more heavily than had McGregor on the Londonderry colonists' identity, reputation, and loyalty. 'We could bear the many scandalous & unjust reflections which [our critics from Boston and Haverhill] cast upon us by saying we are romans and not good Subjects to his present Majesty,' McMurphy wrote, 'being well assured your Hon[our] well knows to the Contrary [that] ... many of us Resolutely opposed both ['romans' and 'bad Subjects'] while in our own Country[.] Witness the

---

5   The only extant 'original' copy of McGregor's petition, in the Jeremy Belknap Papers at the Massachusetts Historical Society, Boston, is dated 27 February 1720. However, a semi-legible marginal note suggests McGregor may have written it in late 1719. In the petition's title, the settlement's name is spelled 'Nutfeild'.

6   Londonderry was denominated a 'town' according to colonial New England usage, but it was analogous to what in Pennsylvania was called a 'township'. Londonderry had no urban centre and, although it contained storekeepers, millers, weavers, and other full- or part-time craftsmen, it was an overwhelmingly rural community dominated by farmers.

Trubles in Ireland at the Comeing in of King William of Blessed memory,' McMurphy urged, when 'our Present Minister & Severall of our People [were] at the Seige of Derry & had no small shear in that Glorious Defence of Our religion & Country'.[7]

In 1740 London finally confirmed New Hampshire's ownership of the upper Merrimac Valley. Meanwhile, despite the troubles with Haverhill, Londonderry had flourished. By 1740 it was the second-largest settlement in the province: by 1767 it had 2,400 inhabitants, and its growing population, augmented by modest but steady migration from Ulster, had spawned other communities in the Merrimac and Connecticut valleys. Although Londonderry's farms produced goods primarily for local exchange and consumption, as in Ulster its townspeople also developed a regionally unique and thriving industry in the household manufacture of linen yarn and cloth that were marketed throughout New England.

After the American Revolution, new Ulster migration to New Hampshire virtually ceased, and by the late 1700s observers sometimes claimed, albeit wrongly, that save for unusual emphases on flax cultivation and linen production, little distinguished the farmers of Londonderry and its satellite towns from neighbouring Congregationalists. However, in the early and mid-1800s the descendants of New Hampshire's Ulster Presbyterian settlers formally emerged as a distinct ethnic group, particularly in a series of centennial celebrations and authorized town histories, whose orators and authors, usually clergymen, staked their ancestors' claims to 'founding father' status. Most important, they argued vehemently that their forebears had not been 'Irish' — although that had been the term most commonly applied to, and acknowledged by, Ulster Presbyterians in late eighteenth-century America. Instead, their eulogists contended, the founders of Londonderry and all other Ulster Presbyterian immigrants had been members of the 'Scotch-Irish race', a group distinct in its Scottish origins and Protestant faith, and consequently superior in habits and morals to the 'native Irish' Catholics with whom their ancestors had contended in the North of Ireland.

Since then, the controversy between the celebrants and the critics of what the latter often called the 'Scotch-Irish myth' has been unceasing and often acrimonious. Of importance here is the fact that 'Scotch-Irish' spokesmen such as the Rev. Edward L. Parker, the author of Londonderry's first town history, almost invariably buttressed their arguments by drawing on early statements such as those in the foregoing petitions, particularly on the Rev. James McGregor's strenuous objection to the application of the 'Irish' label to his people.[8] Hence, an analysis of the precise content and context of these petitions may be useful.

7   McMurphy's petition, dated 17 March 1730, is catalogued as CO5/871 ff.186–87 in the New England correspondence of the Papers of the Board of Trade and Secretaries of State (America and West Indies) in the PRO, London.
8   Rev. E. L. Parker, The History of Londonderry [New Hampshire] (Boston, 1851). The importance of Parker and his peers in asserting 'Scotch-Irishness' was first argued by R. S. Wallace, 'The Scotch-Irish of Provincial New Hampshire' (PhD diss., University of New Hampshire, 1984).

It is important to note that neither McGregor nor McMurphy identified their countrymen as 'Scotch-Irish'. Indeed, the petitioners essayed no positive ethnic identifications,
but focused on statements of what their people were *not*, thus illustrating an uncertainty
or fluidity in their early ethnic identity that later generations, in an era of nationalist
fervour, would find unacceptable. There were several specific reasons why McGregor, in
his 1719-20 message to Boston, took pains to deny that his parishioners were 'Irish'. Of
course, he desired to draw a sharp distinction between the Nutfield settlers and the native
Irish, a few of whom had already come to New England as poor indentured servants
and who were associated with a Catholicism that was abhorred ideologically and feared
practically — especially in the danger it posed from French Quebec — throughout
England's colonies. However, even McGregor's supporters in the New Hampshire
government referred favourably to his flock as 'a company of Irish at Nutfield', so it
was already clear that disinterested or sympathetic observers would *not* confuse Irish
Presbyterian and Catholic immigrants.[9] Thus, there may have been additional reasons
for McGregor's statements.

First was the fact that many, perhaps most, of McGregor's followers had migrated
from Scotland to Ulster only during the reigns of James II (1685–88) and William III
(1689–1702), and in the Bann Valley allegedly 'they had kept together in church relations,
as well as in residence, more closely than most of the Scotch settlers' in northern
Ireland.[10] If true, it would be natural if they had little identification with Ireland, even as
a place, when they re-migrated to New England scarcely twenty or thirty years later. In
length of residence, then, the Nutfield colonists were certainly far less 'Irish' than other
Presbyterians whose ancestors had come to Ireland in the Ulster Plantation (c. 1611–41),
the Cromwellian era (1650s), or even the reign of Charles II (1660–85). Likewise, their
identification with Ireland as homeland was far less secure than for the great majority
of Ulster Presbyterians who would emigrate to America in the mid- and late 1700s and
in the early 1800s — often three, four, or more generations after their ancestors had
left Scotland.

Ironically, one of the truly 'Irish' characteristics of the New Hampshire colony was
its eventual name, Londonderry. Indeed, one wonders why, if the first settlers wished
to distinguish themselves clearly as non-Irish, they did not name their community, say,
'Argyle' or 'Ayrshire', after their most common Scottish places of origin, or 'Glasgow' in
honour of Scottish Presbyterianism's ecclesiastical and educational centre? Or why they
did not name their settlement after one of the Bann Valley congregations, whence most
of them had emigrated? The traditional explanation is that Nutfield's settlers 'naturally'

9   Likewise, Rev. James MacSparran, an Ulster-born clergyman of Scottish parentage and the author of the
    first Irish emigrants' guide, *America Dissected* (Dublin, 1752), referred to Londonderry's inhabitants —
    indeed, to all Ulster Presbyterian settlers in the New World — as 'Irish'. See Miller, *et al.*, *Irish Immigrants
    in the Land of Canaan*, 55–72; and Kerby A. Miller, 'Rev. James MacSparran's *America Dissected* (1753): 18th-
    Century Emigration and Constructions of "Irishness"', *History Ireland*, 11, 4 (winter 2003), 17–23.
10 Rev. A. L. Perry, *Scotch-Irish in New England* (Boston, 1891), 21.

renamed their township to commemorate the walled Irish city in which many of them had fought and suffered during the siege of 1688–89. Allegedly McGregor himself had fought on Derry's walls, although but a boy of twelve years old, and supposedly others had done so as well. True or not, there is no doubt that the siege already had assumed mythic proportions and become a symbol with which all Ulster Presbyterians wished to associate — perhaps especially in view of Irish Anglicans' denial of their prominence in the city's defence. Yet given Londonderry's totemic significance, why did Nutfield's first colonists not rename their community at once, rather than four years after its initial settlement and a year after its incorporation?

Perhaps there were very pragmatic reasons for McGregor's and his people's choice of name and for their precise timing. As McGregor (probably) and Wentworth (certainly) were aware — and as Boston and London authorities were not — the Nutfield settlers' hold on their New Hampshire lands was extremely tenuous, not only because of Haverhill's competing claims, but because the old 1629 Wheelright patent that McGregor's followers purchased in 1719, and which he defended in his 1719–20 petition, was a forgery, cleverly executed only a dozen or so years earlier by Portsmouth politicians. Hence, to reinforce their shaky title, Nutfield's leaders promulgated what became the traditional (albeit fallacious) explanation of their grant — namely, that it had been a 'free gift of King William', promised to the 'faithful champions of his throne in the siege and defence of Londonderry'.[11] Thus, the renaming of Nutfield not only symbolized its inhabitants' loyal Protestantism, but also implied and justified an 'ancient' title to their new possessions. The name 'Londonderry' signified a northern fortress, not only against the Catholic French and their Indian allies above, but also against counterclaims from Haverhill and Boston below, as even after its incorporation in 1722, the new community remained as besieged by 'outsiders' as its settlers had formerly been threatened — first by Irish Catholics and then by contemptuous Anglicans — in Ulster itself.

It may also be significant that, in his early petition from 'Nutfield', McGregor did not specifically evoke the siege of Derry or 'King William of Blessed memory'. Not until after the township's rechristening, McGregor's death in 1729, and his replacement as Londonderry's parson by the elderly Rev. Matthew Clarke, a recent arrival whose scarred face demonstrated his military service on Derry's walls, did those themes emerge and become prominent, as in John McMurphy's petition of 1730. Likewise, it may be illuminating that McMurphy did not repeat McGregor's denial that the Nutfield/ Londonderry settlers were 'Irish'. (Indeed, one wonders whether the date of McMurphy's petition, St. Patrick's Day, was merely an ironic coincidence.) Instead, he stated only that they were not 'romans', apparently assuming that the distinction between 'Irish' Protestants and Catholics would be clearly understood. In his tactical shift, McMurphy may have presumed for his intended audience a greater sophistication than McGregor had credited, or the change may have reflected the sentiments of later settlers whose

11 Perry, Scotch-Irish in New England, 23.

families had lived for generations in Ulster and who therefore regarded themselves as 'Irish' at least in geographical origin.[12]

Nevertheless, the religious distinction and political loyalty that McMurphy emphasized were crucial, and not only because of the virulent anti-Catholicism prevailing in the colonies, but for another reason peculiar to Londonderry. During all the French and Indian wars that ravaged the northern frontiers from 1722 to 1760, Londonderry was never attacked, allegedly — as the townspeople believed — because McGregor and the Marquis de Vaudreuil, governor of Quebec in the 1720s, had been schoolmates and friends in the Netherlands and maintained a cordial correspondence in America, and so the marquis persuaded the Jesuits in Canada 'to charge the Indians not to injure' McGregor's people, 'as they were different from the English'. If true (and Vaudreuil's address was purportedly found in McGregor's papers after his death), this was a remarkably fortuitous circumstance for Londonderry's inhabitants. However, it was also a coincidence which, if widely known outside the community, would have provoked intense suspicion and hostility at a time when Anglo-American colonists, and especially New England Congregationalists, regularly confused or conflated Protestants and Catholics from Ireland and often charged that 'Irish papist' traders in the backcountry were inciting the Indians to war 'in the French Interest'.

Yet it is equally revealing that neither McGregor nor McMurphy described their people as 'Scotch-Irish', for that term's origins and associations — both in the British Isles and in America — were highly problematic. In the late 1500s and the 1600s, apparently its most common British and Irish usage was pejorative, as both Irish Anglicans and Lowland Scots Presbyterians labelled as 'Scotch-Irish' the Catholic, Gaelic-speaking McDonnells and other Highlanders who migrated back and forth between Argyll, the Western Isles, and the north Antrim glens, causing political and military problems for Protestant officials in Edinburgh and Dublin alike. By contrast, Scots Presbyterian settlers in Ireland were then and well into the early 1700s more commonly described as 'Ulster-' or 'northern Scots', as the 'Scottish Interest' or 'Nation' in Ireland, or occasionally as 'British' — not in the later, inclusive sense, but to distinguish them from the 'English'.

It is true that Ulster Presbyterian students at the universities of Glasgow and Edinburgh were often individually registered as 'Scottus Hibernicus', and some scholars have suggested this was the origin of the modern term 'Scotch-Irish', with its exclusively Protestant and positive connotations. In fact, however, Scottish university officials, faculty, and local magistrates almost invariably referred to such students as 'Irish' — and often linked their 'Irishness' to negative attributes (stupidity,

---

12 During the 1700s the populations of Londonderry and its satellite towns became more diversely 'Irish'. For example, nearby Bedford's Revolutionary War casualties included John Callahan and Valentine Sullivan — 'native Irish', whatever their religion.

drunkenness, insubordination) traditionally associated with their 'papist' countrymen.[13] Moreover, by the mid-1700s Presbyterian spokesmen in Ulster itself were referring increasingly to their people as 'Irish' — a development that reflected longer residence in Ireland, feelings of greater security from Catholic rebellion, and, as among Irish Anglicans, a growing 'national' identification with the economic and political interests of 'Ireland' versus 'England'.

Spurring the latter development was the steady divergence between Scottish and Ulster Presbyterian political conditions that began after the Glorious Revolution and widened after the Act of Union between England and Scotland. In Scotland after 1690 Presbyterianism was the legally established religion, and after the Union of 1707 the upper and middling ranks of Scottish Lowlands society rushed to seize the economic benefits of full membership in the empire, strove to emulate the alleged superiority of English 'civilization', and gloried in a new 'North British' identity that obscured the realities of English contempt and their country's economic and political subordination to its larger, wealthier, and more powerful partner. By contrast, Ireland's Presbyterians endured and bitterly resented their legal inferiority, and, ignored politically by their Scottish co-religionists (and unable, for religious reasons, to sympathize with Catholic-Jacobite opponents to the new Scots establishment), many became increasingly receptive to the rhetoric of Dublin's Patriot politicians who promoted a vague but inclusively 'Irish' colonial nationalism that subsumed denominational differences and promised economic and political reform. Consequently, Ulster Presbyterians' political interests and identities were increasingly oriented to Ireland's capital rather than to Edinburgh or London. Thus, although eighteenth-century Scottish and Ulster Presbyterians shared similar political cultures — both based heavily on the works of Ulster-born Francis Hutcheson, the 'father of the Scottish Enlightenment' — the very different contexts in which Scottish and Ulster Presbyterians' political ideas operated determined equally distinct applications and conclusions.[14]

In eighteenth-century America Ulster Presbyterian identities appear to have developed along lines somewhat parallel to those in Ireland. From the early 1700s Anglo-American colonists normally described Ulster Presbyterian immigrants as 'Irish' — as New Hampshire officials had labelled Londonderry's settlers. By contrast, the term 'Scotch-Irish' was less common and often had profoundly negative socio-cultural and political connotations. Thus, in 1767 the (probably Irish) Anglican missionary Charles Woodmason described backcountry South Carolina's inhabitants as 'a Sett of the most lowest vilest Crew breathing — Scotch-Irish Presbyterians from the North

---

13 Indeed, Professor Thomas Reid, Scotland's famous 'common sense' philosopher, scorned Ulster Presbyterian students at his Glasgow University as 'stupid Irish teagues'. See Ian McBride, 'The School of Virtue: Francis Hutcheson, Irish Presbyterians and the Scottish Enlightenment,' in D. G. Boyce, et al., eds., Political Thought in Ireland since the Seventeenth Century (London, 1993), 89.

14 All this began to change after 1800, of course, when the Act of Union between Ireland and Great Britain dramatically reconfigured the political context; see below, Chapter 8.

of Ireland', and during the revolution American General Charles Lee condemned the people of the Shenandoah Valley as 'a Banditti of Scotch-Irish Servants or their immediate descendants'.[15]

By contrast, to be 'Irish' in a broad, ecumenical sense was meanwhile becoming useful, even fashionable, among wealthy or ambitious Irish Protestant immigrants. From the early mid-1700s, for example, Ulster Presbyterian merchants and professionals in New York, Philadelphia, and other American seaports had joined with Anglican and even Catholic compatriots in celebrating St. Patrick's Day and in organizing specifically 'Irish' or 'Hibernian' associations. (Conversely, Scottish-born Presbyterians congregated separately in St. Andrew's societies.) Moreover, the American Revolution appears to have accelerated Ulster Presbyterian immigrants' tendency to embrace — and of Anglo-Americans to perceive — a generic and positive 'Irish' identity. Both native- and Irish Americans, whether rebels or loyalists, commonly viewed 'Ireland's' proverbial discontent with English rule — now identified with the Protestant-led Patriot movement — as virtually synonymous with the American struggle for self-government. Correctly or not, the 'Irish' in America were associated with wholehearted support for the revolution, whereas Scottish immigrants were perceived as obsequiously loyal to the Crown, as well as selfish and avaricious.[16] Thus, perhaps it was not surprising that, for a while after the revolution, the 'Scotch-Irish' designation, already infrequent, almost disappeared from public print. It is surprising, therefore, that in the nineteenth century the term 'Scotch-Irish' reappeared and soon became commonplace, and in the eyes of Protestant native Americans and Ulster Americans, it now enjoyed associations that were much more unambiguously favourable than in previous centuries.

For scholars 'Scotch-Irish' could be a serviceable label, designating valid distinctions among Ulster Presbyterian immigrants (and their descendants) of Scottish origin, other Irish Protestants (Anglicans, Quakers, etcetera) of largely English ancestry, and Irish Catholics (and Protestants) of Gaelic, Hiberno-Norman, and other backgrounds. During the nineteenth century, however, the term broadened to embrace all Americans of Irish birth or descent who were not currently Catholic, regardless of their religious or ethnic antecedents. Meanwhile, among Irish-American Catholics, 'Scotch-Irishness' became a source of grievance and resentment — primarily because the term allegedly re-emerged from obscurity during the Great Famine, when many Ulster-American Protestants reportedly rushed to distinguish themselves as 'Scotch-Irish' and, hence,

---

15 R. J. Hooker, ed., *The Carolina Backcountry on the Eve of the Revolution: The Journal and Other Writings of Charles Woodmason, Anglican Itinerant* (Chapel Hill, NC, 1953) 14; Lee cited in F. H. Hart, *The Valley of Virginia in the American Revolution, 1763–1789* (Chapel Hill, NC, 1942), 109.

16 For example, in 1774 James Caldwell, a young merchant in Philadelphia, informed his brother in north Antrim that, although 'Scotch' immigrants were characterized negatively by 'unbounded loyalty' to the British crown, 'nine-tenths' of the 'Irish ... espouse[d] the American cause': significantly, as 'Irish' Caldwell included Presbyterians (like himself), Anglicans, and Catholics, with all of whom he associated in the city's Friendly Sons of St. Patrick and other ecumenically 'Irish' social, political, and military organizations. See Miller, et al., *Irish Immigrants in the Land of Canaan*, ch. 58.

as different from and superior to the overwhelmingly Catholic, impoverished, and often Irish-speaking Famine refugees.

However, the modern meanings of 'Scotch-Irish' — its 'Protestant' and 'positive' connotations, its strident reassertion of an impermeable, quasi-racial division between its members and the now once more exclusively Catholic 'Irish' — began to take shape much earlier, in the 1790–1820 period, long before Irish Catholics or their Church became significant factors in American society. Hence, it is likely that the new 'Scotch-Irish' ethnicity had other, subtler origins — that initially it was generated, not by an external threat (real or perceived) from Irish Catholic immigration, but rather by Ulster-American society's internal dynamics and by its relationship to Protestant Anglo-America's socio-economic, cultural, and political hierarchies. Specifically, it is arguable that modernized 'Scotch-Irishness' was largely the product of an intra-communal contest for political and cultural hegemony — a contest led in New England (as elsewhere) by Ulster America's politically conservative clergy and 'respectable' laymen. And although this was an American contest, it mirrored a parallel struggle in contemporary Ulster, between Presbyterians who embraced or rejected the ultra-democratic and ecumenical ideals of the United Irishmen.

Genteel Ulster Americans, eager for acceptance and influence in an Anglo-American 'society' that in New England was dominated by Federalist merchants and Congregational ministers, needed to expunge from their own communities the radical political tendencies and the 'backward' socio-cultural traits that both offended genteel American sensibilities and were embarrassingly similar to those traditionally associated with the Catholic 'Irish'. In the 1790s Federalist party polemicists applied the term 'wild Irish' — laden with historical connotations of Catholic Irish 'barbarism', 'treachery', and rebellion, as in the 1641 Ulster rising — to all Irish Americans who opposed the Washington and Adams administrations, sympathized with the French Revolution, and supported the Jeffersonian Republicans. Federalists knew well that the overwhelming majority of their 'wild Irish' adversaries were not Catholics but Ulster Presbyterian farmers, weavers, and radical journalists. However, the message was clear: if Ulster Presbyterians wished to avoid 'wild Irish' associations, their putative leaders should follow and expand on McGregor's precedent and identify themselves and 'their people' as the 'Scotch-Irish' antitheses of the proverbially uncivilized, drunken, and rebellious 'Irish'. Not coincidentally, it was New Englander Jeremy Belknap — Congregational clergyman, staunch Federalist pamphleteer, and future Harvard president — who, by resurrecting and publishing McGregor's old petition in his History of New Hampshire (1784–92), first pointed those leaders towards a 'Scotch-Irish' resolution of their political and cultural dilemmas.

Their problem was that ordinary Ulster Presbyterians in New England (and elsewhere) often behaved in ways that seemed suspiciously 'Irish'. From the start, Londonderry's settlers were confused with Irish 'papists' and embroiled in violent conflicts over land titles with colonial officials and Anglo-American élites — as were their countrymen on the

Maine, Pennsylvania, and Carolina frontiers. Although the revolution forged a political
alliance between New England's Ulster Presbyterian farmers and Anglo-Congregational
leadership, in the 1780s that disintegrated rapidly as the region's Presbyterian clergy
joined the Federalists in espousing law and order, deference and hierarchy, whereas
most of their parishioners vociferously demanded greater democracy and fairer taxes.
In winter 1786–87 the inhabitants of Pelham and other Ulster settlements in western
Massachusetts supported Daniel Shays's rebellion against the Boston government.
In 1787–88 most Ulster Presbyterian farmers in Londonderry and elsewhere opposed
ratification of the US Constitution. In 1794, the year of the largely Ulster-Presbyterian
'Whiskey Insurrection' in western Pennsylvania, New Englanders of northern Irish
ancestry staged their own protests against Alexander Hamilton's excise. Afterwards,
most enlisted in the Republican party, and by 1797 Vermont's Irish-born congressman,
Matthew Lyon, a former indentured servant, epitomized everything New England's
Federalists feared and hated about Jefferson's 'wild Irish' adherents.[17] In the 1820s
most of New England's Presbyterians of Ulster descent were still voting for Republican
candidates — and in the 1830s for Jacksonian Democrats.

New England's genteel Presbyterians were alarmed as well by the apparent cultural
similarities between 'their people' and Irish Catholic peasants. Given their recent
origins in parts of western Scotland where Scots Gaelic was common, it is likely that
many of Londonderry's first settlers were linguistically alien from New England's
Congregationalists, provoking the latter's suspicion and contempt. Well into the late
1700s the immigrants' offspring, as well as more recent arrivals, still spoke Ulster Scots
(the dialect or language — scholars dispute which — common in much of rural Ulster
and akin to that of the Scots Lowlands) or at least English in a 'broad Scotch' accent
that Yankees found almost unintelligible. Likewise, in the late 1700s the inhabitants
of Londonderry and other Ulster settlements remained notorious among their
Anglo-American neighbours for their alleged uncleanliness, aversion to bathing bodies
or clothes, indifference to sanitary facilities, and slovenly farmsteads. They also had a
notorious reputation as heavy drinkers, and their marriages, wakes, and funerals were
proverbially sodden, boisterous affairs that scandalized polite contemporaries. Finally,
by virtue of Londonderry's 1722 charter its farmers enjoyed a uniquely 'Irish' institution,
semi-annual fairs that, like Catholic Ireland's Donnybrook, had by the mid-1700s
become infamous for their 'scenes of vice and folly'. Even the fairs' dates, 8 November
and 8 May, were suspiciously akin to those of two ancient and pagan Celtic festivals,
Samhain and *Bealtaine.* [18]

17 In 1797 Lyon, a Protestant, outraged opponents by spitting on a Connecticut Federalist during a
   Congressional debate; in 1798 a Federalist judge sentenced Lyon to a $1,000 fine and four months'
   imprisonment for libelling president John Adams under the newly passed Sedition Act.
18 Perry, *Scotch-Irish in New England*, 42–43. On ancient Celtic festivals, see Alwyn Rees and Brinley Rees,
   Celtic Heritage: Ancient Tradition in Ireland and Wales (London, 1961).

Perhaps it was little wonder, then, that McGregor and McMurphy had been so defensive — especially the former, given his own record of intemperance. Or that 100 years later the Rev. Parker and other 'Scotch-Irish' eulogists would blame what they described as their people's temporary deviations from Scots-Protestant virtue, order, and sobriety on their ancestors' brief but contaminating exposure to Ulster's Catholics. Inadvertently, however, their argument revealed that modern 'Scotch-Irish' ethnicity was rooted ultimately in neither ancestral origin nor even religion, but instead was based on relatively new 'middle-class' behavioural standards. The thrifty, law-abiding, sober, respectable 'Scotch-Irish' that Parker and his peers invented and celebrated had been common in neither seventeenth-century Scotland nor eighteenth-century Ulster. Nor were they representative of the great majority of Ulster Presbyterian immigrants or even their descendants in eighteenth- and early nineteenth-century America. Rather, their new image reflected the hegemonic imperatives of an emergent Ulster-American bourgeoisie whose goals and ascendancy remained woefully incomplete even in the early 1800s.

Not coincidentally, the local clergy's first attempt to tame Londonderry's raucous fairs occurred in 1798, the year of the Federalists' Alien and Sedition Acts in America as well as the United Irishmen's rebellion in east Ulster and elsewhere in Ireland. However, not until 1839, in the midst of a region-wide religious revival and temperance crusade, would they finally suppress what had long been an integral expression of their ancestors' traditional culture. Yet between those dates the poems of Robert Dinsmoor (1756–1836), grandson and great-grandson of two of Londonderry's first settlers, from Ballywattick, County Antrim, heralded the changes that commercialization, evangelicalism, and the urge for gentility eventually wrought among New England's Ulster Presbyterians. The few scholars who have studied New Hampshire's self-styled 'Rustic Bard' have portrayed him as an American analogue to the 'Rhyming Weavers' of late eighteenth- and early nineteenth-century Ulster. Linguistic similarities aside, however, in fact they were strikingly different.

Like their Scottish hero Robert Burns, many — perhaps most — of Ulster's Rhyming Weavers were liberal or sceptical in religion, radical in politics, and defiant of genteel conventions. Because they wrote in the vernacular of Lowland Scotland and Presbyterian Ulster, some scholars in Northern Ireland have claimed them as cultural markers of a unique 'Ulster Scots' cultural and political identity — distinctly non-'Irish' and hence the equivalent of 'Scotch-Irish' ethnicity in America. In fact, many of the Rhyming Weavers' compositions evince strong Irish nationalist sentiments, and more than a few of these plebeian poets, such as James Orr of Ballycarry, joined or sympathized with the United Irishmen and the 1798 rebellion. By contrast, and despite his humble persona, Dinsmoor was an orthodox Calvinist and a fiercely conservative Federalist for whom the French Revolution and Jeffersonian republicanism (as well as Roman Catholicism) literally represented the many faces of the Antichrist. In his poems, published in New England newspapers, Dinsmoor linked American religious and political conservatism to both his Presbyterian heritage and his Scottish ancestry. 'The highest pedigree I plead,' he wrote, is a 'Yankee born' of 'true Scottish breed'.[19]

Thus, McGregor's and McMurphy's early eighteenth-century search for a definition — and for Anglo-American recognition — of their followers' non-'Irish' identity was realized in New England, a century later, in part through the poetry, hagiography, and sermons of Ulster-stock Presbyterians such as Robert Dinsmoor and the Rev. Edward L. Parker. Indeed, so successful were Dinsmoor's and Parker's efforts, and those of their counterparts in Pennsylvania[20] and elsewhere, that soon their people's ambiguous origins and embarrassing 'Irish' interludes were all but forgotten in the subsequent scramble for a purportedly timeless and respectable 'Scotch-Irish' ancestry that eventually nearly all non-Catholic Americans of Irish descent would eagerly claim.

---

19 Robert Dinsmoor ['The Rustic Bard'], *Incidental Poems Accompanied with Letters, and a Few Select Pieces, Mostly Original, for their Illustration, Together with a Preface, and Sketch of the Author's Life* (Haverhill, Mass., 1828).

20 On parallel developments in Pennsylvania, 1780s–1820s, see Miller, *et al.*, *Irish Immigrants in the Land of Canaan*, chs. 62–64 and 67; and Peter Gilmore and Kerby A. Miller, 'Searching for "Irish" Freedom — Settling for "Scotch-Irish" Respectability: Southwestern Pennsylvania, 1780 to 1810', in Warren Hofstra, ed., *Ulster to America: The Scots-Irish Migration Experience, 1680s–1830s* (Knoxville, Tenn., forthcoming). In Pennsylvania, Belknap's role was played more abrasively by Hugh Henry Brackenridge, a Scottish immigrant and conservative judge, who in his serialized novel *Modern Chivalry* (1792–1815) satirized his radical Jeffersonian political opponents, William Findley and William Duane, by transforming them, in their turn, into the blundering, inebriated, and politically absurd 'stage-Irish' character of Teague O'Regan, although in fact Findley was an Ulster-born Presbyterian and Duane was an American-born Episcopalian of Irish parentage. For Brackenridge and his readers, it was Findley's and Duane's lowly social origins and, especially, their demotic political opinions and style, not their religion or birthplace, that made them stereotypically 'wild Irish'. Likewise, western Pennsylvania's equivalent of Dinsmore was the Scottish-born Federalist propagandist David Bruce, who in the 1790s signed his dialect poems, published in local newspapers, 'A Scots-Irishmen'. The strategy appears to have become effective early on: by 1812 even Republican Congressman William Findley — now elderly, 'respectable', and politically more 'moderate' — designated his own ancestry as 'Scotch-Irish', although in the 1780s and 1790s he had been universally known, by friends and enemies alike, as an 'Irish' politician; see 'William Findley of Westmoreland, Pa.', *Pennsylvania Magazine of History and Biography*, 5, 4 (1881), 440–50.

7 'Scotch-Irish', 'Black Irish', and 'Real Irish': Emigrants and Identities in the Old South

In 1804 Thomas Addis Emmet, exiled leader of the United Irishmen, sailed from his temporary haven in Napoleonic France and disembarked in New York City.[1] Shortly thereafter, Richard McCormick, a former comrade who had preceded him to the United States, wrote to Emmet from Georgia, urging him to settle in the 'Old South', that is, in one of the American states or territories that lay south of Pennsylvania and the Ohio River and whose socio-economic and legal systems were dominated by the institution of African-American slavery. Emmet declined his friend's invitation, despite the South's admitted attractions, refusing on principle to reside where his family would be dependent on coerced labour.[2]

Emmet's scruples were not universally shared, and other Irish political exiles managed to accommodate republican principles and American slavery.[3] Indeed, during the eighteenth century and the first several decades of the nineteenth century, there was a substantial Irish migration to and settlement in the Old South. David N. Doyle, Ireland's premier historian of the American Irish, has analysed the first US census of 1790 and concludes that approximately one-fifth of the white population of the southern states, over a quarter-million Southerners, were of Irish birth or descent. The Irish-stock proportions of the populations of individual southern states ranged from 17 to 18 per cent in Delaware, Maryland, Virginia, and North Carolina to as high as one-third in

---

1   This chapter was originally published, under the same title, in Andy Bielenberg, ed., *The Irish Diaspora* (Harlow, 2000), 139–57. I wish to thank the editors of Longman publishers, an imprint of Pearson Education Ltd., for permission to republish the essay here, with minor revisions.
2   Thomas A. Emmet, *Memoir of Thomas Addis and Robert Emmet*, 2 vols. (New York, 1915), vol. 1, 227.
3   David A. Wilson, *United Irishmen, United States: Immigrant Radicals in the Early Republic* (Ithaca, NY, 1998), ch. 7.

Kentucky and Tennessee, while in Georgia and South Carolina the Irish comprised slightly over one-fourth of their white inhabitants. Doyle estimates that roughly two-thirds of these early Irish-American Southerners were what later generations would usually call the 'Scotch-Irish' — that is, the descendants of Scottish Presbyterians who, in the seventeenth and early eighteenth centuries, had settled in Ulster before re-migrating later to North America. However, Doyle contends that this group also included many whose northern Irish ancestors had been Anglicans or Catholics but who had converted to Presbyterianism, either before or after their migrations to the New World, and who subsequently were absorbed into what he calls the 'Ulster-American' community. Finally, Doyle concludes that in 1790 the other one-third of the 'Irish' in the Old South represented families whose members or ancestors had been born in the South of Ireland; originally most had been Catholics, but, given the dearth of priests and chapels in eighteenth- and early nineteenth-century America, the great majority also joined Protestant congregations and eventually merged into the so-called 'Scotch-Irish' group.[4]

Yet despite the size and significance of this early Irish migration to the Old South, by the late 1830s and 1840s most Irishmen and -women were avoiding the southern states, primarily for economic reasons that included a reluctance to compete with slave labour. And when Irish immigration peaked during and immediately after the Great Famine, relatively few newcomers settled in the Old South. Thus, although in 1860 there were in the entire United States about 1.6 million Irish-born inhabitants, representing roughly 6 per cent of the nation's white population, only 11 per cent of these immigrants — fewer than 200,000 — resided in the slave states, where they comprised merely 2.25 per cent of the South's white population. Moreover, nearly 70 per cent of these Irish-born Southerners were concentrated in a handful of exceptionally urbanized 'border states' — in Louisiana, Delaware, Maryland, Kentucky, and Missouri — and primarily in cities such as New Orleans, Wilmington, Baltimore, Louisville, and St. Louis. In the long-settled and overwhelmingly rural states of the Southeast, Irish immigrants were very rare; for instance, in 1860 fewer than 5,000 Irish immigrants lived in South Carolina and only about 6,600 in Georgia, comprising merely 1.7 and 1.1 per cent of their respective white populations.[5]

In 1860 the comparatively few Irishmen and -women enumerated in the Old South were predominantly Catholics, part of the immense Famine exodus that primarily flowed to and settled in the northern United States or in Canada.[6] And by 1860, of course, the overwhelming majority of the eighteenth- and very early nineteenth-century Irish-born settlers in the Old South had died, and since the 1860 census did not record parental birthplaces, the ancestral origins of their living descendants also went untallied.

4   David Noel Doyle, *Ireland, Irishmen and Revolutionary America, 1760–1820* (Dublin and Cork, 1981), 51–76.
5   United States Census Office, *Population of the United States in 1860; Compiled from the Official Returns of the Eighth Census* (Washington, DC, 1864).
6   Kerby A. Miller, *Emigrants and Exiles: Ireland and the Irish Exodus to North America* (New York, 1985), ch. 7.

Recently, however, the 1990 US census recorded some rather curious statistics. In 1990 some 38.7 million Americans responded to a question concerning their ethnicity by listing 'Irish' as their response. Remarkably, 34 per cent of these self-described 'Irish Americans' (approximately 13.3 million) resided in the South — more than triple the mere 11 per cent of all the Irish immigrants reported in the 1860 census as resident in the southern states. Put another way, in 1990, 20 per cent of white Southerners identified their ancestry as Irish, although in 1860 merely 2 per cent of white Southerners had been Irish-born. However, what is most surprising is that, although the respondents to the 1990 census questionnaire were given the option of designating 'Scotch-Irish' as their ancestry, relatively few southern whites did so. Only 2.6 million whites in the South — less than 4 per cent of all southern whites — stated their ethnicity as 'Scotch-Irish', compared with the 20 per cent of white Southerners who simply claimed to be 'Irish'. For example, 21 per cent of Georgia's whites in 1990 claimed 'Irish' ancestry, whereas only 4 per cent labelled themselves 'Scotch-Irish', and in South Carolina the respective figures were 20 per cent 'Irish' compared with fewer than 7 per cent 'Scotch-Irish'.[7] Thus, given the paucity of Famine migrants in the Old South, it would appear that by 1990 a surprisingly large number of the remote descendants of the South's early Irish Protestant settlers — of those who had immigrated prior to the America Revolution or, at the latest, prior to the mid-1830s — were not only willing to identify themselves with the birthplace of ancestors who had left Ireland 200 or even 250 years earlier, but even to designate their ethnic identity as 'Irish' rather than as 'Scotch-Irish', although the overwhelming majority of their forebears had been Ulster Presbyterians.

Ultimately, of course, the question of ethnicity is not one of ancestral birthplace or religious affiliation but one of individual and collective identification, which in turn is subjective and variable, shaped by a multitude of shifting social, cultural, political,

7   Bureau of the Census, 1990 *Census of Population. Social and Economic Characteristics. United States*, vols. CP–2–1 through CP–2–52 (Washington, DC, 1993). The 2.6 million southern whites who claimed 'Scotch-Irish' ancestry in 1990 represented 47 per cent of all American whites who did so. The regional variations in the 1990 responses are also interesting. In sharp contrast to South Carolina and Georgia, for example, a large majority of the relevant respondents in Alabama chose 'Scotch-Irish' rather than 'Irish' as their ethnic designation. There are no doubt several historical reasons for this, but it may be pertinent that, in the early twentieth century, all social and political relationships in Alabama were extremely tense; that nativist pressures in the class, ethnic, and racial conflict-ridden industrial city of Birmingham were so acute that even genteel Irish Catholic immigrants felt obliged to change their names to disguise their ethno-religious identities; and that in 1920 the response (orchestrated by the Ku Klux Klan) to Eamon de Valera's visit to Birmingham was unusually hostile and violent, culminating in the murder of a local priest; see the letters of Patrick [pseud. 'Frederick'] J. Monks, 1909–15, in the Joseph Halloway Papers (Ms. 22,406, NLI); and David B. Franklin, 'Bigotry in 'Bama: De Valera's Visit to Birmingham, Alabama, April 1920', *History Ireland*, 12, 4 (winter 2004), 30–34. For alleged contemporary associations between 'Scotch-Irishness' and reactionary politics in Alabama and elsewhere (coincident with the South's neo-Confederate movement), see James Webb's *Born Fighting: How the Scots-Irish Shaped America* (New York, 2004).

and psychological circumstances.[8] To provide an extreme example, at least through the 1960s, St. Patrick's Day in New York City was celebrated by an association named the Loyal Yiddish Sons of Erin, whose founders were the Irish-born children of Lithuanian and Polish Jews for whom Ireland was merely a brief interlude in a multistaged migration from eastern Europe to America.[9] This suggests that, within certain limits, ethnicity can be a matter of individual choice — as well as an extremely complex, situational, multilayered phenomenon. This may be especially true in the United States, at least for whites, and indeed one of the purported benefits of migration from Europe to America was that it allowed the newcomers to create identities that might differ significantly from the categories imposed by public officials, landlords, clergy, or even kinsmen in their former homelands.

Usually, however, there are 'certain limits' within which immigrants, their descendants, or even 'impartial observers' can define ethnicity or nationality, and these constraints are often political in nature: overtly so in places like the North of Ireland, where sectarian and political affiliations are commonly both synonymous and inherited; but covertly even in the United States and, during the nineteenth and early twentieth centuries, particularly among Irish immigrants and their offspring. For instance, from at least the 1830s on, celebrants of what the early Irish-American historian Michael O'Brien called the 'Scotch-Irish myth' made sharp and often invidious comparisons between their Irish Protestant ancestors and Irish Catholic immigrants. Ignoring Ulster Presbyterian immigrants whose economic distress or political activities did not exemplify group prosperity or conventional patriotism, they projected the 'faults' of their own unfortunates and 'malcontents' onto Irish Catholic migrants, implying that the Scotch-Irish could not have been failures or 'disloyal' because, by definition, the virtues inherent in their religion and British origins guaranteed their moral, cultural, and hence economic superiority and political probity.[10]

Arguably, as the scholar James Leyburn wrote, 'Scotch-Irish' is 'a useful term ... express[ing] a historical reality', and, if employed carefully and neutrally, it could reflect objective differences between Ulster Presbyterians and other Irish immigrants. As noted in the preceding chapter, however, use of the term 'Scotch-Irish' — by contemporaries or by Ulster Presbyterians themselves — was not common in eighteenth-century America (Leyburn found only a handful of documented instances), and its connotations were

---

8   The scholarly literature on ethnicity is voluminous. On Irish-American Catholic ethnicity, see Chapter 11 in this volume.

9   Memoir of Emmanuel Steen (courtesy of Mr. Steen, River Edge, NJ, and Professor Emeritus Arnold Schrier, University of Cincinnati).

10 Michael J. O'Brien, 'The "Scotch-Irish" Myth', *Journal of the American Irish Historical Society*, 24 (1925), 142–53. Invidious comparisons between Irish Catholic and 'Scotch-Irish' emigrants can be found in the historical and popular literature on the latter from the early nineteenth through the early twentieth centuries; e.g., in Rev. E. L. Parker, *The History of Londonderry* [New Hampshire] (Boston, 1851); *The Scotch-Irish in America: Proceedings of the Scotch-Irish Congresses*, 10 vols. (Cincinnati, Ohio, 1889–1901); and Maude Glasgow, *The Scotch-Irish in Northern Ireland and in the American Colonies* (New York, 1936).

ambiguous and not always flattering.[11] Yet the label was reborn and sanitized in the 1790s and the early 1800s, initially as a Federalist party strategy designed to demobilize Presbyterian 'Irish' support for Thomas Jefferson, and also in the context of the early nineteenth-century religious revival known as the Second Great Awakening, in the initial stages of which politically conservative Presbyterian clergymen played prominent roles. The conventional explanation, however, is that 'Scotch-Irish' really became popular at mid-century, particularly among middle-class Americans of Ulster Presbyterian descent who were appalled by the prospect of damnation by association with the Irish Catholic paupers who inundated American seaports during the Great Famine. Whatever its origins, the term soon lost any scholarly utility, for by the late nineteenth and early twentieth centuries, if not before, its usage had expanded to include all Americans of Irish birth or descent who were not *presently* Catholic, regardless of their actual antecedents. Thus, the authors of county histories in states as far afield as South Carolina and South Dakota blithely designated as 'Scotch-Irish' the ancestors of Methodist merchants and Baptist farmers bearing names like O'Hara, O'Brien, and O'Callaghan.[12]

In the eighteenth and very early nineteenth centuries, however, designations such as 'Irish Protestants', 'north Irish', or, most frequent and most vaguely inclusive of all, simply 'Irish' (with or usually without religious or regional qualifiers), were much more common than 'Scotch-Irish'. But what did it mean to be 'Irish' in Ireland and in America during that era? In some respects, ethnic identification among the Irish-born had both more and less significance than it does today. It had more significance because, prior to the American Revolution and the repeal of the Irish Penal Laws, a person's religious affiliation determined the extent of his civil rights and economic opportunities, to the benefit of Protestants (especially Anglicans) and to the detriment of Catholics. Yet, it also had less significance because, on local and personal levels, the boundaries of these ethno-religious communities were often much more permeable than they later became, and a remarkable degree of ethnic and religious fluidity prevailed in eighteenth-century Ireland and especially among early Irish immigrants in America. In Ireland, for example, it now appears that religious conversions, particularly (but by no means exclusively) from Catholicism to Protestantism, were considerably more common

---

11 James G. Leyburn, *The Scotch-Irish: A Social History* (Chapel Hill, NC, 1962), 327–34.

12 For South Dakota, for example see the *Memorial and Biographical Record of Turner, Lincoln, Union and Clay Counties* (Chicago, 1897). In response, Michael O'Brien and other critics of the 'Scotch-Irish myth' either contended that Ulster Presbyterians' long residence in Ireland had made them 'Irish', despite their religion, or they searched assiduously for the latter's 'real' (i.e., 'native' and 'Catholic') Irish antecedents. O'Brien's 'Scotch-Irish' adversaries were equally enterprising: one late nineteenth-century historian ethnically cleansed the early history of Virginia's Upper Shenandoah Valley by 'Scotch-Irishizing' every 'native' or 'Catholic' Irish name that appeared in the region's earliest records; see O'Brien, 'The "Scotch-Irish" Myth'; and Kerby A. Miller, *et al.*, *Irish Immigrants in the Land of Canaan: Letters and Memoirs from Colonial and Revolutionary America, 1675–1815* (New York, 2003), ch. 20.

at all social levels than was later acknowledged.[13] On the other side of the Atlantic, the earliest Irish-American organizations — the St. Patrick's and Hibernian associations in seaports such as Philadelphia and New York — included merchants and professionals of all denominations, expressing a tolerance that reflected shared business interests as well as Enlightenment rationalism.[14] Among poorer migrants, the relative frequency of intermarriage and conversion reflected a pragmatic understanding that ethnic and religious affiliations were not absolute but contingent on local economic and social circumstances. Early Irish immigrants appear to have been relatively nonchalant about what subsequent generations would regard as religious apostasy or ethnic treason. The result, as noted earlier, was the absorption of nearly all early Irish Catholic (and also most Irish Anglican) immigrants into the Presbyterian faith of the great majority.[15]

Furthermore, contemporary scholars generally acknowledge that, in terms of political discourse, the boundaries of eighteenth-century Irish 'nationality' were relatively fluid and expansive, and that especially after mid-century new, secular, and inclusive definitions of 'Irishness' temporarily promised to subsume Ireland's different religious and ethnic strains. Ultimately, of course, the era of Henry Grattan and Theobald Wolfe Tone was cut short by rebellion and reaction, and both the old popular and the new political traditions of tolerance faded — rapidly in Ireland, more slowly in the United States. Ireland's future would generally belong to those who practised the politics of ethno-religious polarization, but among the immigrants in America the ecumenical ideals of the United Irishmen flourished through the Jeffersonian and into the Jacksonian era, as most Irish Protestant and Catholic migrants subsumed their religious differences under the banner of a shared Irish-American republicanism.[16]

Of course, as early as the 1820s, some Irish Protestant newcomers, often former members of the Loyal Orange Order (founded in mid-Ulster in 1795), were conspicuously prominent in American nativist movements, temperance associations, and street mobs that demonized and assaulted Irish Catholic immigrants. And by the 1850s, nearly all Irish-American Protestants and Catholics in the northern United States were mobilized in opposing political camps — the former in the Whig-cum-Know-Nothing-

13 Doyle, *Ireland, Irishmen and Revolutionary America*, chs. 1–2; Thomas P. Power, 'Converts', in Power and Kevin Whelan, eds., *Endurance and Emergence: Catholics in Ireland in the Eighteenth Century* (Blackrock, Co. Dublin, 1990), 101–28; and the relevant chapters of Desmond Bowen, *History and the Shaping of Irish Protestantism* (New York, 1995), and Roger Blaney, *Presbyterianism and the Irish Language* (Belfast, 1996).
14 John H. Campbell, *A History of the Friendly Sons of St. Patrick and of the Hibernian Society* (Philadelphia, 1892); Richard C. Murphy and Lawrence J. Mannion, *The History of the Society of the Friendly Sons of St. Patrick in the City of New York, 1784 to 1955* (New York, 1962).
15 Doyle, *Ireland, Irishmen and Revolutionary America*, chs. 3–4.
16 On Ireland: Joep Leerssen, *Mere Irish and Fíor Ghael: Studies in the Idea of Irish Nationality, Its Development and Literary Expression prior to the Nineteenth Century* (Cork, 1997), chs. 7–8; and Kevin Whelan, *The Tree of Liberty: Radicalism, Catholicism and the Construction of Irish Identity, 1760–1830* (Cork, 1996), chs. 3–4. On Irish America: Doyle, *Ireland, Irishmen*, ch. 7; Miller, *Emigrants and Exiles*, chs. 5–6; and Chapter 11 in this volume.

cum-Republican parties, the latter in the Democratic party coalition.[17] However, the old traditions of tolerance and sociability, and the new tradition of ecumenical nationalism, seem to have lingered longer in the Old South than elsewhere in the United States. For example, during the first three or four decades of the nineteenth century, the most flourishing Hibernian and Irish-American nationalist societies were situated not in Boston or New York but in southern cities, such as Charleston and Savannah, where they were usually led by Protestants of Ulster birth or descent.[18] In part, this apparent anachronism may reflect the institutional weakness of the Catholic Church in the Old South — its consequent inability either to mobilize its own flock or to frighten Irish-American Protestants away from secular alliances with their Catholic countrymen.[19] It may also reflect the general tendency of all southern whites to downplay internal differences for the sake of solidarity against the region's large and potentially rebellious black population — for slaves outnumbered whites by a ratio of 3:2 in South Carolina, by 9:1 in the coastal districts around Charleston and Savannah.[20]

It may be inaccurate to conclude that early Irish Protestant and Catholic immigrants or their descendants ever comprised a single, homogeneous, or harmonious group in the Old South, much less in the rest of eighteenth- and early nineteenth-century America. However, considerable evidence suggests that during this period 'Irish' ethnic identity was much more varied, flexible, and inclusive than it would later become, and that the social and political issues that engaged the attention of Irish immigrants, and that caused them to define themselves, often transcended the religious divisions that later became so prominent. Keeping this argument in mind, the next section of this chapter briefly sketches the history of early Irish migration to the Old South, relying primarily on the emigrants' own letters, memoirs, and other writings, before returning at the end to employ similar sources to provide some biographical illustrations of the complexity and mutability of Irish ethnic identities in that region.

Of the one-quarter to one-third of a million Irish who emigrated to North America between 1700 and the American Revolution — most of them Presbyterians from the North of Ireland — perhaps half settled eventually in the southern colonies: *eventually* because, while a minority arrived directly from Ireland, aboard ships that disembarked

17 Miller, *Emigrants and Exiles*, chs. 6–7.
18 Michael F. Funchion, *Irish-American Voluntary Organizations* (Westport, Conn., 1983), 117, 141–45, 239.
19 Jay P. Dolan, *The American Catholic Experience: A History from Colonial Times to the Present* (Garden City, NY, 1985), ch. 4; Randall M. Miller and Jon L. Wakelyn, eds., *Catholics in the Old South: Essays on Church and Culture* (Macon, Ga., 1983).
20 United States Census Office, *Population of the United States in 1860*.

at southern ports, the majority first landed at or near Philadelphia and then moved west and then south, often over several generations, down the Great Wagon Road into the backcountries of Maryland, Virginia, the Carolinas, and Georgia — where they mingled with the smaller streams of immigrants coming up the rivers from Charleston and Savannah. In addition, during the fifty years or so after the American Revolution perhaps as many as 100,000 Irish — again, primarily Ulster Presbyterians — migrated to the southern states. Increasingly, they disembarked at New Orleans or Mobile, rather than at Charleston or Savannah, and settled in new southwestern states such as Alabama, while others landed in Philadelphia and Baltimore and moved westward via the Ohio River into Kentucky, Tennessee, and Missouri.[21]

In the eighteenth century, their motives for leaving Ireland were a subject of controversy. Ulster Presbyterians, especially the clergy, usually claimed that emigration was motivated primarily by religious and political persecution. Thus, Robert Witherspoon, who in 1734 migrated from Belfast to Charleston, later recorded that his family's exodus was determined by his grandfather's resolution 'to seek relief from civil and ecclesiastical oppression' in Ireland.[22] In the nineteenth century, 'Scotch-Irish' eulogists expanded upon this theme, likening the early immigrants to the English 'pilgrims' who settled early seventeenth-century Plymouth, Massachusetts, in order to claim 'founding father' status for their ancestors.[23] However, although religious zeal coloured and justified their departures, the primary motives for early (as well as for later) Irish emigrants were economic. High rents, tithes, and taxes; low wages and periodic depressions in the linen trade; poor harvests and outbreaks of livestock disease: such conditions, operating in a context of small farms and large families, contrasted unfavourably with a vision of unlimited acres, cheap homesteads, high wages, and seemingly boundless opportunities in the New World. As James Lindsey of Desertmartin, County Derry, wrote at mid-century to his cousins in Pennsylvania:

> The good bargains of the lands in your country do greatly encourage me to pluck up my spirits and make ready for the journey, for we are now oppressed with our lands set at eight shillings per acre and other improvements, cutting our land in

21 For the contours of eighteenth- and early nineteenth-century Irish (especially 'Scotch-Irish') emigration and settlement, as described in this and the following paragraphs, see: Doyle, *Ireland, Irishmen and Revolutionary America*; Miller, *Emigrants and Exiles*, chs. 4–6; and Miller, *et al.*, *Irish Immigrants in the Land of Canaan*.
22 Robert Witherspoon, Memoir, copy in Mary S. Witherspoon, 'Genealogy of the Witherspoon Family', 1894 (Ms. in South Caroliniana Library, University of South Carolina, Columbia, SC; hereafter SCL/USC). As per the wish of the editor of the collection in which this essay appeared originally, all quotations from Irish emigrants' letters, memoirs, and other documents have been modernized in spelling, punctuation, and capitalization.
23 Richard S. Wallace, 'The Scotch-Irish of Provincial New Hampshire' (PhD diss., University of New Hampshire, 1984), ch. 1.

two-acre parts and [hedging] and only two years' time for doing it all — Yea, we cannot stand more![24]

After the American Revolution, the failure of the 1798 Irish rebellion, and the election of the Virginian Thomas Jefferson as president in 1800, the new United States became doubly attractive as both an economic and political asylum. This may have been particularly true of the Old South, where, as Ulsterman John Joyce reported from staunchly republican Virginia, '[t]hey are very fond of Irish emigration here, ... it is given as a toast often at their fairs', and the people 'much applaud the Irish for their resolution and spirit of independence'.[25] Thus, writing shortly after the revolution, Andrew Gibson, a farmer in Lisnagirr, County Tyrone, told his brother-in-law in North Carolina:

I think you are blessed living in a land of liberty and free from the great oppression of landlords and everyone in authority which indeed poor Ireland labours under at present. ... The gentlemen are laying on so great taxes ... that it is hard to live here. I pay upwards of £1.10 per year and I have come to great losses these three bad seasons by overflowing of floods and some loss of cattle...

'My wife and I are too old to undertake the danger,' Gibson lamented, but 'our young folk would fondly go to America'.[26]

Letters such as those received by Andrew Gibson undoubtedly provided the primary encouragement for emigration to the Old South. However, there were other inducements as well. On several occasions prior to the revolution, the South Carolina and Georgia governments offered land grants, tools, provisions, and religious freedom to Irish Protestants willing to settle in the southern backcountry — to create a buffer against Indian attacks and to reduce the danger of slave revolts by increasing the white population, thus replicating their ancestors' assigned role in the Ulster Plantation. Private land speculators also encouraged Irish emigration. For example, in 1765 John Rea, an Ulster-born Indian trader, advertised in the *Belfast News-Letter* for 'industrious' emigrants from the North of Ireland to settle at Queensborough township, on his 50,000-acre land grant in the Georgia backcountry, promising the newcomers 100 acres per family, plus horses, mules, and other supplies:

24 David Lindsey, near Desertmartin, County Derry, to his cousins, Pennsylvania, 19 March 1758 (T.2269, PRONI); for a full transcript and discussion of this letter, see Miller, *et al.*, *Irish Immigrants in the Land of Canaan*, 28–30.
25 John Joyce, 24 March 1785, in 'Virginia in 1785', *Virginia Magazine of History and Biography*, 23 (1915), 407–14.
26 Andrew Gibson, Lisnagirr, County Tyrone, to Robert Love, *c.* Gastonia, NC, 22 September 1789 (T.3610, PRONI).

The land I have chosen is good for wheat, and any kind of grain, indigo, flax, and hemp will grow to great perfection, and I do not know any place better situated for a flourishing township than this place will be. ... People that live on the low land near the sea are subject to fever and agues [that is, malaria], but high up in the country it is healthy [with] fine springs of good water. The winter is the finest in the world, never too cold, very little frost and no snow.

Rea candidly admitted that he would not

advise any person to come here that lives well in Ireland, because there is not the pleasure of society [here] that there is there, [nor] the comfort of the Gospel preached, no fairs or markets to go to. But we have greater plenty of good eating and drinking, for, and I bless God for it, I keep as plentiful a table as most gentlemen in Ireland, with good punch, wine, and beer.

Rea concluded with the clinching enticement that, '[i]f any person that comes here can bring money to purchase a slave or two, they may live very easy and well'.[27]

Yet emigration to the Old South was not without hazards, as both Gibson and Rea implied. Before the revolution, voyages from Belfast to Charleston and Savannah normally took from eight to ten weeks. By the 1830s the average voyage was merely six to eight weeks, but fear of Atlantic storms and shipboard epidemics still made many Irishmen and -women quail at the prospect. Also, during the era's frequent Anglo-French wars, Irish emigrants had to brave the danger of attacks by French naval vessels and privateers — and, during the French revolutionary and Napoleonic wars, of seizures by British ships and impressment into the British navy. In 1806–07, for example, John O'Raw, a young emigrant from north County Antrim, experienced an unusually miserable voyage to Charleston that combined all these hazards. After his vessel was nearly shipwrecked on the coast of Donegal, he wrote:

[w]e encountered the most dangerous storms and head winds for three weeks and was driven into the Bay of Biscay off the coast of France. A great many of our passengers now took the bloody flux and one child died of it. The weather continued most dreadful for six weeks, during which we were frequently carrying away our yards and rigging in dangerous storms of thunder and lightning. The captain said he never was at sea in such [a storm] before. I was for four weeks ... almost reduced to the point of death by sickness.

27 John Rea, 15 May 1765, in *Belfast News-Letter*, 3 September 1765 (Ulster Linen Hall Library, Belfast); for full transcript, etc., see Miller, *et al.*, *Irish Immigrants in the Land of Canaan*, 82–86.

After nearly two months being blown back and forth across the Atlantic, O'Raw's ship was wrecked on the coast of Bermuda. The emigrants were saved, but nearly all their possessions were lost and most of his friends were forcibly conscripted into the British navy when they went to the island's capital — a fate which O'Raw escaped by hiding in the remote parts of the island until he and his remaining companions were able to charter another, smaller vessel to convey them to Charleston. After more violent storms that nearly sank his second ship, O'Raw finally reached South Carolina, more than five months after he had left Belfast.[28]

Even after disembarking in southern ports, early Irish immigrants had to endure unaccustomed hardships. Usually landing in summer, they found the climate oppressively hot, and they were assailed by diseases, such as malaria and yellow fever, which were virtually unknown in Ireland. Historians estimate that the great majority of the Irish (and other) indentured servants transported to the southern colonies and the West Indies during the seventeenth century died within a few years of arrival. By the eighteenth century conditions were less lethal, but yellow fever epidemics as well as malaria remained common. In the early nineteenth century southern ports such as New Orleans and Mobile still had well-deserved reputations as Irish immigrant graveyards, and migrants to Charleston and Savannah had to survive a 'seasoning' process of six months or more before they were fit to work. For example, although John O'Raw took care, soon after his arrival, to leave Charleston and the lowlands for the healthier South Carolina upcountry, he took ill for four months at Newbury and nearly died of 'fever' before he could resume his occupation of schoolmaster.[29]

Even healthy immigrants were often discouraged, at least initially, by what John Rea had described as the primitive state of southern society, especially in the eighteenth century. To be sure, in 1768 Hester Wylly from Coleraine found her new home in Savannah quite congenial, as she wrote to her sister:

> My dear Helen, I am sure it will give you pleasure to hear that this place agrees with me as well as Ireland. I have not found any difference. It's true in the heat of summer the people that is exposed to the sun is subject to what they call fever and ague, but it soon leaves them and is seldom dangerous. ... As for the people here, they are extremely polite and sociable. We form a wrong notion of the [American] women for I assure you I never saw finer women in any part of the world, nor finer complexions in my life. They are very gay and spritely, [and] we have constant assemblies and many other amusements to make the place agreeable.[30]

28 John O'Raw, Charleston, SC, to Bryan and Nellie O'Raw, c. Ballymena, County Antrim, 1 April 1809 (D.3613/1/2, PRONI); for a full transcript, etc., see Miller et al., *Irish Immigrants in the Land of Canaan*, 94–103.
29 John O'Raw, 1 April 1809.
30 Hester Wylly, Savannah, Ga., to Mrs. Helen Lawrence, Coleraine, County Derry, 14 December 1768 (D.955/11, PRONI).

Of course, as the wife of a wealthy planter and slave-owner, and as sister of the speaker of Georgia's colonial legislature, Mrs. Wylly rarely socialized with the great majority of 'the people that is exposed to the sun'. More typical was the response of Robert Witherspoon, who penned quite a different account of his family's first years (in the 1730s and 1740s) on the banks of the Black River in backcountry South Carolina. After travelling upriver from Charleston, he wrote:

> my mother and we children were still in expectations of coming to an agreeable place, but when we arrived and saw nothing but a wilderness, and instead of a comfortable house, no other than one of dirt, our spirits sank. ... We had a great deal of trouble and hardships in our first settling [for w]e were also much oppressed with fear ... , especially of being massacred by the Indians, or torn by wild beasts, or of being lost and perishing in the woods, of whom there were three persons [in our party] who were never found. ... [M]any were taken sick with ague and fever, some died and some became dropsical and also died.[31]

The initial hardships were the worst, and those who survived, and acquired legal title to farms and sufficient capital to purchase slaves, often prospered. Thanks to slave labour and a flourishing market for indigo, when Robert Witherspoon's father died in 1768 (the same year Hester Wylly arrived in Savannah), he inherited an estate worth $25,000, including a substantial planter's house built on the 'English' or 'Virginia' model.[32] The steady expansion of market agriculture into the southern backcountry transformed many of the Irish who had settled there from subsistence farmers and cattle-drivers into planters and slave-owners, especially after 1791 when the invention of the cotton gin enabled the spread westward of short-staple cotton production. By the early nineteenth century, the Carolina and Georgia backcountries had spawned their own aristocracies of Irish-stock planters, such as the family of John C. Calhoun, the future architect of southern Secession, and also by this time Irish newcomers such as John O'Raw could count on assistance from dense networks of well-established kinsmen and friends who had preceded them.[33] However, the conditions that Robert Witherspoon had described in the 1730s — and the semi-barbarous society that the Anglican missionary Charles Woodmason lamented in the Carolina backcountry in the early 1770s[34] — were replicated time and again on the retreating margins of the southern frontier.

31 Robert Witherspoon, Memoir.
32 William W. Boddie, History of Williamsburg (Columbia, SC, 1923); Joseph B. Witherspoon, The History and Genealogy of the Witherspoon Family (Ft. Worth, Tex., 1979).
33 Rachel N. Klein, Unification of a Slave State: The Rise of the Planter Class in the South Carolina Backcountry, 1760–1808 (Chapel Hill, NC, 1990).
34 Richard J. Hooker, ed., The Carolina Backcountry on the Eve of the Revolution: The Journal and Other Writings of Charles Woodmason, Anglican Itinerant (Chapel Hill, NC, 1953).

Moreover, a large number, perhaps a majority, of early Irish settlers in the Old South did not become successful planters, even in the backcountry regions where land was relatively cheap. In the 1780s, for example, over half the adult males were landless in the 'Scotch-Irish' strongholds of Augusta and Rockbridge counties, in Virginia's Upper Shenandoah Valley, and during the next fifty years such men and their families migrated further west or south, on a trek that often found economic dead-ends in the Appalachian foothills, the Piney Woods of Mississippi, or the Ozark Mountains of Missouri and Arkansas.[35] Even before the American Civil War, falling cotton prices, and the boll weevil ravaged the southern economy, northern visitors such as Frederick Law Olmsted were appalled by the slovenly and culturally as well as economically impoverished conditions prevailing among the Old South's 'yeoman' farmers.[36] And, belying their eulogists' claims of inherent superiority, by 1900 the 'Scotch-Irish' of the southern states were generally poorer and less-educated than the Catholic Irish who had settled in the urban-industrial North during the previous century.[37]

A final, closer examination of the careers of four late eighteenth- and early nineteenth-century Irish emigrants to the Old South illustrates this chapter's opening argument concerning the variety and mutability of early Irish and Irish-American identities. The first and perhaps the most fascinating story is that of Samuel Burke, who, for several technical reasons, was not precisely an Irish *emigrant*, although culturally and linguistically he was arguably more 'Irish' than most of those who migrated from Ireland to America during this period. Burke was actually born in Charleston about 1755, but he was taken back to Cork as a mere infant, christened and raised there. In 1774, when he was about twenty years old, Burke left Ireland and returned to America, as personal servant to an Anglo-Irish official, Montford Browne, the newly appointed royal governor of the recently established British colony of West Florida. When the American Revolution broke out, both Browne and Burke were seized by the rebellious colonists and sent to prison in Hartford, Connecticut. After their release through a prisoner exchange, they went to the British military base in New York City, where Burke married a widow with

35 Robert D. Mitchell, *Commercialism and Frontier: Perspectives on the Early Shenandoah Valley* (Charlottesville, Va., 1977). Also see Russell L. Gerlach, 'Scotch-Irish Landscapes in the Ozarks', in H. Tyler Blethen and Curtis W. Wood, Jr., eds., *Ulster and North America: Transatlantic Perspectives on the Scotch-Irish* (Tuscaloosa, Ala., 1997), 146–66.

36 Frederick Law Olmsted, *The Cotton Kingdom*, ed. A. M. Schlesinger (New York, 1953). Also see, Grady McWhiney, *Cracker Culture: Celtic Ways in the Old South* (Tuscaloosa, Ala., 1988).

37 David N. Doyle, *Irish-Americans, Native Rights and National Empires: The Structure, Divisions and Attitudes of the Catholic Minority in the Decade of Expansion, 1890–1901* (New York, 1976), 48–49, 59–63.

a small fortune and employed his fluency in the Irish language to assist Browne and other officers in persuading Irish Catholic dock workers to join a loyalist regiment in the British army. Burke himself enlisted in the regiment he helped recruit and, accompanied by his wife, served under the now Brigadier General Browne in the southern campaign of the revolutionary war, during which he was wounded on several occasions. Burke hoped to settle in his native South Carolina, on property that the British confiscated from American rebels, but the British defeat dashed his hopes, and in 1782 he and his wife evacuated Charleston with the British navy. By 1785 Burke was living in London and employed in an artificial flower garden for one shilling per day, although he was scarcely able to work because of his war wounds. In great distress, he applied to the British government for compensation for his military service and lost possessions.[38]

Outside Pennsylvania and the other middle colonies, where Irish-American enthusiasm for independence was virtually unanimous, a large minority of Irish immigrants were loyalists during the American Revolution.[39] Indeed, in the Carolinas and Georgia the conflict degenerated into a vicious, bloody civil war between rival Ulster-American factions, some motivated by political ideals, others by greed and revenge.[40] For example, most of John Rea's Ulster settlers in Queensborough township remained faithful to their king, and in reprisal the victorious patriots confiscated their lands and obliterated the very name of their settlement. Likewise, the rebels seized the great plantations owned by Hester Wylly's kinsmen, who fled to the West Indies, although eventually they recovered part of their former possessions.[41] Thus, it is not Samuel Burke's political allegiance that is surprising. Rather, given the fact that Burke was 'Irish' in nearly every meaningful respect, what is mind-boggling — and what clearly perplexed the British commissioners in London who, rather grudgingly, granted him a small pension — was that Burke was what the commissioners described as 'a Black' in their official documents.[42]

The second biography is that of John O'Raw, the young emigrant from near Ballymena, in County Antrim, who in 1806–07 endured the long, miserable voyage to Charleston described above. Unlike most contemporary Ulster emigrants, O'Raw was Catholic, not Presbyterian. In 1798, although merely fifteen years old and despite the admonitions of his priest, O'Raw had joined his Presbyterian neighbours and fought with the United Irishmen. Clearly, in the late eighteenth century Presbyterian–Catholic

---

38 Samuel Burke petition and testimony, in 'American Loyalists: Transcripts of the Manuscript Books and Papers of the Commission of Inquiry into the Losses and Services of the American Loyalists' (Mss. in the New York Public Library), vol. 41, 539–46 (microfilm edn., London Examinations, reel 13).

39 Wallace Brown, The King's Friends: The Composition and Motives of the American Loyalist Claims (Providence, RI, 1965).

40 Klein, Unification of a Slave State; Jerome J. Nadelhaft, The Disorders of War: The Revolution in South Carolina (Orono, Me., 1981); and Robert S. Lambert, South Carolina Loyalists in the American Revolution (Columbia, SC, 1987).

41 E. R. R. Green, 'Queensborough Township: Scotch-Irish Emigration and the Expansion of Georgia, 1763–1776', William and Mary Quarterly, 3rd ser., 17 (1960), 183–99; Wylly Correspondence (D.955, PRONI).

42 Samuel Burke petition and testimony.

relations in north Antrim were much more congenial than was later the case. Members of both denominations generally felt oppressed by an Anglican aristocracy, and the Catholic O'Raws and O'Haras socialized and intermarried with Presbyterian Moores, McCauleys, and Boyds, whose kinsmen gladly assisted John O'Raw when he came to South Carolina.[43]

After a short tenure as a schoolmaster in the Carolina backcountry, O'Raw decided to try his fortunes in Charleston. By 1820 he had progressed from the position of store clerk to the ownership of a moderately prosperous grocery on Meeting Street and also of two slaves. In addition, he was a member of St. Mary's Catholic church and also of the city's interdenominational Hibernian Society. However, although O'Raw became an American citizen and served in the Anglo-American War of 1812–15, in the late 1820s he returned to County Antrim and died there in 1841.[44] Perhaps his eventual return 'home' suggests how O'Raw resolved the tensions inherent in an 'Irish-American' identity, but even more intriguing is what O'Raw and other Irish Catholics did in 1815–19 during the so-called 'Charleston schism'. During those years, Archbishop Leonard Neale of Baltimore tried to impose an ultra-royalist French priest, a refugee from the French Revolution, on the Catholics of St. Mary's. Despite the archbishop's charge that they were 'disloyal' to the Church and faced excommunication if they did not submit to his authority, O'Raw and St. Mary's other Irish parishioners (most of them, like O'Raw, formerly associated with the United Irishmen) refused to accept Neale's nominee. Significantly, their objections were not to the French priest's nationality but to his outspoken animosity to the republican principles for which they and their Protestant countrymen had fought in Ireland.[45] Fifty to 100 years later, very few Irish-American Catholics (particularly men as 'respectable' as O'Raw and his friends) would have dared defy their bishop so openly and vigorously, for by then Irish Catholics on both sides of the ocean regarded religious loyalty as paramount and integral to their conceptions of Irish identity and nationalism. However, as noted above, in the late eighteenth and early nineteenth centuries, Irish Catholics (and Protestants) often defined 'Irishness' in predominantly political — rather than religious — ways that united rather than divided them.

43 John O'Raw, 1 April 1809; biographical data from Brian Moore O'Hara, Ballylesson, Ballymena, County Antrim.

44 Traces of O'Raw can be found in: James W. Hagy, ed., *People and Professions of Charleston, 1782–1802* (Baltimore, Md., 1992); Brent H. Halcomb, comp., *South Carolina Naturalizations, 1783–1850* (Baltimore, Md., 1985); Kenneth Scott, comp., *British Aliens in the United States during the War of 1812* (Baltimore, Md., 1979); Arthur Mitchell, *History of the Hibernian Society of Charleston, South Carolina, 1799–1981* (Barnwell, SC, 1982); *Charleston Directory and Stranger's Guide* (Charleston, SC, 1816–25; titles vary slightly); and 1820 US Census, unpublished Ms. schedules, Charleston, South Carolina (microfilm), p. 36A. Information from Brian Moore O'Hara on O'Raw's return to and death in County Antrim.

45 For opposing views of the 'Charleston schism', see: Patrick Carey, *People, Priests and Prelates: Ecclesiastical Democracy and the Tensions of Trusteeism* (Notre Dame, Ind., 1987); and Peter Guilday, *The Life and Times of John England, First Bishop of Charleston* (New York, 1927). O'Raw's role on the side of the Charleston 'schismatics' was confirmed by his signature on petitions from the rebellious trustees to Archbishop Neale; for this information, I am grateful to the Rev. Paul K. Thomas, archivist of the Archdiocese of Baltimore, Md.

O'Raw tried to adapt his religion to his political principles, but the third subject is a Catholic immigrant whose ambitions and circumstances in the Old South persuaded him to abandon his faith and embrace the Protestantism of his neighbours. Andrew Leary O'Brien was born in County Cork in 1815, the son of a strong farmer who intended him to become a priest and thereby enhance the family's spiritual and social status. In 1837, after years of expensive schooling in Ireland, O'Brien's parents sent him overseas to finish his clerical studies at Chambly seminary in Quebec. O'Brien's erotic shipboard dreams, recorded in his memoir, of beautiful and seductive blonde-haired women, probably suggested his unsuitability for a celibate life, and so perhaps he was fortunate when in 1837 the Canadian Rebellion against the British colonial government shut down the seminary and cast him adrift. O'Brien made his way south to Pennsylvania, where he found work as a stonemason in the building of the Susquehanna canal. There, surrounded by hundreds of what he described as uncouth, illiterate, frequently drunken, and often violent Irish Catholic canal workers, O'Brien discovered for the first time that, in his words, 'I felt mean at the thought that I was an Irishman'. Despite his father's entreaties that he return to Ireland and resume his studies, O'Brien concluded to escape both his current associates and, one suspects, his entire past. He took his earnings and sailed from New York to Charleston. For several years, he taught school in Barnwell district, South Carolina, where he married into a Methodist family whose church he joined after attending a camp meeting. In 1848 he moved to Cuthbert, Georgia, where in 1854 he founded what was then called Randolph — now Andrew — College. Today, very few of its faculty or graduates are aware that their college, still piously Methodist, was established by an Irish Catholic seminary student and canal worker who had concluded that acceptance and respectability in an overwhelmingly Protestant southern society were more important than the retention of his ethnic and religious heritage.[46]

The last biography is that of William Hill, who lived in Abbeville district, South Carolina, from 1822 until his death, aged eighty, in 1886.[47] Hill was born in 1805 in Ballynure parish, County Antrim, into a Presbyterian family that had been implicated in the 1798 rebellion. According to family tradition, Hill disliked his stepmother and so, at age seventeen, emigrated to Charleston, bearing letters of introduction to a Major John Donald, an earlier emigrant from Ballynure who had settled in Abbeville and fought in the war of 1812. At first Hill clerked in Donald's store, but within two years he had married his employer's daughter, Anna, and commenced farming land that his father-in-law gave him as a wedding present. By the late 1820s Hill had begun concentrating on trade, selling goods in his own country store, although he always retained ownership of about 360 acres that he usually planted in wheat, oats, and Indian

46 Annette McDonald Suarez, The Journal of Andrew Leary O'Brien (Athens, Ga., 1946).
47 Unless otherwise cited, biographical data on William Hill in this and the following paragraphs are derived from information either contained in his obituaries in the Abbeville Medium, 21 January 1886, and especially the Abbeville Press and Banner, 20 January 1886, or communicated by Dr. and Mrs. William G. Hill of Abbeville, SC, whose assistance I very gratefully acknowledge.

corn.[48] Sometime in the 1840s, he moved into Abbeville town, population 400, where he prospered as a merchant. Although Hill had no formal legal training, he gained a reputation as an honest, competent adviser in probate law and estate administration, and in 1852 he was elected to the first of eight successive terms as Abbeville district's judge of the court of ordinary. The 1860 census listed Hill as possessing $20,000 worth of real and personal property, in addition to fifteen slaves.[49] As for many southern whites, the Civil War and its immediate aftermath were disastrous for William Hill and his family. Two of his sons-in-law died of wounds or disease while serving in the Confederate army, and his own eldest son was severely wounded. As a result of the South's defeat, Hill claimed to have lost over $30,000 in slaves, in Confederate bonds and currency, and in the general depreciation of real estate, while the advent of Radical Republican rule in South Carolina deprived him of his office of probate judge.[50] Hill continued to dabble in trade until about 1871 when he retired to his farm outside Abbeville town, where he died fifteen years later.

Throughout his life, Hill wrote regularly to his brother, David, back in Ballynure, and, using his correspondence in conjunction with what is known about his career in South Carolina, we can try to reconstruct the changes in his sense of ethnic identity. One of Hill's obituaries described him as 'a most enthusiastic Irishman, never being entirely weaned of his love for his native land'.[51] Certainly, Hill's emotional identification with Ireland comes through most strongly in his *earliest* surviving correspondence. In one letter, for example, he chides his brother for not writing more often: '[t]here is little or nothing here [in South Carolina] to concern you,' he admonished, but 'every nook and corner of the neighbourhood of Ballynure teems with absorbing interest to me. Although it is upwards of thirty-two years since I left "the green hills of my youth", I can still luxuriate in fancy, ... young again, strolling over the old green sod.' Repeatedly in such letters, Hill declared his longing to return to his native land, if only for a visit.[52]

There are several probable reasons for Hill's profound homesickness for Ireland. One is the circumstance of his emigration: at a relatively young age, and impelled not so much by ambition as by a deteriorating relationship with his stepmother. Another is his romantic attachment to a woman he left behind in Ireland and to whom he referred in one of his early letters, when he remembered 'whispering words of artless love to her who was — most beautiful, most lovely, but now alas, how changed'. Hill asked

48 United States Agricultural Censuses, 1850, 1860, 1880: Abbeville District, South Carolina (Mss. in the South Carolina Department of Archives and History, Columbia, SC).
49 1860 US Census, unpublished Ms. schedules, Abbeville Court House, South Carolina (microfilm), p. 21.
50 William Hill, Abbeville, SC, to David Hill, Ballynure, County Antrim, 8 September 1865 (William Hill Correspondence, SCL/USC).
51 *Abbeville Press and Banner*, 20 January 1886.
52 William Hill, Abbeville, SC, to David Hill, Ballynure, County Antrim, 24 January 1855 (William Hill Correspondence, SCL/USC; and T.1830/3, PRONI). Also, see Hill's letters of 14 July 1847 (William Hill Correspondence, SCL/USC; and T.1830/1, PRONI), and of 21 January 1858 (William Hill Correspondence, SCL/USC), both written in Abbeville to David Hill in Ballynure.

his brother, '[d]o you surmise to whom I allude? — Well then, tell me of her. Although the vase is long broken, yet still the fragrance of the once sweet flower remains.'[53] By contrast, in not one of his six extant letters written before 1867 did Hill ever refer to his wife in South Carolina. Thus, although Hill's obituary referred in formulaic fashion to his 'beloved wife' and their 'happy union for nearly sixty years', it appears that his deepest affections long centred on someone back in Ballynure.[54]

Indeed, if Hill had not married so young and so soon after his migration, it is not unlikely that he might have returned to Ireland permanently, as did John O'Raw. For although Hill's first twenty years or so in South Carolina are shrouded in relative obscurity, they appear to be characterized by a lack of both material success and personal commitment to his adopted country. For example, it may be significant that Hill did not apply for American citizenship until 1834,[55] twelve years after his immigration, and he took no part in public life until 1836, when he joined Abbeville's militia company for service in the Seminole War. Significantly, it was just *before* those years, in 1832–33, that John C. Calhoun and South Carolina's other political leaders precipitated the so-called Nullification Crisis and first challenged the Federal government's authority. During and after that episode, white South Carolinians were under intense pressure to demonstrate communal loyalty and solidarity. Since Hill's obituaries made no mention of any participation in the Nullification crusade, as they surely would have done had he been involved, it is probable that Hill was included in the one-third of Abbeville district's voters (mostly poor men, as was Hill at that time) who opposed Nullification — and so he may have hastened thereafter to conform to 'communal' (that is, local élite) standards. Certainly, it was during the twenty years following the Nullification Crisis that Hill rose in prosperity and public esteem: by acquiring the military credentials, the membership in Abbeville's Presbyterian church, and the ownership of slaves that marked his entrance into the second tier of the district's élite and that made him electable to public office. By 22 November 1860, Hill's eminence was signalled by his membership, alongside the kinsmen of the late John C. Calhoun and other wealthy planters, of the local committee that organized Abbeville's public meeting that in turn selected delegates to South Carolina's fateful Secession convention.[56]

---

53 William Hill, 24 January 1855.
54 *Abbeville Press and Banner*, 20 January 1886.
55 Halcomb, *South Carolina Naturalizations*.
56 On the Nullification and Secession crises, and antebellum South Carolina politics, generally, see: Lacy K. Ford, *Origins of Southern Radicalism: The South Carolina Upcountry, 1800–1860* (New York, 1988), and 'Republics and Democracy: The Parameters of Political Citizenship in Antebellum South Carolina', in David R. Chesnutt and Clyde N. Wilson, eds., *The Meaning of South Carolina History: Essays in Honor of George C. Rogers, Jr.* (Columbia, SC, 1991), 121–45; William W. Freehling, *Prelude to Civil War: The Nullification Controversy in South Carolina* (New York, 1965); and Steven A. Channing, *Crisis of Fear: Secession in South Carolina* (New York, 1970). Information on Hill's organization of Abbeville's Secession meeting from Dr. and Mrs. William G. Hill, Abbeville, SC.

During the same decades that Hill was becoming more 'American' (which, in Abbeville, meant more 'Southern'), several specific developments in both Ireland and South Carolina operated to lessen or qualify Hill's identification with his homeland. During the Nullification Crisis, South Carolina's only Irish-American newspaper, the Charleston *Irishman and Southern Democrat*, was 'violently anti-nullification',[57] and the consequent association of 'Irishness' and 'disloyalty' to South Carolina in the minds of many local whites may have shaken Hill's attachment to Ireland. More certainly, in the early 1840s Daniel O'Connell, political leader of Ireland's Catholics, joined with Irish, British, and Yankee abolitionists in denouncing southern slavery, urging all 'true Irishmen' in America to work for immediate emancipation. In response, Hibernian societies throughout the South either shut their doors or repudiated O'Connell's leadership — particularly after he also declared his opposition to US annexation of Texas as a slave state.[58] Indeed, one of William Hill's own letters to his brother David, vehemently denying that 'slavery and Christianity were inconsistent', indicates the growing gap between the anti-slavery sentiments that prevailed in Ireland and his own commitments — not merely to his propertied interests, but to the safety of the white minority in a district where, between 1820 and 1850, the proportion of slaves in the local population had risen from 40 to 60 per cent.[59]

Another crucial development in the late 1840s and 1850s was the arrival in South Carolina of several thousand Irish Catholic peasants, impoverished refugees from the Great Famine. Hill's 'Irish' identity was ecumenical in theory, shaped by the United Irishmen's republican ideals, which forbade invidious distinctions between Irish Protestants and Catholics. Hill was true to that legacy: he named one of his sons Robert Emmet Hill; and in his letters he denounced England's 'oppressive' rule over Ireland, expressed his detestation of Irish Orangemen for their loyalism and anti-Catholic activities, refused to consider allowing his son to attend the Queen's College of Belfast, because of its royalist associations, and gleefully predicted that the British would lose the Crimean War (1853–56).[60] However, Hill's sense of 'Irishness' had been shaped by his local, native environment, and that environment had been almost exclusively Protestant, as well as relatively genteel. In Ballynure parish, 85 per cent of the inhabitants had been Presbyterians, only 5 per cent Catholics.[61] As a result, Hill was shocked and embarrassed by what he described as the 'poverty and want, rags, squalor, and wretchedness'

57 Freehling, *Prelude to Civil War*, 181–82.
58 Gilbert Osofsky, 'Abolitionists, Irish Immigrants, and the Dilemmas of Romantic Nationalism', *American Historical Review*, 80, 4 (October 1975), 889–912.
59 William Hill, 24 January 1855; demographic data from Ford, *Origins of Southern Radicalism*, 45.
60 William Hill, 24 January 1855; William Hill, Abbeville, SC, to David Hill, Ballynure, County Antrim, 7 March 1872 (courtesy of Dr. and Mrs. William G. Hill, Abbeville, SC).
61 In 1766 Ballynure parish contained 383 Protestant and 8 Catholic families (T.808/15,264, PRONI). According to the 1831 Irish religious census, 3,380 of Ballynure's 3,549 inhabitants were Protestants, of whom 3,004 were Presbyterians; see *Report of the Commissioners of Public Instruction, Ireland*, in BPP, HC 1835, vol. 33. On society in early nineteenth-century Ballynure, see: Angélique Day and Patrick McWilliams,

of the Famine Irish who came to South Carolina at mid-century and who, in his words, 'reflect discredit on the better class of their countrymen'. Although acknowledging that 'most of the [new Irish] emigrants ... never had opportunity of polish', for the first time he was obliged to distinguish between his own people and what he called 'the real Irish, of papist stock'.[62] Hill's fear of guilt by association was not imaginary, for in the mid-1850s the American (or Know-Nothing) party, pledged to halt the Irish influx and curtail immigrants' political rights, briefly flourished in South Carolina. Indeed, in 1857 Hill himself was nearly defeated for re-election as probate judge by a Know-Nothing candidate who denounced him for his 'Irish' background.[63]

On the one hand, white South Carolina's defeat and devastation in the Civil War, plus the partial wreck of his own fortune, rekindled Hill's nostalgia for Ireland and made him yearn to 'go back even in my old age to the dear land wherein I first drew breath'.[64] On the other hand, however, Hill's real commitment to the South — and his real estrangement from Ireland and from most of its people — were increasingly evident. For example, in his post-war letters Hill blamed the Confederacy's defeat on the 'tens of thousands' of Irish 'mercenaries' in the victorious Union army, who had helped the 'accursed' Yankees 'crush a people struggling for self-government regardless of anything but their filthy pay', and he was appalled that the Irish-American soldiers stationed in Abbeville allegedly 'mingle[d] with the Negroes with as much affinity as if of the same blood'.[65] In 1867 Hill did visit Ireland briefly, for the first and only time since his emigration forty-five years earlier. But the letter he wrote to brother David, on his return to Abbeville, was so uncharacteristically devoid of sentiment as to suggest that his visit had been deeply disappointing, memorable only for 'the cough [with] which [he] had been so much troubled' in the damp, cold Irish climate to which Hill was now unaccustomed. Significantly, it was only in this and subsequent letters that Hill first made reference to his wife of forty years.[66]

Perhaps in 1867 William Hill finally came 'home' to South Carolina, in a psychological as well as in a physical sense. Given the evolution of his own ethnic identity and nationalist sympathies — from Irish to white Southern — perhaps it was no wonder that, in the early twentieth century, his granddaughter would write in a school essay that she was not of 'Irish' but 'of Scotch-Irish descent', although neither Hill himself nor the authors of

eds., *Ordnance Survey Memoirs of Ireland*, Vol. 32. *Parishes of County Antrim XII, 1832–3, 1835–40: Ballynure and District* (Belfast, 1995), 31–73.

62 William Hill, Abbeville, SC, to David Hill, Ballynure, County Antrim, 7 July 1859 (William Hill Correspondence, SCL/USC).

63 William Hill, Abbeville, SC, to David Hill, Ballynure, County Antrim, 21 January 1858 (William Hill Correspondence, SCL/USC).

64 William Hill, 8 September 1865.

65 William Hill, 8 September 1865.

66 William Hill, Abbeville, SC, to David Hill, Ballynure, County Antrim, 15 August 1867 (William Hill Correspondence, SCL/USC).

his obituaries ever employed the term.[67] What may be even more significant, however, is that over a century after Hill's demise, according to the 1990 census, the descendants of most early Ulster Protestant settlers in the Old South had come full circle and once again proclaimed themselves to be inclusively, if vaguely, 'Irish'.

67 Mary Hill, 'Who I am' (undated school essay, courtesy of Dr. and Mrs. William G. Hill, Abbeville, SC).

8 Forging 'the Protestant Way of Life': Class Conflict and the Origins of Unionist Hegemony in Early Nineteenth-Century Ulster

In 1817 Henry Joy, one of Belfast's most prominent Presbyterian laymen, stated that no 'occurrence of much importance' had transpired in his town since the passage of the Act of Union in 1800. Almost 200 years later, historian Ian McBride notes that scholars still know little about Ulster Presbyterians' political opinions in the early nineteenth century, in part because of official and unofficial repression, and of self-censorship among those who had sympathized with the United Irishmen's 1798 rebellion or opposed the Act of Union itself.[1] This chapter suggests, however, that Irish emigrant correspondence can dispel some of the darknesses implied by both Joy's and McBride's remarks. Letters sent from America — albeit written from the perspective (and safety) of the New World — provide insights into the motives and attitudes of ordinary Ulster Presbyterian (and other Irish) emigrants. Moreover, missives sent from Ireland to emigrants overseas can illuminate Irish events and developments that most contemporaries preferred to ignore — and, in consequence, that historians have not noticed or have failed to

---

1 This chapter was originally published, with the same title, in Mark G. Spencer and David A. Wilson, eds., *Transatlantic Perspectives on Ulster Presbyterianism: Religion, Politics and Identity* (Dublin, 2006), 128–65. I wish to thank Four Courts Press for permission to republish it in this volume, with a few minor revisions, as well as Liam Kennedy, Ted Koditschek, Mark Spencer, and David Wilson for their helpful comments. An earlier and considerably shorter version, entitled 'Belfast's First Bomb, 28 February 1816: Class Conflict and the Origins of Ulster Unionist Hegemony,' was published in *Éire-Ireland: An Interdisciplinary Journal of Irish Studies*, 39, 1–2 (2004), 262–80.

   [Henry Joy], *Historical Collections Relative to the Town of Belfast: From the Earliest Period to the Union with Great Britain* (Belfast, 1817), xiv; Ian McBride, 'Ulster Presbyterians and the Passing of the Act of Union', in Michael Brown, *et al.*, eds., *The Irish Act of Union, 1800: Bicentennial Essays* (Dublin, 2003), 69; also see McBride, 'Memory and Forgetting: Ulster Presbyterians and 1798', in Thomas Bartlett, *et al.*, eds., *1798: A Bicentenary Perspective* (Dublin, 2003), 478–96.

investigate fully. Such is the case with a letter, written by William Coyne in Belfast on St. Patrick's Day, 1816, describing what may have been 'Belfast's first bomb'.[2]

Coyne was probably a master-cooper, and he may have been in his mid-forties when he wrote this, his only surviving letter, to his brother in Duchess County, New York. Very likely Coyne was a Protestant and perhaps a member of the legally established Church of Ireland. Early nineteenth-century Belfast was a rapidly growing city of migrants, principally from east Ulster's Lagan Valley, and, given the reference in his letter, it is probable that Coyne had moved to Belfast from the predominantly Anglican parish of Magheragall, in the barony of Massareene Upper, in southwest County Antrim.[3] In the

2   The author would like to thank Roger Hayden of Ithaca, NY, for providing photocopies and transcripts of Coyne's letter and for granting permission to publish it.
    The violent incident that Coyne described is omitted from the standard histories of Belfast — J. C. Beckett and R. E. Glasscock, eds., *Belfast: Origin and Growth of an Industrial City* (London, 1967); George Benn, *A History of the Town of Belfast: from the Earliest Times to the Close of the Eighteenth Century*, 2 vols. (London, 1877–80); and W. A. Maguire, *Belfast* (Keele, 1993) — but is mentioned briefly in Jonathan Bardon, *A History of Ulster* (Belfast, 1992), 259; John W. Boyle, *The Irish Labor Movement in the Nineteenth Century* (Washington, DC, 1988), 15–16; E. R. R. Green, *The Lagan Valley, 1800–50* (London, 1949), 101; and R. B. McDowell, *Public Opinion and Government Policy in Ireland, 1801–1846* (London, 1952), 62 — and described in more detail in Andrew Boyd, *The Rise of the Irish Trade Unions*, 2nd edn. (Dublin, 1985), 30–32.
3   According to the *Belfast Street Directory* (c. 1813) and *Bradshaw's Belfast Directory* of 1819, William Co[y]ne (or Cain), cooper, lived at 10 Bluebell Entry, off Waring Street. Perhaps he was the same 'Mr. William Coyne' who died, aged seventy-five, on 31 August 1846, at his home on the Falls Road. *Belfast News-Letter* (hereafter BNL), 4 September 1846; from the death records in the Linen Hall Library, Belfast, which also contains the BNL on microfilm.
    'Coyne' may be an Anglicization of the Irish surname Ó Cadhain, common in Mayo and elsewhere in Connacht, as well as in south Ulster counties such as Cavan; conversely, it may be a variant of (Mac) Coan (or Cone, commonly Cowan), found in County Armagh and likely derived from the Irish (or Scots Gaelic) Mac Comhdhain. The Northern Hiberno-English of Coyne's letter is in mid-Ulster dialect, with few if any Ulster Scots characteristics, as would be expected from his possible origin in southwest Antrim, lying outside the Ulster Scots linguistic domain. In Ulster, however, both language and surname are largely irrelevant to religious identity, and my suggestion that Coyne was likely a Protestant (and affiliated with the Church of Ireland) is based on early census data from Magheragall parish, to which Coyne refers in his letter.
    In 1766 Magheragall contained 420 households, 365 (86.9 per cent) of which were Protestant, 55 (13.1 per cent) Roman Catholic. Employing the eighteenth-century households-to-persons multiplier devised for Ulster by Dickson, Ó Gráda, and Daultrey, in 1766 Magheragall probably contained about 1,840 Protestants and 277 Catholics. By 1831 Magheragall's population included 2,279 Anglicans (67.0 per cent of the total, 74.6 per cent of the parish's Protestants), 646 Presbyterians (20.8 and 23.2 per cent), 63 'other Protestants' (2.0 and 2.3 per cent), and 314 Catholics (10.1 per cent of the total). Thus, by 1831 the Protestant proportion of Magheragall's inhabitants had risen to nearly 90 per cent. However, owing to heavy migration to America, Britain, or nearby industrial towns such as Belfast and Lisburn, between 1766 and 1831 the annual growth rates of Magheragall's populations had been extremely low: merely 0.64 among the parish's Protestants, and much less (0.19) among local Catholics.
    Religious census data for Magheragall in 1766 is in T.808/14,900, in PRONI; and for 1831 in the *First Report of the Commission of Public Instruction, Ireland*, in BPP, HC 1835, xxxiii. Also see D. Dickson, C. Ó Gráda, and S. Daultrey, 'Hearth Tax, Household Size, and Irish Population Change, 1672–1821', *Proceedings of the Royal Irish Academy*, 82C, 6 (1982), 125–50. For surname origins, see Edward MacLysaght, *The Surnames of Ireland*, 6th edn. (Blackrock, Co. Dublin, 1991). For his analysis of the language of Coyne's letter, I

early 1800s transatlantic mail was expensive and its delivery uncertain. Consequently, Irish immigrant correspondence was filled primarily with information that was vitally important to its authors and recipients but which often seems mundanely personal or familial to contemporary scholars. The principal subjects of Coyne's letter, however, were very public and quite dramatic, and his missive's exceptional character indicates that he and his neighbours in Belfast considered the developments he described to be extraordinarily significant — and that he assumed his brother in faraway America would consider them equally so. Social and political historians of early nineteenth-century Ulster should also find Coyne's letter of considerable interest.

William and E. Coyne, Belfast, to Henry Coyne, Pleasant Valley, Duchess County, New York, 17 March 1816[4]

Belfast 17th March 1816

Dear Brother

I have rec[d] your Letter of the 24th Dec[r] which give us great Satisfection to hear that you and your Familey were in good health; my aunt also rec,[d] one from you and She and Nancy desires to be remembred to you   they are both well and would have wrote but as they had nothing particular to mention they thought the one Letter would do us both,   I Showed your Letter to all your acquentainces that is here who was all particularly happy to heare from you, but John Mullan and Michal Roney is both in Scotland; and M[r] M'Pharson,[s] Congregation is disolved   his wife Died here and he is in England   his Church is Converted into a Muslin ware-house and ocupied by an old acquentaince of yours W[m] Shaw[5] who is an acting Partner in a Concern that is doeing a good dale of business at present   however trade is in general but verry flat[6] yet thank God I have had the best of work Since I went to M[r] Bell[7] and the two oldest boys Henry and John is doeing pretty well at the Loom.

am grateful, as always in linguistic matters, to Professor Emeritus Bruce D. Boling of the University of New Mexico.

4   The following transcript reproduces William Coyne's original punctuation and spelling — the latter often indicating his pronunciation, e.g., **dale** (deal), **attact** (attack), **extronary** (extraordinary), **rachedness** (wretchedness), **laveing** (leaving), etc. Occasionally the text is emended by explanatory footnotes or by the insertion of square-bracketed words or letters in the text itself. This minimal editing may cause readers some difficulty, in part because Coyne frequently abbreviated words and/or omitted vowels or entire syllables; thus, **rec**[d] (received); **Dec**[r], **Feb**[y] (December, February); **Covred, covring** (Covered, covering); **evry** (every); **modrate** (moderate); etc. Also, Coyne often employed commas to replace apostrophes — e.g., **M'Pharson,**[s] (M'Pharson's), **Ruth,**[s] (Ruth's), **Subscriber,**[s] (Subscriber's), etc. — or, less commonly, to indicate contractions or abbreviations, as in **rec,**[d] (received) and **per C,**[t] (per Cent).

5   **W**[m] **Shaw**: according to Bradshaw's Belfast Directory, in 1819 William Shaw was a merchant at 24 James's Street, off Waring Street.

6   **but**: only. **trade is in general but very flat**: i.e., in general, trade is only very poor.

7   **M**[r] **Bell**: Bradshaw's Belfast Directory of 1819 lists several merchants, bleachers, and cotton manufacturers named Bell — most prominently John Bell & Co., cotton spinners and manufacturers at John Street,

We have now and then a little Stir as usual between the Weavers and Manifecturiers particularly Thomas How[8] and Frank Johnson[9]   Several voilant attacts have been made on the praperty of these 2 individuals but the most dareing of all was on the night of the 28th of Feby on the House of M[r] Johnson   as his place had been twice Set on fire before he was well prepaird for a third attect haveing the out Side of his windows and door Covred with Sheet Iron and well prepaird in the inside to meet his asealants   however notwithstanding they made the attact about 3 Oclock on the morning of the 28th by forseing off the iron Shutters while he[10] and his inmates with Small arms from the uper windows of the House attected the Guards that was covring the working party at the windows when a havy fireing Commenced on both Sides to[11] the party that was at work forsd the Shutters and entroudeced either a bomb Shel or Some other extronary Combustable preperation that Soon

off Donegall Street and Waring Street; and John Bell, Richard Bell, & Co., muslin bleachers, also at John Street — many of whom could have employed Coyne's coopering skills. After the cotton weavers' attack on Francis Johnson's house (see below), John Bell joined the 'Committee of twenty-one Gentlemen', primarily cotton and muslin manufacturers, appointed to assist Belfast's magistrates and constables to 'seek for and receive information, collect subscriptions [for the rewards offered in return for 'information'], and transact all matters arising out of this disgraceful transaction' (BNL, 1 March 1816).

8 **Thomas How**: According to *Bradshaw's Belfast Directory*, in 1819 Thomas How (or Howe) was a muslin manufacturer with business premises in Long Lane, adjacent to his house on Church Street. He was also listed, at 12 Long Lane and 11 Church Street, in *Pigot's Provincial Directory* (London, 1824). According to Mr. M'Cartney, one of the attorneys who prosecuted those charged with attacking Francis Johnson's house (see below), the accused weavers had earlier targeted Thomas How, 'whose webs they cut, and [had] attacked those persons who worked [for] him' (BNL, 13 August 1816). Thomas How — like John Bell (see n. 7 above) and Johnson himself — was also a member of the 'Committee of twenty-one' appointed to apprehend Johnson's assailants (BNL, 1 March 1816). On 29 June 1838, the BNL recorded the death, eight days earlier, of 'Thomas How, Esq., merchant, aged 56 years'.

9 **Frank Johnson**: Francis Johnson, a leading muslin manufacturer at North Street, on Peter's Hill. According to Jonathan Bardon's *History of Ulster*, 259, Johnson was a 'hated employer' whose home had been attacked at least once before (as Coyne's letter states), in the summer of 1815, by '[d]esperate weavers' who daubed his front door with tar and set it on fire. According to Boyd, *Rise of the Irish Trade Unions*, 30–31, Johnson twice reduced his weavers' wages — the second time in retaliation for their previous assault. At the trial of those accused of bombing his house on 28 February 1816, one of the prosecuting attorneys charged that, before their final assault on his home, the weavers had also threatened Johnson with anonymous letters, 'made attacks on his person', and 'even went so far as to warn the Insurance Offices' against insuring his property, 'as they had determined to burn it' (BNL, 13 August 1816).

On 2 January 1818, the BNL printed a lengthy announcement of 'the death of our worthy and lamented townsman, Mr. FRANCIS JOHNSON, another victim to the dreadful scourge, Typhus Fever, with which our town is so severely visited'. According to his obituary, Johnson's 'character was held in the most elevated range by his fellow-citizens. ... for he was honest, ingenuous, and single-hearted; possessing a cultivated mind, talent, and integrity. In religion and morality, a bright example — in politics, liberal and constitutional — as a merchant, useful and intelligent — and for firmness and unshrinking determination, a man scarcely to be equalled. To his resolute conduct, the country is indebted for the preservation of its most useful manufactures. He was cool, dispassionate, and humane, and amidst difficulties that might have paled a less determined heart, he succeeded in putting down a system of combination which threatened to subvert the very basis of every principle of commercial good order.'

10 **he**: i.e., **Frank Johnson**; see n. 9 above.

11 **to**: until.

exploded and rent the House from top to bottom not a wall nor inside partation that was not torn to pices   yet despirate as it was and wounderfull to relate not a life was lost on either Sides,[12]   large rewards are offerd for aprehending any one Concernd no less than £2000 for prosacution and £500 for private information, four quiet well disposed men have been taken[13] on Suspecion but it is hoped there is nothing against them that will affect their lives. Jonathan Gardner Stood a trial at our last Assises for murder and is Still Confind on account of Some [f]arenciable[14] evidences not comeing forward,   the nature of the Circumstance was thus   he haveing kept a public House down Street about 4 Months [ago] he Shut the doar in [debt for] £700 and it was in an atempt of the Creditors to arest his person that the above accident haptned,[15]   how Soon one trouble Succeeds an other   his Son John who was Clarke in the Bottle House haveing Commited a breach of trust was turnd out and haveing inlisted a few days after onley got the lenth of England when he died[16] laveing a wife and 2 Children   Ruth,s fortune has been little better She maried a man of the name of aken and after gowing throw a Considerable property in a Short time She and her man is in the Antrim Militia   thus the whole Family is reduced to rachedness and distress   I have very little particulars to mention only as I am writeing[17] I have no doubt it will be a Saticefection to you to hear any thing interesting to the place,   among many valuable institutions that has been established here Since your departure none deserves more general approbation than the Saveing Bank   this is instituted for the Saveings of the poor and is Conducted by the foremost of the place   a Comettee of 25 is appointed as directors and manager Consisting of the principle Magastrates and Bankers of the town who meets every Friday Evning to receive deposites from evry discription of working people male and female young and old and each Contributer puts in

---

12 On the night of the weavers' attack, Johnson's large three-storey house was occupied by himself, his wife, six children, two servant women, and one male servant, John Lewis, whom Johnson had recently hired, as a watchman, to guard against nocturnal assaults. Indeed, Lewis's bravery, in carrying the smouldering 'bomb' from the front parlour into the kitchen at the rear of the house, may have saved Johnson, his family, and servants from death; in the event, Lewis and Johnson's wife were the only occupants to suffer even minor injuries.

13 **taken**: arrested.

14 **[f]arenciable**, i.e., 'forensiable': perhaps a hitherto unattested dialect variant of 'forensical' = 'forensic': 'items of evidence suitable for introduction into court proceedings' (see *OED*, s.v.). (An alternative reading of the word might be **parmiciable**, i.e. 'permissible'.) Thanks again to Professor Bruce D. Boling for his assistance in this matter (see n. 3 above).

15 See the BNL of 5 March 1816 for an account of the travails of Gardner, a publican on William Street. **haptned**: happened.

16 **Clarke in the Bottle House**: clerk in a glass bottle manufactory or a bottling plant, perhaps for whiskey. **his Son John ... was turnd out and haveing inlisted a few days after onley got the lenth of England when he died**: i.e., John Gardner was dismissed (**turned out**) from his former employment, and a few days afterwards (**after**) he enlisted in the British army; however, he had travelled only as far as (**the len[g]th of**) England when he died (presumably on his way to military service overseas).

17 **only as I am writeing**: i.e., but since I am writing anyway.

from 10 pence up according as they find it Convenient and as no fines is levied off any member every one makes their payments Convenient to their Silver[18] and when any Subscriber,s payments amounts to 10s they draw interest at the rate of 5 per C,^{t} this is one of the most valuable institutions ever invented for the benifet of the lower Class of the Community and you may guess the general aprobation it meets with from the Sum alredy Colected in 12 nights onley Since its Commensement amounting to £1256–14–9   I must draw this Letter to an end but I cannot Conclude dear Henry without expressing our Sorrow at your determination in gowing to the Indian teritories   if there was any posibelity that you Could get home I think it would be much better than to exile your Self and your Family into Such an uncertain and in all probility uncomfortable Situation for things are [not] altogether So bad here but working people can live in my openion as Comfortable and Contented as they can do in america[19]   for all those that has to earn their Bread by the Sweat of their Brow has to work there as well as here and the rate[20] of our provisions is likely to be very modrate   we have not Seen the oat Meal these 2 years more than 15^s per C,^{wt,21} and the rent of Land and Houses is falling in praportion   Land in general is down from 25 to 35 per Cent;   the rate of victuling at present is Meal from 9^s–6^d to 10^s per C,^{wt} Patatoes from 15^d to 19^d per do[22]   Beef from 3½^d to 6^d per lb   fresh Butter from 1^s to 1^s–3^d per lb   Eggs from 3½ to 5^d per doz   Sweet Milk 2^d per quart and other things in praportion. Ann Coyne was here last week from Magheragell   they are all well there and desires to be remembred to you,   Wm Witherops Familey is also well and likewise Sends their Love,   Jery Lee,^{s} Sister lives here and desires to let you know that he is dead he was wounded at the Battle of Waterloo and died Shortly after,   the name of the man that tom,^{s} wife bore the Child to is John Johnson,[23]   I Can add no mor but remains your affectionate Brother and sister

Wm & E Coyne

18 **Convenient to their Silver**: i.e., according to their means (whatever they can afford).

19 **things are [not] altogether So bad here but working people can live in my openion as Comfortable and Contented as they can do in america**: i.e., conditions are bad here, but in my opinion they are not so bad that working people cannot live as comfortably and contentedly (in Belfast) as they can in America.

20 **rate**: cost.

21 **we have not Seen the oat Meal these 2 years more than 15^s**: i.e., during the last two years we have not seen oatmeal priced at more than fifteen shillings. **per C,^{wt}**: per hundredweight (a unit of measurement equal to 112 lb.). On the prices of oatmeal, potatoes, etc., however, see below, n. 30.

22 **per do**: per ditto (i.e., **per C,^{wt}**); see n. 21 above.

23 **the name of the man that tom,s wife bore the Child to is John Johnson**: this line likely reflects a family scandal. **tom** may be Thomas Coyne, probably William and Henry's brother, who (like William) was listed as a cooper, living at 3 Edward Street (off Patrick Street), in *Bradshaw's Belfast Directory* (1819). Likewise, the **John Johnson** reputed to be the father of **tom,s wife**'s child may have been the same John Johnson, whitesmith, who in 1813 resided at 15 Bluebell Entry, only a few houses removed from William Coyne's abode on the same street (*Belfast Street Directory* [c. 1813]; see n. 3 above).

The urban assault that Coyne described was made against the house of Francis Johnson, one of east Ulster's most prominent manufacturers and merchants, who employed at least 450 cotton weavers (primarily on the putting-out system) and other workers in and around Belfast. Johnson was also a 'resolute' opponent of 'combinations' — the illegal unions that weavers, printers, and other artisans organized to regulate wages and working conditions in the various trades.[24] Indeed, it was Johnson's recent reduction of his employees' wages (or piece rates) that prompted Belfast's unionized weavers to attack his house. It was not surprising, therefore, that the town's leading citizens mobilized at once to express their 'indignation', 'horror and detestation' at what they and the *Belfast News-Letter* denounced as 'this foul deed', this 'unprecedented outrage', 'this most atrocious offence, the equal of which', they claimed (conveniently forgetting the legalized butchery that Belfast and east Ulster had witnessed in 1797–98 and in the aftermath of the 1798 rebellion), 'had never before occurred in this district of the country'.[25]

On the day following the assault, the town's 'principal inhabitants' met at the stock exchange and appointed a 'Committee of twenty-one Gentlemen', principally 'in the cotton and muslin trades', to assist the magistrates and constables in apprehending the 'monsters' 'concerned in this dreadful outrage'. As Coyne's letter attested, the committee subscribed rewards of £2,000 to anyone who would 'discover on, and prosecute [the assailants] to conviction' and of £500 for 'Private Information as may lead to the[ir] discovery and conviction' — plus the promise of 'his Majesty's most gracious Pardon for any Person or Persons implicated ... who shall give such information'. Within a week, total subscriptions soared to nearly £8,000, and from Dublin the lord lieutenant pledged to pardon anyone willing to 'discover [the culprits'] accomplices'.

At least 2,000 printed notices, advertising the rewards, were 'circulated through town and country', and by mid-May they had proved effective. The first fugitive to be apprehended was William Gray, a muslin weaver from the east Belfast suburb of Ballymacarrett, across the Long Bridge over the River Lagan, although originally from Portadown in north Armagh. Gray turned state's evidence, and by 5 July the authorities had arrested five of his alleged accomplices: John Doe, John Magill, Joseph Madden,

---

24 The description of Johnson is from his obituary in BNL, 2 January 1818. The descriptions of the meeting of Belfast's leading citizens, the advertisement for the apprehension of Johnson's assailants, and the weavers' trial, sentencing, execution, etc., recounted in the subsequent paragraphs, are in the following issues of the BNL: 1 March 1816 (the meeting and advertisement); 5 March, 8 March, and 15 March (the advertisement and the lord lieutenant's proclamation); 7 May (the 'hue and cry' for William Gray); 13 August (the trial); 16 August (Judge Day's address to the jury and his sentencing of Johnson's assailants [and of other prisoners]); 3 September (Madden's pardon); and 10 September (the executions). On the illegality of Irish 'combinations', see Patrick Park, 'The Combination Acts in Ireland, 1727–1825', *Irish Jurist*, 14, 2 (1979), 340–59, in addition to Boyle, *Irish Labor Movement*, 7–16, and Boyd, *Rise of the Irish Trade Unions*, 23–26.

25 The floggings and executions that occurred during Belfast's 'Reign of Terror' are detailed in Benn, *History of the Town of Belfast*, vol. 1, 662, and vol. 2, 20; and in [Joy], *Historical Collections Relative to the Town of Belfast*.

James Dickson, and James Park. All were cotton weavers from Belfast or north Down, and probably members of the Belfast Muslin Weavers' Society. As far as can be determined, all were Protestants.[26]

Their day-long trial took place on 12 August 1816, before the County Antrim assizes at Carrickfergus. By today's standards, the proceedings could fairly be described as a 'show trial', as the prosecutors and the judge clearly were determined to condemn not only the alleged culprits but also their 'ruinous ... conspiracies' and 'evil system of combinations'. The prosecution's opening statement skilfully combined eulogies of Ulster's cotton industry — as patriotic as well as profitable — and of the economic benefits conferred on Ireland by the Act of Union, with dire warnings of the awful consequences for the property rights and public safety of Belfast's citizens if the prisoners were not convicted and punished. As for the latter, the prosecution compared their actions and their 'infernal machine' (the bomb that destroyed Johnson's house) to the savagery of 'the tomahawk and scalping knife' and to the bloody scenes enacted in Paris during the 'Terror' of the French Revolution. 'If this kind of conduct is permitted,' the prosecutor warned, 'this country will soon be not safe to live in.'

After William Gray's testimony, implicating the prisoners in varying degrees, the defence attorney argued that Gray had testified solely for the reward money and to escape punishment — thinking 'it would be better ... to hang others than be hanged [him]self'. The defence also alleged that Gray had a long history of petty thievery in both Ireland and Scotland, and hence his word was doubly untrustworthy, whereas those whom Gray accused were 'honest, ... industrious, hard-working m[e]n', at least one of whom, as a witness testified, had been asleep in his home on the night of the attack. Yet most critical for the defence was its argument that, under the law, a defendant could not be convicted solely on the testimony of a single informer. Therefore, since Gray's identification of the accused men could not be corroborated, and since all other evidence against them was circumstantial, the jury must acquit.

At this point, however, the prosecuting attorneys made a crucial intervention, later seconded by Judge Day in his address to the jury, forcefully arguing not only that Gray was an exemplary witness but, more important, that criminals in capital cases could indeed be hanged on the word of only one informer. The judge then charged the jury members to do their duty, pausing only to praise 'the fortitude [and] manly firmness' displayed by Francis Johnson and by the other manufacturers whose efforts had secured the prisoners' apprehension.

After two hours' deliberation, the jury declared that Doe, Magill, and Madden were guilty of attacking Johnson's house, but that Dickson and Park could be found guilty

---

26 On the likelihood that the accused were members of the Belfast Muslin Weavers' Society, see Boyd, *Rise of the Irish Trade Unions*, 30. On their probable religious affiliations, see below, n. 63. It is intriguing that although as many as two dozen men reportedly were involved in the attack on Johnson's house, as far as I can determine only Doe, Magill, Madden, Dickson, and Park were ever tried and condemned for the crime.

only of conspiracy to plot the assault. Although the jury recommended mercy, Judge Day sentenced Doe, Magill, and Madden to be hanged for their 'malignant and atrocious outrage ... against a Gentleman who was benefiting his country by promoting its manufactures' — and to be hanged in Belfast, rather than in Carrickfergus, 'in order that the[ir] example might have a more powerful and lasting effect in deterring others from engaging in such unlawful associations'. The judge then sentenced Dickson and Park to the 'severest punishment' allowed for their crime — public whippings on the Belfast town scaffold and eighteen months' imprisonment — '[i]n order to teach their associates the impropriety of their conduct and the necessity of obedience to the laws'. Concluding his remarks, Judge Day expressed his trust that the trial's results would bring east Ulster's weavers 'to a sense of their duty, and show them the value of peaceable and industrious habits, and the danger of those unlawful combinations which would vainly usurp the law of the land; they will see,' he declared, 'that however secretly or numerously they associate for their lawless purposes, ... the strong arm of the law will always be found superior to their utmost efforts'.[27]

For unknown reasons, the lord lieutenant commuted Joseph Madden's death sentence to transportation for life, but on 6 September 1816 John Magill and John Doe were hanged, on Belfast's High Street, in an 'awful spectacle' designed to 'display the power and the terror of the law in the most impressive manner'. Whether to overawe the 'immense multitude of spectators' or to prevent expressions of sympathy (or rescue attempts) by the crowds, a 'strong military guard' escorted the prisoners from Carrickfergus jail to Belfast, where they joined yet another 'strong detachment of military, both horse

---

27 Magill, Doe, Madden, Dickson, and Park were not the only prisoners tried and sentenced at the Antrim assizes on 12 August 1816. Dominick M'Ilhatton and William Eggleston were sentenced to be hanged for breaking into a farmer's house; Michael M'Anally, Patrick M'Kenna, and Peter Doran were condemned to transportation for life for robbing bleach-greens (another common crime against Ulster's manufacturing and mercantile interests); and Owen Donnelly was sentenced to transportation for seven years for stealing a hat.

Interestingly, most of these 'ordinary criminals' had traditionally 'Catholic' names, although they resided in a county (Antrim) that was overwhelmingly Protestant (and Presbyterian), whereas the 'victims' of their crimes were Protestants, principally manufacturers and merchants — and at least two of them, John Sinclair and Colonel Foster Coulson, were members of the 'Committee of twenty-one Gentlemen' who had organized the apprehension of Francis Johnson's assailants. Thus, although this essay argues for the existence at this time of something resembling 'class war' within east Ulster's Protestant community — as evidenced in part by the language employed by the judge, the prosecution, and the BNL in the 'Belfast's first bomb' episode — clearly an alternative pattern already existed whereby 'serious' criminal behaviour, punishable by death or transportation, could 'normally' or 'naturally' be attributed to Catholics. For an example of contemporary popular convictions that Ulster Protestants, especially Presbyterians, rarely committed major or violent crimes, see John Gamble, Views of Society and Manners in the North of Ireland, in a Series of Letters Written in the Year 1818 (London, 1819), 326, 366–67. By mid-century, this folk belief had become an integral feature of unionist ideology, fundamental to the conviction that 'the Protestant way of life' was superior to that of Irish Catholics; e.g., see D. George Boyce, 'The Making of Unionism', in Boyce and Alan O'Day, eds., Defenders of the Union: A Survey of British and Irish Unionism since 1801 (London, 2001), 23; and Catherine Hirst, Religion, Politics and Violence in Nineteenth-Century Belfast: The Pound and Sandy Row (Dublin, 2002), 27–28, 32, 36.

and foot', from the city's army barracks. At least four clergymen were present at the hangings, before which the condemned men prayed and made speeches (designed for publication) of confession and repentance. Both prisoners played the contrite and pious roles expected in such rituals, albeit in quite different ways. John Doe, a member of an evangelical sect, attributed his transgressions solely to personal, moral failings: to his 'cohabitation' with 'a woman of bad character', by whose influence he was 'cut off from the Church' and led 'step [by] step' to 'the awful deserved chastenings of the Lord'. By contrast, John Magill addressed the socio-political issues involved and expressed sorrow that he had 'acted under the influence of mistaken views'. 'I now see the evil of all such combinations and outrages', he concluded, 'I see I have offended God, dishonoured religion, and injured society, for which I am sincerely sorry'. After Magill's presentation, the prisoners were 'launched into eternity', meeting their deaths with 'manly fortitude' and 'calm resignation', each leaving 'a wife and child to lament their untimely fate'.[28]

Thus was smashed what the *Belfast News-Letter* later called 'a system of combination which threatened to subvert the very basis of every principle of commercial good order'.[29] Yet in truth, commerce and industry in early nineteenth-century Belfast and in Ulster, generally, were scarcely in 'good order'. Indeed, the assault on Johnson's house and business premises can be understood only in the contexts of the profound economic dislocations and often severe distress that afflicted northern Irish society in the decades following the Act of Union.

Between 1782 and 1800 Belfast's population had increased from about 13,000 to 22,000, and by 1831 it rose to more than 53,000, as men and women from rural Ulster migrated to the city or its hinterland to work as handloom weavers or as spinners in cotton factories and, increasingly after 1830, in linen mills. In 1800, according to the Rev. John Dubourdieu, the cotton industry employed about 13,500 people in Belfast alone, plus another 27,000 within ten miles of the city. However, economic growth was unsteady and its rewards were distributed very unevenly. The American Non-Importation and Embargo Acts of 1806 and 1807, respectively, followed in 1812 by the outbreak of the Anglo-American War, cut off Belfast's cotton supplies and caused bankruptcies and unemployment. In 1815 the return of peace precipitated a depression in the textile industry, the effects of which on the labouring poor, in town and country alike, were exacerbated by poor harvests, rising food and fuel prices, outbreaks of typhus, and the return to the labour market of thousands of demobilized soldiers and sailors. In the following year (when Belfast's weavers attacked Johnson's home) the city's poor were ravaged by starvation and fever, falling wages and rising unemployment, responding with food riots and a wave of 'normal' crimes against property. In the mid-1820s the economic situation again deteriorated sharply, as severe industrial depression throughout the United Kingdom

---

28 A week after their comrades' executions, Park and Dickson endured their public floggings. Park received 314 lashes, Dickson 269; both fainted during their ordeals, after which they were returned to Carrickfergus jail to serve their eighteen-month sentences; see Boyd, *Rise of the Irish Trade Unions*, 32.

29 BNL, 2 January 1818.

coincided with parliament's withdrawal of tariff protection for Irish cotton goods. By the early 1830s Ulster's cotton industry had been eclipsed by linen manufacturing, but although the latter expanded rapidly, most of its new factories and economic advantages were concentrated in the province's eastern corner. Beyond the vicinity of Belfast and a few other east Ulster towns, cottage wages and industries collapsed. Rural spinners could not compete with cheap, factory-spun thread, and country weavers could rarely survive far from eastern supplies of yarn and the industry's principal markets. Social conditions among the North's rural poor markedly deteriorated.[30]

Moreover, according to many contemporaries, living standards among weavers in Belfast and other towns also declined sharply. In 1802 a visitor to Belfast reported that its cotton weavers earned at least 18 shillings per week, but their wages had begun to decline before 1815, and by the mid-1820s, when one-third of the city's weavers were unemployed, wages had fallen to merely 7 shillings per week. In 1827 William Ritchie, when petitioning the British government on behalf of 200 Belfast-area weavers desperate to emigrate, described a house-to-house survey, which revealed that 'three fourths of the operative weavers' had weekly wages of only 2 to 4 shillings, while the remainder earned merely 4 to 5 shillings. 'We have no prospect in future of ever paying our rents,' Ritchie lamented; hence, '[we] are completely in the power of our Landlords, who can at pleasure take from us our little all. It is with the greatest difficulty [even] the best workmen can procure subsistence for their families, and we could produce instances of those who have lately died here in a state of starvation.'

Considerable testimony suggests that conditions for east Ulster's weavers improved little, if any, during the following decade — despite the rapid shift from cotton to linen manufacturing and the latter's much-vaunted 'prosperity'. In the early 1830s the *Belfast News-Letter* reported that the weavers in Ballymacarrett were obliged to eat 'oatmeal unfit for cattle' and were 'reduced to skeletons from overwork and lack of sleep'. In 1838 local weaver James Boyd claimed that he and his peers laboured daily from fourteen to eighteen hours for as little as 3s. 6d. per week, while others testified that Belfast's

---

30 On Belfast's population, see Benn, *History of the Town of Belfast*, vol. 1, 300, and vol. 2, 82. For contemporary accounts of the Ulster cotton and linen industries, see: Rev. John Dubourdieu, *Statistical Survey of the County of Antrim* ... (Dublin, 1812), 389–411 (1800 employment data on p. 404), and *Statistical Survey of the County of Down* ... (Dublin, 1802), 235–36; Gamble, *Views of Society and Manners in the North of Ireland*, 415–16; H. D. Inglis, *Ireland in 1834: A Journey throughout Ireland, during the Spring, Summer, and Autumn of 1834*, 2 vols. (London, 1835), vol. 2, 224–63 passim; and Edward Wakefield, *An Account of Ireland, Statistical and Political*, 2 vols. (London, 1812), vol. 1, 680–708. See also the secondary sources cited in n. 31 below.

On the Belfast food riots of 1816, see Boyd, *Rise of the Irish Trade Unions*, 31. The cost-of-living indexes compiled by Professor Liam Kennedy of Queen's University, Belfast, indicate steeply rising prices for oatmeal, potatoes, and other necessities in 1816–17; thereafter prices generally declined but rose sharply again in 1824–27, 1831–32, and 1837–42; my thanks to Professor Kennedy for sharing this data.

In the early nineteenth century, many of the thousands of Irish petitions sent to the British Colonial Office, begging for assisted emigration, were written by or on behalf of demobilized soldiers and sailors, now landless and unemployed, who had served in the British forces during the French Revolutionary and/or Napoleonic Wars (see below, n. 31).

working-class neighbourhoods were 'a mass of filth and misery'. In 1840 Caesar Otway contended that the 'physical condition of [Ulster's] weavers' was 'worse ... than that of any [other] class of Irishmen'. Throughout the pre-Famine decades, British officials were besieged by similar reports — not only from Belfast but also from Ballymena, Moy, Newry, Rathfriland, and other towns in east and mid-Ulster, as well as from places such as Dunnamanagh and Ballyshannon in south and west Ulster — penned by weavers who complained that low wages and uncertain employment rendered it nearly 'impossible [for them] to make a living'.[31]

One would expect that such severe distress might engender conflicts between Ulster's Protestant weavers and their employers — as well as among Protestant landlords, tenants, subtenants, and labourers, generally — and, indeed, examples of such strife had been common at least since the Oakboy and Steelboy uprisings of the 1760s and early 1770s. In the 1780s poor northern Protestants' affiliations with the violent activities of the Peep of Day Boys and, in the 1790s, of the United Irishmen and the Loyal Orange Order also had stemmed, at least in part, from economic anxieties. In the same decades, struggles between Belfast's cotton weavers and their employers appear to have been particularly

---

31 Bardon, *History of Ulster*, 259–60; Beckett and Glasscock, *Belfast*, 82–87; Boyd, *Rise of the Irish Trade Unions*, 24–25; Boyle, *Irish Labor Movement*, 28; F. Geary, 'The Rise and Fall of the Belfast Cotton Industry: Some Problems', *Irish Economic and Social History*, 8 (1981), 30–49; Green, *Lagan Valley*, 100–02; Maguire, *Belfast*, 31; and, more broadly, Liam Kennedy and Philip Ollerenshaw, eds., *An Economic History of Ulster, 1820–1939* (Manchester, 1985), chs. 1–2; and Eoin O'Malley, 'The Decline of Irish Industry in the Nineteenth Century', *Economic and Social Review*, 13, 1 (October 1981), 30–32.

   W. P. Ryan, *The Irish Labour Movement* (Dublin, 1919), 78–111, contains much testimony by and about weavers in Belfast and elsewhere in Ulster during the 1830s; much of this qualifies H. D. Inglis's highly favourable impressions in 1834, but even he acknowledged that, over the previous fifteen years, the condition of rural weavers and spinners had deteriorated; see Inglis, *Ireland in 1834*, vol. 2, 220. The best general work on the North's linen weavers is W. H. Crawford, *The Handloom Weavers and the Ulster Linen Industry* (Belfast, 1994). An excellent local study of socio-economic changes in Belfast's western hinterland is Marilyn Cohen, *Linen, Family and Community in Tullylish, County Down, 1690–1914* (Dublin, 1997), which includes Cæsar Otway's observation on p. 75; Cohen notes (83–84) the weavers' testimony that their conditions were worse when they were employed by manufacturers — i.e., on the putting-out system and/or in weaving shops, as were Francis Johnson's assailants — than when they worked independently. (By the time of the Great Famine, however, this situation was reversed; see n. 71 below.)

   A unique primary source of testimony about socio-economic conditions in Ulster (and elsewhere in Ireland) is the 384 series of Colonial Office (CO) Papers, vols. 1–75, in PRO, London, which contains thousands of letters written by (or on behalf of) weavers, farmers, and others who, between 1817 and the mid-1840s, petitioned the British government for information about, assisted passages to, and/or land grants in British North America (primarily in Upper Canada — now Ontario). Quoted in this and the preceding paragraph are the petitions of weavers William Ritchie, *et al.*, Belfast, 13 April 1827 (CO 384/14), and of John Tovil, Kinnary, near Moy, County Tyrone, 16 April 1842 (CO 384/69). Similar weavers' petitions include: John Shaw, Belfast, 17 January 1817 (CO 384/1); James Smily, *et al.*, Bracky, County Armagh, n.d. [recd. 19 August 1823] (CO 384/9); John Burton, Cookstown, County Tyrone, 13 April 1827, and David Kennedy, Clough, County Down, 21 June 1827 (CO 384/16); J. Beatty, Rathfriland, County Down, 28 March 1831 (CO 384/24); Hugh McComb, Newry, County Down, 6 January 1831, and Daniel Lunney, Dunnamanagh, County Tyrone, 18 March 1831 (CO 384/25); Robert Ritchey, Galgorm, Ballymena, County Antrim, 13 May 1833 (CO 384/31); and John Moore, Belfast, 6 August 1842 (CO 384/69).

intense, provoking condemnation from Presbyterian businessmen and editors of all political persuasions. After the Act of Union, the unsettling processes and inequitable results of industrialization (including the de-industrialization of most of Ulster's countryside) generated among the North's poor — especially among proletarianized weavers in and around Belfast — new waves of anger, organization, protest, and reprisal against perceived exploitation. As early as 1802–04 the *Belfast News-Letter* expressed mounting concern about renewed trade unionism among the city's workers — 'How would trade go on or the town improve,' asked the paper's editor, 'if such actions were permitted?' — and applauded the trials and punishments of workers who combined and went on strike for higher pay. Yet in 1811 cotton weavers in Lisburn, a principal manufacturing town near Belfast, formed another union and destroyed the webs and looms of those who would not work for what its members deemed 'fair wages'. In March 1815 a 'mob of apprentice lads' rioted in Belfast against rising food costs, and in April a march on the city by Lisburn's weavers, protesting wage reductions, ended in tumult and bloodshed when police tried to arrest their leaders.[32]

Thus, in 1816 the north Down weavers' attack on Francis Johnson's house was only one of the most dramatic examples of contemporary class conflict. Indeed, the execution of Johnson's assailants seems to have had no immediate effects. Throughout 1816 the *News-Letter* continued to bewail the 'outrages' — rivalling in frequency and severity those in proverbially 'disturbed' Catholic Munster — committed largely by Presbyterian weavers and other poor Protestants on the persons, livestock, homes, and businesses of east Ulster's landlords, agents, bailiffs, strong farmers, and manufacturers.

On 5 August 1816, for instance, the *News-Letter* lamented the numerous 'outrages' that recently had 'disgraced' the neighbourhood of Ballynahinch, County Down, in the parish of Magheradroll (roughly three-fourths of whose inhabitants were Protestants — of whom the same proportion were Presbyterians).[33] During the winter and spring, 'property to a very considerable amount, consisting of dwelling-houses and offices, a bleach-mill, a flaxmill, a corn-mill, and kilns, [had] been destroyed by fire', in addition to 'cattle shot and mutilated — notices posted up, threatening death and destruction to individuals if they took certain farms, or went beyond a certain rent for their lands — houses attacked and fired into'. As late as July, 'notices were posted, ... calling for a reduction of rents, and breathing vengeance against several individuals'. The same issue of the *News-Letter* also reported the County Antrim grand jury's 'great concern ... at finding [before it] a list of so many unprecedented and atrocious crimes, ... written in characters of blood', that had been committed in that overwhelmingly Protestant and

---

32 Benn, *History of the Town of Belfast*, vol. 2, 22, 36, 47; Boyd, *Rise of the Irish Trade Unions*, 23–32; Boyle, *Irish Labor Movement*, 15–16; Green, *Lagan Valley*, 101; McDowell, *Public Opinion and Government Policy*, 62; and Hirst, *Religion, Politics and Violence in Nineteenth-Century Belfast*, 26–27.

33 In 1831 nearly 72 per cent of the inhabitants of Magheradroll (or Magheradrool) parish were Protestants; of the latter, almost 73 per cent were Presbyterians. See above, n. 3, for the source of 1831 religious census data.

allegedly law-abiding county. In response, Judge Day 'emphatically' asked the grand jury's members whether the local gentry were prepared to allow Antrim to 'become the Tipperary of the North'.[34]

Judge Day's analogy was suggestive, for the minds of élite Irish Protestants and British officials could easily associate Ulster's class conflicts with much wider and more profound threats to law and order. The upper- and middle-class British and Irish Protestant rhetoric of class was virtually identical to that of anti-Catholicism, as both 'papists' and the poor were stigmatized as lazy, immoral, and dangerous. Revealingly, the term 'combinations' signified not only the largely or exclusively Protestant trade unions in Belfast and Dublin, but also the equally illegal Whiteboys and the other Catholic secret agrarian societies that 'terrorized' Tipperary and other counties in southern Ireland. Members of both organizations challenged capitalist relations — for instance, the Thrashers of County Mayo tried to regulate weavers' wages as well as rents — hence, George Cornewall Lewis's characterization of the Whiteboys as 'a vast trades union for the protection of the Irish peasantry'. And in varying degrees both were suspected, by Dublin Castle and affluent Irish Protestants alike, of harbouring subversive political ideas and intentions. It was feared, for instance, that Belfast's weavers had been radicalized by the ideals of the French Revolution, spread by the writings of Thomas Paine and the activities of the United Irishmen, and the city's historian John Gray even speculates that old ideological links between radical politics and the weavers' combinations might have informed their violent activities in 1816 — or at least inspired the government's savage repression. In that light, moreover, alarmed officials could regard such assaults on property not only as implicit threats to the Union — still insecure after only fifteen years — but also as part of a broader, 'Jacobinical' pattern of escalating labour unrest and demands for sweeping political reform that, in the immediate post-war years, quite explicitly threatened the social and political order in Great Britain itself. Thus, the treatment of the Belfast weavers accused of destroying their employer's house must be viewed in light of the government's 'deliberate policy of enforcing exemplary punishments' to quell lower-class 'outrages' and political dissent on both sides of the Irish Sea.[35]

---

34 BNL, 5 August 1816 (the Antrim grand jury met on 3 August); additional reports of crimes and 'outrages' appear in later issues, for instance in that of 6 September 1816. James G. Patterson has noted the continuance in east Ulster of rural violence, perpetrated by disaffected Presbyterians, in the years after the 1798 rebellion; however, his study ends with Robert Emmet and Thomas Russell's abortive rising in 1803, whereas the evidence presented here indicates that certain kinds of unrest either persisted well into the first two decades of the nineteenth century or at least resurged after the Napoleonic Wars. See James G. Patterson, 'Continued Presbyterian Resistance in the Aftermath of the Rebellion of 1798 in Antrim and Down', *Eighteenth Century Life*, 22, 3 (November 1998), 45–61.

35 On the rhetoric of class in early and mid-nineteenth-century Ireland and Britain, see Margaret Preston, 'Discourse and Hegemony: Race and Class in the Language of Charity in Nineteenth-Century Dublin', in Tadhg Foley and Seán Ryder, eds., *Ideology and Ireland in the Nineteenth Century* (Dublin, 1998), 101–02. On secret agrarian societies, generally, and their similarities to workers' combinations, see: George Cornewall Lewis, *Local Disturbances in Ireland* (London, 1836; repr. Cork, 1977); Kerby A. Miller, *Emigrants*

In Britain, workers' unrest and political protests would continue to mount through the 1840s. In Belfast, however, the cotton weavers' combination collapsed in the 1820s, and wages fell so low that Scottish manufacturers began sending cotton yarn to be woven there, rather than in Glasgow or Paisley, both to reduce labour costs and to break the Scottish weavers' unions. Occasional strikes by cabinetmakers, printers, and others still occurred in the next decade.[36] But by the 1830s, evidence of serious or violent social conflict among Protestants in Belfast and elsewhere in Ulster seems to have virtually disappeared — along with any lingering suspicions of the Protestant lower classes' fidelity to the Union and the Crown. The mass actions that had marked the Oakboys' and Steelboys' agitations in the east Ulster countryside never recurred, for example, and in 1837 Jonathan Binns, a member of the recent parliamentary Poor Law Inquiry Commission, described class relationships among rural Protestants in east Ulster as entirely quiescent, despite the extreme competition for land and leases. In Belfast, James Campbell, a local manufacturer, testified in 1838 that weavers' combinations had been extinct for more than a decade; ever since 1825, Campbell reported, 'labour [was] perfectly free' — that is, non-unionized — in the city's textile industries, and he rejoiced that, even when faced with wage cuts, his workers' behaviour was 'very respectful and proper'. In the same period a Belfast weaver, also testifying before a parliamentary committee, pleaded that the government maintain low Irish wages in order to afford 'protection and encouragement to capital'. Likewise, although in Belfast and elsewhere in Ulster the franchise (especially after 1829) was extremely restricted, and political power monopolized by a wealthy few, the 1830s witnessed in Protestant Ulster no workers' movement for equal rights that was remotely comparable to the Irish-led Chartist agitation in Britain itself.[37]

and Exiles: Ireland and Irish Emigration to North America (New York, 1985), 61–67; and George O'Brien, The Economic History of Ireland from the Union to the Famine (London, 1921; repr. Clifton, NJ, 1972), 398. On the radicalism of Belfast's weavers, see John Gray, The Sans Culottes of Belfast: The United Irishmen and the Men of No Property (Belfast, 1998), 29–38; and, generally, Jim Smyth, The Men of No Property: Irish Radicals and Popular Politics in the Late Eighteenth Century (Dublin, 1992). On contemporary labour and political unrest in Britain, and the official panic and repression produced thereby, the classic work is E. P. Thompson, The Making of the English Working Class (New York, 1963); while the official responses in London and Dublin are detailed in Brian Jenkins, Era of Emancipation: British Government of Ireland, 1812–1830 (Kingston and Montreal, 1988), e.g., 123–25; and in Stanley H. Palmer, Police and Protest in England and Ireland, 1780–1850 (Cambridge, 1988). Jenkins notes (68) that, in the language of Robert Peel and his Tory associates in Dublin Castle, 'illegal combinations' also included the upper- and middle-class Catholic associations that campaigned for emancipation.

36 Gray, Sans Cullottes of Belfast, 37–38; Boyd, Rise of the Irish Trades Unions, 29, 40–43; McDowell, Public Opinion and Government Policy, 62–63.

37 Jonathan Binns, The Miseries and Beauties of Ireland, 2 vols. (London, 1837), vol. 1, 54 and passim; Boyle, Irish Labor Movement, 26–27; E. Strauss, Irish Nationalism and British Democracy (London, 1951; repr. Westport, Conn., 1975), 76. On politics in early nineteenth-century Ulster, see Peter Jupp, 'County Down Elections, 1783–1831', Irish Historical Studies, 28, 70 (September 1972), 177–206; Brian Walker, 'Landowners and Parliamentary Elections in County Down, 1801–1921', in Lindsay Proudfoot, ed., Down: History & Society (Dublin, 1997), 297–307; and especially Frank Wright, Two Lands on One Soil: Ulster Politics before Home Rule

Of course, there were still complaints that workers' *attitudes* often remained less than fully satisfactory. As late as 1833, for instance, the co-owner of Belfast's enormous York Street Mill lamented that many of his workers, often recent migrants from the Ulster countryside, were 'as yet scarcely accustomed' to the demands of the new 'factory system'. However, it was precisely during this period that middle-class visitors to Belfast and to east Ulster, generally, became lavish in their praise for the 'industriousness' and 'steadiness' exhibited by the city's and the region's inhabitants. Significantly, observers, native as well as foreign, almost invariably associated this 'spirit of commercial enterprise' with Protestantism, the benign effects of the Act of Union, and other equally salutary 'British' influences. Thus, in 1834 H. D. Inglis reported that, because of its 'Scottish' character, the North had 'nothing in common with the rest of Ireland', and in 1843 the Halls concluded that Belfast was full of 'English virtues — "so much bustle, such an aspect of business, a total absence of all suspicion of [that] idleness"' — 'improvidence' and 'insubordination', as other observers decried — that allegedly characterized the Catholic populace of southern Ireland.[38]

Such testimony suggests that it was these pre-Famine decades that witnessed the emergence and elaboration of what unionists often called 'the Protestant way of life': a complex of pious, loyal, and resolutely bourgeois norms that became the touchstone of modern Ulster Protestant identity and of Ulster unionist political culture. In this now familiar formula, Protestant religion, British ethnicity, loyalty to the Crown, obedience to the laws, respect for property, sturdy self-reliance, and steady, sober, industrious behaviour were allegedly inextricable. Protestantism, unionism, and respectability, in short, were supposedly synonymous. Thus, by 1854 a Protestant missionary in Belfast naturally equated 'respectable' behaviour with Protestantism and found it difficult to believe that the people he encountered in Sandy Row, who did not behave 'respectably', could possibly be Protestants.[39]

Yet how and why had this remarkable transformation supposedly occurred? How had Ulster's turbulent Protestant underclass allegedly been transformed into exemplars of industry and deference? Put another way, how had Protestant Ulster's upper and middle classes, so beleaguered in the early 1800s, succeeded in forging a sense of pan-Protestant identity and community, characterized by unionist verities and capitalist values, that ideally transcended social and denominational divisions? To what degree was the

(New York, 1996), chs. 2–3; and on the Irish role in British Chartism, see Dorothy Thompson, *Outsiders: Class, Gender and Nation* (London, 1993), ch. 4.

38 Cormac Ó Gráda, *Ireland: A New Economic History, 1780–1939* (Oxford, 1994), 329; Inglis, *Ireland in 1834*, vol. 2, 217–18, 249–51; Maguire, *Belfast*, 33. As early as 1825 the conservative *Belfast News-Letter* claimed that the city's mechanics were much more interested in scientists and inventors such as Newton, Boyle, and Arkwright than in martyred United Irishmen like Emmet, Russell, and Tone; McDowell, *Public Opinion and Government Policy in Ireland*, 58–59.

39 The phrase became ubiquitous in unionist rhetoric; see Charles Townshend, *Ireland: The Twentieth Century* (London, 1998), 58. A useful summary of unionist ideology is in Boyce, 'The Making of Unionism', 23. Hirst, *Religion, Politics and Violence in Nineteenth-Century Belfast*, 36.

alleged transformation reflective of an altered reality? Was 'the Protestant way of life' merely a bourgeois aspiration, itself rooted in Protestant Ulster's class relationships, which obscured as much as it revealed? Why and how did it become a communal badge, integral to Ulster Protestants' cultural and political identity?

Unionist spokesmen often argued that the industry, sobriety, and loyalty they attributed to Ulster Protestants were virtually primordial — inherent in their religion and British heritage. In the late eighteenth century, however, observers had been hard-pressed to discover anything resembling a 'Protestant ethic' at work among the great majority of the North's tenants, craftsmen, and labourers. In 1776–79, for example, Arthur Young, an enthusiast for capitalist development, complained that the Protestant small farmers and weavers in and around the east Ulster towns of Antrim, Hillsborough, Lurgan, Newry, and Warrenspoint were 'in general apt to be licentious and disorderly'. Despite the consequent 'misery and inconvenience', they subdivided their smallholdings, repeatedly and 'universally', to enable their sons to marry young. Moreover, they refused to 'work more than half what they might do, owing to the cheapness of provisions making them idle, as they think of nothing more than the present necessity'. '[W]hen meal is cheap, they will not work', but instead they 'spend much of their time in whiskey houses' or hunting hares; 'a pack of hounds is never heard,' Young lamented, 'but all the weavers leave their looms, and away they go after them by hundreds'. In the early decades of the nineteenth century, both foreign and native observers continued to make similar remarks. In 1810 John Gamble, a Presbyterian from Strabane, County Tyrone, bemoaned the notorious uncleanliness of his co-religionists' bodies, homes, clothes, and eating and cooking utensils, and two years later Edward Wakefield noted that northern Presbyterians were as fond of holidays and whiskey, and as averse to the law, as their Catholic neighbours. As noted above, even in the 1830s some middle-class observers commented that Belfast's weavers often still entertained 'erroneous opinions of the relations of employers and labourers, of masters and servants'.[40]

Also, during the late 1700s landlords and officials had complained incessantly about the rampant 'insubordination' and 'disloyalty' among east Ulster's Protestants — especially among its Presbyterians — and with good reason: in the 1760s and early 1770s, the Oakboys and the Steelboys were predominantly Presbyterians, and in the 1790s the United Irishmen were more thoroughly organized in north Down, the Route, and in other disproportionately Protestant and Presbyterian parts of east Ulster than anywhere else in Ireland. And, again, well into the early 1800s observers such as Wakefield and Gamble (the latter now in 1818) remarked on Ulster Presbyterians' continued alienation from — even marked hostility to — their landlords, the Church of Ireland, and the laws. Indeed, in 1812 Wakefield alleged that northern Dissenters remained

40 Arthur W. Hutton, ed., *Arthur Young's Tour in Ireland (1776–1779)*, 2 vols. (London, 1892), vol. 1, 120, 127, 130–34, 150–51; John Gamble, *Sketches of History, Politics, and Manners, in Dublin, and the North of Ireland, in 1810*, 2nd edn. (London, 1826), 262–63; Wakefield, *An Account of Ireland*, vol. 2, 739–40; Hirst, *Religion, Politics and Violence in Nineteenth-Century Belfast*, 28.

'Republicans in principle ... [and] in their hearts decided enemies to the established government'. Thus, the historian Ian McBride concludes that, for some time after the Act of Union, Ulster 'Presbyterian political attitudes remained almost instinctively anti-government in character'.[41]

Of course, for unionist spokesmen, such as the Rev. Henry Cooke, Presbyterian champion of religious orthodoxy and political loyalism, by the 1830s and after it was Belfast's and east Ulster's celebrated economic growth that largely explained their Protestant inhabitants' growing contentment with both the Union and élite rule, and their all-class unity in the face of Catholic nationalist agitation. But as we have seen, the North's prosperity was by no means widespread, even among Protestants. Another explanation for Protestant workers' apparent docility was put forth by Alexander Moncrieffe, a Belfast manufacturer, who in 1838 testified before a parliamentary commission that 'Catholic and Orange rivalries made trade unionism impossible and ensured a supply of cheap labour'.[42] Yet Moncrieffe's explanation was too simple and superficial. It reflected an assumption that lower-class Protestant–Catholic animosities were, if not primordial and inevitable, at least always sufficient in *themselves* to mitigate intracommunal class conflict and to ensure that poor Protestants would defer to the leadership and embrace the capitalist values of their wealthier co-religionists.

The processes by which Ulster's Protestant élites achieved socio-cultural and political hegemony over the Protestant poor were in fact much more complex than either Cooke's or Moncrieffe's explanation implied. Rather, it is arguable that the construction of the 'Ulster unionist community', united in defence of 'the Protestant way of life', had many of its most important origins neither in shared Protestant prosperity nor in Protestant-Catholic strife (local or national), but instead in the upper- and middle-class resolutions of the class struggle revealed by the violent incident described in William Coyne's 1816 letter.

For example, in the early 1800s it was by no means certain that Ulster's predominantly Anglican upper class and its largely Presbyterian middle classes (themselves bitterly divided over contemporary political and religious issues, including the United Irishmen's legacy) could join to present a united front to their own subtenants and labourers.[43]

41 On the United Irishmen in east Ulster, see Nancy J. Curtin, 'Rebels and Radicals: The United Irishmen in County Down', in Proudfoot, ed., *Down: History & Society*, 267–96; Curtin, *The United Irishmen*; *Popular Politics in Ulster and Dublin, 1791–1798* (Oxford, 1994); and A. T. Q. Stewart, *The Summer Soldiers: The 1798 Rebellion in Antrim and Down* (Belfast, 1995). Wakefield, *An Account of Ireland*, vol. 2, 546–47 (I am grateful to Professor David W. Miller of Carnegie Mellon University for this reference); Gamble, *Views of Society and Manners in the North of Ireland*, 87, 191, 197–98, 211–12, 367–69; and McBride, 'Ulster Presbyterians and the Passing of the Act of Union', 75.

42 Boyle, *Irish Labor Movement*, 28–29; Moncrieffe's statement is also summarized in Boyd, *Rise of the Irish Trade Unions*, 25, and in Ryan, *Irish Labour Movement*, 84.

43 Significantly, the BNL's campaign against east Ulster's lower-class Protestant combinations occurred simultaneously with a movement (orchestrated by the Cabinet and Dublin Castle, but spearheaded by local Presbyterian conservatives) to purge the city's Academical Institute of faculty and students who allegedly harboured 'disloyal' and 'heretical' opinions; e.g., see the issue of 7 May 1816. On this controversy,

Yet in the aftermath of the weavers' assault on Francis Johnson's home, Belfast's and east Ulster's gentry, magistrates, merchants, and manufacturers — Anglicans and Presbyterians, Tories and Whigs — united as 'Gentlemen' and mobilized their considerable resources against the workers' threat to property and order. This was not an isolated instance of such convergence. Given the prevalence of lower-class unrest and violence in the early 1800s, the mobilization of élite opinion, if not overt power, concerning class issues must have become semi-permanent and self-perpetuating, creating common interests and sympathies that could transcend other differences.[44]

Equally important is that after 1800 a re-formed Ulster Protestant élite could no longer rely solely, or even primarily, on its *own* legal and military resources to confront lower-class insubordination. Whereas in 1792 Belfast's gentry and businessmen had relied on the city's own Volunteers to suppress workers' combinations — and even to evict a defiant tenant who lived twenty miles from town — after the Union both statutory power and its ultimate enforcement were now centred in London and Dublin Castle. Of course, Ulster Protestant landlords and magistrates often chafed at British reforms that, by professionalizing the Irish legal and policing systems, reduced their autonomy and increased their dependence on British authority. In the crisis of the early 1800s, however, when it appeared that 'commercial good order' teetered on the brink of collapse, their own spokesmen cried out for strong, effective action that could emanate only from Westminster and Dublin. Thus, in late 1816 the *Belfast News-Letter*'s exasperated editor announced that, since 'declarations, resolutions, and subscriptions have been tried and found unavailing[, new] energy must be infused, [new] measures must be matured and acted upon to reclaim the misguided multitude'. If landlords and manufacturers could not convince their tenants and workers by traditional means of 'the illegality of their proceedings, ... stronger [methods] will have to be resorted to'; for otherwise, he warned, 'the turbulent [will only] become more audacious'.[45]

In short, Ulster's Protestant upper and middle classes were obliged not only to unite but also to rely heavily on the coercive mechanisms of the post-Union British state to

---

see Peter Brooke, *Ulster Presbyterians: The Historical Perspective, 1610–1970* (Dublin, 1987), 137–45; and Finlay Holmes, *Henry Cooke* (Belfast, 1981), 14–15.

44 BNL, 1 March 1816. Mary McNeill's *The Life and Times of Mary Ann McCracken, 1770–1866: A Belfast Panorama* (Dublin, 1960) is particularly revealing of such convergence. Although Henry Joy McCracken, the executed leader of the United Irish rebels in Antrim, lamented that 'the rich always betray the poor', after the rebellion his own brothers, prosperous cotton manufacturers, were quick to join his former political foes in condemning Belfast workers' illegal combinations; see 241–44.

45 Gray, *Sans Cullottes of Belfast*, 15–17, 21–22. BNL, 5 August 1816. In 1816 the BNL also lobbied intensively for the creation of a more effective police force in Belfast; e.g., the issue of 6 September; in the same year the British parliament responded with a Police Act that increased the authority of the city's police commissioners. On the period's police and magisterial reforms, and élite Irish opposition to them, see Jenkins, *Era of Emancipation*, and Palmer, *Police and Protest in England and Ireland*; also useful are the early sections of Brian Griffin, *The Bulkies: Police and Crime in Belfast, 1800–1865* (Dublin, 1997); and Virginia Crossman's *Local Government in Nineteenth-Century Ireland* (Belfast, 1994), and *Politics, Law and Order in Nineteenth-Century Ireland* (New York, 1996).

regain authority over their refractory inferiors. In the process, they inevitably developed a community of interest both among each other and with the Union that was now their first and last reliance in their efforts to tame the nocturnal armies of 'idle vagabonds' who assailed them.[46] After all, the Union not only protected Irish Protestants, generally, by submerging Ireland's Catholics in a British Protestant majority, it also protected propertied Irish Protestants against Protestant 'men of no property' by merging the interests of the smaller, weaker, and more vulnerable Irish élite with those of Britain's ruling classes — then perhaps the most dynamic and powerful in the world.

In 1817 the old Belfast Presbyterian liberal Henry Joy expressed the conviction of most propertied Protestants that the Union was their best and only security. In return, for example, the historian Peter Jupp has noted the 'slavish support' that Irish MPs gave the British government in 1800–20, and the works of Brian Jenkins illustrate numerous instances of élite Irish dependence, ranging from patronage to economic policies. Among the latter, and of special relevance to the issues discussed in this chapter, are Irish Chief Secretary Robert Peel's successful efforts, in 1812, to persuade the Cabinet to veto the Board of Trade's proposal to remove the tariff on foreign linen goods, as well as his support for the Corn Laws, enacted (1815) in part at Irish landlords' behest. Equally notable is visitor H. D. Inglis's vague but tantalizing reference in 1834 to 'the peculiar favour and protection which the north of Ireland has enjoyed from the [British] state'. Of course, British support for the Irish landlord and commercial élites was designed primarily to serve imperial interests, and both Peel and his successor in Dublin Castle, Henry Goulbourn, believed that the Union could best be maintained by keeping Ireland's Protestants and Catholics divided — 'I hope they will always be disunited,' Peel wrote, and the 'great art is to keep them so ...' — a strategy that ensured both Protestant dependence on British power and what scholar Frank Wright calls 'reactionary dominance throughout the nation', including 'the metropolis itself'. In the eyes of propertied Protestants, the internal and external, the social and political, projects were inseparable, since a 'valuable employee' was regarded per se as 'a more loyal subject to the British Empire'.[47]

Thus, unlike Ireland's propertied Catholics, who felt alienated and betrayed when denied their promised emancipation for three decades after 1800, their Protestant peers soon enjoyed every reason to be loyal to a British government that long proved able, in Ireland and Britain alike, to protect essential upper-class privileges, to placate middle-class (Protestant) demands, and to suppress or neutralize lower-class challenges.

---

46 BNL, 6 September 1816.

47 McBride, 'Memory and Forgetting: Ulster Presbyterians and 1798', 485–86; P. J. Jupp, 'Irish M.P.s at Westminster in the Early Nineteenth Century', in *Historical Studies VII* (London, 1969), 73; Jenkins, *Era of Emancipation*, and 'The Chief Secretary', in Boyce and O'Day, eds., *Defenders of the Union*, 49, 55; Inglis, *Ireland in 1834*, vol. 2, 218; on Castle officialdom and patronage, also see Edward Brynn, *Crown and Castle: British Rule in Ireland, 1800–1830* (Dublin, 1978), e.g., 80, 119; Wright, *Two Lands on One Soil*, 53; Preston, 'Discourse and Hegemony', 108.

For seventy years after the Act of Union, Westminster denied Ulster farmers' every plea for the legalization of tenant-right, passing instead a series of laws that facilitated evictions, forbade tenants' subdivision of their farms, and in other ways augmented landlords' authority over the occupants of their estates. Ulster's manufacturers were no doubt equally gratified, as in 1803, for example, when parliament legislated for Ireland a special anti-combination Act, the terms of which were 'decidedly harsher' than the draconian measures that applied only to British workers.[48] In addition, the Union's alliance of Irish and British property buttressed Ulster's Protestant élite in its self-interested interpretation and enforcement of such laws. For example, in late 1816, only a few months after Doe and Magill were hanged in Belfast for bombing Johnson's home, John McCann, a manufacturer in Lisburn, was acquitted of murdering his own employee, Gordon Maxwell, the leader of the muslin weavers' union, on Belfast's Malone Road, despite Maxwell's dying declaration that McCann was his killer. And of course it was ultimately by British authority that thousands of Irishmen and -women were transported to the Australian penal colonies — nearly 6,000 between 1825 and 1835 alone — usually for challenging the 'principle[s] of commercial good order'.[49]

Many mechanisms of élite persuasion, however, depended neither on overt force nor on British legislative or administrative authority, although those constituted both the ultimate resort and the essential context. Indeed, if ordinary Ulster Protestants were to internalize the lessons that their superiors wished to inculcate, the latter needed to initiate a variety of measures offering rewards as well as punishments. It was significant, of course, that 1816 witnessed not only the weavers' assault on Johnson's premises but also the establishment in Belfast of a House of Correction — a new prison with a strict work regimen designed to instil 'morals and industry' among its 75 to 100 inmates.[50]

48 J. Dunsmore Clarkson, *Labour and Nationalism in Ireland* (New York, 1925), 55–56; and Park, 'Combination Acts in Ireland', 356.
49 Bardon, *History of Ulster*, 259; Boyle, *Irish Labor Movement*, 15–16, 37; Green, *Lagan Valley*, 101; and BNL, 2 January 1818. Much cheaper and more effective than transportation, of course, was the 'voluntary' mass emigration of the 'disaffected' or of those likely to become either disaffected or a burden on upper- and middle-class charity. Indeed, it is arguable that the British government's relaxation in the late 1820s of its prior restrictions on Irish (and British) emigration was determined not only by the growing popularity of 'free labour' theories and Malthusian apprehensions but also by the recognition, particularly during that decade's severe industrial depression, that mass lower-class emigration could relieve severe social and political pressures on the upper and middle classes in Ireland and Britain alike. Of course, the 'problem' with which British officials wrestled in the 1820s was that, without massive financial assistance from government or landlords, many of the Irish deemed particularly 'superfluous' or 'dangerous' could not afford — or were not willing — to emigrate. See Chapter 2 in this volume; and on assisted migration, generally, see Gerard Moran, *Sending Out Ireland's Poor: Assisted Emigration to North America in the Nineteenth Century* (Dublin, 2004), chs. 1–2.
50 *Bradshaw's Belfast Directory, 1819* (Belfast, 1819), xx. Significantly also, Belfast's House of Industry, to relieve and discipline the poor, was founded in 1809, partly in response to the effects of severe recession in the city's cotton industry; see Dubourdieu, *Statistical Survey of the County of Antrim*, 410, 544–45. Yet, as Margaret Preston notes, applying historian Gareth Stedman Jones's insights to the sponsors of nineteenth-century Irish charity and missionary work, 'The policeman and the workhouse were not sufficient. The respectable

At least equally important, however, was the sort of initiative that William Coyne described in his eulogy of the new Belfast Savings Bank, 'instituted for the Saveings of the poor and ... Conducted by ... the principle Magastrates and Bankers of the town'. Such charitable and morally instructive efforts by Ulster's upper and middle classes were most obvious in cities such as Belfast but were not confined there, as during the early 1800s benevolent loan societies, almost invariably sponsored by local landlords and Protestant clergymen, sprang up in towns and villages throughout the island. Visiting Ireland in 1834, Inglis noted approvingly how such loan societies engendered both dependence and 'good moral effects' among the grateful debtors: 'Habits of punctuality are encouraged,' he observed, 'and so is sobriety' — 'since this virtue is essential to obtaining a loan'.[51]

At least equally pervasive and effective were the pan-Protestant revivals of the so-called Second or New Reformation and the host of charitable and educational institutions that were established or transformed and invigorated under their inspiration. The financial, political, and ideological linkages between Irish revivalism and upper- and middle-class Irish (and British) Protestant loyalism and conservatism are well known, as all sought to purge Protestant (as well as Catholic) Irish society of the Jacobin 'French diseases' of political radicalism, religious infidelity, and lower-class insubordination. In this respect, the new Hibernian Sunday schools that flourished in east and mid-Ulster were but one example of the new forces that contributed to what historians David Hempton and Myrtle Hill have described as 'the inculcation of religious respectability which was so prominent a feature of nineteenth-century Ulster life'. Thus, the historian Mary McNeill contends that Mary Ann McCracken, sister of the United Irish leader, was typical of Belfast's Presbyterian middle classes in channelling the political reformist zeal of the late 1700s into charitable and benevolent activities, targeting the city's poor, in the early and mid-1800s. Yet although McNeill argues for continuity between the old and new reform impulses, it seems clear that the overwhelming majority of McCracken's efforts were conducted under new evangelical auspices and control, and that, whereas the late eighteenth-century activities had *challenged* a hierarchical order that was loyal/aristocratic, the 'busy benevolence' of the post-Union era *confirmed* a new one that was loyal/bourgeois.[52]

Also of major importance were the quasi-charitable and material benefits of lower-class Protestant membership in the Orange Order and in Ulster's disproportionately large Yeomanry corps. Despite its 'plebeian' rank-and-file membership, reportedly drawn (as in County Armagh) from 'the lowest orders', the historian K. Theodore Hoppen concludes that Ulster's Anglican gentry and magistrates were in the forefront of the

---

and the well-to-do had to win the "hearts and minds" of the masses' as well; Preston, 'Discourse and Hegemony', 107.

51 Inglis, *Ireland in 1834*, vol. 1, 37–38.

52 David Hempton and Myrtle Hill, *Evangelical Protestantism in Ulster Society, 1740–1890* (London, 1992), 59–60; see also Cohen, *Linen, Family and Community in Tullylish*, 15. McNeill, *Life and Times of Mary Ann McCracken*, 257–87; McDowell, *Public Opinion and Government Policy in Ireland*, 30.

Orange Order, and that 'the heart of the movement' was supplied by 'the substantial farmers who predominated as local leaders' in the countryside, supplemented in the towns by men in managerial (for example, foreman) or clerical posts.[53] Thus, the Orange Lodges were uniquely able to execute what surely were some of their most vital functions: to ensure ordinary Orangemen received preferential legal treatment, of course, but also — and at least equally important — to insulate them against the dangers of eviction, unemployment, and emigration.[54] The Yeomanry was also a hierarchically controlled, 'property-based force', and hence a means by which landlords exercised discipline over their tenants. During the economically distressed early 1800s, moreover, for ordinary Yeomen it was no doubt crucial that they received *pay*, as well as preferential treatment, for their services. Both affirmed their sense of status, as rewarded for their commitment to the Union and to their élite officers' definitions of law and order.[55]

53 K. Theodore Hoppen, *Elections, Politics and Society in Ireland, 1832–1885* (Oxford, 1984), 320–21. Scholars who emphasize the sometimes contentious relationships between élite and plebeian Orangeism may question this chapter's implicit argument as to the importance of the Orange Order's role in enforcing upper- and middle-class hegemony. I believe, however, that the distinctions and tensions some historians discern between the two phenomena have been greatly overdrawn.

54 On Orangeism and emigration, see n. 75 below.

55 Martin W. Dowling, *Tenant Right and Agrarian Society in Ulster, 1600–1870* (Dublin, 1999), 99, paraphrasing Frank Wright's argument concerning Orangeism in his *Two Lands on One Soil*. On the Yeomanry, see Allan Blackstock, *An Ascendancy Army: The Irish Yeomanry, 1796–1834* (Dublin, 1998); e.g., 222–24; quotation on 271.

  Blackstock notes that '[o]nly in Ulster were there sufficient numbers of yeomen to make an impact on internal disorder, *yet there they were needed least*' (251; my emphasis). Blackstock suggests that this discrepancy between numbers and need reflected the Yeomanry's function as an engine of Protestant patronage in the province where Protestants were most numerous. I agree, yet, if we conceptualize Ulster society not merely according to a simplistic 'Two Traditions' (Protestant versus Catholic) model, but also in terms of intra-Protestant class and denominational divisions, then the heavy concentration of Yeomen in Ulster (especially in overwhelmingly Presbyterian east Ulster) also seems a logical response to the kinds of social-control problems dramatized by the Belfast weavers' 1816 assault on Francis Johnson's house, as well as providing a Castle-funded and an Anglican gentry-led means by which the region's Presbyterians could be managed by — if not integrated within — a pan-Protestant Tory–Orange bloc.

  The Orange Order and the Yeomanry had other symbiotic relationships that greatly benefited their overlapping memberships. For instance, Yeomen enjoyed easy legal and financial access to firearms, which in turn gave Orangemen an enormous advantage over their Catholic competitors and combatants; note the generally huge discrepancies between Protestant and Catholic casualty rates resulting from early nineteenth-century Orange-Green clashes, as chronicled in Sean Farrell's *Rituals and Riots: Sectarian Violence and Political Culture in Ulster, 1784–1886* (Lexington, Ky., 2000). At the risk of cynicism, moreover, it may be conjectured that one of the Orange Order's important, if unacknowledged, functions was to provoke what would be denominated as 'Catholic aggression' against the 'Protestant community' or 'rebellious conspiracy' against the Union, either of which demanded the Yeomanry's mobilization and hence extra service pay for its members. Naturally, evidence to corroborate such conjectures is extremely difficult to uncover, but Dublin Castle officials often expressed suspicions that many of the Irish gentry's and magistrates' pleas for military intervention, to suppress alleged Catholic insurrections in their districts, were motivated by either paranoia or material self-interest. 'Before we became acquainted with the true state of affairs,' complained one British soldier in 1814, 'they [Irish local notables] made us complete hacks, calling us out to assist in every drunken squabble which took place, often through their own insolent behaviour'; cited in Crossman, *Politics, Law and Order in Nineteenth-Century Ireland*, 41.

Like the Petty Sessions Courts (established in 1827), such bodies reinforced hierarchy and deference on local levels and connected those local relationships with supra-local or metropolitan rules, institutions, and power structures. In Ulster especially, perhaps, they not only strengthened traditional, cross-class social bonds but also instilled, encouraged, and rewarded new proto-bourgeois habits and outlooks compatible with the needs of commercialization and industrialization.[56] Equally important, in the process, they sifted Ulster's and Ireland's inhabitants into two broad, dichotomous groups — the 'loyal' versus the 'disloyal', the 'respectable' versus the 'disreputable', the 'worthy' versus the 'unworthy' of patronage and respect.

Of course, those who formulated and benefited from this Manichaean scheme ultimately determined that the most vital and enduring distinction between the two opposing groups, as 'characterized' in 'moral' terms, would almost invariably be made on an allegedly 'natural' sectarian (and even quasi-racial) — Protestant versus Catholic ('British' versus 'Irish') — basis. Yet in 1816 Belfast's Protestant magistrates and élites were willing, perhaps even eager, to enrol the city's parish priest and future Catholic archbishop, William Crolly, as a member of the Committee of Gentlemen that arranged the capture of Francis Johnson's assailants. And no doubt both Crolly and many affluent Protestant liberals would have been happy, on that and similar occasions, to enlist other 'respectable' Catholics among the 'friends of order'.[57] However, a combination of external and internal circumstances aborted any chance for the emergence of the sort of interdenominational, class-based alliance of 'men of property' that the Protestant liberal Henry Grattan had promoted in the late 1700s, or that the southern Catholic bishop, James Doyle of Kildare and Leighlin, continued to advocate — as a 'union of the good and the virtuous' — as late as the 1820s.[58] Instead, for three crucial decades

---

56 *Bradshaw's Belfast Directory* ... 1819, xix. For a unique study of these processes, focusing on Thomastown, County Kilkenny, see Marilyn Silverman, *An Irish Working Class: Explorations in Political Economy and Hegemony, 1800–1950* (Toronto, 2001), esp. 119–41.

57 On Crolly, see Ambrose Macaulay, *William Crolly: Archbishop of Armagh, 1835–49* (Dublin, 1994). As far as can be determined, Fr. Crolly was the only Catholic member of the 'Committee of twenty-one Gentlemen', appointed on 29 February 1816 to raise money and otherwise arrange for the capture of Johnson's assailants (BNL, 1 March 1816). However, Crolly's name disappears thereafter from the BNL's record of the case, presumably because those arrested and convicted turned out to be Protestants; for example, Crolly was *not* among the clergymen who attended Doe's and Magill's executions on 6 September (see BNL, 10 September 1816).

58 Grattan's career is described in many sources, e.g., James Kelly, *Henry Grattan* (Dundalk, 1993), but particularly relevant to the arguments in this chapter is Maurice O'Connell's 'Class Conflict in a Pre-Industrial Society: Dublin in 1780', *Dalhousie Review*, 9, 1 (fall 1963), 43–55. On Bishop James Doyle, see Miller, *Emigrants and Exiles*, 82–83, 89, and passim; as well as Doyle's own *Letters on the State of Ireland; Addressed by J. K. L. to a Friend in England* (Dublin, 1825), esp. 14 and 169–75. As W. P. Ryan notes, 'Bishop Doyle, and priests of his diocese, were in favour of the organizing of "respectable" citizen patrols, accompanied by some police and military', to counter the Whiteboys in south Leinster. 'Among other activities, it was suggested that they should call at night at the houses of suspected persons to see if they were at home. Dr. Doyle desired that the counter-associations should be armed in order to "terrify evil-doers", who should also be dismissed from their employment'; Ryan, *Irish Labour Movement*, 27.

after 1800 the Tories largely controlled the British government and Dublin Castle. The Tories' alliance with Irish ultra-Protestantism and the Orange Order, and their refusal to grant Catholic Emancipation, ensured the adversarial growth of Catholic alienation and nationalism, which in turn effectively guaranteed that Irish unionism would develop as an almost exclusively (and militantly) Protestant phenomenon. Yet the internal factor may have been even more crucial. Given the rampant class conflict of the early 1800s, and in the context of the long depression following the Napoleonic Wars, the Protestant élite's successful imposition of capitalist relationships and mores on Ulster's Protestant poor virtually necessitated the creation and continual reinforcement of a sectarian 'moral economy' that paradoxically combined 'free labour' ideology with the selective reality, or at least the seductive rhetoric, of Protestant privilege and patronage.[59]

Discrimination of various kinds was present of course in the operations of charitable and other institutions, as well as in many less formal social relationships: most obviously in instances of Protestant preferment or in blatant manifestations of anti-Catholic prejudice, as implemented or expressed by ultra-Protestant landlords, magistrates, and employers, and/or by ordinary Orangemen and Yeomen (the two often synonymous). Thus, Catholic spokesmen complained bitterly that in the Protestant-controlled town corporations in Ulster and elsewhere, '[e]very species of Catholic industry and mechanical skill is checked, taxed, and rendered precarious' by 'uncertain and unequal ... justice' and by 'fraud and favouritism daily and openly practised to their prejudice'.[60]

At least initially, however, both élite and plebeian Protestants made important distinctions between the 'loyal-respectable-worthy' and the 'disloyal-disreputable-unworthy' *within the Protestant population itself*. First, and for much longer than unionist mythology would later allow, critical discriminations were made among Protestants on denominational grounds: between proverbially 'loyal' Anglicans and reputedly 'disaffected' and hence 'untrustworthy' Presbyterians.[61] As a result, during the 1798 rebellion, liberal (but loyal) Protestant Dissenters in Donegal and elsewhere were fearful that the Orangemen, then overwhelmingly Anglican, were 'Sworn to Distroy all Prisbitearans' as well as 'Rommans': an apprehension that helps explain Presbyterians' subsequent, if still markedly underrepresented, membership in both the Orange Order

---

59 On the ideological and practical tensions in unionism between sectarian privilege and free-market capitalism, see Chapter 9 in this volume.

60 Miller, *Emigrants and Exiles*, 89; this particular complaint was made in 1812 by Daniel O'Connell, but see similar remarks by ordinary pre-Famine emigrants cited in Miller, *Emigrants and Exiles*, e.g., 244–45. Sympathetic Protestants concurred; for criticisms of Tory–Orange perversion of the legal and judicial systems in Ulster, for instance, see Thomas Reid, *Travels in Ireland, in the Year 1822, Exhibiting Brief Sketches of the Moral, Physical, and Political State of the Country* (London, 1823), 193–94. For one historian's assessment of Orange bias in Ulster's 'notoriously partisan judicial system', see Farrell, *Rituals and Riots*, 44–45.

61 Historians as varied in perspective as Ian McBride and Kevin Whelan concur that Ulster Presbyterian alienation, and Presbyterian–Anglican divisions, lasted long after the Act of Union; see McBride, 'Ulster Presbyterians and the Passing of the Act of Union', 75; and Whelan, *The Tree of Liberty: Radicalism, Catholicism and the Construction of Irish Identity, 1760–1830* (Cork, 1996), 155.

and the Yeomanry. Suspicions about Presbyterian fidelity to the Union lingered long, however, and officials in Dublin Castle feared that many Presbyterians' enrolment in Ulster's Yeomanry corps was merely expedient or even 'insincere'. For their part, as Edward Wakefield, John Gamble, and others testified, ordinary Presbyterians remained socially and politically alienated: resenting the rents they paid to Anglican landlords; despising tithes and regarding the Church of Ireland clergy with 'sovereign contempt'.[62] It is more difficult, of course, to discern whether similar animosities were common between Anglicans and Presbyterians who shared the same social status.[63] In the circumstances, however, perhaps it was no wonder that, at least by the 1820s, most loyal Protestants —

62 James Steele, Raphoe, County Donegal, 15 May 1797, cited in Miller, Emigrants and Exiles, 230. Blackstock, Ascendancy Army, 129. Also see McBride, 'Ulster Presbyterians and the Passing of the Act of Union', 80, where he argues that, although the Yeomanry offered 'propertied Protestants' a 'route to rehabilitation' after 1798, Presbyterians remained greatly underrepresented and, as one Anglican magistrate feared, may have joined Yeomanry corps (and the Orange Order) primarily to 'screen themselves' from loyalist suspicions and reprisals. Wakefield, An Account of Ireland, vol. 2, 548.

At least into the 1830s, Ulster's leading Whig-Presbyterian newspaper, the Belfast Northern Whig, continued to denounce tithes on the Presbyterians' behalf; see Flann Campbell, The Dissenting Voice: Protestant Democracy in Ulster from Plantation to Partition (Belfast, 1991), 145–53. There is evidence, however, that suggests a lessening of Presbyterian animosity toward tithes between the early 1800s, when Presbyterians in Aghaloe parish, County Antrim, murdered a tithe-proctor (c. 1822), and the 1830s and 1840s, when some observers claimed that tithes no longer agitated east Ulster's Dissenters because the region's landlords allegedly had assumed responsibility for paying them — even before the 1838 Tithe Act mandated they do so. If the latter is true, perhaps such landlord paternalism was a significant cause or consequence of the creation of a pan-Protestant unionism, which the effects of the 1838 Act itself might also have promoted. See Reid, Travels in Ireland, in the Year 1822, 221; Inglis, Ireland in 1834, vol. 2, 206–07; and Binns, Miseries and Beauties of Ireland, vol. 1, 77.

63 Nevertheless, it may be revealing that, judging from their respective domiciles, William Gray, the weaver-conspirator turned informer in 1816, was probably an Anglican, whereas those who suffered from his betrayal were most likely Presbyterians. The BNL's detailed account of the trial testimony makes clear that William Gray, although then a resident of Ballymacarrett (in Knockbreda parish, north County Down), was originally from the neighbourhood of Portadown, County Armagh, where his father and sister still resided. Portadown is in Drumcree and Seagoe parishes, the total populations of which were c. 54–57 per cent Protestant in 1766 and 70 per cent Protestant in 1831, and whose Protestant populations in 1831 were each slightly more than 88 per cent Anglican. (In 1766 Anglicans comprised roughly 77 per cent of Seagoe's Protestants; no comparable 1766 data exists for Drumcree.)

By contrast, the condemned weavers were all described as residents of Belfast or adjacent areas in north Down, and Doe and Magill were buried in Knockbreckan, a townland located in the north Down parishes of Drumbo and Knockbreda. No 1766 census figures survive for either parish, but in 1831 Drumbo's and Knockbreda's total populations were 97 and 94 per cent Protestant, respectively, and their Protestant populations were 83 per cent (Drumbo) and 78 per cent (Knockbreda) Presbyterian. For the sources of this religious census data, see above, n. 3.

It may also be significant that one of the other prisoners, James Park, who was sentenced only to flogging and imprisonment, had almost certainly been a member of the Yeomanry before his arrest. See BNL, 16 August 1816, in which Judge Day, while sentencing Park and Dickson, remarked that the former 'had evinced his guilt by resisting a magistrate, with a musket which had been committed to him ... for the protection of [the law]'. Unfortunately, the connections that Joseph Madden enjoyed, to persuade the lord lieutenant to commute his death sentence to transportation for life, can only be conjectured, since the BNL was unusually reticent on the matter. Intriguingly, extensive research by Dr. Jennifer Harrison, of the University of Queensland, was unable to discover any evidence that Madden was ever actually transported

with increasing numbers of Presbyterians — felt obliged to 'all show themselves' in the annual Twelfth of July parades, for, as one Orangeman demanded, 'how [else] could we tell whether they are of the right or wrong sort?' As Thomas Reid, a visiting Scottish reformer, concluded, 'it is not the poor Catholics alone whose allegiance is suspected; poor Protestants are also thrown into the back ground; none but Orangemen are the "right sort"'.[64]

Moreover, as Reid's employment of the term 'poor Protestants' suggests, a second set of intra-Protestant pressures was imposed hierarchically, across class lines, often overlapping or reinforcing those imposed on a denominational basis. Protestants of property and influence, Anglicans and Presbyterians alike, also stigmatized as 'unworthy' those Protestants of lesser wealth and status, regardless of their church affiliations, who did not conform to the emerging bourgeois unionist order. During the social crises of the early 1800s, for example, Irish municipal authorities often instructed parish relief committees not to grant charity even to Protestant applicants who lacked certificates of 'good character' from their landlords, clergymen, or employers — testifying, for example, to the petitioners' non-membership in working-class combinations.[65] In the same period, east Ulster's few remaining 'rhyming weavers' — formerly the heralds of socio-political discontent and religious liberalism — learned, often from bitter experience, that élite patronage and publication prospects were generally closed to those who resisted the tides of convention. Likewise, and especially after 1831, the North's Protestant schoolmasters increasingly fell under the sway of conservative clergymen. Meanwhile, the Prebyterian clergy's own ranks were successively purged of 'disloyalty' and 'heresy' by Tory allies, such as the Rev. Robert Black and the Rev. Henry Cooke, who increasingly dominated the Ulster Synod and other religious bodies and who distributed government bounties and the Synod's own resources according to political and doctrinal criteria, to ensure what one critic called a 'pious and loyal servility'.[66]

---

to Australia, as he does not appear in the pertinent colonial and ship records (communication to author, 22 October 2004); my thanks to Dr. Harrison for her efforts in this regard.

64 Reid, *Travels in Ireland, in the Year 1822*, 189, 368. Similarly, in 1810 John Gamble noted that the Orangemen in Newtown-Stewart, County Tyrone, despised the Protestant (mostly Presbyterian) populace of nearby Strabane — as 'worse than Catholics', as 'renegadoes who had deserted the good old cause' — because they had showed, in Gamble's view, 'good sense' and charity to their Catholic neighbours by refusing to allow the Order to march through the town on 12 July; in revenge, the Orangemen invaded Strabane in force and terrorized its inhabitants; Gamble, *Sketches of History Politics, and Manners*, 269–70.

65 Boyle, *Irish Labor Movement*, 18–19.

66 On the rhyming weavers, generally, see John Hewitt, *Rhyming Weavers and Other Country Poets of Antrim and Down* (Belfast, 1974). Frank Wright argues that it was the debate over implementation of the Irish National Education Act (1831) that forged the alliance between Presbyterian orthodoxy (with its demand for the 'open [i.e., Protestant] bible' in the schoolroom) and an 'Anglican landlord conservatism [that] was employing its political and institutional resources to link opposition to national "Godless" education to a generalized opposition to the Whig government and all its works'; see Wright, *Two Lands on One Soil*, 67. On the political and doctrinal struggles in Ulster Presbyterianism, generally, see Brooke, *Ulster Presbyterianism*, 129–74; and, on the selective distribution of the *regium donum* to create a conservative clergy, also see

Over time such formative influences, and other modes of conditioning less obvious but continuous and increasingly pervasive, were instrumental in shaping the *mentalité* of ordinary Protestants in the economically unstable and socially stratified world of pre-Famine Ulster. Surely it was critical, for example, that such influences were brought to bear initially and most insistently during the four decades immediately following the Act of Union — decades marked by escalating competition and heightened insecurity wrought by a lethal combination of explosive population growth, severe economic hardships, and profound dislocations and capitalist 'modernizations' in agriculture and manufacturing alike: all operating in a society that yet remained rigidly hierarchical and characterized, even among Protestants, by a strikingly unequal distribution of power and resources. As Robert Peel noted with satisfaction during the economic crisis of 1816–17 (when the Belfast weavers launched their ill-fated attack on Johnson's house), severe distress eventually 'promoted peace and good order', because, he wrote, 'The lower classes became in many parts completely dependent upon the bounty of their wealthier neighbours, and soon found the policy of fortifying their claims to compassion by peaceable behaviour'.[67]

On the provincial level, certainly, after 1798 Ulster's ordinary Protestants had no lawful political alternatives to docility and loyalty. In parliamentary elections (on the rare occasions when contests among competing candidates actually occurred), the North's Protestant voters (most of whom were disfranchised in 1829) simply concurred in their landlords' choices, either from deference or coercion, and parliamentary seats in Antrim, Down, and nearly all other constituencies were the virtual monopoly of a handful of Ulster's wealthiest magnates. Of course, some of east Ulster's most powerful families, such as the Downshires, were Whigs; and Belfast itself was a centre of Whig party strength. However, although traditionally the 'Presbyterian party', the Whigs were scarcely more sympathetic to lower-class Protestants' economic grievances than their 'Church and King' adversaries among the Conservatives. At least Tory landlords, especially those affiliated with the Orange Order, offered ordinary Protestants the prospect — or the comforting illusion — of upper-class paternalism. By contrast, Ulster's Whigs — especially the Presbyterian haute bourgeoisie (including most of Belfast's leading merchants, bankers, and manufacturers) — espoused a free-market capitalism that, however potent a rhetorical weapon against 'Tory aristocracy', translated into attitudes and legislation at least as prejudicial to working-class combinations and to Ulster's poor, generally, as anything Tory landlords could devise. Moreover, the Whigs' chronic political weakness in the North — in part a result of their inability or unwillingness to address poor Protestants' economic concerns — made the party heavily dependent on support from British Whigs and (in return for championing emancipation)

McBride, 'Ulster Presbyterians and the Passing of the Act of Union', 75 (quotation in text); and Holmes, *Henry Cooke*, 14–15.
67 Jenkins, *Era of Emancipation*, 132.

on Irish Catholic voters and the Catholic hierarchy: dependence on British political allies naturally reinforced Irish Whigs' own commitment to the Union and to Britain's ruling classes, whereas reliance on Irish Catholic support only made them more vulnerable to the pan-Protestant appeals of the Tory–Orange alliance.[68]

The lack of regional or national alternatives meant that local circumstances would be instrumental in determining the future of Protestant Ulster's social ethos and political culture. And on local levels, what were no doubt most crucial and pervasive were a multitude of everyday signals, hierarchically imposed but laterally reinforced, that conformity to 'respectable' and 'loyal' norms of behaviour and opinion — the two at least rhetorically indivisible — were essential prerequisites for favourable leases, steady employment, decent wages, extended credit, rapid promotion, and charity during hard times — as well as for the subtler comforts of social and religious fellowship, for a sense of 'community', that lessened the sting of poverty in psychological if not material ways. The most important signals, especially at first, were made by those who had the greatest resources and power to bestow or withhold rewards, but eventually they were reinforced by sub-élites, social intermediaries, and, in the end, by all those

68 On Ulster politics in the early nineteenth century, see: Hoppen, *Elections, Politics and Society in Ireland,* 265–66; the three following works by Peter Jupp, *British and Irish Elections, 1784–1831* (Newton Abbot, 1973), 153–60; 'County Down Elections, 1783–1831', 177–206; and 'Irish M.P.s at Westminster in the Early Nineteenth Century', 65–80; Brian M. Walker's 'Landowners and Parliamentary Elections in County Down, 1801–1921', 297–307, and his *Ulster Politics: The Formative Years, 1868–86* (Belfast, 1989), chs. 1–3 and pp. 47–49; and Wright, *Two Lands on One Soil,* chs. 2–3.

    Whig party loyalties offered few rewards even to Ulster's middle-class Presbyterians; the Conservatives dominated electoral politics in nearly all constituencies, as by 1850 the Tories were 'enthroned as the "natural" party of Protestantism' (Hoppen, 266). Moreover, the Whig party itself rarely rewarded Presbyterians with seats in parliament; in 1832–57 only 4 of 25 Ulster Whig MPs were Presbyterians, with Anglicans (and 1 Quaker) comprising the remainder (Hoppen, 265). Nor did party power at Westminster translate into local influence and patronage for Ulster's Whig Presbyterians; as late as 1884 nearly three-fourths of the province's justices of the peace were members of the Church of Ireland (Walker, *Ulster Politics,* 23). In addition, although Irish and especially Ulster Whigs were strongly opposed to tithes, save for a few mavericks like W. Sharman Crawford they were lukewarm or at best ineffective in protecting tenant-right. And on issues directly affecting the welfare of Ulster's Protestant poor, they generally espoused classic 'liberal' positions in support of property rights, 'free labour', and 'scientific' charity; e.g., in 1816 and in 1825–26, Irish Whig MPs led demands for the Tenants' Recovery Act (facilitating evictions) and the Subletting Act, respectively, and their support for Catholic Emancipation was accompanied by their willingness, if not eagerness, to disfranchise Ireland's forty-shilling-freehold voters (who included thousands of Ulster Protestants); see McDowell, *Public Opinion and Government Policy in Ireland,* 74, 99. Likewise, Belfast's middle-class Whigs were particularly energetic (on both economic and moral grounds) in their support for the government's campaign to eradicate illegal whiskey distillation, a vital income source for poor rural Protestants (as well as Catholics) in de-industrializing west and south Ulster; see Wright, *Two Lands on One Soil,* 75. For Belfast's beleaguered workers, Francis Dalzell Finley, editor of the *Northern Whig,* must have appeared a quintessential middle-class Liberal, as he negated the popular effect of his criticisms of landlordism with strident opposition to unions, even after they became legal in 1825; in 1836 he broke the city's printers' union by importing scab printers from Dublin and Scotland, and, when that failed, by training pauper children from local charity institutions to replace his workers; see Boyd, *Rise of the Irish Trade Unions,* 42–43; Gray, *Sans Culottes of Belfast,* 37–38; McDowell as above, 58–91; and Brian Inglis, *The Freedom of the Press in Ireland, 1784–1841* (London, 1954), 216.

who, consciously or unconsciously, acknowledged their legitimacy and thus adhered
— however sincerely, pragmatically, or superficially — to the norms demanded by 'the
Protestant way of life'. Thus, the early and mid-nineteenth-century transformation of the
Harshaws, Presbyterian farmers in west Down, from open sympathizers with Catholic
Emancipation and repeal of the Act of Union into staunch unionists and Orangemen,
was instructive and perhaps typical, as its younger members were enmeshed in webs
of credit and other obligations to members of the Orange Order, while the older ones
were publicly attacked by local clergymen for refusing either to join the Order or to
acknowledge the unionist dictum that Protestantism, loyalty, and respectability were
synonymous and interdependent.[69]

Indeed, some pressures for conformity may have been even more intimate and
intense. As the historical sociologist Marilyn Cohen has noted, whereas the evangelical
Protestantism of the Second Reformation offered Ulster's upper classes what scholars
David Hempton and Myrtle Hill call '"a creed which reaffirmed old values and supplied
a rigorous defense of social and political conservatism"', it also sanctified bourgeois
family relationships and enshrined the special roles of wives and mothers in propagating
and guarding the norms of 'respectability' (industry, cleanliness, piety, sobriety, chastity)
that were allegedly associated with Protestantism, threatened by Catholicism (and by
the 'improvident' lower classes, generally), and hence protected by the Union with
Protestant Britain. In this context, it may be accurate to speak of the domestication and
even the feminization of unionism, complementing the latter's 'outdoor' and overtly
masculine expressions in the Orange Order. Indeed, from the 1870s on, Orangeism
itself would become more respectable, domesticated, and to a degree even feminized
through the adoption of the Orangemen's now 'traditional' 'marching uniform' (suits
and bowler hats) as well as of 'ladies' auxiliaries'. Arguably, however, it was in the early
nineteenth century, with the rise of the bourgeoisie in tandem with evangelicalism,
that unionism and its associations became embedded in the heart of Ulster Protestant
family culture.[70]

---

69 For the Harshaws' story, I am grateful to Marjorie Harshaw Robie, of Ipswich, Mass., who generously
   shared the results of her then unpublished research on her family's roles in the local dynamics of east
   Ulster Protestant society, early to mid-1800s; many of her findings are now published in Robie, *Dwelling
   Place of Dragons: An Irish Story* (n.p., 2006).
70 Cohen, *Linen, Family and Community in Tullylish*, 15 (citing Hempton and Hill, *Evangelical Protestantism in
   Ulster Society*, 43) and *passim*. To my knowledge, no scholars have examined the development of Ulster
   unionism through these perspectives. My arguments are extrapolated from research into the Johnston
   family correspondence from Ballymahon, County Longford (see Chapter 9 in this volume), and by analogy
   with scholarship on industrialization, evangelical religion, middle-class domesticity, and gender in early
   and mid-nineteenth-century America; e.g., Paul Johnson, *A Shopkeeper's Millennium: Society and Revivals
   in Rochester, New York, 1815–1837* (New York, 1978); Colleen McDannell, *The Christian Home in Victorian
   America, 1840–1900* (Bloomington, Ind., 1986); and Mary P. Ryan, *Cradle of the Middle Class: The Family in
   Oneida County, New York, 1790–1865* (New York, 1981). For information about the Orangemen's marching
   attire and women's auxiliaries, I am grateful to Professor Donald MacRaild of the University of Ulster,
   Coleraine.

Finally, the success of these hegemonic pressures was both revealed and ensured by two other critical factors that historians of Ulster society and political culture have largely ignored: namely, the massive size and the selective character of early and mid-nineteenth-century Ulster Protestant emigration. Between the end of the American Revolution and the beginning of the Great Famine, at least one-quarter of a million and probably much closer to half a million Protestants left an Ulster which, near its demographic peak in 1831, contained less than 1.1 million Protestants.[71] Moreover, both denominational and social class factors heavily determined which Protestants would emigrate and which would not. Modern analyses of census data confirm contemporary reports that Ulster's Protestant emigrants were disproportionately, indeed overwhelmingly, Presbyterians as well as predominantly cottage artisans (principally weavers) and small to middling tenant farmers or their children.[72]

No doubt, eighteenth-century links with America encouraged much northern Protestant emigration in the early 1800s. So allegedly did competition with Catholics for land and employment — perhaps especially in Protestant-minority areas in south and west Ulster — in part because many landlords merely paid lip-service to the 'moral' claims of 'Protestant community' and leased farms on their estates to the highest bidders, as Protestant tenants often complained.[73] Yet more important causes

71 According to computations of the parish data in the First Report of the Commission of Public Instruction, Ireland (see n. 3 above), in 1831 Ulster contained approximately 1,077,500 Protestants (and 1,197,100 Catholics). Strictly speaking, the nine-county North would not become 'the Protestant Province of Ulster', as unionists liked to call it, until 1871. On contemporary Ulster emigration, see Miller, Emigrants and Exiles, chs. 5–6; Ó Gráda, Ireland: A New Economic History, 76; and William Forbes Adams, Ireland and Irish Emigration to the New World from 1815 to the Great Famine (New Haven, Conn., 1932).

72 See above, n. 49. For evidence as to the 'character' of pre-Famine emigration from Ulster and elsewhere in Ireland, taken from contemporary observers' reports and ships' passenger lists, see Miller, Emigrants and Exiles, ch. 6. I plan to publish a full, census-based analysis of the denominational and social composition of early and mid-nineteenth century Ulster emigration, but some preliminary conclusions can be found in: Kerby A. Miller, et al., Irish Immigrants in the Land of Canaan: Letters and Memoirs from Colonial and Revolutionary America, 1675–1815 (New York, 2003), Appendix 2: 'Irish Migration and Demography' (with Liam Kennedy); in Chapter 10 in this volume; and in May Kao Xiong, 'Shadows in the Land of Eoghain: The Great Irish Famine in County Tyrone, 1845–50' (MA thesis, University of Missouri-Columbia, 2003), which examines census data for 1821–41 as well as for 1841–51. It may be notable as well that, at least in the post-Famine period, Ulster Protestant emigration (especially from east Ulster), in contrast to the Catholic exodus from the three southern provinces, appears also to have been disproportionately male; see Miller, Emigrants and Exiles, 371.

73 In the nineteenth century, the allegation that 'unfair' Catholic competition was a — or even the — primary cause of Irish Protestant emigration became an integral aspect of unionist mythology and rhetoric; e.g., see Boyce, 'The Making of Unionism', 23. However, in the 1700s it had rarely featured in Ulster Presbyterian discourse on emigration, and in the 1800s it rarely appeared as a cause of complaint in Ulster Presbyterian emigrants' correspondence. In both, by contrast, attributions of emigration to 'landlord tyranny', tithes and taxes, and (after 1800) to British misgovernment were much more common. Although instances of Catholic competition displacing Ulster Presbyterians (and other Protestants) undoubtedly occurred, and although the latter's fears of such competition became widespread (as attested by relatively impartial observers such as John Gamble and Jonathan Binns), the demographic evidence indicates that widespread Catholic displacement of Presbyterians in the North did not take place (see text below).

are strongly suggested by the overall differences between the high rates of Ulster Presbyterian emigration and the low rates of Ulster Anglican emigration that can be inferred from the significant disparities between their respective annual growth rates in 1766–1831 and in 1831–61. Furthermore, it is striking that those disparities were greatest in the mid-Ulster region, in the so-called linen triangle, centred on north and central Armagh but also including west Down and east Tyrone. Of course, in the late 1700s and early 1800s this religiously mixed district experienced Ulster's highest population growth, the most intense competition over land and employment, and the most profound socio-economic dislocations. But at least equally important, perhaps, is the fact that mid-Ulster was also the epicentre of Anglican loyalism and, after 1795, of Anglican loyalism as institutionalized, mobilized, and well-armed in the Orange Order. Indeed, in many parts of mid-Ulster the denominational balance between Anglicans and Presbyterians changed so radically in the early and mid-1800s that it is difficult to avoid the conclusion that formal or informal, overt or subtle, forms of discrimination practised by Anglican landlords, employers and magistrates, as well as by ordinary Orangemen,

It is therefore arguable that Ulster (and Irish) unionists, and many ordinary Protestants, embraced the 'Catholic competition = Protestant emigration' thesis for several closely related ideological and practical reasons. Ulster Presbyterian emigrants' traditional self-portrayal — as oppressed 'victims' of landlord oppression, Anglican clerical avarice, and British misgovernment — was incompatible with unionism's demand for pan-Protestant solidarity and loyalty; indeed, it was dangerously similar to Irish Catholic nationalists' argument that emigration was forced 'exile'. By contrast, blaming Protestant emigration on Catholic competition reinforced Protestants' traditional 'settler ideology', portraying the latter as 'victims' once more under 'siege' by the 'natives'. That contention also reinforced notions of Protestants' inherent 'respectability' and 'superiority', because, in contrast to their Catholic competitors, who allegedly were content to live in filth and misery in order to pay rack-rents, Protestant tenants deserved and proudly demanded 'decency and comfort' (Boyce, 'The Making of Unionism', 23). In addition, the explanation enabled Protestant tenants to employ against their landlords the standard unionist appeals for Protestant solidarity; although tenant spokesmen's frequent complaints suggest that such pleas may at best have enjoyed only partial success, ordinary Protestants (having abandoned the Steelboys' option) had no lawful alternative to their insistent, Orange-dressed reiteration (see Chapter 9 in this volume; also Wright, Two Lands on One Soil, 28). Indeed, it may be that the 'Catholic competition' argument's most important function, especially in Ulster, and its most crucial contribution to pan-Protestant unionism, was in deflecting attention from the intra-Protestant social-class and denominational conflicts that the actual patterns of northern emigration both reflected and revealed (see text below).

Surprisingly, no scholar has investigated the social or political consequences in Ulster of the disfranchisement of Protestant forty-shilling freeholders, despite widespread claims that large numbers of former Catholic voters were evicted after 1829. For evidence (or allegations) of Ulster landlords replacing Protestant tenants with Catholics, however, see Whelan, Tree of Liberty, 51 (shortly after Waterloo, in Armagh and Cavan); Gamble, Views of Society and Manners in the North of Ireland, 421–22 (1818, west Ulster); and Binns, Miseries and Beauties of Ireland, vol. 1, 78–79 (late 1830s, in Down); but see also Binns, vol. 1, 315, for evidence of Ulster landlords (especially evangelical leaders and/or Orange district masters) evicting Catholics to replace them with 'loyal' Protestants — a complaint made frequently by Catholic nationalists and priests in the pre-Famine decades, and probably with at least equally good cause.

may have been critical in stimulating such disproportionately high rates of Presbyterian (as well as Catholic) out-migration.[74]

Of course, whether Ulster Presbyterian (and other) emigrants left Ireland primarily from ambition, frustration, intimidation, or desperation is problematic. Historians' judgements as to the relative importance of 'push' and 'pull' factors — of economic, cultural, religious, or political causes and motivations — are often based as much on their own ideological predilections as on the emigrants' actual circumstances. Yet whatever the reasons, the fact is that in early and mid-nineteenth-century Ulster, generally, and in mid-Ulster particularly, Presbyterians were most liable to emigrate, whereas Anglicans were most likely to stay.[75]

74 For example, in Moira parish, in west Down, between 1766 and 1831 the Presbyterian proportion of the population fell from 34 per cent to merely 19 per cent, while the Anglican share soared from 34 to 54 per cent (the Catholic proportion declined from 32 to 27 per cent); likewise, in the combined Armagh parishes of Loughgilly and Killevy, the annual growth rates 1766–1831 were 4.03 per cent among Anglicans, 1.91 among Catholics, and only 1.17 among Presbyterians; for these and other mid-Ulster data, see Miller, et al., *Irish Immigrants in the Land of Canaan*, Appendix 2, esp. 663–68. See also Miller, 'Ulster Presbyterians and the "Two Traditions" in Ireland and America', in Terry Brotherstone, Anna Clark, and Kevin Whelan, eds., *These Fissured Isles: Varieties of British and Irish Identities* (Edinburgh, 2005), 260–77 (data on 273–74), and reprinted in J. J. Lee and Marion R. Casey, eds., *Making the Irish American: History and Heritage of the Irish in the United States* (New York, 2006), 255–70.

   Significantly, Anglican–Presbyterian differentials in rates of population decline and hence of emigration continued into and beyond the Famine era, again suggesting that patronage from Anglican landlords, magistrates, etc., plus membership in the Orange Order, may have sheltered poor Anglicans in large part from the economic pressures that encouraged emigration — and in 1845–52 caused severe suffering — among less-favoured Protestants; see Chapter 10 in this volume.

   Also noteworthy is Marilyn Cohen's conclusion that the poor Protestant weavers in west County Down who best survived the Famine crisis were those who had become fully proletarianized and hence totally dependent on their employers, whereas the yet-independent or even semi-independent farmer-weavers with 5–10 acres fared far worse. Although Cohen scarcely mentions the Orange Order or denominational distinctions in her study, her data suggest the inextricable nature of socio-economic, ethnic, religious, and political factors in determining who persisted, emigrated, or perished during the Great Famine; Cohen, *Linen, Family and Community in Tullylish*, 134–55.

   Intriguingly, also, it was not until the 1880s that Ulster Presbyterian and Anglican population decline and emigration rates converged, becoming virtually identical through 1926; moreover, it was in 1881–1926 that Presbyterian numbers declined at rates significantly lower than those of Ulster's Catholics, whereas before 1881 the North's Presbyterians and Catholics had shared very similar demographic experiences. Not coincidentally, perhaps, historians contend that it was in the mid-1880s that Ulster's Presbyterians finally joined the Orange Order en masse, thereby not only demonstrating pan-Protestant solidarity in opposition to Home Rule but perhaps also acquiring whatever relative immunity from emigration Orangeism had traditionally conferred on the province's Anglicans. Of course, it may also be the case that, by the 1880s, decades of heavy emigration had so restructured and 'simplified' Ulster Presbyterian society that, despite the rural crisis of the 1880s, there remained relatively few lower-class Presbyterians on whom pressures to emigrate could operate. Denominational rates of population decline, 1881–1926, computed from the data in W. E. Vaughan and A. J. Fitzpatrick, eds., *Irish Historical Statistics: Population 1821–1971* (Dublin, 1978), 57–73.

75 In the mid-1830s, the Rev. Mortimer O'Sullivan, Anglican rector of Killyman parish (straddling counties Armagh and Tyrone, in the heart of the linen triangle), testified before a parliamentary commission that five-sixths of Killyman's Protestants were members of the Orange Order because Orangeism

Certainly, in the circumstances any Ulster Protestants — Anglicans or Presbyterians (and perhaps especially the latter) — who hoped to *avoid* emigration altogether (or to emigrate on the most advantageous terms — with landlord or government assistance, perhaps even with free land grants or jobs waiting in a British colony) knew that their chances of success would be immeasurably enhanced if they proclaimed themselves — as in their petitions to the Colonial Office — to be 'Protestants from time immemorial', 'Loyal and submissive to their government', as well as 'industrious [and] peaceably ... inclined'. It would be even better if they could 'prove' their claims, for example by reference to Catholic 'persecutions' they had suffered for their loyal service, as in the Yeomanry, and by producing written 'characters' from what one petitioner called 'the highest toned protestants in Ireland': landlords, magistrates, clergymen, employers, and/or Orange Lodge masters. Sadly, of course, the images conjured up by grovelling missives such as that of James Gibson, who 'cast [him]self at the feet of [his lordship's] protection', scarcely comported with the 'sturdy, independent' self-image of Ulster Protestant and unionist mythology.[76]

'gave Protestants courage to stay rather than emigrate', despite their alleged fears of being 'exterminated' by their Catholic neighbours, who numbered roughly half the parish's inhabitants. Religious demographic data, however, illuminate and cast doubt on O'Sullivan's claims. It is intriguing that the proportion of Killyman's Protestants whom O'Sullivan claimed to be Orangemen was almost identical to the proportion that was composed of members of the Church of Ireland. Yet O'Sullivan's allegation that, prior to the advent of the Orange Order, Protestants had fled Killyman because of competition from, or fear of, Catholics is highly questionable, since between 1766 and 1831 the parish's Protestant population had increased by about 276 per cent, whereas the number of Catholic inhabitants had risen only 126 per cent. Finally, between 1831 and 1861 it appears that in Killyman (as in the rest of Ulster) only Anglicans (not 'Protestants' generally) gained through Orangeism sufficient 'courage' (or economic advantage?) not to emigrate, for although the local Church of Ireland population declined merely 12 per cent between 1831 and 1861 (compared with Catholic losses of nearly 34 per cent), the number of the parish's Presbyterian inhabitants fell almost 26 per cent. (The figures for 1831–61 in County Armagh, generally, were Anglicans -8 per cent, Catholics -16 per cent, and Presbyterians a remarkable -31 per cent.) For O'Sullivan's testimony, see Wright, *Two Lands on One Soil*, 97. Percentages computed from population data for Killyman parish in 1766 (T.808/15,266, PRONI); in 1831 (*First Report of the Commission of Public Instruction, Ireland*; see n. 3 above); and in 1861 (Irish Census, 1861, BBP, HC 1863, liv [vol. 3, Ulster]). For demographic patterns in the entire province, particularly in mid-Ulster, see the sources cited in nos. 72 and 74 above.

76 Of course, the great majority of the petitions written and sent between the 1810s and 1840s by Irish Protestants (and Catholics) to the Colonial Office in London, begging for free passages to, and/or land grants in, British North America (and later, Australia), expressed loyal sentiments in varying degrees. My arguments, however, are: first, that Ulster (and other Irish) Anglicans were greatly advantaged in that usually they could rely on traditional, recent, and contemporary 'proofs' of their loyalty, as in 1798 or simply by virtue of Church of Ireland (and often Orange Order) membership; second, that to gain comparable leverage Ulster Presbyterians — both traditionally and (often with good reason) recently under suspicion from landlords and magistrates — needed at least to match their Anglican neighbours in demonstrations of fidelity to the established order; and, third, that Catholics, proverbially suspect and unable to join either the Orange Order or (usually) the Yeomanry corps, would inevitably become the 'other': the foils against whom both Anglicans and Dissenters could contrast their own 'love and veneration for, and obedience to, his majesty's Government', as well as their claims to superior industry, sobriety, and respectability.

By contrast, from the early 1800s to mid-century the letters written by Ulster Presbyterians who emigrated to the United States often breathed alienation and even 'manly' defiance, as they perceived or at least portrayed themselves as economic and even political refugees from an inequitable and repressive society. Many such emigrants, for example, were like David Robinson, a farmer's son from County Derry, who from his Kentucky refuge declared he 'could never brook the idea of cringing to a despotic tyrant', or like John McBride, a weaver from County Antrim, who declared he had left Ulster so he would not 'have to stand like a beggar at a manufacturer's door'.[77] Others included the predominantly Presbyterian small farmers and craftsmen whom John Gamble observed, shortly after the Napoleonic Wars, who explained their decisions to emigrate in language that mixed bitter criticism of landlordism and of post-Union Ulster's social and political inequities with republican dreams of the political 'freedom' and socio-economic 'independence' they hoped to enjoy in America. 'Borne down by poverty and oppression,' Gamble wrote of his Presbyterian countrymen, 'they carry their industry, talents and energy, to a distant and happier land, and never think of the one they have quitted but with loathing, and of its government, with a feeling, for which hatred is but a feeble word.'[78] And, finally, still others were the weavers and labourers who migrated to northern England's industrial towns, where, in the early 1800s, they became notorious for the radicalism of their trade unionism and political activities, and where — in another revealing example of Irish and British élite convergence — they often fell victim to spies and informers whom the British government recruited among yet other Ulster migrants who were members of the Orange Order.[79]

The petitions quoted in this paragraph of the text (and above) are: James Campbell, Portadown, County Armagh, 5 April 1819 (CO 384/4); William Burroughs, Magherafelt, County Derry, 22 March 1822 (CO 384/8); James Smily, et al., Bracky, County Armagh, n.d. [recd. 19 August 1823] (CO 384/9); James Gibson, Omagh, County Tyrone, 12 April 1828 (CO 384/19); Patrick Clark, Dunleer, County Louth, 5 November 1829 (CO 384/21); and Robert Ritchey, Galgorm, County Antrim, 13 May 1833 (CO 384/31).

Other petitioners testifying to their Protestantism and/or their loyal service (in the Yeomanry or the police, as informers, etc.), offering 'character' references from clergymen, Orange Lodges, etc., and/or alleging their victimization at the hands of 'disloyal' Catholics, include: James McConnel, Enniskillen, County Fermanagh, 12 January 1824 (CO 384/10); Rev. Alexander McEwen (on behalf of his Presbyterian congregation), Kirkcubbin, County Down, n.d. [1826] (CO 384/14); David Kennedy, Clough, County Down, 21 June 1827 (CO 384/16); James Rogers, Bailieboro, County Cavan, 6 October 1830 (CO 384/23); and John MacRay, Butler's Bridge, County Cavan, 23 May 1844 (CO 384/75). See above, n. 31, for the full citation to the Colonial Office petitions.

It should be noted that Orange Lodge transfer certificates, signifying membership in good standing, were invaluable aids for many Irish Protestant emigrants, especially those intending to settle and find employment in British North America; see Cecil J. Houston and William J. Smyth, *The Sash Canada Wore: A Historical Geography of the Orange Order in Canada* (Toronto, 1980).

77 David Robinson, Lexington, Ky., 4 May 1817, full text in Miller, et al., *Irish Immigrants in the Land of Canaan*, 681–83; John McBride, Watertown, NY, to James McBride, Derriaghy, County Antrim, 9 January 1820 (T.2613/3, PRONI).

78 Gamble, *Views of Society and Manners in the North of Ireland*, 191; also see 197–98, 202, 367–68, 421.

79 Kevin Haddick-Flynn, *Orangeism: The Making of a Tradition* (Dublin, 1999), 202–08. See also Boyd, *Rise of the Irish Trade Unions*, 37–40; Strauss, *Irish Nationalism and British Democracy*, 125–26; and Thompson, *Outsiders*:

In conclusion, what might be termed the 'taming' of Ulster's Protestant lower classes would be a prolonged, uneasy, and even transatlantic development. It would involve the transformations of 'wild Irish' in America and in the United Kingdom into respectable 'Scotch-Irish' and 'loyal Britons', as well as the creation of staunch unionists in northern Ireland itself.[80] Even the latter process would remain bedeviled by intracommunal conflicts — over tenant-right and industrial relations, for example — as Ulster's Protestant upper, middle, and lower classes sought to define unionism's practical implications — and distribute its material rewards or burdens — in different ways. In the end, of course, as at the beginning, their residents' loyal defence of 'the Protestant way of life' would have quite different outcomes in Belfast's upper-, middle-, and working-class Protestant neighbourhoods. Yet from at least the middle of the nineteenth century, such issues would be contested almost invariably within the 'unionist family': within a hegemonic framework of shared political, social, and cultural assumptions that had been forged, disseminated, and at times quite harshly imposed by Ulster's Protestant élites in the early 1800s. Thus, 'Belfast's first bomb' in 1816 was by no means the most destructive that would be exploded during the next two centuries. To historians, however, it may signal the importance of a hitherto unappreciated intracommunal social conflict, the resolution of which was of momentous importance for the future of Ulster and Irish society.

Class, Gender and Nation, chs. 4–5.

80 With regard to the development of 'Scotch-Irish' identity and community in late eighteenth- and early nineteenth-century America, this argument is elaborated in Miller, *et al.*, *Irish Immigrants in the Land of Canaan*, esp. in chs. 49–68; also see Chapters 6 and 7 in this volume. On the creation of 'loyal Britons', see Linda Colley, *Britons: Forging the Nation, 1707–1837* (New Haven, Conn., 1992).

9 The Lost World of Andrew Johnston:
Sectarianism, Social Conflict, and Cultural Change in Southern
Ireland during the Pre-Famine Era

Since the Reformation, sectarianism has been deeply rooted in both Protestant and Catholic Irish cultures, expressed in songs and folklore as well as in politics and violence.[1] This is hardly surprising, given that the British conquests and colonizations of Ireland were both promulgated and resisted in the political and cultural frameworks of the Protestant Reformation and the Catholic Counter-Reformation. Yet although religious prejudices may therefore always be latent in Irish popular culture, it is arguable that often their most strident expressions and violent manifestations occur when one or both of the two religious communities are themselves sharply divided by socio-economic and cultural antagonisms, and when Catholic and/or Protestant leaders therefore have special needs to mobilize their respective followers against the 'traditional' enemy.

1 This chapter, under the same title, was originally published in James S. Donnelly, Jr., and Kerby A. Miller, eds., *Irish Popular Culture, 1650–1850* (Dublin, 1998), 222–41; and I wish to thank Irish Academic Press, in Dublin, for permission to republish it in this volume, with minor revisions. A considerably shorter version, entitled 'No Middle Ground: The Erosion of the Protestant Middle Class in Southern Ireland during the Pre-Famine Era', appeared a decade earlier, in *The Huntington Library Quarterly*, 49, 4 (autumn 1986), 295–306.

   I would like to thank Sharon Fleming and Patricia Miller, whose painstaking transcriptions of the Johnston letters made this research possible; Professor Liam Kennedy of the Queen's University, Belfast, for generous sharing of ideas, office space, and research tasks; Dr. Fergus O'Ferrall, for allowing me to read his masterful doctoral thesis on early nineteenth-century Longford politics; the Research Council of the University of Missouri-Columbia, the American Council of Learned Societies, the Huntington Library, and the National Endowment for the Humanities for funding the research. Thanks as well to Mr. and Mrs. S. Bothwell of St. Angelo, Trory parish, Count Fermanagh, and especially to the late Paddy Whelan, Marian Keaney, Fr. Owen Devaney, Jude Flynn, and the other members of the County Longford Historical Society who made my enquiries into south Longford history both productive and enjoyable.

In southern Ireland, for example, during the early nineteenth century an ambitious Catholic middle class and an anxious Protestant Ascendancy were locked not only in political conflict with each other but also, less overtly but no less significantly, in social conflicts with their own inferiors. In the pre-Famine decades both the Catholic bourgeoisie and the Protestant landlord class sought to rationalize Irish agriculture, increase profits, and impose a free-market ethos on their poorer co-religionists. Both Catholic peasants and at least some members of the rural Protestant middle and lower classes resisted the blandishments of liberalism — the former through the violence of the secret agrarian societies, the latter as members of the Loyal Orange Order and in anguished letters to Tory newspapers — for both regarded the spirit of the marketplace as inimical not only to their economic survival but also to archaic beliefs in an organic, paternalistic, and hierarchical society.[2] Thus to deflect popular resentment within their own communities, as well as to challenge their rivals more effectively, Catholic and Protestant leaders alike employed political and religious symbols to marshal their co-religionists into all-class alliances and crusades for sectarian advantage. Faced with economic depression, a burgeoning population, and fierce competition for land and employment, most ordinary Catholics and Protestants faced the options of enlisting in those crusades or emigrating abroad — of supporting their own socio-economic exploiters or sailing to North America. As a result, both the triumph of liberal capitalism and the consequent sectarian and political struggles shaped a modern Ireland, which became both profoundly bourgeois and deeply divided. For better or worse, in the process, a way of life — an older world of different values and relationships — was lost forever. The trials and betrayals of Andrew Johnston, an insignificant but perhaps not an ignoble figure in the maelstrom of Irish history, illustrate how that process occurred.

After the partition of Ireland in 1921 and during the remainder of the century, violent conflict between Irish Catholics and Protestants was confined almost exclusively to Northern Ireland. But in the last third of the eighteenth century and the first half of the nineteenth, various kinds of 'outrages' frequently occurred throughout the island. Most of these were social or political, not strictly sectarian, in inspiration, but, given Irish society's essential alignment of class, political, and religious authority, Protestants usually perceived or advertised any challenges to the 'established order' — even the Whiteboys' largely intracommunal violence — as ultimately if not immediately sectarian. Moreover, the suppression of such challenges by the overwhelmingly Protestant agents

---

2   On pre-Famine emigration generally, see Chapter 2 in this volume. As argued in Chapters 8 and 10 in this work, in Ulster the principal intracommunal conflicts generating sectarianism were within Protestant society and were both social and denominational in nature. In general, Ulster's Catholics, relative to those in the South (especially in Leinster and east Munster), were too beleaguered, poor, and socially homogenous to develop the kind of politically assertive and economically exploitive lay middle class that was characteristic of southern counties like Longford. Consequently, middle-class Catholic leadership in Ulster was confined largely to a Church hierarchy and clergy that usually (and especially before the Famine) pursued a much more 'accommodationist' policy towards Protestant power than did most of their peers in the Catholic-majority parts of the island.

of what most Catholics regarded as a hostile Protestant state almost invariably coloured Catholics' social or political protests, and Protestants' responses in support of 'law and order', with sectarian animosity.

In any case, to judge from the thousands of Irish petitions sent to the British Colonial Office between 1817 and the early 1840s, a desire to escape from violence was second only to the goal of economic 'independence' in explaining why an estimated 500,000 Irish Protestants (with an approximately equal number of Catholics) emigrated during the pre-Famine decades (1815–44). The same motive may have impelled significant numbers of Protestants and Catholics to migrate within Ireland, seeking safety in areas dominated by their co-religionists. Although the Protestant proportion of the future Northern Ireland was not appreciably diminished by emigration,[3] and may have been enhanced slightly by internal migration, the effects of these population movements on the much smaller Protestant communities in the counties of southern Ireland were very significant. The haemorrhage of southern Irish Protestants both resulted from and greatly contributed to the rise of middle-class Catholic political and economic ascendancy in those counties, and also contributed to a weakening of landlord control and British authority, which eventually proved fatal to both.

For example, in 1831 County Longford contained c. 10,612 Protestant inhabitants, almost all members of the legally established Church of Ireland, about 9.5 per cent of the county's population. But between 1831 and 1861 Longford's Protestant population fell by 35 per cent, only slightly less than the 36 per cent Catholic decline despite the much more severe impact of the Great Famine on the county's predominantly Catholic lower classes of smallholders and labourers. Prior to the Famine one major cause of Protestant decline was the attrition of Protestant middlemen — head tenants who leased several hundred acres or more, most of which they sublet to a multitude of undertenants. Once prominent members of County Longford society, Protestant middlemen were not only pillars of the Protestant Ascendancy, but they also — in their roles as subletters, investors, employers, and magistrates — served as vital mainstays for the humbler ranks of Protestant small farmers, shopkeepers, artisans, and labourers. Consequently, their disappearance during the pre-Famine decades eroded the infrastructure of Protestant society and ultimately weakened landlord and British power. This chapter will investigate the causes of the middlemen's decline in County Longford by focusing on the fate of the Andrew Johnston family, whose remarkable letters to their emigrant children are preserved in the Huntington Library in California.[4]

3 However, the Presbyterian proportions of Ulster's overall and Protestant populations were certainly reduced by mass migration; see Chapters 8 and 10 in this volume.

4 On County Longford's population, see: W. E. Vaughan and A. J. Fitzpatrick, eds., *Irish Historical Statistics: Population, 1821–1971* (Dublin, 1978), 6 and 51; and Liam Kennedy and Kerby A. Miller, with Mark Graham, 'The Long Retreat: Protestants, Economy and Society, 1660–1926', in Raymond Gillespie and Gerard Moran, eds., *Longford: Essays in County History* (Dublin, 1991), 31–62, esp. 40 and 49; the data on the declines of Longford's Protestant and Catholic populations between 1831 and 1861 were calculated from the *First Report of the Commissioners of Public Instruction, Ireland*, in BBP, HC 1835, xxxiii, and from the Census

Andrew Johnston, his wife Eliza, his sister-in-law Alicia Welsh, and Johnston's twelve children (five of whom emigrated in the 1830s) resided in a large, two-storey house in the town of Ballymahon, located on the River Inny, in the parishes of Shrule and Noughaval in south Longford. In 1841 Ballymahon had 1,229 inhabitants, about 90 per cent of whom were Catholics, the remainder parishioners of the local Church of Ireland. Although consisting primarily of only one main street, Ballymahon was blessed with a combined courthouse and market house, where markets were held every Thursday; large flour and corn mills; four annual fairs, one of which — the May cattle fair — was considered second only to the great Ballinasloe fair, in east Galway, in regional importance; two schools; a dispensary; and a constabulary barracks. The town was also the residence of the Catholic bishop of Ardagh. The countryside surrounding Ballymahon was fertile and considered ideal for grazing, although prior to the Famine the land was still devoted primarily to tillage, especially to conacre (the short-term rental of potato ground), owing to its dense population of peasants and labourers. Ballymahon had a nearby dock on the Royal Canal, which provided cheap transport to Dublin, and it was surrounded by an unusually large number of gentlemen's 'Big Houses' and demesne lands. The proprietor of two of those houses, Ballymulvey and Moigh House, was William Molyneux Shuldham, who owned all of Ballymahon and most of the adjacent parishes — in all about 2,600 acres, later valued at nearly £2,700 per year.[5]

Andrew Johnston was a younger, non-inheriting son of a small proprietor, Peyton Johnston, from mid-Longford. From at least 1804 onwards, Andrew Johnston was a head tenant and middleman on the Shuldham estate. By the late 1820s and early 1830s Johnston was leasing about 30 per cent of the Shuldham property — over 800 statute

of Ireland for the Year 1861, in BBP, HC 1863 [3204-III], lix, as summarized in Vaughan and Fitzpatrick, eds., Irish Historical Statistics, 51. On middlemen generally, see: David Dickson, 'Middlemen', in Thomas Bartlett and D. W. Hayton, eds., Penal Era and Golden Age: Essays in Irish History, 1690–1800 (Belfast, 1979), 162–85; L. M. Cullen, The Emergence of Modern Ireland, 1600–1900, paperback edn. (Dublin, 1983), 99–107, 128–31; and Cormac Ó Gráda, Ireland: A New Economic History, 1780–1939 (Oxford, 1994), 31–33, 125–27.

   The Johnston family letters, formally titled the Peyton Johnston Mss., form part of the Robert Alonzo Brock collection at the Huntington Library, San Marino, California. A typescript of most of the letters has been deposited in the Longford-Westmeath County Library Headquarters in Mullingar, County Westmeath. Unless otherwise stated, all the letters cited below that were written by Andrew Johnston, his wife Eliza Johnston, or his sisters-in-law Alicia Welsh and Anna Cox, were sent from Ballymahon, County Longford, to his son, Peyton Johnston (although sometimes co-addressed to Peyton's siblings) in Richmond, Virginia.

5 Information on Ballymahon from: The Traveller's New Guide through Ireland (Dublin, 1815), 184–85; William Shaw Mason, A Statistical Account, or Parochial Survey of Ireland, vol. 3 (Dublin, 1819), 337–67; James Johnston, map of 'The town of Ballymahon, 1825' (Longford-Westmeath County Library); H. D. Inglis, Ireland in 1834: A Journey throughout Ireland, during the Spring, Summer, and Autumn of 1834, 2 vols. (London, 1835), vol. 1, 338 and passim; T. MacManus, 'One Hundred Years Ago', Longford Year Book, 1931 (Longford, 1931), 9–13; Thom's Directory of Ireland (Dublin, 1846), citation courtesy of Paddy Whelan, Ballymahon; Report of the Commission on Public Instruction, Ireland, in BPP, 62–63; Parliamentary Gazetteer of Ireland (Dublin, 1844), vol. 1, 182; Land Owners in Ireland. Return of Owners of Land of One Acre and Upwards, in the Several Counties, Counties of Cities, and Counties of Towns in Ireland (Dublin, 1876), 52–55.

acres with an annual value of nearly £500 — usually on leases running for three lives or thirty-one years. Sixty of these acres were in Ballymulvey townland, immediately adjacent to Ballymahon, and in the town itself Johnston rented eight more acres, divided into four lots, on which were located the town market house, his flour and corn mills, a flax-dressing concern, and his own residence — the latter situated in the shadow of his landlord's town house, Inny View, and just across the narrow bridge that spanned the river and separated Johnston's house and mills from the bulk of the town. On paper at least, Johnston's holdings made him one of Ballymahon's most affluent and influential citizens. In 1837 Johnston was fifty-six years old; during the preceding decades he had served as a vestryman, churchwarden, and tithe assessor in the local Anglican church; in 1821 he had registered to vote as a £50 freeholder (in 1832 as a £20 freeholder); and he and his family participated on equal terms in the social life of the lesser gentry of the south Longford–Westmeath border region. As will be seen later, Johnston also enjoyed one other species of property, also leased from Shuldham, which brought him unusual income, power, and ultimate disaster.[6]

The great crisis in Andrew Johnston's life began on Thursday, 21 September 1837. That evening about seven o'clock, one of his employees, a somewhat simple-minded and often inebriated Protestant named John Frayne, got into a fight with a young Catholic, a candidate for the priesthood named Thomas Ferrall, while the two men were crossing Ballymahon bridge in front of the Johnston residence. Andrew Johnston and his eldest son, John, moved to intervene, as did a sizeable number of Ferrall's friends. The result was a small but fatal riot. Before the constabulary arrived to restore order, Johnston and his son were badly beaten, and Ferrall was mortally wounded when stabbed twice in his side. As a result of the testimony of several witnesses, including the accusation of the dying Thomas Ferrall, Andrew and John Johnston were arrested. The coroner's inquest was held over the next two days, and the coroner's jury concluded that Ferrall had been murdered — stabbed to death by John Johnston, aided by his father. Accordingly, the two men were arraigned for trial at the March 1838 assizes on the charge of murder, although both were soon released on bail. Their trial was later postponed until the July assizes, and the charge was reduced from murder to manslaughter. Prior to the trial, in late November 1837, Andrew Johnston barely escaped assassination when four bullets fired by unknown assailants struck the gig in which he was riding while inspecting his farms.

6 James Johnston, map of 'James Dowdall's part of ... Ballymahon, 1804' (Ms. 16F. 15, NLI); Tithe Applotment Books, County Longford, 1826 (National Archives of Ireland, Dublin; formerly in the Public Record Office of Ireland); James Johnston, map of 'Town of Ballymahon'; Lease of Derrynagalagh, L. Warren and W. Barton to Andrew Johnston, 2 April 1822 (Ms. 805/475/542, 810, in the Irish Registry of Deeds, King's Inn, Dublin); Andrew Johnston, 15 October 1837 (Peyton Johnston Mss.); Shrule Parish Vestry Minute Book (Representative Church Body Library, Dublin); Lists of Freeholders, County Longford (Irish Genealogical Office, Dublin), copy courtesy of Dr. Kevin Whelan, now director of the Dublin campus of the University of Notre Dame's Irish studies programme.

The Johnstons' trial was held at Longford town on 16 July 1838 before Judge Edward Pennefather. At the conclusion of the testimony the judge instructed the jury to acquit Andrew Johnston since the blows he had struck during the riot obviously had not been fatal. He then charged the jury that 'with respect to John Johnston they must be satisfied that the blows as stated, inflicted by him [on Thomas Ferrall,] were in the defence of his father's life, at that time endangered, before such stabs could be justified' and the defendant acquitted; 'if they had a doubt,' he concluded, 'they should give the prisoners the benefit of it, for the criminal law requires every charge to be fully proven'. After briefly retiring, the jury acquitted both prisoners. Shortly afterward, however, Andrew Johnston relinquished or sold the interest in all his holdings, packed up his family and goods, and left Ballymahon and County Longford forever.[7]

It is impossible to determine what really transpired during the riot of 21 September 1837, for the specific issue of the Johnstons' guilt or innocence was entirely submerged in bitter political and sectarian interests that have coloured all the surviving evidence. The three provincial newspapers that served County Longford covered the riot, the coroner's inquest, and the Johnstons' trial extensively. According to the O'Connellite journal, the *Athlone Sentinel*, the affair was 'THE BALLYMAHON MURDER' — committed in cold blood by John Johnston. But the Tory newspapers, the *Athlone Conservative Advocate* and the *Westmeath Guardian and Longford News-Letter*, called Thomas Ferrall's death 'justifiable homicide' and hailed the Johnstons as 'innocent men, whose only crime has been the defence of their lives from the fury of ... priest-ridden and furious mobs'. The Conservative weeklies, the constabulary reports, and the Johnstons' own letters claimed that the coroner's inquest was conducted unfairly, in an atmosphere of public excitement and intimidation; that the Johnstons were prevented from calling a single witness on their behalf; that the Catholic witnesses lied under oath; and that the coroner's jury which charged the Johnstons with murder was packed with ten Catholics against two Protestants. For their part, local Catholics accused the magistrates of Orange bias when they released the Johnstons on bail, and the *Athlone Sentinel* ignored the subsequent attempt on Andrew Johnston's life, whereas the Tory papers featured it prominently.[8]

At the trial itself the prosecution witnesses claimed that the Johnstons had been the aggressors on Ballymahon bridge and that Andrew Johnston had beaten Ferrall senseless

---

7   See Johnston family letters of 22 June 1835 (on Frayne), 20 December 1837, and 12 January 1838 (Peyton Johnston Mss.); Report of Samuel Alworthy, 22 September 1837 (Chief Secretary's Office Registered Papers, Outrage Papers 1837/19/197, National Archives of Ireland; formerly in the State Paper Office, Dublin); *Athlone Sentinel*, 22 and 29 September 1837, 20 July 1838; *Westmeath Guardian and Longford News-Letter*, 28 September and 2 November 1837, 8 March and 19 July 1838; *Athlone Conservative Advocate*, 28 September 1837 (all newspapers cited here and below are in the British Newspaper Library, London). The contrasts between the judges' interpretations of the law, and their instructions to the juries, in the 1816 trial of the Belfast weavers and the 1838 trial of the Johnstons, are stark and revealing; see Chapter 8 in this volume.

8   See note 7 above, and also A Resident of Longford, 'Insurrectionary State of the County of Longford', *Dublin University Magazine*, 2 (January 1838), 121–23.

with a poker before John Johnston stabbed him with a dagger in front of sober, peaceful, and horrified Catholic bystanders. By contrast, the defence witnesses testified that the Johnstons had carried no weapons; that before they could even touch Ferrall they had been set upon and badly beaten by a mob of drunken Catholics who had emerged from an adjacent public house; and that John Johnston had already fled into another house before Ferrall received his mortal injuries — presumably inflicted accidentally by other members of the crowd who were attempting to stab the Johnstons. (It is fruitless to attempt a reconciliation of such totally contradictory evidence, although it may be significant that Andrew Johnston's private account of the affair, conveyed in letters to his emigrant sons, largely corroborated the story later told by his defence witnesses.) Needless to say, the *Athlone Sentinel*'s editor was disgusted with the Johnstons' ultimate acquittal by a jury allegedly containing nine Protestants and only three Catholics, while the *Westmeath Guardian* and other Conservative journals rejoiced at the Johnstons' narrow escape from 'Popish persecution'.[9]

Of course, the Ballymahon riot was merely one of many 'outrages' that occurred in pre-Famine Ireland, especially during the anti-tithe campaigns of the 1830s. Moreover, violence seems to have been unusually prevalent in County Longford. As early as 1793 Ballymahon itself was the venue of a major anti-militia riot, and in 1798 the final, horrific scenes of the United Irish rising were played out at Granard and Ballinamuck: the massacres of surrendered rebels after both battles, by British troops and loyalists, engendered lasting bitterness. Because of a combination of circumstances — economic depression, tension over land-use between commercial and subsistence cultivators, high population density, and the presence of a significant Protestant minority — Longford was wracked with agrarian and sectarian conflict during the pre-Famine decades. From 1806 through the mid-1840s local secret agrarian societies were almost continuously active, and according to police reports, the Ribbonmen were unusually strong among the county's lower-middle- and labouring-class Catholics, especially among townsmen and workers on the Royal Canal.[10]

Most important, beginning with the Catholic Emancipation crisis of the late 1820s, political activity by the county's middle-class lay Catholics and clergy served to legitimate or at least to corroborate violent expressions of popular grievances against Longford's local Tory/Protestant ascendancy. By the early 1830s Longford's Catholics were effectively mobilized in support of the perennial Liberal candidates for parliament,

9   See the sources cited in note 7 above.
10 *Parliamentary Gazetteer of Ireland*, vol. 1, 182; H. A. Richey, *A Short History of the Royal Longford Militia, 1793–1893* (Dublin, 1894), 10–12; Sean Murray, 'A Short History of County Longford' (Ms. in Longford-Westmeath County Library), 57; James P. Farrell, *Historical Notes and Stories of the County Longford* (Dublin, 1886), 204; Michael R. Beames, *Peasants and Power: The Whiteboy Movements and Their Control in Pre-Famine Ireland* (Dublin, 1983), 43, 85–86, 132, and 'The Ribbon Societies: Lower-Class Nationalism in Pre-Famine Ireland', *Past and Present*, no. 97 (November 1982), 129, 140; Tom Garvin, 'Defenders, Ribbonmen and Others: Underground Political Networks in Pre-Famine Ireland', *Past and Present*, 96 (August 1982), 133–55, esp. 151; Report of Capt. Edward Hill, R.M., 31 January 1842 (CO 904/9, PRO, London).

Luke White and his brother, Colonel Henry White, while the Conservatives rallied Protestant voters behind the ultra-Tory Anthony Lefroy, Viscount Forbes, and after Forbes's death in 1836, behind Charles Fox. Unhappily, the county witnessed almost constant political strife during the 1830s, for there were no fewer than six general elections or by-elections in the decade, and nearly all were extremely close contests, since the restrictive £10 freehold franchise heavily favoured the more affluent Protestant minority. As mentioned earlier, the Catholic bishop of Ardagh, Dr. William Higgins, resided in Ballymahon: he and many of his priests were ardent supporters of O'Connell, and their sermons and political activities helped to make south Longford a centre of pro-Liberal and anti-tithe agitation. For their part, the county's Conservatives relied heavily on the Anglican clergy and the resurgent Orange Order to mobilize Protestant voters; during the 1830s Longford contained at least nine Orange Lodges, with an alleged total of 5,000 members. According to their critics, the local Tories also utilized the magistracy, the constabulary, and the prerogatives of landlordism to intimidate or punish enfranchised Catholics. Indeed, it appears that several of the wealthiest landlords, especially Lord Lorton, systematically cleared Catholic tenants from their estates and replaced them with Protestants. The result was further bitterness and a convergence of political protests and agrarian violence that culminated in the so-called Ballinamuck land war of 1835–39. Despite these Tory efforts, the Protestant cause in Longford was ultimately a losing one. Liberal election victories in 1832 and 1836 were thwarted by successful Tory petitions to parliament, but the last election of the decade in the summer of 1837 witnessed a great Liberal–Catholic triumph: Longford sent both Whites to parliament, and at Dublin Castle the newly appointed Whig administration began what the defeated Tories called the 'Mulgravization' of County Longford's magistracy and constabulary. As Andrew Johnston's sister-in-law despaired in early 1837, 'nothing is now given to Protestants but left to the mercy of Papists, who are ruling them with a rod of iron'. As her comment suggests, by 1837 County Longford was bitterly polarized.[11]

11 Irish Liberals comprised the reform wing of the Whig party in Ireland; hence, as in Longford, they were more likely than conservative Irish Whigs to ally with O'Connell in parliament and to court electoral support from the local Liberal Clubs that he had established in the late 1820s, to support the campaign for Catholic Emancipation; in the early 1840s some Irish Liberals became Repealers. What the Irish Tory press called 'Mulgravization' referred to the efforts of the Whig Party, in power in 1835–41 through alliance with O'Connell's Irish Liberals, to reform Ireland's administrative, legal, judicial, and police systems, by purging them of Tory-Orange bias and personnel; Lord Mulgrave (Irish lord lieutenant in 1835–39) was the nominal head of the reform administration in Dublin Castle, but its most forceful figure was Thomas Drummond, Irish under-secretary in 1835–40. See Angus Macintyre, *The Liberator: Daniel O'Connell and the Irish Party, 1830–1847* (London, 1965), esp. 96–98. On Longford, see: Fergus O'Ferrall, 'The Struggle for Catholic Emancipation in County Longford, 1824–29', *Teathbha: Journal of the Longford Historical Society*, 1 (October 1978), 259–79; 'The Ballinamuck "Land War", 1835–39,' *Teathbha*, 2 (March 1983), 104–09; and 'The Growth of Political Consciousness in Ireland, 1824–1848' (PhD thesis, University of Dublin, 1978), 485–676. C. Moloney, 'Parliamentary Returns, 1830–80: A Thesis' (Ms. in the Longford County Library, Longford), no pagination; B. M. Walker, ed., *Parliamentary Election Results in Ireland, 1801–1922* (Dublin, 1978), 228–29, 298–99; James Joseph MacNamee, *History of the Diocese of Ardagh* (Dublin, 1954), 458–59; James Monahan, *Records Relating to the Diocese of Ardagh and Clonmacnois* (Dublin, 1886), 160–68; Donal Kerr,

Much evidence indicates that nearly all Longford's Protestants feared for their lives and fortunes in the 1830s — and especially after the Whites' 1837 victory — at the hands of what the *Westmeath Guardian* called a 'brutal and unintelligent' and now unrestrained 'peasantry'. Indeed, early in September 1837, a week prior to the Ballymahon riot, a crowd of Catholics attacked a Protestant farmer and his labourers near the town, and a few months later a member of the Irish Constabulary, an Ulster Protestant, was murdered near Longford town. Nevertheless, although this climate of agitation and animosity provided the general context of the Ballymahon riot, it does not explain why Andrew Johnston and the Tory press believed that he and his family had been singled out as *specific* targets of 'Popish persecution'. Of course, Johnston no doubt voted Tory, but so did nearly all Longford Protestants, and neither his letters nor the local newspapers suggest that he was prominent or even especially interested in either politics or the Orange Order. Likewise, the *Athlone Sentinel* failed to levy the common charges that Johnston was a rack-renter or an 'exterminator', and what little evidence survives suggests that his relationships with his own Catholic subtenants and labourers were remarkably good. Moreover, in 1829 — at the very height of the Catholic Emancipation crisis — Johnston had founded in Ballymahon a Masonic Lodge that welcomed and contained many Catholic as well as Protestant members, perhaps in an attempt to create a social bridge between the otherwise divided religious communities in the region. Thus, in order to understand the popular animosity towards Johnston, it is necessary to examine more closely both his own position in Ballymahon and the dynamics of Catholic agitation in south Longford.[12]

Andrew Johnston not only leased 800 acres of farmland from the Shuldham estate, but he also leased the local mills and, more important, the right to levy and collect the 'tolls of markets' and the 'customs of fairs' held in Ballymahon. Since the weekly market was reportedly 'well-attended', and since the town's cattle fairs were of considerable regional significance, Johnston's monopoly of the 'tolls and customs' brought him substantial profits. The *Westmeath Guardian* alleged that the tolls and customs amounted to £600 annually, and Johnston himself claimed that he made 'upwards of £200 a year' from them. Truly, Johnston was a 'middleman' in more than the usual sense of the term, for the leasing of both the local mills and the tolls and customs placed him in an economically strategic and intermediate position between the Catholic farmers and

Peel, Priests, and Politics: Sir Robert Peel's Administration and the Roman Catholic Church in Ireland, 1841–46 (Oxford, 1982), 8; *Report from the Select Committee to Inquire into the Nature ... of the Orange Lodge Associations*, in BPP, HC 1835, ix, Appendix, *passim*; Grand Orange Lodge, Book of Warrants, no date, and Book of New Warrants, 1875 (Library, Grand Orange Lodge Headquarters, Belfast); Resident of Longford, 'Insurrectionary State', 123; Alicia Welsh, 8 February 1837 (Peyton Johnston Mss.).

12 *Westmeath Guardian and Longford News-Letter*, 24 August, 14 and 21 September 1837, and 4 January 1838; Masonic Lodge Warrant Books (Library, Grand Lodge of the Order of Masons, Dublin), with assistance from Paddy Whelan in identifying Ballymahon Lodge members.

cottiers of the south Longford countryside and the Catholic dealers and shopkeepers of Ballymahon. It was a highly lucrative position, but it was also a fatally vulnerable one.[13]

In pre-Famine Ireland generally, Catholic political agitation on the local level was led by representatives of an aspiring bourgeoisie: strong farmers, professionals, shopkeepers, publicans, and priests of middle-class origins. County Longford was no exception, and its conflicts between middle-class Catholics and Protestants may have been especially fierce because in numerical terms the two groups were so evenly balanced. In his doctoral thesis Fergus O'Ferrall identified over thirty of the Liberal activists in and around Ballymahon during the pre-Famine decades. For our purposes the most important of these men were Fr. Peter Dawson, the administrator of Shrule parish in the years 1835–40 and an ambitious would-be bishop; Owen Maxwell, a grocer, and his brother, Thomas Maxwell, a draper; George Corcoran, a physician; and Valentine Dillon, a substantial tenant on the Shuldham estate. Another prominent Liberal was H. Wilson Slator, a member of an affluent Protestant mercantile family, who nominated Luke White for parliament in 1837.[14]

Among such men, liberal principles nicely converged not only with their own economic and political interests but also with their lower-class followers' traditional prejudices against both the *Sasanaigh* and 'parasitical middlemen' (such as the hated 'tithe-farmers'). As a result, it was not difficult for O'Connell's local champions to mobilize popular crusades, under the banner of 'Catholic liberalism', against what they called the 'artificial monopolies' that denied Catholics both equal political rights and equal opportunities to compete economically with Protestants. Of course, there were certain inconsistencies in Catholic liberalism. Lower-class Catholics in the secret agrarian societies, often engaged in an intra-communal class war over conacre rents and wages, knew that many members of the Catholic bourgeoisie were at least as exploitive as their Protestant counterparts. Likewise, the policy of 'exclusive dealing' (later known as 'boycotting'), which Catholic merchants often employed against their Protestant peers, certainly violated the liberal 'free-market' ethos. Nevertheless, in a county as polarized along sectarian lines as Longford, a middle-class Catholic campaign against Protestant privilege could command widespread support. Moreover, a crusade against a *specific* Protestant's monopoly of tolls and customs could unite Catholics of all classes in both town and countryside behind middle-class leadership — and thus serve both the broad hegemonic and the personal economic interests of that leadership.[15]

---

13 *Westmeath Guardian and Longford News-Letter*, 19 July 1838; *Parliamentary Gazetteer of Ireland*, 182; Andrew Johnston, 20 December 1837 (Peyton Johnston Mss.).

14 Tom Garvin, *The Evolution of Irish Nationalist Politics* (Dublin, 1981), 34–52; Fergus O'Ferrall, *Daniel O'Connell* (Dublin, 1981), *passim*, and 'Growth of Political Consciousness in Ireland', 484–86, 499–501, 518, 530–39, 548–49, 595, 603–05, 675–76, 687–88; on Slator, see *Athlone Sentinel*, 19 August 1837.

15 On Liberal–Catholic ideology, see O'Ferrall, *Daniel O'Connell, and Catholic Emancipation: Daniel O'Connell and the Birth of Irish Democracy* (Dublin, 1985). The literature on secret agrarian societies is voluminous; see especially Samuel Clark and James S. Donnelly, Jr., eds., *Irish Peasants: Violence and Political Unrest,*

Interestingly, the *Athlone Sentinel* never alluded to the possibility that the Ballymahon riot might have been sparked by middle-class Catholic hostility to or jealousy of Johnston's control of the tolls and customs, though this Liberal newspaper often reported and applauded Catholic assaults on that peculiar monopoly which occurred elsewhere in Ireland. However, according to the Tory press, the Johnstons' own letters, and some of the testimony that emerged at their trial, the riot of 21 September could not be understood except in such a context. According to this evidence, shortly after the Liberal victory in the 1837 election, Ballymahon's Catholic activists determined to punish Johnston, ostensibly for his Tory convictions, by denying him his profits from the tolls and customs. In late August or early September some of the Whites' chief supporters, led by Fr. Dawson, erected three public 'cranes' or weighing scales and directed their followers to use these, instead of Johnston's, on market days. This boycott was extremely effective: in a letter to his son, Johnston complained that he 'never rec[eive]d a penny for anything since' that 'vilinous priest Dawson put up' the new cranes. Moreover, the incident that precipitated the Ballymahon riot, the fight between Thomas Ferrall and Johnston's employee John Frayne, seems to have occurred as a direct result of the strain and humiliation consequent on this boycott. Not only did the fight occur at the end of a market day, when popular tensions surrounding the issue were at their height, but Ferrall seems to have been one of Fr. Dawson's more active and boastful adherents, while Frayne's major duty (perhaps the only one of which he was capable) was the management of Andrew Johnston's now deserted crane. Finally, although it is unlikely that the riot — *as it actually occurred* — was premeditated, there were indications in the trial testimony, brought out under examination by the defence counsels, that a public meeting or a popular protest of *some kind* against Johnston's monopoly had been planned for that very evening.[16]

Of course, Ferrall's death and the Johnstons' subsequent arrest, trial, and hasty departure from Ballymahon could not have been foreseen. Nevertheless, there is strong circumstantial evidence that local Catholic activists were quick to take advantage of the Johnstons' sudden vulnerability. For example, it may be significant that the presiding magistrate at the coroner's inquest, which refused to hear the Johnstons' witnesses and which charged Andrew and John Johnston with murder, was none other than Luke White — though surely under ordinary circumstances such a minor affray would not have commanded personal attention from an MP and a newly appointed lord lieutenant of the county. Perhaps more telling, during the inquest itself both Thomas Maxwell

1780–1914 (Madison, Wisc., 1983); and George Cornewall Lewis, *Local Disturbances in Ireland* (London, 1836), as well as Beames, *Peasants and Power*.

16 On Catholic-Liberal protests against tolls and customs elsewhere in Ireland, see *Athlone Sentinel*, 27 April 1838 (Moate, County Westmeath), 1 June 1838 (Ballyboy, King's County), and 24 August 1838 (Nenagh, County Tipperary). *Westmeath Guardian and Longford News-Letter*, 28 September 1837 and 19 July 1838; *Athlone Conservative Advocate*, 21 and 28 September 1837; Resident of Longford, 'Insurrectionary State', 121–23; Alicia Welsh, 1 October 1837, and Andrew Johnston, 15 October 1837 (Peyton Johnston Mss.).

and Dr. George Corcoran gave especially damning testimony, swearing that Thomas Ferrall, in a dying declaration before Fr. Dawson, had branded John Johnston as his murderer. Corcoran later repeated his testimony at the Johnstons' trial, and although Maxwell did not testify again on that occasion, another witness for the prosecution — James Armstrong, whom the *Athlone Sentinel* described as 'a wretched, ragged creature' — hinted under cross-examination that Maxwell and others might have rewarded him for his testimony. Indeed, according to Andrew Johnston's sister-in-law, among all of Ballymahon's leading Catholics only Valentine Dillon, a member of the coroner's jury, 'behaved handsomely' during the crisis, perhaps because — of all the Catholic leaders involved — only he was also a member of Andrew Johnston's Masonic Lodge.[17]

At this distance, of course, it is impossible to be as certain as were the Tory newspapers and Johnston's sister-in-law that, in her words, 'all this ha[d] been planned'. Nevertheless, south Longford's middle-class Catholics certainly benefited in general from the Johnstons' downfall, for no one dared henceforth to lease or enforce Shuldham's tolls and customs, and 'free trade' — largely in Catholic hands — became the order of the day in Ballymahon. In addition, it may have been more than fortuitous that some local Liberal leaders benefited personally from the Johnstons' discomfort and departure. For example, almost immediately, the family of H. Wilson Slator, the Liberal Protestant ally of Luke White, secured Johnston's old lease of the town's corn and flour mills. More significantly, in 1839, in what was surely a sale forced by his distress, Andrew Johnston transferred his lease of Derrynagalliagh, a townland of 320 acres, to Owen Maxwell in a transaction witnessed by Dr. George Corcoran. Indeed, within a few years the Catholic Maxwells — scarcely mentioned in the 1826 tithe-applotment lists — seem to have supplanted the Protestant Johnstons in Ballymahon. By the mid-1840s Owen Maxwell was a member of the local Poor Law Board of Guardians and rented at least 24 acres of land within and immediately adjacent to Ballymahon; according to local historian Patrick Whelan, by mid-century Owen Maxwell owned or rented 'half the town'. Similarly, his brother Thomas became secretary of the local loan fund and by 1871 he owned outright nearly 570 acres in south Longford. Clearly, for such men patriotism in the service of Catholic Ireland could be more than spiritually rewarding.[18]

17 *Athlone Sentinel*, 29 September 1837; *Westmeath Guardian and Longford News-Letter*, 19 July 1838 (revealingly, James Armstrong's reference to Maxwell was omitted from the *Athlone Sentinel*'s transcription of the trial testimony — one of several curious discrepancies between the two newspapers' reports of the trial); Alicia Welsh and Anna Cox, 28 September–1 October 1837 (Peyton Johnston Mss.) on Valentine Dillon, and see Masonic Lodge Warrant Books, cited in n. 12 above.

18 Alicia Welsh, 1 October 1837 (Peyton Johnston Mss.); on Shuldham's tolls and customs and the tenancies of the Slators and Maxwells, see *Valuation of Land [Griffith's]*, *Ballymahon Union* (Dublin, 1872; copies in the NLI, Trinity College, Dublin, and in the National Archives of Ireland); Lease of Derrynagalliagh, Andrew Johnston to Owen Maxwell, 5 April 1839 (Ms. 1839/6/219, Irish Registry of Deeds). Fr. Peter Dawson never attained a bishop's mitre but he did become vicar-general of Ardagh diocese. When Thomas Maxwell died in the 1870s, he bequeathed £1,000 plus 'a large farm' (one of Andrew Johnston's?) and house to provide for the establishment of a convent of the Sisters of Mercy. On Owen Maxwell I have also relied on O'Ferrall, 'Growth of Political Consciousness', 587–88, 675, and on information from Paddy Whelan,

Yet it would be misleading to attribute Andrew Johnston's downfall solely to Catholic pressure and to sectarian conflict. Johnston's economic position had been deteriorating long before the Ballymahon riot, and, most important, the Protestant middle class in Longford and more generally in southern Ireland was being eroded by socio-economic and cultural conflicts within the Protestant community itself.

In part Andrew Johnston's economic problems reflected the long post-war depression, which afflicted Ireland in general and the middleman class in particular. In 1819 the Anglican curate of Shrule parish had described Ballymahon as 'thriving', but twenty years later scholar John O'Donovan, working in south Longford for the Ordnance Survey, observed that 'little business is carried on'. In 1834 Johnston himself wrote that 'it was a fortunate day' when his emigrant sons 'left Ballymahon as there is nothing to be done in the country'. After the Napoleonic Wars domestic industry in north Leinster counties collapsed, while prices for both livestock and tillage products contracted sharply. Still, according to British traveller H. D. Inglis, Longford's burgeoning population and intense competition for land kept rents exceptionally high, and for head tenants like Johnston, whose long leases had been negotiated during the prosperous war years, the results were catastrophic. '[E]very thing the landholder has to dispose of is low' in price, Johnston complained, but 'the landlords [were] not making any [rent] reduction[s]'.[19]

Johnston's letters indicate that he struggled heroically to avoid falling into arrears, but by 1837 what Johnston's wife called his 'enormous' rents, plus the failure of some ill-judged speculations in grain futures, forced him to advertise his beloved farm, Highlands, on the shores of Lough Ree. But Johnston was unable to find a purchaser prior to the Ballymahon riot and his farm's subsequent, forced sale. Thus in March 1837, six months before the fatal incident on Ballymahon bridge, his wife admitted that 'wee are at present in a very precarious state as to our affairs'. Certainly, by that summer Johnston was exceptionally vulnerable to any assault on the tolls and customs, which had now become the primary source of his declining income.[20]

Johnston's economic situation was not unique in southern Ireland, for middlemen specifically — and middle-class Protestants, generally — appear to have suffered acutely during the depressed pre-Famine decades. For example, the Johnstons' own letters reveal that most of their relatives and acquaintances were living shabbily, in genteel poverty — 'struggling ... to keep up an appearance upon very little'. Some of their kinsmen suffered dramatic declines in status, and Johnston's own niece — heir to his brother's now bankrupt estate — married a gardener's son and worked in Dublin as a servant or,

Ballymahon. On Thomas Maxwell, see *Slator's National Commercial Directory*, 11; *Land Owners of Ireland*, 52–55; and MacNamee, *History of the Diocese of Ardagh*, 766–68 (also on Fr. Dawson).

19 Mason, *Statistical Account, or Parochial Survey*, vol. 3, 337; John O'Donovan cited in MacManus, 'One Hundred Years Ago', 9; Andrew Johnston, 20 January 1834 (Peyton Johnston Mss.); Inglis, *Ireland in 1834*, vol. 1, 348–53.

20 Eliza Johnston, 27 January 1834, 24 October 1835, 4 October 1836, and 20 March 1837; also see Andrew Johnston, 20 January 1834, and Alicia Welsh, 9 May 1837 (Peyton Johnston Mss.).

at best, a governess. The Johnstons' correspondence also suggests that under the impact of economic distress middle-class Protestant society was crumbling from within, just at the moment when solidarity in the face of Catholic assaults was most essential. According to the letters, ties of kinship and mutual assistance were dissolving rapidly in a welter of acrimonious disputes and lawsuits, most of which stemmed from the unwillingness or inability of relatives to honour family settlements and other legal obligations that had been incurred in more prosperous times. Likewise, young Protestants often found it difficult or impossible to secure employment or other assistance from relatives who still possessed some wealth and influence. Thus, despite Johnston's past generosity to his own and his wife's kinsmen, he was unable to secure similar financial aid when his fortunes faltered in the mid-1830s.[21]

But a more important source of Johnston's troubles — and perhaps the key reason why local Catholics felt by 1837 that they could attack him with impunity — was that Johnston's own landlord had turned against him and was undermining his social status. According to the local Protestant curate, in the late eighteenth and early nineteenth centuries the relationship between Captain John Brady Shuldham and his tenants had been characterized by generous paternalism from above and grateful deference from below. The people of south Longford regarded Captain Shuldham with affection, he wrote, for their landlord's 'family had been endeared to them and their ancestors by countless acts of kindness for many generations'. 'If every Irish landlord ... would follow the example of Captain Shuldham', the curate concluded, 'Ireland would be happy and contented.' During those happier times Andrew Johnston had even named one of his sons Shuldham in his landlord's honour, and he and the captain's other tenants had celebrated Shuldham's victory in a protracted lawsuit as if it had been their own triumph, parading through Ballymahon and illuminating the neighbourhood with bonfires.[22]

Unfortunately, however, Captain Shuldham died unmarried in 1832, and his Longford estate then passed to his brother, William Molyneux Shuldham. Whether for personal, economic, or ideological reasons, the new proprietor displayed a much more clinical and exploitive attitude towards his estate and its tenants. Indeed, in 1833 Shuldham became a semi-permanent absentee, residing primarily at his new wife's estate at Bellaghy, County Antrim, and visiting his Longford properties only occasionally. Meanwhile, he employed a salaried agent to manage his south Longford estate — hence bypassing Andrew Johnston and his other middlemen — and began to press his lessees for rent, to deny lease renewals when old contracts expired, and to evict long-standing tenants for non-payment of arrears. Thus in 1834 the Johnstons complained that since

21 Cullen, *Emergence of Modern Ireland*, 99–107, 128–31; L. M. Cullen, *An Economic History of Ireland since 1660*, paperback edn. (London, 1976), 100–33. Eliza Johnston, 19–20 March 1834 and 22 June 1835; Alicia Welsh, 22 June 1835 and 20 March 1837 (Peyton Johnston Mss.). On the plight of Andrew Johnston's niece, see Mary Johnston, Dublin, to Peyton Johnston, Sr., County Longford, 9 January 1835 (Peyton Johnston Mss.).
22 Mason, *Statistical Account, or Parochial Survey*, vol. 3, 367.

the Shuldhams had left Ballymahon, there was 'no word, no talk of [their] return, but writing every day to the agent for money is the[ir] cry'. Moreover, the income raised thereby was invested in County Antrim, not on the Longford properties. There is 'no order for leases, no order for building, no order for any one thing to improv[e] the tenants since' Shuldham's departure, Johnston's wife complained; 'it is folly to live here strugling to make rent for such a man'. Travelling through south Longford in the same year, Inglis noted the unhappy consequences: Ballymahon and its environs, he wrote, were 'utterly neglected by the proprietor, who grants no leases, and acts ... as if he had no interest in the permanent improvement of his property'. '[B]ad as this town looked when you saw it', Andrew Johnston wrote to one of his emigrant sons, 'it is fifty times worse now: houses falling out of the face and no sign of loans or any encouragement what ever.'[23]

Johnston himself suffered immediately from Shuldham's new policies, which led to a growing personal estrangement between himself and his proprietor. 'Mr Shuldham is grown more and more every day dark and darker to your father and shows no intention to renew' his leases, wrote Johnston's wife in 1835; 'times are sadly altered [since the days] when a Johnston was supposed to have a first claim on a Shuldham', but now 'every one thinks he [Shuldham] wishes to thro[w] of[f] the old tenants' — that is, the middlemen — and let his lands directly to the Catholic farmers at higher rents and on shorter leases or even annual tenancies. By the spring of 1837 Johnston was desperate to sell the interest in his holdings, for he now knew — as his embittered sister-in-law declared — that he could expect nothing but 'enmity from his landlord ... , as he is grinding his tenants to the dust'. Indeed, no sooner had the Ballymahon riot and the coroner's inquest occurred than Shuldham served Andrew Johnston with eviction notices for all his tenancies. Neither Johnston's ultimate acquittal nor the intercession of mutual friends and local Tory leaders could dissuade Shuldham from his cruel course, and in the end Johnston left Ballymahon with only 'about £500 to begin the world anew'.[24]

Johnston's fate serves to highlight the contradictory economic and political strategies that landlords in County Longford and elsewhere in Ireland pursued in the pre-Famine decades. On the one hand, Irish Protestant leaders had long recognized the relationships between population and power, and their periodic inquiries into the demographic 'progress of popery' clearly demonstrated what they most feared: that ever since the early eighteenth century the Protestant population of southern Ireland had declined in proportional if not absolute terms. In County Longford itself, for example, the Protestant percentage of the population had shrunk from 15 per cent in 1731 to 13 per cent in 1766

23 Information on the Shuldham family from: *Burke's Genealogical and Heraldic History of the Landed Gentry of Ireland*, new rev. edn. (London, 1912), 638–39, and the research of Paddy Whelan, Ballymahon. Eliza Johnston, 27 January 1834, and Andrew Johnston, 27 January 1834 (Peyton Johnston Mss.). Inglis, *Ireland in 1834*, vol. 1, 343.

24 Eliza Johnston, 24 October 1835; Alicia Welsh, 9 May 1837, 1 October 1837, and 20 December 1837 (Peyton Johnston Mss.).

and to merely 9 per cent by 1831. Primarily, this decline was due to emigration (and to a lesser extent, conversions to Catholicism) among middle- and lower-class Protestants. And according to historian L. M. Cullen, the Protestant community's demographic decline was attributable especially to the economic downfall and emigration of Protestant middleman families: 'the accelerating decay of the middleman's world', Cullen wrote, 'greatly weakened the Protestant interest in the [Irish] countryside'; 'the central pockets of rural Protestants fell apart', and Protestant society in southern Ireland began an inexorable decline. In turn, of course, reduced Protestant numbers inevitably meant diminished Tory power and a consequent weakening of support for the Union with Britain, for the Established Church, and for landlordism.[25]

Therefore, in hindsight at least, Shuldham's harsh treatment of Andrew Johnston and the other Protestant middlemen on his estate would appear to have been detrimental to his own long-term interests and to those of the entire Protestant Ascendancy. Indeed, Johnston's sister-in-law immediately recognized the implications of Shuldham's policies: 'your papa was the person [who] should stand between Shuldham and the people,' she wrote to her nephew in America, 'but that is all over now. He [Shuldham] must fight the battle now himself'. However, Shuldham's actions were by no means unique, and landlord policy generally in the pre-Famine period was to clear middlemen from their estates, thus abolishing economic niches that hitherto had sheltered Protestants of middling wealth and rank. Likewise, ordinary Protestant tenant farmers, who might previously have expected preferential treatment from their landlords, also were becoming victims of rent-maximizing leasing policies. For example, in 1837 the staunchly Tory *Westmeath Guardian* admitted that the 'gentlemen of the county have ... taken their lands out of the hands of Protestant tenants' and leased those farms to Catholics willing to pay higher rents. Letters to the same newspaper indicated that many middling and poor Protestants felt bitterly betrayed by their proprietors' new policies, and they asked how Tory landlords expected to maintain their party's political strength if they continued to take advantage of the 'ruinous spirit of competition' for leases that was driving the Protestant 'yeomanry' out of the island. Indeed, given the likely conditions of sectarian hiring practices, a loss of Protestant farms would in turn result in a contraction of labouring opportunities for the poorer categories of Protestants. The effect of this negative multiplier would not have stopped there, but would also have extended to shopkeepers, artisans, and others servicing Protestant farmers and labourers.[26]

What we appear to be seeing, therefore, in the case of Andrew Johnston and others is the dissolution of earlier patterns of paternalism and preference in favour of classic liberal, free-market principles of maximizing the returns to landownership — even at the expense of straining or even destroying the social bonds that extended vertically through

25 Kennedy and Miller, 'Long Retreat', 38–40; Cullen, *Emergence of Modern Ireland*, 106–07, 128–31.
26 Alicia Welsh, 1 October 1837 (Peyton Johnston Mss.); *Westmeath Guardian*, 28 September 1837, 2 November 1837, and 5 July 1838; Kennedy and Miller, 'Long Retreat', 44–45.

Protestant communities. Those bonds, rooted in the original colonial settlements and in pre-modern notions of hierarchy and organic community, had drawn sustenance from shared religious and political affiliations. But in an increasingly commercialized Irish society, conflicts of interest across class lines now cut across community solidarity. Thus, just as the Catholic bourgeoisie raised the banners of religion and repeal to mobilize peasants and labourers behind middle-class leadership, so also did many of County Longford's Protestant landlords and clergy try to compensate for the increasing instrumentality of their class's economic policies by sponsoring the spread of the Orange Order, by financing the evangelical enthusiasm of the Second Reformation, and by mobilizing the Protestant electorate in the Brunswick Clubs. In addition, a few Protestant proprietors, such as Lady Rosse and Lord Lorton, renewed their ancestors' sectarian leasing policies in order to generate what the *Westmeath Guardian* termed 'a spirit of encouragement ... to those [Protestants] who for some years past have been too much neglected and driven from these shores to seek protection in foreign lands'.[27]

Through such strategies upper-class Protestants successfully redefined the terms of Protestant solidarity and thereby renegotiated their cultural hegemony over their poorer co-religionists. By themselves, however, such largely symbolic actions could not stem the steady attrition of southern Ireland's Protestant communities. For all its notoriety, 'exclusive leasing' in favour of Protestants was practiced inconsistently and by only a minority of proprietors. Whether resident or absentee, too many landlords were either short-term profiteers or sincere champions of a free-market ethos that challenged the maintenance of an artificial, sectarian marketplace. Despite their demands for Protestant loyalty and deference, most landlords pursued economic policies that gave their middle- and working-class co-religionists little option other than emigration. Ironically also, the increasingly visible Orangeism, evangelicalism, and abrasive politics sponsored by Longford's leading Tories only invited Catholic reprisals on more vulnerable middle- and working-class Protestants, which in turn stimulated their further emigration. For example, in the late 1830s the Crown solicitor of the county noted that Longford's population had become so religiously and politically polarized that Catholics considered all 'the lower population who are Protestants' to be bitter Orangemen, 'whether they [really] are so or not'. Thus Andrew Johnston testified that the members of the mob that had attacked him on Ballymahon bridge had cried out, '[H]ere he is again the Orange rascal. [N]ow is our time to mas[s]acre them all' — despite the fact that Johnston's

27 Kennedy and Miller, 'Long Retreat', 44–50; O'Ferrall, 'Ballinamuck "Land War"', 104–09; *Westmeath Guardian*, 28 September 1837. Established after the passage of Catholic Emancipation (1829), the Brunswick Clubs were the Tory Party's counterparts in Ireland of O'Connell's Liberal Clubs; in social terms, the Brunswick Clubs represented a Protestant-élite version of the Orange Order; their main political functions were to choose Tory candidates for office and to marshal Protestant funds and voters for parliamentary elections.

sponsorship of an interdenominational Masonic Lodge strongly indicated his aversion to Orangeism and its intolerant spirit.[28]

Sadly, by the late 1830s Johnston was an anachronism, whether viewed from the perspective of a Protestant landlord class that preached traditional Toryism yet generally practised free-market liberalism, or from the perspective of an aspiring Catholic bourgeoisie that waved the banner of anti-monopoly capitalism but used it to cloak sectarian warfare against their Protestant competitors. Even Johnston's own sister-in-law recognized the hopelessness of his position in an era when neither his traditional loyalty to the Shuldhams nor his customary paternalism towards his Catholic undertenants was any longer rewarded by 'an ungrateful, treacherous people'.[29]

Furthermore, the conflicts within Protestant society were cultural as well as economic, internalized as well as overt, and in these respects Johnston was also a 'middleman', trapped in an increasingly untenable position, whose own kinfolk mirrored his community's internal tensions. For example, although both Johnston's and his wife's families originally came from County Cavan, they represented very distinct epochs of Protestant social and cultural history. Johnston's ancestors had migrated to Longford in the 1740s, when his grandfather married a local heiress from east Connacht. What can be reconstructed of his family's history tends to characterize the males as stereotypically eighteenth-century, southern Irish 'squireens', with the easy-going, hard-drinking, but relatively tolerant habits that were described nostalgically by Sir Jonah Barrington and critically by Arthur Young. For example, by the 1830s it appears that Johnston's older brother had long since frittered away the family estate in mid-Longford, perhaps by contracting a second marriage to a Catholic woman less than a third his age, and Johnston himself frequently joined his Catholic subtenants and labourers to drink illegally distilled poitín at cockfights and harvest festivals — and fled alongside them from the raids of the revenue police. In sharp contrast Johnston's wife had come from Cavan much more recently, and most of her relatives still lived in south Ulster where they were small proprietors, Church of Ireland clergy, enthusiastic evangelicals, and prominent Orangemen. In short, the Welsh family was resolutely Protestant, bourgeois, and respectable in nineteenth-century terms, and Eliza Johnston was 'much fretted about' her husband's behavior and enjoined her children to avoid 'idleness', 'drink, and high living'. The Johnston correspondence leaves no doubt that both Eliza and her resident sister Alicia revered Johnston, but it is equally obvious that they regarded him as a champion of a vanishing era, whose customs and attitudes were dysfunctional in an increasingly instrumental and intolerant age. Thus, while Johnston long resisted the necessity of abandoning Ballymahon, his sister-in-law was more realistic: between their

28 Kennedy and Miller, 'Long Retreat', 59; Andrew Johnston, 15 October 1837 (Peyton Johnston Mss.).
29 Alicia Welsh, 1 October 1837 (Peyton Johnston Mss.).

'heartless landlord' and 'a rabble of papists', she wrote, there no longer existed a 'middle ground'. Instead, 'the country is in such a state [that] each now stick to their *party*'.[30]

When one's traditional 'party' was no longer led by paternalistic landlords, but instead dominated by rural capitalists of convenient convictions, there were few options to migration or militant Orangeism. Ironically, as Longford's Protestant middle class and demographic strength steadily waned, local landlords had to rely more and more heavily on formal instruments of British power — the magistracy, the constabulary, and ultimately the army — to maintain their authority. But in the late 1830s that recourse failed during Lord Mulgrave's reform administration, and even the Tories' return to power in 1841 under Robert Peel did not signal the return to Orange ascendancy that Alicia Welsh and other ultra-Protestants had anticipated. Subsequently, some prominent local Tories, such as Samuel Blackhall and Richard Maxwell Fox, openly deserted their erstwhile followers and joined the Liberal camp. In such a climate of expediency it was no wonder that in the years 1841–43, when Johnston and his relatives begged the Tories in Dublin Castle for government appointments, their well-founded claims that they had been 'driven to beggary for [their] exertions in the Conservative cause' went unheeded. Once an obstacle to the economic ambitions of his landlord and his Catholic

---

30 The background of the Johnston family was traced to the 1740s in the deeds and wills located in the Registry of Deeds, King's Inn, Dublin; in E. S. Gray, 'Some Notes on the High Sheriffs of Co. Leitrim, 1701–1800', *Irish Genealogist*, 1, 10 (October 1941), 301–09; and in the research of Paddy Whelan, Ballymahon. On the Welsh family in south Ulster and their evangelical and Orange connections, see: James B. Leslie, *Clogher Clergy and Parishes* (Belfast, 1928), 101, 268, and *Raphoe Clergy and Parishes* (Enniskillen, 1940), 85; *Report of the Proceedings of the Grand Orange Lodge of Ireland, 1851* (Dublin, 1851); *Report of the Proceedings of the Grand Orange Lodge of Ireland, 1852* (Dublin, 1852); and *The Grand Orange Lodge of Ireland for the Year 1853* (Dublin, 1853), 16 (all three volumes in the Library of the Loyal Orange Lodge Headquarters, Belfast). For Eliza Johnston's and Alicia Welsh's bourgeois critiques of Andrew Johnston and 'squireen' society in south Longford, see: Eliza Johnston, 8 December 1834, 22 June 1835, and 24 October 1835; and Alicia Welsh, 22 June 1835, 29 October 1835, and 8 February 1837 (Peyton Johnston Mss.).

   Issues of gender are not specifically addressed in this chapter. However, it is apparent that the bourgeois norms and evangelical ethos that undermined the social, cultural, and political fabric of Andrew Johnston's world also provided the ideological perspective and the cultural vocabulary that enabled his wife and sister-in-law to criticize his lifestyle and values — and in the process to undermine patterns of patriarchy which had been central to eighteenth-century society. In this context, as noted in the preceding chapter, we might speak of a *feminization* as well as an embourgeoisement of much of early nineteenth-century Irish Protestant culture — a process that largely confined overtly 'masculine' behaviour (once expressed in Ulster, for example, in the *intra*-communal, class-based violence of the Oakboys and Steelboys) to the Orange Lodges, whose sectarian conflicts with Catholics served to reconsolidate the Protestant community across class lines and under landlord hegemony. Likewise, the evangelical piety and anti-Catholic prejudices revealed in the letters of Eliza Johnston and Alicia Welsh, far exceeding the expressions of Andrew Johnston, suggest that Irish Protestant women — through their domestication of evangelicalism and bourgeois values — played a major role in the creation of nineteenth-century Irish Protestant identity, enshrining a more intense and pervasive sectarianism in the heart of Irish Protestant family culture.

competitors alike, Johnston — like the archaic worldview he represented — was now merely an embarrassment to his former friends and political spokesmen.[31]

Whatever happened to middle-class, southern Irish Protestant families such as the Johnstons? At least a few converted to Catholicism, as some of Johnston's poorer relatives seem to have done. A very much larger number emigrated, particularly to British North America, where they could attempt to re-create past securities in a new, yet culturally familiar and politically congenial environment. Finally, an unknown number, perhaps chiefly from border counties like Longford, followed the bitter path Johnston took from Ballymahon to the safety of strong Protestant-majority areas in the future Northern Ireland. By 1839 Johnston's economic problems were still considerable, but he was now leasing a farm from the deputy grand master of the Orange Order, on the shores of Lough Erne, in a County Fermanagh parish, the inhabitants of which were over 50 per cent Protestant. Whether Johnston actually found happiness, as opposed to mere physical security, among his co-religionists in the 'Black North' is another matter, and his sister-in-law's last surviving letters suggest that he had more trouble dealing with Protestant Ulster's 'clever' business practices than with the waterlogged and weed-choked pastures of his new farm. What is more certain is that Johnston's move to Ulster symbolized the accelerating erosion of any 'middle ground' between Ireland's increasingly polarized worlds of Protestants and Catholics, landlords and tenants. The increasing congruence of religion, politics, and geography prefigured Ireland's ultimate partition into two hostile, sectarian, petty-bourgeois, and culturally oppressive states, neither of which, one suspects, would Andrew Johnston have found very congenial. Likewise, whether Johnston's former subtenants and labourers in south Longford benefited from his downfall and departure is problematic. But as one of the few apologists for the old order lamented, 'if the middleman had been his tenant's master, he was also his ... protector', and now 'there is no link between the highest and the lowest'. By the eve of the Famine, wrote another, more critical, observer, the formerly 'large and prosperous, albeit parasitic class' of Protestant middlemen had virtually disappeared, and with its disappearance fell one of the pillars of landlordism, of Protestant society, and of an older, unequal, yet perhaps less bitterly sectarian society in Longford and elsewhere in southern Ireland.[32]

---

31 O'Ferrall, 'Growth of Political Consciousness', 708–16; Eliza Johnston, St. Angelo, Trory parish, County Fermanagh, to Peyton Johnston, Richmond, Va., 20 June 1841, and Alicia Welsh, same address, to same, 23 September 1841 (Peyton Johnston Mss.). See petitions to Dublin Castle on the Johnstons' behalf, in Index to Registered Papers, 1842, Second Division, CSORP Z15,732, 17 December 1841; 1843, Second Division, CSORP Z7426, 31 May 1843; and in Registered Papers, Second Division, 1843, Item 2910, 24 February 1843, and Z9716, 14 July 1843 (all in the National Archives of Ireland, formerly in the State Paper Office).

32 Kennedy and Miller, 'Long Retreat', 41–44 on Protestant conversions and out-migration. The Johnstons' new farm was St. Angelo, in Srahenny townland, Trory parish, County Fermanagh, and was leased from Edward Archdall of Riversdale; Trory parish population data in 1831 have been recalculated from the First Report of the Commissioners of Public Instruction, Ireland, in BBP, HC 1835, xxxiii. Other information on the

·

Johnstons' new residence is from 'The Johnstons of St. Angelo' (typescript in the possession of Mr. and Mrs. S. Bothwell, St. Angelo). On Archdall's Orange associations see: *Report from the Select Committee to Inquire into the Nature ... of the Orange Lodge Associations*, in BPP, HC 1835, xv, 42; and *Report of the Proceedings of the Grand Orange Lodge ... 1852*. Alicia Welsh, St. Angelo, to Peyton Johnston, Richmond, Va., 3 September 1839 and 21 September 1841, and Eliza Johnston, same address, to same, 20 June 1841 (Peyton Johnston Mss.). Kerby A. Miller, *Emigrants and Exiles: Ireland and the Irish Exodus to North America* (New York, 1985), 46–49, 210–11.

10 The Famine's Scars:
William Murphy's Ulster and American Odyssey

Until very recently scholars have neglected the Great Famine's impact on the northern Irish, nine-county province of Ulster and especially its impact on Ulster's Protestant inhabitants.[1] This neglect stemmed in part from historians' reading of published census and other data that indicate that the North's *general* experience of excess mortality and emigration in 1845–52 was indeed less catastrophic than that of southern and western Ireland. Thus, whereas between 1841 and 1851 the populations of Munster and Connacht declined by 22.5 and 28.8 per cent, respectively, that of Ulster fell by 'only' 15.7 per cent.[2]

---

1   This chapter was first published, with the same title, in *Éire-Ireland: An Interdisciplinary Journal of Irish Studies*, 36, 1–2 (spring–summer 2001), 98–123, a 'Special Issue on Irish America', edited by Professor Kevin Kenny of Boston College. It was subsequently reprinted in Kenny, ed., *New Directions in Irish-American History* (Madison, Wisc., 2003), 36–60. Both were formally listed as co-authored by Dr. Bruce D. Boling of the University of New Mexico, who helped me research the Murphy family in Belfast, and as 'with' Professor Liam Kennedy of Queen's University, Belfast, with whom in 1985–86 I began collecting some of the pre-census Irish demographic data that appear in this work. Re-publication here provides an opportunity to again thank Boling and Kennedy, but neither scholar is responsible for the interpretations herein. I would also like to thank the editors of *Éire-Ireland* and of the University of Wisconsin Press for permitting me to republish the essay, with some revisions (see below), in this volume.

    Several years after this chapter's initial publication in *Éire-Ireland*, I was contacted by Mrs. Mary Calaba Weston of Rancho Palos Verdes, California, who generously provided much additional information about her ancestors — members of the Murphy/Ritchie families described herein — much of it from her own genealogical research, the rest from Norma and Robert Moore Grainger of London, Ontario, also descendants of William Murphy's mother. Accordingly, I have revised this chapter in light of this new information (and also corrected mistakes in earlier data calculations), and I am very grateful to the Graingers and especially to Mrs. Weston for their kind assistance.

2   W. E. Vaughan and A. J. Fitzpatrick, eds., *Irish Historical Statistics: Population, 1821–1971* (Dublin, 1978), 15–16. Also see Liam Kennedy, et al., *Mapping the Great Irish Famine: A Survey of the Famine Decades* (Dublin, 1999).

Although Joel Mokyr and other scholars have noted that several counties in south or 'outer' Ulster — particularly Cavan and Monaghan — witnessed high rates of Famine mortality, this is commonly understood by reference to the fact that their populations were composed predominantly of poor Catholic smallholders and cottier labourers.[3] By contrast, conventional wisdom holds that northeast Ulster or, even more broadly, the six counties — Antrim, Down, Armagh, Londonderry, Tyrone, and Fermanagh — that later became Northern Ireland, and particularly their Protestant inhabitants, escaped the Famine with comparatively minimal damage, whether measured in excess mortality or in abnormally heavy out-migration. To explain this apparent phenomenon, historians often have cited socio-economic and cultural factors relatively unique to northeast Ulster, such as industrialization and urbanization, the prevalence of tenant-right and comparatively congenial landlord–tenant relations, and, among the rural populace, a greater variety of income sources and less dietary dependence on potatoes than prevailed in Munster and Connacht.[4]

Inadvertently, however, some scholars may have unconsciously repeated contemporary and subsequent claims by Irish unionists, who argued that 'Ulster' — that is, its Protestant inhabitants — eluded the Famine because of the province's superior 'character' for industry, virtue, and loyalty. But in reality, many Protestant as well as Catholic Ulstermen and -women suffered grievously. Between 1841 and 1851 Ulster's population fell by nearly one-sixth — slightly more than the 15.3 per cent decline that occurred in heavily Catholic Leinster. During the same period the number of inhabitants of the future Northern Ireland fell by 14.7 per cent (or 13.0 per cent if Belfast's burgeoning population is included), and in the four northeastern counties that in 1861 had Protestant majorities (Antrim, Armagh, Down, and Derry), the comparable decline was 12.1 per cent (or, including Belfast, nearly 10 per cent).[5] Of course, it is likely that northeastern Catholics suffered more severely than did Protestants, and it is probable that population losses in the region, particularly among Protestants, were primarily due to out-migration rather than to the effects of starvation and disease.[6] However, as David Miller has argued, in the pre-Famine decades the contraction of rural weaving and spinning had created

3   Joel Mokyr, *Why Ireland Starved: A Quantitative and Analytical History of the Irish Economy, 1800–1850*, paperback edn. (London, 1985), 267. Also see Cormac Ó Gráda, *Ireland Before and After the Famine: Explorations in Economic History, 1800–1925* (Manchester, 1988), 87. Between 1841 and 1851, counties Cavan and Monaghan lost 28.4 and 29.2 per cent of their respective populations; see Vaughan and Fitzpatrick, eds., *Irish Historical Statistics*, 11, 13. In 1831 Cavan's and Monaghan's populations were 82 and 73 per cent Catholic, respectively; calculated from the religious census data in the *First Report of the Commission of Public Instruction, Ireland*, in BPP, HC 1835, xxxiii.

4   On socio-economic developments in pre-Famine Ulster, especially in the northeastern counties, that generally stemmed the Famine's effects on the region, see the relevant chapters of: Jonathan Bardon, *A History of Ulster* (Belfast, 1992); L. M. Cullen, *An Economic History of Ireland since 1660* (London, 1972), and ed., *The Formation of the Irish Economy* (Cork, 1969); and Liam Kennedy and Philip Ollerenshaw, eds., *An Economic History of Ulster, 1820–1939* (Manchester, 1985).

5   Calculated from the data in Vaughan and Fitzpatrick, eds., *Irish Historical Statistics*, 5–16.

6   Cormac Ó Gráda, *Black '47 and Beyond: The Great Irish Famine* (Princeton, NJ, 1999), 110.

in Ulster an impoverished Protestant underclass whose members' vulnerability to the crisis of 1845–52 can be compared with that of Catholic cottiers and labourers in the South and West. Furthermore, Miller points out, some poor Protestants in northeast Ulster did perish of malnutrition or 'famine fever', even in areas adjacent to busy industrial centres, and Mokyr's estimated excess mortality rates for heavily Protestant County Antrim, as well as for the roughly half-Protestant counties of Armagh, Fermanagh, and Tyrone (all four in the future Northern Ireland), exceed those in most parts of Leinster.[7]

Unfortunately, not until 1861 did the official Irish censuses record religious affiliations, and so it is impossible to gauge precisely or compare population losses among Ulster's Protestants and Catholics between 1841 and 1851. And although the Irish Commissioners of Public Instruction compiled parish-based religious censuses in 1831 and 1834, scholars rarely have tried to correlate these data with those of 1861.[8] Thus, the authors of a recent comprehensive study of the Famine in Ulster made few attempts to distinguish between Protestant and Catholic experiences, and the subject awaits detailed research in church, estate, and other records.[9] Yet much evidence indicates that Protestants suffered heavy losses, primarily through emigration but also to a degree from disease and malnutrition, in many areas of northeast Ulster.[10] For example, David Miller concludes that between 1845 and 1861 the Presbyterian population of Maghera, County Derry, fell by about 30 per cent.[11] Likewise, between 1841 and 1851 the number of inhabitants in ten heavily Protestant, contiguous parishes in east and mid-Antrim declined overall by more than 14 per cent, and losses in some parishes were comparable to those in parts of Munster and Connacht.[12] For example, in 1841–51 the population of Glenwhirry parish (92 per cent Protestant in 1831) fell by nearly 23 per cent, in Raloo (84 per cent Protestant)

7 David W. Miller, 'Irish Presbyterians and the Great Famine', in J. Hill and C. Lennon, eds., *Luxury and Austerity: Historical Studies XXI* (Dublin, 1999), 168; and Mokyr, *Why Ireland Starved*, 267. Also see Christine Kinealy, *This Great Calamity: The Irish Famine, 1845–52* (Dublin, 1994), 233–34.

8 For the 1831 and 1834 religious censuses, see the *First Report of the Commission of Public Instruction, Ireland*, in BPP, HC 1835, xxxiii. In 1985–86 Professor Liam Kennedy of Queen's University, Belfast, and I embarked on a project to organize and compare the 1831 religious census figures with earlier and subsequent demographic data; for some preliminary results, see Kennedy and Miller, 'The Long Retreat: Protestants, Economy, and Society, 1660–1926', in Raymond Gillespie and Gerard Moran, eds., *Longford: Essays in County History* (Dublin, 1991), 31–61; and Kerby A. Miller, et al., *Irish Immigrants in the Land of Canaan: Letters and Memoirs from Colonial and Revolutionary America, 1675–1815* (New York, 2003), Appendix 2; also see Chapter 8 in this volume.

9 Christine Kinealy and Trevor Parkhill, eds., *The Famine in Ulster: The Regional Impact* (Belfast, 1997).

10 Ó Gráda, *Black '47 and Beyond*, 89.

11 Miller, 'Irish Presbyterians and the Great Famine', 168.

12 The parishes surveyed were: Ballycor (including Doagh Grange and Rashee), Ballynure, Carncastle (including Solar), Glenwhirry, Glynn, Inver, Killyglen Grange, Kilwaughter (see below), Larne (not including its workhouse inhabitants in 1851), and Raloo; 1841–51 data in the 1841 and 1851 Irish censuses, published in BPP, HC 1843, xxiv, and HC 1852–53, xcii (vol. 3, Ulster).

by more than 24 per cent, and in Killyglen Grange (81 per cent Protestant) by nearly 21 per cent.[13]

Significantly, the Protestant inhabitants of these Antrim parishes were in 1831 overwhelmingly Presbyterians: for instance, nearly 100 per cent in Glenwhirry; 92 per cent in Raloo; and 97 per cent in Killyglen Grange. Indeed, much evidence suggests that the Famine's effects were *not* evenly distributed among Ulster's Protestants, and that Presbyterians experienced substantially greater attrition than did members of the legally established Church of Ireland. For example, during the measurable period 1831–1861, spanning the Famine crisis, Ulster's Presbyterian population fell by nearly 18 per cent, compared with a less than 13 per cent decline among Anglicans (and a 19 per cent decrease among Catholics).[14] In 1831–61 Presbyterians suffered greater proportional losses than did Anglicans in eight of Ulster's nine counties; only in Fermanagh, with its miniscule Presbyterian population, did the percentage decline among communicants of the Church of Ireland exceed that experienced by Presbyterians (and by Catholics). Moreover, only in Antrim (excluding Belfast) and in Down were Presbyterian attrition rates slightly less than those of Catholics. In Antrim (excluding Belfast), for instance, between 1831 and 1861 the Presbyterian and the Catholic populations declined by 7 and 10 per cent, respectively, but the number of Anglicans increased by more than 12 per cent. Likewise, Armagh's Anglican population fell by merely 7.8 per cent, compared with a 31 per cent decline among Presbyterians (and a 16 per cent decrease among Catholics); and in County Londonderry the number of Anglicans rose by nearly 1 per cent, while that of Presbyterians fell by 28.5 per cent (and of Catholics by 13.3 per cent). Even in the predominantly Catholic 'outer' Ulster counties of Cavan, Donegal, and Monaghan, proportional losses among Presbyterians in 1831–61 exceeded those among Anglicans and Catholics alike.

To be sure, between 1831 and 1861 the Catholic proportion of Ulster's total inhabitants declined from 52.6 to 50.5 per cent. However, whereas the Famine and the emigrations immediately preceding and following that crisis made Ulster more heavily Protestant, they also made the North and its Protestant populace less Presbyterian and more Anglican. Thus, between 1831 and 1861 the Presbyterian proportions of Ulster's overall and Protestant populations declined from 27 to 26 per cent and from 57 to 53 per cent, respectively. In northeast Ulster, the heartland of the future Northern Ireland, the changes in the balance between Presbyterians and Anglicans were more striking. For instance, in Antrim (excluding Belfast), the Presbyterian percentage of the Protestant population declined from 76 to 70.5, while the Anglican proportion rose from less than 22 to more than 24 per cent; in Armagh the comparable Presbyterian decrease was

13 The Protestant proportions of the parishes' populations in 1831 were calculated from the 1831–34 religious censuses, in the *First Report of the Commission of Public Instruction, Ireland*, in BPP, HC 1835, xxxiii. Even greater losses occurred in Kilwaughter parish (see below).

14 These and the following percentages are based on comparisons of data in the 1831 religious census (see n. 13 above) and in the official 1861 Irish census in BPP, HC 1863, liv (vol. 3, Ulster).

from 40.5 to 32 per cent, and the Anglican rise from 58 to 60 per cent; in Down the Presbyterian decline was from 71 to 66 per cent, and the Anglican increase from 27 to 30 per cent; and in Londonderry the Presbyterian decrease was from 73 to 64 per cent, while the Anglican share of the county's Protestants rose from 25 to 31 per cent.[15] These trends would continue for at least the next half-century: between 1861 and 1926 the Protestant share of the total population in the area that became Northern Ireland rose from 59 to 66.5 per cent, whereas the Presbyterian proportion of the future statelet's Protestant

15 It is noteworthy that the Presbyterian proportion of Belfast's Protestant population also declined between 1831 and 1861 — from 57 to 53 per cent — whereas the comparable Anglican percentage fell from 40 to 37.5 per cent, while 'other Protestants' increased their share of Belfast's non-Catholic population from 3 to 9.5 per cent. In the same period, the Catholic proportion of the city's inhabitants rose slightly from 33 to 34 per cent.

   In nine-county Ulster as a whole between 1831 and 1861, the 252 per cent increase in the number of members of 'other Protestant' denominations — primarily of evangelical churches such as the Methodists and Baptists — is a complicating factor. However, it is likely that the actual increase was less dramatic, because in 1831 Methodists were often counted as members of the Church of Ireland, from which their separation was yet incomplete. In addition, and despite the Murphy family's experience (see below), in general there is no reason to assume that in 1831–61 Presbyterians were more susceptible to the lures of evangelicalism than were members of the Church of Ireland.

   On the other hand, in the eighteenth century it was common for wealthy, ambitious, or upwardly mobile Presbyterians to convert to the legally established Church. If this trend continued during the nineteenth century (and Presbyterian spokesmen frequently lamented that it did so), it would help explain the shifting balance between the two denominations. Also, conversions to Anglicanism among ordinary Presbyterians may have increased during times of unusual political or economic stress, as during the loyalist repressions of suspected United Irishmen in the 1790s. Did the Great Famine have similar effects? To my knowledge, no historians have investigated whether northern Presbyterians, as well as western Catholics, were subject to the blandishments of 'souperism' — and, if so, whether their susceptibility might have been due to disproportionate Anglican/Orange influence — exerted by Ulster landlords, clergy, and magistrates — in local relief distribution.

   Although I believe that major differences in emigration rates, rather than conversions to Anglicanism, were the principal reason why northern Presbyterians in 1831–61 experienced much greater demographic decline than did Anglicans, those differences were rooted in socio-economic, cultural, and political factors that were inextricable and that could foster conversion or emigration. Put another way, although an Ulster Presbyterian suffering or anticipating social distress or dislocation (e.g., eviction, unemployment) had a range of possible responses, the extreme logical alternatives were conversion to the Church of Ireland (and/or membership in the Orange Order) or emigration to the American republic. Each alternative involved a self-conscious decision with political as well as economic connotations — the former signifying loyalty to the established order, the latter at least implying its rejection.

   Of course, adherence to the Church of Ireland and/or to the Orange Order did not always preclude the necessity or desirability of emigration. Indeed, such adherence was often a prelude to — or prerequisite for — favourable migration to, and successful settlement in, an Anglican-dominated British colony, such as 'Orange Ontario'. It was not coincidental that, relative to their shares of Ireland's population, Irish emigrants to Canada, Australia, New Zealand, and South Africa were disproportionately Protestant, Anglican, and Methodist. However, the great majority of Ireland's overseas emigrants went to the US, and the different rates of Ulster Anglican and Presbyterian population decline in 1831–61 (indeed, from 1766 to 1881), indicate that Anglicans (and Orangemen) generally experienced fewer pressures to emigrate. See Chapter 8 in this volume.

inhabitants declined from 55 to 47 per cent; meanwhile the percentage of Protestants who were members of the Church of Ireland rose from 39 to 40.[16]

Scholars have scarcely examined these demographic trends, although the shifting balance between Ulster's Presbyterians and Anglicans probably began in the early eighteenth century with the onset of heavy Presbyterian emigration to North America. Nor have historians considered their possible political ramifications — for example, for the consolidation of Ulster Protestant loyalism and conservatism, both traditionally Anglican projects — although the remarkable attrition of Presbyterians in many mid-Ulster parishes between 1766 and 1831, accompanied by equally startling proportional increases among the area's Anglicans, suggests that local Dissenters, no less than Catholics, may have been severely affected by the rise of Orangeism and the triumph of loyalism in the 1790s and early 1800s.[17] More pertinent to this study, however, is that quantitative as well as qualitative evidence indicates that many of Ulster's Protestants, especially its Presbyterians and even in its most economically 'advanced' counties, did not escape the horrors of Black '47 and other Famine years.

But how did ordinary northern Protestants, particularly Presbyterians, respond to the travails they endured and witnessed between 1845 and 1852? In the aftermath of the crisis contemporaries observed, and historians subsequently have confirmed, that the Famine — and Irish and Irish-American nationalists' Anglophobic interpretations of that crisis — engendered lasting bitterness among Irish Catholics both at home and in the United States, fueling desires for vengeance against the British government and Ireland's Protestant landlords that found expression, from the 1860s through the early 1920s, in Catholic Irish and Irish-American support for the Fenian, Home Rule, Land League, and Sinn Féin movements. In addition, this author and other scholars have argued that such expressions also served hegemonic and psychological functions, enabling Catholics in Ireland and overseas to project onto alien 'others' feelings of anger and shame: anger that might have been directed against wealthier co-religionists — merchants, shopkeepers, and, perhaps especially, 'land-grabbers' — who benefited from the plight of starving peasants and evicted neighbours; and shame — for their

16 By 1961 the Presbyterian share of Northern Ireland's Protestant population had fallen to only 44.5 per cent. All figures in text calculated from the 1861 and 1926 data in Vaughan and Fitzpatrick, eds., *Irish Historical Statistics*, 4, 10–13, and 69–73. Again, the increasing proportion of 'other Protestants' — comprising 12.4 per cent of Northern Ireland's non-Catholic inhabitants in 1926 — is a complicating factor, as is the possibility of Presbyterian conversions to the Anglican faith (see n. 15 above). In Belfast, between 1861 and 1926 the Presbyterian proportion of the city's Protestant inhabitants declined from 53 to 43 per cent, but the Anglican share rose from 37.5 to 42 per cent, and the proportion of 'other Protestants' increased from 9 to 15 per cent. Between 1861 and 1926 the Catholic percentage of Belfast's total population fell from 34 to 23.
17 See Miller, *et al.*, *Irish Immigrants in the Land of Canaan*, Appendix 2; and also Chapter 8 in this volume.

poverty, humiliation, and self-saving violations of communal obligations — which, if not externalized, might have had destructive personal consequences.[18]

During the Famine years some Ulster Presbyterian emigrants did write letters that revealed anti-British and anti-landlord sentiments comparable to those expressed by Irish and Irish-American Catholic nationalists. Thus, from the safety of New Orleans in 1849, young John Kerr cried 'Down with landlordism' and told his uncle in County Antrim that he prayed for a revolution that would overthrow 'the vile British Government', establish an Irish 'Republick', and banish 'all the pampered aristocracy from the country'. Likewise, in 1854 another recent emigrant from Antrim, Robert McElderry, echoed from Virginia the opinions of fellow Ulster Presbyterian John Mitchel, the radical and now exiled Young Ireland polemicist, and urged Irish Protestants and Catholics to unite and 'rise up and by force break off that accursed union with England which Keeps you in bondage'.[19] Thus, the Great Famine could rekindle the United Irishmen's spirit among at least a few Ulster Presbyterians.

In general, however, northern Protestants' political culture, as it had developed on both sides of the Atlantic since the Act of Union, allowed for neither a nationalist nor a class-based interpretation of the Famine experience. In Ulster itself, for example, although Anglican–Dissenter and landlord–tenant conflicts remained common, between the early 1800s and the 1840s a combination of socio-economic, religious, and political factors (not least of which was mass emigration by disaffected Presbyterians) seemingly had eradicated among most northern Protestants the ecumenical radicalism of the 1790s — creating instead a pervasive, hegemonic loyalty to the Union with Britain and to its Irish upper- and middle-class Protestant champions, as well as a corresponding hostility to Irish nationalist movements that were now almost exclusively Catholic in composition and identity. Likewise, by the mid-1800s Irish-American Protestant political culture was dominated by what later critics would call a 'Scotch-Irish myth' that encompassed nearly all non-Catholic Irish immigrants and their descendants in a shared sense of social and cultural superiority.[20]

18 On Irish Catholic responses to the Famine, generally, see Kerby A. Miller, *Emigrants and Exiles: Ireland and the Irish Exodus to North America* (New York, 1985), ch. 7; and Chapters 3 and 12 in this volume. This argument does not imply, however, that Irish and Irish-American Catholics were unjustified in attributing most Famine suffering to landlords and to grossly inadequate or hardhearted British government relief policies.

19 John Kerr, New Orleans, to James Graham, Newpark, County Antrim, 29 January 1849 (MIC 144/1/13, PRONI); likewise, in another letter to his uncle, dated 26 November 1845 from Perrysville, Pennsylvania, Kerr denounced the Orange Order as '[t]he most tyrannical Society in the world' (MIC 144/1/7, PRONI). Robert McElderry, Lynchburg, Va., to Thomas McElderry, Ballymoney, County Antrim, 31 May 1854 (T. 2414/16, PRONI). Most immediately, Kerr and McElderry may have been influenced by John Mitchel's revolutionary 'Letters to the Protestant Farmers, Labourers, and Artisans of the North of Ireland', originally published in his newspaper, the *United Irishman* (Dublin), 28 April and 13 May 1848; reprinted in *An Ulsterman for Ireland*, Introduction by Eoin Mac Neill (Dublin, 1917).

20 e.g., see Miller, *Emigrants and Exiles*, 68–69, 84–88, 228–35; Kerby A. Miller, '"Scotch-Irish" Myths and "Irish" Identities in Eighteenth- and Nineteenth-Century America', in Charles Fanning, ed., *New Perspectives*

Indeed, it is arguable that the Famine in Ulster played a crucial role in the consolidation of unionist ideology (just as Famine immigration, heavily Catholic and generally impoverished, undoubtedly spurred Irish-American Protestants' efforts to distinguish themselves as 'Scotch-Irish').[21] This was because Ulster Protestant distress during the Famine belied unionists' most basic assumptions in at least three crucial respects. First, it contradicted their fundamental conviction that Protestantism and its associated social virtues would inevitably produce material rewards, win God's favour, and thus shield its adherents from poverty, famine, and eviction — that is, from the 'natural' consequences of the social and moral degradation that Irish Protestants conventionally attributed to Irish Catholics, especially to the peasantry, and from the divine punishment that Catholics allegedly deserved for their wickedness and disloyalty to the Crown. Second, Ulster Protestant suffering in 1845–52, and especially the deficiencies of official relief, had the potential to call into question the practical value of the Union with Britain even among the queen's most proverbially dutiful subjects. Not only revolutionaries like John Mitchel saw that possibility; for instance, in 1849 the Ulster Protestant MP William Sharman Crawford warned the British government that its Rate-in-Aid Bill, which levied extra taxes on solvent Poor Law unions in east Ulster for relief of bankrupt unions in western Ireland, might dissolve the ties of loyalty that bound the North's Protestants to the 'British connexion'.[22] And third, Famine conditions and the inadequacy of local relief exposed and exacerbated the overlapping class and denominational conflicts within Ulster Protestant society itself.

Thus, ideological and political imperatives converged with economic and social concerns to ensure that Anglican landlords, clergymen, and other Ulster Protestant spokesmen would interpret or 'explain' the Famine by escalating unionist and sectarian rhetoric so as to counteract the divisive and educational potential of the crisis. For example, as rents fell and relief costs and poor rates rose, Protestant proprietors and middle-class rate-payers became less likely to be charitable and more prone to contend that, thanks to 'Ulster's' thrifty, Protestant character, there was no Famine in 'their province' at all. Moreover, unionist pronouncements not only denied the Famine's very existence in loyal, industrious, and Protestant 'Ulster', but ascribed hunger and misery only to the 'lazy, vicious and indolent' Catholics of southern and western Ireland, and

on the Irish Diaspora (Carbondale, Ill., 2000), 75–92; and Chapters 6–7 in this volume.

21 But see Chapter 6 in this volume, where it is argued that the modern, formal expression of 'Scotch-Irish' identity first emerged in late eighteenth-century America.

22 James Grant, 'The Great Famine and the Poor Law in Ulster: The Rate-in-Aid Issue of 1849', Irish Historical Studies, 105 (May 1990), 35–36. Also on the rate-in-aid, see James S. Donnelly, Jr., 'The Administration of Relief, 1847–51', in W. E. Vaughan, ed., A New History of Ireland, V: Ireland under the Union, I, 1801–70 (Oxford, 1989), 328; Peter Gray, Famine, Land and Politics: British Government and Irish Society, 1843–50 (Dublin, 1999), 317; and Kinealy, This Great Calamity, 257–60.

attributed the latter's plight to 'the almighty's wrath' against 'idle', 'feckless', and 'sabbath-breaking repealers'.[23]

Such arguments — repeated in Protestant newspapers, speeches, sermons, and public resolutions — helped justify the exceptionally parsimonious relief measures implemented (or denied) by many northern Poor Law boards, especially in eastern Ulster. Those measures won high praise for 'efficiency' and 'frugality' from Whig officials in London, but must have exacerbated distress among lower-class Protestants as well as Catholics. Hence, public works, soup kitchens, and outdoor Famine relief, generally, were employed less often in Ulster (especially in its northeastern counties) than in any other province, while local landlords and Poor Law guardians publicly rejected accusations of misery and starvation among their dependants as malicious slanders on 'the peaceable and industrious inhabitants of the north of Ireland'.[24]

This rhetoric of course obscured the harsh realities of contemporary experience for poor northern Protestants, but it also served to cloak the actions of many Anglican landlords — and of affluent Protestant head tenants and employers — who, in east Ulster as elsewhere, often evicted insolvent farmers, cottiers, and labourers or, at the least, viewed with equanimity the Famine's demographic 'thinnings' of their properties.[25] Furthermore, as David Miller has argued, unionist rhetoric during the Famine also reflected Ulster Presbyterianism's contemporary transformation from 'an inclusive communal faith' to a bourgeois, 'class-based denomination' — and, in consequence, its clerical and lay leaders' increasing tendencies to ignore poor, unchurched Presbyterians and to interpret 'class' problems, such as posed by the crisis of 1845–52, in crudely sectarian terms.[26] Finally, therefore, it may be very significant that the greatest outpouring of unionist and sectarian rhetoric occurred in the Famine's latter years and coincided not only with the controversy over the rate-in-aid, which threatened upper- and middle-class Ulstermen with higher taxation, but also with the beginnings of Sharman Crawford's tenant-right movement, designed to mobilize ordinary Presbyterian farmers against the authority of landlords and their middle-class allies.

In short, Ulster Protestant victims of famine, evictions, and parsimonious relief measures could not express their pain, their grievances and resentments, within the context of a hegemonic religious and political culture that denied their very existence. Consequently, whereas the letters of some Famine immigrants suggest that the crisis of 1845–52 scarred them psychologically and adversely affected their adjustment to American life, this may have been particularly true of those who were poor Protestants.

23 e.g., see Bardon, A History of Ulster, 299; Grant, 'The Great Famine and the Poor Law in Ulster', 36, 43; Kinealy, This Great Calamity, 259; Kinealy and Parkhill, eds., The Famine in Ulster, 11–12; and Miller, 'Irish Presbyterians and the Great Famine', 174.
24 Grant, 'The Great Famine and the Poor Law in Ulster', 31–33; Bardon, A History of Ulster, 287; and Kinealy and Parkhill, eds., The Famine in Ulster, 11–12.
25 Kinealy, This Great Calamity, 218; and Cahal Dallat, 'The Famine in County Antrim', in Kinealy and Parkhill, eds., The Famine in Ulster, 28.
26 Miller, 'Irish Presbyterians and the Great Famine', 167–75.

In contrast to Irish Catholic immigrants, Protestant migrants from Ulster generally lacked large, cohesive, and supportive working-class ethnic communities and subcultures in a mid- and late nineteenth-century America where the prevalent 'Scotch-Irish myth' also denied that Irish Protestant immigrants might be chronically destitute. More crucially, as loyalists to both the British Crown and the ideology of Protestant superiority, Ulster Protestant immigrants could only internalize feelings of anger and shame that Irish Catholics could project outwards on their traditional oppressors.[27] Such may have been the situation of William Murphy, a skilled or semi-skilled Protestant labourer from County Antrim, who never fully settled physically or psychologically in the United States. Often homesick, burdened by guilt, and a frequent sufferer from severe depression, Murphy was unable to form close attachments to persons or places to replace the relationships that had been tragically sundered in his formative years. Other Famine emigrants no doubt shared similar problems, but Murphy was unusual in his ability to articulate a sense of *anomie* or spiritual exile, which others felt but could not express so eloquently.[28]

William Murphy, the son of a boot- and shoe-maker, was born in 1841 and spent his childhood in the townland of Rory's Glen, in Kilwaughter parish, County Antrim, adjacent to the seaport and manufacturing town of Larne, just north of Belfast.[29] His

27 Alternatively, they could follow the logic of Ulster Protestant mythology, rooted in communal 'memories' of settler conflicts with Catholics, and blame their plight not on Protestant landlords and relief officials, but on fellow sufferers who were Irish 'papists'. Of course, in parts of mid- and outer Ulster, where Protestant–Catholic competition for land was keen, such sentiments were often grounded in the realities of sectarian strife. Yet as noted above, in general it was not Catholics but members of the Church of Ireland who were most likely to inherit Ulster from the Presbyterians, who, in proportion to their numbers, were most commonly subject to displacement before, during, and after the Famine. See also Chapter 8, esp. n. 73.
    Nevertheless, it is possible that unionist interpretations of the Famine, as described above, heightened anti-Catholic and loyalist sentiments among Irish Protestant emigrants to America (just as the nationalist interpretation intensified Irish Catholics' animosities to the British government and to Irish landlordism). The single reference to Irish Catholics (specifically to Fenians in the United States) in the Murphy brothers' surviving letters *might* be construed to reflect such sentiments (albeit in a very muted way). From their Famine experiences in Kilwaughter, however, perhaps the Murphys knew better, as it may be significant that their letters never expressed the anti-Irish Catholic and anti-Home Rule sentiments that were increasingly common in Ulster Protestant emigrants' letters during the late 1800s and early 1900s; see notes 28 and 50 below.
28 The remainder of this chapter is based largely on the immigrants' letters of William, Robert, and James Murphy, catalogued as D. 3558/1/21 in PRONI. The collection also contains a certified copy of the since destroyed 1851 Irish census schedule for the Murphy household in Bradbury Place, Belfast. I wish to thank PRONI and W. R. Thompson, Esq., for permission to publish in full several of William Murphy's letters. Thanks also to Jennifer Altenhofel, then a PhD candidate at American University, Washington, DC, for her efforts (albeit unsuccessful) to locate William Murphy's military and pension records in the US National Archives.
29 The information about Rory's Glen, Kilwaughter parish, the Agnew estate, and County Antrim contained in this and the following paragraphs was derived from the following sources: the 1831, 1841, and 1851 Irish censuses, the 1831–34 Irish religious censuses, the Irish Poor Law reports of 1837–38, and the 1841 and 1851 Irish agricultural returns, all published in the BBP; Samuel Lewis, *A Topographical Dictionary of Ireland*,

parents, Alexander Murphy and Anne Ritchie Murphy (born in 1806 and 1807, respectively) resided on the Agnew estate, a property of nearly 10,000 acres, which included the entire parish. Married in 1832, by 1851 Alexander and Anne Murphy had at least eight children, three older and four younger than William. Alexander Murphy was a Presbyterian, but his wife's Ritchie family was Methodist; somewhat surprisingly, most of their children seem to have espoused their mother's religion, although Methodists were only a tiny minority among Kilwaughter's residents. In 1831 Protestants comprised 76 per cent of Kilwaughter's inhabitants, and the Presbyterians — described in 1840 as 'very bigoted in their religious opinions' — made up 96 per cent of the parish's Protestants, nearly three-quarters of its total population.[30]

Prior to the mid-1820s Kilwaughter parish, like nearby Larne, was a centre of cotton manufacturing, but the industrial depression of that decade bankrupted the local mills, and by 1841 a majority of the local families were engaged exclusively in agriculture. Only one-third of the parish was arable, the rest 'mountain and waste land', dominated by bogs and the imposing mass of Agnew's Hill, which loomed over the landscape. Consequently, the area was more suitable for large grazing farms than for tillage,

vol. 2 (1837; Baltimore, 1984 repr.); Angelique Day and Patrick McWilliams, eds., *Ordnance Survey Memoirs of Ireland, Vol. 10: Parishes of County Antrim III, 1833, 1835, 1839–40: Larne and Island Magee* (Belfast, 1991), 106–22; *Land Owners in Ireland ... , 1876* (1876; repr. Baltimore, 1988); Classon Emmet Porter, *Congregational Memoirs of the Old Presbyterian Congregation of Larne and Kilwaughter* (orig. in *Christian Unitarian* monthly, c. 1864; repr. Larne, 1929); George Rutherford, comp., and R. S. J. Clarke, ed., *Old Families of Larne and District* (Belfast, 2004); and Vaughan and Fitzpatrick, eds., *Irish Historical Statistics*. Information as to the birth dates and literacy of William Murphy and his parents is included in the 1851 census schedule, located in D. 3558/1/21, PRONI. The above sources are now supplemented by information provided by Mrs. Mary Calaba Weston (see n. 1).

30 Day and McWilliams, eds., *Ordnance Survey Memoirs*, 114. In 1831 the population of Kilwaughter parish included 1,476 Presbyterians, 484 Catholics, 25 members of the Church of Ireland, and only 31 other Protestant Dissenters, including Methodists — among whom the Ritchies must have predominated.

Alexander Murphy seems to have been a lone figure in the family's history: his children's letters from America never mention Murphy relations, although they are full of references to the Ritchies and their kin; and that may help explain the Murphy children's adherence to their mother's religion. Another likely explanation is that Anne Ritchie Murphy's parents, James and Elizabeth Ritchie, were by local standards quite comfortable farmers and, as such, must have enjoyed unusual status in the parish. Shortly after the Famine, Arnott Knowe, the Ritchie farm in Rory's Glen, comprised some 81 acres, with an annual valuation of £20, and the family also rented grazing or turbary rights in another townland; the Ritchie home and farm buildings were valued at £14. Also, there was no formal place of worship, of any kind, in Kilwaughter parish (Anglicans attended church in Carncastle; Presbyterians and Methodists in nearby Larne town; Catholics in Larne or Ballygowan), which would have strengthened the influence of Anne Murphy's father, James Ritchie (described as 'a dedicated Local Preacher'), over his extended family. Despite James Ritchie's efforts, however, the 1831 religious census recorded only 31 'other Protestant Dissenters' (including Methodists) in Kilwaughter, and by 1861 their number had only risen to 35, including merely 12 Methodists (although the latter numbered 127 in nearby Larne town); hence, this chapter's focus on Kilwaughter's Presbyterians seems fully merited. Information on the Ritchies, their farm, etc., from Mrs. Mary Calaba Weston (see n. 1); also see G. Knox, *A History of Larne Methodist Church, 1885–1985* (Larne, 1985), a copy of which Mrs. Weston located in the Larne public library. On local Presbyterianism, see Porter, *Congregational Memoirs*.

but in 1841 over 87 per cent of the holdings were still devoted to raising oats and potatoes, and most farms were too small to employ paid labourers. Before the Famine the average-sized farm on the Agnew estate was merely 20 acres, and over 80 per cent of the occupiers inhabited one- or two-roomed thatched cottages. Nevertheless, half the men and almost one-third of the women in the parish could read and write, and local literacy rates were significantly higher than in County Antrim, generally.

William Murphy's father and mother were both literate, and his father's skilled trade and his parents' superior education not only maintained the Murphys above poverty but also ensured them a certain stature in the parish, no doubt enhanced by the ability of at least one family branch, which emigrated to Upper Canada, to prepare its sons for the ministry.[31] Moreover, in 1840 the Ordnance Survey memoirist recorded an Alexander Murphy as a butler at Kilwaughter Castle, the Agnew estate house, and as superintendent of a Sunday school which boasted a lending library of 100 religious books.[32] If this was William Murphy's father, then his family indeed enjoyed relatively high status during his formative years — which makes his parents' subsequent descent into poverty more traumatic, and his own sense of loss and maladjustment in America even more comprehensible.

The documentary evidence, and hints in his own letters, suggest that the security of William Murphy's childhood crumbled dramatically during and shortly after the Great Famine. In the late eighteenth and early nineteenth centuries, Edward Jones Agnew, Kilwaughter's landlord and one-time member of the Irish parliament, had granted his tenants leases of twenty-one years and two 'lives', one of which was his own; thus, his death in 1834 meant that the expiration of most leases would coincide with the onset of the potato blight. Margaret Jones, Agnew's successor as proprietor, enjoyed a benevolent reputation and may not have evicted her dependants during the Famine's early years.[33] She died in 1848, however, and the prior collapse of cottage spinning, the

31 This was the Moore branch of the family, descended from Anne Ritchie Murphy's younger sister, Jane (or Jannet) Ritchie, who in 1837 married John Moore, a Kilwaughter Presbyterian. John and Jane Moore emigrated in 1839 and settled in Ingersoll, Upper Canada, where he became a prosperous iron manufacturer. On 12 July 1847 Jane Moore wrote to her parents in Kilwaughter, expressed alarm at news of 'the distress in Ireland', and hoped that 'non of our friends ar suffering under it'. One of her sons, William (1838–1915), was educated at Princeton Theological Seminary and became the foremost Presbyterian minister in Ottawa; in 1897 he was elected Moderator of the Presbyterian General Assembly in Ontario. Information from Mrs. Mary Calaba Weston (see n. 1).
32 Presbyterians, Independents, and Methodists preached on alternating Sundays in the school that Alexander Murphy superintended; undoubtedly, his father-in-law, James Ritchie, would have been a regular preacher for the Methodists.
33 The Agnews' reputed benevolence reflected an archaic paternalism: this was evinced in ample charity to the local poor but also in the preservation, well into the mid-1800s, of a number of 'ancient customs' on the estate, including requirements that tenants grind their corn only at the Agnews' mill and that they give 'duty days' cutting and hauling the family's turf. In 1840 the Ordnance Survey memoirist reported that 'Miss Jones ... will not allow any undertenants. All must pay rent to her. Neither will she allow any farmer to keep more than 1 labourer or cottier'; Day and McWilliams, eds., *Ordnance Survey Memoirs*, 111–17. After she died in 1848, her heirs nullified her will's charitable bequest of £700 in Famine relief 'to the

introduction of power looms in Belfast factories at mid-century, and the overcrowded and impoverished conditions that characterized Kilwaughter's smallholdings made the parish highly susceptible to the same processes that operated in the poor, mountainous districts of mid- and south Ulster during the Great Famine. Thus, whether forced or 'voluntary', wholesale clearances of smallholders, cottiers, and weavers must have occurred, perhaps soon after Jones's death, for between 1841 and 1851 the populations of Kilwaughter parish and Rory's Glen declined by a remarkable 36.4 per cent and 35.6 per cent, respectively, compared with merely a 9 per cent decline in County Antrim, generally (not including Belfast). By 1851 nearly a third of Kilwaughter's families, enumerated in 1841, had disappeared, including almost half of those that had occupied the poorest houses and cabins.[34] As noted above, population losses in 1841–51 cannot be distinguished by religion. However, between 1831 and 1861, in the three decades spanning the Famine crisis, the size of Kilwaughter's majority Presbyterian community fell by 36 per cent, almost precisely the same as the 1831–61 decline in the parish's entire population. In 1831–61 only Kilwaughter's small and extremely poor Catholic community had a higher rate of population loss. And although the numbers of local Anglicans and 'other Protestant Dissenters' (including Methodists) increased, they were so few that they scarcely affected the overall pattern of catastrophic decline.[35]

As a result of Famine depletion alone, by 1851 a consolidation of holdings had radically altered the local landscape: nearly half of Kilwaughter's farms were now over 30 acres in size, and more than three-fourths of the parish's arable land had been converted to grazing. Relatively few of the inhabitants may have perished in the Famine from actual malnutrition or disease, but out-migration from the parish — hitherto rare — was extensive. If Alexander Murphy had indeed been a butler at Kilwaughter Castle, one can only speculate how or why he lost or relinquished his position, but apparently he suffered the same fate as his poorer neighbours. Given the family's size, the Murphys could not afford to emigrate overseas, but with many others they moved to the growing industrial city of Belfast.

Between 1851 and 1854 the Irish census and the Belfast city directories list Alexander Murphy, 'boot and shoemaker', his wife and eight children, as living in south Belfast

Poor of the Parish of Kilwaughter, without distinction of religion', and probably commenced wholesale evictions and clearances — the results of which were evident in the 1851 census; see Porter, *Congregational Memoirs*, 91.

34 Between 1841 and 1851 the number of persons in Kilwaughter parish fell from 2,164 to 1,376, and in Rory's Glen from 228 to 147. The total number of families in Kilwaughter declined from 376 to 257; the number of families that occupied third-class houses fell from 168 to 155, and the number in fourth-class dwellings declined from 136 to 0. Meanwhile, the number of unoccupied houses more than doubled.

35 Between 1831 and 1861 the number of Presbyterians in Kilwaughter fell from 1,476 to 945, while the number of Catholics declined from 484 to 261 (-46 per cent). During the same period, the number of Anglicans in the parish increased from 25 to 58, and the number of 'other Protestant Dissenters' rose from 31 to 35. Nearly all of Kilwaughter's Catholics were concentrated in Mulloughsandall townland; their general destitution is attested in Day and McWilliams, eds., *Ordnance Survey Memoirs*, 114.

alongside other petty craftsmen at 9 Bradbury Place, a terrace of houses and shops on the west side of the roadway, near the present Shaftsbury Square. In 1851 young William Murphy was attending a school taught by James McMullen at 24 Fifth Street, in the virtually all-Protestant Shankill neighbourhood. Perhaps it was McMullen who taught William and his brothers the lines by Thomas Hood and other popular poets, which the Murphys later would quote in their letters from America. However, in 1854 Alexander Murphy moved his family yet again: across the Lagan River to the industrial suburb of Ballymacarrett, in east Belfast, where until 1862 he resided at Wheeler Place and was first listed as a 'mechanic', later as a 'mechanic and grocer', in city directories.[36] Thus, expelled from the relatively homogenous and even bucolic environs of Rory's Glen, William Murphy spent his late childhood and adolescent years in a city that was grossly overcrowded with poor migrants from the Ulster countryside, riven by violent sectarian conflict, and beset by severe problems of sanitation and disease.

Between 1841 and 1851 Belfast's population increased by almost one-fourth, to 87,000 inhabitants.[37] Many of the newcomers were Famine refugees; in 1847 alone, 14,000 persons gained admission to the city's workhouse, while hundreds of others perished in the streets. By 1861 Belfast's inhabitants numbered 122,000, a rise of nearly 40 per cent in ten years, and in 1861–71 the population grew by another 43 per cent, to 174,000. Many migrants found employment in the city's expanding linen factories and shipyards, and by Irish or even British standards, mid-nineteenth-century Belfast was relatively prosperous. However, wages were low, and both Protestant and Catholic workers, not yet fully segregated into discrete neighbourhoods, expressed their grievances in fierce competition and sometimes violent conflict with each other, rather than in co-operation against their employers. In 1861 Presbyterians comprised 35 per cent, members of the Church of Ireland 25 per cent, Methodists and other Protestants 6 per cent, and Catholics 34 per cent of the city's inhabitants. Protestant street preachers such as the Presbyterian minister, 'Roaring' Hugh Hanna, acted as catalysts of sectarian strife; the Murphys would have witnessed the Rev. Hanna's anti-'papist' harangues and the consequent riots of 1857, when Catholic and Protestant workers — many of the latter members of the Loyal Orange Order — engaged in bloody street battles throughout the summer.

However, the aspect of life in working-class Belfast that apparently affected the Murphys most severely was the prevalence of disease. In 1833–40 the Ordnance Survey had described Kilwaughter parish and its inhabitants as remarkably healthy. By contrast, mid-nineteenth century Belfast had the highest death rate in Ireland and probably in the entire United Kingdom: water and sewage systems were grossly inadequate; epidemics of cholera, typhus, and typhoid were frequent; tuberculosis and bronchial disorders were chronic; and infant mortality rates were so high that the average life expectancy

36 Information derived from: *Henderson's Belfast Directory and Northern Depository* (Belfast, 1852); *Belfast and Province of Ulster Directory* (Belfast, 1852–62).
37 Information on Belfast in this and the following paragraph derived from: J. C. Beckett and R. Glasscock, eds., *Belfast: Origin and Growth of an Industrial City* (London, 1967); and W. A. Maguire, *Belfast* (Keele, 1993).

at birth was merely nine years. Although the Murphys do not appear to have resided in neighbourhoods that were unusually congested or squalid, all working-class areas suffered from impure water, filth (25,000 houses had no privies or sewer lines), and endemic disease. After 1862 Alexander Murphy's name disappears from the city directories, and his son's later letters (especially that of 1880) strongly suggest that in the late 1850s or early 1860s both of William Murphy's parents and four of his siblings died within a relatively short time, perhaps from the effects of their unhealthy environment.[38] Meanwhile, another brother, James, contracted the tuberculosis that would shorten his life in America.

Murphy himself emigrated c. 1862–63, in his early twenties, apparently alone and perhaps in a manner that justified some of his American relations in accusing him of deserting his orphaned and only surviving sister, Eliza (Elizabeth Jane, born c. 1849–50) — to whom he wrote his later letters, often in an exculpatory vein. We do not know Murphy's motives for emigrating, but it may be credible to speculate that his traumatic early experiences, the losses of community (twice) and family, and perhaps a drinking problem (hinted in his American letters) drove him to leave his homeland in search of a security and identity lost forever in Ireland. Sadly, however, his correspondence indicates that those same traumas made it impossible for him to form close or permanent associations in America — or even to identify with any place or anyone except the scenes and the few relatives he had left behind, and the comrades, living and dead, by whose side he fought during the American Civil War. Moreover, the fragmentation and fatalism of his personality, the latter perhaps conditioned by his father's Calvinism,[39] may have been exacerbated by his participation in the carnage of that terrible war, which he described in his first surviving letter, written from one of Pittsburgh's industrial suburbs.

William Murphy, Lawrenceville, Pennsylvania, to his brother, James Murphy, Belfast, 8 November 1865

Lawerenceville Nov 8th 1865
Dear Brother
I suppose youl think it strange that I didnt answer your letter sooner but I have tramped a good deal since I got your letter and I hope you will pardon me not writeing sooner   I couldnt go to work for a long time after I wrote to you last   I doctered till my money was about all gone and I had given up all hope of ever being well when I met with an old Indian docter who gave me some herbs and two weeks

38 When Anne Ritchie Murphy's father, James Ritchie (b. 1783), made his will and died in early 1865, both Anne and her husband Alexander Murphy were already deceased; information from Mrs. Mary Calaba Weston (see n. 1).
39 Apparently Murphy's father was an orthodox Presbyterian, as Alexander Murphy's Sunday school in Kilwaughter parish originated when local Calvinists seceded from another school dominated by 'Unitarians', i.e., by 'New Light' Presbyterians.

affter I begun to take them I was abel to go to work and to day I beleve I am stouter
and better than I ever was. I went to work in Erie [Pennsylvania] but I hadnt worked
long before they took down our wages and there was a genreal[40] strike amongst
the hands   I might have stoped in Erie as long as I had a mind to for I have lots
of friends there but I didnt want to stop when I couldnt get work so I started on
tramp   I tramped all over ohio and hauled up at last in the far famed Iiron City
of Pittsburgh Pennsilvania   the reason I have my letter headded Lawrencevill is
becaus the part of city I work in goes by that name[41]   however when you answer
this drect to Erie Wm Murphy box 207 because I cant tell how long I may be in this
place but I have [a] friend in Erie who will send all letters to me no matter where I
be   his name is Alex maxwell   him and I shiped in the Navy to gather and stuck
by [each] other like brothers through it all[42]   if ever you should come across him
and let him know you were a brother of mine there would be nothing to good
for you   times are rather dull here but for all that dear James I wish that you and
robert were here for if you were here and the three of us stick to gather we could
make lots of money   I dont know how it is but I cant get along myself at   if have
had[43] good chances many a time but some how luck always went againest   no
matter   there is a good time comeing yet. I often in my black moods have wished
that some Southern bullet had strecthed me along side my fallen Shipmates on the
banks of the Cumberland Tennesee or Missisippy river but Im getting over all that
I wish I had that letter of Elizas   I will write to aunt Eliza as soon as I get settled
down again   tell W^m McCoulloh and Hugh Nelson that I will give theme a long
decription of the war Millatary and political some day   if I knew roberts adress I
would write to him   James when you write please let me know your plans   give
my best respects to hugh Nelson[,] W^m McCoulaugh and all the rorysglen follk

40 **genreal**: general. With few exceptions (noted below), when Murphy's misspellings or omitted words and
   letters might confuse readers, this chapter presents Murphy's correspondence with minimal editorial
   insertions and annotations, and in strict accordance with the original manuscripts.
41 Lawrenceville (population 3,260 in 1860) was one of several industrial villages east of Pittsburgh that were
   annexed to the city in 1868; after annexation the Lawrenceville district comprised Pittsburgh wards 17 and
   18. In 1870 about one-fourth of Lawrenceville district's population was Irish-born, increasing to over a
   third by 1880, when nearly 70 per cent of its Irish inhabitants were unskilled labourers, primarily in the
   iron and steel mills. See Victor A. Walsh, 'Across "The Big Wather": Irish Community Life in Pittsburgh
   and Allegheny City, 1850–1885' (PhD diss., University of Pittsburgh, 1983).
42 William Murphy enlisted in the US Navy, at Erie, Pennsylvania, on 28 July 1864; his enlistment papers
   described him as a 'seaman', age twenty-three, with blue eyes, dark hair, fair complexion, 5ft. 9in. tall,
   with a 'large mole on right arm'; Murphy served in the Mississippi Squadron, principally aboard the
   gunboat *Silver Lake*, from which he was mustered out at Mound City, Illinois, in June 1865. In 1885 Murphy
   requested his enlistment records from Washington, DC, so he could join Post 4 of the Grand Army of
   the Republic (GAR) in Deer Lodge, Montana. **Alex**ander **Maxwell**: perhaps an emigrant from William
   Murphy's neighbourhood (a Maxwell boy was a labourer on the Ritchie farm in Kilwaughter); served
   as quarter master on the *Silver Lake* and other US Navy gunboats during the Civil War; drew his military
   pension in 1886, and died in 1923 in Erie, Pa. Information from Mrs. Mary Calaba Weston (see n. 1).
43 **I cant get along myself at   if have had ...**: i.e., I can't get along myself at it   I have had ... .

remember me to Charlie Jonson   give my love to Grandmother Aunt Eliza and our own Eliza and robert[44]   God bless and keep you

> Your affectionate
> brother William Murphy

Murphy's subsequent 'black moods', suggesting manic depression, may never have been as severe as in the war's immediate aftermath, but the letter above exposes several contradictions at the heart of this immigrant's career and personality. On the one hand, for example, Murphy craved comradeship and guidance, especially from his remaining kin and even from younger brother James (born c. 1843–44). Indeed, in his next letter, written in early 1866 from Pittsburgh to his older sibling Robert (born c. 1837–38),[45] William expressed his own needs and inadequacies more explicitly and poignantly, practically begging his brothers to join and look after him in America:

> ... I thought I would write you these few lines merely to let you know that I [am] well and expecting to see you both before long   there [is] some mistake about me Id like to do well but I cant   the fact of the matter is this bob I want you here to lead me   I have no thought for the future and soon forget the past   I form good resolutions but soon forget them and if you and James dont come here and kick me along I'll[46] never be worth ten cents ...[47]

However, although his brothers did emigrate in 1866–67, William Murphy spent only a relatively few months with them during all their years in America. During part of 1867–68 William and Robert apparently worked together in Pittsburgh and Chicago, and in 1869–70 he and James laboured for a ship's captain in the Hudson River port of Poughkeepsie, but after that date, he rarely saw them — although they wrote sporadically and affectionately to each other. In part, such separations reflected the exigencies of unmarried life for immigrant artisans and labourers, as all three brothers were involved in the carpentry and building trades, and as Robert admitted, 'a wife is rather an expensive

---

44 **Grandmother:** Elizabeth Ritchie (1782–1866), James Ritchie's widow and mother of Anne Richie Murphy, William Murphy's deceased mother. **Aunt Eliza:** Elizabeth Ritchie Johnston (1823–1909), younger sister of Anne Ritchie Murphy, who had married Samuel Johnston; she and her husband inherited the Ritchie farm on her father's death. **our own Eliza:** Elizabeth Jane Murphy, William's youngest and only surviving sister; apparently Eliza was then living with the Ritchies/Johnstons on the farm in Rory's Glen. **robert** (also **bob**): Robert Ritchie Murphy, William's older brother. Information from Mrs. Mary Calaba Weston (see n. 1).
45 In 1868 the *Belfast and Province of Ulster Directory* listed Robert Murphy, of Wheeler's Place, Ballymacarrett, east Belfast, as a labourer, although by this time he had emigrated to America.
46 **I;ll** Murphy frequently employed semi-colons instead of apostrophes in his correspondence; in such instances and for readers' convenience, apostrophes have been silently restored.
47 William Murphy, Pittsburgh, to Robert Murphy, Belfast, 27 January 1866.

luxury in this country'.[48] Nevertheless, after 1870 Robert and James were inseparable during their travels in the Far West, until the latter's death from consumption in San Francisco in 1879, and William's social and spiritual isolation seems more a function of personality than occupation.

Likewise, despite his avowed affection for fellow ex-soldiers, and his subsequent career as a member of sizeable, albeit transient, workgroups, close-knit by necessity, William remained remarkably disconnected from the overlapping ethnic and working-class associations, both formal and informal, that structured the lives of most Irish immigrants, Protestants as well as Catholics. For instance, during the 1870s, 1880s, and 1890s Murphy was either headquartered or permanently resident in or near Pittsburgh, over a tenth of whose inhabitants were Irish immigrants, over 20 per cent of whom were skilled and semi-skilled workers (plus over 50 per cent unskilled), and about one-fourth of whom were Ulster Protestants.[49] However, judging from his letters, the tumultuous events that shook that city in those decades and which involved so many of its Irish workers (the temperance crusade of 1876, led by Francis Murphy, an Ulster Protestant immigrant; the great railroad strike and riots of 1877; the rise of the Knights of Labor, the Greenback-Labor party, and the Irish American Land League in the late 1870s and 1880s; the struggles of the Amalgamated Iron and Steel Workers' Union, culminating in the violent Homestead strike of 1892) made no impression upon him, save perhaps to confirm his alienation from what he called 'this Wicked World'.[50] Moreover, Murphy never resided in any of Pittsburgh's Ulster Protestant enclaves (Lawrenceville's Irish were primarily Munster and Connacht Catholics), and in his letters he never

48 Robert Murphy, San Francisco, to David and Eliza Gilmore, Belfast, 29 November 1875. Between 1875 and 1889, Robert Murphy wrote ten surviving letters to the Gilmores, primarily from San Francisco and from Butte and Anaconda, Montana, where he alternated between carpentry and unrewarding attempts at gold mining. Although he was more sociable than his brother William, Robert's letters express much the same sense of fatalism, especially with regard to his occupational failures ('I am very unlucky', he wrote on 18 March 1889), which may reflect their father's Calvinism as well as their common childhood experiences of famine, privation, and loss.
49 The information on Pittsburgh and the Irish in that city, contained in this and subsequent paragraphs, is derived from: Walsh, 'Across "The Big Wather"'; Francis G. Couvares, The Remaking of Pittsburgh: Class and Culture in an Industrializing City (Albany, NY, 1984); Leland D. Baldwin, Pittsburgh: The Story of a City (Pittsburgh, 1937); Stefan Lorant, ed., Pittsburgh: The Story of an American City (Garden City, NY, 1964); Erasmus Wilson, Standard History of the City of Pittsburgh (Chicago, 1888); and G. M. Hopkins, Atlas of the County of Allegheny, Pennsylvania (Philadelphia, 1876).
50 William Murphy, Guyandotte, Va., to David and Eliza Gilmore, Belfast, 31 December 1871. The sole exception to Murphy's apparent disinterest in Irish-American political activities was his facetious remarks on the Fenian movement, written from Pittsburgh in 1866: 'the fenians are fighting amongst themselves here   the[y] have got two Presedents for the Irish republic   at a late Government sale of condemned Muskets warented to kill at every shot (if they dont kill the man the[y] shoot at theyl kill the man that shoots them off) one party of the finnegans bought 80,000 of these Muskets but whether they are going [to] use them against the English or themselves it dont state'; William Murphy, 27 January 1866; parentheses added. Perhaps most striking, although many, perhaps most, Irish Protestant immigrants adapted to life overseas in large part through participation in North American churches and/or revival meetings, William Murphy's letters never mentioned joining or even attending any churches or revivals in the US.

remarked on the ethnic or religious affiliations of any non-relations he encountered in America. Indeed, in his later correspondence specific references to wartime comrades or fellow workers disappeared almost entirely, and he seemed to attain psychological equilibrium by an almost total emotional detachment from people and places in the United States and by projecting his affections and hopes overseas to his sister Eliza and her husband, David Gilmore.[51] Thus, in early 1869, from Poughkeepsie, New York, Murphy wrote plaintively:

[D]ont think Eliza, that either him [brother Robert] or me have ever forgot our Sister   for I tell you Eliza and I tell you truely in some of the hardest fought battles of the late war when men fell like grain before the sickel, above the roar and din of battle above the wild cheers of the combatants the heartrending shrieks of the wounded and dying something seemed to whisper in my ear never fear your little Sister prays for you and I sometimes think that although she has got to be a big married woman she sometimes prays for me yet, [even] if I shouldnt be quite as good as I ought to be.[52]

By 1870, after a short career aboard a coastal steamer, Murphy had settled into what would be his livelihood for at least the next decade, working for a Pittsburgh-based bridge-building firm, probably Andrew Carnegie's Keystone Bridge Manufacturing Company, travelling in crews throughout the country, constructing iron bridges to accommodate the enormous contemporary expansion of the nation's railroad system.[53]

51 Eliza (Elizabeth Jane) Murphy married David Gilmore, 'grocer', in St. Matthew's church (Church of Ireland), in the Shankill, on 24 October 1868; see: Civil Register of Marriages, 1868, vol. 16, 397 (General Register Office, Belfast; on microfilm in the library of the Church of Jesus Christ of Latter Day Saints, Holywood, Co. Down).
    Eliza Murphy's husband was a son of the David Gilmore listed in the Belfast city directory as a baker, living in 1865–68 at 27 Welwynne Street, in the area between the Crumlin and Shankill roads. From 1868 to 1870 the Welwynne Street address was occupied by a Mrs. John Gilmore, listed in 1870 as a mill worker. Between 1870 and 1899, David Gilmore, Eliza's husband, was listed as a grocer or a provision dealer at various Belfast addresses: 101 Old Lodge Road, north Belfast (1870–76); M'Millen's Buildings, 81 Albert Bridge Road, east Belfast (1877–84, and again in 1894); and 203 Grosvenor Street, west Belfast (1894–99). See Belfast and Province of Ulster Directory (1865–84); Slater's Ulster Directory (Belfast, 1870–94); and Slater's Belfast Directory (Belfast, 1894). David Gilmore also had some success as an inventor of machines. He and Eliza had at least three children: Ann, David, and Florence. Information from Mrs. Mary Calaba Weston (see n. 1).
52 William Murphy, Poughkeepsie, NY, to Eliza and David Gilmore, Belfast, 22 March 1869.
53 Between 1860 and 1890, the nation's railroad track expanded from less than 31,000 to nearly 160,000 miles. This generated an enormous demand for railroad bridges — as well as for timber, iron, and steel, generally — which specialized bridge-manufacturing companies formed to supply. In 1865 Andrew Carnegie organized the Keystone Bridge Company of Pittsburgh, which built the superstructure of the famous Eads Bridge at St. Louis (1868–74), among many others. In 1888 Keystone employed about 600 workers and was one of the nation's major bridge-building firms. However, in the late 1880s and 1890s, American bridge-building, hitherto highly competitive among numerous companies (which often led to cheap, shoddy construction with unreliable wooden and iron trusses), shifted to steel and became

In the following letter, Murphy described his new trade and rationalized his personal anomie, expiating his guilt and evading responsibility for leaving his orphaned sister in Belfast, by sentimentalizing his homesickness and, ironically, by conforming (albeit in non-politicized ways) to what were generally Irish Catholic conventions of involuntary 'exile' from the 'old country'.

William Murphy, Poughkeepsie, New York, to David and Eliza Gilmore, Belfast, 5 April 1870

April 5th 1870.
Dear Brother & Sister
after a long silence I sit down to write you a few lines   I hardly know how to excuse myself for not writeing to you sooner but the truth is I have contracted such a habit of moveing from place to place that I am never in one place long enough to here from the old country   when I wrote to you last I was sailing on an American coaster   in that trade I have been all along the seaboard from Maine to Mexico I have seen the ornge groves of Cuba   yes Dave I have seen all the glourious beauties of the Sunny South and a great many of her horrors to[o] but after all many a time I have thought as I trod the deck in the lonely watchs of the night or gaezed on the dark bleu waters of the Gulf how much better and happier I was when I took my first trip down the bay to bangor[54]   the people at home think that we exiles in a forigen land soon forget the home and freinds of our youth but the[y] are greatly mistakeing   abesence makes the heart grow fonder   I have seen many a sunbrowned wanderer drop a tear as he told some little anicdote of his boyish days in his far distant Island home   yes Dave I have made some good freinds and true in this country yet I have never forgoten my old freinds at home and far above them all my little sister   I know there is plenty around her to tell her that I am not worthy to be her brother. now David I know I have done wrong often   I have been acused of not helping Eliza when she was battling with the world alone but circumstances over which I had no control prevented me for God knows I would give my hearts blood to aid Eliza if it was required   the reason I have writen this is because I have seen a relative of mine[55] sometime ago who called me a scoundrel

consolidated under control of the railroad companies. The consequent transitions, both technological and organizational, may have cost Murphy his job c. 1890 (see below). See George Rogers Taylor and Irene Neu, *The American Railroad Network, 1861–1890* (Cambridge, Mass., 1956); J. A. L. Waddell, *Bridge Engineering* (New York, 1941); and Llewellyn N. Edwards, *History and Evolution of Early American Bridges* (Orono, Me., 1959).
54 **bangor:** Bangor, a minor seaport on Belfast Lough, about ten miles from the city, in County Down.
55 Murphy's reference was to his uncle Robert L. Ritchie (or the latter's wife Sarah), whom he visited unsuccessfully, in Newburgh, New York, sometime in the late 1860s. This branch of the Ritchie family had emigrated and settled in Newburgh c. 1838–39. Robert L. Ritchie was a 'local minister' for over forty years at Newburgh's Trinity Methodist church and a patron as well of the local African Methodist Episcopal

and a reprobate and among other thing[s] cast up to my teeth that before Eliza was married I did'nt care wether she starved or not   alas for the raririty of christan charity under the sun. I felt for Eliza keenly the more so because I could'nt help her. but let us drop this and take up something else   well I have given up Salt water and taken to bridge biulding   dont think that I have turned stone mason bridges here and the long bridge[56] diffrs   here the[y] are built of iron or wood as the case may be and it takes only a few weeks to put one up so that I am traveling around from place to place with a bridge company helping to put up New ones and pull down old ones   I am at present in the State of Pennsilvania but I cant tell what state I'll [be] in when you get this   perhaps the State of matrimony   I sometimes think it would be better for me if I was but however I'll think it over and let you know some other time   I suppose you have a dozen bouncing boys and girls by this time   I hope so at any rate   I would like to be called uncle once to see what it was like but I must stop this nonsense   answer this as soon as you can and I wont be so long of writeing again [no signature]

Despite his speculations, Murphy never married and for the next decade, at least, he roamed the country building bridges, primarily in the South and West. Between construction jobs, he boarded with various families in the Lawrenceville district of Pittsburgh, where his neighbours were a mixture of Irish, German, and British ironworkers, artisans, and saloonkeepers congregated along Butler Avenue between 40th Street and 42nd Street. Interestingly, in 1880 Murphy boarded with the family of a German shoemaker: on the one hand, a reflection of his lack of close ties to his fellow bridge-builders or to other Ulster immigrants; on the other hand, perhaps an unconscious effort to replicate the vanished securities of his shoemaker father's Irish household.[57] However, during the 1870s Murphy apparently became reconciled to having no fixed abode: 'the wide world is my home now,' he wrote to his sister and brother-in-law on New Year's Eve, 1871;

if I had settled in one place at first it might have been different but I was bound to see the world   well i have seen it and I must confess I feel no happier for the sight   the bad far outweighs the good as far as my experience goes[58] and it is wide and varied. there is some times I think I will settle down   then the old yearning to

congregation. According to family tradition, he was 'very religious and strict'; at least four of his nine children never married, and another child — a rebellious daughter — apparently faked her own murder and absconded from Newburgh to San Francisco. Information from Mrs. Mary Calaba Weston (see n. 1).

56 **the long bridge**: Murphy was probably referring to the Queen's Bridge, over the Lagan River in Belfast, which replaced the old Long Bridge in 1842.

57 The house in which William Murphy lived in 1880 was located in the microfilmed schedules of that year's US census for Pittsburgh. Unfortunately, his transience, plus the commonness of his name, made it impossible to locate Murphy himself in any US censuses or Pittsburgh city directories.

58 **gois**.

see more comes over and I drop the idea at once   in fact Davy I have got a rovers commison and do my best I cant get rid of it.[59]

However, in 1880 news of James's death in San Francisco, and the prospect that his sister's family might join him in America, forced Murphy to abandon, at least temporarily, the pretence that his transient, solitary life was either voluntary or more than tolerable.

William Murphy, Keokuk, Iowa, to David and Eliza Gilmore, Belfast, 18 December 1880

Keokuk Iowa   Dec 13th 1880
Dear Brother & Sister
I hardly know how to commence a letter to you it is so long since I heard from you direct   I here from you right along thru Robert but that would scarcly excuse me from writeing to you   I wrote to you last winter from Indiana but Bob informed me you never got my letter   the fact is Dave & Eliza I have to knock around so much at the work I follow that I hardly know what to do very often. I am hardly ever more than a week or two in one place and I make up my mind to write every place I go but when I get there I think this way well I'm not going to be long here perhaps the next place I go I can wait and get an answer and so it gos   but I hope you will forgive me and I know you will for my neglect. I asure you I never for a moment forget you. no doubt you think why dont I settel down like other peopel I have asked myself that question a thousand times,   I have went further   I have tried to do so   I know that I can make as good a liveing perhaps better by staying in one place all the time but when I try it I soon get tired and the restless spirit gets the best of me all the time. the fact is traveling is so natural to me that I might as well try to live without eating as withou[t] wandering around   but what diffrence does it make[?]   life is but a dream and although I know that my last days will be spent in all propability amongst strangers, I almost wish sometimes the dream was over   Dear Brother & sister dont think for a moment that I am despondent or downhearted for I am anything but that   but just think for a second of the past that has gone never to be recalled. it seems but yesterday since we were a happy and United famly Mother Father Brothers and Sisters   where are they now. they grew togather side by side   they filled one hall with glee   there graves are scaterd far and wide by mountain stream and sea   six of that once happy family sleep the last long sleep beneath the Green sod of their native land and James the latest of our loved and lost laid him down to rest in the far away Calaifornia   he like thousands more tried to find a fortune and instead he found a grave   but where could he find

59 William Murphy, 31 December 1871.

a more fitting resting place than in lone Mountain   the last rays of the setting Sun
kiss his grave as it sinks behind the waters of the Great pacific, and his spirit has
crossed the great divide and joined the others in that better land beyond   there
are but three left now and thousands of miles of land and sea seperate them three
robert is away up on top of the rocky mountains whilst I like the wandering jew
cannot call one spot of earth my home, and you dear Sister (and I thank God from
the very bottom of my heart for it) are a happy wife and mother   although you
may think me cold hearted because I dont write oftner still I never forget my littel
Sister and if you only knew how my heart yearns to see you once again you would
forgive my aparient neglect but I will promise to do better in the future   I have
made arrangements with a freind so that letters will be forwarded to me no matter
where I am   I had a letter from Robert a day or two since   he says you were
wanting [to] know something about the Climate &c of Colrado   well Dave my
boy Southren Colrada has a splended Climate dry and warm not to[o] warm   the
princple biusness in the state is mineing although there is considreble farming
done in some parts of the state but as a genrel thing the Climate is to[o] dry for
farming   Northren Colrado is very montainous and the winters are very severe the
thermomenter going way down to 40 below zero   but Dave if you have any notion
to leave old played out Europe and come to this live and pogreseve land I would
advise you to go to some of the older states   California has the finest Climate in
the world nither to[o] hot nor to[o] cold but nearly a uniform temprature all the
year round   in fact with a few exceptions in some of the Southren and middel
Westren States the Climate of this country is healthy   but I must come to a close
this time but next time I write I will give you all the information I can   I hope you
are both well and happy   give my love to aunt Eliza and let me know [how] she
gets along   also to Lizzey Martin[60]   I dont know her name now but that makes
no diffrenc   I suppose she is a sedate old married woman now but I think of her
only as the lively littel girl she used to be   and Dear Brother and Sister may God
bless and perserve you is the ernest Prayer of your affectionate Brother —

William

in care F Smith   N° 4018 Butler Street
Pittsburgh Pennselvaina

After the above there is a ten-year gap between William Murphy's surviving letters.
In summer 1885 he was living in Deer Lodge, Montana, where he applied to Washington
for copies of his navy service records, and in March 1889 his brother Robert reported
(also from Montana) that William was then in North Carolina, still building bridges.[61]

60 **Lizzey Martin**: probably William Murphy's cousin and a child of his aunt Margaret Ritchie, who married
   William Martin. Information from Mrs. Mary Calaba Weston (see n. 1).
61 Robert Murphy, Anaconda, Montana, to David and Eliza Gilmore, Belfast, 18 March 1889.

However, on 17 August 1891 William wrote from Braddock, a grimy steel town just east of Pittsburgh, that he had been unemployed for an unspecified length of time and forced to work at 'common labour', probably at the mammoth J. Edgar Thomson steelworks that dominated Braddock, alongside what he called 'the very lowest scum of Europe Itilians & Hungarians as filthy and ignorant a class of people as God ever put the breath of life into'.[62] Seven years later, according to his last surviving letters, also from Braddock, Murphy was again working, probably for a steel mill or a coal gas company, but a coal miners' strike made his employment 'rather ticklish', and, buoyed by remittances from the Gilmores, he hoped to return at last to Ireland in the fall.[63] Indeed, sometime after August 1897 William Murphy finally resigned his 'rovers commison' and returned to die amid the scenes of his childhood. Thus, the 1911 Irish census recorded him as living, with his brother and fellow sojourner Robert, in a four-room, slate-roofed house in Kilwaughter parish's Ballykeel townland, only a short walk from Rory's Glen and from the homes of his now elderly Ritchie cousins and their children.[64]

Recent studies of late nineteenth- and early twentieth-century Pittsburgh describe a city which, especially after 1890, was increasingly dominated by economic and political forces beyond the individual or collective control of the Irish and other old-stock workers who, in the 1870s and 1880s, had struggled with some success against corporate power. The technological and managerial revolutions associated with the displacement of iron by steel and of numerous competing firms by industrial giants such as Carnegie Steel and its successor, the United States Steel Corporation, plus the huge influx of black migrants from the South and of so-called 'New Immigrants' from eastern and southern Europe, proletarianized and fragmented the city's workforce, weakening labour solidarity and

62 William Murphy, Braddock, Pa., to David and Eliza Gilmore, Belfast, 17 August 1891. On Braddock, see George H. Lamb, ed., *The Unwritten History of Braddock's Field* (Braddock, Pa., 1917). Ironically in view of its future as a citadel of corporate capitalism and industrialization, in 1794 Braddock was the scene of some of the bloodiest strife occasioned by the predominantly Ulster-Presbyterian Whiskey Insurrection against the policies of Alexander Hamilton.

63 William Murphy, Braddock, Pa., to Eliza Gilmore, Belfast, 23 August 1897; this letter is accompanied by another, of the same date, to one of Eliza's daughters. By this time, Eliza's husband, David, may have died, for Murphy's 1897 letters do not mention him.

64 The 1911 Irish census schedule describes William Murphy, aged seventy, as a Methodist and US military pensioner. (In 1910 Murphy had sought confirmation of his birth date from the Irish Public Record Office, in order to gain the Civil War pension which hitherto had eluded him.) The schedule also lists Robert Murphy, age seventy-one, as a 'Carpenter, unemployed'. Interestingly, William is recorded as the 'landholder' and as 'head' of the 'family' occupying the house in Ballykeel, suggesting that William's long years of labour in America had been more remunerative than his brother's. Not far from the Murphy's house was the Ritchies' old farm in Rory's Glen, still held by the descendants of their mother's sister, 'Aunt Eliza' Ritchie Johnston, who had died in 1909; this branch of the family (although not Eliza herself) had returned to Presbyterianism. Also nearby was the separate house of William and Robert's cousin, Samuel Johnston, a farm labourer, as well as the home of William's childhood friend (mentioned in his 8 November 1865 letter), Hugh Nelson, a 62-year-old farmer. Unfortunately, we have been unable to discover when or where William or Robert Murphy died, but neither appears in the 1926 census of Northern Ireland. Information in the 1911 Irish census schedules from Mrs. Mary Calaba Weston (see n. 1).

often destroying union power, as in the great Homestead strike of 1892. In Lawrenceville and other districts, the Irish were displaced from their old jobs and neighbourhoods, and it seems likely that in 1889–97 William Murphy was one of many victims of these developments. Ironically, for personal reasons centred in Ulster, Murphy had already undergone the often severe psychological consequences that the degradation of status and the atomization of community wrought among many American workers. And for that reason perhaps he was better able to cope with what was, for him, only another round of potentially devastating change and loss — from which he could again escape by re-crossing the Atlantic.

Thus, although Murphy's experience of the Great Irish Famine — and his inability to externalize its psychological impact within the religious and political constraints of Protestant Ulster's dominant culture — may have inhibited his ability to adjust to American society, that same experience may have helped to cushion him emotionally from the 'future shocks' that corporate capitalism dealt him in his adopted land. Unfortunately, once he returned to northern Ireland, we can only speculate how well Murphy (in Pittsburgh a self-described 'rabid democrat'[65] — despite his ethnic prejudices) was able to readjust to an Ulster Protestant society that in the early 1900s was not only rigidly stratified but in which unionist mythology was even more hegemonically powerful and pervasive than it had been in the late 1840s and 1850s — when its upper- and middle-class purveyors had effectively erased from public memory the Famine's harrowing effects on the poor inhabitants of Rory's Glen and of similar northern Protestant communities.

65 William Murphy, 17 August 1891.

III Irish Immigration and the Creation of Irish America

11 Class, Culture, and Ethnicity:
The Construction of Irish America in the Nineteenth Century

On 4 July 1805 William James Macneven, scion of an old Irish gentry family, arrived in the United States. Literally a political exile, Macneven had spent four years in British prisons for his prominence in the leadership of the United Irishmen, but, exceptionally well educated, he quickly became one of New York City's most eminent physicians and honoured citizens.[1] More than a half century later, Frank Roney left his native Belfast to avoid prosecution for his involvement in yet another Irish revolutionary movement — the Fenian, or Irish Republican, Brotherhood. After landing in New York in 1866, Roney worked his way across the continent before settling permanently in San Francisco, where he found employment in a local iron foundry.[2] More typical in their economic

---

1 The bulk of this chapter, as initially written, was condensed from my book, *Emigrants and Exiles: Ireland and the Irish Exodus to North America* (New York, 1985). Consequently, to save space, I cited only quotations and those books, articles, etc., specifically consulted. For fuller references and a more detailed exposition of this chapter's primary themes, see *Emigrants and Exiles*, esp. 312–44 and 492–555 on the Irish in mid- and late nineteenth-century America.

    I would like to thank Charles Tilly and William Zeisel, of the New School for Social Research in New York City, for their advice and assistance in preparing the original paper, titled 'Class, Culture, and Immigrant Group Identity in the United States: The Case of Irish-American Ethnicity', and published in Virginia Yans-McLaughlin, ed., *Immigration Reconsidered: History, Sociology, and Politics* (New York, 1990). I am also grateful to Oxford University Press for permission to re-publish the essay, with some revisions, in this volume. Thanks as well to David N. Doyle of University College, Dublin, and Patricia Kelleher of Kutztown University of Pennsylvania for generous sharing of information and insights.

    On Macneven, see Victor R. Greene, *American Immigrant Leaders, 1800–1910: Marginality and Identity* (Baltimore, Md., 1983), 25–27; and Jane M. Macneven, 'Memoir of William James Macneven', in the R. R. Madden Papers (Ms. 873, Trinity College, Dublin).

2 Ira B. Cross, ed., *Frank Roney: Irish Rebel and California Labor Leader: An Autobiography* (Berkeley, Calif., 1931); Neil L. Shumsky, 'Frank Roney's San Francisco — His Diary: April 1875–March 1876', *Labor History*, 17 (spring 1976), 245–64.

motives for leaving Ireland were Patrick Dunny and Mary Ann Rowe. Dunny departed County Carlow during the Great Famine and spent his long life as a railroad porter in Philadelphia, whereas Rowe, the non-dowered daughter of a farmer in County Kilkenny, left home in the late 1880s, worked as a domestic servant in a middle-class household near Boston, married an Irish immigrant labourer, and died shortly after the birth of her only child.[3]

Macneven, Roney, Dunny, and Rowe were Irish by birth and Catholic by religion, all part of what contemporary Americans and later historians regarded as the Irish-American ethnic community.[4] However, the associational ties and perceptions that shaped and expressed the ethnic identities of these and other Irish immigrants were remarkably diverse. For example, although Macneven mixed confidently in upper-class American society, he remained deeply interested in the welfare of poor Irish immigrants and loyal to the ideal of an independent Ireland; thus, he played leading roles in early Irish immigrant charitable societies as well as in the first Irish-American nationalist movements. By contrast, economic exploitation in San Francisco persuaded Roney to jettison both his religious and his Irish nationalist faiths, and to submerge ethnicity almost entirely in an inclusive working-class struggle against corporate capitalism. Again, Dunny and Rowe were more conventional, seeking identity and fellowship through their respective affiliations with local representatives of the Democratic party and the Catholic Church, as well as in various social organizations. These four instances, of an estimated 5 million Irish Catholics who settled in the United States during the nineteenth century, demonstrate the great variety of that immigration and of Irish-American society. They also suggest the diversity and complexity of ethnic associations and identities even within a single immigrant group.

This chapter examines ethnicity, its origins, development, and consequences, with specific reference to Irish immigration and Irish America, although perhaps the theoretical framework and conclusions herein will be useful to students of other immigrant and ethnic communities. Traditionally, most historians and historical sociologists have interpreted the immigration experience in terms of assimilation and acculturation or of ethnic resilience.[5] The assimilation interpretation implies that as

3 Patrick Dunny, Philadelphia, to his parents and siblings, Sleaty, County Carlow, 30 December 1856 and 22 October 1861 (from the Schrier collection); Mary Ann Rowe, Dedham, Mass., to James Wallace, Ballintee, Dunnamaggan, County Kilkenny, 29 October 1888 (letter and background information courtesy of Mrs. Brid Galway, Barrowsland, Thomastown, County Kilkenny); on Rowe, also see Chapter 13 in this volume.

4 Despite the fluid and problematic nature of the terms 'Irish' and 'Irish American', in this chapter these ethnic labels will refer exclusively (as they usually did contemporaneously) to Catholics of Irish birth or descent. On questions of 'Irish' (and 'Scotch-Irish') identities and religion, see Chapters 6–7 in this volume, plus the references therein to my other published works that explore these issues.

5 Even in 1986–87, when this chapter was initially composed, the literature on assimilation and ethnicity was enormous. Among other works, I found these overviews helpful: Nathan Glazer, 'Ethnic Groups in America: From National Culture to Ideology', in Morroe Berger, et al., eds., Freedom and Control in Modern Society (New York, 1964); Nathan Glazer and Daniel P. Moynihan, Beyond the Melting Pot: The Negroes, Puerto

immigrants experience greater degrees of socio-economic integration into their adopted country, they shed Old World social customs and cultural traits for those prevailing in the host society. From this perspective, the existence in American society of ethnically distinctive socio-cultural patterns reflects a transitional or temporarily arrested stage in the assimilation process; moreover, such patterns are viewed primarily as products of that process, owing more to the American environment than to transplanted institutions and values. By contrast, the ethnic resilience interpretation stresses the persistence, if not permanence, of at least some imported socio-cultural patterns, practices, and beliefs that provide structure, continuity, and meaning in an alien and often alienating New World. Thus, whereas in the former scenario mutable traits encounter an inexorable and ultimately consensual process, in the latter, highly resilient characteristics contend and create an ethnically pluralistic society.

Each model, however, oversimplifies the processes of migration, adaptation, and social formation in both donor and host societies. Assimilation theory implies the interaction of individual immigrants with American society, yet as many scholars have noted, individuals migrate and settle as members of social groups or networks that interact *collectively* with new socio-economic structures and cultural norms.[6] Likewise, historians who focus on ethnic persistence sometimes pay insufficient attention to the socio-cultural complexity of the donor societies and the diversity of their emigrants, sometimes implying that ethnic subsocieties and subcultures are relatively homogenous as well as 'un-meltable' transplants from the Old World, not fundamentally transformed by conditions in the New. Conversely, although scholars stressing assimilation do describe ethnicity as dynamic and situational, their overriding stress on American determinants tends to downgrade or even deny the importance of overseas origins. In addition, most historians have analysed assimilation (at least implicitly) in the context of transatlantic 'modernization' or 'progress' from 'traditional' (rural or pre-industrial) to 'modern' (urban-industrial) society. Such an approach often homogenizes both donor and host societies; in particular, it obscures the socio-economic and political (and consequent ethnic) stratification of American society and implies that assimilation to bourgeois-capitalist institutions and norms was the only historical possibility. Indeed, and partly in response to that implication, there has emerged yet a

Ricans, Jews, Italians, and Irish of New York City, 2nd edn. (Cambridge, Mass., 1970); Nathan Glazer and Daniel P. Moynihan, eds., *Ethnicity: Theory and Experience* (Cambridge, Mass., 1975); Andrew Greeley, *Ethnicity in the United States* (New York, 1974); Milton Gordon, *Assimilation in American Life* (New York, 1964); John Higham, 'Current Trends in the Study of Ethnicity in the United States', *Journal of American Ethnic History*, 2 (fall 1982), 5–15; Fred Matthews, 'Cultural Pluralism in Context: External History, Philosophic Premise, and the Theories of Ethnicity in Modern America', *Journal of Ethnic Studies*, 12 (summer 1984), 63–79; Howard F. Stein and Robert F. Hill, *The Ethnic Imperative* (University Park, Pa., 1977); Werner Sollors, 'Theory of American Ethnicity', *American Quarterly*, 33 (fall 1981), 257–83; Stephen Steinberg, *The Ethnic Myth: Race, Ethnicity, and Class in America* (New York, 1981); and Robert P. Swierenga, 'Ethnicity in Historical Perspective', *Social Science*, 52 (winter 1977), 31–44.

6 Charles Tilly, 'Transplanted Networks', in Yans-McLaughlin, *Immigration Reconsidered*, 84ff.

third approach, offered recently by historians of American labour, which sees immigrant assimilation in the context of a distinct working-class subculture.[7] Although satisfying in many respects, this model also obscures crucial social and cultural developments, as argued in this chapter's final section.

Thus, despite the efforts of the assimilation and ethnic resilience schools, and those of recent labour historians, we still lack a means of analysing ethnicity, over the *longue durée*, that takes account of the intricate and fluid social structures and cultural patterns in the donor society, the immigrant stream, the host society, and the ethnic subsociety, and that explores the complex relationships among and within those groups. Seeking this more dynamic approach might begin with Charles Tilly's observation that 'identity' — ethnic or otherwise — is a shared cultural construction, a set of usages, that people adopt in their relationships with one another.[8] In the process of immigration, those relationships or networks, on which identities are based, change and generate new explanations and expressions or reinforce old ones. Whether these social constructions are residual, 'ethnic', or assimilationist depends on numerous contextual factors, which in turn help shape the nature of the interactions among the various elements of both the immigrant group and the host society. In other words, ethnic identity is the result of the dynamic conjunctions of social structures and relationships and cultural patterns in the old country and the new. Ethnicity evolves from a complex dialectic that exists between an immigrant group and a host society but also among the immigrants themselves and among members of the host society. Most important, these interactions must be interpreted within the context of a vast international development: the growth of a transatlantic capitalism that shaped the social structures and cultures of both donor and host societies in ways that impelled, encouraged, and accommodated the enormous nineteenth-century migrations.

Understanding Irish immigration to the United States and the nature of the Irish-American community within the world-capitalist context requires a mediating analytical tool that can explain how ideologies are created that may deflect or transcend profound socio-economic conflicts, such as the tension between capital and labour. In Chapter 4, Gramsci's theory of cultural hegemony was employed to analyse political

---

7 David Brundage, 'Irish Land and American Workers: Class and Ethnicity in Denver, Colorado', in Dirk Hoerder, ed., *'Struggle a Hard Battle': Essays on Working-Class Immigrants* (DeKalb, Ill., 1986), 46–67; Eric Foner, 'Class, Ethnicity, and Radicalism in the Gilded Age: The Land League and Irish America', *Marxist Perspectives*, 1 (summer 1978), 7–55; Michael Gordon, 'Studies in Irish and Irish-American Thought and Behavior in Gilded Age New York City' (PhD diss., University of Rochester, 1977); Herbert Gutman, 'Work, Culture, and Society in Industrializing America, 1815–1919', *American Historical Review*, 78 (June 1973), 531–87; David Montgomery, *Beyond Equality: Labor and the Radical Republicans, 1862–72* (New York, 1967), and 'The Irish and the American Labor Movement', in David N. Doyle and Owen Dudley Edwards, eds., *America and Ireland, 1776–1976: The American Identity and the Irish Connection* (Westport, Conn., 1980), 205–18.
8 Tilly, 'Transplanted Networks'; Charles Tilly, New York City, letter to the author, 2 December 1986.

culture in Ireland itself, especially with respect to the external and internal 'projects'[9] of the Catholic bourgeoisie in the post-Famine period (1856–1929). This chapter applies Gramscian insights to Irish-American society and particularly to the development of middle-class Catholic socio-cultural authority over the Irish-American working classes. Mass migration of course linked the evolutions of Irish and Irish-American societies; the self-conscious construction of the Irish bourgeoisie was a transatlantic phenomenon, and its members faced similar obstacles in their quests for power on each side of the ocean. Therefore, a brief review of Irish history, and of the Catholic bourgeoisie's construction of hegemony in Ireland itself, is necessary before focusing on parallel developments among the Irish in the United States.[10]

As described in previous chapters, nineteenth-century Catholic Ireland was an overwhelmingly rural society.[11] Before the Great Famine more than four-fifths of all farmers held fewer than 30 acres, and over half of all rural-dwellers were cottiers, with 2 acres or less, or landless labourers; as late as 1911 two-thirds of farmers still held less than 30 acres, while a third of the rural population remained cottiers and farm workers. These conditions were among the legacies of past British and Irish Protestant conquests, confiscations, and penal legislation — the latter finally repealed in 1829, although Catholics (and Dissenters) still paid tithes to a legally established Protestant Church until 1869, and although Protestant landlords controlled rural society and local government until the end of the century. Despite these impositions, Irish Catholic society was of course neither static nor homogeneous. From the late eighteenth century, Ireland experienced dramatic economic 'development', under imperial and capitalist auspices, and consequent social and cultural changes as well. Likewise, Irish population increased markedly, from about 4 million in the late 1700s to over 8 million on the Famine's eve. On the one hand, a Catholic middle class expanded in size and ambition, based on commercial (or 'strong') farming, especially cattle-raising, and trade with British markets. On the other hand, and especially with the onset of severe economic depression after the Napoleonic Wars, the peasant or subsistence sector of rural society increased both in size and in depth of poverty and desperation.

9 Terminology borrowed from sociologist Michael Peillon's *Contemporary Irish Society: An Introduction* (Dublin, 1982).
10 On cultural hegemony theory and its application to Irish society, see Chapter 4 in this volume and, for relevant citations, nos. 4–5.
11 For a more detailed exposition of the material in this section, see Chapter 4 in this volume. In the present chapter, I exclude consideration of the Protestant-dominated, urban-industrial counties of northeastern Ireland (Ulster), but see Chapters 8 and 10 in this volume.

This in turn generated mass migration (in 1815–44 c. 500,000 Catholics went to North America alone) but also the formation of secret agrarian societies (generically known as Whiteboys or Ribbonmen), whose violent conspiracies aimed to protect peasants from the negative effects of the commercialization of agriculture. Despite official repression and clerical condemnation, before 1845 the Whiteboys' struggles — against Protestant landlords and clergy certainly, but principally against Catholic graziers, strong farmers, and shopkeepers — slowed the pace of evictions and other effects of rural 'modernization'. However, the Great Famine caused the death of 1 million Irish and the immediate emigration of about 2 million more; by eradicating much of the peasantry, the Famine also eviscerated the secret agrarian societies, thus enabling the Catholic bourgeoisie and the Catholic Church to extend their authority over a much-diminished and culturally deracinated society. These trends persisted throughout the post-Famine period. The numbers of small farmers and labourers continued to decline through emigration, with perhaps 5 million more departures before 1929, as rural and industrial employment shrank (outside east Ulster) and as the custom of impartible inheritance, formerly practised only by commercial farmers, became universal, obliging farmers' non-inheriting children to emigrate.[12]

Thus, sharp economic or class conflicts were often blatant (pre-Famine) and always latent (post-Famine) in Irish Catholic society. These were accompanied, most obviously before the Famine, by social and cultural conflicts: between, on one side, peasants who clung to the Irish language, to archaic social and religious customs, and to either traditional or revolutionary modes of political thought and expression; and, on the other side, middle-class Catholics — both laymen and Catholic clergy — who were 'Anglicized' in language, 'Roman' in religion, 'genteel' in their tastes, and usually 'moderate' or 'constitutional' in their political aspirations and activities. Yet, as noted in earlier chapters, nearly all Irish Catholics shared beliefs that expressed a common identity, based on religious affiliation and fortified by bitter resentment against the *Sasanaigh* for remembered cruelties and current indignities. Likewise, they also shared elements of a traditional worldview — expressed through a variety of secular, religious, and even linguistic media — through which contemporary conditions were viewed as in conformity or in conflict with communal and pre-capitalist norms, such as continuity and mutuality, which ideally devalued innovative, individualistic, and competitive behaviour. Thus, traditionally negative ways of describing emigration — as *deoraí* or exile — reflected broader cultural emphases, attributing emigration to impersonal fate or to British/landlord tyranny, rather than to individual volition.[13]

---

12 On emigration and the Irish family, see Chapter 5 in this volume.
13 On Irish emigration as exile, see above, Chapter 1, and also Miller, *Emigrants and Exiles*, 102–30. For other interpretations of Irish emigration (and of the United States as 'promised land'), see Chapter 5 in this volume as well as Kerby A. Miller and Bruce D. Boling, 'Golden Streets, Bitter Tears: The Irish Image of America during the Era of Mass Migration', *Journal of American Ethnic History*, 10, 1–2 (1990–91), 14–35.

Yet because of the real socio-economic conflicts in a rapidly 'modernizing' Irish Catholic society, the question of how to define, interpret, and apply traditional beliefs and symbols was at the centre of a struggle by the Catholic bourgeoisie for cultural hegemony vis-á-vis both British power and their own subordinate classes. The Catholic middle class's position mandated a dual struggle, for although its members embraced British commitments to capitalist institutions and processes, they could not wrest self-government from Britain unless they mobilized large numbers of ordinary Catholics (including emigrants), whose experiences of — and attitudes towards — capitalism's effects on rural Irish society (including emigration) were at best deeply ambivalent. Their solution to this problem was threefold. First, in the pre-Famine period, under Daniel O'Connell's leadership the middle classes allied with the Catholic Church, thus acquiring for their nationalist project a 'spiritual' and purportedly timeless authority from what Gramsci called society's 'traditional' intellectuals, as well as access to the institutional Church itself. Second, after the Famine had decimated Ireland's poorest classes, the Catholic bourgeoisie embraced the slogan 'The Land for the People!', thus allying with the farmers' and peasants' traditional hunger for the land that all Catholics believed had been stolen from their ancestors. Finally, and partly to resolve the ideological contradictions and practical tensions inherent in those alliances, the middle classes and their clerical allies refashioned elements of the peasants' traditional worldview into an ideological framework that obscured capitalism's operations and effects on Irish society — especially the complicity of the bourgeoisie and the Church in Irish 'modernization'. At the centre of this new hegemonic culture was the pre-capitalist image of 'holy Ireland': a deeply traditional Christian commonwealth — organic, familial, and patriarchal — from which emigration would be unnecessary if not for British misgovernment, landlord oppression, and the corrosive cultural effects of Anglicization (or 'Anglo-Saxonism').[14] Crucially, the notion of 'holy Ireland' required the reification of traditional beliefs in Irish emigration as exile: as resulting from extra-communal pressures (or internal 'subversion'), rather than from the actual processes of Irish capitalism as operated by Catholic graziers, land-grabbers, and traders — many of whom profited, directly or indirectly, from lower-class migration. Thus, within the parameters of this hegemonic culture, achievement of the middle-class project — Irish self-government, ostensibly to defend 'holy Ireland' but in fact to empower 'native' capitalists — was the only permissible solution to Irish poverty

---

14 The 'holy Ireland' ideal took shape in the early nineteenth century, primarily under clerical auspices, but its outlines were sharpened in the 1840s by the impact of romantic nationalism, imported from the Continent, on middle-class, urban Catholics, some of whom formed the Young Ireland movement and staged an abortive revolution in 1848. Although O'Connell, conservative Catholic laymen, and the bishops abhorred Young Ireland's secular republicanism and revolutionary activities, in subsequent decades middle-class nationalists drew heavily on the movement's sentimental literature. See Chapter 4 in this volume.

and mass migration (not the wholesale restructuring of Irish society, as some radicals argued).

The notion of 'holy Ireland' demanded even (indeed, especially) the emigrants' loyalty to family, Church, and 'sacred cause' — their fealty as expressed in sorrow at the American wakes when departing but, more important, through remittances to parents, faithful observance of religious duties overseas, and financial donations to both clerical and nationalist projects at 'home'. Yet cultural hegemony by its very nature — 'open' as it was 'at both ends' to residual beliefs and subaltern experiences alike[15] — could never be complete, especially when the prospect of emigration itself posed alternatives to the 'holy Ireland' mythology. In the early nineteenth century, for example, many Irish emigrants left home to achieve what they called an 'independence', and although for poor artisans, small farmers, and labourers that term usually connoted pre- or proto-capitalist ideals of 'comfortable self-sufficiency', under appropriate conditions — before departure or once abroad — it could develop into acquisitive, individualistic ambitions for upward mobility through marketplace competition.[16] In the post-Famine era, business-minded young Irishmen found Catholic society's pseudo-traditional strictures stifling to personal enterprise, while at the other end of the social spectrum, the children of impoverished farm labourers, urban workers, and disinherited female emigrants, generally, often viewed emigration as release from more overt forms of social repression. Of course, the process of chain migration — Catholic Ireland's predominant mode of emigration — linked the departed to the society left behind, its demands and norms. However, as Tilly and other scholars make clear,[17] chain migration involved the transplantation of social groups or networks, and many of these groups — because of poverty or socio-cultural marginality — had been imperfectly assimilated to Catholic Ireland's dominant culture and institutions before their departures. In other words, even prior to emigration the contradictions between the hegemonic Catholic culture and the norms or experiences of the most traditional-minded or exploited members of Irish society were often too blatant to ignore. Consequently, the emigrants' resentment against the actual and immediate material (versus the general and idealized) causes of their departures often informed their attitudes towards emigration and, especially after residence in the United States, towards both their adopted and abandoned homelands.[18]

---

15 T. J. Jackson Lears, 'The Concept of Cultural Hegemony: Problems and Possibilities', *American Historical Review*, 90 (June 1985), 571–73.

16 On pre-Famine emigrants' varying interpretations of 'independence', see Chapter 2 in this volume.

17 Tilly, 'Transplanted Networks', 84ff.

18 Even the successful assimilation of intending emigrants into the Irish nationalist bloc meant that they would 'see' and expect resolution of their ideals and material grievances through specific programmes of political liberation. When pragmatic or socially conservative middle-class leaders failed those expectations, one possible result was apostasy from nationalism or even from Catholicism (not uncommon in the United States), but more frequent were 'purist' schisms that produced new, more extreme varieties of Irish

Because Catholic Irish emigration to the United States — unlike, say, Polish or Italian — remained at high levels for more than a century, the formation and incorporation of the ultimately dominant Catholic culture was a long, slow process, variously affecting the successive waves of emigrants to American shores according to their timing, regional origins, social composition, and cultural backgrounds. The pre-Famine emigrants were relatively diverse, socially and culturally, and at mid-century the masses of Famine refugees included large numbers of impoverished, illiterate, unchurched, and Irish-speaking emigrants. Although in general the post-Famine emigrants were far more culturally homogeneous, politically and religiously engaged, and assimilated to bourgeois norms than most members of previous waves, they also included large numbers of proletarianized labourers, provincial Irish-speakers from Ireland's West, and female fugitives from an oppressive patriarchy. The point is that these varied groups, coming throughout the 1800s and carrying different kinds of socio-cultural baggage, adapted to sundry and dynamic American environments, and interacted with native-born Protestant Americans and one another, in diverse ways. Although these tremendous migrations helped ensure bourgeois hegemony in Ireland, middle-class Irish Americans met difficulties in exerting a like influence over the immigrant masses in the United States. Nevertheless, given the not dissimilar impacts of nineteenth-century capitalism on Irish, American, and Irish-American societies — creating regional variants of a transatlantic bourgeoisie — it is not surprising that by 1900 the dominant cultures and group identities of Irish Catholics on both sides of the ocean were remarkably similar.

Irish Catholics who immigrated to the United States during the nineteenth century exchanged a society in economic and (after 1845) demographic decline for another characterized by explosive growth. Between 1800 and 1840 the US population more than tripled, from 5.3 million to 17.1 million, and between 1840 and 1900 — while Ireland's population shrank from 8.2 million to only 4.5 million — that of the United States soared to 76 million. While urban growth in Catholic Ireland stagnated, the proportion of Americans living in cities and towns rose from 11 per cent in 1840 to 40 per cent in 1900. This urbanization resulted from industrialization and immigration, as well as from the commercialization of agriculture and internal migration. In 1850 the United States officially contained 1.2 million white, foreign-born inhabitants (about 1 million of them Irish-born), and in 1900 the comparable figure was 5.5 million (including 1.6 million Irish-born, plus another 3.4 million US-born children of Irish immigrants). Between

and Irish-American nationalism, such as Fenianism in 1858–67, Sinn Féin in 1916–23, and anti-Treaty republicanism in 1922–23 and thereafter.

1820 and 1900 the proportion of the American workforce engaged in non-agricultural occupations increased from 28 per cent to 62 per cent, and the percentage employed in manufacturing and construction grew from 12 per cent to 28 per cent. Irish Catholic immigrants were on the cutting edge of this urban-industrial growth. For example, in 1870 nearly 95 per cent of the Irish-born population was concentrated in just twenty states, mostly in the heavily urbanized and industrialized New England, Middle Atlantic, and Upper Midwest regions. The 1870 census also revealed that less than 15 per cent of the nation's Irish-born workforce laboured in agriculture (compared to 54 per cent of the native-born, and 27 per cent and 26 per cent of German and English immigrants, respectively).[19]

The Irish concentration in US cities and in many of the most dynamic economic sectors — especially construction, transportation, and heavy manufacturing — eventually paid off; scholars such as David Doyle argue that by 1900 the Irish-born and, especially, their children were at least approaching, or had even achieved, relative occupational parity with native white Americans in all fields except agriculture. At the century's end, roughly the same proportions of male Irish Americans were engaged in white-collar (35 per cent), skilled and semi-skilled (50 per cent), and unskilled (15 per cent) jobs as were white Americans of native birth and parentage. In addition, by 1900 skilled Irish-American male workers were disproportionately concentrated in the best-paid, most highly unionized trades, and US-born Irishwomen were moving rapidly into teaching, nursing, and clerical occupations.[20] Nevertheless, such an overview obscures the terrible poverty and insecurity that had haunted most Irish immigrants — especially the ragged Famine refugees — at mid-century, when from 60 to 80 per cent (varying by region) were semi-skilled or unskilled labourers, as well as the crippling setbacks experienced during the severe economic depressions of 1873–78, 1883–85, and 1893–97.

---

19 *Historical Statistics of the United States: Colonial Times to 1970* (Washington, DC, 1975), 8–14, 116–18; *United States Census*, 1870, vol. 1, 698–702. Information on Irish-America's regional and urban concentration from David N. Doyle, University College, Dublin, later published as 'The Irish as Urban Pioneers in the United States, 1850–1870', *Journal of American Ethnic History*, 10, 1–2 (1990–91), 36–59. Doyle's research also shows that, in 1870 and in those twenty states, nearly 70 per cent of Irish immigrants resided in merely 146 counties (out of 1,090 total) that were characterized by urbanization or mining; moreover, nearly 45 per cent of all Irish immigrants lived in the nation's 50 largest cities, 34 per cent in the largest 15.

20 David N. Doyle, *Irish Americans, Native Rights, and National Empires: The Structure, Divisions, and Attitudes of the Catholic Minority in the Decade of Expansion, 1890–1901* (New York, 1976), 48–49, 59–63. On Irish-American women, see Janet R. Nolan, *Ourselves Alone: Women's Emigration from Ireland, 1885–1920* (Lexington, Ky., 1989), and *Servants of the Poor: Teachers and Mobility in Ireland and Irish America* (Notre Dame, Ind., 2004).

The nineteenth century's earliest Irish Catholic immigrants experienced relatively little difficulty in adapting to Jeffersonian society. During this era, Catholics were only a small minority of a relatively few Irish immigrants, and — like their Irish Protestant peers — a large proportion were of middle-class or at least artisanal origins.[21] Their talents and skills were in great demand, and the goals they sought through immigration — 'independence' as either upward mobility or comfortable self-sufficiency — complemented the still undifferentiated emphases of the new American nation's broad republican culture. Early US republicanism was based on the optimistic assumption that, thanks to the revolution and America's democratic institutions, 'equal opportunities' (to compete in the marketplace) and 'equal rights' (implying a rough equality of access to the marketplace, and of the results of such competition) would not conflict and produce new 'aristocracies' similar to those overthrown in 1776.[22] In the Anglo-American mind, of course, Catholic authoritarianism (linked to Old World monarchism) always threatened republican values and polities, but in 1780–1820 the Catholic Church in the United States was so small and uninfluential that most Americans regarded it as merely a curiosity rather than a threat to Protestantism or to democratic ideals and institutions. Moveover, the political ideals of the (largely Protestant) United Irish exiles both unified most early immigrants across class and religious lines, and won group acceptance from most of their American hosts. As one Ulster immigrant reported, 'The Irish in America are particularly well recvd. and looked upon as Patriotic republicans, and if you were to tell an American you had flyd your country or you would have been hung for treason against the Government, they would think ten times more of you and it would be the greatest trumpet sounded in your praise.'[23] Thus, the congruence of Irish and American republicanism enabled men such as Macneven to play varied yet complementary roles — as Republican politicians and journalists, as employers of both Irish and non-Irish labour, as founders and trustees of Catholic churches, and as leaders and patrons of both ethnic and inclusive benevolent and patriotic associations — without compromising their status in either mainstream American or Irish-American societies.

21 During the century's earliest decades, Irish immigrants from professional, entrepreneurial, and commercial farming backgrounds may have composed 20–25 per cent of the exodus, in addition to perhaps 40 per cent who were artisans, principally weavers. Most of these early immigrants were Protestants, primarily Presbyterians from Ulster. See Chapter 2 of this volume.

22 Even in 1986–87 the historical literature on republican political culture and the American working class was large and growing; see especially, Sean Wilentz, *Chants Democratic: New York City and the Rise of the American Working Class, 1788–1850* (New York, 1984). Of course, early nineteenth-century US republicanism and optimism were underlain by unique economic circumstances: by the availability of millions of acres of relatively cheap land, expropriated from the 'Indians', and, in the South, by the expropriation of unpaid labour from (in 1830) more than 2 million slaves, principally in the production of cotton, by far the nation's most valuable export, and the profits from which stimulated the entire economy and financed the development of much of the nation's urban-industrial and transportation infrastructures.

23 James Richey, Hopkinsville, Ky., to his parents, Moyrusk, Lisburn, County Antrim, 2 March 1826, in Richey family letters (from the Green collection; now deposited in PRONI).

That happy period was brief and anomalous. After the Panic of 1819, the first major financial crisis in the United States, and especially from the 1830s through the 1850s, the position of the Irish in the United States became much more complex and controversial, and, in consequence, the role of the Irish-American middle class became much more precarious. After about 1820, under the impacts of the transportation and industrial 'revolutions', the American society to which Catholic Irish immigrants were obliged to adapt changed rapidly and radically. Manufacturers and ambitious artisans responded to widening markets for industrial goods by abandoning the old household method of production for new systems of subcontracting, putting-out, and factory production. Only about one-third of artisans and journeymen commanded sufficient capital to become even small-scale employers under the new order; the remainder fell to the ranks of pieceworkers or wage-labourers, forced to compete with semi-skilled and unskilled migrants from the American and European countrysides.

Under these and other strains, the American republican concensus fragmented along class lines (as, for broader socio-cultural, regionalist and political reasons, did the Jeffersonian Republican party itself). The now-dominant version of American republicanism was shaped largely by the imperatives of the new middle classes generated by industrialization, and organized workers were unable to create an effective counter-hegemony to the bourgeois-capitalist norms evoked by the employer classes — at least not before the rise of the Knights of Labor in the 1880s. The workers' 'producer' ideology was essentially a petty-capitalist version of the old republican culture, and, consequently, both employers and employees shared similar terms of reference — such as individual freedom, faith in progress, the sanctity of private property, opposition to 'artificial monopolies', and contempt for the unskilled, 'undeserving' poor — which bourgeois spokesmen employed to obscure the social differentiation wrought by industrialization. Moreover, the entrepreneurial and producer ideologies of native-born Protestant employers and workers alike were permeated by religious beliefs that also obscured or tempered the social conflicts between them. Although organized workers sometimes tried to unite around Dissenting visions of a Christian commonwealth, the middle class advanced its ideals more successfully through a series of religious revivals that convulsed Protestant America from the 1830s on. Evangelical ministers perfectly complemented bourgeois norms, suffusing them with a timeless, spiritual authority, and providing the moral imperative around which the new middle class would coalesce. Thus, evangelical religion, like republican political rhetoric, provided cultural cohesion for an otherwise conflicted society, providing Protestant workers with new avenues to success, security, or at least symbolic affinity with the governing classes through 'proper' behaviour and shared notions of respectability.[24]

24 Mike Davis, *Prisoners of the American Dream: Politics and Economy in the History of the US Working Class* (London, 1986), 7–21 and *passim*. Nineteenth-century bourgeois evangelicalism was a transatlantic phenomenon, and so revivalism and 'benevolent' reformism, e.g. in the Second Great Awakening in the US and the Second or New Reformation in Ireland (especially in Ulster), played similar roles in accommodating

Significantly, it was during this very period—when economic dislocations, Protestant revivalism, and political tensions were at their height — that the socio-cultural composition of Irish immigration changed markedly, and Irish Catholic immigration turned from a trickle into a flood tide. Even prior to the Great Famine, in the 1830s and early 1840s, Irish immigration to the United States was increasingly dominated by rural Catholics who lacked capital, education, and marketable skills. During the late 1840s and the 1850s, American cities were inundated by waves of impoverished peasants, many of them from the most 'backward', least Anglicized regions of southern and western Ireland.[25]

These arrivals now clashed with American society and culture in a variety of complementary ways. Even before 1820, anti-Catholic and anti-Irish prejudice was an important component of Anglo-American Protestantism, albeit obscured by an optimistic, secular republicanism. After that date convictions that the Irish belonged to 'a race of savages'[26] — lazy, superstitious, drunken, and violent — became widespread as the new influx of immigrants and the consequent growth of the Catholic Church exacerbated and epitomized growing fears for the social stability, political purity, and cultural homogeneity of the new republic. Skilled and unskilled Irish labourers competed increasingly with native-born Protestant workers at precisely the moment when the latter felt least secure. Although skilled Irish Catholic immigrants often shared the same independent-producer ideology as native-born craftsmen, and sometimes helped organize trade unions and labour federations, as in Philadelphia during the 1830s, fierce competition for jobs and housing and frequent economic depressions converged with Protestant revivalism to aggravate ethnic and religious tensions and forestall working-class solidarity. Thus, Philadelphia's General Trades Union collapsed after the Panic of 1837; by 1844 native Protestant and Irish Catholic workers were engaged in pitched battles on the city's streets; and during the 1850s hostility towards Irish Catholics assumed national proportions, formalized in the so-called Know-Nothing party and, after its collapse, incorporated in the new Republican party coalition.

For their part, many Irish Catholic immigrants were equally at odds with American society and culture. An imported worldview emphasizing communal and even pre-capitalist values permeated much of Irish-American society — shaping the outlooks and strategies even of middle-class immigrants who often encountered a much more prejudiced and ruthlessly competitive environment than anticipated. Among Irish Catholic artisans, although their traditions of mutuality and craft integrity may

---

their adherents to industrial-capitalist norms and practices as well as in heightening anti-(Irish) Catholic sentiments. On the Second Reformation, see Chapter 8 in this volume.

25 By the 1830s and early 1840s, only about one-third of an increasingly Catholic Irish immigration was composed of migrants who possessed significant degrees of capital, education, business experience, or marketable skills. This proportion continued to decline during the periods of Famine and post-Famine immigration, when middle-class arrivals probably never exceeded 5–6 per cent annually, plus another 10–12 per cent of skilled workers.

26 John Chambers, New York City, to Robert Simms, Belfast, 12 February 1822 (D.1739/3B, PRONI).

temporarily have united them in trade unions with their Protestant peers, that very unity and its public expressions exacerbated class and ethnic conflicts between the native-born middle class and skilled-worker Catholics — the latter already concentrated in rapidly mechanizing and downwardly mobile occupations, such as handloom weaving and shoemaking. Thus, skilled Irish Catholic prominence in organized labour (real or exaggerated) provided employers and evangelical preachers with additional incentives and opportunities to stigmatize trade unions and strikes as 'un-American', which in turn encouraged Protestant craftsmen to repudiate inter-ethnic, working-class alliances. Meanwhile, the poorest, unskilled Irish immigrants were often bewildered by and alienated from an American capitalism that barely provided subsistence wages and violated traditional norms of communal justice and reciprocity.

Under such circumstances, although many Irish Catholics still favourably contrasted American opportunity and freedom to Irish poverty and British oppression, large numbers became angry and disillusioned. '[S]lighted and despised' — viewed by many native-born Americans as 'animals ... utterly unfit for ... the common courtesies and decencies of civilized life' — they fell back 'into the circle of [their] fellow countrymen':[27] thus retaining or adapting boisterous and sodden peasant customs to the harsh realities of Irish-American neighbourhoods and public works sites, forming secret societies like those they had known in Ireland, and reverting to the traditional belief that emigration was involuntary exile to explain their homesickness and alienation. Such social and cultural defences reified and homogenized Irish immigrant identity, yet they also widened the gulf between the immigrants and middle-class Americans.

As a result, by the 1840s and especially in the wake of the massive Famine migration, the Irish-American Catholic bourgeoisie was doubly disadvantaged: increasingly marginal with respect to both Protestant America and the general Irish immigrant population. Although the bourgeoisie had grown numerically through immigration and some upward mobility, in proportional terms it had become an even smaller minority within a largely peasant-proletarian mass that was feared and stigmatized by the native-Protestant middle classes — in part because the Famine influx itself had only intensified Anglo-Americans' traditional anti-Catholicism. As the Irish immigrant lawyer John Blake Dillon discovered in the early 1850s, 'Although in this country all religions enjoy perfect equality *before the law*, in society it is far otherwise. In this latter respect,' he concluded, 'this country may be said to be eminently Protestant, and the inconveniences to which persons of strong Catholic convictions are subjected are neither few nor inconsiderable.'[28] Similar complaints were voiced throughout the nineteenth and well into the twentieth century.

27 Douglas V. Shaw, *The Making of an Immigrant City: Ethnic and Cultural Conflict in Jersey City, New Jersey, 1850–1877* (New York, 1976), 77–82; Thomas C. Grattan, *Civilized America* (1859; repr. New York, 1969), vol. 2, 8–9.
28 John Blake Dillon, New York City, to William Smith O'Brien, Port Arthur, Van Diemen's Land (later Tasmania), 12 December 1852 (Ms. 445, NLI).

Middle-class Irish Catholics were likewise well aware of the other major cause of the opprobrium they shared with their poorer countrymen. After all, one bourgeois immigrant admitted at mid-century, 'to judge of Ireland and Irishmen from the *enchantillon* which the United States presents, one would be forced to regard the former as the fruitful home of incorrigible ignorance and incurable superstition'.[29] The Famine influx, especially, had transferred a large proportion of lower-class Irish society to America's shores, conspicuously concentrating most of its poverty and problems of adjustment in a relatively few urban-industrial areas. As noted earlier, residual aspects of Irish peasant culture experienced renewed vigour in Irish-American slums, mining camps, and construction sites. Irish immigrants' whiskey drinking became more notorious in the United States than in contemporary Ireland, where Fr. Theobald Mathew's temperance crusade had sharply (if temporarily) reduced alcohol consumption. Also infamous were Irish immigrants' frequent episodes of intracommunal violence — between the 'Corkonians' and 'Far Downs' on US public works sites, for example — but most frequently condemned were their oft-brutal conflicts with non-Irish workers or with exploitive employers — the former epitomized by the New York City Draft Riots of 1863, the latter by Pennsylvania's Molly Maguires in the 1860s to 1870s—although by mid-century traditional faction fighting and Whiteboyism had largely been suppressed in Ireland itself.

Middle-class Irish immigrants felt deeply embarrassed by such activities. The group's overwhelmingly lower-class composition not only lowered the status of the middle-class minority but, equally important, made it extremely difficult for that minority to exercise even the fragile hegemony over the Catholic Irish masses that the Irish bourgeoisie was creating in the old country. Moreover, in their roles as employers, subcontractors, and tenement owners, middle-class Irish Americans often found themselves attacked by their own resentful countrymen. Until recently, historians have paid little attention to class conflicts *within* the Irish-American community. However, such conflicts were frequent

---

Theoretically, Victorian America's dominant culture promoted acceptance of middle-class Irish Catholics on meritocratic grounds, but the fact that its liberal values were viewed as both inseparable from Protestantism and threatened by Catholicism and by Irish Catholic immigration guaranteed that even men such as Dillon would face at least some prejudice and proscription. By contrast, nineteenth-century Irish Protestant immigrants generally encountered no such barriers. During the 1800s perhaps 1 million Irish Presbyterians, Anglicans, Methodists, and other Protestants settled in the United States. Relatively few were impoverished or illiterate, and many came from bourgeois or at least from commercial-farming or urban-industrial backgrounds. Many of them also shared evangelical and anti-Catholic convictions, and in general they adapted fairly readily to American society, largely through membership in local Protestant churches and fraternal organizations. Indeed, some of them played prominent roles in American nativist movements. The sole designation — 'Scotch-Irish' — cultivated by some of the group's spokesmen was intended primarily to distinguish the group from the Catholic Irish, not from native American Protestants. On the 'Scotch-Irish', see Chapters 6–7 in this volume, and more extensive discussion in Kerby A. Miller, et al., *Irish Immigrants in the Land of Canaan: Letters and Memoirs from Colonial and Revolutionary America, 1675–1815* (New York, 2003).

29 Anonymous immigrant's letter, in *Cork Constitution*, 12 March 1857 (Schrier collection).

and often violent, as in Philadelphia's Kensington district in 1842–43, when organized Irish weavers conducted bloody strikes against Irish Catholic bosses and slumlords; in Worcester, Massachusetts, during the same decade, when railroad labourers and recent Famine refugees assaulted Irish contractors and merchants; and in Denver and in Butte, Montana, during the late nineteenth and early twentieth centuries, when strife between Irish miners and Irish foremen and mine owners wracked those communities. Significantly, the intensity of such conflicts often stemmed from Irish workers' bitter recognition that, as one immigrant put it, in America '[a]n Irishman was the worst boss you could have' — 'slave-driving all the time'.[30]

Thus, in the eyes of native-born Protestants, middle-class Irish Catholic immigrants were by religion and association not 'good Americans', but in the opinion of many of their own transplanted countrymen, they were not 'good Irishmen' either. To surmount their dilemma, the immigrant middle class needed to create and lead a new ethnic society that would include all Irish Catholic immigrants and their offspring, and that would embody a new, dominant ethnic culture. This new, hybrid culture would adapt some transplanted norms and symbols to both the Irish immigrant experience and the institutions and ideals of middle-class America, creating in the process a novel but doubly derivative identity that could transcend the divisions within Irish America and between that subsociety and native-born America.

In the attempt to surmount its dually marginal status, the Irish-American middle class, like its counterpart in Ireland, had to pursue two separate but complementary projects. Because in the New World the Irish nationalist goal of group autonomy was unattainable and, from a middle-class perspective, undesirable, the Irish-American bourgeoisie had to gain acceptance from and access to the classes and institutions that governed native society; more immediately, it also had to assert a social and cultural hegemony over its own lower classes. As in Ireland, the success or failure of the twin projects was highly interdependent. Middle-class immigrants could not gain status in American society until they had both mobilized the Irish-American masses, to demonstrate their political leverage, and imposed bourgeois norms on them, to reassure the host society's governing classes that the group was sufficiently 'civilized' to warrant incorporation. Moreover, only the prospect of such assimilation would enable the Irish bourgeoisie to provide 'successful models' for lower-class immigrant emulation, which in turn would enable them to exercise effective hegemony.

The process of reconstructing hegemony in the New World was fraught with perils and contradictions. On the one hand, the erosion of immigrant provincialism — the replacement of parochial loyalties to specific Irish locales by a broader, collective identification — was an essential concomitant of group mobilization. However, new ethnic identities shaped by poverty, exclusion, and proletarianization — and expressed through labour unions and secret societies, violent strikes and mob actions, or

30 Ms. 1409, p. 327 (DIF/UCD).

homesickness for Ireland and alienation from the United States — were not compatible with the Irish-American bourgeoisie's norms and aspirations. For instance, although many ambitious immigrants became saloonkeepers in Irish-American neighbourhoods, the social authority and political patronage they gained thereby were offset partly by the fact that communal whiskey drinking — and Irish bourgeois complicity in group intemperance — only reinforced native-born Americans' negative image of all Irish Catholics as thriftless, inebriated, and undisciplined. Yet, if middle-class Irish Americans sought to appear as censorious as native Protestants, unsympathetic to the problems, yearnings, and customs of the immigrant masses, they stood to forfeit their fellow countrymen's respect and allegiance. Although Irish-American newspaper editors sometimes urged their readers to 'take pattern by the Yankee ... [and] imitate the energy, patience, and prudence of his character', they also realized that most of their potential audience was yet unable or unwilling to 'flow into' what one middle-class immigrant eulogized as 'the great current of American life'.[31] Consequently, until the very end of the nineteenth century, most Irish-American periodicals generally 'left the impression that the United States was a suburb of Ireland' because their owners and editors understood that the Irish-Catholic road to respectability would have to follow its own course. That road would in fact follow three principal, complementary paths: the Democratic party, the Catholic church, and Irish-American nationalism.[32]

Constitutional and demographic considerations determined that in the United States, unlike Ireland, the Irish middle class could not create an effective political movement of its own. Thus, the Democratic party of Andrew Jackson and his successors became the principal native-American institution through which middle-class Irish Americans gained access to power, expressed their values, and engaged their adherents. To some extent, the Democracy merely inherited Irish Catholics' fealty to the Jeffersonian Republicans — from whom the Democrats claimed direct descent — with Jackson's Irish parentage and military victories over the hated English easing the transition. In the fierce party competition of the Jacksonian era, Democratic politicians offered patronage in return for votes; in their roles as employers, subcontractors, and saloonkeepers, middle-class and ambitious working-class Irish Americans happily reciprocated. Likewise, Democratic politicians championed a pluralistic vision of American society that could

31 George Potter, *To the Golden Door: The Story of the Irish in Ireland and America* (Boston, 1960), 282; J. F. Fitzgerald, Columbus, Ohio, to his cousin Joseph, Castletroy, County Limerick, 21 August 1860 (courtesy of Alan Kennedy, Castletroy).
32 Robert Ernst, *Immigrant Life in New York City, 1825–1863* (1949; repr. Port Washington, NY, 1965), 150–53.

accommodate Irish Catholics' needs for protection against native Protestant hostility, while the rhetoric of party spokesmen often incorporated (however insincerely) the ideals and grievances of small producers and disadvantaged workers. Hence, the Democrats could appeal to Irish voters as immigrants, Catholics, and labourers, whereas the Whig party and its Republican successor tended to attract the new native-Protestant employer classes, especially in manufacturing, as well as Protestant farmers and workers 'burned over' by evangelical revivalism. The Democracy's support for slavery and its inveterate racism at the least did not offend most Irish Catholic immigrants, for whereas the Whig, Know-Nothing, and Republican parties promised to shelter 'True American' (that is, native Protestant) workers and institutions from Irish competition and Catholic subversion, the Democrats pledged to protect Irish immigrants from Abolitionists and evangelicals who would free the slaves and force the Irish to compete with 'degraded' black labour. Finally, and especially after the Civil War, Democratic control of urban political 'machines' and state governments generated vast patronage, legal and illegal, such as lucrative liquor licenses, construction contracts, and steady employment for the party's Irish-American 'bosses' and their ethnic constituents.[33]

Thus, through integration into the Democratic party, middle-class Irishmen gained perquisites for themselves, rewards for their followers, and a forum for raising ethnic, religious, and cultural issues, such as those concerning restrictive liquor laws or Protestant influence in the public schools, that engaged ordinary Irish immigrants and obscured intra-ethnic class conflicts. Thus, although Philadelphia's Irish Catholic manufacturers lost control over their immigrant workers during the textile weavers' strikes of 1842–43, after two more years of Protestant revivalism, nativist agitation, and mob violence against Irish Catholics and their churches, they emerged as Democratic champions and protectors of an embattled ethnic community, commanding their employees' political allegiance while simultaneously slashing the latter's wages to pre-strike levels. The coincidence of Irish urban and neighbourhood concentrations with the territorially fragmented nature of American urban government, particularly with the ward system, facilitated Irish entry into the Democratic party en bloc, and aided the Irish-American middle class's dual strategies: individual and bourgeois access to native society's governing institutions and ethnic integrity and solidarity across class lines. Hence, for a recently (and illegally) naturalized immigrant such as Patrick Dunny, membership in the Democracy enabled him to be both a 'good American' and a 'good Irishman' — the two identities conflated as 'loyal [Irish-American] Democrat'. Dunny, like thousands of other Irish immigrants, found in the Democratic party a communal bulwark and a real and symbolic source of pride and acceptance in a large swath of native society. 'James Buchannon is Elected President on the Democratic ticket by an overwhelming Majority,' Dunny exulted in 1856; 'there neverr was [such] excitement ... before at an Elections nor the [nativist] Americans never got a home blow before the

33 Davis, *Prisoners of the American Dream*, 25–29.

Irish Came out victorious and now Clame as good right here as americans themselves.'[34] Of course, as one fastidious immigrant admitted, Democratic party politics was often 'a filthy pool of shabbiness[,] falsehood and corruption',[35] and Irish immigrants' identification with the party of Tammany Hall and southern Secession did nothing to enhance their reputations among northern Protestant Whigs and Republicans. Indeed, the fears evinced by many middle-class immigrants of the Democracy's moral deficiencies and alleged working-class biases, plus the disproportionately small size of the Irish-American middle class, determined that the latter would also be obliged to pursue the same strategy in the United States as in Ireland: heavy reliance on the Catholic Church's 'traditional' intellectuals to disseminate and sacralize the principles of respectability, deference, and group cohesion.

In the nineteenth century's earliest decades, Catholicism was merely one facet of Irish-American identity in a society where the Church was institutionally insignificant.[36] When new Catholic parishes were created and churches built, it was often at the initiative of affluent Irish-American laymen, who retained a large measure of control over priests and church finances through the so-called trustee system, which in turn restricted lay influence to middle-class pew renters. Irish-American Catholics successfully demanded their own ethnic parishes and Irish-born priests from early on, but they contended that their congregations' semi-democratic organization and relative freedom from hierarchical authority made the Catholic Church in the United States fully compatible with republican norms. During the Jacksonian era, however, the relationship between the Irish-American bourgeoisie and an increasingly ultramontane Church began to change radically. The Catholic immigrants of the 1830s and, especially, the 1840s and 1850s contained large numbers of lower-middle- and working-class Irish, who, thanks to Daniel O'Connell's alliance with the Irish Church, were more amenable to clerical leadership and whose identities had been shaped at home by a resurgent, even militant Catholicism. The new Irish arrivals also included a substantial majority of peasants, from southern and western Ireland, who were devout but 'customary' and (by Roman standards) irregularly-practising Catholics. These presented the American Catholic hierarchy and the Irish-American bourgeoisie alike with tremendous problems of social

34 Patrick Dunny, 30 December 1856.
35 Richard O'Gorman, New York City, to William Smith O'Brien, [Dromoland, Cahirmoyle, County Clare?], 1 January 1859 (Ms. 445, NLI); on Richard O'Gorman, see Chapter 12 in this volume.
36 When this essay was first written, the best general history of the American Catholic Church was Jay P. Dolan's *The American Catholic Experience: A History from Colonial Times to the Present* (Garden City, NY, 1985); it remains a standard work on the subject.

control but also enormous opportunities for mobilization in an all-class ethnic and religious alliance. To meet this challenge, Rome appointed more American bishops of Irish birth or descent, who in turn imported thousands of priests and teaching nuns from Ireland. Soon American Catholicism was rapidly expanding its institutional infrastructure under a largely Irish hierarchy and clergy. The Church's growth and new ethnic complexion increased clerical influence over both ordinary immigrants and the Irish-American middle class, whose old trustee system was now dismantled by an alliance of forceful bishops and dutiful new parishioners — the latter trained to believe, as one immigrant wrote, that 'you Will not fret for bng in A strange Country [if] you … mind your duty to god and go to your priest A[nd] consult With him'.[37] Despite clerical fears of widespread apostasy in America, such immigrants were more likely to formalize and intensify than to de-emphasize or abandon their religious commitments abroad. Moreover, the nativist assault on Irish immigrants and their Church further conflated secular and religious identities, enabling aggressive Irish bishops, such as New York's Archbishop John Hughes, to rally Irish-American Catholics around issues, such as education, that were Church-defined and Church-centred but also of community-wide symbolic as well as practical importance. Indeed, in circumstances that demanded abandonment of so many aspects of traditional group identity, such as the Irish language, Catholicism became the primary expression of Irish-American consciousness, a development parallel to that taking place in an Anglicizing but also Romanizing Ireland.

The consequence was that the Irish-American bourgeoisie had no choice but to form an unequal alliance with an Irish-dominated American Catholic Church, despite the qualms of a few over the loss of the United Irishmen's brand of secular and ecumenical 'Irishness', as well as their sometimes privately expressed fears that clerical militancy only enflamed nativism and so retarded assimilationist ambitions. In general, however, Irish-American bishops and priests (themselves usually of middle-class origins) pursued strategies that complemented and furthered those of their bourgeois allies, as they laboured to transform an inchoate mass of Irish immigrants into 'good Catholics', who, they sought to prove, were by virtue of their very Irish Catholicity 'good Americans'.

Through sermons, parochial schools, moral-uplift societies, and other means, Catholic clerics selectively adapted and accommodated middle-class norms, peasant ideals, and the diverse realities of Irish immigrant experience to the Church's own institutional goals and traditional teachings. Like its Irish counterpart, the American Church preached the twin gospels of respectability and resignation. Through the former, Churchmen encouraged ambitious Irish Americans to practise industry, thrift, sobriety, self-control, and domestic purity — bourgeois habits that would prevent spiritual ruin as well as shape 'good citizens' and successful entrepreneurs. Conversely, through the

---

37 Judith Phelan, Raheen, Queen's County, to Teresa Lawlor Gallagher, Memphis, Tenn., 24 January 1851 (Teresa Lawlor Letters, California Historical Society, San Francisco).

gospel of resignation, they offered religious consolation to the impoverished and the alienated by expressing the church's own deep suspicions of materialism, progress, and individual ambition, associating the last with selfishness and potential apostasy to creed and community. Like the eulogists of 'holy Ireland' across the ocean, Irish-American Churchmen offered a morally controlled capitalism in an idealized, organic, and hierarchical society congenial to transplanted peasant parishioners: poverty, part of God's plan, was to be accepted with patience and resignation; charity, not violence or radical change, was its only solution. Convinced that 'Irishness' (as clerically defined) was an essential bulwark of religious faith, the Irish-American clergy homogenized and reinforced immigrant group identity and integrity, for instance, through ethnic parishes and clerically controlled St. Patrick's Day celebrations, by disowning religiously 'mixed' marriages, and by teaching pride in a sanitized, Church-centred version of Irish history in parochial schools, which were themselves designed to insulate Irish-American and other Catholic children from pernicious 'Anglo-Saxon' (that is, Protestant) influences. Simultaneously, however, the Church assiduously cultivated American patriotism and countered nativist criticisms by proclaiming that 'good Irish Catholics' made the very best American citizens because they came to the New World seeking the same civil and religious liberties that allegedly had inspired America's 'founding fathers'; because the Church's teachings conformed its parishioners to bourgeois norms of uplift and respectability and commanded their obedience to the laws and their social superiors; and because conservative Catholic values allegedly protected an inherently unstable American society from social fragmentation and political radicalism.

In short, the ideals and strategies of Irish-American Churchmen broadly coincided with those of the ethnic middle class. On the one hand, the clergy lauded and demanded religious freedom and civil equality in a pluralistic and voluntaristic society, but on the other hand, they exercised that freedom to create an ethno-religious *imperium in imperio* — an Irish-American Catholic 'ghetto' — whose solidarity and collective purpose could provide its middle-class representatives both the political bases and the economic networks necessary for ultimate access to American power structures. Moreover, the material basis for the alliance between 'brick-and-mortar' Churchmen and the nascent Irish-American bourgeoisie cannot be under-estimated, as the construction, furnishing, and maintenance of the American Church's vast physical infrastructure (including parochial schools, convents, hospitals and other charitable institutions, as well as churches and cathedrals) generated innumerable and profitable opportunities in contracts and employment, while in turn a network of new Catholic universities, colleges, law and medical schools, as well as seminaries, promoted both upward mobility and ethno-religious solidarity among the children of the Irish immigrant middle- and skilled working classes.

More broadly, of course, the Church promoted bourgeois interests by staunchly defending the institutions of American capitalism, such as private property, while simultaneously incorporating and defusing the resentments of poor, frustrated immigrants by criticizing the materialistic, individualistic values that informed that system. Not surprisingly, perhaps, in the 1880s to 1890s the inherent contradictions between those positions engendered heated controversies among the clergy themselves: between liberal (or 'Americanist') and conservative bishops over the Church's proper relationship to American society. Although most members of Irish America's growing upper middle class embraced the liberals' more assimilationist thrust, by the end of the century the conservatives were victorious, partly because of Rome's condemnation of modernist ideas, but primarily because the conservatives' ethnocentric and traditionalist emphases best suited Irish-American society and the dualities of its dominant culture.

After 1880 Irish America was composed primarily of the native-born and (at least in hindsight) of the relatively secure and even the upwardly mobile. Almost immediately, however, the coincidence of economic depressions, renewed nativist attacks, and job competition from waves of New Immigrants from southern and eastern Europe again placed Irish Americans on the defensive and increased or reinforced the attractions of ethnic solidarity. This was particularly true for the Irish Catholic immigrants who arrived during those decades. All had been shaped by the Irish Church's pervasive devotional revolution; many were impoverished peasants — often Irish-speakers — from the western counties; and both their piety and lack of skills, education, and prior urban-industrial experience made them particularly susceptible to the influence of conservative Irish-American Churchmen. Likewise, most middle-class Irish Americans — confronted by these new arrivals as well as by upsurges of intra-ethnic class conflict (1880s) and of nativism (1890s) — perforce relied on an authoritative, traditionalist Church that could assert its (and their) hegemony over the Irish-American working class. After all, wondered one middle-class immigrant, 'If the priest has no influence, what would guide the people?'[38] Indeed, well before the century's end, Irish America's hegemonic culture had become a constraining force, and although some members of the middle class might chafe at traditional Catholicism's moral restraints on usury, blatant profiteering, and social-climbing, few could forgo regular mass attendance, membership in religious societies, or other Church-centred indices of ethnicity and respectability that justified and sanctified bourgeois authority over their social inferiors. Moreover, by the century's latter decades, if not earlier, nearly all members of the Irish-American bourgeoisie had themselves internalized the spiritual values and contradictory impulses that informed their dominant culture and shaped their communal identity. Thus, a successful immigrant like the Irish Californian Michael Flanagan could lament that in the United States secular concerns 'monopolize a man ... body and soul, to the banishment of what every Christian man should be'; and even John Boyle O'Reilly, Yankee Boston's 'token Irishman' and a fervent apostle of immigrant entrepreneurship and assimilation, poured out his private doubts in poems that longed

38 Patrick Flanagan, Napa, Calif., to Michael Flanagan, Tubbertoby, Clogherhead, County Louth, 16 August 1891 (courtesy of Peter and Mary Flanagan, Tubbertoby).

for 'holy Ireland's' imagined innocence and critiqued the American notion that 'the only meaning of life is to barter and buy'.[39]

Irish-American nationalism was the final principal medium through which the immigrant middle classes inculcated their values and forged a united ethnic community. In the early 1800s, Irish-American nationalist organizations had been small and ephemeral, confined largely to the middle class, and heavily dependent on native-born American sympathy and support. Although middle-class Irish Americans rallied in support of Young Ireland's prospects for Irish revolution in the mid-1840s, that movement quickly collapsed under the impacts of heavy Famine immigration, public embarrassment over Young Ireland's pathetic failed 'rising' of 1848, and Irish-American clerical condemnation of the 'red republicanism' and infidelity that purportedly characterized Young Ireland's exiled leaders in the United States. In the second half of the nineteenth century, however, Irish-American nationalism experienced a great resurgence. During the 1860s the Fenian movement — which aimed to overthrow British rule with Irish-American military aid — gained some 50,000 members, many of them Irish soldiers in the Civil War, plus hundreds of thousands of ardent sympathizers. Although Irish-American nationalism was moribund for a decade after Fenianism's failure, it revived again in the early 1880s, when over half a million Irish Americans joined the Irish National Land League of America to support the contemporary Land War against Irish landlordism. From 1883 through 1916 smaller but still significant numbers joined organizations and donated money to aid the constitutional-nationalist campaign for Irish Home Rule (provincial self-government), while some 10,000 more were members of the Clan na Gael and other clandestine groups that supported violent revolution and total Irish freedom. Finally, in 1916 Irish Americans responded so vehemently to British suppression of the Clan-aided Easter Rising in Dublin that between that date and 1921 some 800,000 joined nationalist organizations and remitted over $10 million to support Sinn Féin and the Irish Republican Army (IRA) in their partly successful War of Independence. On the national level, all these groups were led by bourgeois Irish Americans, and although working-class immigrants predominated among the rank and file, particularly in the local chapters of the more radical organizations, usually middle-class membership was disproportionately large.

39 Michael Flanagan, Napa, Calif., to John Flanagan, Tubbertoby, Clogherhead, County Louth, 14 April 1877 (courtesy of Peter and Mary Flanagan, Tubbertoby). On John Boyle O'Reilly, see John Duffy Ibsen, 'Will the World Break Your Heart? An Historical Analysis of the Dimensions and Consequences of Irish-American Assimilation' (PhD diss., Brandeis University, 1976), 106–20, since published (New York, 1990).

In some respects it was natural that middle- as well as working-class Irish immigrants and their children should identify with Ireland's political struggles. Before emigration their sense of group consciousness had already been shaped either by the mass political mobilizations that characterized Catholic Ireland from the 1820s on, or by communal traditions of resentment and rebellion. Evicted farmers and the Famine immigrants, generally, were especially likely to perceive themselves as victims of British and landlord tyranny, and, as noted earlier, peasant traditions and bourgeois strategies converged to reinforce the common notion that essentially all Irish emigration was political exile. Finally, not only were nationalist ideas already internalized by many arrivals — and kept fresh in the New World through contacts with Ireland via letters, chain migration, and newspapers — but in addition poverty, frustration, alienation, and homesickness only strengthened many immigrants' emotional identification with the old country and their allegiance to those who promised to liberate Ireland and abolish emigration's purported causes.

Yet while middle-class immigrants benefited from the cultivation of nationalist sensibilities, they also incurred risks. Irish nationalism was frequently associated with violent assaults on life, property, and constituted authority, and often with various modes of social radicalism. Sometimes, Irish nationalism was also associated with an anti-clericalism — or at least resistance to Church control — that defied and disturbed the Catholic clergy, and yet also with past (and propagandistically exaggerated) sectarian massacres, as in 1641 and 1798, that only reinforced the group's reputation for 'savagery' among Anglo-American Protestants. Indeed, Irish-American support for even peaceful, constitutional nationalism offended many Protestant Americans, who were increasingly Anglophile and forgetful of their own country's past struggle against British rule. In addition, organized immigrant devotion to Ireland inevitably provoked nativist accusations that Irish Americans were less than fully loyal to the United States: 'There can be no such thing as a divided national allegiance,' warned an American judge at mid-century,[40] presaging President Woodrow Wilson's later attacks on Irish-American 'hyphenates' who obstructed Anglo-American rapprochement. More broadly, the nationalists' interpretation of emigration as forced exile, implying that the Irish were in America by compulsion rather than by choice, seemed to epitomize the group's ambiguous status in the New World.

Except for a few of the most ardent revolutionaries, Irish-American nationalist spokesmen generally made tortuous efforts to reconcile Irish and American patriotism and to reassure the American middle class — as well as hesitant middle-class Irish Americans (and Catholic clergy) — that Irish-American nationalism was fully compatible with aspirations to assimilation and respectability (as well as devotion to the Church).

---

40 Oliver MacDonagh, 'Irish Emigration to the United States of America and the British Colonies during the Famine,' in R. Dudley Edwards and T. Desmond Williams, eds., *The Great Famine: Studies in Irish History* (New York, 1957), 382.

Irish-American politicians and journalists continued to insist that democratic political ideals and a shared history of struggle against British monarchism still united Irish and American traditions. As one editor put it, 'The strongest and best hater of England is sure to prove the best American.'[41] Perhaps the most contrived and tragic attempt at such self-serving synthesis occurred in the Civil War's early years, when Irish-American spokesmen — eager to demonstrate the group's patriotism — urged their countrymen to enlist and join the slaughter to gain military training for subsequent use against England. Likewise, the Fenians' post-war attempts to conquer Canada reflected desires to merge Irish animosity against the British Empire with the long-standing American aspiration to annex that valuable 'speculation' in northern 'real estate'.[42] And in 1916–21 Irish-American leaders justified agitation for Irish independence in light of their adopted country's contemporary (if specious) wartime 'crusade' for democracy and self-determination for small nations.

Middle-class Irish Americans usually explained nationalist aspirations in bourgeois and assimilationist terms. They asserted, for example, that the creation of a free and prosperous Ireland was a necessary precondition for Irish Americans to gain respect in the New World — an argument that appealed to ambitious entrepreneurs and striving craftsmen such as New York's Patrick Taggart, who hoped 'that ere long Irish men will have a flag of their own to shelter and protect them' from nativist aspersions.[43] Also, the mobilization of Irish immigrants in nationalist movements dissolved parochial loyalties in a common consciousness and united the group in ways conducive to their leaders' domestic goals. For instance, nationalist spokesmen such as Young Irelander Thomas Francis Meagher and Fenian leader Patrick Collins, later governor of Montana Territory and mayor of Boston, respectively, used the reputations and followings created through their championship of Ireland's 'sacred cause' to advance their own political careers. Similarly, local nationalist clubs were often merely stepping-stones to power for ambitious ward heelers like Boston's James Michael Curley. In addition, Irish-American entrepreneurs and politicians alike realized that 'patriotic' leadership of nationalist

---

41 William L. Joyce, *Editors and Ethnicity: A History of the Irish-American Press, 1848–1883* (New York, 1976), 77.

42 Montgomery, *Beyond Equality*, 133.

43 Patrick Taggart, New York City, to Robert Humphreys, [London or Windsor, England?], 14 June 1869 (Fleming-Humphreys Papers, Cornell University Archives, Ithaca, NY).

Some historians, most notably Thomas N. Brown in his *Irish-American Nationalism, 1870–1890* (Philadelphia, 1966), contend that the primary, if not only, purpose of Irish-American nationalism was to promote its middle-class adherents' goals of acceptance and upward mobility in American society. That interpretation is too one-sided, however, for the most loyal followers of nationalist movements, especially those most radical, were usually alienated labourers and homesick peasants, recently arrived; likewise, many of the most dedicated leaders — particularly of revolutionary organizations such as the Clan na Gael — were relatively indifferent to their personal prospects in American society. However, although Irish-American nationalism was a multifaceted phenomenon, it was precisely through its incorporation of Irish America's socio-economic and ideological dualities that its predominately middle-class leaders were able to employ it to exercise hegemony in the United States as well as to promote Irish self-government or independence.

movements could obscure or even deflect intra-ethnic class conflict; sometimes, as in Denver in 1879–81, garnering them support from Irish workers who formerly had been militantly class-conscious. From the perspective of Irish-American social conservatives, even extreme Irish-American nationalist societies like the Clan na Gael performed the valuable function of diverting immigrant workers' radical resentments away from more dangerous domestic channels. Nationalist movements would be successful, middle-class leaders admonished, only if Irish Americans took care to 'be faithful, be Catholic, be practical, be temperate, be industrious, [and] be obedient to the laws';[44] and the nationalist rhetoric of emigration-as-exile itself obscured internal differences by implying that all Irish Americans shared similar, externally imposed reasons for their or their parents' emigrations. Likewise, the demands of Irish-American nationalists that the immigrants remain faithful to the 'motherland' — like clerical injunctions to fidelity to 'mother Church' — coincided with the popular imagery and material needs of Irish families in both Ireland and America, thus imposing strong communal pressures for ethnic solidarity and conformity on ambitious or assimilation-minded individuals.

The success in employing nationalism as a medium for cultural hegemony was demonstrated by its thorough integration with the other means of incorporation: the Democratic party and the Catholic Church. Democratic politicians quickly learned to 'twist the British lion's tail' for Irish-American voters; and although Ireland's cause gained few practical benefits from such rhetorical exercises, the symbolic assimilation of Irish and native-American political traditions both legitimated the former and opened up the latter for middle-class Irish Americans. Likewise, Irish-American Churchmen soon understood that a clerically recognized and tamed Irish-American nationalism could strengthen religious faith, that clerical expressions of 'sympathy with the national aspirations of the race' helped cement Irish loyalties to the Church in the United States as in Ireland.[45] Thus, Irish-American nationalism was conflated with American patriotism, loyalty to the Democracy, and fidelity to Catholicism in a synthetic ethnic identity. The success of that synthesis largely explains both the last, remarkable resurgence of nationalism in 1916–21 — when the group was composed overwhelmingly of second- and third-generation Irish Americans — and the fact that Irish America retained its ethnic identity despite the nearly total disintegration and disappearance of organized Irish-American nationalism after the creation of the Irish Free State and the outbreak of the Irish Civil War in 1922.

44 Rev. Thomas N. Burke, *Lectures on Faith and Fatherland* (London, n.d. [c. 1872–77]), 235. Burke (1830–82), an Irish priest, was a popular lecturer among the American Irish in the post-Civil War decades. For a synopsis of Thomas Francis Meagher's career, see Chapter 12, n. 25.
45 James P. Gaffey, *Citizen of No Mean City: Archbishop Patrick Riordan of San Francisco* (Hawthorne, Calif., 1976), 144.

※

As noted in the first section of this chapter, some US labour historians, particularly Eric Foner and David Montgomery, have put forth a different interpretation of Irish-American ethnicity, contending that it derived primarily from the stratification and segmentation of Irish workers in the United States.[46] Most Irish immigrants adapted not to bourgeois models of individual respectability and upward mobility, they argue, but to an American working-class subculture, in which Irish pre-industrial and craft traditions merged with the ideals of native and other immigrant workers to forge a militant American working-class consciousness that both incorporated and transcended parochial ethnic identities. As a result, during the late 1860s, 1870s, and especially the 1880s, there developed a 'symbiotic relationship'[47] between Irish immigrants' traditional oppositions to landlordism and British imperialism, and American labour leaders' contemporary crusades against plutocracy and 'wage slavery'. The two strands of protest were conflated by spokesmen such as the Irish-American newspaper editor Patrick Ford, whose *Irish World and Industrial Liberator* — the nation's most popular Irish weekly in the 1870s and 1880s — offered a working-class road to assimilation via a radical brand of Irish-American nationalism that demanded fundamental socio-economic reforms on both sides of the Atlantic. Once his readers understood, as Ford put it, that 'the cause of the poor in Donegal is the cause of the factory slave in Fall River',[48] then Irish-American nationalism broadened and prepared its working-class adherents for their increasingly prominent position in militant trade unions, the Knights of Labor, and the third-party efforts — such as Henry George's 1886 campaign for mayor of New York — that characterized the 1880s.

Ideologically and emotionally, this interpretation is very appealing. An assessment of its validity must begin by acknowledging that mass participation by Irish immigrants and their sons (and daughters, as in Chicago's radical teachers' union[49]) in the late nineteenth- and early twentieth-century American labour movement is incontrovertible, as is their disproportionately large role in the Knights of Labor and later in the American Federation of Labor (AFL). Indeed, Terence Powderly, the Knights' national leader, was an Irish-American Catholic (and active as well in the Clan na Gael), and in 1890–1920 workers of Irish stock were 'incredibly dominant' among both the leadership and the rank and file in most of the craft unions affiliated with the AFL, which then accounted

46 For references to works by Foner, Montgomery, etc., see above, n. 7.
47 Foner, 'Class, Ethnicity, and Radicalism', 26–27.
48 Brown, *Irish-American Nationalism*, 108.
49 See Nolan, *Servants of the Poor*, esp. ch. 5.

for 75 per cent of all organized labourers.[50] Nor is there any doubt that the bonds forged among Irish immigrant workers in iron mills, construction sites, mining camps, and working-class neighbourhoods simultaneously heightened a consciousness of class as well as of ethnicity, at least insofar as the two coincided. Despite group upward mobility, on at least cultural and psychological levels, that link persisted well into the twentieth century. Thus, even wealthy Irish-born entrepreneurs, such as Montana's Hugh Daly (whose mansion's walls were adorned with green shamrock wallpaper), expressed deep resentment against their continued exclusion from Anglo-America's economic and political élites, employing rhetoric that tinged ethno-religious consciousness with working-class terminology to 'explain' — defensively or defiantly — their imposed or perceived status as 'outsiders' in American society.[51]

Yet despite Irish America's persistent 'underdog' mentality, the particular interpretations of Foner, Montgomery et al., have been overstretched. Indeed, it is arguable that the 'symbiotic relationship' they identify between Irish Catholic immigrants and working-class organizations worked in ways opposite to these labour historians' contentions, serving over time to diminish proletarian consciousness among both the Irish and the labour movement, and assimilating them instead to the 'quasi-middle-class' values that characterized the dominant cultures of Irish America and native-born Protestant America alike.[52]

Unfortunately, with few and quite transitory exceptions, Irish-American working-class neighbourhoods were not the crucibles of radical proletarianization that some scholars have hypothesized. In cities such as Fall River, Massachusetts, where the workforce was distinctly segmented and residentially segregated on ethnic lines, job competition and the socio-cultural, territorial, and political divisions between 'Irish wards', 'Irish parishes', and other, non-Irish neighbourhoods only intensified ethnic consciousness and insularity.[53] More important, in most such instances it is only superficially accurate to speak of Irish working-class neighbourhoods, as if that phrase indicated either social or ideological homogeneity. Most such districts were dominated, socially and politically, by petty entrepreneurs and employers — such as saloonkeepers, grocers, contractors — and although such men were often former factory workers or even unskilled labourers, and although they often supported strikes by local residents and customers, their functions and lifestyles oriented their neighbourhoods towards 'broader', bourgeois-dominated associations and values that undermined both parochial and proletarian identities. Thus, studies such as one

50 David N. Doyle, 'The Irish and American Labour, 1880–1920', Saothar: The Journal of the Irish Labour History Society, 1 (1975), 42–53.
51 Hugh O'Daly, 'Life History', 1867–1945 (courtesy of David M. Harney, Los Angeles, and Rev. Patrick Daly, Monaghan, County Monaghan).
52 Doyle, 'Irish and American Labour', 50–51.
53 On the Irish in Fall River, see John Cumbler, Working Class Community in Industrial America: Work, Leisure, and Struggle in Two Industrial Cities, 1880–1930 (Westport, Conn., 1979).

of Worcester, Massachusetts, in the mid-1800s demonstrate that after a brief period of severe social dislocation and conflict precipitated by the Famine influx, the actual working-class inhabitants of most Irish neighbourhoods were over time increasingly subject to the socio-cultural and political influence of families that a historian of Worcester in a later period, Roy Rosenzweig, describes as 'working-class respectables' and 'settled livers', in opposition to those among whom traditional peasant or radical proletarian characteristics still prevailed.[54] Significantly, 'working-class respectables' included the families of Irish-American policemen, who were crucial, albeit ultimately coercive, intermediaries between the Irish working class and the legal, judicial, and political systems that enforced capitalist 'rules' and bourgeois standards — stringently in the case of threats to 'property' or 'law and order', selectively with respect to drinking and 'vice'. As a result, the denizens of Irish-American working-class neighbourhoods generally viewed 'their' local policemen with deep ambivalence — admiring their status, although resenting their social apostasy — while the latter's reputation among non-Irish workers was proverbially (and often justifiably) negative.[55]

Moreover, the relative ease of Irish family re-formation in the United States may have been crucial to Irish America's comparative insularity from other predominantly working-class groups, as well as to its social transformation. Unlike the situations of immigrants from southern and eastern Europe, endogamous marriage patterns and the family's central importance in Irish America were ensured early on by an unusually high proportion of female Irish immigrants (about 50 per cent in 1840–1900). It is arguable that family bonds and responsibilities alone tended both to encourage ethnic exclusivity and to discourage proletarian militancy. Likewise, the increasing segregation of workers' lives between home and workplace (or saloon) tended to foster a cult of domesticity that converged with middle-class norms and found physical expression in the stereotypical lace curtains adorning the windows of 'respectable' working-class Irish homes.[56]

In this regard, the particular role of the Irish immigrant woman may have been very significant.[57] Most Irish immigrant women, who commonly left home in their late teens or early twenties, emigrated at least in part to gain what one called 'love and liberty'[58] — in reaction against the stifling personal and social conditions they had experienced

54 Vincent E. Powers, '"Invisible Immigrants": The Pre-Famine Irish Community in Worcester, Massachusetts, from 1826 to 1860' (PhD diss., Clark University, 1976), since published (New York, 1989); Roy Rosenzweig, Eight Hours for What We Will: Workers and Leisure in an Industrial City, 1870–1920 (Cambridge, 1983), esp. 65–90.

55 e.g., see Charles Fanning, Finley Peter Dunne and Mr. Dooley: The Chicago Years (Lexington, Ky., 1978).

56 On the privatization of workers' lives, see Susan E. Hirsch, Roots of the American Working Class: The Industrialization of Crafts in Newark, 1800–1860 (Philadelphia, Pa., 1978).

57 On Irish immigrant women, see: Hasia R. Diner, Erin's Daughters in America: Irish Immigrant Women in the Nineteenth Century (Baltimore, Md., 1983); Carol Groneman, 'Working-Class Immigrant Women in Mid-Nineteenth Century New York: The Irish Woman's Experience', Journal of Urban History, 4 (May 1978), 255–73; and Nolan, Ourselves Alone and Servants of the Poor. Also see Chapter 13 in this volume.

58 Mary Brown, New York City, to Mary Brown, Tomhaggard, County Wexford, 20 January 1859 (Schrier collection; original in Ms. 1408, DIF/UCD).

in highly patriarchal families and in rural Irish society, generally. Ironically, however, one of their few avenues to status or expression in Ireland was through an equally patriarchal Catholic Church, which exalted female piety, purity, and domesticity; as a result, most Irishwomen in America, although often personally assertive, remained extremely attentive to religious devotions. As a consequence of these mixed experiences, Irish immigrant women tended to be ambitious and pragmatic, even 'tough-minded', yet also family-centred and devout. Their letters suggest, for example, that generally they were more prone than their brothers to regard emigration to the United States as economic opportunity (even as escape) rather than as exile, and once abroad they tended to embrace American consumerism and its underlying assumptions — concerning, for instance, the relationship between domestic furnishings (as well as personal appearance and behaviour) and family 'character' and status. Also, before marrying (almost exclusively to other Irish Americans), most of these women laboured as domestic servants in upper- or middle-class American households, where they gained further exposure to bourgeois standards (of 'niceness', for example) and to the material symbols of the domestic comfort and stability to which they aspired. Finally, Irish-American women's proverbial piety enabled them to draw on and represent the moral and institutional authority of 'mother Church' in their relationships with other family members, thus sacralizing standards of 'proper' behaviour. Together their experiences, ambitions, and religious devotions — plus the crucial fact that in the United States they married by *choice* rather than under the rural Irish dowry system — enabled many Irish immigrant women to play vital roles as interpreters of middle-class norms and as advocates of 'Irish-American Catholic' versions of respectability and advancement in their working-class families.

These factors, combined with the desire of transplanted peasants for security in a highly unstable and harshly competitive new environment, may help explain why working-class Irish families seem to have been especially assiduous and successful in acquiring property and, particularly, in becoming homeowners, once streetcars and other forms of cheap intra-urban transport opened up American city peripheries to suburban development. An index of status and permanence, homeownership itself fostered conservative attitudes. In addition, although the overall (if inconsistent) expansion of the American economy in 1850–1900 was most important, the centrality of the Irish-American family and, especially, of the mother's role also may help explain the occupational mobility and diversity that characterized the entire ethnic group by the century's end, when 'most Irish American families were fluid in their kinship and communal status relationships'. The result, as the historian David Doyle has recorded, was that 'the railroad worker, switchman or maintenance worker, would have a cousin a grocer, a brother a small official, a son a teacher or a train-driver' — and, perhaps even more likely, a daughter a teacher or a nurse or a clerical worker or telephone operator in a downtown office building.[59] Consequently, most Irish immigrants, and especially

---

59 Doyle, 'The Irish and American Labour', 50–51; and Nolan, *Servants of the Poor*.

their US-born children, would not identify with a 'closed' socio-economic community but, rather, with ethno-religious associations and formal institutions that encompassed those fluid relationships and that were the very media through which the Irish-American bourgeoisie disseminated its hegemonic culture.

From the late 1860s on, nearly all Irish-American neighbourhoods not only were dominated by Catholic churches and Democratic party organizations but also were replete with branches of national ethnic and religious benevolent and fraternal societies, such as the Irish Catholic Benevolent Union, the Catholic Total Abstinence Union (CTAU), the Ancient Order of Hibernians, and, by the century's end, the Knights of Columbus — as well as by a host of smaller, locally based associations (for example, the Irish county clubs, reflecting members' origins in Cork, Kilkenny, etcetera).[60] These societies' leadership cadres and membership lists often interlocked on both national and local levels, and, most important, their leaders were predominantly middle-class, often second-generation Irish Americans (especially in the national organizations), while the bulk of their members were either of petty bourgeois or skilled-worker status. Consequently, although these associations expressed the full range of emphases allowed by the dominant ethnic culture — from 'Irish Chauvinism' to 'Catholic Americanism', to employ the terms of historian Timothy Meagher[61] — they all espoused an ostentatious American patriotism and preached a gospel of progress and individual uplift through self-discipline, industry, thrift, and, especially, sobriety. '[T]he Irish people should never touch liquor or beer in America ... if they are desirous of becoming good Citizens,' declared one Irish-born CTAU officer; 'total abstinence ... is the golden lever which will guide our weak machinery to a successful goal.'[62]

Hence, like the Democratic party, the Catholic Church, and organized Irish-American nationalism, these ethno-religious institutions provided supplemental media that also served the hegemonic imperatives of the Irish-American bourgeoisie, forging group solidarity across class divisions and incorporating middle-class norms with working-class sensibilities in a synthetic ethnic culture. Of course, Irish immigrant workers who joined these societies recognized that self-discipline and temperance were

---

60 There was a brief period during and shortly after the Famine influx when many Irish immigrant neighbourhoods lacked formal, middle-class, political, religious, and social institutions, which may help explain the 1860s phenomenon of Fenianism, with its unique promise to return large numbers of unattached (and often alienated) Irish-American males to Irish soil. By the 1870s and 1880s, however, a typical working-class immigrant in a city such as Philadelphia could observe that 'Irishmen are pretty well organized here ... . This is a great place for societies'; Owen O'Callaghan, Philadelphia, Pa., to his parents, Fallagh, Kilmacthomas, County Waterford, 12 December 1884 (courtesy of Eugene O'Callaghan, Fallagh).

61 Timothy J. Meagher, '"The Lord is not Dead": Cultural and Social Change among the Irish in Worcester, Massachusetts' (PhD diss., Brown University, 1982), since superbly revised, expanded, and published as *Inventing Irish America: Generation, Class, and Ethnic Identity in a New England City, 1880–1928* (Notre Dame, Ind., 2001).

62 William H. Downes, Brooklyn, NY, to James Shaughnessy, Pallaskenry, County Limerick, 13 October 1887 (courtesy of William O'Shaughnessy, Pallaskenry).

as necessary for conducting successful strikes as they were likely to enhance personal chances for job stability or promotion.[63] Nevertheless, even in the late 1860s the future of the Irish-American working class already belonged to devout, aspiring labourers such as Patrick Taggart, who proudly avowed his 'abstinence from those mixtures which ... debases man lower than the beast'; after all, he concluded, 'a man cannot have a good reputation without soberiety'.[64]

In light of the above, how to reassess the relationship between Irish America and organized labour? There is no doubt that ethno-religious affinities informed and solidified Irish workers' efforts to organize and protest. However, the strong ethnic base of such 'class' alliances tended to separate Irish Catholic from native-born Protestant workers as well as from those of other immigrant origins. This was especially true by the 1880s and 1890s, when class and ethnicity were *dis*-integrating for various reasons.[65] First, as described earlier, Irish-American workers were increasingly drawn into formal, bourgeois-dominated ethnic associations that transcended class divisions and disseminated middle-class outlooks. As a result, organized Irish workers had competing allegiances to political, religious, and social institutions that in practice were often hostile to organized labour but whose rhetoric appealed to proletarian as well as ethnic sensibilities. This helps to explain why, in the 1880s, Irish-American Democratic politicians were successful in co-opting or, when necessary, crushing Irish and other workers' third-party challenges, and also why Terence Powderly was obliged to expend a disproportionate amount of time and energy protecting the Knights of Labor from condemnation by reactionary Irish-American bishops and priests, whose pulpit denunciations and powers of excommunication threatened to force Irish workers to quit the organization.[66] Both Tammany patronage and hierarchical condemnation were instrumental in defeating Henry George's bid for New York's mayoralty in 1886, as the secular and clerical wings of the Irish-American bourgeoisie united publicly to stamp out oppositional, proletarian interpretations of Irish ethnicity. Like the

63 Likewise, Irish-American nationalists knew that temperance was as essential to effective conspiracies against British rule in Ireland as it was to their individual prospects in US society.

64 Patrick Taggart, 14 June 1869; **sobereity** as spelt in ms.

65 It is true that some Irish-American workers maintained into the early 1900s the radical ideals and affiliations first shaped in the 1870s and 1880s. Frank Roney's story, however, suggests that such workers often disassociated themselves from the institutional and cultural indices of 'Irishness' as conventionally defined through the processes described here. For example, Elizabeth Gurley Flynn, later a leader of the American Communist party, wrote that her Irish-born father abandoned the Catholic Church in response to its role in defeating Henry George's bid for New York's mayoralty in 1886, and James Connolly, who sojourned in early twentieth-century America and worked as an organizer for the radical Industrial Workers of the World, lamented that the few Irish-American socialists usually rejected Irish-American nationalism for 'internationalism' and became 'more anti-Christian [and, especially, more anti-Catholic] than the devil'. On Roney, see above, n. 2; on Flynn and Connolly, see Miller, *Emigrants and Exiles*, 530–31.

66 See Davis, *Prisoners of the American Dream*, 29–40; Leon Fink, *Workingman's Democracy: The Knights of Labor and American Politics* (Urbana, Ill., 1983); and Henry J. Browne, *The Catholic Church and the Knights of Labor* (1949; repr. New York, 1976).

mass executions of Molly Maguires in 1877, Tammany's theft of the 1886 election, and the Church's excommunication or 'exile' (to remote rural parishes) of its few radical priests, clearly marked the boundaries of permissible action and debate imposed by the hegemonic (and mutually reinforcing) cultures and institutions of both the national and the Irish-American bourgeoisies.

In addition, the connections, both coercive and co-optational, between the Democracy, the Church, and the Knights of Labor alienated many of the Knights' native-born, Protestant-Republican members and facilitated their incorporation into another manifestation of all-class nativism, the American Protective Association, which emerged in the late 1880s and peaked during the economic crisis of the next decade. Likewise, it is arguable that, despite Patrick Ford's efforts, in the long run the connection between Irish-American nationalism and the labour movement also may have diminished working-class consciousness and solidarity, in part by heightening Irish workers' own ethno-religious awareness and by incorporating them into nationalist alliances with bourgeois Irish employers and reactionary clerics, but also by providing native-born Protestant businessmen and workers with excuses and opportunities to characterize Irish labourers as disloyal to 'American' institutions and values and therefore as undesirable employees, workmates, or comrades in labour organizations. Thus, in regions where Irish ethnicity and class consciousness did coincide most closely — for example, in the Pennsylvania anthracite fields and in Troy's iron industry — militant labour's intimate identification with Irish Catholics enabled native-Protestant employers and their legal, clerical, and journalistic allies to brand strikes, boycotts, and other forms of labour protest as stereotypically 'Irish' and hence 'un-American'.[67]

Second, the early Irish dominance of many urban-industrial occupations meant that by the 1880s and 1890s the increasing stratification of the American workforce, coupled with Irish mobility from the unskilled ranks, had placed the organized vanguard (by 1900 a majority) of Irish-American workers in a relatively privileged but highly tenuous position. On the one hand, skilled Irish workers were threatened by employers' efforts to reduce production costs through wage cuts and mechanization, and on the other hand, such workers faced new sources of job competition from waves of unskilled immigrants from southern and eastern Europe, from the so-called Black Belt of the US South, and even — in California and elsewhere in the Far West — from China. According to Irish labourers, these newcomers 'work cheaper & are more submissive than the English-speaking working man',[68] and, indeed, employers often

---

67 On the Irish in Troy, see Daniel J. Walkowitz, *Worker City, Company Town: Iron and Cotton-Worker Protest in Troy and Cohoes, New York, 1855–84* (Urbana, Ill., 1978), esp. 219–44. Ironically, Irish-American conservatives (lay and clerical) would later employ similar rhetoric to denounce, as 'foreign' and 'un-American', strikes and political protests by New Immigrants — especially when led by Church-condemned radicals, as in the Lawrence, Massachusetts, textile workers' strike of 1912, spearheaded by the Industrial Workers of the World; see Donald Cole, *Immigrant City: Lawrence, Massachusetts, 1845–1921* (Chapel Hill, NC, 1963).

68 Patrick McKeown, Philadelphia, Pa., to Andrew Cosgrove, Belfast, 11 September 1904 (Schrier collection).

used the new arrivals to slash wages, defeat strikes, and break Irish-dominated unions. The point is that the defensive posture of the heavily Irish craft unions made their leaders and members job- or craft-concious, rather than class-conscious, and to the extent that skilled jobs as machinists, bricklayers, and so on, were monopolized by the Irish, that coincidence reinforced ethnic consciousness as well. In fact, many trade unions became Irish-American bastions or enclaves, perpetuating their ethnic complexion through exclusive apprenticeship programmes and other forms of nepotism — by such means incorporating not only their members' sons but also recently arrived nephews and other kin from Ireland. As Richard Oestreicher and other historians have pointed out, Irish (and other) 'craft conservatives' ultimately rejected the Knights of Labor's utopian reformism and undermined its efforts to create an all-inclusive working-class movement, instead embracing (and shaping) the job- (and perforce ethnic-) conscious and 'class-collaborationist' strategies of the AFL.[69]

Finally and ironically, the assimilation of Irish-American workers into the mainstream of the American labour movement only made them more exposed and vulnerable to middle-class norms. For example, to the extent that strikes or legislative pressure *were* successful in raising wages or shortening work hours, such material improvements facilitated Irish families' suburbanization and incorporation to a culture of consumerism and respectability. As in the early nineteenth century, the ideologies of most American labour organizations were in many respects at least implicitly conservative. Both the Knights of Labor and the AFL fostered a belief in 'American exceptionalism' as well as an abhorrence of degraded, 'servile' labour: the former reinforced Irish immigrants' imported (albeit sorely tested) faith in American institutions, whereas the latter converged with their economic resentments and cultural prejudices against their New Immigrant, African-American, and Chinese competitors. Even the Knights' efforts to create a nearly all-inclusive co-operative commonwealth blurred class distinctions between workers and so-called 'good' employers, whereas AFL leaders explicitly disavowed both reformism and independent labour politics, striving instead to form pragmatic coalitions with those sectors of the bourgeoisie sympathetic to Samuel Gompers's argument that higher wages would generate increased consumerism, larger corporate profits, and industrial harmony.

Perhaps most important, the increasing coincidence of Irish ethnicity and the boundaries of organized labour not only reinforced the former but also brought the trade unions themselves into intimate contact — and, eventually, tacit alliances — with those bourgeois-dominated institutions that defined Irish-American ethnicity. Marc Karson has demonstrated the extensive influence in the late nineteenth and early twentieth centuries of the Catholic Church on the AFL, shaping the conservative

---

69 Richard J. Oestreicher, *Solidarity and Fragmentation: Working People and Class Consciousness in Detroit, 1875–1900* (Urbana, Ill., 1986), esp. 30–67 and 172–214; Davis, *Prisoners of the American Dream*, 40–45.

policies of its predominantly Irish-stock leaders.[70] Likewise, Gwendolyn Mink has argued that racist opposition to New Immigrants, Chinese labourers, and black migrants united Irish-American labour leaders and politicians, and facilitated the AFL's incorporation into an all-class, nativist coalition under the Democratic party of William Jennings Bryan and Woodrow Wilson.[71] Ironically, although Irish Americans themselves remained subject and extremely sensitive to Yankee prejudice, both their middle- and working-class spokesmen embraced a fashionable racism through which they could both emphasize their ethnic distinctiveness and simultaneously claim affinity with — and preferential treatment from — America's governing classes. In many cities unorganized semi-skilled and unskilled Irish labourers were particularly dependent on the Democratic party, specifically on Irish-dominated political machines, to provide jobs as street pavers, tram-drivers, gas workers, and so on in the face of competition from Italians, Poles, and French Canadians. In numerous urban parishes the links between Irish-American contractors, politicians, city employees, priests, and trade-union leaders were so intimate and inextricable (and mutually profitable) that members of other immigrant groups turned to Yankee-Protestant, business-Republican leadership — which in turn only further reinforced Irish workers' many-sided allegiance to their own ethnic group. Often the relationship between organized labour and Irish-American nationalism was also close and important; for example, AFL conventions regularly issued statements supporting Irish freedom, and on occasion, as in the 1894 convention, Irish craft-union leaders cynically manipulated nationalist issues to defeat socialist motions emanating from the federation's German- or native-American constituents.

As a result, through both direct and indirect influence on Irish workers and their organizations, the Irish-American bourgeoisie was able to incorporate many of its key values and implement its hegemonic strategies even via an ostensibly 'proletarian' institution such as the AFL. Of course, such an incorporation (like the Irish nationalists' embrace of poor tenants' land hunger) inevitably broadened the dualities of the dominant subculture, but it both solidified the ethnic ideological bloc across class lines and opened new avenues for collective and individual access to influence and power — strengthening, for instance, the positions of Irish-American politicians and bishops in their relationships with native-Protestant Americans and New Immigrants, as well as with their own Irish constituents.

Thus, a complex, multifaceted, but virtually all-inclusive Irish-American Catholic ethnicity was now complete, adapting Irish traditions and American experiences to both the hegemonic imperatives of the Irish-American bourgeoisie and the assimilable needs and beliefs of their social inferiors. By 1900 Irish ethnic identity had achieved

70 Marc Karson, *American Labor Unions and Politics, 1900–1918* (1958; repr. Boston, 1965), 212–84.
71 Gwendolyn Mink, *Old Labor and New Immigrants in American Political Development: Union, Party, and State, 1875–1920* (Ithaca, NY, 1986).

ultimate synthesis: a 'good Irish American' was at least one if not all of the following: a good Democrat, a faithfully practising Catholic, a good family man (or devoted wife and mother), in most cases a loyal union member, and nearly always at least a passive supporter of Ireland's freedom. As a result, actual transatlantic family ties — increasingly remote in most instances — were no longer necessary to sustain Irish-American ethnicity. Rather, Irish-Americans' identifications with Catholicism, with Irish nationalism, and with middle-class values, generally, linked Irish Americans at least symbolically to Catholic Ireland and its hegemonic culture, especially to the romanticized, 'parlour' renditions of that culture, as retailed in the US by postcards, lithographs, and sentimental 'Tin Pan Alley' songs like 'My Wild Irish Rose'.[72] Most important, all the bourgeois-defined traits and associations that characterized 'good Irish Americans' also enabled them to assert that they were 'good Americans' as well: indeed, so much so that cultural affinity with the governing classes legitimized the group's intermediate position and allowed its leaders to play 'Americanizing' (and policing) roles for the New Immigrants. Ironically, whether as foremen, politicians, union leaders, bishops, or merely as fellow guardians of American capitalism, 'family values', and 'racial purity', by the early twentieth century Irish Americans had earned Henry Cabot Lodge's designation of 'honorary Anglo-Saxons' through the very process of creating a bourgeois-defined Irish ethnic identity.

---

72 On late nineteenth- and early twentieth-century Irish-American music and popular culture, generally, see: William H. A. Williams, 'Twas Only an Irishman's Dream: The Image of Ireland and the Irish in American Popular Song Lyrics, 1800–1920 (Urbana, Ill., 1996), especially chs. 9–11 on the 'Tin Pan Alley' songs produced in turn-of-the-century New York City by Irish-American composers and lyricists such as Chauncey Olcott and George M. Cohan.

12 The Pauper, the Politician, and the Creation of Irish America

The lives and correspondence of few Famine immigrants were as disparate as those of Mary Rush, a poor peasant woman from County Sligo, and Richard O'Gorman, an affluent lawyer from Dublin.[1] Their stories and letters, detailed below, are interesting in their own right. More important, they illustrate the diversity of the Irish immigrant experience and the creation of a new Irish-American society. Richard O'Gorman and Mary Rush were linked, not only by a shared Catholicism and by the Great Famine, which directly or indirectly spurred their separate flights to America, but also through the symbiotic and hegemonic relationships between the Irish-American bourgeoisie and proletariat. In the middle and later decades of the nineteenth century, those relationships produced an Irish-American political culture that was shaped by the interaction between the imperatives of the bourgeoisie and the sensibilities of the immigrant masses. Irish-American politicians, businessmen, clerics, and other professionals, such as Richard O'Gorman, dominated this political culture, but it could not flourish without the conscious or unconscious acquiescence of poor Irish immigrants like Mary Rush. As a result, it expressed and inculcated a new and comprehensive sense of Irish-American identity that largely obscured or controlled the socio-economic differences

---

1   This chapter was originally published, as 'The Pauper and the Politician: A Tale of Two Immigrants and the Construction of Irish-American Society', in Arthur Gribben, ed., *The Great Famine and the Irish Diaspora in America* (Amherst, Mass., 1999), 196–218. I am grateful to the University of Massachusetts Press for permission to republish this essay, with slight revisions, in this volume. For research aid and advice, I wish to thank Claude Bourguignon of St. Columban, Quebec; Dr. Marion Casey of the Irish Studies programme at New York University; Professor David Fitzpatrick of Trinity College, Dublin; John C. McTernan of the Sligo County Library; Marianna O'Gallagher of Quebec city; Angie O'Gorman of St. Louis, Mo.; and especially Professor Emeritus Bruce D. Boling, of the University of New Mexico, who was listed as co-author in the essay's original publication in grateful acknowledgement of his efforts to trace the Rush family in County Sligo records.

and conflicts among Irish immigrants, uniting them in loyalty to a Democratic party and a Catholic Church that reinterpreted and institutionalized 'Irishness' and assimilated it to bourgeois American norms.

The Pauper's Plight

Mary Rush and her husband, Michael, were typical Famine emigrants to North America — at least three-fourths of whom were poor labourers and servants — except in one respect. Whereas the vast majority left no written records of their travails, a single letter from Mary Rush, sent from County Sligo to her father, Thomas Barrett, in the province of Quebec,[2] survived because it entered the public domain as evidence in the contemporary debates over British policies concerning Irish Famine relief and Irish emigration. Penned in early September 1846, the letter passed from Canadian to London officials and was published the following year in the British Parliamentary Papers. Rush's remarkable testament and its accompanying documents illustrate both the panic that impelled much Famine emigration, particularly among the rural poor who faced destitution and death if they remained at home, and the failure of British officialdom to respond adequately either to the Famine itself or to the Irish peasantry's desperate need for financial assistance to emigrate overseas.[3]

Sometime in the early 1820s Thomas Barrett had emigrated from the townland of Dromore, in Kilmacshalgan parish, Tireragh barony, in west County Sligo in the province of Connacht. He was accompanied by his wife, Bridget (née O'Doherty), and several of their children, but he left behind his daughter Mary, who later married Michael Rush, a cottier in nearby Ardnaglass. During this period, Irish departures for the New World averaged between 15,000 and 20,000 annually. Most of these emigrants went (at least initially) to British North America and primarily sailed from Ulster ports such as Belfast and Londonderry, but about 1,000 to 2,000 per year embarked from Sligo harbour, usually aboard small timber ships bound for Quebec or the Maritime provinces. In the 1820s most of the emigrants who took ship at Sligo port had left homes in southwest Ulster, as prior to the Famine relatively few of County Sligo's Catholic inhabitants emigrated. Most were still relatively insulated from North America's published attractions by their poverty and illiteracy and by the prevalence of the Irish language.

In 1831 nearly 97 per cent of the heads of households in Tireragh barony were labourers, cottiers, or farmers too poor to hire labourers themselves; and in 1841 over 90 per cent of

2 In 1846, when Mary Rush wrote her surviving letter to Thomas Barrett, the province of Quebec was officially known as Canada East. In the early 1820s when Barrett had emigrated, however, its official name was Lower Canada.

3 The Rush letter and accompanying petitions, letters, and memoranda by C. J. Forbes, Fr. John Falvey, Lord Elgin, and Earl Grey are printed in 'Further Papers Relative to Emigration to the British Provinces in North America [June 1847]', in the BBP, HC 1847 (824), xxix, 70–77.

the families in Kilmacshalgan parish lived in one- or two-room thatched cabins made of mud or dry stones. Thus, although later Canadian censuses recorded Thomas Barrett and his wife as illiterate, they could not have been among Sligo's very poorest inhabitants, for passages to Quebec still cost £4 to £6 per adult, plus other expenses. It is likely they were small farmers of 5–10 acres, who had grazed a few livestock and raised oats and potatoes on soil reclaimed from the mountainy bog that dominated the landscape, and who had paid rents largely from the proceeds of spinning and weaving linen before the depression of the 1820s virtually destroyed north Connacht's once flourishing cottage industries. Probably they left County Sligo to avoid a decline in status, a descent into landless poverty, which apparently befell the daughter they left behind. Between 1821 and 1841 the proportion of Kilmacshalgan's parishioners working in industry and other non-farm pursuits fell from 57 per cent to merely 18 per cent. Yet, as Sligo's poor became almost exclusively dependent on the land and the potato for employment and sustenance, the county's population continued to increase, from 146,000 in 1821 to nearly 200,000 by the Famine's eve.[4]

Most Irish immigrants who landed at Quebec city during the early nineteenth century either pushed on to Ontario,[5] if they had sufficient capital to purchase land and begin farming, or migrated southwards to the United States, if they sought employment as artisans or labourers. Only a small minority remained in the former French colony, most visibly in cities such as Quebec and Montreal where by 1845 the Irish comprised the largest 'English-speaking' minorities. However, most of the Irish who stayed in Quebec province settled on farms, often after several years of saving wages earned by working on urban waterfronts, in canal construction, or for timber companies. By the Famine's eve discrete Irish Catholic (and Protestant) farming communities were scattered from the Gaspé peninsula on the Atlantic coast to the Eastern Townships bordering Ontario. Unfortunately, farming the richest soils along the St. Lawrence was precluded by prior French settlement, so Irish immigrants turned to marginal, uncleared lands such as those on the hilly slopes of the Laurentian Shield north of the St. Lawrence. There, in

---

4 Demographic and socio-economic data on Kilmacshalgan parish and Tireragh barony, County Sligo, are taken from the Irish censuses of 1821, 1841, and 1851, and from the Irish Poor Law Commission Reports (1836), vols. xxx–xxxiii, both also in the BBP. Thanks to John C. McTernon of the Sligo County Library for demographic and other data on the Barrett-Rush families and their townlands from County Sligo's parish, tithe, land, and other records.

   For general surveys of Irish emigration to British North America in the 1820s and during the Famine, see: William Forbes Adams, *Ireland and the Irish Emigration to the New World* (New Haven, Conn., 1932); Kerby A. Miller, *Emigrants and Exiles: Ireland and the Irish Exodus to North America* (New York, 1985), esp. chs. 6–7; Cecil J. Houston and William J. Smyth, *Irish Emigration and Canadian Settlement: Patterns, Links, and Letters* (Toronto, 1990); and Donald McKay, *Flight from Famine: The Coming of the Irish to Canada* (Toronto, 1990).

5 During the first half of the nineteenth century, Ontario was officially known first as Upper Canada and later as Canada West.

the early and mid-1820s, along the banks of the small Rivière du Nord, Barrett and other Irish Catholic families settled what became known as the parish of St. Columban.[6]

St. Columban was part of the Lac des Deux-Montagnes region. In 1717 the French Crown had granted the area, under the seigneurial system, to the missionary Order of St. Sulpice. However, it was not until the early 1800s that the Order, headquartered in Montreal, devised a plan for the area's survey and settlement, and the first grants were not made until 1819. Although most immigrants to British North America, such as the Loyalist refugees from the American Revolution, rejected both the seigneurial system and French Catholicism and settled elsewhere than Quebec, at least some poor Irish Catholics apparently found seigneurial fees and clerical paternalism unobjectionable. Thus, in the early 1820s Irish-born Sulpician priests in Montreal succeeded in persuading many of the Irish in Montreal's Griffintown slum to leave the city and colonize the Rivière de Nord. In 1825 the Order formally granted the northernmost portion of the seigneurie to the Irish, and in 1830 the settlers were formally organized into the separate parish of St. Columban.

Among the Irish colonists were Thomas Barrett and his family, as well as a William Barrett, also from Sligo, who may have been the former's brother or cousin. On 27 February 1826 Thomas Barrett received a *concession* or grant of Lot 183, containing c. 70–75 acres in a long, narrow strip, one end of which fronted the river on the Côte St. Paul. Sometime in the 1850s, Barrett also acquired adjacent Lot 184 from another early Irish settler, and by 1861 the Canadian agricultural census recorded his possession of 130 acres.

At first St. Columban grew rapidly, from merely 219 inhabitants in 1825 to 1,015 in 1846. Nearly all were Irish Catholics, mostly from counties in Leinster and north Munster. However, the settlement never flourished economically; instead, St. Columban became the poorest parish in Deux-Montagnes County. The settlers could not even persuade a priest to remain among them until 1840; nor could they afford to build a permanent church until 1860. In many respects, life for the Irish in St. Columban was very similar to what it had been at home. The farms were considerably larger than those left behind in Ireland, but once cleared of dense forests most of St. Columban's soils proved thin and stony, which ensured that potatoes and oats, raised for subsistence, were the farmers' primary crops. Most of the initial settlers had so little capital that the government had to supply them with farm implements as well as blankets and house utensils. Potash, made from the ashes of cleared trees, long remained the farmers' major income source, yet roads were so poor and the long winter weather so severe that markets were often inaccessible. At first, farm animals were few and needed constant protection from wolves, although between 1842 and 1851 the numbers of

6   On Irish settlement in Quebec, see: Houston and Smyth, *Irish Emigration and Canadian Settlement*; and the essays by Marianna O'Gallagher and by D. Aidan McQuillan in Robert O'Driscoll and Lorna Reynolds, eds., *The Untold Story: The Irish in Canada*, 2 vols. (Toronto, 1988), vol. 1, 253–70.

livestock, especially cattle and sheep 'of an inferior quality', increased as the danger from predators declined and as the shallow soils became too exhausted for tillage crops. Only a handful of St. Columbans held non-farm occupations — for example, as artisans or as labourers in the parish's few gristmills or sawmills — but many farmers had to work on the Beauharnois canal and other public works to earn the cash needed to purchase necessities and pay seigneurial fees.

Thomas Barrett's economic condition was no better than that of most St. Columbans. As late as 1861 his family still lived in a one-storey log house; only 16 of his 130 acres were cleared for tillage or pasture; and the total value of his agricultural produce, livestock, and farm implements was merely $128. Moreover, neither Thomas nor William Barrett's names appear prominently in local records, for example as contributors to the parish church or as petitioners to the bishop in Montreal, and it appears that families from more commercially developed mid-Ulster and south Leinster counties such as Tyrone and Kilkenny predominated socially and politically over their less literate, Irish-speaking neighbours from Munster and Connacht.[7]

St. Columban's straitened situation may explain why Barrett's daughter and son-in-law did not leave County Sligo to join him before potato blight and famine struck Ireland in 1845–46. Either Barrett had sent them remittances insufficient to pay their passages, or the information they had received from the Rivière du Nord suggested they would scarcely improve their condition by exchanging Sligo for Quebec. However, by early September 1846 even the forests and snows of St. Columban seemed preferable to unprecedented misery and almost certain death in Ireland. In August the Irish potato crop failed for the second year in a row and, unlike that of 1845, the failure of 1846 was nearly total, which presaged economic ruin, probable eviction, and dire starvation for poor farmers and labourers alike. Since the overwhelming majority of both men and women in the barony of Tireragh were illiterate, many of them monolingual Irish-speakers, it is uncertain whether either Mary or Michael Rush actually penned or merely dictated the following letter, which no doubt was edited before its eventual publication in London. However, the document's authenticity seems unquestionable. Panic and despair; resentment against local landlords and rich graziers, whose cattle throve while children starved; and anger at a relief system that was already proving tragically inadequate: all these emotions of the Irish poor fairly scream from the lines addressed to Thomas Barrett:

> Ardnaglass, 6th September 1846
> Dear Father and Mother,
> I received your kind and affectionate letter dated 24th May, which gave us great pleasure to hear of your being in good health, as it leaves us at present; thank God

---

7   On the Irish settlement of St. Columban, see: Claude Bourguignon, *Saint Columban: Une épopée irlandaise au piédmont des Laurentides* (Chambly, Quebec, 1988). I am grateful to Claude Bourguignon for his generous sharing of data on the Barretts from his research in St. Columban's land, tax, census, and church records.

for his mercies to us. Dear father and mother, pen cannot dictate the poverty of this country, at present, the potato crop is quite done away all over Ireland and we are told prevailing all over Europe. There is nothing expected here, only an immediate famine. The labouring class getting only two stone of Indian meal for each days labour, and only three days given out of each week, to prolong the little money sent out by Government, to keep the people from going out to the fields to prevent slaughtering the cattle, which they are threatening very hard they will do, before they starve. I think you will have all this account by public print before this letter comes to hand. Now, my dear parents, pity our hard case, and do not leave us on the number of the starving poor, and if it be your wish to keep us until we earn at any labour you wish to put us to, we will feel happy in doing so. When we had not the good fortune of going there, the different times ye sent us money; but alas, we had not that good fortune. Now, my dear father and mother, if you knew what hunger we and our fellow-countrymen are suffering, if you were ever so much distressed, you would take us out of this poverty Isle. We can only say, the scourge of God fell down in Ireland, in taking away the potatoes, they being the only support of the people. Not like countries that has a supply of wheat and other grain. So, dear father and mother, if you don't endeavour to take us out of it, it will be the first news you will hear by some friend of me and my little family to be lost by hunger, and there are thousands dread they will share the same fate. Do not think there is one word of untruth in this; you will see it in every letter, and of course in the public prints. Those that have oats, they have some chance, for they say they will die before they part any of it to pay rent. So the landlord is in a bad way too. Sicily Boyers and family are well; Michael Barrett is very unwell, this time past, but hopes to recover. John Barrett is confined to his bed by rheumatism. The last market, oatmeal went from 1£. to 1£.1s. per cwt.[8] As for potatoes there was none at market. Butter 5£ per cwt., pork 2£.8s. per cwt., and every thing in provision way expected to get higher. The Lord is merciful, he fed the 5000 men with five loaves and two small fishes. Hugh Hart's mother is dead; he is in good health. So I conclude with my blessings to you both and remain your affectionate son and daughter.

Michael and Mary Rush

For God's sake take us out of poverty, and don't let us die with the hunger.

Too poor himself to pay the passages of his daughter's family, Barrett appealed for aid to the Hon. C. J. Forbes, Deux-Montagnes County's representative to the Canadian parliament. After consulting with Fr. John Falvey, St. Columban's Irish-born priest, Forbes proposed to Lord Elgin, Canada's governor general, that relief funds from the British Treasury be used to bring out from Ireland not only Thomas Barrett's poor relations but also those of St. Columban's other Irish inhabitants. In turn, the latter

---

8   **Cwt.** See Chapter 8 in this volume, n. 21.

promised to feed, house, and employ the newcomers. Unfortunately, both Lord Elgin and his superior in London, Earl Grey, secretary of state for the colonies, rejected Forbes's and other proposals for government-assisted emigration from Ireland. Like most Whig statesmen a firm disciple of laissez-faire, Elgin feared that government subsidization of emigration would not only prove expensive and compete with private enterprise, but would also discourage individual industry, thrift, and prudence among Irish Canadians, thereby causing a reduction in the flow of private remittances from Canada to Ireland. Lord Grey was equally concerned to minimize government expenditures, and although in 1847 the Whig administration appropriated an additional £10,000 for the relief of sick emigrants who managed to reach British North America without government aid, he warned the Canadian authorities to 'in no degree … relax … the strictness of their economy' or 'their vigilance in resisting ill-founded claims to assistance'.

Sadly, the same spirit of cold, calculating, and niggardly charity characterized the British government's relief efforts in Ireland as in Canada, with especially fatal results in poor western counties like Sligo, where an unusually large proportion of the population depended on potatoes for subsistence. Thus, between 1841 and 1851 the county's population fell 29 per cent, and in the barony of Tireragh, where over half the families lived in one-room mud cabins, the population declined by 34 per cent due to deaths and emigration. The Barretts' parish of Kilmacshalgan fared slightly better, but still lost 28 per cent of its inhabitants.

Despite their poverty and the lack of government aid, apparently the Rush family succeeded in escaping starvation and plague, for on 15 May 1847 the ship *Garrick* from Liverpool disembarked at New York City a veritable tribe of thirteen related Rush and Barrett kin, ranged in age from one to sixty and led by Michael Rush, recorded in the passenger lists as a 'labourer', aged forty. Perhaps they had received financial assistance from other American relatives, from their landlord, or from local charities, which enabled them to emigrate; or perhaps they were not quite as destitute as Mary and Michael Rush's letter had indicated. In any event, the Rush family cannot be traced beyond the docks of New York. However, it is virtually certain they did not join Thomas Barrett and settle in St. Columban, for there is no trace of them in the parish's detailed records. Like most Famine immigrants, the Rushes no doubt chose to explore the more dynamic economy of urban-industrial America.[9]

9　On the Rush family's 1847 voyage to New York, see: Ira A. Glazer and Michael Tepper, eds., *The Famine Immigrants: Lists of Irish Immigrants Arriving at the Port of New York, 1846–1851*, 7 vols. (Baltimore, Md., 1983), vol. 1, 492–93.

　　The Rush family's decision to avoid Quebec was a sound one, for in 1847 the Irish settlement on the Rivière du Nord was already in economic and demographic decline. Indeed, its ability to absorb new immigrants had been exhausted by the late 1830s, when many of the sons of the original settlers began to abandon St. Columban and seek employment in Montreal and, increasingly, in American cities like Boston — their migrations merging almost indistinguishably with the general exodus of French Canadians to the United States in the late nineteenth and early twentieth centuries. As a result, St. Columban's population fell from about 1,000 in 1850 to merely 324 in 1901. Among those who disappeared from the

Perhaps the Rushes settled in New York City, the hub of America's commercial, financial, and transportation systems, alongside thousands of other impoverished refugees from the 'Great Hunger'. By 1855 New York City contained nearly 176,000 Irish-born inhabitants, about 28 per cent of the total population, and it was during this era that the tip of Manhattan Island became the socio-economic, political, and cultural capital of a new social entity called Irish-America, a development that was due not only to the sheer numbers of Famine Irish settlers, but also to the influence of a few, much more advantaged newcomers, such as Richard O'Gorman.

The Politician's Progress

In the early nineteenth century, the United Irishmen who had fled to New York City after the failed rebellion of 1798 found sanctuary in a Jeffersonian-republican polity and political culture that invited Irish immigration and supported Irish nationalism. However, by mid-century American urban society was less confident and more fragmented along socio-economic, ethnic, and religious lines. Increasingly fearful of pauper immigrants, organized labour, and the Catholic Church, many Protestant Americans — especially the Whig merchant élite whose members had long dominated New York's social and political systems — no longer welcomed either Irish Catholic immigrants at home or the prospect of Irish revolution abroad. Consequently, the fugitive leaders of the Young Ireland revolution of 1848 (and of the Fenian revolt of 1867) often had to make what was, for most of them, a relatively easy choice. One alternative was to pursue careers as single-minded and radical Irish-American nationalists, thereby marginalizing their personal prospects in the conservative mainstreams of both Irish- and native-born American societies. The second and more attractive option was to become Irish-American politicians. In that role, they could capitalize on Irish rhetoric and reputations to unite Irish immigrants, under their leadership, into a formidable political force — in the process, winning approval from the Irish-American Catholic hierarchy, grudging respect from the native-Protestant American establishment, and money and power for themselves.

Richard O'Gorman was a supreme example of an idealistic Irish revolutionary turned pragmatic American politico.[10] The son of a prosperous woollen merchant and Catholic

banks of the Rivière du Nord were the Barretts, for between 1898 and 1903 the last of the line, Michael, a day-labourer in Montreal and probably the nephew of Thomas Barrett, sold to French-Canadian farmers what remained of his family's *concessions*.

10 On Richard O'Gorman and the Young Irelanders in Ireland and America, see: Charles Gavan Duffy, *Young Ireland* (New York, 1881); Richard Pigott, *Personal Recollections of an Irish National Journalist* (Dublin, 1883); T. F. O'Sullivan, *The Young Irelanders* (Tralee, 1945); Kevin B. Nowlan, *The Politics of Repeal* (London, 1965); Blanche M. Touhill, *William Smith O'Brien and His Revolutionary Companions in Penal Exile* (Columbia, Mo., 1981); Rebecca O'Conner, *Jenny Mitchel: Young Irelander* (Dublin, 1988); Richard Davis, *The Young Ireland Movement* (Dublin, 1987); and Brendan O'Cathaoir, *John Blake Dillon, Young Irelander* (Dublin, 1990), which makes extensive use of the Dillon letters at Trinity College, Dublin, quoted in this chapter.

politician, O'Gorman was born in Dublin in 1821, educated at Trinity College, and trained in London to become a barrister. In 1844 he joined Daniel O'Connell's Repeal Association and soon became a secondary leader of the association's so-called Young Ireland faction, composed primarily of young Trinity-educated Protestant and Catholic intellectuals, such as Thomas Davis, John Mitchel, and John Blake Dillon. Despite his later scholarly reputation, O'Gorman's primary value to this band of romantic nationalists lay in his social status and in his powerful and florid oratory. Ironically in view of his subsequent American political career, O'Gorman and other Young Irelanders criticized O'Connell and his followers for their alleged demagoguery, political opportunism, place-hunting, mismanagement of Repeal funds, and subservience to the Catholic hierarchy, especially concerning the issue of interdenominational or 'mixed' education, which the Young Irelanders favoured and which O'Connell and most bishops strenuously opposed.

Shortly before and during the Great Famine, the Young Irelanders' disagreements with O'Connell and their increasing disaffection from Britain split the Repeal movement and precipitated their abortive 'revolution' of 1848. The government arrested the rebellion's reluctant leader, the Protestant landlord William Smith O'Brien, as well as Mitchel, Thomas Francis Meagher, and several others, and sentenced them to exile in Van Diemen's Land. However, many of the Young Irelanders, including Dillon and Michael Doheny, eluded arrest and fled to America. Despite a £300 reward for his capture, O'Gorman, who had attempted to raise the farmers of Limerick and Clare in revolt, escaped to Europe, whence he sailed to New York on 1 June 1849. Ten days earlier, from his temporary refuge in Belgium, O'Gorman wrote Smith O'Brien a letter that declared his ambitions and prefigured his American career: 'I am determined,' he wrote, 'to ... win some higher character than that of an Irish agitator — I think the keeping up an Irish party in America is a fatal mistake, and if I chance to gain any influence over my countrymen, I will seek to induce them rather to blend and fuse their interests with American parties ...'[11]

On arrival in the United States, O'Gorman first settled in St. Louis, but in 1850 he returned to New York City, where he resided for the rest of his life. Through the patronage of Robert Emmet, scion of 1798 exile Thomas Addis Emmet, O'Gorman and Dillon joined the élite Society of the Friendly Sons of St. Patrick, were admitted to the New York bar, and formed a successful legal partnership that lasted until the latter's return to Ireland in 1855.[12] Both were cynical about the future prospects of Irish nationalism ('I will believe in the resurrection of Irish nationality when I see dead

---

11 Richard O'Gorman, Bruges, Belgium, to William Smith O'Brien, Dublin, 21 May 1849 (Ms. 443, no. 2547, NLI); Smith O'Brien was not sent into exile in Van Diemen's Land until 9 July 1849. The O'Gorman letters cited in this chapter are included among the William Smith O'Brien Papers, Mss. 443–47, NLI.

12 On O'Gorman, see: David McAdam, et al., History of the Bench and Bar of New York, 2 vols. (New York, 1897), vol. 1, 437–38; Richard C. Murphy and Lawrence J. Mannion, History of the Society of the Friendly Sons of Saint Patrick in the City of New York (New York, 1962); and John K. Sharp, History of the Diocese of Brooklyn, 1853–1953, 2 vols. (New York, 1954), vol. 1, 215.

men rising from their graves', Dillon wrote)[13] and dissociated themselves from most of the other Young Ireland exiles in New York. Thus, in another letter to Smith O'Brien, O'Gorman ridiculed his former comrade (and future Fenian leader) Michael Doheny for the futility of his 'warlike and choleric' efforts to stoke the fires of Irish revolution among New York's immigrants.[14]

Despite growing American nativism during the mid-1850s, neither O'Gorman nor Dillon had great difficulty, as the latter put it, 'in making ourselves quite at home in [this] heretical society',[15] as they prospered in both their legal practice and their business investments. Now married and domesticated in Brooklyn, O'Gorman was more than reconciled to spending the rest of his life amidst the 'rush and progress' of New York: 'Commercial[,] cosmopolitan and a[d]venturous,' he wrote to Smith O'Brien of his adopted city; 'I like it extremely, because I suppose, it likes me.' Very occasionally, he acknowledged, 'I remember my old Home and there comes sometimes, a sting, and I dream of old times   But I shake it off soon   Its all useless — There is no going back for me — I have staked too much here to think of another change — For the rest of my life, I am American.' Indeed, by 1857 O'Gorman was convinced that the 'Destiny of our Race' lay not in Ireland but in the United States, for 'The moment it touches this soil, it seems to be imbued with miraculous energy ...' The eventual result, he believed, was that 'this northern continent will fall into the hands of Men whose composition will be four fifths Celtic'.[16]

In 1849 O'Gorman had rationalized his assimilation to American political life as a way 'to serve Ireland' — winning 'the American mind ... for her cause' not by 'foolish boasting ... but by silently working on American society and guiding its sights to that island, which was once home of so many of its citizens'.[17] However, as Dillon had recognized, Irish-American politics could easily descend into 'a mere piece of acting' for 'financial speculations', and although Dillon declared himself 'not sufficiently yankeefied to be reconciled to the notion of converting sham patriotism into dollars',[18] O'Gorman and many other self-styled Irish 'exiles' readily embraced the heady temptations which he described in his 1859 letter to Smith O'Brien,[19] by now released from captivity and residing in Ireland.

13 O'Cathaoir, John Blake Dillon, 117.
14 Richard O'Gorman, New York City, to William Smith O'Brien, Port Arthur, Van Diemen's Land, 12 December 1852 (Ms. 445, no. 2842, NLI).
15 O'Cathaoir, John Blake Dillon, 129–30.
16 Richard O'Gorman, Brooklyn, NY, to William Smith O'Brien, [Dromoland, Cahirmoyle, County Clare?], 17 May 1857 (Ms. 445, no. 2958, NLI); in 1854 the British government released Smith O'Brien from his capitivity in Van Diemen's Land, but did not allow him to return to his home in Ireland until 1856; in the interim he resided in Brussels.
17 Richard O'Gorman, 24 May 1849.
18 O'Cathaoir, John Blake Dillon, 138.
19 Richard O'Gorman, New York City, to William Smith O'Brien, [Dromoland, Cahirmoyle, County Clare?], 1 January 1859 (Ms. 446, no. 3082, NLI).

January 1, 1859

Dear friend,

I heard some ten days ago, from home, that you proposed paying a visit to the United States, and I determined to write you by the next mail   Other matters drove this out of my head, and now while I sit recalling my various sins of commission and omission during the year 1858, my conscience disturbs me about you — I hope you will come — and whenever you do come, be sure that you will find one friend at least to welcome you. Indeed the chances are that you will find more friends here, and a more affectionate welcome than you desire[20]

Every man that can, should see the United States — although from such seeing, as a passing traveller Can get — no very reliable information can be obtained, — However, you have by this time learned the art of seeing — for it is an art — and will not be satisfied with the mere surface   At this time too, when Bright[21] and Cobden[22] are talking up American Institutions, it is well to understand something about their working — Cobden and Bright, I think would be the better of a little more Knowledge on that Score — It is quite easy to be an enthusiastic admirer of the United States and its style of government —

The progress of the country in all matters of material wealth is miraculous — There is in the Yankee — wondrous energy — self reliance — power of combination — readiness in the use of all his powers — He has rough and ready work to do, and he does it — The business of the day is to till land — cut down timber — drain swamps — get rid of Indians — build railways, cities, states — and our Yankee does it with surprising speed — and what he can't do himself, he knows how to get others to do for him — This, I suppose, is all that is to be expected — all that is wanting — and we should be satisfied —

And yet, there is another side to the picture — not quite so agreeable to look at — not on bread alone, does man live — Railways and steam ploughs are great — but not the greatest —

The tone of Political morality — in some respects of social morality — is not high — As to Politics, and government, I firmly believe that American progress is in spite of the government and the Politicians. I am not perhaps quite entitled to consideration in my opinion on this point — I feel myself intolerant and violent

20 In 1859 Smith O'Brien made an extensive tour of the United States, his impressions of which he described in *Lectures on America, Delivered in the Mechanics Institute, Dublin, November 1859* (Dublin, 1860).

21 John Bright (1811–89): British statesman, orator, and radical land, tax, and political reformer; leader of the Anti-Corn Law League (1838–46); fervent admirer of American institutions and supporter of the Union during the Civil War; advocated Protestant disestablishment and peasant proprietorship in Ireland, but opposed Gladstone's Irish Home Rule Bill of 1886.

22 Richard Cobden (1804–65): British statesman, political economist, and radical reformer; advocate of free trade and perhaps the most prominent leader of the movement to repeal the Corn Laws, 1838–46; visited the United States in 1835 and 1859; like his close friend, John Bright, a staunch supporter of the Union during the Civil War.

in my contempt for the Diplomacy — government — governors and politicians of the United States — The whole thing seems to me a filthy pool of shabbiness falsehood and corruption. It has grown worse in ten years — I have watched — Ten years ago, we had great men in high places — Webster — Clay[,] Calhoun — Benton[23] — each in his own way, a strong man — They are gone, and we have *adroit* men in their place — *smart* men.

New York is the head Quarters of political corruption — It is here organized — a sort of University for educating the rising generation in the endless variety of means of cheating the public out of their votes and places of Emolument — Here, and for the present, no one can say that Universal suffrage works well — There is only the name in fact — a few leaders — and a few subordinates rule — choose candidates — bring up their armies of voters — and the thing is somehow done as they command — Respectability fears for its eyes and the integrity of its nose, and keeps away from the Polls — For some of our leading politicians are men of Science and strike from the shoulder — and wealth, meekly stays away and consents to be taxed —

There have been various most energetic efforts at Reform made during my time — the results were funny — great struggle — infinite speechmaking — denunciation — detection &c great victory — virtue triumphant at last — new men rule us — and when we come to look at the bills for the year, we are robbed and Cheated and taxed worse than before — I am told this is the boiling and effervescing of the vat — the wine will come in time — I hope so — Time will tell — For the present however — the thing is neither pleasant nor good — It is refreshing however to find that in this effervescing process, our Countrymen have their share — in all political proceedings — primary Elections — smashing Ballot boxes — [im]personating citizens — filling minor offices of all Kinds, and plundering the Public for the Public good — in readiness to gull others or be gulled themselves — the children of our Native Land are Eminently successful. The astuteness of these Citizens in grasping at any man or anything that can serve their end is surprising —

The honest fellow, I left behind me in Ireland a 'cheque clerk' on the road, is now owner of a corner grocery in new York and covets the post of alderman, and scents plunder from afar — When you arrive, this potentate will get up a meeting in his own house — thereby securing — 1st the sale of unlimited Drinks — 2nd the position of an original and creative genius — The seed thus sown will germinate — You will be invited by the city fathers to a reception in the City Hall — Nay, if you choose it — they will have you conveyed thereto in a coach with six white horses

---

23 US senators Daniel Webster of Massachusetts (1782–1852), Henry Clay of Kentucky (1777–1852), John C. Calhoun of South Carolina (1782–1850), and Thomas Hart Benton of Missouri (1782–1858) were the acknowledged giants of antebellum American politics.

— the same poor Kossuth[24] was shown in to an admiring multitude — People will shake you by the hand — the form is settled by long usage — and there's an end of it. I saw the thing done to Kossuth and Meagher[25] and Mitchel[26] and I abhor the ghastly operation —

New York itself will be in 50 years the finest City on this Earth — barring Paris — if even that excels it — It is only *being* built now — yet, its situation is glorious — As to '*society*' here, I have had no concern with it for some years past — I had worn out my taste for it, before I came and never sought much of it — But I Know it nevertheless — It is an unsettled — eager — unsatisfied sort of thing — There is no position permanent here — wealth is all fairy gold — and turns to slate in due course — There is scarcely any family pride or recollection — If you chance to sit at any good mans feast — and he warms into Communicativeness, he tells you that he came into the City of new York twenty years ago, without a shoe to his foot — got on by his *own* exertions[,] owes *no one* any help he; and you begin to think at last — the man grew out of the Earth and never had a father or mother — so utterly is *self* the leading idea.

These men however are most generous — liberal — while the money comes, it goes — we don't hoard — we are too young to be misers yet — of course, in all I write — I write of classes — There are of course here, noble fellows — genial households — pleasant Clubs — a generous manly scorn for all that is base around us — all that you find here — I would not give up my own friends here for any I have ever met — But the general tone of society is not very high — or very refined   The value of gentlemen is in some places, perhaps, overrated — it may be — but it might not hurt America if its system allowed of some hereditary certainty

---

24 Lajos Kossuth (1802–94): radical Hungarian nationalist and fiery orator; leader of the Hungarian revolution against Austria in 1848; after defeat and exile, in 1851 he visited the United States seeking support; was lionized by Democratic politicians but denounced as an 'infidel' and 'red republican' by the Irish-American (and other) Catholic clergy.

25 Thomas Francis Meagher (1822–67): Young Ireland journalist and orator, noted for his bellicose speeches; transported to Van Diemen's Land after the July 1848 rising; escaped to the US in 1853 and became a popular lecturer, Irish-American newspaper editor, and Democratic party politician; in the Civil War he became brigadier-general of the New York Irish Brigade, which suffered heavy casualties at the battles of Fredericksburg and Chancellorsville; after the war, was appointed acting governor of Montana Territory, where he died in mysterious circumstances.

26 John Mitchel (1815–75): radical Young Ireland journalist, although an Ulster Protestant; arrested for treason-felony and sentenced to exile in Van Diemen's Land in May 1848, before the July rising; escaped to the US in 1853; first settled in New York, where he published an Irish-American nationalist newspaper that outraged local Catholic clergymen; in the late 1850s Mitchel moved to Knoxville, Tenn., later to Richmond, Va., where he espoused slavery, southern Secession, and the Confederate cause in the Civil War; after the war he was imprisoned by the US government, then went to Paris where he served as agent for the Fenians; returned to Ireland in 1874 and was twice elected MP for North Tipperary, on a radical-nationalist platform, but parliament invalidated Mitchel's elections on the grounds that he was an escaped felon.

of position — some class that could sit on the benches and look on at the dust & din and sweat and passion of the arena —

And now I have written you a stupid letter I am sure — nothing in it that you did not Know before. It will let you Know in what mood you may expect to find me — I want you to write me at once — say when you are coming — Don't come till April at all Events — There will be no travelling unless in the south until then — I propose going over in July — Good by my dear friend —

I am yours faithfully
Rich^d O'Gorman

Perhaps when writing to Smith O'Brien, a gentleman of noble lineage and formidable integrity, or in his 1867 oration on the death of his old comrade, Meagher, O'Gorman could pay fleeting tributes to his own former idealism. Otherwise, as the old Fenian John O'Leary later observed, 'O'Gorman seems to have exhausted his whole stock of [Irish] patriotism in '48' and took 'little part in Irish [nationalist] affairs' thereafter, 'save in what may be called the ornamental, oratorical [St.] Patrick's day line of business'.[27] However, that 'line of business' paid very well. As O'Gorman's career attested, the opportunities in New York politics were boundless for a man who could trade on his nationalist past and oratory to win the allegiance of his fellow immigrants, curry the favour of the local Irish-American Catholic hierarchy — privately, over dinners with Archbishop Hughes, and politically, by championing Church interests, as in gaining tax support for parochial education — and yet mix confidently with the city's wealthiest merchants and lawyers, gratifying their need for 'culture' with erudite addresses on Shakespeare and Goldsmith, while exalting their patriotism in more bombastic speeches on the Fourth of July.[28]

Thus, despite his disclaimers to the fastidious Smith O'Brien, O'Gorman had already plunged headlong into the 'filthy pool' of New York City politics. Before 1859 O'Gorman had joined Tammany Hall, the city's chief Democratic party organization, and had begun his political career as the Hall's chief 'ornamental' Irishman. Thanks to the Famine, by 1855 over one-fifth of New York City's voters were Irish-born, and during the next two decades Tammany naturalized (often illegally) thousands more immigrant voters — over 41,000 in 1868 alone. Moreover, the collapse of the nation's party system in the 1850s created unprecedented political fluidity and opportunities. The local Democrats themselves were divided between rival 'machine' politicians Fernando Wood and William Tweed, each of whom angled for Irish support, while the party's 'Swallowtails' — the wealthy merchants, bankers, and developers who financed the Democracy —

27 John O'Leary, *Recollections of Fenians and Fenianism*, 2 vols. (Dublin, 1896), vol. 1, 95.
28 O'Gorman's political and social career can be followed most easily in the indexed, albeit usually hostile, articles and editorials in the *New York Times*.

looked askance at both and demanded low taxes, social peace, and a city government favouring their business interests. In addition, New York's skilled and unskilled labourers (many of the former, and most of the latter, Irish-born) were mobilizing, formally and informally: organizing unions and third-party movements; striking for higher wages and shorter workdays; demanding favourable legislation; and, in times of depression, petitioning the city government for 'work or bread' in mass meetings that frightened all men of property, both native- and Irish-born. Finally, the advent of the Civil War threatened a loyalty crisis in the city, especially within the Democratic party, many of whose leaders (Wood, for example) and Irish adherents opposed the war itself, as well as the Republican administration, military conscription, and the abolition of slavery. The horrific Irish-led Draft Riots of July 1863 only epitomized the political, class, and ethnic conflicts that rent New York City in the 1850s and 1860s. Yet those very conflicts made O'Gorman an invaluable component of the Democratic coalition, based largely on Irish votes, which Tweed put together to rule the city between 1865 and 1871.[29]

During the Civil War, O'Gorman echoed Tammany policy by rallying the Irish to fight for the Union, while criticizing Republican policies, especially emancipation. The vigorously anti-Irish *New York Times* called O'Gorman's public criticisms of the Lincoln administration 'Copperhead speeches',[30] but in fact they were designed to divert Irish immigrant frustrations away from violence and into safe, Democratic channels. O'Gorman's reward came in late 1865, when all the city's Democratic factions, plus the élite reformers in the Citizens Association, secured his election to the first of two terms as corporation counsel. Despite his promises to the reformers, O'Gorman soon became a pivotal figure in the infamous 'Tweed Ring', which looted the city's finances during the next six years. As New York's chief law officer, O'Gorman allegedly authorized payment to Ring henchmen of at least $1 million in fraudulent claims against the city, while charging the taxpayers over $500 a day for his and his associates' legal services. O'Gorman also was intimately involved in lucrative frauds involving the opening, widening, and improving of city streets, and he intentionally mismanaged city lawsuits against influential Democrats, even foiling the prosecutions of many Ring leaders after the *New York Times*'s revelations of fraud, the subsequent collapse of the city's bond market, and public outrage over the 1871 Irish Orange–Green riot caused Tweed's fall from power that year.

---

29 On the Irish in mid- and late nineteenth-century New York City politics, see: Robert Ernst, *Immigrant Life in New York City, 1825–1863* (New York, 1949); Florence E. Gibson, *The Attitudes of the New York Irish Toward State and National Affairs, 1848–1892* (New York, 1951); Alexander B. Callow, *The Tweed Ring* (New York, 1965), esp. 135–43 on O'Gorman; Jerome Mushkat, *Tammany: The Evolution of a Political Machine, 1789–1865* (Syracuse, NY, 1971), and *Fernando Wood* (Kent, Ohio, 1990); David C. Hammack, *Power and Society: Greater New York at the Turn of the Century* (New York, 1982); Amy Bridges, *A City in the Republic: Antebellum New York and the Origins of Machine Politics* (Ithaca, NY, 1987); Steven P. Erie, *Rainbow's End: Irish-Americans and the Dilemmas of Urban Machine Politics, 1840–1985* (Berkeley, Calif., 1988); and Iver Bernstein, *The New York City Draft Riots: Their Significance for American Society and Politics in the Age of the Civil War* (New York, 1990).
30 *New York Times*, 19 November 1865.

Apparently, O'Gorman's close relations with leading Swallowtail Democrats, such as Samuel Tilden and Charles O'Conor, saved him from Tweed's disgrace. Although no longer corporation counsel, he remained president of the state's immigration commissioners, expanded his lucrative private law practice, and, ironically, by 1876 had become a leading spokesman for one of the city Democracy's anti-Tammany or 'reform' factions. The Times's personal hostility continued, but neither its frequent reiteration of old scandals, nor its new charge in 1877 that O'Gorman had swindled orphans whose estate he managed,[31] prevented his nomination by all Democratic factions for a superior court judgeship and his election in 1882. O'Gorman's elevation to the bench, bastion of property and order during the class-conflict ridden 1880s, evidently stifled even the Times's virulent criticisms — perhaps especially after 1886, when O'Gorman helped elect as mayor the wealthy Swallowtail and Tammany nominee Abram S. Hewitt, by persuading at least some Irish Catholics not to support the independent candidacy of Henry George, radical reformer and hero to class-conscious Irish workers.

In any case, after 1882 and until his death the Times reported only the 'society' weddings of O'Gorman's children and the lavish testimonial dinners at Delmonico's and the Lotos Club occasioned by his retirement from the superior court in 1890.[32] By the time of O'Gorman's death in 1895, the Times recalled only his 'patriotism' during the Civil War and described him as a 'distinguished jurist and orator'.[33] Even after the panic of 1893 and the distribution of much of his wealth to his four married children, O'Gorman's estate at death still amounted to over $75,000.[34] His funeral at fashionable St. Francis Xavier church, like his children's weddings and his testimonial dinners, was attended by a cross-section of the city's Anglo- and Irish-American political, social, and religious leaders, the latter including Archbishop Michael Corrigan, banker Eugene Kelly, jurist Charles P. Daly, and William R. Grace, shipping magnate and New York's first Irish Catholic mayor, as well as a host of lesser politicians, the trustees of the Irish Emigrant Industrial Savings Bank, and representatives from Irish-American societies ranging from the élite Friendly Sons of St. Patrick to more plebeian veterans' and militia companies.[35] In 1858 his old Young Ireland comrade Michael Doheny had described O'Gorman as 'sharp as a chisel and equally keen in his race for money'.[36] Financially as well as politically, O'Gorman had won his race. Clearly, the course had turned out to be much more devious than he had imagined as an idealistic and rebellious youth, but, as he wrote to Smith O'Brien in 1859, O'Gorman had left that 'honest fellow' far 'behind [him] in Ireland'.

31 e.g., New York Times, 5 September 1877.
32 New York Times, 28 December 1888, 1 March 1889, 21 and 24 December 1890, 23 January 1891, and 12 April 1893.
33 New York Times, 2 March 1895.
34 New York Times, 6 March 1895.
35 New York Times, 5 March 1895.
36 Michael Doheny, New York City, to William Smith O'Brien, [Dromoland, Cahirmoyle, County Clare?], 20 August 1858 (Ms. 446, no. 3058, NLI).

The Rushes and the O'Gormans in the Making of Irish America

Ordinary Irish immigrants, especially western peasants such as Mary and Michael Rush, brought to America a culture that was in rapid, even traumatic transition between tradition and modernity. On the one hand, their sense of identity was profoundly localistic and familial, bound to specific communities, landscapes, and folkways that were expressed primarily in the Irish language and were often pre-Christian in origin. On the other hand, since the late eighteenth century even the townlands of western Ireland were increasingly assimilated into an international capitalist economy and a cosmopolitan religious and political culture. The steady commercialization of Irish agriculture and the spread of markets, fairs, shops, branch banks, and cottage industries had all made Irish country folk more dependent on a cash economy; the growing influence of the Catholic clergy had begun to formalize and institutionalize rural religious practices and beliefs; and the political agitations of the United Irishmen (1790s), of Daniel O'Connell (1823–47), and of Young Ireland (1842–48) had broadened and sharpened the peasants' archaic resentments against Protestant landlords and British officials.

Yet the results of change were mixed and often contradictory. The violent activities of the Whiteboys and other secret agrarian societies stemmed primarily from the growing socio-economic conflict over land-use *within* the rural Catholic community: a conflict that ranged poor subsistence cultivators and landless labourers like Michael Rush against relatively affluent, profit-seeking strong farmers, graziers, and their middle-class urban and clerical allies — many of whom, like Richard O'Gorman, were active Irish nationalists. By contrast, although nationalist rhetoric played upon the peasants' material grievances, as well as on their centuries-old resentments against the *Sasanaigh*, bourgeois nationalists and their clerical auxiliaries sought to unite all Irish Catholics across social divisions and under middle-class leadership. Indeed, Young Irelanders such as O'Gorman even tried to assimilate Catholics and Protestants in a comprehensive Irish identity that would suppress sectarian as well as class conflicts.

Popular attitudes towards emigration, even to the 'promised land' of the United States, were equally diverse. Thomas Barrett's departure in the early 1820s indicates that many rural Catholics, like their Ulster Protestant predecessors, were beginning to accept the imperatives of an international labour market and coming to view emigration to the New World as escape or opportunity. Likewise, despite the political circumstances that compelled his own voyage overseas, clearly Richard O'Gorman — like most middle-class Irish — personally viewed emigration in positive, materialistic terms. By contrast, Mary Rush's long hesitation may have reflected most country folk's traditional belief that Irish emigration was unwilling exile, forced by cruel fate or English oppression, which epitomized communal tragedy and likely produced only personal sorrow. During the Great Famine, rural Irish experiences of mass evictions and starvation, and of inadequate or injurious British government policies, easily corroborated the old popular conviction that Irish emigration was tantamount to political banishment. In America, likewise, the high mortality rates and the poverty and prejudice the Famine Irish suffered in New York and elsewhere threatened to confirm their worst fears and alienate the newcomers from the land of their adoption — or at least from its Protestant ruling classes — while in turn the peasants' religion and transplanted customs, even their physical appearance, only fuelled American nativist prejudices and political movements.

In a sense, the dilemma of the Irish immigrant bourgeoisie in mid-nineteenth-century America was similar to the one their peers had to resolve in Ireland itself. In the face of Protestant prejudice and exclusion, middle-class Irish Americans learned they could not gain status in their adopted country until they had organized the immigrant masses both politically and culturally: the former to gain leverage in the US political and economic arenas; the latter to impose on them bourgeois norms in order to reassure America's Anglo-Protestant élites that the Irish as a group were sufficiently 'civilized' to merit such influence. Conversely, if members of the Irish-American bourgeoisie were to establish cultural authority over the Irish-American working class, the reality, or at least the prospect, of their own acceptance in native society was essential. For not until they were themselves empowered could members of the Irish-American middle class offer 'successful models' for lower-class immigrants' emulation and provide benefits to the latter trickling downwards: either material benefits, in the forms of employment, subcontracts, minor offices, charity, and other kinds of economic and political patronage; or at least the psychological satisfaction that ordinary immigrants might derive from watching their alleged 'champions' surmount the barriers erected by the defenders of Yankee Protestant privilege.

Thus, the project of bourgeois Irish Americans such as Richard O'Gorman was to break the cycle of alienation and conflict: to both mobilize and 'tame' the Mary and Michael Rushes by uniting them politically behind middle-class leadership and by 'uplifting' them socially and culturally according to middle-class standards. In these respects, O'Gorman was an ideal ethnic leader for a people in transition. As a figure of inherited Irish status, he could marshal the residual deference of transplanted peasants, and as a lawyer and politician, he could command the legal knowledge and the sources of patronage that the immigrants needed to survive or succeed in a hostile environment. As a corrupt opportunist, O'Gorman not only reflected his own complete assimilation to the social mores of Gilded Age America, but he also demonstrated to poor but ambitious immigrants a way to adapt to nineteenth-century capitalism, so as to exploit in New York the economic and political opportunities denied them in Ireland.

Perhaps most important, as a real political exile, as well as a practising Catholic, O'Gorman could symbolize and speak to the poor Famine immigrants' resentments against England and the Irish and American Protestant establishments alike, while demonstrating through his achievements that the legacy of English and Ascendancy oppression in Ireland, and the burden of nativist hostility in America, could be overcome. For despite his literal banishment, and unlike fellow fugitives such as Doheny, O'Gorman was typical of most middle-class Irish Americans who desired upward mobility and assimilation to American bourgeois society, and who, like the Irish-American Catholic clergy, regarded real or radical (versus rhetorical or opportunistic) manifestations of Irish-American nationalism — as well as class conflict and traditional peasant customs — with studied aversion, aware as they were that such practices offended Anglo-American sensibilities and, by association, impeded their own prospects for advancement. Consequently, O'Gorman's function was to utilize traditional-peasant and tribal symbols to mobilize ordinary immigrants for distinctly modern-bourgeois and ultimately assimilative ends. Ideally, in return Mary Rush and other members of the Irish-American working classes would gain, materially at best or vicariously at least, from the social and political ascent of the bourgeoisie and from the entire group's consequent integration into native American society and culture. Redefined and sanitized, 'Irishness' would be reaffirmed yet made fully compatible with being 'American'.

Of course, the immigrant bourgeoisie faced great difficulties in creating a self-conscious Irish America, while also winning acceptance in native society. In New York itself, for example, on the one hand, their initial success under Boss Tweed collapsed in ruin and increased group opprobrium that threatened even O'Gorman's status. On the other hand, the Draft and Orange–Green riots, as well as continued class conflict, demonstrated the dangers of group mobilization and the fragility of middle-class influence over the city's Irish-American proletariat. However, formal political organizations, such as Tammany Hall, increasingly institutionalized, deflected, and tempered ethnic and other social conflicts; in 1886 Henry George's failed mayoralty campaign was the last major Irish working-class challenge to bourgeois and clerical hegemony; and by the time of O'Gorman's death in 1895 the Irish-American middle class had succeeded in safely assimilating Irish symbols and interests to the imperatives of the American socio-economic and political order and, more specifically, of the Democratic party and the Catholic Church, which represented that order to the immigrant masses. In turn, the growing influence of those increasingly Irish-dominated institutions channelled Irish working-class aspirations, nationalist dreams, and (sanitized) residual customs into forms that most native-Protestant Americans considered legitimate, harmless, or quaint. It is fair to speculate as to the implications of O'Gorman's shady example for the deeper meanings of both American and Irish-American societies, cultures, and identities. However, his eulogy by the New York Times, and the gathering at his funeral by representatives of the native-Protestant and Irish-American élites alike, clearly indicated that, by the time of O'Gorman's death, the despised children of the Famine had become, at least by association, whatever it meant to be called 'good Americans'.

13 For 'Love and Liberty':
Irishwomen, Migration, and Domesticity in Ireland and America,
1815–1929

Before the late 1970s, few historians had studied women's roles in the history of Ireland, of Irish migration, or of Irish America. Since then, however, scholars such as Joseph Lee, Mary Cullen, David Fitzpatrick, Rita Rhodes, and Joanna Bourke have written about women in nineteenth- and twentieth-century Ireland, and Hasia Diner and Janet Nolan have published important books about Irishwomen's emigration and their lives in the United States.[1]

1   This chapter was published originally, with the same title, in Patrick O'Sullivan, ed., *The Irish World Wide: History, Heritage, Identity. Volume 4: Irish Women and Irish Migration* (London, 1995). I am grateful to Paddy O'Sullivan for his editorial work on the original essay, and to Leicester University Press for permission to republish it, enlarged and revised, in this volume. Thanks also to Joanna Bourke, Malcolm Campbell, Hasia Diner, Deirdre Mageean, and to the late Susan Porter Benson for their helpful comments on the initial drafts. I am particularly grateful to professors David Fitzpatrick of Trinity College, Dublin, Patricia Kelleher of the Kutztown University of Pennsylvania, and David N. Doyle of University College, Dublin, for ideas, information, and research leads that contributed greatly to the interpretations and evidence presented here; hence the formal authorship of the first published version as 'with' Doyle and Kelleher. Finally, I am grateful to Dr. Patricia Trainor O'Malley of Bradford, Massachusetts, for allowing me to include in this revision quotations from her ancestors' correspondence — unavailable when the original essay was written.

For a review of the historical literature on Irishwomen, see David Fitzpatrick, 'Women, Gender and the Writing of Irish History', *Irish Historical Studies*, 28, 107 (May 1991), 267–73. Two important works, published after Fitzpatrick's survey, are: Rita M. Rhodes, *Women and the Family in Post-Famine Ireland: Status and Opportunity in a Patriarchal Society* (New York, 1992); and Joanna Bourke, *Husbandry to Housewifery: Women, Economic Change, and Housework in Ireland, 1890–1914* (New York, 1993). On Irish-American women, see Hasia R. Diner, *Erin's Daughters in America: Irish Immigrant Women in the Nineteenth Century* (Baltimore, Md., 1983); and Janet R. Nolan, *Ourselves Alone: Women's Emigration from Ireland, 1885–1920* (Lexington, Ky., 1989).

Several major themes and debates have emerged from this scholarship. First, with regard to the 'push factors' or Irish causes of female emigration, most scholars conclude that the reason comparatively few women left Ireland between 1815 and 1844 was that their status in pre-Famine rural society was relatively favourable. For example, although women's waged labour was less varied, extensive, and remunerative after the Napoleonic Wars than during the relatively prosperous half-century prior to 1815, their economic contributions to their families' incomes and welfare were still very significant and highly valued. Thus, despite the rapid mechanization and urbanization of flax spinning, which sharply curtailed rural women's waged work in cottage industry, spinning for local consumption continued to earn crucial shillings in many poor households. More important, female labour in waged fieldwork and in dairying, pig- and poultry-raising was vitally necessary on the multitude of small, semi-subsistence farms where tenants engaged largely in the production of potatoes and other tillage crops. Among farm labourers, who comprised the largest classes in pre-Famine society, women's economic contributions were even more substantial. Mary Cullen estimates that the earnings of labourers' wives from spinning, farm work and, in hard times, begging accounted for at least 15 per cent of their families' incomes, rising to over 35 per cent when their husbands lacked steady employment — as was usually the case.[2] Also, prior to the Famine small farmers and cottier tenants commonly practised partible inheritance, which, coupled with the high value placed on wives' wage-earning abilities, ensured ample opportunities for marriage — and at relatively early ages — for rural women among all but a small minority of affluent tenants, strong farmers and graziers, who practised impartible inheritance and restricted marriage through the dowry system. For instance, Kevin O'Neill's analysis of the 1841 census data from Killashandra parish, County Cavan, an area dominated by smallholdings, indicates that on average farmers' wives had married at the age of 21.7, labourers' wives at 22.3.[3] Furthermore, although the average marriage age was rising during the depressed pre-Famine decades (David Fitzpatrick estimates that the average marriage age of Irishwomen born in 1821 was 26.2), celibacy rates were low, relative to post-Famine patterns. In 1841 only 12.5

This revised essay is also informed by recent work, especially: Patricia Kelleher, 'Young Irish Workers: Class Implications of Men's and Women's Experiences in Gilded Age Chicago', in Kevin Kenny, ed., *New Directions in Irish-American History* (Madison, Wisc., 2003), 185–208; Janet Nolan, *Servants of the Poor: Teachers and Mobility in Ireland and Irish America* (Notre Dame, Ind., 2004); and Margaret Lynch-Brennan, 'Ubiquitous Biddy: Irish Immigrant Women in Domestic Service in America, 1840–1930' (PhD diss., University of Albany, State University of New York, 2002), a summary of which is in J. J. Lee and Marion Casey, eds., *Making the Irish American: History and Heritage in the United States* (New York, 2006), 332–53.

2 Mary Cullen, 'Breadwinners and Providers: Women in the Household Economy of Labouring Families, 1835–36', in Maria Luddy and Cliona Murphy, eds., *Women Surviving: Studies in Irish Women's History in the 19th and 20th Centuries* (Dublin, 1990), 98–99, 106–11.

3 Kevin O'Neill, *Family and Farm in Pre-Famine Ireland: The Parish of Killashandra* (Madison, Wisc., 1985), 178–84.

per cent of Irishwomen aged 45–54 had never married.[4] The result, most historians
conclude, was that rural women were generally able, encouraged, and content to remain
in early nineteenth-century Ireland, and so, prior to the Great Famine, Irish emigration
to North America was predominantly (about two thirds) male.[5]

However, nearly all scholars also argue that after mid-century, in the post-Famine
period, 1850s–1920s, a great increase in female emigration occurred because the
socio-economic status of rural Irishwomen deteriorated dramatically. High rates of
mortality and emigration during and immediately after the Famine decimated the
poorest classes which had practised partible inheritance and to whose economic
survival women had contributed most heavily. Likewise, after mid-century women's
wage-earning opportunities contracted sharply because of the continued de-
industrialization of the Irish countryside and because economic pressures and
demographic change caused major shifts from subsistence to commercial agriculture
and from tillage to pasture farming, both trends coupled with a fall in the production
and consumption of potatoes, which were increasingly replaced by bread and other
store-bought goods in the farmers' diets. Accompanying these economic changes was a
shift among small-farm families from partible to impartible inheritance, which, linked
to their declining wage-earning capacities, meant that women (and men) were not only
obliged to marry less frequently and at later ages than in the pre-Famine past, but that
their choices of marriage partners were determined and restricted by the dowry system,
enforced by their fathers and reinforced by codes of female subordination and sexual
repression purveyed by a patriarchal Catholic Church. Thus, according to Fitzpatrick,
'after the famine the daughters and wives of farmers steadily retreated from the process
of production'; their socio-economic status declined commensurately, to the point
where the dowry 'may be treated as a fine for the transfer of a redundant dependent
female from one family to another'.[6] As a result, between 1845 and 1914 Ireland's annual
marriage rate fell from 7 to 4 per 1,000; by 1926 the average marital age had risen to 29
for women (to 35 for men), and nearly a fourth of Irishwomen aged 45–54 had never
married.[7] In addition, by eradicating customary, magical, and often female-centred
expressions of popular religion, the increasing institutionalization of post-Famine
Catholicism, within the confines of a male-dominated Church, likely eroded rural
women's traditional status in less tangible ways. The consequence of all these changes
was massive post-Famine emigration by young, unmarried women, whose numbers

4 David Fitzpatrick, 'The Modernisation of the Irish Female', in Patrick O'Flanagan, Paul Ferguson,
   and Kevin Whelan, eds., Rural Ireland, 1600–1900: Modernisation and Change (Cork, 1987), 167–69.
5 On pre-Famine Irish society and emigration, generally, see Kerby A. Miller, Emigrants and Exiles: Ireland and
   the Irish Exodus to North America (New York, 1985), 26–101, 193–252; as well as Chapter 2 in this volume.
6 Fitzpatrick, 'Modernisation of the Irish Female', 166–69.
7 Miller, Emigrants and Exiles, 403–04. Irish celibacy in 1926 computed from W. E. Vaughan and
   A. J. Fitzpatrick, eds., Irish Historical Statistics: Population, 1821–1971 (Dublin, 1978), 91.

equalled and often exceeded those of Irish emigrant males in the late nineteenth and early twentieth centuries.[8]

Second, with regard to the 'pull factors' in Irishwomen's emigration, all scholars agree that late nineteenth- and early twentieth-century America's attractions — as advertised in emigrants' letters, for example — exacerbated Irishwomen's dissatisfaction with their limited economic and marital opportunities at home and accelerated their migration overseas. However, American historians disagree as to which specific motives and goals were preeminent. Hasia Diner argues that Irish females consciously rejected Irish male domination and emigrated as ambitious individuals seeking economic independence through waged labour, usually as domestic servants in American cities. In evidence, she demonstrates that Irishwomen in the United States had significantly lower marriage rates, and married at older ages, than did other immigrant women. According to Diner, these Irish-American marital patterns not only reflected cultural continuity with rural Ireland but, more important, indicated that 'economic motives for migration were paramount. Irishwomen did not migrate primarily to find the husbands they could not find at home.' Otherwise, Diner argues, Irishwomen would not have settled so often in eastern US cities where they so heavily outnumbered Irishmen as to inhibit their opportunities for endogamous marriage.[9] In contrast, Janet Nolan contends that Irishwomen did indeed emigrate principally to recover overseas the lost opportunities for frequent, early marriage that their grandmothers had enjoyed in pre-Famine Ireland. Ironically, to support her interpretation Nolan employs two assertions which Diner made but downplayed in her earlier work: that in the United States Irish immigrant women's marital rates were higher, and marriage ages and celibacy rates were lower, than among females who remained in post-Famine Ireland; and that Irish-American marital patterns were little different from those of native-born Americans.[10]

Yet Diner and Nolan provide little or no evidence to prove either of those assertions. Diner's Irish-American data is fragmentary, often contradictory, and drawn primarily from studies of small northeastern mill towns whose Irish-born populations were unusually female-dominated. For example, although Diner's evidence from late nineteenth-century Pittsburgh indicates that Irish celibacy rates in that city were much lower than in contemporary Ireland, and although she cites statistical surveys of Massachusetts in 1890–1900 that suggest the essential similarity of Irish-immigrant and native-born marital behaviour, her data from other locales, such as Cohoes, New York,

---

8   On post-Famine Irish society and emigration, generally, see Miller, *Emigrants and Exiles*, 345–426. However, this is not to say that the ratio of female to male emigrants rose consistently after the Great Famine. Professor David Fitzpatrick of Trinity College, Dublin, concludes that that ratio was 100 in the early 1850s, falling to 74 by 1870, rising to 116 by 1900, and then declining to 90 on the eve of the First World War; Fitzpatrick believes that these data suggest that changes in sex-specific demands for migrant workers were at least as influential as changes in post-Famine Irishwomen's socio-economic status (Fitzpatrick, Dublin, letter to author, 12 February 1992).

9   Diner, *Erin's Daughters in America*, 50 and *passim*.

10 Nolan, *Ourselves Alone*, 74–75 and *passim*; Diner, *Erin's Daughters in America*, 46–47.

in 1880, suggest that in factory towns with Irish workforces that were overwhelmingly female, Irish immigrant women married less often and at later ages than their sisters in Ireland.[11] Moreover, Nolan's argument for greater marital opportunities in America is scarcely supported at all, except by a dubious analogy with Irish practices in mid-nineteenth-century London and by a handful of personal reminiscences by elderly Irish-American women.[12]

Thus, despite their apparently universal acceptance, the assumptions that post-Famine Irishwomen married more often and earlier in the United States than in Ireland, and that Irish female immigrants' marital patterns were converging with those of native-born Americans, must be considered highly likely but as yet unproven.[13] Rather than attempt the broad statistical study necessary to prove either hypothesis conclusively, this chapter will employ other kinds of evidence, primarily Irish female emigrants' letters and memoirs, to interrogate both the accepted and the contested interpretations of the causes and goals of Irishwomen's emigration. This is still a novel field of study, and the following arguments are by no means definitive but hopefully will suggest alternative perspectives and new avenues of research.

The first and broadest point is that no single model or interpretation can apply to all female emigrants from Ireland, either before or after the Great Famine. Arguably, the ultimate determinants of gender roles and relationships are sexual divisions of labour, which in turn vary greatly among different socio-economic classes and cultures.[14] If Irish and Irish-American historians had access to the detailed documentation available

---

11 Diner, *Erin's Daughters in America*, 46–49.

12 Nolan, *Ourselves Alone*, 74–75.

13 The only detailed statistical comparison of Irish and Irish-American (and of Irish-, German-, and white native-born American) marriage and celibacy patterns is Timothy Guinnane, 'Marriage, Migration, and Household Formation: The Irish at the Turn of the Century' (PhD diss., Stanford University, 1989); since published as *The Vanishing Irish: Households, Migration, and the Rural Economy in Ireland, 1850–1914* (Princeton, NJ, 1997). However, Guinnane focuses primarily on male nuptiality, concluding that Irish celibacy in the United States (1900) was well below that for Ireland (1901), but significantly higher than for German- or white native-Americans. According to David Fitzpatrick, among women aged 45–54 in 1900, 13 per cent of Irish-born women in the United States were unmarried, compared with 22 per cent of those who remained in Ireland; yet only 3 per cent of similarly aged German-born women and 8 per cent of white native-born women in America were not married. However, these statistics apply to women born shortly before and after 1850, who emigrated *c.* 1870, and the marital experiences of later cohorts of Irish-born women are still unknown (Fitzpatrick, Dublin, letter to author, 12 February 1992).

14 Nancy A. Hewitt, 'Beyond the Search for Sisterhood: American Women's History in the 1880s', in Ellen Carol DuBois and Vicki L. Ruiz, eds., *Unequal Sisters: A Multicultural Reader in U.S. Women's History* (New York, 1990), 11 and *passim*.

to Scandinavian scholars, and could they trace large numbers of specific women from rural Ireland to the United States, it is highly probable they would discover that women from different class, regional, and cultural backgrounds in Ireland had significantly different patterns of and motives for emigration and significantly different work and marital experiences in different regions of the New World. Lacking such evidence, historians have inadvertently homogenized the lives and attitudes of the daughters of commercial farmers in south Leinster, landless labourers in north Munster, mill workers in east Ulster, and Irish-speaking peasants in west Connacht — thereby obscuring these and other crucial distinctions that governed relationships and shaped outlooks in a highly localistic, family-centred, and status-conscious society.[15] For example, even in the early 1900s marital rates remained higher, and marriage ages and celibacy rates were lower, in Ireland's impoverished western counties than in the rest of the island.[16] Thus, it is possible that women from those counties married abroad less frequently and later than females who remained in western Ireland, especially if they settled in the northeastern United States where economic and marital prospects were comparatively poor. By contrast, females from eastern Ireland, where celibacy rates were highest, almost certainly improved their marriage opportunities by emigrating, particularly if they moved to midwestern or western US cities where both economic conditions and gender ratios favoured matrimony. Also, it is very likely that important differences would emerge if scholars could determine the relative positions of emigrant women in the structures and dynamics of their respective Irish families. For instance, whether a woman was an older or younger daughter, or whether she had many — or any — male or female siblings, might determine her expectations and outlooks as to marriage and emigration. Equally crucial, such issues might determine her age at emigration, or her educational attainments and work experiences prior to emigration, which in turn would affect her economic and marital chances overseas.

A more specific issue is whether rural women in the early nineteenth century indeed enjoyed a social status so favourable as to explain the relative paucity of female emigration from pre-Famine Ireland. Mary Cullen contends that no one paradigm of pre-Famine gender relations clearly applies — 'whether that of an oppressor–oppressed relationship between men and women or of a one-to-one relationship between economic contribution on the one hand and status on the other'.[17] However, much evidence suggests that the condition of rural women, married or unmarried, was far from advantageous. Contemporaries remarked repeatedly that both in

---

15 This point is also made by Rhodes, in *Women and the Family in Post-Famine Ireland*, 126–81, where she distinguishes among the experiences and expectations of women in three types of rural families in post-Famine Ireland: those of commercial farmers; of subsistence smallholders, especially in the western counties; and of agricultural labourers.

16 Damian F. Hannan, 'Peasant Models and the Understanding of Social and Cultural Change in Rural Ireland', in P. J. Drudy, ed., *Irish Studies 2. Ireland: Land, Politics and People* (Cambridge, 1982), 150–51.

17 Cullen, 'Breadwinners and Providers', 114.

agriculture and in cottage industry pre-Famine Irishwomen worked 'more like slaves than labourers', treated by their menfolk as 'beasts of burden'.[18] Judging from a variety of sources, ranging from parliamentary commission reports to William Carleton's short stories, It seems obvious that prior to the Great Famine Irishwomen made major economic contributions to their households' survival because they had no other choice. Small farmers' and labourers' families, roughly 70 per cent of the rural population, were struggling for mere subsistence, and many Irishmen were underemployed or unemployed and, by many accounts, often failed to embrace bourgeois norms of exertion and sobriety. Thus, Ann McNabb, a Famine emigrant from County Londonderry, later remembered that her father's alcoholism had obliged her mother to thatch the family's peat-walled cabin, a task normally considered 'men's work'; in addition, she recalled, 'My mother an' me an' [my sister] Tilly we worked in the field for Squire Varney ... plowin' an' seedin' an' diggin' — any farm work he'd give us. We did men's work, but we didn't get men's pay.'[19] Likewise, the evidence on the favourable character of pre-Famine marriages is very insubstantial. Contemporaries described the wives of small farmers and labourers as drudges and slaves, 'oppressed by their husbands and living in affectionless marriages',[20] and the era's emigrant letters reveal far more romantic sentiments among men and women in the urban and even the rural middle classes than among ordinary farmers and peasants, and far more cold calculations as to matrimony among the latter than the former. Among the rural poor, too, alcoholism and its socio-economic consequences, including wife-abuse and desertion, appear to have been common, which makes it unsurprising that in the 1830s and early 1840s Irishwomen enthusiastically embraced Fr. Mathew's temperance crusade, perhaps finding more consolation and protection in the institutional Church than in popular religion's eroding folkways. Moreover, when poor, pre-Famine Irishwomen were unable to contribute positively to family incomes, they simply reduced their intake of food, allowing their husbands and sons to consume a disproportionate share of their families' meagre diets.[21] In short, most evidence indicates that women's status in pre-Famine Ireland was one of subjugation and that their economic contributions were inseparable from grinding poverty and backbreaking toil. If women in these conditions had any economic power, it was largely by default, and the only alternative power — that of Carleton's fictional 'big lump' of a peasant woman, who physically beat her husband in return for his abuse — was available only to an unusually strong and well-nourished few.

Indeed, the failure of pre-Famine women to emigrate in greater numbers may have been a direct or indirect result of their subjugated condition in early nineteenth-century Ireland, rather than a reflection of their allegedly high status and contentment.

18 Miller, Emigrants and Exiles, 58, 406.
19 'The Story of an Irish Cook', Independent [New York], 58, no. 2939 (30 March 1905), 715.
20 Cullen, 'Breadwinners and Providers', 112.
21 Rhodes, Women and the Family in Post-Famine Ireland, 24–25.

For example, in Irish experience there is a strong, positive correlation between literacy and emigration, and as late as 1841 Irish females (above age 5) were over two and one-half times more likely to be illiterate than were Irish males. Among those aged between 15 and 24, the most likely years of emigration, less than 27 per cent of Irishwomen were literate, compared to over 47 per cent of Irishmen. Not until after 1850 would female literacy and emigration rise in tandem, eclipsing male rates in both respects by the century's end. Also, before the Famine there appears to have been a high, negative correlation between Irish-speaking and emigration, and as late as 1861 Irishwomen were twice as likely as Irishmen to be bilingual or monolingual Irish-speakers.[22] As noted previously, both illiteracy and Irish-speaking insulated Irishwomen from America's advertised attractions. Both also reflected women's markedly inferior educational opportunities in pre-Famine Ireland, and both probably reinforced a cultural conservatism that may also have inhibited emigration. In addition, illiteracy and ignorance of English may have made pre-Famine Irishwomen less marketable in America than were their menfolk, for whom such deficiencies mattered little when applying for jobs as unskilled labourers digging canals or loading cargoes. By contrast, except among southern slaves, female strength in rough, outdoor labour was reportedly less utilized in the United States than in Ireland; indeed, one Irish-American farmer even claimed that 'It would be considered a wonder to see a woman in the States Carry water or milk Cows.'[23] Furthermore, early nineteenth-century America's urban-industrial economies were not yet sufficiently large or mature to generate the huge demand for great numbers of unskilled Irish female domestic servants and factory workers that would begin to develop around mid-century. And, finally, not until the 1840s and 1850s did massive Irish Catholic immigration and urban settlement begin to create the large and relatively stable Irish-American Catholic communities that could absorb great numbers of unmarried Irishwomen into familial and institutional networks.[24]

That last point raises a related and central issue. Save for runaways, Irish emigration was usually based on *family* — not *individual* — decisions: for example, choices by Irish parents as to which of their children to send or allow to go abroad first; and choices by Irish Americans as to which of their siblings, cousins, or other relatives to encourage and assist to emigrate and join them.[25] The cautious tone of early nineteenth-century emigrants' letters indicates that such decisions were more crucial in the pre-Famine era than later, because in these decades Catholic emigration from most parts of Ireland was

---

22 Fitzpatrick, 'Modernisation of the Irish Female', 164–65, 174–76. Data on Irish-speakers compiled from the 1861 Irish census, part 2: Report and Tables on Ages and Education, vol. 1, BBP, HC 1863, lvii, 49.
23 Miller, *Emigrants and Exiles*, 407.
24 Miller, *Emigrants and Exiles*, 263–79. Also see David N. Doyle, 'The Irish in North America, 1776–1845', in W. E. Vaughan, ed., *A New History of Ireland, V: Ireland under the Union I, 1801–1870* (Oxford, 1989), 682–725.
25 Rhodes, *Women and the Family in Post-Famine Ireland*, esp. 257–70, also argues that Irish migration decisions should be viewed as strategic choices, made primarily by parents within the context of the rural family economy.

just beginning, and most Irish families' first beachheads in America were just being established. Consequently, and given the female disabilities mentioned above, Irish parents or other relatives already settled in the United States were much more likely to send or bring over the strongest, most highly skilled, best-educated, and hence most marketable male emigrants — those deemed most likely to survive, succeed, and, most important to those who remained in Ireland, send back the remittances that would pay rents, purchase necessities, and establish the patterns of chain migration that would enable nearly all future Irish Catholic departures. From her parents' perspective, not only was it riskier to send a daughter to America because of her relatively limited economic marketability, but also the likelihood of her dropping quickly out of the marketplace by marrying into one of early nineteenth-century America's predominantly male Irish communities was very high. From the viewpoint of her parents and of others waiting at home to emigrate, that might be disastrous, for marriage abroad usually would end a woman's willingness or ability to remit money to relatives in Ireland. Thus, as a later emigrant warned her mother, 'when I do get married I Suppose I will be like the rest [and] not write at all and as little as I send home now you will get nothing then'.[26] In light of these circumstances, it is surprising that no scholars have interpreted the low rates of Irish female emigration in the early nineteenth century as evidence that pre-Famine Ireland was a *more* repressively patriarchal and male-dominated society than it later became — a society in which unmarried women and would-be emigrants like Margaret Wright, a poor spinster in County Tyrone, felt trapped by 'dependen[ce] on the[ir] mercenary and covetous [male relations] for a miserable and wretched support'.[27]

Conversely, it is questionable whether the massive emigration of young, unmarried women from post-Famine Ireland indeed reflected a marked deterioration in their status since the early nineteenth century. To be sure, after the Famine Irishwomen's wage-earning opportunities and economic contributions to household incomes greatly declined both outside and inside the home, in agriculture and cottage industry alike. As a result, increasingly their contributions to the family economy were confined to unpaid housework and to the bearing and rearing of future heirs and emigrants. Certainly, too, the dearth of waged employment for women, coupled with the shifts among nearly all landholding families to impartible inheritance and the dowry system,

26 Julia Lough, Winsted, Conn., to her mother, Meelick, Queen's County, 3 September 1893, in the Lough family letters, 1876–1927 (courtesy of Edward Dunne and Mrs. Kate Tynan, Portlaoise, County Laois, and Canice and Eilish O'Mahony, Dundalk, County Louth). Similarly, domestic servant Hannah Collins wrote that, although she wanted to marry, 'I have to send some money to my dear Parents once and a while and if I get married I can't send them any'; Hannah Collins, Elmira, NY, to Nora McCarthy, Haverhill, Mass., 21 February 1900 (courtesy of Dr. Patricia Trainor O'Malley, Bradford, Mass.; hereafter O'Malley collection).
27 Margaret Wright, Aughintober, County Tyrone, to Alexander McNish, Salem, NY, 27 May 1808 (McNish Papers, Cornell University Library, Ithaca, NY); since published in Kerby A. Miller, *et al.*, *Irish Immigrants in the Land of Canaan: Letters and Memoirs from Colonial and Revolutionary America, 1675–1815* (New York, 2003), 45–50.

made it much more difficult for rural women (and men) to marry, to marry early, and to marry spouses of their own choosing. Likewise, it would be mistaken simply to reverse established interpretations by arguing that post-Famine women's emigration signified their liberation from pre-Famine repression. For in the late nineteenth century, as before, most decisions concerning emigration were made in the contexts of international labour markets and of Irish and Irish-American families' economic strategies, the terms of which now encouraged, as formerly they had discouraged, women's migration overseas. The result, as Annie O'Donnell from west Galway lamented, was that '[a]s soon as a boy or girl gets big enough to help the house, he [or she] is *forced* to leave ...'[28]

However, whereas it may be fruitless to debate whether rural women's status was higher or lower, or their subordination greater or lesser, in pre- or post-Famine Ireland, what is certain is that the parameters — and perhaps rural women's own definitions — of status and/or repression had been altered significantly. Thus, by applying to Ireland the insights of nineteenth-century women's history in the United States and other 'modernizing' societies, Joanna Bourke, a New Zealand scholar, argues persuasively that what most historians have regarded as post-Famine Irishwomen's increasing 'confinement' to a separate and inferior domestic sphere in fact enabled them — or at least those who were married — to exercise new and greater influence over their husbands and children than had been hitherto possible. Indeed, according to Bourke, women in post-Famine Ireland consciously and eagerly chose unpaid housework as wives and mothers precisely because it bestowed greater status and authority than any form of paid labour available to them (or to their pre-Famine predecessors).[29]

Bourke contends that the concentration of post-Famine women in housework reflected not only a decreased demand for female waged and/or rough outdoor labour, but, more important, it reflected rising rural incomes and the socio-cultural and psychological embourgeoisement of an Irish rural society that was increasingly dominated in all respects by affluent or aspiring farmers and shopkeepers.[30] As farming became more commercialized (and mechanized) and as middle-class or 'Victorian' tastes and aspirations spread, the home became more separate, special, and important. More capital was now available for investment in the home. Livestock and agricultural implements, formally quartered in the farmer's house, were relegated to barns and sheds. Thatched roofs were covered with slate; new rooms were added and old ones were floored and wallpapered; furniture became more ample and comfortable; and many families built new stone houses to replace mud-walled dwellings. Perhaps

28 Annie O'Donnell, Pittsburgh, Pa., to James Phelan, Indianapolis, Ind., 5 May 1902, in Maureen Murphy, ed., *Your Fondest Annie: Letters from Annie O'Donnell to James P. Phelan, 1901–1904* (Dublin, 2005), 65 (emphasis added).
29 Joanna Bourke, '"The Best of All Home Rulers": The Economic Power of Women in Ireland, 1880–1914', *Irish Economic and Social History*, 18 (1991), 24–37. The author wishes to thank Dr. Bourke for allowing him to see an earlier version of her article.
30 On post-Famine Irish society, generally, see Miller, *Emigrants and Exiles*, 380–424.

most striking were the new parlours that post-Famine farmers added to their houses. In their expensive furnishings, conspicuously displayed religious objects, and proverbially spotless cleanliness, the parlours embodied and projected to visitors their owners' new pretensions to respectability and gentility.

Contemporary literature describes post-Famine Irishwomen as dominating parlour activities, but they assumed primary responsibility for the functions and ethos of the entire domestic sphere, in the process marginalizing their husbands' influence. Of course, housework was tedious, even exhausting, and many farmers' wives also raised poultry and performed other chores outside the home.[31] For the most part, however, their new duties required not physical strength but managerial skills and a ceaseless attention to efficiency, order, cleanliness, and decorum. For example, as consumption and shop-purchases became more central to the household economy, women played more active roles in managing the increased proportion of the family earnings that was devoted to domestic needs. Likewise, the housewife's tasks expanded as the farm family's diet became more varied and elaborate. And the mother's role as nurturer of children became more crucial due to the protraction of childhood and adolescence, itself caused, in turn, by the declining need for children's labour and by the new trends towards delayed or averted marriage among both male and female offspring. Indeed, emotional ties between mothers and children in post-Famine Ireland were proverbially close, smotheringly so between mothers and sons, allegedly because of the increasing age difference and consequent emotional distance between husbands and wives — which in turn may have reinforced both the ideal and the reality of separate spheres for spouses, as well as the desexualized, 'passionless' image of the Irish mother. As a result of these developments, housework in all its varied aspects became more central to the life and self-image of Irish farm families than ever before, and married women's status and authority were enhanced by their dominion over the home and their guardianship of its values and integrity.

Of course, only the wives of fairly substantial farmers were fully able to create and rule a 'Victorian home'. Poor farmers could only approximate that goal, and among landless labourers it largely remained elusive. Nevertheless, although the new domesticity was imperfectly available, the ideal was widely disseminated through all social classes and legitimated through the cultural hegemony of the Catholic bourgeoisie, especially as incorporated in education, employer–employee relations, and religion. Bourke and other scholars have demonstrated that after the Famine, greatly expanded opportunities for women's education accompanied their withdrawal from the marketplace. The daughters of affluent farmers imbibed order and refinement in new convent schools, often staffed by nuns from France, but even girls from poorer families became literate

---

31 Joanna Bourke, 'Women and Poultry in Ireland, 1891–1914', *Irish Historical Studies*, 25, 99 (May 1987), 293–310.

and learned domestic skills and bourgeois values from exposure to public education.[32] Likewise, domestic service in middle-class households was an important stage in the lifecycle of many adolescent females in the Irish countryside.[33] This institution served at least two functions: it exposed the daughters of poor farmers and labourers to bourgeois norms and habits of domesticity; and the regulation of lower-class servants confirmed middle-class women's 'superior' status and values, especially through the enforcement of Victorian codes of sexual morality on their dependants.[34] Most important of all was the influence of the Irish Catholic Church. As described in earlier chapters, the clergy's goal was to create and defend a 'holy Ireland' against pernicious Protestant and secular influences. They accordingly eulogized the farm family as the foundation stone of their pious ideal — the Sacred Family, in which Mary was the central figure. Tony Fahey suggests that 'it was primarily as wife and mother that the Irish Catholic church drew on and utilized the support of laywomen, and that the church in return propped up and glorified those roles'.[35] By far the most numerous and important women's organizations in post-Famine Ireland were sodalities and other Church-centred associations. Thus, whereas most Irish historians have viewed the post-Famine Church — with its emphases on women's purity and self-sacrifice — as an engine of female subordination, from these women's perspective the Church's ideology and institutional network sanctified and hence reinforced their domestic hegemony. Their practical authority as housewives and mothers was fortified by a moral authority derived from the most powerful and pervasive institution in Irish society. It was no coincidence that when the priest came to visit an Irish farm family he was always entertained in the parlour: symbolic of the tacit alliance between the Church and the women to 'uplift' Catholic society, sacralize the home, and guard against the potential immorality or irresponsibility of their menfolk — for whom the village pubs became a last retreat.

Bourke contends that all women in post-Famine Ireland, even those who never married, were empowered to a degree by the increased importance and status of unwaged housework and the domestic sphere. Otherwise, she suggests, it is difficult to explain why so many single women remained in Ireland, instead of emigrating. However, other scholars have argued more persuasively that older, unmarried women in Ireland were generally objects of pity or scorn, despite the Church's ennobling of female self-sacrifice

32 Anne V. O'Connor, 'The Revolution in Girls' Secondary Education in Ireland, 1860–1910', in Mary Cullen, ed., Girls Don't Do Honours: Irish Women in Education in the 19th and 20th Centuries (Dublin, 1987), 31–54. Also see David Fitzpatrick, '"A Share of the Honeycomb": Education, Emigration and Irishwomen', in Mary Daly and David Dickson, eds., The Origins of Popular Literacy in Ireland: Language Change and Educational Development, 1700–1920 (Dublin, 1990), 167–87.
33 Fitzpatrick, 'Modernisation of the Irish Female', 166.
34 For example, see Mary Carbery, The Farm by Lough Gur (1937; repr. Cork, 1973). Also, Judith L. Newton, Mary P. Ryan, and Judith R. Walkowitz, eds., Sex and Class in Women's History (London, 1983), 6–9.
35 Tony Fahey, 'Nuns in the Catholic Church in the Nineteenth Century', in Cullen, Girls Don't Do Honours, 27–28; Miller, Emigrants and Exiles, 463–65.

and exaltation of celibacy, as among nuns.[36] Unmarried women may have enjoyed some respect as homeworkers in parentless 'families' of middle-aged siblings, but as unmarriageable housekeepers who had forsaken emigration to care for elderly parents, awaiting the latter's deaths to release them from perpetual adolescence, their situations were commonly viewed as pathetic. Indeed, the failure of many unmarried women to emigrate should be considered, not as evidence of their empowerment at home, but rather as indicating their subordination to their male relatives' economic strategies and, more broadly, to a cult of family and domesticity that could entrap women as well as glorify their housekeeping roles. Thus, when west Kerrywoman Peig Sayers rejected an opportunity to emigrate by concluding she would be 'more favoured with grace' if she stayed to comfort her parents' old age, she demonstrated that women's separate sphere could become a gilded cage for unmarried as well as for married women.[37]

Limited as it was, in order for a woman to exercise and enjoy the full status and authority of housework, it was essential for her to have a house and family of her own, which could be acquired only through marriage and child-bearing. These were the goals to which nearly all women aspired — both because of the enhanced and sanctified roles of wife/mother/houseworker, and because the waged alternatives for women in post-Famine Ireland were so few and bleak. Hence, it is arguable that the dowry should be viewed in part as the price a woman's parents had to pay to secure for her a marriage and domestic sphere of her own — a price paid in part to compensate her new husband's mother and unmarried sisters, whose position and authority as houseworkers she would now supplant or, from their perspective, usurp.

For post-Famine Irishwomen, the greatest disadvantage of the dowry system was not the fact (if it is a 'fact', for concrete evidence is sorely lacking) that marriages were more arranged or loveless than heretofore. Rather, the disadvantages were, first, given escalating dowry costs (itself perhaps a reflection of the increased value placed on housework),[38] most rural families could not afford the price of marriage for more than one of their several or many daughters; and, second, usually dowries or 'matches' could be arranged only between families of comparable wealth and reputation. If housework and family conferred status and authority on a woman, then the 'better' the house and family she could marry into, the more status and authority she would enjoy in a social system that linked prestige with property and propriety. However, upward mobility under the dowry system was rare (although perhaps no rarer than in pre-Famine Ireland), as few labourers' daughters were allowed to marry farmers' sons, and few smallholders' daughters could wed the offspring of graziers or strong farmers.

36 For example, see Joseph J. Lee, 'Women and the Church since the Famine', in Margaret MacCurtain and Donncha Ó Corráin, eds., Women in Irish Society: The Historical Dimension (Dublin, 1978), 37–45.
37 Miller, Emigrants and Exiles, 475.
38 It must be noted that Cormac Ó Gráda has argued that dowry costs declined between 1870 and 1910; see Ó Gráda, Ireland Before and After the Famine: Explorations in Economic History, 1800–1925 (Manchester, 1988), 167; but see Fitzpatrick, 'Women, Gender and the Writing of Irish History', 271–72.

*

It was the women whom the dowry system could not accommodate who poured overseas into American cities in the late nineteenth and early twentieth centuries: the non-dowered daughters of small farmers and the daughters of agricultural labourers, generally. However, did they emigrate primarily for economic opportunities, as Diner argues, or to secure husbands and families, as Nolan contends?

In one sense, posing the question in this way is misleading. As Rita Rhodes has written, two factors comprised the principal and 'initial impetus' for female emigration from post-Famine Ireland: economically based decisions made by patriarchal Irish families, and daughters' 'duties' (to relieve financial burdens at home and to send remittances from abroad) as conceived in traditional, self-sacrificial terms. Thus, 'Go where you will earn good money, you have wasted your time too long here' was Irish parents' archetypical injunction to daughters who, like Annie O'Donnell from Connemara, had to acknowledge, however reluctantly, that 'life was duty' and therefore they had to emigrate — although, in O'Donnell's case, 'it placed the Atlantic between me and those I loved' and 'stamped a mark on my life never to be forgotten'. Yet Rhodes also points out that many young women left home willingly, even eagerly, because female emigration stemmed as well from 'the gradual growth of a limited individualism on the part of daughters themselves' — reflected, for example, in Irishwomen's oft-expressed desires to escape the drudgery of unpaid farm work and to seek 'independence' overseas. Thus, in most instances emigration enabled young Irishwomen to reconcile traditional obligations with new individual motivations. Ironically, however, even the latter were shaped by familial values and goals that could no longer be realized in rural Ireland.[39]

In this light, Bourke's portrait of Irishwomen, of their motives and aspirations, suggests that Nolan's hypothesis appears to be the more accurate: that young Irishwomen emigrated to establish families in which they could enjoy the status and moral authority of homemakers in the separate, domestic sphere, which was eulogized in Victorian America, as in Ireland, and which was as idealized by the American Catholic Church and the emergent Irish-American bourgeoisie as by their native-born Protestant counterparts.[40] Although Irishwomen frequently migrated to eastern US cities and mill towns, where the preponderance of Irish-born females lessened their marital opportunities, such patterns do not necessarily reflect an indifference or aversion to matrimony, as Diner contends. Rather, they reflect continued patterns of earlier Irish settlement and the fact that nearly all post-Famine emigration was channelled

39 Rhodes, *Women and the Family in Post-Famine Ireland*, 257–77, quotation on 259; Annie O'Donnell, Pittsburgh, Pa., to James Phelan, Indianapolis, Ind., 25 August 1901, in Murphy, *Your Fondest Annie*, 39.
40 Diner, *Erin's Daughters in America*, 67; Colleen McDannell, *The Christian Home in Victorian America, 1840–1900* (Bloomington, Ind., 1986), 52–76, 108–55.

by existing *family* networks, as uncles and aunts, sisters and brothers sent remittances that brought Irishwomen (and men) to communities where employment opportunities for single Irish *males* (but not for females) were atrophying during the late nineteenth and early twentieth centuries.[41] After arrival in such locales, single Irish males tended to be more venturesome and mobile in search of employment or better wages, but female Irish immigrants tended to remain, under the protection of Irish relatives, unless they received specific invitations from other relations who had settled further west, in cities where Irish-American sex ratios were more favourable to endogamous marriage.

Moreover, at least according to both Diner and Nolan, Irishwomen in the United States generally married more often and at younger ages than did those who remained in Ireland. Also, the most significant impression that emerges from their American data c. 1900 is not that Irish immigrants' marital rates and ages were so different from those of Italian, Polish, or French-Canadian immigrants, but rather that they were increasingly similar to the marriage patterns of native-born Protestants. This indicates the growing convergence of bourgeois lifestyles and norms in Ireland and America, as already suggested, and also of native-Protestant and Irish-American societies in the United States. David Doyle and other scholars have already demonstrated that in the late nineteenth and early twentieth centuries Irish Americans had among the lowest rates of residential segregation and among the highest rates of suburbanization and homeownership of all ethnic groups; furthermore, by 1900–20 Irish America's occupational structure and rates of school attendance and educational achievement were almost identical to those of native-born Protestants.[42] Likewise, the fact that nearly all post-Famine immigrants spoke English, were literate to some degree, and adapted to American society through the medium of bourgeois-dominated and fervently patriotic associations (for example, the Catholic Church, the Democratic party, and Irish-American benevolent and temperance associations) also promoted Irish acculturation — as did unmarried Irish immigrant women's concentration in domestic service.[43] Thus, it is little wonder that Irishwomen's marital patterns were increasingly similar to those of native-born Protestant Americans, or dissimilar from those of southern and eastern Europeans. It was primarily in their patterns of marital fertility that Irish- and

41 Diner, Nolan, and other historians of Irishwomen's migration contend that female relatives overseas sent most of the remittances that brought their sisters, nieces, etc., to America; however, male Irish emigrants commonly sent passage tickets to their female kin, and, in reading over 6,000 emigrants' letters, I discern no gendered patterns in the remittance process.
42 Miller, *Emigrants and Exiles*, 492–501; David N. Doyle, *Irish Americans, Native Rights, and National Empires: The Structure, Divisions, and Attitudes of the Catholic Minority in the Decade of Expansion, 1890–1901* (New York, 1976), 48–49, 59–63.
43 On Irish domestic service and acculturation, see below in this chapter. On Irish-American affiliations with the Catholic church, the Democratic party, etcetera, see above, Chapter 11 in this volume. With respect to post-Famine emigrant literacy, David Fitzpatrick's research indicates that merely 29 per cent of Irish emigrant females (and 40 per cent of Irish emigrant males) were literate in 1851–60; however, by the end of the century literacy was nearly universal among the age-cohorts most prone to emigration (Fitzpatrick, Dublin, letter to author, 12 February 1992).

native-born white women still differed greatly — perhaps reflecting Irishwomen's view of large families as enhancing their domestic status and providing social insurance, as well as Church teachings regarding motherhood and the evils of contraception. However, some evidence suggests that by 1900 even Irish-American birthrates were beginning to converge with Anglo-American norms.[44]

Thus, according to Irish newspapers such as the *Cork Examiner*, during the post-Famine era 'Every [Irish] servant-maid thinks of the land of promise ... where husbands are thought more procurable than in Ireland.'[45] Moreover, the letters written by Irish immigrant women themselves indicate that the desire to marry, to marry men of their own choosing, and to have families and households of their own was a primary motive for coming to the United States. In their letters, for example, Nora McCarthy's many correspondents — all immigrants from west Cork, now domestic servants in the northeastern states — regularly expressed strong desires for matrimony. And no wonder, declared another servant, an Ulster immigrant in New York City, because 'it's the happiest time ever ... when under your own roof in [your] own house'. Likewise, young female immigrants often wrote bantering and, as they put it, 'foolish' (that is, romantic) remarks about their and their girlfriends' suitors.[46] Indeed, many young Irishwomen, such as Mary Ann Landy, Minnie Markey, and Mary Brown, were positively entranced by the liberal courtship patterns and romantic possibilities available in what Landy called 'the free lands of America'.[47] 'You would not think I had any beaux but I have a good many,' wrote New York servant Mary Brown to her envious cousin in County Wexford; 'I got half a dozen now   I have [become] quite a yankee and if I was at home the boys would all be around me.'[48]

Nevertheless, the distinction that Nolan and Diner make between Irishwomen's marital and economic motives for emigration is drawn too sharply. Female Irish emigrants desired what Mary Brown called 'love and liberty':[49] that is, they wanted both economic opportunity *and* domestic bliss in America — and they viewed the successful appropriation of the former as the key to the successful acquisition of the latter. That

44 For example, see the suggestive data in 'Fecundity of Immigrant Women', *Reports of the Immigration Commission* (Dillingham Commission), 61st Congress, 2nd Session, Senate Documents, 65 (Washington, DC, 1911), 731–826; my thanks to Professor David N. Doyle, of University College, Dublin, for bringing this source to my attention.

45 Miller, *Emigrants and Exiles*, 408.

46 e.g., Hannah Collins, Elmira, NY, to Nora McCarthy, Haverhill, Mass., 1 December 1898, 16 December 1898, and 24 May 1899 (O'Malley collection); Mary Hanlon, New York City, to Bernard Hanlon, Ballymote, County Down, n.d. [autumn 1871] (D. 885/13, PRONI).

47 Mary Ann Landy, Philadelphia, to Ellen [Landy], Balbriggan, County Dublin, n.d. [1884–85] (courtesy of Eileen McKenna, Balbriggan, County Dublin); Minnie Markey letters, 1889–94, among the Carroll family letters, 1847–1932 (courtesy of Kathleen McMahon, Martinstown, Togher, Drogheda, County Louth).

48 Mary Brown, New York City, to Mary Brown, Tomhaggard, County Wexford, 11 March 1858 (the Schrier collection; original in Ms. 1408, DIF/UCD).

49 Mary Brown, New York City, to Mary Brown, Tomhaggard, County Wexford, 20 January 1859 (Schrier collection and otherwise as in n. 48).

was one major reason why Irishwomen emigrated at an increasingly early age, usually in their late teens or early twenties: so they could work in the United States for six, eight, or even ten years — if as servants, as most of them were, honing their skills at domesticity; earning sufficient money to send remittances home; and, most important, accumulating the capital equivalents of dowries so they could attract and marry the most promising Irish immigrant males available and secure the status and moral authority of Irish-American homemakers and mothers before they passed beyond an age when matrimony and childbearing became difficult or unlikely.

Examine, for example, the career of Julia Lough, a farm labourer's daughter from Queen's County, who emigrated in 1884 at age thirteen to Winsted, Connecticut, where she joined four of her older sisters, all of whom already had married in America. During her first several years in Winsted, Julia Lough worked as a seamstress for one of her sisters and in the neighbourhood. At age nineteen she was an unpaid dressmaker's apprentice, as well as a member of the young women's sodality at St. Leo's Catholic church, and two years later she was a salaried employee in a dressmaker's shop. By age twenty-three she was an independent dressmaker, with an establishment of her own on Main Street, travelling frequently to New York City to purchase material and new patterns. However, three years later Julia Lough sold her business and married an Irish-born railroad engineer (a 'good match' in socio-economic terms), bearing him six children in a home dominated by feminine piety and gentility until she and her husband died in 1959. Thus, although she had exulted in the economic 'independence' that her hard work and business acumen had achieved, for her and most Irishwomen the 'good marriage' and the status and authority of wife/mother/houseworker represented their ultimate ambitions. Early emigration and successful economic strategies could make possible both capital accumulation and marriage, as in the case of Julia Lough, who was still not quite twenty-six when she wed Thomas McCarthy.[50]

Of course, most unmarried Irishwomen in America were domestic servants, not small entrepreneurs like Julia Lough. As late as 1900, over 70 per cent of employed Irish-born women in the United States were engaged in domestic and personal service, and in the late nineteenth and early twentieth centuries single Irishwomen dominated household service in most American cities outside the Deep South.[51] Diner has argued that Irish immigrant women viewed domestic service, like other waged employment, as an alternative to marriage. However, in light of its central importance in the lives of nearly all Irish female immigrants, including the great majority of those who eventually married, it would seem more pertinent to enquire into the conditions specific to that occupation which either encouraged or discouraged matrimony.

50 Biographical information on Julia Lough from the Lough family letters, 1876–1927 (see n. 26), and from her daughter, Mrs. Jenny Rasmussen, and her son-in-law, Hartford, Conn.
51 Miller, *Emigrants and Exiles*, 449–500; Nolan, *Ourselves Alone*, 68; Rhodes, *Women and the Family in Post-Famine Ireland*, 299; Diner, *Erin's Daughters in America*, 80–105.

First, both in Ireland and America, Catholic writers viewed domestic service for young women as a valuable preparation for housewifery, and at least some Irishwomen appear to have viewed it in that light.[52] As noted above, many Irish females had worked as household servants prior to emigrating, and most had been exposed to the cult, if not the reality, of bourgeois domesticity in Ireland. Thus, the criticism offered by James Reford, an Ulster Protestant immigrant, of newly arrived Irish Catholic servants 'from the bogs of Conoght', implies that they already expected and demanded middle-class comforts and conveniences from American employers: 'if you want a girl to do house work' in the United States, Reford complained, 'the[ir] first question is have you got hot and cold water in the house [and] Stationary wash tubs, [and] wringer[s?]   is my Bed room carpeted [with] Bureau Table wash stand and chairs and what privileges?'[53] On the other hand, many Irishwomen's letters indicate that domestic service in middle-class American households certainly increased and refined, if they did not create, bourgeois aspirations both material and socio-cultural. 'I would far rather live here than In Ireland,' wrote Mary Ann Sinclair, a house servant in San Francisco; 'The ways and customs of the people are so different   the[y] are all so polite and for who will talk the prettiest.'[54] Similarly, another young woman from Ulster was almost overwhelmed by her first exposure to the comforts and manners of a Victorian home. '[I]t is a very nice place to live in,' wrote Annie Gass from Attica, Indiana:

> it seams to bee the nicest place that I ever sean ... [It] Contains 11 Rooms all carpeted with Ritsh Carpet all mehogny furniture also silver dishes nives and forkes and every thing in proportion   you could have no idea how things looks ... the people are very Clean in their habits   the[y] are all well bread and very fine dress ... [and] the Children ... are so nise in their manner. ... [At dinner] there hands and fase must bee washed Clean and hair nicely Comed   their Behaveour is very good.[55]

If only to keep their situations and increase their wages, Irish domestic servants had to conform to — and help maintain — such standards, and indeed the letters of many indicate clearly that they accepted and even internalized Victorian values of cleanliness, punctuality, and efficiency.[56] Often, like Mary Clear of Utica, New York, Maggie Hennessy of Hartford, Connecticut, and Minnie Markey of Chicago, they criticized

---

52 McDannell, *Christian Home in Victorian America*, 62.

53 James A. Reford, Bloomfield, NJ, to Frances Reford, Greystone, Antrim, County Antrim, 9 April [1873] (T. 3028/B9, PRONI).

54 Mary Ann Sinclair, San Francisco, to Mary Ann Graham, Six Towns, Draperstown, County Derry, 3 June 1882 (D. 1497/2/2, PRONI).

55 Annie Gass, Attica, Ind., to Mary Gass, Markethill, County Armagh, 8 January 1872 (T. 1396/7, PRONI).

56 For example, see Mary Ann Sinclair, 3 June 1882; Ann Jane Sinclair, San Francisco, to Mary Ann Graham, Six Towns, Draperstown, County Derry, [24?] December 1879, and (from Oakland, Calif.), 9 February 1881 (D. 1497/4/2 and /7, PRONI); Mary Clear [Cleer/Clare], Utica, NY, to William Bennett, Enniscorthy, County Wexford, 14 May 1899, in 'Letters from Robert Eugene O'Neill', *The Past* [Wexford] (1964),

harshly the absence of such standards in rural Ireland or among their less 'respectable' Irish-American neighbours.[57] More important, as historian Colleen McDannell suggests, 'When these domestics married and started their own families, ... they sought to establish homes of similar quality.' Although they may not have 'consciously believed that Victorian domesticity was a way of inching into the middle class', they aspired to create 'the "right" kind of home ... which then would make them into the "right" kind of people'.[58] Expressions of such aspirations were often subtle but pervasive: 'Take that bottle off the table', one former servant would demand of her husband and children, 'This isn't Mulligan's Flats!' — referring to a popular song that satirized lower-class life in the tenements from which ambitious Irish Americans strove to escape.[59] Visiting Irish priests noted the results approvingly; thus, Fr. Pius Devine, while inspecting working-class Irish-American neighbourhoods, discovered as early as the 1870s that, despite their plain exteriors, 'the little wooden houses had each a parlour & a carpet into which nobody got entrance except very respectable visitors'.[60]

Also, domestic service provided an ideal economic as well as cultural foundation for achieving a 'good marriage' and a home in the United States. Although domestic service offered virtually no opportunities for occupational mobility (except within the large servant staffs employed by the very rich), the possibilities of modest but significant capital accumulation were substantial. For domestic servants demand was greater, unemployment far less frequent, and real wages — including room, board, and often clothes and presents — were higher than in any other occupation available to unskilled (and most skilled) women in late nineteenth and early twentieth-century America.[61] Thus, in 1894 the Ulsterman Patrick McKeown, a street-paver in Philadelphia,

115–18; and Maria Sheehan, Brookline, Mass., to Mary Hayes, Kinsale, County Cork, 5 April 1921 (M. Hayes Papers, Kinsale Regional Museum, Kinsale, County Cork).

57 Mary Clear, 14 May 1899; Minnie [Mary] Markey, Chicago, to Mary Carroll, Martinstown, Dunleer, County Louth, 23 October 1889 (Carroll family letters; see n. 47); Maggie Hennessy, Hartford, Conn., to her uncle, New Ross, County Wexford, ? July 1882 (courtesy of Victor Hennessy, New Ross, County Wexford; thanks to Dr. Kevin Whelan, then with the National Library of Ireland, Dublin, for facilitating acquisition of copies of the Hennessy letters).

58 McDannell, Christian Home in Victorian America, 73.

59 Murphy, Your Fondest Annie, 22; Annie O'Donnell's reference to 'Mulligan's Flats' may be an unconscious conflation of Ned Harrigan's popular 'Mulligan Guards' musicals with another popular song and show (and later a comic strip) titled 'McFadden's Row of Flats', all produced in the late nineteenth century and later the subjects of attacks by the Ancient Order of Hibernians, the United Irish Societies, and other Irish-American organizations that sought to counter 'defamatory' with 'respectable' communal images. I thank Professor William H. A. Williams of the Union Institute and University, in Cincinnati, Ohio, for this insight; on Irish-American popular culture, generally, see his superb 'Twas Only an Irishman's Dream: The Image of Ireland and the Irish in American Popular Song Lyrics, 1800–1920 (Urbana, Ill., 1996).

60 Fr. Pius Devine, CP, 'Journal of a Voyage to America', 1870; and 'Adventures and Misadventures of a Jolly Beggar', 1872–75 (Mss. in the archives of St. Paul of the Cross Retreat, Mount Argus, Dublin; copies courtesy of Fr. Declan O'Sullivan, CP, archivist).

61 Diner, Erin's Daughters in America, 90; David M. Katzman, Seven Days a Week: Women and Domestic Service in Industrializing America (Urbana, Ill., 1978), 311–14.

reported enviously that Irish domestic servants 'seem to be the most successful and save more money than any class of working girls, as they are at little or no expence, and get a great many presents if they are fortunate in getting into a good house'.[62] Indeed, comparisons between 'good places' and 'bad places' to work were a constant refrain in the letters of Irish-American servants, who changed households frequently, much to their employers' displeasure, in search of higher wages, better working conditions, and kind mistresses who would bribe them to remain with gifts and other indulgences. Through such strategies, they often amassed savings of $1,000 or more before they quit work altogether for marriage.[63]

Of course, domestic service was an arduous occupation, and historians such as David Katzman and especially Faye Dudden have shown that overwork, long hours, constant supervision, demeaning treatment, and profound loneliness and alienation were the lot of many unhappy servants.[64] In such respects, the record revealed by Irish immigrant servants' correspondence is mixed. Nora Hayes, Kate Monohan, Mary Ann Donovan, Hannah Collins, and other servants from west Cork, complained frequently in letters, written in Massachusetts and New York, about their employers' onerous demands and their own exhausting labours, especially when they were the only servants in large households: 'I have not had a week's vacation in two years,' Collins lamented; 'I work all the time and feels tired.'[65] 'Manny a night I dont [even] feel like writing' home, bewailed a worn-out Katie O'Sullivan from the other side of the continent; 'tis work work all the time'.[66] Similarly, Mary Hanlon in New York City protested that her employers 'scrutinized & commented' on her 'every act'; while Nora Hayes was desperate to escape her Boston household — 'this confounded whol,' she called it — because her mistress allowed her 'no privileges whatsoever' — 'not even any company' — and so Hayes felt she was 'in imprisonment'.[67]

Yet is not difficult to find contrasting evidence, as even Hannah Collins admitted that her employers were 'very nice' to her.[68] Ann Jane Sinclair's employer in Oakland,

62 Patrick McKeown, Philadelphia, to his sisters, Lisburn, County Antrim, 22 April 1894 (Schrier collection).

63 Katzman, Seven Days a Week, 3, 270; Diner, Erin's Daughters in America, 80–105; e.g., see the letters of Hannah Collins of Elmira, NY, 1898–1900 (O'Malley collection).

64 Katzman, Seven Days a Week, 7–14, 267–69; Faye E. Dudden, Serving Women: Household Service in Nineteenth-Century America (Middletown, Conn., 1983), 193–235.

65 Nora Hayes, Dorchester, Mass., 9 January 1896 and n.d. [postmarked 21 January 1897]; Kate Monohan, Dorchester, Mass., 9 October 1896; Mary Holland, Boston, 11 April 1897; Mary Ann Donovan, Lowell, Mass., 20 April 1897; and Hannah Collins, Elmira, NY, 27 May 1898, 30 June 1898, 29 July 1898 (quotation in text), 7 September 1898, 16 October 1898, 1 December 1898, and 24 May 1899: all to Nora McCarthy, Haverhill, Mass. (O'Malley collection).

66 Katie O'Sullivan, San Jose, Calif., to her brother, c. Finuge, Lixnaw, County Kerry, 5 December 1906 (Schrier collection).

67 Mary Hanlon, [autumn 1871]; Nora Hayes, Dorchester, Mass., to Nora McCarthy, Haverhill, Mass., 9 January [1896] (O'Malley collection).

68 Hannah Collins, Dorchester, Mass., to Nora McCarthy, Haverhill, Mass., 5 April 1900 (O'Malley collection).

California, gave her free piano lessons; her sister in San Francisco received from her mistress 'a beautiful silver thimble for a christmas present'; and although Maggie Murphy's first employer in Jersey City was 'a perfect Devel [who] wanted every thing to perfection', she quickly abandoned her harsh mistress for another who gave her dresses and was 'as nice as you could get'.[69] Likewise, some evidence suggests that household service in America was less arduous or demeaning than the work to which small farmers' and labourers' daughters were accustomed at home, and many Irish servants in America remarked upon the relatively egalitarian treatment they received from their employers.[70] Thus, Mary Clear wrote that her 'rich' employer in Utica was 'nice to his help', and Annie Heggarty reported from Iowa that she had 'a good home', where her master 'makes no differ with me more than aney of his own daughters'.[71] In addition, the letters of Mary Clear, Hannah Collins, James Reford, and others suggest that Irish-American servants did not shrink from confrontations with their employers, who often complained of their 'impudence'.[72] 'The cook is a very nice girl,' wrote Mary Clear of one of her fellow house servants; 'she is a Murphy, Irish-American, about the size of a doll, but as smart a piece as I ever saw. She makes the Boss think that she is just as good as him — she wouldn't take a word from the best of them, nor neither will I.'[73]

More important was that, for the great majority of Irish immigrant women, domestic servitude was only temporary, a means to achieve another goal, and the extent to which Irishwomen resented its negative aspects only encouraged their escape to what they regarded as the shelters of husband and homemaking. Thus, Catharine Ann McFarland of Philadelphia was so ashamed of 'liven at service' and so tired of what she had 'to put up with in ane ones kitchen' that she eagerly embraced 'an offer of Marige from a very respectable Man' — an Irish-born carpenter; 'you [k]now that i never had mutch plesur in my young days', she wrote to her mother in Derry city, 'sow i hope to have som now'.[74] 'I hope someday will come when I won't have to work so hard,' wrote Hannah Collins, and 'that is when I will be Mrs [Tom] Cloak' — married to her long-time Irish-American

69 Ann Jane Sinclair, 9 February 1881; Mary Ann Sinclair, San Francisco, to Mary Ann Graham, Six Towns, Draperstown, County Derry, 11 February 1880 (D. 1497/4/7, PRONI); and Maggie [Murphy?], Jersey City, NJ, to Nora Murphy, Lissarulla, Claregalway, County Galway, 22 June [1924?] (Green collection).
70 Rhodes, *Women and the Family in Post-Famine Ireland*, 305, also makes this argument.
71 Mary Clear, 14 May 1899; Annie Heggarty, Ottumwa, Iowa, to Mr. and Mrs. Michael McFadden, Kilcar, County Donegal, 19 July 1884 (Schrier collection).
72 Mary Clear, 14 May 1899; and James A. Reford, 9 April [1873]. Thus, Hannah Collins left her 'very nice' employers when they asked her to 'mind' their children in the evenings, after completing her house-cleaning chores, telling them bluntly that 'I was not a nurse girl to be taking care of kids   they are old enough to mind themselves'; Hannah Collins, 5 April 1900.
73 Mary Clear, 14 May 1899.
74 Catharine Ann McFarland, Philadelphia, to her mother, Londonderry city, 5 March and 25 June 1855 (D. 1665/3/6–7, PRONI); by the time of her 25 June 1855 letter, the writer's married name was Hutchinson.

suitor.[75] Likewise, although Mary Ann Rowe in Dedham, Massachusetts, admitted that, like Collins, she too was employed by 'a very nice family', she also turned to matrimony — in her case to escape unbearable loneliness and longing for the home and family she had left in County Kilkenny.[76] Finally, Lizzie McCann, an Ulster Catholic and hotel servant in Minneapolis, confided to her sister in Belfast that 'it is pretty hard life for us to work out all those years   we are just tired out with hardwork   So i am not going to be so hard to soute in a husbant as i have been   i am going to Make a home for my self this time. I will not wait any longer ... i Expect to get Married in May' — and she did so, in a sumptuous working-class wedding, which, judging from her enthusiastic description, was the high point of her young life.[77]

As far as can be known, Catharine Ann McFarland's, Hannah Collins's, and Lizzie McCann's experiences of immigration, like those of Julia Lough's, culminated happily, according to their own aspirations. However, there were others who, by those standards at least, were less fortunate. First, there were those already mentioned whose situations or whose families' strategies allowed them neither to emigrate nor to marry nor to find a respected, 'independent' niche (for example, as nuns, teachers, or postal workers) in post-Famine Irish society. Second, there were at least a few young immigrants whose overly literal pursuit of 'love and liberty' — in defiance of bourgeois conventions, Irish traditions, and religious sanctions — brought them only the disgrace of unwed motherhood and the likely poverty of prostitution. 'It was my fortune to witness an excommunication ... yesterday ... [of a] young girl,' wrote one sanctimonious Irish American, Hugh Harlin from Jackson, Michigan:

> There is not a community of Irish in America but what there is always one or more houses where the lower class of servant girls associate. Of course they meet some company of the opposite sex and ... they frequently have a 'drop' by way of friendship. Of course such conduct will run to extremes, particularly at the saturday night dances. ... [So, i]s it to be wondered at that under the influence of the ... bottle or pitcher, their coarser natures are excited and they become passive

---

75 Hannah Collins, 24 May 1899; Collins eventually married Thomas Cloak, a mill worker of Irish parentage in Elmira, NY.

76 Mary Ann Rowe, Dedham, Mass., to James Wallace, Dunnamaggan, County Kilkenny, 29 October 1888 (courtesy of Mrs. Brid Galway, Barrowsland, Thomastown, County Kilkenny).

77 Lizzie McCann, Minneapolis, Minn., to Mrs. Mary McKeown, Belfast, 20 March and 17 July 1888 (T.1456/7 and /4–6, PRONI).

to the fulsom adolations of the vilest scamps that ever left Ireland. When they reach this point they are lost.

In fact, the object of Hugh Harlin's censure apparently escaped 'the fate worse than death': she married her lover and appears to have been excommunicated less for her sexual transgressions than because her husband was a Protestant and their wedding took place in an Episcopal church.[78] However, it is unlikely that this woman's problems ended happily at the altar, for third, and far more common than unwed mothers, were those immigrants whose eagerness to become Irish-American wives and houseworkers blinded their judgements and led them to enter the abusive, drunken, and often broken marriages that Diner describes in horrifying detail and which, sadly, became the fates of Mary Ann Rowe and Minnie Markey, blighting their dreams of romance and their hopes of ascent from drudgery to security and respectability.[79] Such pathological examples were evident everywhere in Irish America, but probably were most common in eastern cities and mill towns, where Irishwomen's endogamous marital choices were quantitatively fewer and, perhaps, qualitatively lower than further west.

Fourth were those female immigrants who never married in America, for although some became successful 'women of property', purchased with hoarded savings, others ended their lives in almshouses or asylums.[80] No doubt many unmarried Irishwomen consciously chose to remain single, and Diner may be correct in her contention that Irish socio-cultural patterns and/or Irish-American experiences made women from Ireland more hesitant to marry, or at least more aware of alternate survival strategies, than were females in other ethnic groups.[81] Irish immigrant women knew too well, for example, that even the best of husbands could suffer prolonged bouts of unemployment, or turn to drink at least temporarily, as did the spouse of Marion McCarthy in 1870s Chicago; and they were also aware, as her stepmother, Mary Kelly Malone, warned, 'what a burden children is in America' for working-class families: 'people at home have no idea all it

78 Hugh Harlin, Jackson, Mich., to John Harlin, New York City, 19 April 1858 (courtesy of Robert J. Fitzgerald, Rouses Point, NY; thanks to Dr. Gerry Moran, then in Rathfarnham, Dublin, for initiating the acquisition of copies of the Harlin letters).
79 Diner, Erin's Daughters in America, 53–65. Biographical information on Mary Ann Rowe from Mrs. Brid Galway (see n. 76). Biographical information on Minnie Markey from Annie Carroll's letters, from Chicago, dated 1895–1898, in the Carroll family letters (see n. 47).
80 Dudden, Serving Women, 208.
81 Patricia Kelleher, Durham, NH, letter to author, 16 July 1991. For example, between 1898 and 1900 Hannah Collins continually vacillated among dreams of matrimony ('I am getting tired of this single life'), her financial duties to her parents in west Cork, and desires to remain independent ('I hates to get married and you know I am young enough yet'); Hannah Collins, Elmira, NY, to Nora McCarthy, Haverhill, Mass., 1 December 1898 and 21 February 1900 (O'Malley collection). Annie O'Donnell was equally hesitant to abandon her 'kind' and affluent employers (a branch of Pittsburgh's fabulously wealthy Mellon family) for the uncertainties of matrimony with a tram-car driver from County Kilkenny; Murphy, Your Fondest Annie, 10, 19.

costs to support a family,' she wrote, especially before the children could go 'to work so young and for small pay [so] that we can just get along'.[82]

Moreover, if marriage postponement was a peculiarly Irish Catholic device to limit family size without recourse to birth control, as some scholars suggest, it is easy to imagine how the accompanying code of female chastity and sexual repression could discourage matrimony and make postponement permanent; indeed, at least one immigrant's letter implied that the lack of sexual instruction given by Irish mothers prior to their daughters' emigration may have inhibited the latter's sense of confidence regarding marriage and male–female relationships, generally.[83] Also, given the intimate connections among property, security, and female self-identity in rural Irish and Victorian American cultures alike, perhaps it would not be surprising if, over time, steady employment and capital accumulation became ends in themselves for many Irishwomen abroad, especially for domestic servants who feared that those achievements — as well as the genteel standards imbibed in their employers' households — might be forfeited, at least temporarily, through marriage to working-class Irish Americans.[84] At least a few Irish servants must have made quite rational decisions not to forsake their employers' comfortable homes and kind treatment for the uncertain bliss of matrimony.

Dudden and Katzman identify additional aspects of domestic service that could discourage marriage. As Nora Hayes complained, some employers — perhaps fearful of the dangers Hugh Harlin described — denied servants the leisure time and personal freedom necessary for social life and courtship rituals.[85] Furthermore, Katzman argues, 'many mistresses encouraged servants to express their nurturing and loving instincts on the employing family. In exploiting the emotional needs of the domestic, the employer might be winning a faithful and loyal servant, one who lost her own vision of an independent life and instead adopted the family she worked for as a substitute for her own.'[86] Such appears to have been the case with Ann McNabb, the labourer's daughter from County Derry, who, atypically, worked as cook and nurse for one family for twenty-two years and never married. 'Mrs. Carr's interests was my interests,' she stated proudly; 'I took better care of her things than she did herself, and I loved the childer as if they was my own.'[87]

However, there were other Irish immigrant spinsters who had never enjoyed the opportunity or the choice of matrimony. For some, this may have been due to the

82 Marion McCarthy, Chicago, to Anne Doyle, Pollerton, Carlow, County Carlow, n.d. [1879–81?]; Mary Kelly Malone, Chicago, to John and Anne Doyle, same, n.d. [1874–75], 7 May 1877, and 11 November [1885?] (courtesy of Seamus Murphy, Pollerton Little, Carlow, County Carlow).
83 Ann [Nan] Lough McMahon, Winsted, Conn., to her mother, Meelick, Queen's County, n.d. [c. 1890?], in the Lough family letters (see n. 26).
84 Dudden, Serving Women, 228–30.
85 Dudden, Serving Women, 211; Katzman, Seven Days a Week, 7–14; Nora Hayes, 9 January [1896].
86 Katzman, Seven Days a Week, 269.
87 'Story of an Irish Cook', 715–17.

gender imbalance that prevailed among the Irish in many American cities. Many others may have emigrated too late in life, obliged by their families' economic and inheritance strategies to postpone their departures until one brother married (since his wife's dowry might finance his sisters' emigrations) or until their parents' deaths.[88] Thus, the historian Deirdre Mageean finds that a large proportion of the unmarried, middle-aged and elderly Irish-born domestic servants in early twentieth-century Chicago had not emigrated until their late twenties or early thirties.[89] By the time they had laboured five to ten years to accumulate much capital in America, they were pressing against the outer limits of marriageability and childbearing. Also, the Irish cult of domestic duty could inhibit immigrants' marriage by burdening them with obligations to send home remittances, thus depleting their savings and stifling their social opportunities in order to finance their siblings' emigrations or to support their families in Ireland. 'I have to think of my dear Parents and send them a little money,' declared one dutiful immigrant; and besides, she wrote, her siblings 'Maggie and Patsey are older than I am so they have to [marry] first.'[90] In general, however, the greatest impositions may have fallen on older daughters who were the first of their siblings to emigrate: not only were they expected to pay their younger brothers' and sisters' passages, but also they would have to wait longest in America before their parents' deaths released them from obligations to the home farm. Such appears to have been at least part of the explanation for Annie Carroll's impoverished spinsterhood. Despite her often bitter complaints, she faithfully sent home large sums, earned at service in Chicago, to finance her brother's emigration and to pay the rent of her mother's farm. Unfortunately, Annie Carroll's mother did not die until 1891, eight years after her emigration; two years later she lost her only suitor to a younger rival; and in 1896 she developed the chronic foot ulcer that would terminate her employment. For a time she lived with her bachelor brother, but by 1915 she was residing in an asylum.[91]

Finally, it is likely that many Irishwomen who never married abroad had grown up in small farmers' or labourers' households that were so poor and primitive that they had never been exposed to the new standards and skills of middle-class housework — which may have made them relatively unmarketable in America, both as domestic servants and as wives. One such case was Mary Malone from County Waterford, a 'lonseom and down harted' scrubwoman in Fairport, New York, who explained in a letter to her brother that 'my wages is so little' because 'I am not capble of earning big

88 Fitzpatrick, 'Modernisation of the Irish Female', 174.

89 Deirdre Mageean, 'Irish Women in Chicago' (paper, 'Women in the Migration Process' conference, Worpswede, Germany, 4–7 November 1990), material from which has since been published in Mageean's 'Making Sense and Providing Structure: Irish-American Women in the Parish Neighborhood', in Christine Harzig, ed., Peasant Maids — City Women: From the European Countryside to Urban America (Ithaca, NY, 1997), 223–60.

90 Hannah Collins, Elmira, NY, to Nora McCarthy, Haverhill, Mass., 10 June 1899 (O'Malley collection).

91 Annie Carroll letters, from Chicago, 1883–1906, in the Carroll family letters (see n. 47); additional biographical information from Roberta Fosdal, Jefferson, Wisc.

wages like other girls who can cook and [do] the large washings and fine ironings   I cannot do this   you know I was not brought [up] to any such thing [for] I was sent away frum my Mother when young to the farmers to work out in the fields and I never got much in sight about house keeping or to be handy to sew.'[92] Of course, most young 'greenhorns' from similarly impoverished backgrounds, such as Ann McNabb, 'larned hand over hand' from their first employers how 'to cook and bake and to wash and do up shirts — all American fashion'.[93] 'America revolutionizes them,' one observer wrote, referring contemptuously to Irish domestic servants' often pathetic early attempts to adapt to American bourgeois standards.[94] However, apparently some Irishwomen never overcame their initial deficiencies. Thus, Maggie Black, an Irish housewife in late nineteenth-century Chicago, described the plight of an inept or 'lazy' immigrant relative:

> Margaret has been rather unfortunate in her situation lately. She is likely to be out [of work] this week again. She was getting 3 dols per week in the last month. She was expected to do the Shirts but she cannot please the lady in doing them, so she loses a dollar a week for that & her mistress thinks she is not worth more than 2 dollars ... I think she is not worth 1 *dollar a week*. She's awfully slow & that won't do here, & they won't wait on a girl here, just if she does not suit pay her off without much ceremony. I dont think she will ever be any better.[95]

Like Catharine Ann McFarland, the unhappy Mary Malone and Maggie Black's incompetent kinswoman might have been eager candidates for hasty matrimony. However, their lack of domestic skills and savings may have fatally reduced their marital prospects or, even worse, consigned them to 'unfortunate' marriages scarred by poverty, alcoholism, and abuse.

92 Mary Malone, Fairport, NY, to her brother, Glenmore, County Waterford, 24 January 1877 (Schrier collection). It is revealing that the elaborate socio-cultural and status hierarchies among the large servant staffs in wealthy American families often mirrored those in post-Famine Irish society. Thus, upper-class Protestant employers generally preferred, for the high-status and best-paid positions, servants who were not only skilled in household duties and reasonably well-educated, but who also behaved genteelly and spoke 'the King's English'. Unfortunately, the children of poor Irish farmers and farm labourers (especially from western Ireland) usually lacked such attributes, and as a result were generally assigned, like Mary Malone, to the dirtiest, most exhausting, and lowly-paid tasks. For the same reasons, it is probable that similar immigrants, from the 'worst' socio-cultural backgrounds, were obliged to take the 'worst' jobs available in the domestic-servant marketplace — as the sole affordable servants in lower-middle-class Yankee households. Such servants were most likely to report overwork and bad treatment, and their mistresses were most likely to complain of their 'stupidity' — i.e., of their inexperience and unfamiliarity with bourgeois norms and practices — thus offering apparent validation of 'Bridget's' harsh stereotype in the contemporary American press. On 'the King's English', see Murphy, Your Fondest Annie, 10.
93 'Story of an Irish Cook', 715–17.
94 James A. Reford, 9 April [1873].
95 Maggie Black, Chicago, to Annie [Hall?], County Armagh, 12 February 1891, and to Adela [Hall?], County Armagh, 16 March 1891 (D. 2041/Bundle 13, PRONI).

In conclusion, emigration brought the Julia Loughs and Lizzie McCanns of Ireland all they had hoped for: economic achievement sufficient to secure 'respectable' marriages and the status and authority of homemakers. Indeed, by the late 1890s even the once impoverished Marion McCarthy could report that, despite her and her husband's travails, their Chicago home was finally 'secure[d]', and their married children now boasted pianos in their own houses.[96] Yet for Ireland's Annie Carrolls and Mary Malones, such goals proved more elusive, and for Ireland's Ann McNabbs, the means to achieve matrimony ultimately became the ends in themselves. In the last analysis, it is difficult to say which were the most fortunate. Maggie Black, the lower middle-class wife of an Irish-born dry goods salesman, worked herself into a state of nervous exhaustion 'constantly cleaning & dusting' her nine-room house, cooking for several boarders as well as her own family, attending missionary society and ladies' prayer meetings, and fretting over Chicago's moral dangers to her offspring.[97] Across town, Marion McCarthy doubtless never forgot that — in contrast to her now 'stylish' daughter — she 'could never afford to put on style either before or after marriage': 'from a sense of duty,' she recalled ruefully, 'I always managed to dispose of any little I had to spare after Common necessities'.[98] Likewise, Annie O'Donnell may have longed always for her Irish youth, 'when my heart was light and happy' and when 'I slept and dreamt that life was beauty', before she 'woke from that sleep' to the harsh realities of an American adulthood.[99] And although Ellen Flinn, wife of a day labourer in Barrytown, New York, 'purchased a house and lot that cost her fourteen hundred dollars' earned as a laundress, her Sisyphean efforts to push her family up the road to respectability left her 'very thin and old looking'.[100] Perhaps 'love and liberty' was a dream only for the young, and perhaps in old age even the Julia Loughs sometimes wondered if they had sacrificed too much on the altars of duty and domesticity.

96 Marion McCarthy, n.d. [1895–96].
97 Maggie Black, Chicago, to Annie [Hall?], County Armagh, 25 September 1890, and to Adela [Hall?], County Armagh, 23 October 1890 (D. 2041/Bundle 13, PRONI).
98 Marion McCarthy, n.d. [1879–81].
99 Annie O'Donnell, 25 August 1901, in Murphy, Your Fondest Annie, 39.
100 Mary Quin, Barrytown, NY, to her sister, Stewartstown, County Tyrone, [1873?], and Arthur Quin, same address, to same, 18 September 1876 (D. 1819/3 and /6, PRONI).

14 Assimilation and Alienation:
   Irish Immigrants' Responses to Industrial America, 1870s–1920s

Between the 1870s and the onset of the Great Depression in 1929, at least 2.5 million Irishmen and -women emigrated to the United States, more than a third of the estimated entire exodus of c. 6–7 million who crossed the Atlantic after 1607 to settle in what eventually became the American republic.[1] Nevertheless, this great post-Famine migration from Ireland has been slighted by historians — compared to their concentrations on the Irish emigrants to colonial and revolutionary era America (c. 7–8 per cent of the 1607–1929 total), the pre-Famine emigrants of 1815–44 (c. 15 per cent), and the Famine emigrants of 1845–55 (c. 28 per cent) — perhaps because the late-nineteenth and early twentieth-century emigrants seemed absorbed in an already well-established and, after 1880, largely US-born Irish-American society. This chapter attempts to redress the balance, but less by focusing on Irish America's institutional development (the subject of Chapter 11) than on the post-Famine migrants' extremely varied circumstances in and responses to the New World. As reflected primarily in their personal letters and memoirs, among other sources, those responses reveal turn-of-the-century Irish America as a remarkably heterogeneous and deeply ambivalent society: on the one hand, progressing rapidly towards middle-class status and full assimilation in the 'triple melting pot' outlined by sociologist Will Herberg, yet, on the other hand, still rooted firmly in proletarian conditions and distinctively Irish origins

1   This chapter, with substantially the same title, was first published in P. J. Drudy, ed., *Irish Studies 4: The Irish in America: Emigration, Assimilation and Impact* (Cambridge, 1985). I am grateful to Cambridge University Press for permission to republish the essay in this volume, with some revisions. Thanks also to Liam Kennedy of Queen's University, Belfast, and to David N. Doyle of University College, Dublin, for their helpful comments on the original essay, and to Bruce D. Boling, now professor emeritus at the University of New Mexico, for his graceful translations of the works in the Irish language that are cited in the text.

and concerns. Thus, whereas in 1914 President Woodrow Wilson's gratuitous attack on Irish-American 'hyphenism' demonstrated that native-born Protestant champions of '100 per cent Americanism' remained unsatisfied, in 1919–21 Eamon de Valera's disillusionment with many of his Irish-American hosts revealed how irretrievably 'American' the latter had become.[2]

Since post-Famine migrants' situations and outlooks overseas were partly determined by their material and cultural baggage, a brief look at the composition of the 1870s–1920s exodus is in order. At least 75 per cent of these emigrants were Catholics, and considerations of space mandate this chapter's almost exclusive attention upon them. Between 75 and 91 per cent annually stated their occupations to be either labourer or servant, although in fact many were not the children of landless workers but instead the non-inheriting sons or dowerless daughters of middling and small farmers. They carried little capital overseas — an average of only £2 15s. in 1900, for example — and the great majority emigrated on remittances sent by their predecessors. About 60 per cent were between the ages of 15 and 24; most were unmarried and travelling alone or with siblings, cousins, etcetera (rather than with parents or children); and a slight majority were females. After 1880 about half the Catholic emigrants came from the impoverished western counties along the Atlantic seaboard; perhaps a third were Irish-speakers (albeit usually bilingual to some degree), and many of the rest could be described as ill-educated (although rarely completely illiterate) and imperfectly Anglicized. However, thanks to the era's almost constant nationalist agitation and the Irish Catholic Church's devotional revolution, the 1870s–1920s emigrants were the most thoroughly politicized and formally devout in Irish history. Finally, of course, it must be remembered that, between 1845 and 1870 alone, the United States had already provided havens for some 2.5 million Irish immigrants, and the survivors and their children comprised a large majority of the nearly 5 million Irish Americans recorded in the 1900 US census. Consequently, the Irish America that the 1870s–1920s emigrants joined was an extraordinarily varied society, exhibiting a great diversity of situations and perspectives.[3]

2 Will Herberg, *Protestant-Catholic-Jew: Essay in American Religious Sociology*, 2nd rev. edn. (Garden City, NY, 1960); John O'Dea, *History of Ancient Order of Hibernians*, 3 vols. (Philadelphia, 1923), vol. 3, 1482–86; Francis M. Carroll, *American Opinion and the Irish Question, 1910–23* (New York, 1978), 156–62. For an expanded treatment of the issues considered here, and more detailed citations, see Kerby A. Miller, *Emigrants and Exiles: Ireland and the Irish Exodus to North America* (New York, 1985), ch. 8, section 4; as well as Chapters 1, 4–5, and 11 in this volume.

3 Information based primarily on: W. E. Vaughan and A. J. Fitzpatrick, eds., *Irish Historical Statistics: Population, 1821–1971* (Dublin, 1978), 269–353; Cormac Ó Gráda, 'Some Aspects of Nineteenth-Century Irish Emigration', in L. M. Cullen and T. C. Smout, eds., *Comparative Aspects of Scottish and Irish Economic and Social History* (Edinburgh, 1977), 68–71; Brinley Thomas, *Migration and Economic Growth: A Study of Great Britain and the Atlantic Economy*, 2nd edn. (Cambridge, 1973), 74, 348; Robert E. Kennedy, Jr., *The Irish: Emigration, Marriage, and Fertility* (Berkeley, Calif., 1975), *passim*; and Arnold Schrier, *Ireland and the American Emigration, 1850–1900* (New York, 1970 edn.), 110–11, 167–8.

By the early 1870s, for example, a small but significant class of wealthy Irish Americans had already emerged from the prevalent poverty of the Famine decades, led by a handful of millionaires such as shipping magnate William Grace, New York City's first Catholic mayor, and flanked by a growing number of affluent professionals and businessmen. Below this rarefied atmosphere, an increasingly large petty bourgeoisie of 'lace-curtain' Irish furnished parlours with pianos and strove to keep the still omnipresent 'tenement' and 'shanty' Irish at arm's length. Remarkably, and despite the crippling depressions of 1873–78 and 1893–97, by 1900 Irish America (the Irish-born and their children) had achieved 'relative occupational parity with native white America'. As noted in Chapter 11, outside the economically stagnant Yankee fiefdom of New England, roughly the same proportions of Irish-American males were employed in white-collar (35 per cent), in skilled and semi-skilled (50 per cent), and in unskilled occupations (15 per cent), as were white Americans of native birth and parentage; only in agriculture were Irish Americans underrepresented. Moreover, whereas in the mid-nineteenth century the relatively few middle- and upper-working-class Irish Americans had based their success largely on advantages (capital, education, skills) brought from Ireland, by the early twentieth century the Irish-American bourgeoisie was primarily the product of upward mobility from the labouring ranks. On occasion the Irish-born had experienced dramatic social ascent; however, most immigrants still ended their American careers as manual labourers or, at best, small proprietors, and it was their American-born children who took fullest advantage of the mushrooming growth of corporate staffs and public service bureaucracies.[4]

Irish-American success often astounded post-Famine migrants, who discovered that their kinsmen lived in dwellings that, at least by rural Irish standards, seemed 'richly' furnished, with well-stocked dinner tables. Similarly, the Irish rise to respectability helped assuage native-born Protestants' fears, ubiquitous at mid-century, that Irish Catholic immigrants constituted a permanent and unassimilable proletariat. In 1887 a Boston Brahmin declared that 'What we need is not to dominate the Irish but absorb them. ... We want them to become rich, and send their sons to our colleges, to share our prosperity and sentiments.' Only nine years later the prestigious *Atlantic Monthly* rejoiced that such goals were nearly achieved, that 'the Irish will, before many years are past, be lost in the American and ... there will be no longer an "Irish question" or an "Irish vote", but a people one in feeling, and practically one in race'. However, Irish Americans' new status as 'honorary Anglo-Saxons' was condescending at best, and most middle-class Irish were painfully aware that their position in American society remained marginal. For example, most Irish-American businessmen remained economically — and thus socially — dependent on a clientele composed largely of working-class Irish, often recent

4 David N. Doyle, *Irish Americans, Native Rights and National Empires: The Structure, Divisions and Attitudes of the Catholic Minority in the Decade of Expansion, 1890–1901* (New York, 1976), 48–49, 59–63. Studies of Irish occupational mobility and property acquisition in late nineteenth-century America are listed in n. 46 of ch. 7 and n. 186 of ch. 8, in Miller, *Emigrants and Exiles*.

and relatively 'uncouth' immigrants. Moreover, problems of social and cultural marginality may have been even greater for those middle-class Irish Americans who mixed in native-Protestant society: with few exceptions, not only did they remain under-represented in their respective fields — and generally excluded from financial, manufacturing, and professional élites — but they often still endured irritating, if not economically-harmful, prejudices and slights from native employers and co-workers. For instance, when Peter Murphy worked in downtown Chicago he learned quickly that 'some bigotry towards Catholics' was 'taken for granted', and during times of depression — as in the 1890s — prejudice became widespread and virulent. Finally, although lower-middle-class Irish Americans — clerks, teachers, sales personnel — enjoyed higher status than manual workers, their wages were considerably lower than those of skilled labourers in unionized trades. During economic depressions their struggles to purchase homes often proved unavailing, and even the successful usually were burdened with second mortgages on modest brick or frame houses located in inner suburbs, which were often precariously near their recently abandoned, working-class tenement districts.[5]

In short, underrepresentation in native power structures, the precariousness of status in rapidly changing economies, unwelcome proximity to the unsuccessful, and, perhaps most important, Anglo-American non-recognition of Irish-American accomplishment — all served to embitter the Irish middle class and to keep fresh old wounds inherited from the Famine decades. Thus, James Michael Curley, many times Boston mayor and once governor of Massachusetts, never forgot what he learned as a poor Irish-speaking boy in Roxbury — that he 'belonged to an Irish-Catholic minority who were despised socially and discriminated against politically'. '[O]ften unconscious of their too frequent vulgarity', as one critic put it, the Irish-American bourgeoisie tended to be morbidly sensitive to real or imagined snubs, invariably attributed to Protestant prejudice, and to any perceived threats to their tenuous grasp on respectability. Crippled emotionally by deep-seated feelings of inferiority and insecurity, having learned too young what Eugene O'Neill called 'the value of a dollar and the fear of the poorhouse', they sometimes became compulsive hoarders or rack-renting slumlords — 'more American than the Americans', as another witness observed. However, others more reflective wondered whether the game was worth the candle. It was not only struggling labourers like Michael Kilcran, a slaughterhouse worker on Chicago's South Side, for example, but also 'comfortable' Irish immigrants, such as Michael Flanagan, William Downes, and even John Boyle O'Reilly, editor of the *Boston Pilot*, Irish America's premier newspaper, who privately lamented the harsh disjunctions between the ethos and exigencies of American capitalism and their idealized memories of Irish social life and their notions

5   Annie Gass, Attica, Ind., to Mary Gass, Markethill, County Armagh, 8 January 1872 (T. 1396, PRONI); Katherine Donovan, 'Good Old Pat: An Irish-American Stereotype in Decline', *Éire-Ireland: An Interdisciplinary Journal of Irish Studies*, 15, 3 (1980), 6–14; Peter Murphy, East Islip, NY, to Philip Loe, Chicago, 23 April 1954 (Frank Conlan Mss., Chicago Historical Society).

of 'what the ideal Christian man should be'. Generally, such misgivings and conflicts were internalized, but as historian John Duffy Ibsen speculates, 'the tensions sewn into the lace curtain' may have reinforced Irish propensities to drink, and many immigrants' accounts of the period portray an Irish-American bourgeoisie whose aspirations and achievements were ravaged by an alcoholism born of debilitating self-doubt.[6]

In the early twentieth century the working classes still held a majority of Irish Americans, but since 1870 their overall situation had improved significantly and their circumstances were extremely diverse. Indeed, most were now skilled or semi-skilled workers, the former concentrated in the best-paid, most highly unionized trades; only in Massachusetts did unskilled outnumber skilled Irish workers — a dramatic contrast with 1850 when at least two-thirds of all Irish-American males held semi-skilled or unskilled jobs. Also, within many heavy industries (iron, steel, mining), Irish Americans increasingly dominated blue-collar managerial posts, leaving the heaviest, lowest-paid labour to newly arrived Slavs, Hungarians, and Italians. Even in 1900, however, 25 per cent of Irish-born males, and 17 per cent of the American-born, still held unskilled, poorly paid, and usually non-unionized jobs; as late as 1904 Irish Americans still composed a disproportionately large share (11 per cent) of the nation's casual labourers, and although American-born Irishwomen usually escaped the drudgery of domestic service, a substantial majority of Irish immigrant females still laboured as servants or in textile factories and sweatshops.[7]

Thus, by 1900 the conditions of working-class Irish America varied enormously, although overall trends were encouraging. Early Irish predominance in factory labour, construction, and transportation had proved advantageous as those sectors expanded in the late nineteenth and early twentieth centuries: for example, enabling Irish-born building contractors to amass small fortunes and employ growing and reasonably well-paid workforces of fellow immigrants and their children. Likewise, Irish-dominated trade unions, such as those in the AFL, protected the wages of skilled Irish Americans and transmitted invaluable union cards to members' sons and to nephews from the old country. In addition, even unskilled immigrants benefited from

6 James Michael Curley, *I'd Do It Again: A Record of All My Uproarious Years* (Englewood Cliffs, NJ, 1967), 32; Thomas Beer, *The Mauve Decade: American Life at the End of the Nineteenth Century*, intro. Frank Freidel (1926; New York, 1960), 111–16; Alice Stopford Green, draft essay on the American Irish (Ms. 10,455, NLI); Michael Kilcran, Journal 1880–90 (courtesy of John and James Kilcran, Carrick-on-Shannon, County Leitrim); Michael Flanagan, Napa, Calif., to John Flanagan, Tubbertoby, County Louth, 14 April 1877 (courtesy of Peter and Mary Flanagan, Togher, Clogherhead, County Louth); William H. Downes, Brooklyn, NY, to James Shaughnessy, Pallaskenry, County Limerick, 13 October 1887 (courtesy of William O'Shaughnessy, Pallaskenry); John Duffy Ibsen, 'Will the World Break Your Heart? An Historical Analysis of the Dimensions and Consequences of Irish-American Assimilation' (PhD diss., Brandeis University, 1976), 56, 106–20, 214, 304–05; since published (New York, 1990).

7 David N. Doyle, 'The Irish and American Labour, 1880–1920', *Saothar: Journal of the Irish Labour History Society*, 1 (1975), 42–43, and 'Unestablished Irishmen: New Immigrants and Industrial America', in Dirk Hoerder, ed., *American Labor and Immigration History, 1877–1920s* (Urbana, Ill., 1983), 195–96; David M. Katzman, *Seven Days a Week: Women and Domestic Service in Industrializing America* (Oxford, 1978), 66–70.

the relative maturity of Irish-American societies, as by 1900 urban parishes could provide newcomers with a wide range of kinship networks and a host of formal social, political, and charitable institutions. Consequently, as one Irish American wrote home, immigration, unlike mid-century, was no longer 'like going into a City where you dont know anybody'. Thanks to these developments, in the context of a generally expanding American economy, many working-class Irish did well in the late nineteenth and early twentieth centuries. American wages were significantly higher than in Ireland, and for the children of Irish farm labourers and small farmers virtually any jobs in America connoted improvements in status and condition. Thus, Michael Kinney rejoiced that, by contrast to the farmers who had employed him in County Kerry, his new bosses in a Pittsburgh steel mill 'paid me what was coming to me', while apprentice seamstress Julia Lough reported that her 'new life' was 'getting along splendid' as she would 'soon have a trade and be ... independent'. A few immigrants achieved spectacular upward mobility, such as David Lawlor from County Waterford, who advanced from a Massachusetts textile mill to a highly successful career as an advertising executive. Such achievement was exceptional, but many unskilled immigrants were able to accumulate modest property and/or raise their children to skilled-manual or even low white-collar status. For example, although Ulsterman Patrick McKeown remained a casual labourer throughout forty years in Philadelphia, his children entered the ranks of plumbers, steamfitters, stenographers, and elevator operators.[8]

   Given this general improvement, it is at first glance remarkable that most surviving letters and memoirs written by working-class Irish immigrants, from the 1870s through the 1920s, reflect a generalized unease — indeed, often a deep dissatisfaction — with urban-industrial life in their adopted country. Although most Irish Americans offered assistance to impending emigrants, sending passage tickets to relatives at home, only rarely did they actually encourage departures by praising America's economic opportunities, as had been common during the eighteenth and early nineteenth centuries. Instead, most letters written during the period conveyed cautionary or even negative information about the United States and the newcomers' likely prospects: their typical messages were that 'this America is not what it used to be', and so 'any person who can make a fair living at home are better stay theire'. In large part, such letters accurately reflected the difficult realities of working-class life in a generally expanding but highly unstable, stridently competitive, and even physically brutal industrial economy. Financial panics and crippling economic depressions were

8 Doyle, 'The Irish and American Labour', 42–44; James J. Harte, New York City, to Kate Connolly, [Aughnafineguar, County Roscommon?], 21 April 1922 (courtesy of Nuala Simon, Boyle, County Roscommon); Michael Kinney's and other Irish immigrants' memoirs in Joan Morrison and Charlotte Fox Zabusky, eds., *American Mosaic: The Immigrant Experience in the Words of Those Who Lived It* (New York, 1980), 48–49, 61–62; Julia Lough, Winsted, Conn., to her sister, Meelick, Queen's County, 18 January 1891 (Schrier collection); David S. Lawlor, *The Life and Struggles of an Irish Boy in America: An Autobiography* (Newton, Mass., 1936), 25–36 and *passim*; Patrick McKeown, Philadelphia, to his sisters, Lisburn, County Antrim, 8 December 1901 (Schrier collection).

common, and skilled as well as unskilled immigrants suffered grievously at such times: 'our hopes become tinctured with despair ... [and] we feel as if there was no use further to struggle,' wrote Belfast-born Frank Roney, an unemployed iron moulder in San Francisco, during the dark depression winter of 1875–76. During the next major crisis of 1893–97, over a fifth of the entire workforce was unemployed, including 55 per cent of building tradesmen, 44 per cent of miners, and 30 per cent of textile workers — fields where Irish Americans were heavily concentrated. The consequent misery and social dislocation in working-class Irish neighbourhoods became acute, reflected in the black despair and barely suppressed rage that characterized Finley Peter Dunne's 'Mr. Dooley' sketches of contemporary Bridgeport, on Chicago's South Side. Likewise, in the early twentieth century inflated prices alternated with short but sharp recessions, leading the temporary immigrant James Connolly to conclude that the ubiquitous breadlines in New York, Chicago, and other cities, seemed the only uniquely 'American' institutions.[9]

Even during ostensibly 'good times' the lives of Irish-American workers were fraught with insecurity: 'life in America was very trying on a person's nerves,' recalled one returned emigrant, for 'there was always the fear that one might lose his position and become destitute, and destitution in America made life unbearable'. Indeed, after forty years labouring in New England factories, Corkman Timothy Cashman concluded that 'There never was good times for the ordinary *honest worker*.' High living costs frequently offset comparatively high wages, and between inflation and depressions it was 'the same [in America] as in Ireland,' railroad worker James McFadden warned, 'every year something new comes up to make the rich man richer and the poor man poorer'. 'Ireland and America is much all a like,' complained another labourer, ' ther is People to be los[t] in both Places and ther is anuff be hind ...' Fierce competition for jobs exacerbated ethnic and religious animosities, and although in retrospect it appears that the flood of New Immigrants from southern and eastern Europe elevated Irish Americans' status, its effects seemed entirely negative to Irishmen such as Patrick Kearney, James Chamberlain, and Patrick McKeown, who complained in 1904 that his trade of street paving was now monopolized by Italians and Slavs who 'work cheaper & are more submissive'. Moreover, Irish-American 'bosses' and what Frank Roney called 'lick-spittle' foremen also exploited their own countrymen, and ordinary immigrants often had little choice but to be complicit: thus, despite his conviction that 'to deprive

9 Annie Heggarty, Ottumwa, Iowa, to Michael and Mrs. McFadden, Kilcar, County Donegal, 19 July 1884; and James Chamberlain, South Boston, Mass., to his parents, Mitchelstown, County Cork, n.d. [1889–90?] (Schrier collection); Owen O'Callaghan, Philadelphia, to his father and sister Maggie, Fallow, Kilmacthomas, County Waterford, 5 December 1883, and same, from Belmont, Philadelphia, to same, 2 November 1884 (courtesy of Eugene O'Callaghan, Kilmacthomas); Neil L. Shumsky, 'Frank Roney's San Francisco — His Diary: April 1875–March 1876', *Labor History*, 17, 2 (spring 1976), 256; Doyle, 'The Irish and American Labour', 45; Charles Fanning, *Finley Peter Dunne and Mr. Dooley: The Chicago Years* (Lexington, Ky., 1978), 67–104; Carl Reeve and Ann Barton Reeve, *James Connolly and the United States: The Road to the 1916 Irish Rebellion* (Atlantic Highlands, NJ, 1978), 116.

the laborer of his wages' was the 'one sin which cries to the Holy Ghost for vengeance', fear of losing his own job forced the young David Lawlor to help management cheat his fellow Irish mill workers in Fall River, Massachusetts. Unions provided some protection to skilled Irish Americans, but their gains were under constant assault by businessmen and their political allies, and the sheer magnitude of labour unrest in the period (in 1880–1905 the building trades alone engaged in over 9,500 strikes) indicated how tenuous was the status of Irish America's blue-collar élite.[10]

Unskilled Irish Americans suffered most of all, for lack of marketable skills was a serious disadvantage, even for domestic servants, in a highly competitive and uncertain economy. Thus, in 1877 Mary Malone, the Irish-born scrubwoman, complained that in America she could earn no more than '1 Dolard a week', because her parents had consigned her Irish youth to farm work 'out in the fields', thus depriving her of opportunities to learn housekeeping skills: a lament echoed later by Hannah Collins, the overworked servant in upstate New York, who begged her mother in west Cork to send her younger sister to school, so as 'not to have her [become] like I was myself' — poorly educated, ill-trained, and, as Mary Malone put it, 'not cap[a]ble of ... earning big wages'. Many other labourers' and small farmers' children also had little but brawn to market abroad, and in terms of prior social experience and cultural background some were no better prepared than the impoverished Famine immigrants to function in a complex urban-industrial society that demanded work patterns and outlooks antithetical to those prevailing in the Irish-speaking western counties. Most west Kerrymen 'had no business in America', testified one returned emigrant, for 'They had no experience at keeping watch on a clock or at the kind of work that was there, and consequently a lot of them came home again.' However, wages for unskilled workers were so low and uncertain that most could never afford to go home — unless they returned like Tomás Ó Crohan's brother, 'without a red farthing in his pocket ... [t]hough he had not had a day out of work all those long years'. Even in 1900–10 nearly a fourth of male Irish Americans still earned less than family-subsistence wages, and the unmarried drifted about searching for work as harvesters, miners, or factory hands: like west Kerryman Séamus Ó Muircheartaigh, they spent years 'going from place to place, with no company at my side'.[11]

10 Ms. 1409, p. 303 (DIF/UCD); Timothy Cashman, Memoir (courtesy of Patrick Clancy, Youghal, County Cork); James McFadden, Mapleton, Iowa, to Michael McFadden, Kilcar, County Donegal, 17 October 1897 (Schrier collection); Francis Woolsey, Greenpoint, Brooklyn, NY, to Alexander Woolsey, Belfast, 18 June 1877 (Schrier collection); Patrick Kearney, 21 December 1890, in Séamus de Búrca, The Soldier's Song: The Story of Peadar Ó Cearnaigh (Dublin, 1937), 250–53; James Chamberlain, n.d. [1889–90?]; Patrick McKeown, Philadelphia, to Andrew Cosgrove, Belfast, 11 September 1904 (Schrier collection); Ira B. Cross, ed., Frank Roney: Irish Rebel and California Labor Leader: An Autobiography (Berkeley, Calif., 1931), 187; Lawlor, Life and Struggles of an Irish Boy in America, 25–26; Doyle, 'The Irish and American Labour', 46–47.

11 Mary Malone, Fairport, NY, to her brother, Glenmore, County Waterford, 24 January 1877 (Schrier collection); Hannah Collins, Elmira, NY, to Nora McCarthy, Haverhill, Mass., 20 May 1898 (O'Malley

The jobs that post-Famine immigrants did find were often extremely dangerous, for American industrial accident and mortality rates were the world's highest, and Irishmen such as David Lawlor and Seán Ruiséal noted how employers' indifference to their workers' safety brutalized labourers who grew accustomed to replacing killed or injured workmates on assembly lines and pit crews without pause or murmur. Other health hazards were more subtle but equally damaging over time: Lawlor and Seán Ó Gormain reported how the damp air and incessant noise of New England's textile mills produced tuberculosis, permanent deafness, and in Lawlor's case, a nervous breakdown until he resolved 'to quit the mill forever'. Even more galling was the strict discipline imposed by American employers and 'the lean foreman' who 'think ... you're only an ass to be beaten with a stick'. Likewise, despite their greater security, Irish domestic servants such as Elizabeth Dolan chafed under 'hard mistresses' who 'want girls on tap from six in the morning to 10 or 11 at night' and 'boss ... you everlastingly'; 'Whatever you do, don't go into service,' they advised their daughters, for 'You'll always be prisoners and always be looked down upon.'[12]

Given the persistent poverty of a large number of Irish immigrants and their children, it was not surprising that contemporary descriptions of lower-working-class Irish-American neighbourhoods in the 1890s–1920s were often strikingly reminiscent of the destitution and demoralization observed in the 1840s and 1850s. Both residents' and outsiders' accounts of Irish slum life in Boston, New York, Philadelphia, Chicago, and other cities, revealed societies ravaged by chronic unemployment, alcoholism, and disease. In the early twentieth century Irish Americans still contributed a higher proportion of the nation's paupers than any other white ethnic group, and mortality rates, especially from tuberculosis, remained appallingly high: 'It would keep you poor burying your children,' one slum-dweller lamented. Excessive drinking was common among unskilled labourers — in part because they 'could not stand the work', as a Pittsburgh Irishwoman testified of her alcoholic husband — and abused or abandoned wives and children composed an alarmingly high proportion of Irish slum populations. Similarly, Irish immigrants still made up a disproportionately large percentage of patients in public mental institutions: most of them suffering from schizophrenia — an ironic symbol of both the extreme disparities in Irish-American society and the still enormous gaps between new immigrants' often naïve expectations and the unpleasant realities they frequently encountered in the supposed 'land of promise'.[13]

collection); Ms. 1407, 157–88 (DIF/UCD); Ó Crohan cited in Doyle, 'Unestablished Irishmen', 196; Seán Ó Dúbhda, ed., Duanaire Duibhneach (Baile Átha Cliath, 1933), 130–35 (trans. Bruce D. Boling).

12 Ó Dúbhda, ed., Duanaire Duibhneach, 130–35 (trans. Bruce D. Boling); Lawlor, Life and Struggles of an Irish Boy, 25–39; Katzman, Seven Days a Week, 8–9, 38–39, 241.

13 Descriptions include: Alvan F. Sanborn, Moody's Lodging House and Other Tenement Sketches (Boston, 1895), 97–161; Barbara Mullen, Life is My Adventure (New York, 1937); William Z. Foster, Pages from a Worker's Life, 2nd edn. (1939; New York, 1970), 1–20; Fanning, Finley Peter Dunne and Mr. Dooley, 67–104; and Michael Kilcran, Journal 1880–90. Doyle, 'Unestablished Irishmen'; Victor A. Walsh, 'Drowning the Shamrock: The Catholic Total Abstinence Movement in Pittsburgh during the Gilded Age', conference paper (1982),

✳

How did post-Famine immigrants react to the varied circumstances of Irish-American life between the 1870s and the 1920s? How did their experiences alter or confirm expectations and outlooks brought from east Leinster's lush grasslands or west Connacht's bogs and glens? Certainly, their first exposures to urban-industrial America's harsh landscape shocked many newcomers: 'And you mean to tell me ... ,' newly arrived immigrants from County Mayo often exclaimed, gazing in astonishment at Pennsylvania's mining towns and slag heaps, 'Do you mean to tell me that this is America?' However, the prospect and eventual achievement of material improvements helped many such immigrants overcome initial disappointments and decide that, as Annie Lough put it, 'we are better off than if we stayed in Ireland'. Impoverished Connachtmen — often assisted emigrants — and former agricultural labourers especially appreciated that although 'you have got to work hard in America, and work to the clock ... , there is work to be got, and when you do it, you get paid'. Female migrants seemed especially prone to realistic assessments of America's comparative advantages, less likely than husbands or brothers to cling to old customs or romanticize the society left behind: 'Maggie is well and likes this Country,' wrote Thomas McCann of his immigrant sister; 'she would not go back to old Ireland for anny money ... she sayes she had to work to[o] hard when she was there and had nothing for it.' Naturally, those immigrants who achieved success often exulted in the relative fluidity of an American society where, as one Irish American put it, 'labor is prized and rewarded, and where every man is the equal of his fellows'. Such eulogies had been more common during the eighteenth and early nineteenth centuries, and most post-Famine emigrants were less sanguine about claims to American 'exceptionalism' or their own prospects for significant upward mobility. However, most also realized that the New World offered their American-born children opportunities unattainable at home: 'my children is doying first rate,' declared one transplanted Ulsterman, but 'if the[y] were back there [in Ireland] what wood the[y] be?'[14]

since published as '"Drowning the Shamrock": Drink, Teetotalism, and the Irish Catholics of Gilded Age Pittsburgh', Journal of American Ethnic History, 10, 1–2 (1990–91), 60–79; Ibsen, 'Will the World Break Your Heart', 57–58, 229, 286–90.

14 Ms. 1409, 280, and Ms. 1410, 123–5 (DIF/UCD); Ann Lough, Winsted, Conn., to her mother, Meelick, Queen's County, 29 October 1891 (Schrier collection); James Hack Tuke, Reports and Papers Relating to the Proceedings of the Committee of 'Mr. Tuke's Fund' for Assisting Emigration from Ireland during ... 1882, 1883, and 1884 (Dublin, 1883), 158 and passim; Kate Buckley, ed., Diary of a Tour in America by Rev. M. B. Buckley, of Cork, Ireland: A Special Missionary in North America and Canada in 1870 and 1871 (Dublin, 1889), 143–44, 170, 280; Thomas McCann, Minneapolis, Minn., to Mrs. Mary McKeown, Belfast, 18 October 1884 (T.1456/2, PRONI); John S. Sinclair, Healdsburg, Calif., to Margaret Graham, Draperstown, County Derry, 14 December 1883 (D.1497/1/3, PRONI).

Moreover, 'residence under the wings of the American Eagle soon makes people think for themselves', as one migrant reported, and the promptings of their own ambitions and the exigencies of American life often obliged Irish immigrants to alter traditional attitudes and behaviour patterns. Nearly all immigrants quickly assimilated to American norms in superficial matters of speech, dress, and diet, easily persuaded that such adjustments were both means to and symbols of improved status. Thus, former Irish-speakers often took pride in acquired abilities to speak English 'grandly', which belied peasant origins; others rapidly exhibited a 'more developed "acquisitiveness"' by purchasing white bread, first-quality tea, and fashionable clothes from storekeepers who easily exploited their eagerness 'to get ... into "the hang" of the country'. More significant, as James McCauley of County Donegal remembered, was that the immigrants not only had 'to forget a good many of their Irish habits', but also had to 'mind their own business' abroad: behaviour and outlooks compatible with traditional, close-knit rural communities were often dysfunctional in a viciously competitive and individualistic America that obliged a successful migrant such as Michael MacGowan 'to do a lot of things against his will in trying to make a livelihood'. Naïve young immigrants frequently had great difficulties adjusting, but relatives and workmates long-settled in America usually subjected 'greenhorns' to a sometimes brutal process of socialization, often showering newcomers with pitiless ridicule: 'you must work or starve', Michael Kilcran was told after his first day's work in a Chicago slaughterhouse; 'This is not Ireland, this is America and there is no bread for idlers here.' In short, both calculated ambition and the need for sheer self-preservation obliged many immigrants to become 'hard hearted and selfish' in a land where 'it was ... "every man for himself"' and where those who failed to develop self-reliance 'got it in the neck'. 'Every man you meet' in America, advised another returned emigrant, 'take him for a rogue'.[15]

Significantly, post-Famine migrants complained less of harsh treatment from native-Protestant Americans, from whom indifference or exploitation was perhaps expected, than from fellow countrymen. Irish-American 'bosses' and tenement-owners often earned reputations as 'slave drivers' and slumlords, but even more disillusioning for many 'greenhorns' who had migrated to join relatives abroad was the hard-earned lesson that 'A man Cant depend on any friend in this Country ... (however, near in Kin) ...' Consequently, the guiding philosophy of many Irish Americans became 'look out for No.1', for 'it does not pay to have to[o] many ... friends ... in this country': advice echoed by tough-minded women such as Maria Sheehan, who summed up the wisdom of twenty-eight years in America as 'the dollar is your only friend not your relations'. Similarly, many post-Famine immigrants' letters suggest that the ties of family obligation, which

---

15 F. McCosker, Mobile, Ala., to William Cole, Campsey, County Derry, 14 September 1873 (Green collection); James Hack Tuke, 'News from Some Irish Emigrants', *Nineteenth Century*, 25 (March 1889), 432–33; Buckley, *Diary of a Tour*, 151–52. Ms. 1407, 56; Ms. 1409, 300–03 and 327; and Ms. 1411, 349 (DIF/UCD); emphasis added to McCauley quotation. Michael MacGowan, *The Hard Road to Klondike*, trans. Valentin Iremonger (London, 1962), xii, 130; Michael Kilcran, Journal 1880–90.

for decades had sustained chain migration across the Atlantic, were finally beginning to fray and break, in large part because the circumstances of American life often encouraged emotional distance from Ireland. 'Duties' to remit passage tickets, assist newcomers, and support relatives at home were onerous burdens for struggling or ambitious migrants who grew increasingly hardened to kinsmen's pleas and angered at their obstinate assumptions that all immigrants were 'on the pig's back since they were on the other side': 'the people do not like to send money to Ireland', admitted Annie Carroll from Chicago, 'it is all lost'. Echoing such sentiments, in 1883 Irish-American politician Alexander Sullivan declared that the $5 million in annual remittances to Ireland had become an intolerable burden — 'compulsory and of the nature of a tax' — on Irish Americans. Although Sullivan couched his statement in traditionally nationalistic terms, asserting that American dollars shored up Irish landlordism, his argument accurately reflected the growing distance between Ireland and an Irish America two-thirds of whose members were, by 1900, American-born. Whether out of shame for Irish 'backwardness' or pride in their adopted country, many post-Famine immigrants never told their American-born children anything about Ireland: consequently, much evidence suggests that James T. Farrell's fictional Studs Lonigan — a child of American mass culture, bereft of historical consciousness and identity — was a far more typical post-Famine immigrant's son than a dedicated nationalist such as Cincinnati-born Martin Lomasney, who vaporized himself while attempting to dynamite London Bridge. Even among the Irish-born, many labourers' and farmers' children (the latter often forced to emigrate by parents' adverse decisions concerning land inheritance and dowries) were so deeply alienated from impoverished, repressive backgrounds, or so impressed with the necessity to alter totally their personalities in America, that they contemptuously rejected Ireland and its associated folkways. Needless to say, few such immigrants expressed desires to return to Ireland, and many rarely or never wrote home except to vent old resentments and display their newfound superiority to what they called the 'do-nothing and gain-nothing system of going on in the Old Country'. Finally, of course, for most immigrants emotional disengagement from Ireland was less a matter of conscious decision than of time's inexorable processes. When Irish relatives died or emigrated, when the immigrants married and had children of their own, their centres of emotional gravity almost invariably shifted to the New World. And, by the time immigrants reached old age, as millions were doing in the late 1800s and early 1900s, attachments to their adopted country usually proved stronger than faded memories: 'We have been here a long time', explained one elderly Irish American, 'and it is home to us now'.[16]

16 Ms. 1409, 327 (DIF/UCD); Maurice Woulfe, Fort Sedgwick, Colorado Terr., to his uncle, Bruff, County Limerick, 12 May 1867 (Woulfe family letters, courtesy of the late Dr. Kevin Danaher, Dublin; also in microfilm p3887, NLI). James Bredin, Fort Lyon, Colo., to his parents, Kiltyclogher, County Leitrim, 18 November 1887 (courtesy of James Bredin, Birmingham, England); Maria Sheehan, Brookline, Mass., to Mary Hayes, Kinsale, County Cork, 4 August 1914 (M. Hayes Mss., Kinsale Regional Museum, Kinsale);

Nevertheless, despite pressures for assimilation, much evidence indicates that a very large number of post-Famine immigrants regarded themselves as homesick, involuntary 'exiles' — thereby conforming to the biases of a traditional, communal culture as well as to the injunctions of contemporary Irish and Irish-American nationalists and clerics who employed an archaic emigration-as-exile motif as a rallying cry against what they claimed was the British or landlord oppression that had forced the exodus. Of course, for many immigrants the exile imagery was merely rhetorical or ceremonial, a ritual label of community identification. For others, probably the majority, it was internalized but situational, deeply felt at certain stages of the immigrant's life cycle or on particularly emotive occasions, but otherwise suppressed or irrelevant. However, for a large minority, especially for western Irish-speakers and others whose backgrounds ill-fitted them for urban-industrial life, feelings of unhappy exile were so strong that they may have helped shape the immigrants' 'reality' by affecting their responses to American conditions.[17]

Acute homesickness pervaded the letters and memoirs of many post-Famine immigrants. 'Ah Nora,' wrote one woman to her sister in County Galway, 'It makes my very heart break when I think right of home, ... oh Nora I hate to think of it I do be that homesick and lonely'. Usually such feelings were most intense during the immigrants' first months or years abroad, before they 'settled down', but others retained 'that longing' for home throughout their lives and deeply regretted inabilities to fulfil promises to return made at the American wakes held on the eve of departures. Often homesickness was attributable to immigrant poverty, the rootlessness experienced by transient labourers, lack of relatives or friends nearby, and loneliness among the unmarried. Thus, poor Mary Malone, slaving in strangers' kitchens, was 'verry lonseom and down harted' and 'wish[ed] my Sister Margaret was here', while Seán Ruiséal, a self-described 'Spailpín Fánach' (itinerant labourer), complained of 'wandering ... like a helpless cripple / Without a woman to love me'. On the other hand, many immigrants who were comfortably situated, happily married, surrounded by kinsmen and neighbours, also expressed similar sentiments. For all his success and fame, John Boyle O'Reilly 'long[ed]' to lie down in the clover fields of my boyhood', and although Maurice Woulfe acknowledged that America more than satisfied his material needs, he could 'never forget home ... [a]s every Irishman in a foreign land can never forget the land he was raised in'.[18]

Tomás Ó Crohan, The Islandman (London, 1934), 227; Annie Carroll, Chicago, to her cousin, Martinstown, Dunleer, County Louth, 10 May 1890 (courtesy of Kathleen McMahan, Martinstown); Alexander Sullivan, cited in newspaper clipping (HO 45/9635/A29278, PRO, London); Ann Douglas, 'Studs Lonigan and the Failure of History in Mass Society', American Quarterly, 29 (winter 1977), 487–505; Fr. Pius Devine, Journal of a Voyage to America, 1870 (courtesy of Fr. Declan O'Sullivan, St. Paul of the Cross Retreat, Mount Argus, Dublin); Jane Kelly Crowe, Galveston, Tex., to Peter Gaffey, Cregameen, Castlerea, County Roscommon, 10 November 1959 (courtesy of Martin J. Kelly, Celbridge, County Kildare).

17 On emigration as exile, see Chapter 1 in this volume and Miller, Emigrants and Exiles, esp. ch. 3.
18 Katie [Murphy?], Jersey City, NJ, to Nora Murphy, Lissarulla, Claregalway, County Galway, n.d. [1921?] (Green collection); Morrison and Zabusky, American Mosaic, 48; Margaret McGuinness Elliott, Memoir

Most migrants tempered such nostalgia with reason. Thus, although farm labourer J. F. Costello considered Ireland 'the dearest spot in the world', he rationalized that 'home sickness is something that's natural', and despite his desire to be 'home again', if only for 'the short space of one day', Costello — a child of farm labourers — knew well that he and similarly 'poor men' had no chances in Ireland. Others, like Ellen Enright, a former servant from west Cork, now happily married to a saloonkeeper in Washington, DC, realized as well that, because of the effects of mass migration, 'home' no longer existed: 'Dear old Ballinlough,' she sighed, 'no doubt it must be very dreary over there ... . I often set down and picture things that have gone by ... and wonder if there is any fun at all to be had there now but I guess not. All the old fogies remained back and all that had life in [them] left ... . Tell the truth', she asked her friend in Massachusetts, 'are you not glad to be away from there?' However, for some immigrants chronic homesickness crippled ambition and paralysed exertion; thus, Mary O'Donnell from Connemara spent her nights in Pittsburgh sadly remembering 'the days when my heart was light and happy' — as did the Irish-speakers in Chicago whom Michael MacGowan characterized as having 'only one wish and that was to get back to the old country', although most 'would never see the green sod of Ireland again'. Likewise, Mary Ann Rowe, a domestic servant near Boston, 'fe[lt] so bad' that she could scarcely bear to write to her family in County Kilkenny; 'I cannot banish the thought of home out of my mind', she cried; 'no matter where I go is equal to me', and despite her 'very nice' employers, 'nothing could cheer and Strange to say I am growing worse every day'. Indeed, however dubious the prevailing tradition in western Ireland that 'a big number of our boys and girls died of a broken heart' in America, there is no doubt that homesickness sometimes assumed pathological proportions. Many immigrants, like Rowe and Cathy Greene, a young servant in Brooklyn, were tormented nightly by vivid dreams of home: sometimes by 'sweet illusion[s]' but more often by harrowing premonitions of parents' or siblings' deaths, which perhaps reflected guilt felt for having emigrated, as well as consciously repressed longing for home.[19]

c. 1905–20 (courtesy of Alice L. McGuinness, Hampton Bays, NY); on American wakes, see Schrier, *Ireland and the American Emigration*, 84–91, and Miller, *Emigrants and Exiles*, conclusion; on celibacy and postponed marriage in Irish America, see Hasia R. Diner, *Erin's Daughters in America: Irish Immigrant Women in the Nineteenth Century* (Baltimore, Md., 1983), 43–69; Mary Malone, 24 January 1877; Ó Dúbhda, *Duanaire Duibhneach*, 127–29 (trans. Bruce D. Boling); Ibsen, 'Will the World Break Your Heart', 119; Maurice Woulfe, Fort D. A. Russell, Wyoming Terr., to Michael Woulfe, Tralee, County Kerry, 26 January 1870 (Woulfe family letters, see n. 16).

19 J. F. Costello, White River Valley, Washington Terr., to his family, Croagh, County Limerick, 11 January 1883 (Schrier collection); Ellen Enright, Washington, DC, to Nora McCarthy, Haverhill, Mass., 3 July 1900 (O'Malley collection); Annie O'Donnell, Pittsburgh, Pa., to James Phelan, Indianapolis, Ind., 25 August 1901, in Maureen Murphy, ed., *Your Fondest Annie: Letters from Annie O'Donnell to James P. Phelan, 1901–1904* (Dublin, 2005), 39; MacGowan, *Hard Road to Klondike*, 138; Ms. 1410, pp. 104–05, and Ms. 1411, pp. 93, 245 (DIF/UCD); Henry L. Walsh, SJ, *Hallowed Were the Gold Dust Trails: The Story of the Pioneer Priests of Northern California* (Santa Clara, Calif., 1946), 22; Mary Ann Rowe, Dedham, Mass., to James Wallace, Ballintee, Dunnamaggan, County Kilkenny, 29 October 1888 (courtesy of Mrs. Brid Galway, Barrowsland, Thomastown, County

In short, Irish immigrants' homesickness was both consequence and contributing cause of the difficulties experienced abroad, and it resulted from the interaction of characteristics and outlooks brought from Ireland with conditions and situations encountered overseas. Although Costello was correct in asserting that homesickness was 'natural' for nearly all migrants, it was perhaps especially so for many post-Famine Irish because of their marked unpreparedness for urban-industrial society. Thus, recalling his family's immigration to Chicago, Peter Murphy remembered 'how inept we were, how unfitted to battle for a living in a foreign country. ... We were babes in the woods'. Late nineteenth- and early twentieth-century America was 'a surging workshop, displaying incredible marvels at worlds fairs with its spider webs of electricity, its dynamos, its cranes, its transmissions of power, leading to perpetual upheavals and revisions ...'; but what perplexed Kilkenny emigrant Francis Hackett — despite his own bourgeois origins — was his and his countrymen's 'lack of preparation for all this'.[20]

Most post-Famine immigrants were extraordinarily young, in their teens or early twenties, and many — particularly farmers' children who hitherto had led relatively sheltered lives — were even more socially than physically immature. Now they had to endure the tensions of adolescence and migration simultaneously, and while many welcomed their new freedom from prior restraints, others lamented their inexperience and lost innocence and comforts: 'I was too young to know what was good for me / When I left lovely Ireland,' admitted one west Kerryman. In addition, despite the 'modernization' of post-Famine Irish society, most young migrants — especially those from western counties — still came from close-knit, parochial, intensely familial communities, and although an increasing minority expressed alienation from Irish poverty or repression, most remained almost pathetically attached to parents and old neighbours: 'I never knew the good of a Father or Mother [until] I had left them', lamented Patrick Campbell, 'but I never lost that hope nor never will, to be back with them again'. As Sir Horace Plunkett observed from extensive knowledge of both Ireland and Irish America, an Irish countryman had a much broader concept of 'home' than a middle-class Englishman, one which transcended the nuclear family to embrace an entire 'social order' and its physical features: 'these are the things to which [an Irishman] clings ... and which he remembers in exile'. Conveniently forgetting the drudgery and spitefulness of rural life, many immigrants expressed profound nostalgia for their native parishes, creating in memory a 'holy Ireland' that comported with — and was reinforced by — contemporary nationalist and clerical rhetoric. America was 'fine and splendid', acknowledged Batt O'Connor, a Kerry-born stonemason in New England, but 'It has no associations. It is not home'. Indeed, the fact that urban-industrial America was so startlingly different from rural Ireland only heightened immigrants' natural homesickness. Thus, servant

Kilkenny); Cathy Greene, Brooklyn, NY, to Mrs. Catherine Greene, Ballylarkin, Callan, County Kilkenny, 1 August 1884 (Greene/Norris Mss., Archives Department, University College, Dublin).
20 Peter Murphy, East Islip, NY, to Philip Loe, Chicago, 21 April 1954 (Frank Conlan Mss., Chicago Historical Society); Francis Hackett, *American Rainbow: Early Reminiscences* (New York, 1971), 89–90.

girl Anastasia Dowling felt 'very lonesome here' because 'the ways of this place is so different from home', and Seán Ruiséal lamented that although he had 'walked every village and city' in America, 'I never saw a place like the village / I left at the break of day'. The relative anomie of American cities was a frequent cause of complaint in immigrants' letters — 'if we went out in the morning and walked all day we would not meet one face we know', despaired one woman. So also was the harsh American climate — with its 'summer[s] as hot as hell' and its 'winter[s] as cold as the north of the world' — which many immigrants found physically oppressive, indeed often life-threatening, especially compared with Ireland's relatively mild and consistent weather, and thus emblematic of the discontinuity felt by displaced country folk.[21]

In 1872 immigrant William Porter had warned his brother in Ulster 'never [to] come to this Country while you are undecided whether it would suit you better than Ireland, for no body prospers Here that thinks they could do better at home. When you make up your mind to leave Ireland', he concluded, 'do it for good and all ...' Unfortunately, a large proportion of young post-Famine migrants never made such mature, calculated decisions to leave home, but instead merely followed previously established chains of relatives and remittances to the New World. Some were reluctant emigrants who submitted sorrowfully to the exigencies of Irish life, while others who left eagerly did so with naïve expectations based on the fallacious visions of an American paradise — with 'gold and silver out on the ditches, and nothing to do but to gather it' — which were current in rural Ireland, especially in the West. When such visions proved false, and when Irish-American relations proved less 'friendly' than anticipated, the result was often sorrow and regret. 'Alas that I ever came to this land', wrote Séamus Ó Muircheartaigh, 'And that I left my beloved Ireland behind', but

> I got a letter from a relation
> Telling me to hasten across the sea,
> That gold was to be found in plenty there
> And that I'd never have a hard day or a poor one again. ...

> Alas, when I landed
> I made for the city without delay;
> But I never saw gold on the street corners
> Alas, I was a poor aimless person cast adrift.

21 Ó Dúbhda, Duanaire Duibhneach, 127–31 (trans. Bruce D. Boling); Patrick F. Campbell, Journal 1884 (courtesy of Paul Maguire, Ederney, County Fermanagh); Horace Plunkett, Ireland in the New Century (London, 1904), 53–55; Batt O'Connor, With Michael Collins in the Fight for Irish Independence (London, 1929), 14–15; Anastasia Dowling, Buffalo, NY, to Mr. and Mrs. Dunny, Sleaty, County Carlow, 20 January 1870 (Schrier collection); Ellen Wogan, Philadelphia, to Thomas Dunny, Sleaty, County Carlow, 2 September 1870 (Schrier collection); Owen O'Callaghan, Philadelphia, to Thomas O'Callaghan, Fallow, Kilmacthomas, County Waterford, 27 May 1884 (courtesy of Eugene O'Callaghan, Kilmacthomas); Eoin Ua Cathail, Pentwater, Mich., to editor, An Claidheamh Soluis, 4 (26 April 1902), 124–25 (trans. Bruce D. Boling).

Although emigrants who had been most exploited at home — landless labourers and farmers' daughters — generally left Ireland with realistic and minimal goals and so were less prone to disappointment abroad, comfortable farmers' and shopkeepers' sons often held grossly inflated notions of their future prospects and thus were easily disillusioned. Frequently such youths had to work hard for the first time in their lives, often on equal terms with the lower-class Irish whom they had despised at home. Thus, one transplanted Ulsterman admitted that America 'is a good place for men who do manual labour and never feasted on anything better than "Indian buck"', but for himself he could 'see neither comfort nor pleasure' there. 'Ah, Jimmy', complained another pretentious immigrant, 'dacent people and priests' brothers, there's no respect for them' in America.[22]

However, the myth of America as a land of gold was so widely diffused in Irish rural culture that even migrants from the most exploited backgrounds frequently suffered bitter disappointment when they discovered that the United States was not 'a mutual-assistance-doing-unto-others-as-you-would-be-done-by society' but rather, in James Connolly's words, a land where 'human souls are reckoned less than gold'. Indeed, immigrants of peasant origin — unskilled, ill-educated, often Irish-speakers — were especially vulnerable to nativist prejudice and the insecurities of life at the bottom of a society where 'anything you get ... , you sweat blood for'. More than a few western emigrants, such as west Kerryman Tom Brick, had great difficulties conversing in English, and the cultural and psychological barriers to success seem to have been even more formidable than the linguistic. Unprepared by training or perspective for the 'ruthless efficiency' of American life, most prone to nostalgia for intimate, insular communities left behind, such immigrants often proved 'severely out of touch with the American cultural environment to which they were at the same time so vulnerable', as one Yankee noted of the poor Irish huddled in Boston's South End. Francis Hackett drew the same distinctions when he admitted that native-born Americans 'were full of business enterprise, while unenterprise was much more our specialty': 'there was this mind lag', he believed, between traditional Irish and modern American outlooks that hindered his own as well as his poorer countrymen's 'progress' and contentment in the New World.[23]

---

22 William Porter, Chebanse, Ill., to Robert Porter, Dysart, County Down, 25 March 1872 (D. 1152/3/24, PRONI); Maurice O'Sullivan, *Twenty Years A-Growing* (New York, 1933), 239; Ó Dúbhda, *Duanaire Duibhneach*, 132–33 (trans. Bruce D. Boling). On the popular Irish images of America, see Chapter 5 in this volume, and Kerby A. Miller and Bruce D. Boling, 'Golden Streets, Bitter Tears: The Irish Image of America during the Age of Mass Migration', *Journal of American Ethnic History*, 10, 1–2 (1990–91), 16–35. John L. Hall, McDonald, Pa., to Maggie Black, County Armagh, 27 November 1888 (D.2041/Bundle 13, PRONI); Ms. 1407, 43–44 (DIF/UCD).

23 Patrick Blessing, 'West among Strangers: Irish Migration to California, 1850–80' (PhD diss., University of California at Los Angeles, 1977), 128; Reeve and Reeve, *James Connolly and the United States*, 176; Agnes Kelly, Galveston, Tex., to Peter Gaffey, Cregameen, Castlerea, County Roscommon, 22 September 1937 (courtesy of Martin J. Kelly, Celbridge, County Kildare); Tom Brick, Memoir 1881–1904 (courtesy of

The point here is not that cultural legacies predetermined Irish failures abroad, although the cold and 'unnatural' ruthlessness which 'greenhorns' decried among many Irish Americans indicated the drastic personality changes that success or even survival often demanded, but rather that transplanted village outlooks shaped attitudes towards America and the immigration experience that contradicted naïve expectations, and which therefore reinforced or revived traditional perceptions of emigration as unhappy exile. 'Dear Mother,' post-Famine immigrants frequently wrote, 'this country is not what I thought it was', for 'life here is not a bit romantic — it is painfully real'. In such circumstances, expressed desires to return home were commonplace, especially among displaced peasants who longed for lost securities and familiar scenes and faces. 'Go back to Ireland, my modest young girl,' counselled Ó Muircheartaigh,

> Listen to me, little lad and head for home,
> Where you'll have a pound and sixpence on fair day
> And freedom for a carefree dance together on the dew.

Indeed, impressionistic evidence suggests that post-Famine migrants, particularly from the western counties, did return home permanently in comparatively large numbers: in part a reflection of the cheapness of contemporary steamship fares, but also a consequence of the negative impact of American economic depressions and of urban-industrial life generally on Irish-speakers such as Sarah Doherty who were 'never happy' in American cities and who 'never got up in the morning in it, but ... thought how nice it would have been to be rising in Ballighan and seeing the sun' rise over their native mountains.[24]

Of course, the great majority of post-Famine immigrants never returned: some, like the protagonist of Frank O'Connor's story 'Uprooted', because they realized that childhood's idealized and timeless past was irretrievable; others, like Colm Cháit Anna, Máirtín Ó Cadhain's fictional Connemara emigrant, because of lifelong poverty. '[I]f I had the money I would go Back Home again ... in fact I would have been as well if I had never left it', admitted one of Ó Cadhain's non-fictional models, 'but I suppose that will be more than I can ever do'. Many turned to drink for solace, in barrooms awash with broken dreams of lost childhood homes, but most struggled on resignedly against American odds; 'still I hope,' wrote Frank Roney in the depression winter of 1875–76, 'and still will hope while life remains to me'. In this instance, their thorough religious training in Ireland, coupled with the great contemporary expansion of the Catholic

---

Doncha Ó Conchúir, Ballyferriter, County Kerry), and on Brick, see Chapter 15 in this volume; Ibsen, 'Will the World Break Your Heart', 227–28; Hackett, *American Rainbow*, 86–90.

24 Charles Mullen, Brooklyn, NY, to his uncle and aunt, [County Sligo?], 28 December 1883 (T.1866/9, PRONI); John L. Hall, 27 November 1888; Ó Dúbhda, *Duanaire Duibhneach*, 127–33 (trans. Bruce D. Boling); M. 't Hart, '"Heading for Paddy's Green Shamrock Shore": Returned Emigrants in Nineteenth-Century Ireland', *Irish Economic and Social History*, 10 (1983), 96; Ms. 1403, 108–9, and Ms. 1411, 93 (DIF/UCD).

Church in America, served the immigrants well, for internalized faiths in 'God's holy will' saved young Irishmen such as Michael Kilcran and James Hagan from debilitating homesickness and self-pity, as well as from more secular temptations. Likewise, the expanding host of secular institutions that increasingly structured Irish-American life assuaged homesickness and eased adjustments for many newcomers. And, as noted earlier, material improvements, the necessity to repress dysfunctional emotions, and time alone often wrought significant changes in outlook. Nevertheless, homesickness and discontent were remarkably widespread in turn-of-the-century Irish America, particularly among peasant newcomers, and arguably it was those deep-seated emotions of the poor (not a comfortable bourgeoisie's thirst for status) that composed the flickering embers of Irish-American nationalism that Devoy and de Valera fanned into flames in 1916–21.[25]

25 Ruth Sherry, 'Frank O'Connor and Gaelic Ireland', in P. J. Drudy, ed., Irish Studies 1 (Cambridge, 1980), 47–48; Máirtín Ó Cadhain, 'Tnúthán an Dúthchais', in An Braon Broghach (Baile Átha Cliath, 1948), 7–32 (trans. Bruce D. Boling); A. B. McMillan, Pittsburgh, Pa., to Eliza Crossan, Newtownards, County Down, 10 April 1894 (D. 1195/5/39, PRONI); Shumsky, 'Frank Roney's San Francisco', 256; Michael Kilcran, Journal 1880–90; James Hagan, New York City, to Mary Hagan, Dungannon, County Tyrone, 3 October 1884 (MIC 181/33, PRONI).

15 From the Gaeltacht to the Prairie: Tom Brick's Ireland and America, 1881–1979

No doubt it is generally true that the ability to speak English gave Irish migrants to North America certain collective advantages over immigrants from Germany, Scandinavia, and later from southern and eastern Europe.[1] However, there was always a substantial contingent of Irish-speakers among Ireland's emigrants to the New World, and although most were more or less bilingual, many were scarce able to comprehend or converse in English. Ironically, evidence of a Gaelic America is sparse during the pre-Famine decades, when at least half the Catholics in Ireland itself were Irish-speakers, perhaps because in 1815–44 overseas migration remained comparatively rare from the western counties where Irish-speaking from cradle to grave was most prevalent. Nevertheless, Irish-speakers were common wherever in America the poorest immigrants congregated, as in waterfront neighbourhoods, suburban shanty towns, mining and lumber camps, and among the gangs on public works sites. Thus, in the 1820s poet Pádraig Cúndún, a monoglot Irish-speaker from east Cork, laboured on the Erie Canal alongside thousands of other Irish-speakers — communicating with Anglo-America only through his wife and other bilingual migrants — before purchasing his 'snug farm' near Utica, New York.[2]

1 Originally titled 'In the Famine's Shadow: From West Kerry to South Dakota, 1881–1979', this chapter was published initially in Margaret M. Mulrooney, ed., *Fleeing the Famine: North America and Irish Refugees, 1845–1851* (Westport, Conn., 2003), 113–32, a volume created by Dr. Mulrooney in memory of the late Professor Tim Sarbaugh, of Gonzaga University, who initiated the project and invited me to contribute prior to his sudden death. My thanks to Praeger Publishers for permission to republish the essay, with revisions, in this volume. Thanks also to Professor David N. Doyle, of University College, Dublin, for his guidance through the mysteries of the published 1870 and 1900 US censuses and of the Dillingham Commission's reports.
2 Kerby A. Miller, *Emigrants and Exiles: Ireland and the Irish Exodus to North America* (New York, 1985), ch. 6.

It was the Great Famine, however, that stimulated mass migration from the Irish-speaking West and thereby remodelled Irish America and gave its lower-class majority a decidedly Gaelic cast. In 1845–55 between 50 and 60 per cent of Irish emigrants to North America came from regions where Irish was still the majority — or at least a strong minority — language. As a result, at least a fourth and perhaps a third of all Famine migrants to the New World were bilingual or monolingual Irish-speakers. Most Protestant Americans, ignorant of Irish society and fixated on the newcomers' Catholicism, overlooked this phenomenon, although certainly it intensified the alienation felt by élite native-born Americans, like George Templeton Strong, from the Irish labourers whom they encountered on the streets of US cities. Similarly, most middle-class Irish Americans, eager (like their peers in Ireland) to stress their group's adaptability to 'civilized' (that is, English-speaking) society, generally ignored the presence of the Irish language even as they deprecated the transplanted 'peasant' customs with which it was associated. Consequently, most of the few surviving remarks on Irish-speakers in mid-nineteenth-century America came from Irish Catholic priests, who knew that the success of the Church's spiritual mission abroad depended heavily on their ability to preach and administer the sacraments in what was many Famine immigrants' sole or preferred language.[3]

In the decades immediately following the Famine, the Irish-speaking proportion of Irish migrants to North America probably declined. In post-Famine Ireland itself the numbers of Irish-speakers steadily fell, and by 1901 they comprised merely 14 per cent of the island's inhabitants. Also, during the 1856–80 period generally — and despite surges of departures from Galway and other western counties in the early 1860s — over half the overseas migrants came from the most Anglicized Irish provinces of Leinster and Ulster. From the late 1870s, however, a new rural crisis in western Ireland precipitated a political upheaval and — despite the Land War's success — a socio-cultural revolution that made mass migration a permanent, omnipresent feature of western Irish society. As a result, between 1880 and the 1920s more than half of all emigrants departed from Ireland's most culturally and linguistically 'traditional' regions. Nearly all the counties that experienced the period's highest emigration rates — Clare, west Cork, and Kerry in Munster, Donegal in Ulster, and Galway and Mayo in Connacht — were located along Ireland's impoverished and still heavily Irish-speaking western seaboard. Between one-fourth and one-third of these late post-Famine emigrants were Irish-speakers, mostly from areas that in 1891 were officially described as the 'Congested Districts' — so poor and 'backward' they were targeted for special government assistance. Ironically, after Irish independence, the same Irish-speaking regions were legally designated as the Gaeltacht and eulogized as the new nation's cultural and spiritual heartland. As during the Famine, however, many of the new western emigrants were, compared to their peers from northern and eastern Ireland, ill-prepared for American life in their

---

3   Miller, *Emigrants and Exiles*, ch. 7, esp. 297–98.

lack of capital, skills, grasp of English, and basic literacy. Thus, from the 1880s on, just as Irish America as a whole was beginning to attain the kinds of socio-economic and institutional maturity described in Chapter 11, it was obliged to absorb a last substantial wave of peasant immigrants who were generally impoverished, marginally Anglicized, and hence often profoundly embarrassing to the Irish-American bourgeoisie — some of whose spokesmen responded with demands that the US government curtail 'pauper emigration' from the homeland.[4]

Tom Brick, the subject of this final chapter, was quite typical of late post-Famine migrants from the Irish-speaking West, except in one important respect. The great majority settled in urban-industrial enclaves, usually in the Northeast, Middle Atlantic, or Midwest regions. Hence, in mill towns like Holyoke and Springfield, Massachusetts, and in lower-working-class neighborhoods such as South Boston and in Pittsburgh's Point and north Philadelphia's Schuylkill districts, contemporaries often remarked on their largely unskilled and Irish-speaking inhabitants: on their high rates of unemployment, poverty, and social pathology; on their socio-cultural isolation from Irish America's middle classes (as well as from Anglo-America, generally); and on their strong sense of alienation and homesickness.[5] By contrast, Tom Brick's family connections took him from west Kerry to the American Midwest's prairies and plains, and to one of post-Famine Irish America's few Irish-speaking agricultural communities. Fortunately, the latter's 'settled' and prosperous character enabled Brick, despite his own homesickness, to adapt constructively and, eventually, quite prosperously to his adopted country.

It may be true that a large, unknown proportion of pre-Famine Irish immigrants, Catholics as well as Protestants, became farmers in the United States. However, for lack of sufficient capital or skills, and perhaps also for socio-cultural reasons (as contemporaries, Irish and non-Irish, often alleged), that certainly was not true of the Famine and post-Famine immigrants, as US census data clearly demonstrate. In 1870, for instance, only 14.6 per cent of Irish immigrants were engaged in agricultural pursuits, compared with 54.1 per cent of native-born Americans and nearly 23 per cent of all foreign-born persons — including roughly 27 per cent of German, 25 per cent of British, and 46 per cent of Scandinavian immigrants. The 1900 census, supplemented by reports from the so-called Dillingham Commission on US immigration, evinces similar patterns. Thus, in 1900 less than 12 per cent of America's 'Irish stock' inhabitants (that is, the Irish-born and the US-born of Irish parentage combined) were engaged in agricultural occupations, compared with nearly 40 per cent of native-born whites and almost 21 per cent of the members of all white 'ethnic' groups, generally. From a slightly different perspective, in 1900 only 15.3 per cent of Irish-stock 'male breadwinners' (and merely 13.6 per cent of those born in Ireland) were employed in

4 Miller, *Emigrants and Exiles*, ch. 8, esp. 346–53. See also David N. Doyle, 'Unestablished Irishmen: New Immigrants and Industrial America, 1870–1910', in Dirk Hoerder, ed., *American Labor and Immigration History, 1877–1920s: Recent European Research* (Urbana, Ill., 1983), 193–220.
5 Miller, *Emigrants and Exiles*, ch. 8, esp. 397–402 and 492–555; and Doyle, 'Unestablished Irishmen'.

agricultural pursuits, compared with 47.3 per cent of native whites of native parentage, with 23.3 per cent of all whites of foreign parentage (21.2 per cent of all foreign-born), and with 28 per cent, 22 per cent, and 41 per cent of those of German, British, and Scandinavian stock, respectively.

There were, of course, significant regional differences. In some midwestern states, with economies that were overwhelmingly agricultural, their relatively few Irish residents were likewise engaged principally in farming and related occupations. Thus, in 1870 nearly 57 per cent of the comparatively small numbers of Irish immigrants in Iowa and Wisconsin, and nearly 60 per cent of those in Minnesota, were employed in agriculture. Moreover, in those states the great majority of Irish immigrants so employed were farmers rather than agricultural labourers, whereas in eastern, urban-industrial states, such as Massachusetts and New Jersey, Irish farm labourers outnumbered Irish farmers by roughly two to one. In 1900 the same patterns prevailed, and in states like Massachusetts it is very likely that the relatively few Irish immigrant males employed in agriculture (who comprised merely 5.9 per cent of the Bay State's Irish-born males in all occupations) were concentrated heavily among the nearly two-thirds of the Irish so employed who were agricultural labourers rather than farmers. In Iowa, by contrast, in 1900 nearly 87 per cent of the Irish-born males engaged in agriculture were farmers. By then, however, most of Iowa's Irish-born farmers were late middle-aged or elderly, for in the 1890s and early 1900s many once thriving Irish rural communities were thinning or even disintegrating, as Irish immigrant farmers' US-born children and grandchildren, like their young Anglo-American contemporaries, abandoned the countryside for urban employment.[6]

Thus, although Tom Brick's life in America began rather unusually, with farm work on the midwestern prairie, it eventually followed well-worn paths that had been pioneered by his Famine and even pre-Famine predecessors: towards his eventual urbanization, for example, and in his close associations with tightly knit Irish-American families and communities; and also in his progress — based largely on those networks — from unskilled to semi-skilled and skilled labour, and eventually into the ranks of urban proprietors and property owners. Likewise typical of western Ireland's latest immigrants was Brick's close identification with the Catholic Church and the Democratic party, but also his retention of traditional Irish folkways, his political sympathies rooted in bitter Irish memories and in his cohort's doubly 'outsider' status in Irish-American as well as American societies, and his consequent support for the most radical (and least

6 Proportions in this and the preceding paragraph were calculated from the tables in *Ninth Census* [1870] *of the United States: Vol. 1: Population* (Washington, DC, 1872), 669–765; *Twelfth Census* [1900] *of the United States: Special Report, Occupations* (Washington, DC, 1904), clxxxvi–ccxii, 7–83; and *Reports of the Immigration* [Dillingham] *Commission, Vol. 28: Occupations of the First and Second Generations of Immigrants in the United States* (Washington, DC, 1911), 6, 60–69, 216–33, and 328. On the Irish in the 1870 US census, also see David N. Doyle, 'The Irish as Urban Pioneers in the United States, 1850–1870', *Journal of American Ethnic History*, 10, 1–2 (1990–91), 36–59.

'respectable') expressions of Irish and Irish-American nationalism. In such respects, Brick's origins in western Ireland — under the shadow of the Great Famine and of the West's more recent socio-cultural and political crises — were perhaps as important in shaping the character of his long pilgrimage in the United States as was the tiny and singular Irish-American community to which he adapted. Fortunately, Brick's own memoir, written near the end of his long life, provides a unique and intimate perspective on his career's early stages, both in Ireland and on the American prairie, whereas his later decades can be documented through family papers, public records, and other sources.[7]

The Great Famine ravaged most of the poor regions along Ireland's western coasts: hundreds of thousands died of hunger and disease, and roughly equal numbers fled overseas or to Britain. However, many of the Famine's long-term, structural effects were delayed in western Ireland. In remote parts of counties such as Kerry, Mayo, and Donegal, subsistence cultivation and traditional farming patterns, the Irish language and old customs and beliefs, survived the catastrophe; and between 1855 and 1878 western Irish emigration was generally less institutionalized than elsewhere on the island — thanks in part to the continued prevalence of partible inheritance. However, the near-famine of 1878–82, agrarian and political conflicts during the 1880s, and the inexorable advances of commercialization and Anglicization wrought profound changes in the West. Most farmers finally shifted to impartible inheritance, thereby disinheriting a majority of their children; despite the efforts of the Gaelic League, Irish-speaking declined sharply in many areas; and old communal and familial bonds were eroded and reconstituted abroad as the children of western Ireland flocked to America.[8]

Among these emigrants was Thomas or Tom Brick (Tomás Ó Bric) from the clachán village and townland of Gortadoo (Na Gorta Dubha: 'Black Fields') in the parish of

7 Much of the following information about Tom Brick and his family, and all quotations not otherwise attributed in the text or in notes, are derived from the memoir he produced in 1970. For permission to publish selections from Brick's memoir, and for additional biographical and other information, I wish to thank especially James and Kevin Brick of Sioux Falls, South Dakota. I am also very grateful to Doncha Ó Conchúir of Ballyferriter, County Kerry, for first bringing Tom Brick's memoir to my attention and for Irish background data; to James V. Manning of Sioux City, Iowa, who in 1978 first secured permission from his uncle Tom Brick, then still living, to use his memoir in my historical research; to Alice Beck of Mabank, Texas, Professor David Emmons of the University of Montana, Margaret Fortin of Glendale, California, J. Byron O'Connor of Sioux City, Iowa, and Dorothy Walsh of Long Beach, California, for information about the Garryowen, South Dakota, settlement; and to Fayann Hubert of Salix, Iowa, for her prodigious research in census, probate, and other records concerning the Brick family, their relatives, and the Irish in Woodbury County, Iowa, and in South Dakota, generally.

8 On the causes of post-Famine emigration from western Ireland, see: Kerby A. Miller, *Emigrants and Exiles: Ireland and the Irish Exodus to North America* (New York, 1985), ch. 8, sections 2–3.

Dunurlin, Corkaguiney barony, at the tip of the Dingle peninsula in west County Kerry. Born in September 1881,[9] Brick was the youngest of at least eight children born to William Brick (1831–1911) and Ellen (Nell) Sullivan (born 1836; still living in 1925), who, in partnership with eight other families, rented Gortadoo, over 418 acres, from the earl of Cork.[10] The total rent was £111, and William Brick's share, £14 12s. in 1902, suggests that he held about 50 acres divided in traditional rundale fashion among small parcels of tillage, pasture, and rough lands scattered throughout the townland. Although much of their holding was mountain pasture and bog, the family was minimally comfortable by west Kerry standards. Moreover, as the Anglo-Irish writer John Millington Synge observed, not only was Brick's parish a scene of 'indescribable grandeur', but even in the early twentieth century traditional music and dancing, stories, poems, and fairy-belief yet flourished. Most of the people of Dunurlin, like Tom Brick, still spoke Irish as their first and sometimes only language; and Irish was so prevalent that, even before the advent of the Gaelic League, the National School that Brick attended in Ballyferriter taught students to read and write Irish, as well as English — a language that Brick could speak only haltingly until he had lived several years in America.[11]

Yet although culturally enriched, life for the fifteen households in Gortadoo was materially impoverished. Synge noted that typhus often infested such villages, and in 1900 Tom Brick shared his three-room, thatched house not only with his parents and sister Margaret (born 1873) but also with his married brother James (born 1858) and the latter's wife and five children. Indeed, before the emigrations of other siblings, the house had held fourteen persons, and the adjacent farmstead belonging to Brick's

9 Tom Brick never knew his precise birth date — which was not uncommon among Irish country folk at that time — and it was not until 1970 that he wrote to the Catholic priest at Ballyferriter and learned that he had been baptized at the local chapel on 21 September 1881.

10 In 1876 the earl of Cork, who resided in Somersetshire, England, owned 11,531 acres in County Kerry, valued at £2,547, plus another 20,165 acres in County Cork. However, most of the townlands in Dunurlin parish were owned by the earl of Ventry, of Burnham House in nearby Dingle, and in 1876 Lord Ventry held a total of 93,629 acres in Kerry, valued at £17,067. See: *Land Owners in Ireland. Return of Owners of Land of One Acre and Upwards in the Several Counties, Counties of Cities, and Counties of Towns in Ireland* (1876; repr. Baltimore, Md., 1988).

11 Background information about Tom Brick's west Kerry background, which appears in this and the following paragraphs, was derived from data provided by Doncha Ó Conchúir (see n. 7) or from the following sources: Sir Richard Griffith, *Primary Valuation of Ireland*, 1848–64: Dunurlin parish (1852), copy in the NLI; and the updated records in the Irish Land Valuation Office, Dublin; the 1901 Irish census schedules for Gortadoo townland, in the National Archives of Ireland, Dublin, as well as the published Irish censuses, 1841–1911, in the BBP; *Land Owners in Ireland* (see n. 10); Samuel Lewis, *A Topographical Dictionary of Ireland ... with Historical and Statistical Descriptions* (1837; repr. Baltimore, Md., 1984); John Millington Synge, 'In West Kerry', in Robert Tracy, ed., *The Aran Islands and Other Writings* (New York, 1962), 215–67 (quotation and reference to typhus [below in text] on 224–25); Miller, *Emigrants and Exiles*, ch. 8, sections 2–3; and especially Pádraig Ó Siochfhradha, *Triocha-céad Chorca Dhuibhne* (Baile Átha Cliath, 1938); Tomás Mac Síthigh, *Paróiste an Fheirtéaraigh* (Baile Átha Cliath, 1984) and the essays by Éanna Ní Mhóráin and Seán Ó Lúing in Micheál Ó Cíosáin, ed., *Céad Bliain, 1871–1971* (Baile an Fheirtéaraigh, 1973). I am grateful to Professor Emeritus Bruce D. Boling of the University of New Mexico for translating the relevant information from these works in the Irish language.

uncle, Maurice, still housed eleven. In addition, neither Dunurlin nor Gortadoo was immune from the socio-economic and cultural changes that compelled or encouraged emigration. Between deaths and departures overseas, during the Great Famine the parish and the townland had lost 50 per cent and 24 per cent of their respective populations, and these first emigrants had included Brick's aunt, Johanna Sullivan O'Connor (1832–1910), and her husband, Thomas O'Connor (1834–1907). During the 1860s Gortadoo's inhabitants decreased nearly 7 per cent, and among these later emigrants was an uncle, Thomas Sullivan (1836–1913), who left home in 1863.

As elsewhere in western Ireland, in the late 1870s and early 1880s potato crop failures, falling farm prices, and evictions caused a sharp increase in emigration from west Kerry. In 1880 Tom Brick's aunt, Mary Sullivan (1835–1924), left Gortadoo for South Dakota, where she married a cousin, also named Thomas Sullivan; and in the same year (shortly before he was born) Brick's own sister Mary (1861–1943) emigrated to western Iowa and later married Timothy Rohan (1857–1934), who had left west Kerry in 1879.[12] Between 1881 and 1891 Dunurlin's and Gortadoo's populations declined by nearly 11 and 7 per cent, respectively, and in 1892 another of Brick's sisters, Julia (1879–1960), departed to join her relatives in South Dakota, where she married an Iowa-born farmer of Irish parentage, John Manning (1870–1942). Between 1891 and 1901 Gortadoo's population declined less than 2 per cent (while Dunurlin's actually increased slightly), but in 1900 Brick's brother, William (1880–1922), left to join the Mannings in South Dakota, and during the first decade of the twentieth century the townland's population fell by a further 12 per cent. Thus, between 1841 and 1911 the numbers of inhabitants in Dunurlin and Gortadoo declined from 2,145 and 210, respectively, to merely 799 and 99. No wonder that William Long, the assistant schoolmaster in Ballyferriter, counselled Tom Brick and his other pupils 'to study American history and American geography, for "that's where the most of ye are going"'.

For Tom Brick and for many other post-Famine Catholic emigrants, memories of Ireland were coloured by nationalist sentiments that persisted or even grew stronger in the New World, often leading them to interpret their departures as tantamount to political exile forced by British and/or landlord oppression. Certainly, Dunurlin parish contained numerous reminders of Catholic defeat and despoliation: near the strand of Smerwick Harbour, where the Bricks grazed their cattle, were the remains of a fort where in 1580 English troops had massacred over 600 Irish rebels and their Spanish allies; equally close was the ruined castle of Piaras Feirtéir, hanged for rebellion in 1653. In more recent times, Dunurlin's country people had good cause to despise the local landlords, the earls of Cork and Ventry, and especially their agents, the

12 At least two more of Tom Brick's sisters also emigrated. Katherine (1872–1948) was in Salix, Iowa, in 1887, when she witnessed the marriage of sister Mary to Tim Rohan; in 1896 she married Edward Cleary, also in Salix, but she died 'separated' from her husband. In 1925 another sister (b. 1875), first name unknown, was listed as Mrs. John Dowd of Burbank, South Dakota, in her brother William's probate administration. I am grateful to Fayann Hubert of Salix for discovering this information.

Husseys and Rices, for rack-renting and evicting their tenantry during the Famine and afterwards. Yet until the late nineteenth century, nationalist sentiments among western Irish-speakers tended to be rhetorical, fossilized in poetry and songs, and localized, based on parochial resentments; and until the late 1870s the peasants of west Kerry, Mayo, and elsewhere along the Atlantic coast played little part in organized nationalist movements. However, the conflicts and agitations of the 1880s mobilized the West under Davitt's and Parnell's leadership, and although the Land War did not come to Dunurlin and Gortadoo until after the middle of the decade (in the phase known as the Plan of Campaign), Brick's memoirs, written some eighty-five years after the events described, demonstrate how the bitter events and emotions of that period, in this instance set to verse by a local poet, were burned indelibly into the minds of late nineteenth- and early twentieth-century emigrants:[13]

> The one incident I will always remember if I am to live to be one hundred years old … was the morning I got up and got dressed and expecting some breakfast [found instead t]hat Mother and Father [and] the rest of the family were gone … . Looking to find somebody that would tell me where my Father & Mother and everybody were[, t]he only one I found in the whole village was Batt Manning[14] who told me that all the people of the village had gone to the eviction. … [I]t was the two Ferriter families[15] that were being evicted by Lord Ventry for non-payment of rent. I … ran the short distance and got close enough to see the company of English Red Coats[16] and the sheriff leaving the Ferriter place and returning to Dingle … . On the [Ferriters'] land was a very unusual large slate-roofed stone dwelling house which had two open fire places and several other farm houses such as a cow house and horse stable. They usually kept twenty milk cows, two work horses and several stock cattle, some sheep on the rough coast land, where the old tower and old castle stood over the steep … cliffs. The Ferriter place adjoined the land that my father rented from … Lord Cork. Anyway, there was not a living animal on the Ferriter place … [t]hat the Red Coats and sheriff could attach for overdue rent. All of the Ferriters' livestock including the two work horses were distributed among the neighbours the day before the eviction. We … had one of the milk cows and milked it all that summer. The proceeds from that milk was

---

13 Thomas Brick's memoir was initially a tape-recording and then a transcription typed by a relative. In these circumstances, for publication it was necessary to make minor editorial emendations in the transcript.

14 Bartholomew Manning was recorded in the 1901 Irish census as a bachelor farmer and monolingual Irish-speaker, age forty, who lived in a one-room thatched cottage.

15 The Ferriters of Ballyoughteragh townland, adjacent to Gortadoo, had rented jointly with another family some 455 acres from Lord Ventry. In 1852 the entire holding had been assigned an annual valuation of nearly £100; the Ferriters' share was valued at £65 7s. During the 1880s, members of the Ferriter family were prominent in the Ballyferriter Land League agitation, which provoked their landlord's wrath and brought about their eviction from the Ballyoughteragh farm on 21 July 1887.

16 British soldiers were still wearing red uniforms in 1887.

kept separate and given to the Ferriter family. The cow was sold late in the autumn of that year at a regular market day in Dingle and the proceeds given to the Ferriter family. The day after the Ferriters were evicted, ... the men of the parish got together and built a stone house with a thatch roof in one day on some common ground next to the Ferriter Cove Beach for one of the Ferriter family, Michael Ferriter. [T]he other Shawn Ferriter moved into an already vacant house also on the same beach ... . The evicted Ferriter place was not vacant very long when the landlord, Lord Ventry, decided to make use of the good house and land, so he immediately dispatched some fifty or seventy-five stock cattle to graze on the land. ... In charge were two Bailiff caretakers and three or four helmeted policemen from [the] North [of] Ireland to protect [them]. In a matter of a few days the caretaker and four policemen could not buy groceries, milk, bread, butter or potatoes any place because of a boycott started by the people in several parishes west of Dingle. So in order to partially relieve the situation ... Lord Ventry ... dispatched two nice black Kerry milk cows in charge of two special trustworthy bailiffs to deliver the ... cows to the two caretakers and the four policemen protecting the caretakers on the Ferriters' evicted farm.

It was fifteen or eighteen long Irish miles from Burnham [Lord Ventry's demesne] ... to the evicted Ferriter farm. Evidently the dust of the road was affecting the two bailiffs driving the two black Kerry cows ... . [K]nowing that Mrs. John DeHora ... operated a public house with a back yard walled in by the roadside on the west end of the village of Bally Ferriter ... only a mile or two from their destination[,] and no doubt dry and thirsty, they both decided to stop at Mrs. John DeHora's public house where the two cows would be safe in the enclosed backyard while they the two bailiffs would partake of the good thirst-quenching liquids that Mrs. DeHora dispensed ... . Evidently they lingered and tarried at the bar too long[, for] while the police and the bailiffs were taking the[ir] rest, the two cows disappeared for good never to be found.

Brick completed his primary education at Ballyferriter in 1896 and, given his poor mastery of English, had no desire for further schooling. Instead, he and William secured a loan of £16 from the Congested Districts Board to purchase a boat and other fishing equipment. Created by parliament in 1891, the board was designed to develop the economy of the impoverished regions along the western coasts: before its demise in 1923, the board spent £11 million in purchasing and redistributing land to the inhabitants; improving farm methods, buildings, and livestock breeds; and encouraging industries such as lace-making and fishing. The latter was one of the board's greatest successes, and its loans enabled fishermen in west Kerry and elsewhere to purchase the larger boats needed for profitable deep-sea fishing. However, as Brick remembered in his memoir, trolling for mackerel at night along the rugged coasts was dangerous, and the brothers almost drowned on at least one occasion when a steamship nearly ran them down.

Moreover, as Synge noted, marginal economic improvements in western Ireland only generated novel ambitions that the inhabitants could not satisfy at home; and, ironically, the benign efforts of the Congested Districts Board — and the higher living standards that prevailed in the West, generally, after the 1880s — only encouraged more emigration, especially by young men and women whose chances for land and marriage were now thwarted by the restrictions of impartible inheritance and the dowry system.[17]

Thus, in 1902 Tom Brick decided to abandon Ireland and join his relations overseas. In his memoir, he described his fateful decision and departure, demonstrating the interplay between his dissatisfaction with limited opportunities in Ireland (which he blamed partly on 'landlords and British rule'), the romantic and tangible lures of America, and the anxieties and sorrows consequent on actually leaving home:

> ... [F]ishing in Smerwick Harbor was not getting any better and just as dangerous as ever and receiving an occasional letter from my sister Mary Brick at Salix, Iowa, who was married to Timothy Rohan, I am thinking about coming to America. ... I would lay on the bank over the black rocks, adjacent to the sandy beach at Cooltraig and look west towards Ennis Tousgart[18] beyond and wonder how Columbus ever got the courage in his effort to discover America in those three little galleys that Queen Isabella of Spain furnished him. Here I am now close to twenty years of age, living with my father and mother and an older brother Shamus who is married and raising a family and living in the same house ... . According to landlords and British rule at that time, [h]e being the oldest son in the family naturally would fall heir to the landholding,[19] such as it was, ... the grass or pasturage for eight or ten cows[. A]s for me, here I am with only the Curra[20] boat and a string of nets to try and make a living. To get married and settle down under those circumstances was out of the question and to sign up to learn any of the trades which required

17 On the operations of the Congested Districts Board in the West of Ireland, see: Synge, 'In West Kerry'; and, more generally, L. P. Curtis, Jr., *Coercion and Conciliation in Ireland, 1880–1892: A Study in Conservative Unionism* (Princeton, NJ, 1963).

18 Inis Tuaisceart, or the Northern Island, one of the Blasket Islands off the west Kerry coast, still inhabited during most of Tom Brick's lifetime.

19 It is intriguing that Tom Brick blamed 'landlords and British rule' for the practice of impartible inheritance which western farmers adopted wholesale and quasi-voluntarily, under market pressures, in the late nineteenth and early twentieth century. Equally intriguing is Brick's assertion that 'landlords and British rule' mandated primogeniture as the rule of inheritance, since his father's choice of the eldest son to inherit the farm was not only voluntary but also far from universal. Indeed, some studies suggest that western farmers' decisions as to inheritance were random but with a bias towards ultimogeniture: i.e., the youngest sons were more likely to inherit than the oldest — in part because, by the time farmers were willing to retire, their eldest children had already emigrated, leaving only the youngest to care for their aged parents.

20 i.e. curragh: a light, wood-framed, and canoe-shaped fishing boat, commonly employed by fishermen on Ireland's west coast. Traditionally, the hulls were made of sealskins stretched over the frames, but the newer and larger models used oilskins and, less fragile, were better suited to fishing in deep water further offshore.

five or six years of apprenticeship without any pay and not enough to eat much of
the time, that too was out of the question[;] and [to] make matters worse when
the colleen I liked and loved was married and given a dowry by her father, as was
customary to a neighbouring farmer's son, with all this happening at that time,
is making me think and decide on that venture to America. Why not take the
chance Columbus did[?] From day to day it became the greatest thought in my
mind, until finally I made up my mind to go ... , having all the money needed to
pay for my passage to any locality in the United States of America or Australia. ...
[A]s there were many people emigrating from the County Kerry to Australia and
South Africa at that time, I am undecided which venture to take[,] U.S. America or
Australia, giving the matter some thought and some consultation with a neighbour
(a returned Yank as they were nicknamed at that time by the local people).
[It was this] man Jim Higgins[21] who spent eight years in Springfield, Mass. U.S.A.
who really persuaded me to go to America instead of Australia. [Also I had] a fair
knowledge of United States History from a large United States History book that
my sister Mary Brick Rohan had brought home on a visit from Salix, Iowa, ... about
1897 or 1898. The[n] there was another inducement[:] Knowing that I had three
aunts and two uncles all on my mother's side of that family, who had taken and
settled on some government land somewhere in eastern So[uth] Dakota, U.S.A.
about the year 1868 in an Irish settlement ... named Garry Owen ... . Now it is
well I remember because it is many a letter I read and wrote for my mother to her
brothers Tom and Daniel Sullivan of ... South Dakota ... .

Now that I have decided to go to America, the next thing was ... to break the
news to Father and Mother. [I]t was on a cattle market day on the way to Dingle
... driving a few head of cattle to the Dingle market that I told my Father than I
intended to go to Timothy Galvin[,] John's Street, Dingle[,] and register for my
passage to Salix, Iowa, U.S.A. to which Father Bill finally after a time consented.
After selling the cattle and getting the money at the bank on Main Street, Dingle,
Father accompanied me across the little bridge and up to John's Street and
Tim Galvin's shipping agency ... with whom I registered and paid the required fee
... . I then purchased some necessary luggage and was given the date of sailing on
the liner Oceanic from Queenstown, twelve o'clock high noon, ... April 17, 1902.

... I persuaded my Father Bill to break the news to mother that I had registered
and paid for my passage. ... It was late when Father Bill and myself returned home
to Gortadoo that evening walking all the way over the hard, rough mountain
pass, twelve miles [of] road carrying a few household necessities. The following
morning it was when my Father Bill told my Mother, Brother Jim, and the rest of
the remaining Brick family ...

---

21 The 1901 Irish census reported James Higgins, age sixty and bilingual, as a carpenter, living with his wife
and one child in a two-room house in Gortadoo.

... [T]he atmosphere in the Brick Family home was none too cheerful now for the few remaining days until April 15th when I would be leaving [my] home at Gortadoo[, a]s it took one day from there by cart to Dingle, then by narrow gauge railroad to Tralee, from Tralee by rail to Cork and eventually to Queenstown. The evening of the fourteenth there was a farewell party[22] in the old thatch roof Brick Family household. Not all of the fifteen families living in the village of Gortadoo at that time attended the party that evening, but there was enough to fill the spacious kitchen floor. There was singing and dancing, some drink and lots to eat such as we had. The large flagstone in front of the fireplace hearth took a terrific beating that evening while S[h]awneen played 'The Wind that Shook the Barley' on his fiddle for the eight-hand reel for the four boys and four girls dancing it[, t]hen playing the fisher's horn pipe, the ricketts and the sailor's horn pipe for the [t]hree practical step dancers who lived at Gortadoo at that time. [T]he party remained late that night and it was little or no sleep that night until breakfast time the next morning and time to make the rounds of the village to say 'Good-bye' to most of the villagers when leaving home that morning. Many of the villagers ... accompanied us to a certain crossroad about one-third of the way to Dingle, where they all shook hands with me for what might be their last farewell and returned to their homes at Gortadoo[, l]eaving the Brick Family with a few others, to proceed on the rest of the road to Dingle, Father and Mother riding the horse-drawn cart[, t]he rest of the followers afoot[, a]rriving in Dingle in time for the twelve o'clock narrow gauge train leaving Dingle for Tralee a distance of over thirty miles. It was there at the Dingle Railway Station ... that I bid my last farewell to my Father and Mother, Brother Jim, William,[23] and Sister Margaret. A couple of shrill whistles from the Donkey steam locomotive and we were off for Tralee ... . There was some weeping and wailing and tears dropping there at the station by the parents, relatives and friends of the emigrant boys and girls boarding that train ... that day for America.

Brick's trip to Queenstown and his voyage in steerage to New York were unremarkable. Surrounded by west Kerrymen, mostly bound for Springfield, Massachusetts, apparently Brick suffered little homesickness and learned much about his destination from older emigrants returning to America after visits home. Accustomed to the seas from his fishing venture, Brick was spared the seasickness that plagued most emigrants,

22 On the 'farewell parties' held for Irish emigrants, commonly called American wakes, see: Miller, *Emigrants and Exiles*, conclusion; and Arnold Schrier, *Ireland and the American Emigration, 1850–1900* (Minneapolis, Minn., 1958).

23 If Tom Brick's memory of saying farewell to his brother William in April 1902 was accurate, then William had returned temporarily from America, for he had emigrated in 1900 and in that year's US census he was listed as a 'laborer' on the farm of his sister, Julia, and her husband John Manning, in Brule township, Union County, South Dakota. William fared poorly in the US and apparently returned to Ireland at least once before his tragic death in 1922 (see n. 39).

and he passed his time serving as interpreter for a monolingual Irish-speaker, from County Galway's Aran Islands, bound for San Francisco. The *Oceanic* was a new steamship, 'the fastest liner crossing the Atlantic at that time', and it carried Brick and 1,100 other Irish emigrants to New York in merely six days. '[W]e are in sight of land now,' Brick related, 'with special instructions from the naturalized Irish American citizens on board returning to America, who told us what to do coming into New York Harbour[:] ... when passing the Statue of Liberty we were supposed to remove our caps and hats ... and salute that sizeable lady holding that torch, which we all did.' After passing without difficulty through inspection at Ellis Island, Brick proceeded by ferry to Jersey City, where he began the trip by train to Salix, Iowa, via Buffalo (where he visited Niagara Falls), Toledo, and Chicago.

Not until leaving Chicago's Central Station did Brick begin to experience the pangs of emigration. Until then he had been accompanied by large numbers of Irish immigrants, many of them Irish-speakers, but '[a]fter boarding that train [for Salix], the only one left of all the passengers [from] New York City was a red-faced Dane bound for Sargent's Bluff, Iowa, who knew no English ...' Moreover, Brick felt increasingly isolated because his own command of English was weak: 'although I had a fair knowledge of the English language from the school books at Bally-Ferriter, nevertheless it was difficult for me to hold a conversation in the English language'. Not surprisingly, Brick's memories of his train travels are dominated by accounts of his relief in meeting Irish-speakers, such as the policeman in Niagara who shared his tobacco, with whom he could converse freely. Under these circumstances the negative and fearful images of America as 'the Land of the Snakes' or, in Brick's case, 'the land of ... wild Indian natives', which alternated in western Irish folklore with visions of 'the land of promise',[24] became increasingly prominent in Brick's imagination and were exacerbated and seemingly verified by a book he purchased and read on the trip from Chicago to Salix, Captain William F. Drannan's luridly illustrated *Thirty-One Years on the Plains and in the Mountains*.[25] By the time Brick reached Timothy and Mary Rohan's farm near Salix, he was extremely apprehensive and immediately took ill with a severe cold that may have been psychosomatic in origin. 'A matter of a day or two and I am up and around again, but very dissatisfied with my bargain[,] and after completing reading that book that I bought from the newsboy on the train coming from Chicago[, w]ith all its Indian fighting and killing, I was getting homesick and telling my sister I wanted to go back to my old haunts in Ireland.'

Brick's host, Timothy Rohan, had left Ireland in 1879. In 1880 he was a tenant or labourer on a farm in Liberty township, Woodbury County, Iowa, owned by Thomas O'Farrell (1844–1911), another Kerry immigrant (in 1863) and sometime mayor of nearby Salix. In 1887 Rohan married Mary Brick and by 1900 they had five children and owned

---

24 On the images of America in western Ireland, see Chapter 5 in this volume.

25 Capt. William F. Drannan, *Thirty-One Years on the Plains and in the Mountains; or, The Last Voice from the Plains. An Authentic Record of a Life Time of Hunting, Trapping, Scouting, and Indian Fighting in the Far West* (Chicago, 1900).

a corn and livestock farm of about 100 acres in Lakeport township, about a mile from the Missouri River. By Iowa standards, Rohan's farm was small, a good part of it was unproductive marshland, and Brick was probably less than impressed by his sister's limited success in America. Furthermore, although Salix had a Catholic church, St. Joseph's, since 1875, and a parochial school staffed by nuns since 1892, most local Catholics were French Canadians, and in the latter year the once thriving town was devastated by fire and had never recovered. In addition, although the husband of Brick's cousin, Ida McGrath, was a foreman with the street department in nearby and prosperous Sioux City, in 1900 there were fewer than a thousand Irish immigrants in all of Woodbury County, less than 2 per cent of the population.[26] Finally, located just across the Missouri from the Rohan farm was the Winnebago Indian Reservation, and the sounds of the Indians' drums, as they prepared for their annual 'powwows', made Brick even more 'unsettled in my mind about staying'. However, he recalled, 'Mr. Rohan promised me that I could stay and work on his farm that summer cultivating corn and [that he would] pay me regular wages', which Brick could use to return to Ireland, if he wished. In fact, Brick remained on the Rohan farm for over a year. Timothy Rohan pastured his cattle on rented lands in the Winnebago Reservation, and eventually Brick lost his fear of the Indians, especially after Rohan admitted their situation was analogous to that of the Catholics in Ireland, stripped of their land and 'discriminated against by the United States Government and by the white settlers'. But never having ridden a saddled horse or handled modern farm machinery, initially Brick had great difficulty in adjusting to American farm work, as he related in his memoir. However, his memoir also shows how his homesickness was mitigated by an Irish-American social life that flourished even on the midwestern prairies:

> … I find Mr. Rohan working on some kind of a plow that appeared to be different than any plow that I ever saw. It even had two mould boards on it. After some inquiring, Mr. Rohan explained to me that the plow was to be drawn by four horses and used to plant corn with, as it was now that time of the year when corn should be planted. Not being acquainted with Iowa, American farm work, I tried the best

---

26 On Iowa's Woodbury County, the towns of Salix and Sioux City, and their Irish residents, see: J. D. Adams, *Three Quarters of a Century of Progress: The Story of the Growth of Sioux City* (Sioux City, Iowa, 1923); Louis N. Duchaine, *Salix History, Book One and Book Two* (Salix, Iowa, n.d. [1932?]; repr. 1981); *History of the Counties of Woodbury and Plymouth, Iowa, Including an Extended Sketch of Sioux City, Their Early Settlement and Progress to the Present Time*, 2 vols. (Chicago, 1890–91); Constant R. Marks, ed., *Past and Present of Sioux City and Woodbury County, Iowa* (Chicago, 1904); *Standard Atlas of Woodbury County, Iowa* (Chicago, 1902); and Woodbury County Genealogical Society, *The History of Woodbury County, Iowa* (Dallas, Tex., 1984). Demographic information on the Rohans and other Irish families in Woodbury County was located in the manuscript schedules of the 1880, 1900, and 1910 US censuses, as well as in the records of St. Joseph's church in Salix, and the obituary records in the Sioux City Public Library. I am grateful to Fayann Hubert of Salix for her research in these and other sources.

I could to apply myself only as a helper with any of the work[,] at least until I got better acquainted with the way things are done in America.

There is a lot of preliminary preparatory groundwork to be done yet before corn planting, such as my first field work job given me. It was stalk cutting, that is cutting up the old corn stalks remaining in the fields since last year. The work being done with a machine mounted on or between two wheels with a seat for the driver, with framework beneath the driver's seat. It was made to accommodate two cylinders on which was mounted three or four curved shaped sharp blades that revolve on the ground and cut up the old cornstalks. As the machine is drawn by the two-horse team, with the driver riding on that seat between both wheels, to me it was a dangerous outfit on account of those revolving sharp blades[, i]n case the driver would happen to fall off his seat into those ... blades or get any of his clothing caught in them ... . With the stalks all cut ... , the team was hitched on to a hay rake and the stalks raked up into wind rows[, w]hen dry enough to be set afire the first favorable wind that came along[. U]sually the burning was done evenings and provided an interesting sight with so many of the neighbouring farmers doing likewise. With the weather favourable now any day, the four-horse team will be hitched onto that double mold board plow[,] whose other name is corn lister, used to plant the corn with[. T]he day has arrived now and we hitch the four-horse team to that ... plow. [C]orn planting is now under way. I am told that a man with this plow and a good four-horse team could plant ten acres of ground in a ten-hour day, ... the corn seed being planted in the furrows ... .

We are about to start the first process of cultivation, which is done with a two-horse team hitched onto a two-wheel machine, ... on which is mounted two sets of sharp round revolving iron discs[, t]hree discs to the set, revolving on the ground, cutting out any weeds growing close to the corn plants now in the furrows by the pressure applied by the driver's feet on the disc revolving cutters, which requires careful operation ... because extra pressure by one foot, on one set of the disc cutters, might result in forcing one set of the cutters in on the growing plants [and] result in cutting out some of the corn plants[,] as happened to me when first learning to operate the machine.

Now with this first corn cultivation done, we take time to put up or save about fifteen acres of hay needed to feed the horses during the working summer season and throughout the coming winter ... . To mow and save fifteen acres of hayland took only three days using the machinery on hand at that time[:] horse-drawn mower, horse-drawn hay rake, horse-operated hay sweep, and horse-operated stacker lift. With hay all put up now, we start the second process of corn cultivating again, only with those discs on the cultivator reversed and when in operation ... will systematically throw the soil around the growing corn plants now about eight or ten inches in height. This process of corn cultivating is kept up now from day to day on into or about July 10th when the corn plants ... are now too high for the cultivator to go over the rows without breaking some of the plants.

... I must say these were very lonesome days for me out in the cornfield. Some days it was hard for me to keep from crying, but Mr. Rohan always had a cheerful word for me[,] besides Mary, my sister ... , did a lot to persuade me to stay, otherwise I might have gone back to Ireland and my old haunts. The summer and Sunday afternoon crossroad dancing at Bally-Ferriter and an occasional Sunday afternoon rowing about in the Curra across the harbour to Bally David, to take in the dancing on that side of the harbor (being bona fide travelers we [were] entitled to two drinks at Peg Carty's bar)[:] with all this on my mind, it is a wonder that I did not go back, but there was always that spirit of adventure and travel characteristic of the Brick family. And I thought of going back to see the girl I loved, married to a farmer and raising a family, that put a crimp in my idea of ever going back, whatever the future had in store for me.

With the grain harvest about due, the next job due on the Rohan farm was to cultivate and bug the potato patch. With that job done and the Fourth of July coming up next week, Mr. Rohan has promised to take the whole family, with the team and wagon to the Fourth of July picnic at Sargent's Bluff, a distance of fourteen or fifteen miles. ... Arriving at the picnic grounds ... at noon, with some help from all the family, the dinner lunch was served over spreads on the green lawn. With the lunch-dinner consumed now there was plenty of attractions such as is usual at any Fourth of July picnic[:] The shell game man, the roulette man, the trick of the loop man, the man with the big mallet to test your strength ... . There was some other attractions too, before the baseball game started. For instance, a very fancy drill exhibition by the Woodmen of the World with a band playing some patriotic music. One-thirty or two o'clock the ball game began. I do not recollect now what teams played in that ball game[;] with the most of the fans sitting all around on the ground ... , a grounder [came] right into my lap where I was sitting. ... [A]nyway, it was a day well spent. It made quite an impression on me, being [my] first American picnic ... .

From that day on[,] now with the corn stalks growing too high for much more cultivating, we devoted much of our time going through the corn field on foot looking for any weeds growing between the corn rows or among the growing corn stalks. ... [W]ith not much to do for me now on the Rohan farm[,] Sister Mary contacted some of the neighbours[:] result from that day on, the neighbours kept me busy at various work ... between the town[s] of Salix and Sloan. ... In those localities there were divers[e] peoples of various denominations such as French, Scandinavians, Dutch, and Irish. ... [T]he Irish [included] the Cleareys, the Murrays, the Malloys, the O'Farrells, the O'Maras, the Rhines, the Reynolds, the Harringtons, the Joyces, the Harvards, the Smalls, [and] the Mulvihills. Then there was the McDowells and last of my memory, the Manley family, who built a great new barn and to whose house I was invited to attend a party of young Irish boys and native Salix girls at the Manley house[, w]ith one of the Manley boys playing on his violin and one of the Salix girls playing the piano. How they found out that I could step dance I do not know but when Tom Manley, I believe it was, started playing the violin and the fisher's horn pipe, I could not resist[. B]ut to step dance on that beautiful carpet in the Manley house parlor with me still wearing rough brogues was out of the question. However[,] with Mr. Manley's consent ... the rest of the party ... insisted on using the front porch of the house [w]ith the bare board floor, with Anton Manley playing the violin and Mamy Harrington playing the piano[. F]irst on the list was the sailor's horn pipe[; t]hen with me doing the sword dance and other[s] to the tune of the 'Rocky Road to Dublin'. ... I enjoyed the party very much, especially with the father Mr. Manley who spoke fluent (Connaught) Galway Gaelic. ...

Other than an occasional day's work among the neighbors, there is not very much to do now at the Rohan farm. When not working out, we kept busy doing the usual chores, such as is done on most Iowa farms at that time[. W]ith summer ending near now and September, the first school opening on hand[, n]ow my job is hauling the Rohan children forth and back to the Sister's school at Salix. I am still a little homesick, not contented at all with my lot. However, there is always some kind of work to be done on a farm that helps to keep the thoughts of returning off my mind. With the month of October now approaching, I am given a different job. That is going through the corn field to select and pick out the ripest corn ears, leaving some of the husks on them to be hung up ... inside the corn crib to be used the following year for seed corn. Selected, picked, and hung up, we are preparing now for the regular job of corn picking. With only one wagon to get ready, we proceed to put the bang boards on the right side of the wagon. All this procedure is new to me ... , but when the morning arrived to start, after breakfast with the horse team hitched to the wagon, Mr. Rohan had a brand new pair of cotton flannel mittens for me to wear, under which he fastened on to my right hand fingers some sort of an iron gadget with leather straps on it[, t]o hold it fast to the fingers[, and] with a sharp point on it. That was intended to break the husk on the ear of corn[:] the ear of corn to be jerked from under the husk and thrown against the high bank board on the right side of the wagon and into the wagon with the horse team moving slowly until we got to the end of the field[,] to turn around to repeat the operation on the way back towards the house and the corn crib where we scooped the corn with a scoop shovel into the corn crib. For me that was the hardest part of the work. Then to the house for coffee.

This process was kept up daily until the last ear of corn in the field was deprived of its husk and thrown into the wagon and eventually hoisted into the corn crib. As to the number of bushels that corn crib held, that will be determined later when the corn is sold and the man with the corn sheller and his crew comes and shells the kernels of corn from the ear ... . [Then i]t is usually hauled to the nearest town, weighed and unloaded at some grain elevator, [owned by an] operator and buyer of all kinds of grain. It so happened this year that Mr. Rohan fed a good deal of his corn to the cattle that he intended to fatten ... [, t]he cattle to be sold the following spring when the cattle are fattened and ready to be shipped to the Sioux City stockyards in care of some cattle-buying commission firm and eventually to be slaughtered at a packing house there.

During all that winter of 1902 and on into 1903 I helped feed those cattle together with doing other chores[,] such as feeding a number of hogs that run in feed yards with the cattle[,] and hauling the Rohan family school children back and forth to the Sisters' School at Salix. This sort of activity kept up during that fall of 1902 and on into and through the winter, until early spring of 1903 when Mr. Rohan sold his cattle[,] after which there was not much to do but wait for the spring of 1903 to open up. But when the time came for corn planting, spring rains started and the fields got so wet that farmers could not get into their fields to plant the corn until later than usual. The results were a private talk with Mrs. Rohan [my] sister who advised me to go up to Dakota and visit some of my relatives in Garry Owen.

After two weeks visiting his cousin in Sioux City, where he deposited the $100 wages that Rohan had paid him for his year's work, Tom Brick went to his relatives, the Mannings, Sullivans, and O'Connors, in the Garryowen settlement, centred on Spink township in Union County, South Dakota, where he resided for most of the next four years. Garryowen was not a village in the Irish sense, but merely the site of a Catholic church, St. Mary's (established 1879), which in 1903 served about 60 Irish and Irish-American families whose 160-acre homesteads were scattered on both sides of the boundary line between Union and Clay counties and between Brule Creek and the Vermillion River. In a sense, the Garryowen settlement was the western extremity of a migration of Irish immigrants, many of them canal diggers and lead miners, who in the 1830s had moved through the Old Northwest into the prairies of western Illinois and across the Mississippi River into northeastern Iowa, concentrating around Dubuque. Many of them turned to farming, and in 1838–39 Irish immigrants, mainly from Munster, founded a settlement in Butler township, Jackson County, about twenty miles south of Dubuque, which they called Garryowen after the site of a popular fair and parade ground just outside the old walls of Limerick city.[27] This first Garryowen flourished under the patronage of Dubuque's

27 'Garryowen' was also the title of several popular Irish songs, through which the name came to symbolize Ireland among its emigrants overseas — especially those from County Limerick and from Munster, generally. The song's earliest version celebrated the rowdy behaviour of the Royal Irish Lancers, who were stationed in Limerick's Garryowen suburb; later Thomas Moore (1779–1852) adapted the tune to his genteel exile ballad, 'The Daughters of Erin'; and during or shortly after the American Civil War it was adopted, with new words, as the marching song of the Seventh US Cavalry, perhaps at the instigation of its Irish-born lieutenant colonel, Myles Keogh, whose father had been an officer in the Royal Irish Lancers. On 25 June 1876 Keogh and several troops of the Seventh Cavalry perished under Custer's command at

Catholic bishop, Matthias Loras (1792–1858), and the name was later applied to the South Dakota settlement by a member of the Manning family, from west Kerry, who in 1860 moved from the Iowa colony to the southeastern extremity of the newly formed Dakota Territory.[18]

In the late 1850s and early 1860s five railroad companies were building lines across Iowa, bringing with them Irish labourers and settlers to northwestern Iowa, to Sioux City (founded in 1855), and eventually across the Missouri and Big Sioux rivers onto the rich prairie soils of Union and Clay counties in Dakota Territory. During the Sioux Indian wars of 1862–68 the Dakota settlements were nearly abandoned. However, the Laramie Treaty of 1868 ended the Indian threat; in 1868 the completion of the Sioux City and Pacific Railroad gave the settlers in southeastern Dakota access to eastern markets for their crops; and in early 1873 the opening of the Dakota Southern Railroad from Sioux City to Yankton caused a boom in commercial farming and property values in Union and Clay counties, which in turn stimulated migration and settlement by native-born Americans and by immigrants alike. Most of the latter were from Scandinavia and Germany, not Ireland, and despite the efforts of Charles Collins, the eccentric Irish-American editor of the *Sioux City Times*, to promote Fenian colonies in Dakota, nearly all of the relatively few Irish families in the territory arrived independently, attracted by the region's rich soils and the benefits of the Homestead Act of 1862. Despite grasshopper plagues, the adverse effects of the Panic of 1873, and a credit shortage that drove interest rates on farm mortgages up to 24 per cent in the mid-1870s, by the time prosperity and in-migration were renewed in 1878–85, Dakota's population had increased from about 10,000 in 1870 to nearly 250,000 by the middle of the next decade. Of these, in 1880 some 4,104 were Irish-born and 5,486 were the children of Irish immigrants, together representing about 7 per cent of the territory's population, the highest proportion ever achieved. However, most of the Irish had gone to the Black Hills mining settlements, and only 369 Irish immigrants resided in Union and Clay counties, merely 5.3 and 2.3 per cent of their respective populations.[29]

the Little Big Horn. For this information I am grateful to Marion Casey, Eileen Reilly, and Mick Maloney of the Irish Studies programme at New York University.

28 On Irish migrations through — and settlements in — Iowa, see: Alfred T. Andreas, *Illustrated Historical Atlas of the State of Iowa* (Chicago, 1875); Homer L. Calkin, 'The Irish in Iowa', *Palimpsest*, 45, 2 (February 1964), 33–97; Rev. Mathias M. Hoffman, ed., *Centennial History of the Archdiocese of Dubuque* (Dubuque, Iowa, 1938); Sr. M. G. Kelly, 'Irish Catholic Colonies and Colonization Projects in the United States, 1795–1860: Part II', *Studies: An Irish Quarterly Review* (Dublin), 29 (1940), 447–65; *Owen's Gazetteer and Directory of Jackson County, Iowa* (Davenport, Iowa, 1878), on the first Garryowen settlement; Leland L. Sage, *A History of Iowa* (Ames, Iowa, 1974); Charles R. Tuttle, *An Illustrated History of the State of Iowa* (Chicago, 1876); and Mark Wyman, *Immigrants in the Valley: Irish, Germans, and Americans in the Upper Mississippi Country, 1830–1860* (Chicago, 1984).

29 The general data in this and the following paragraphs, on the Irish in South Dakota and in its Garryowen settlement, are derived from: *Atlas of Clay and Union Counties, South Dakota* (Des Moines, Iowa, 1924); Sr. Claudia Duratschek, *The Beginnings of Catholicism in South Dakota* (Washington, DC, 1943) and *Builders of God's Kingdom: The History of the Catholic Church in South Dakota* (Yankton, S. Dak., 1979); *History of Southeastern*

Analysis of the 1880 and 1900 census schedules for Garryowen's Irish-born farmers in Spink and adjacent townships indicates that three-fourths had been born prior to the Famine, primarily in the 1830s and early 1840s, and either had emigrated to the United States as children, with their parents, during or shortly after the Famine, or, more commonly, had come to America as adults in the mid- to late 1860s. About two-thirds settled in South Dakota roughly between 1866 and 1876, and most of the rest (including a large proportion of the American-born Irish settlers, who averaged some twenty years younger than the Irish-born) arrived in the late 1870s. Judging from the birthplaces of their children, the great majority of both the Irish and Irish-American settlers had lived for considerable periods of time in Illinois and/or Iowa, most of the remainder in Canada or New York, before venturing to Dakota. Thus, by the time Tom Brick arrived in Garryowen in 1903, the settlement's Irish-born contingent was an elderly minority; many first-comers had already died, and the average age of the survivors was 57.5 years. However, the first settlers had large families (in 1900 those of the Irish-born averaged 5.12 children still at home, and many had seven or more), and, despite the hardships of the early 1890s, apparently no widespread abandonment of Irish farms had yet occurred. Indeed, between 1880 and 1900 the number of Irish farms in Spink township increased from 19 to 21 — 15 of them still owned by Irish immigrants.[30]

By the early 1900s most of the farms in Garryowen and in Union and Clay counties, generally, were very prosperous, their economies based on a mixture of corn, small grains, stock and dairy cattle, hogs, and poultry. Southeastern South Dakota had

---

Dakota, Its Settlement and Growth ... (Sioux City, Iowa, 1881); J. P. Johansen, 'Immigrants and Their Children in South Dakota', *Bulletin 302 of the South Dakota Experiment Station* (Brookings, S. Dak., 1936); George W. Kingsbury, *History of Dakota Territory and South Dakota: Its History and Its People*, 5 vols., ed. George Martin Smith (Chicago, 1915); *Memorial and Biographical Record of Turner, Lincoln, Union and Clay Counties, South Dakota* (Chicago, 1897); Rex C. Myers, 'An Immigrant Heritage: South Dakota's Foreign-born in the Era of Assimilation', *South Dakota History*, 19 (summer 1989), 134–55; Robert C. Ostergren, 'European Settlement and Ethnicity Patterns on the Agricultural Frontier of South Dakota', *South Dakota History*, 13 (spring–summer 1983); E. Frank Peterson, *Historical Atlas of South Dakota* (Vermillion, S. Dak., 1904); Doane Robinson, *History of South Dakota*, 2 vols. ([Logansport, Ind.?], 1904) and *Encyclopedia of South Dakota* (Pierre, S. Dak., 1925); and Herbert S. Schell, *History of South Dakota* (Lincoln, Neb., 1961) and *History of Clay County, South Dakota* (Vermillion, S. Dak., 1976). Published demographic data came from the *United States Censuses, 1860–1920*; the *1889 South Dakota Statistical, Historical, and Political Abstract* (Aberdeen, S. Dak., 1889); and Doane Robinson, super., *Second Census of the State of South Dakota, 1905* (Aberdeen, S. Dak., 1905).

For general background on farming and ethnicity in the late nineteenth-century Midwest, see: Allan G. Bogue, *From Prairie to Cornbelt: Farming on the Illinois and Iowa Prairies in the Nineteenth Centuries* (Chicago, 1963); Jon Gjerde, *The Minds of the West: Ethnocultural Evolution in the Rural Middle West, 1830–1917* (Chapel Hill, NC, 1997); and Fred A. Shannon, *The Farmer's Last Frontier: Agriculture, 1860–1897* (New York, 1945).

30 Demographic information on the Bricks, Sullivans, O'Connors, Mannings, and other Irish and Irish-American farm families in Garryowen, South Dakota, was derived and/or calculated from the manuscript schedules of the 1880, 1900, and 1910 US censuses (examined on microfilm at the Missouri State Historical Society, Columbia, Mo.), and from the records of the South Dakota Graves Registration Project, 1940 (St. Mary's Cemetery, Garryowen), in the South Dakota State Archives, Pierre. I am grateful to Professor David Emmons of the University of Montana for sharing the results of his research in the St. Mary's Cemetery records.

annual rainfalls of 24 inches or more, and so those who farmed its rich prairie loam had little fear of the devastating droughts that periodically afflicted more recent settlers on the Great Plains in the state's central and western counties. The sod houses and frame shanties of the first settlers had long since been abandoned, replaced in many instances with what observers described as 'unusually attractive' farmhouses that had cost $5,000 to $6,000 to build, and which were now served by rural mail delivery and increasingly by telephone lines. In some parts of Clay County land values had increased from $2 to $5 per acre in 1879 to $50 to $100 in 1904. Furthermore, although the exigencies of the Homestead Act had obliged the Garryowen Irish to scatter their holdings among a large majority of Swedish and Norwegian farmers, there was sufficient contiguity to sustain a rich community social life, centred around the church and local school (established 1870), which was not dissimilar to that which Tom Brick had enjoyed back in Dunurlin. Each year there was a harvest festival; dances and church dinners were frequent; and the community even had its own baseball team. More important, despite the mechanization of farming, the families in Garryowen still shared many tasks, such as threshing and harvesting, and turned them into festivals of neighbourly and ethnic solidarity — analogous to the *meitheal* in rural Ireland. Indeed, as one elderly resident later remembered, Garryowen held so many interrelated Irish kin-groups that a 'family dinner' could host as many as fifty people.

In these circumstances, it was no wonder that the homesick immigrant, Tom Brick, remained in Garryowen for four years, living with his relations and working on their and their neighbours' farms, sometimes as a member of a threshing crew run by a distant cousin, Long Mike O'Connor. In a sense, the Garryowen settlement was an ideal crucible for Brick's successful adaptation to American life. On the one hand, he could converse in Irish and share memories of home with its late middle-aged and elderly Irish-born residents. On the other hand, the vast majority of Garryowen's inhabitants who were his own age were the American-born, English-speaking children and even grandchildren of the original settlers. Of course, religion, music, social activities, and a strong ethnic pride united Garryowen's several generations. However, Brick's interaction with young men and women, who from necessity or desire were — like most rural youth in Hamlin Garland's Midwest[31] — increasingly oriented towards the cities, mass culture, and non-farm occupations, could not help but gently prepare him for a life outside the settlement.

Unfortunately, Brick's memoir concludes in 1904, and in 1907 he left Garryowen and for the next ten years pursued in succession a variety of occupations. In 1907 he worked with his brother William as a carpenter's helper in the copper mines of Butte, Montana

---

31 Hamlin Garland (1860–1940), popular US novelist, short-story writer, and poet. His fictional and autobiographical works deal primarily with the hardships of farm life in the Midwest during the 1890s and early 1900s; his most noted writings are *Main-Traveled Roads* (1891) and *A Son of the Middle Border* (1917).

(a major centre of Irish-speaking immigrants from west Munster),[32] and the following year he accompanied his brother in the latter's ill-fated homesteading venture on the plains of central South Dakota. Between 1909 and 1912 he assembled machinery at an International Harvester factory in Aberdeen, South Dakota,[33] worked as a carpenter and stockyard labourer in Sioux City; and was employed as a millwright in a sawmill in Sturgis, South Dakota. Perhaps tired of wage labour, in 1913 he tried homesteading himself on 160 acres near the White River in Lyman County, South Dakota. However, by this time he may have become too urbanized to endure the loneliness of the Great Plains, where, as he wrote in a preamble to a poem he penned in both Irish and English (thereby continuing, however poorly, the west Kerry tradition of spontaneous poetic composition), the howling of the coyote 'reminded me of the Banshee's lonely croon'. In any event, in 1914 he moved to the town of Vermillion (population 2,187 in 1915), in southern Clay County, where he lived for the rest of his life, traded his homestead claim for a 1910 Hudson touring car, and operated a taxi service between Vermillion and Yankton. In 1917, after working two years as Vermillion's only policeman, Brick was finally ready to settle down. That year he purchased the C. E. Vincent Confectionary, a candy store and ice-cream parlour, and married Bridget Agnes Cavanaugh (1893–1939), an Irish-speaker from Ballywiheen, in Marhin parish, County Kerry, just east of his native Dunurlin. They had five children, two of whom died in childhood.[34] In 1939 Brick sold his business to his eldest son, James, and opened a package liquor store that he operated until 1943.[35] After the Second World War Vermillion's population rose from 3,608 in 1945 to 10,136 in 1980, doubtless increasing Brick's income from his real estate investments. Thus, he spent his long retirement comfortably, repairing hunting guns and woodworking; remarkably, he specialized in making violins, completing the last one at age ninety. On 30 August 1979 Brick died in Vermillion, just a few weeks short of his ninety-eighth birthday.[36]

It is difficult to assess the meaning of immigration for someone as long-lived as Tom Brick. Economically, he was quite successful: in addition to his various business enterprises, he owned considerable real estate and rental property in Vermillion, and

---

32 See David M. Emmons's superb study, *The Butte Irish: Class and Ethnicity in an American Mining Town, 1875–1925* (Urbana, Ill., 1989).

33 Brick received his final citizenship papers on 25 May 1909, while living in Aberdeen. This likely means that Brick did not decide to remain permanently in the US until 1906 or 1907.

34 Tom and Bridget Brick's children were: James T. (b. 1918); Mary Francis (1919–20); Donald W. (1921–29); Kathleen Ann (b. 1925); and William C. (b. 1931). When Tom Brick died in 1979, James was living in Sioux Falls, William in Peoria, Illinois, and Kathleen (now Mrs. A. J. Carlson) in Danbury, Connecticut.

35 In 1933 South Dakota authorized the sale of beer, which had not been legally available in Vermillion for nearly forty years, not in the state since 1917, which helps explain why Tom Brick (legally) merchandised only candy and ice cream until the late 1930s.

36 Tom Brick's post-1904 biographical data, and access to his poems and other writings, are derived primarily from James and Kevin Brick of Sioux Falls, South Dakota, and from James V. Manning of Sioux City, Iowa. On Vermillion's population in 1915 and 1945–80, see Riley Moffat, *Population History of Western U.S. Cities and Towns, 1850–1990* (Lanham, Md., 1996), 229.

was a generous donor to the Knights of Columbus and to the many Irish-American organizations to which he belonged. Likewise, in South Dakota he had achieved the marriage and family denied him in west Kerry, and in old age he was surrounded by innumerable, younger relatives who cherished his memories of Ireland and early Garryowen. Unlike other Irish immigrants in South Dakota, Brick never lost his knowledge of Irish and continued to compose poems in that language throughout his life. His religious beliefs were deeply held and yet also very traditional; although a faithful member of St. Agnes parish in Vermillion, his formal Catholicism was complemented by a fairy-belief retained from his west Kerry childhood, and he may have noted the irony that just north of Vermillion and west of Garryowen was a hill called Spirit Mound, which the displaced Sioux Indians had believed was inhabited by a mysterious and malicious race of 'little people'.

Yet, despite the material success and despite — or perhaps because of — the cultural continuities preserved from west Kerry, a thread of regret and even alienation runs through Brick's life. He remained a fiercely liberal Democrat, voting for George McGovern for president in 1972, for example, when most of the electorate in McGovern's own state deserted him as too 'radical' on both the Vietnam War and social issues. Brick also remained a militant Irish-American nationalist, strongly supporting the IRA in 1916–23[37] and later in the 'Troubles' that erupted in Northern Ireland after 1968. For those reasons — as also for his Catholicism and his sympathy for South Dakota's impoverished Native Americans— Brick was marginalized in a South Dakota political culture that generally was staunchly Republican,[38] conservative, Protestant, Anglophile, hyper-patriotic, and virulently hostile to both the anti-war and the Native American civil rights movements. It is not known whether Brick suffered during the nativist and right-wing hysterias of the First World War and the early 1920s, when persecution of aliens and alleged radicals was especially rabid in South Dakota, but it is likely that Brick's Anglophobia made him suspect to those who advocated American entry into the war on Britain's side. It is known, however, that in mid-1941, during a later neutrality crisis, Brick penned a bitter poetic satire, 'The Battle of the Dem Cross See' (that is, 'The Battle of the Democracy'), which attacked the '100 per cent Americans' who demanded intervention on Britain's side ('Don't loan our guns to foreign bums,' Brick wrote) and sought to exclude immigrants from political office. Unfortunately, what Brick later

---

37 According to family tradition in South Dakota, Tom Brick's kinsmen in west Kerry were members of Sinn Féin and fought with the Irish Republican Army in the War of Independence of 1919–21 and perhaps also with the Anti-Treaty IRA in the Civil War of 1922–23 — the latter suspicion now supported by private information from west Kerry.

38 Indeed, successful Irish Catholic immigrants, whose biographies appeared in late nineteenth- and early twentieth-century South Dakota state and county histories, were almost invariably described as loyal Republicans. Also noteworthy is that many of the prominent farmers and businessmen listed therein, who had 'native Irish' or 'Catholic Irish' names but who were members of local Protestant churches (usually Baptist, Methodist, or Presbyterian), were therefore described as 'Scotch-Irish'; on the development of 'Scotch-Irishness' in America, see Chapters 6–7 in this volume.

thought of Richard Nixon and his administration's persecution of Irish-American IRA-supporters — or, if still alive today, what he would think of the second Bush regime and its Irish-American apologists — can only be imagined.[39]

However, while Brick remained in some respects intransigently 'Irish', the original Irish communities in eastern South Dakota were dying around him. Brick long outlived the Garryowen settlement, where, after the Second World War, only a few Irish families lingered on the old homesteads. Merely a handful of Irish immigrants had come to South Dakota after 1900, even fewer after the First World War. In 1930 the average age of the state's Irish-born inhabitants was nearly 60; and by 1950 Brick was one of only 477 Irish immigrants left in all South Dakota — most of them in the Black Hills counties. Apparently, after about 1904 Brick never seriously considered the possibility of returning permanently to Ireland (his sole visit home in 1929 had ended tragically when his 'favourite son' died accidentally in Cork), but his relatives remember him as stoically homesick, delighting in his increasingly infrequent conversations in the Irish language with a diminishing number of elderly immigrants. To be sure, Brick also wrote poems in Irish that extolled the beauty and bounty of Dakota's prairies, but he revealed his heart when, in 1977, he gave his nephew, Jim Manning, incredibly precise, written directions for the latter's visit to west Kerry, describing in minute and loving detail every twist of the road, each hill and stream, the ruined castles and the Famine graves, between Dingle and Ballyferriter — 're-creating in memory for the thousandth time the scenario of [his] homeland and childhood days,' as Manning later wrote,[40] as well as the route of his own emigration seventy-seven years earlier.

---

39 A personal tragedy also overshadowed Tom Brick's immigration. At least by the early 1920s his brother William, whom Tom had accompanied to work in Butte, Montana, and later to homestead in central South Dakota, had gone insane — perhaps a result of the schizophrenia that was common in west Kerry, perhaps exacerbated by lonely bachelorhood on the High Plains. On 30 December 1922 William wandered twenty-five miles from his farm in Clark County, entered a stranger's farmhouse at two the next morning, and was mistakenly shot and killed as a prowler. Tom Brick retrieved his brother's remains for burial in Vermillion, and William's death was the subject of articles in the *Clark Pilot Review* (4 January 1923) and the *Sioux City Journal* (8 January 1923). On schizophrenia in west Kerry, see Nancy Scheper-Hughes, *Saints, Scholars, and Schizophrenics: Mental Illness in Rural Ireland* (Berkeley, Calif., 1979).

40 James V. Manning, Sioux City, Iowa, to the author, 16 January 1978.

Epilogue
Re-Imagining Irish and Irish Migration History

The essays in this collection represent my best efforts, to date, to reconstruct and reinterpret — to re-imagine, if you will — the histories of Ireland and of Irish migration, particularly to the United States.[1] Of course, my endeavours are by no means unique. Gaelic poets and English conquerors, Catholic and Protestant clergymen, nationalists and unionists, British observers and spokespersons for the Irish overseas: for centuries these and others have contested the facts and interpretations of Ireland's troubled history, interrogating what it means and has meant to be 'Irish' at home and abroad.

Contemporary Irish historians, like their predecessors, have played a major supportive role in this process. From the 1930s and especially since the 1960s, their dominant paradigm has been 'revisionism'.[2] Revisionist interpretations have permeated Irish scholarship as well as Irish education, media, and, despite some resistance, political culture and popular consciousness. Purportedly blessed with unbiased, 'value-free' perspectives and armed with new 'scientific' methodologies, revisionists have claimed to write 'objective' history. Their efforts have been prodigious and in some

---

1   Titled 'Re-Imagining Irish Revisionism', this essay was originally published in Andrew Higgins Wyndham, ed., *Re-Imagining Ireland* (Charlottesville, Va., 2006), 223–43. An abbreviated version is 'Re-Imagining the Imaginary: A Challenge to Revisionist Mythology', in Britta Olinder, ed., *Place and Memory in the New Ireland*, vol. 2 of the publications of the European Federation of Associations and Conferences in Irish Studies (Trier, Germany, forthcoming 2007–08). I would like to thank my colleague, Ted Koditschek, for his insightful comments on early drafts of the original essay.
2   The critical literature concerning Irish historical revisionism is voluminous. Perhaps the most balanced survey is Ciaran Brady, ed., *Interpreting Irish History: The Debate on Historical Revisionism* (Dublin, 1994), and one of the most important short critiques is Luke Gibbons, 'Challenging the Canon: Revisionism and Cultural Criticism', in Seamus Deane, ed., *The Field Day Anthology of Irish Writing*, 3 vols. (Derry, 1991), vol. 3, 561–68.

respects praiseworthy: they have uncovered new evidence, illuminated experiences of hitherto neglected groups, and developed new and challenging ways of understanding Ireland's past.

The revisionists' main objective, however, has been to deconstruct, destabilize, and expel from the realms of 'responsible' discourse (public as well as academic) what they condemn as the 'dangerous myths' of Irish nationalist history: that is, the traditional accounts and interpretations of conquest and resistance that allegedly fostered the Easter rebellion of 1916, the Irish revolutionary and civil wars of 1919–23, the socio-cultural and political inadequacies of independent Ireland, and, most critically, the recent 'Troubles' in Northern Ireland. Indeed, their anti-Irish nationalist sentiments are often so obvious, there is little doubt that many revisionists, if miraculously granted the opportunity to prevent just *one* occurrence in the Irish past, likely would choose the Easter rebellion rather than the conquest, partition, or even the Great Famine. Compromised by that agenda, much revisionist scholarship seems scarcely more objective than the much-maligned nationalist history that it has largely supplanted. Perhaps equally damning is that, after decades of dominance, and despite its practitioners' undeniable sophistication, much revisionist history — once innovative and stimulating — has become tediously predictable.

No history, popular or professional, nationalist or revisionist, is 'value-free', but rather is conditioned, consciously or unconsciously, by the historians' political culture: by the socio-economic, cultural, political, and academic hierarchies — the prevailing systems of rewards and punishments — in which they function. As Fintan O'Toole suggests provocatively, one of the independent Irish state's greatest failures was that, out of parsimony or philistinism, from the 1920s it failed to co-opt many of Ireland's young intellectuals into the state's 'founding' nationalist and Catholic mythologies, thus alienating them and often obliging them to seek nourishment from other sources that were contemptuous of those mythologies and/or of the new state itself.[3] Yet complicating O'Toole's analysis is that after 1921 the Irish state's leaders and apologists were themselves necessarily ambivalent towards at least some nationalist mythologies, as in the wake of partition and the Civil War the logic and emotive power of 32-county republicanism threatened from within the new state's stability and legitimacy.

The 1960s, however, marked the Irish establishment's critical if long-disguised break with traditional nationalism. The state's abandonment of autarchic, Sinn Féin economic policies — 'capitalism in one country' — for total immersion in an international 'free market' controlled by Anglo-American financial and corporate capitalism, plus the explosion of Northern Ireland's smouldering conflict between Irish and British/unionist nationalisms, persuaded most Irish academics to embrace new socio-economic and historical mythologies better suited to the needs of the globalized, 'post-nationalist' future which, Dublin's politicians and pundits now promised, would bring Ireland the

---

3   Fintan O'Toole, *The Ex-Isle of Ireland* (Dublin, 1996), 95–96.

economic prosperity, social stability, and political closure which the old beliefs had failed to deliver.

Revisionist interpretations of Irish history generally reflect this convergence of neo-liberal economic and of (allegedly) post-nationalist political perspectives.[4] Indeed, historical revisionism is somewhat akin to that key neo-liberal project, privatization. In Ireland both revisionism and privatization find their greatest enthusiasts in periodicals like the *Irish Independent* and among Progressive Democrats and other ideological denizens of 'Dublin 4'. Both strip 'property' (material or cultural) from national, public ownership or common understanding and entrust it to privileged, 'cosmopolitan' élites. Both purport to be objective and inevitable processes that 'liberate' individuals from the stultifying effects of 'mistaken' past policies and understandings. Both appropriate liberal or humanistic terms and values — concerning individual 'freedom', 'dignity', and 'agency', for instance — to condemn the alleged dangers of 'paternalism', 'dependency culture', or 'victimization history'. Yet both subvert such terms to validate new forms of economic and cultural domination — and old forms as well: for just as privatization's apostles ignore its consequent inequities of wealth and power, revisionists (despite their post-nationalist pose) rarely critique British nationalism or Ulster unionism with the vigour and asperity they apply to Irish nationalism. Finally, despite their advocates' disdain for nationalist or leftist 'ideologues', both impose degrees of legal, structural, or philosophical conformity designed to preclude policy-reversal or intellectual challenge.

Thus, just as the ascendancy of neo-liberalism has constricted public debate on contemporary socio-economic and political questions, so the hegemony of revisionism has restricted research or marginalized alternative perspectives on many critical issues in Irish history. Yet revisionism itself must be deconstructed and its basic assumptions denied their mystifying authority — not only to restore a healthy equilibrium to Irish historical scholarship, but perhaps also to help Ireland's inhabitants 're-imagine' a more coherent vision of themselves, their past, present, and possible future. In this Epilogue, therefore, I propose to interrogate revisionist interpretations of three historical issues of considerable contemporary importance: Ulster Protestant identities; the causes and consequences of Irish emigration; and Irish relationships, past and present, with empire and imperialism.

---

4   Revisionism is not ideologically homogeneous, however, despite its practitioners' shared aversion to the Irish nationalism of Tone, Mitchel, Pearse, and Connolly. For instance, revisionism tolerates a handful of Marxist-unionist (but not Marxist-republican) practitioners. Also, revisionists include some devoutly Catholic 'traditionalist' scholars, who dislike many aspects of *secular* nationalism (its Enlightenment, Protestant, and sometimes socialist inspirations and/or its revolutionary methods) that, in their view, compete with Church and faith for historical prominence and popular allegiance. Despite profound philosophical differences, secular and clerical revisionists maintain an alliance of convenience, as illustrated by the formers' lavish praise for Fr. Francis Shaw's influential article, 'The Canon of Irish History — A Challenge', in *Studies*, 61, 242 (1972), 113–53, which criticized the Irish nationalism of Tone *et al.* from an essentially theocratic perspective.

✳

In Ireland, historically and currently, questions of ethno-religious or 'national' identities invariably have political connotations. Unfortunately, the prevailing revisionist model of Irish ethnic identities and relationships — the 'two traditions' paradigm — is deficient, even dysfunctional. The term suggests the paramount and permanent existence of only two Irish groups whose adherents have totally distinct historical experiences, antagonistic political cultures, and conflicting material interests. One group is characterized as Gaelic, Catholic, nationalist, and 'Irish'; the other as English/Scottish, Protestant, unionist, and 'British'.

As suggested in this volume, especially in Part II, the two traditions model does not promote a full understanding of the Irish past. By merely substituting a two traditions model for the old unitary nationalist one, revisionists have declined to grasp the complexity they normally celebrate. Ironically, in the guise of 'pluralism' the two traditions paradigm simply reifies what scholar Frank Wright calls the Ulster Protestants' 'settler ideology' as well as the 'natives'' Manichaean analogue.[5] Consequently, the binary model ignores or de-emphasizes similarities, common interests, and instances of co-operation between Protestants and Catholics. Also, it un-historically homogenizes both traditions, slighting the diversity, the complexity, and the socio-cultural and (among Protestants) denominational conflicts within each group. Although the two traditions paradigm purportedly illuminates cultural distinctions, its concept of culture is limited: culture is conceived as an independent variable, divorced from socio-economic and other contexts; thus, culture and cultural conflicts are 'naturalized' as virtually primordial and eternal.

In fact, of course, ethnic cultures and identities are impermanent, situational, contingent on ever-changing historical and environmental factors. Among them, demographic factors are crucial but are often ignored, yet between the early 1700s and early 1900s dramatic population changes undoubtedly conditioned the development of Irish Protestant identities and politics. For example, between 1732 and 1911 the proportion of Ireland's Protestants who lived *inside* the future 26-county Irish Republic fell from nearly 51 to less than 29 per cent, primarily because in the 1700s, long before 1798 or the rise of Daniel O'Connell's Irish Catholic nationalism, southern Ireland's Protestant communities began to decline precipitously, largely due to high emigration rates that exceeded even those among Ulster's Protestants. As a result, by 1920, when the Government of Ireland Act partitioned the island, Northern Ireland's six counties contained almost three-fourths of the island's Protestants. At least equally important, although between 1831 and 1911 the Protestant proportion of those six counties'

5 Frank Wright, *Two Lands on One Soil: Ulster Politics before Home Rule* (New York, 1996), 20, and *passim*.

inhabitants rose from 57 to 67 per cent, between the early 1700s and the early 1900s, as noted previously, the *Presbyterians'* share of that region's Protestants fell from at least three-fifths to less than half.[6] The socio-cultural and political implications of these and other demographic changes were surely momentous — for the rise and fall of the eighteenth-century's Dublin-centred Irish Protestant nationalism, for instance, or for the subsequent consolidation of Orangeism and unionism in Ulster.

But the two traditions paradigm is also unhelpful, at best, for understanding contemporary Northern Ireland — for contextualizing its ethno-religious divisions or imagining their future transcendence. Instead, the two traditions model is a prescription for eternal socio-cultural and political partition in Northern Ireland and between it and the rest of the island. Likewise, the paradigm's most recent elaboration, by those promoting a pan-Protestant 'Ulster Scots' identity, arguably only historicizes and exacerbates ethno-religious polarization by implicitly denying all northern Protestant associations with 'Ireland' and the 'Irish'. Moreover, in its common usage the term 'Ulster Scots' erases from historical consciousness the large and important body of northern Anglicans, primarily of English descent. Although Anglicans long dominated Ulster Protestant society, their crucial historical roles are now obscured, subsumed in an 'Ulster Scots' hegemony, which logically, and falsely, implies Presbyterian primacy in the North's socio-cultural and political history. In reality, however, it was the Ulster Presbyterians' disputatious political culture — once the bane of Anglican bishops, landlords, and officials — that was subsumed in the zealous monarchism and Tory conservatism that traditionally characterized Ulster's Anglicans — as well as in the latter's most distinctive institution, the Loyal Orange Order.

The two traditions model ignores these denominational distinctions, as it also ignores class conflicts, within the Ulster Protestant population, although both the demographic data and Ulster emigrants' own correspondence indicate that Anglicans and Presbyterians often had starkly different experiences and perspectives, based on their different and oft-conflicting positions in the province's socio-economic and political hierarchies. It is certain, for example, that when the poor Presbyterians of Kilwaughter, County Antrim, and similar parishes suffered during the Great Famine, their fates had not been determined by members of the 'other' tradition — by their 'ancient Catholic enemies' — but rather by Ulster's Protestant and largely Anglican upper and middle classes, whose members mythologized the Famine in Ulster as devoid of Protestant suffering and, a few decades later, mobilized the survivors and their descendants to defend a Union that had signally failed to protect their former neighbours or their own ancestors against deprivation and disaster.

6   Demographic data are described and analysed in Chapters 8–10 of this volume. See also Miller, 'Ulster Presbyterians and the "Two Traditions" in Ireland and America', in Terry Brotherstone, *et al.*, eds., *These Fissured Isles: Varieties of British and Irish Identities* (Edinburgh, 2005); and (for data from the late seventeenth century to 1831) Miller, *et al.*, *Irish Immigrants in the Land of Canaan: Letters and Memoirs from Colonial and Revolutionary America, 1675–1815* (New York, 2003), esp. Appendix 2 (with Liam Kennedy).

Thus, in 1848 John Mitchel's revolutionary appeal to 'the Protestant Farmers, Labourers, and Artisans' of Ulster fell largely on deaf ears, for northern Protestants' political culture, as it had evolved since 1798, thanks in part to massive pre-Famine emigration by disaffected Presbyterians, allowed for neither a nationalist nor a class-based interpretation of the Great Hunger.[7] Poor Protestants' pain — as in 1845–52 or in the earlier dislocations wrought by industrialization — could not be expressed within the context of a unionist hegemony that denied their very existence. As a result, the confines of their 'tradition' — the constraints imposed by the so-called 'Protestant way of life' — forbade the Famine's Protestant survivors to support any nationalist movements that challenged the landlord class or questioned the Union — even when such movements wrung from the British government enormous concessions (abolition of tithes, the secret ballot, reduced rents and protection from eviction, the democratization of local government, even the abolition of landlordism itself) that benefited ordinary Protestants, as well as Catholics, and were gained despite fierce opposition from affluent unionists and the Orange Order.

In the 1790s the United Irishmen asked if Ulster (and other Irish) Protestants and Catholics were forever condemned 'to walk like beasts of prey over fields which [their] ancestors [had] stained with blood'?[8] Sadly, the logic of the two traditions paradigm, reflecting in turn the logic of the unionist position, would seem to answer that question affirmatively. Thus, for the past half-century revisionist historians have dissected the Irish nationalist tradition — subjecting it to intense analysis, exposing its contextual nature, its ambiguities, contradictions, contingencies, and inadequacies. Indeed, the critical results of their work logically imply that only the unionist tradition, unscathed by similarly corrosive criticism, retains any credibility or legitimacy. Surely, however, historians' analyses should be impartial if relationships in Northern Ireland, and between northern Protestants and the inhabitants of the rest of the island, are to achieve peaceful and constructive resolution. If the interrogation and deconstruction of Irish nationalist 'mythologies' are healthy, valuable exercises, then it would seem only fair and salutary to scrutinize and dissect those of Ulster unionism as well. Revisionists claim to anticipate the emergence of a post-nationalist Irish society. It is not possible, or permissible, to explore as well the historical case for a 'post-unionist' Ireland?

Hopefully, the two traditions paradigm offers no more infallible a guide to Ireland's future than it does to the realities of Ulster's past. Some of the essays in this collection posit the existence of other, alternative 'traditions' and perspectives — one or more of which might provide better guideposts to a brighter future than the perpetual polarization and partition to which the revisionist model would consign us.

---

7 Mitchel's 'Letters to the Protestant Farmers ...' first appeared in his newspaper, the United Irishman (Dublin), 28 April and 13 May 1848; reprinted in An Ulsterman for Ireland, with an Introduction by Eoin Mac Neill (Dublin, 1917).
8 Cited in Nancy J. Curtin, The United Irishmen: Popular Politics in Ulster and Dublin, 1791–1798 (Oxford, 1994), 21.

✳

At its peak in 1845 the Irish population was about 8.5 million. Remarkably, between 1600 and 2000 roughly the same number of Ireland's inhabitants emigrated, primarily to the United States, but also to Britain, Canada, Australasia, and lesser destinations. Yet if Ireland has been an 'emigrant nursery',[9] to a lesser degree it also has been a migrants' destination: for the Celts in prehistoric times, for Vikings and Normans in the Middle Ages, and for 250,000 to 400,000 Protestant colonists, principally English and Scots, between the 1500s and the early 1700s. More recently, since the 1990s perhaps 100,000 'new immigrants' and refugees, primarily from Eastern Europe, Asia, and Africa, have come to Ireland.

Thus, Ireland's people have for centuries been familiar with what is now called globalization, as geography and history placed their island at the Atlantic crossroads of the emergent Anglo-American economic and political empires. During the nineteenth and early twentieth centuries (and even earlier for northern Presbyterians), most Irishmen and -women enjoyed only a tenuous, temporary grip on 'home'. Even before they emigrated, many became more familiar with 'away' — with the Bostons and the Liverpools whence their relatives sent letters, money, and passage tickets — than with other parts of Ireland itself.

Indeed, O'Toole has suggested that, in recent decades, vastly accelerated changes — rapid travel, instant electronic communications, the globalization (read Anglo-Americanization) of corporate commerce and popular culture — have virtually erased conventional distinctions between 'home' and 'away'. As a result, today's Irish emigrants — especially the well-educated, ambitious, and upwardly mobile — often feel more comfortable in Manhattan, Brussels, or Sydney than in an Ireland which they, unlike their predecessors, can visit easily.[10]

In reality, of course, many recent emigrants have been poor and unskilled, and relatively few have experienced migration in purely positive, painless ways. O'Toole's argument, however, highlights one of this volume's principal theses, namely, that the 'story' of Irish emigration has always been contested. Interpretations of its causes, character, and consequences have long been subjects of controversy for the Irish in Ireland, the non-Irish members of the host societies overseas, and the emigrants and their descendants in the far-flung Irish diaspora. Contending 'meanings' and disputed 'lessons' of Irish emigration have emerged from dialogue and debate both among and within these groups. Invariably the results of these contentions — the voices and interpretations that became dominant — reflected the interests and outlooks of those

9 Jim Mac Laughlin, *Ireland: The Emigrant Nursery and the World Economy* (Cork, 1994).
10 O'Toole, *Ex-Isle of Ireland*, esp. the introductory and final sections.

classes that enjoyed the greatest social and cultural authority. Put simply, the 'meaning' of Irish migration always was, and remains today, a profoundly political question, inextricably related to power relationships in Ireland and among the emigrants and their descendants overseas.

As contended in the first section of this book, Ireland's 'possessing classes'[11] have always 'explained' Irish emigration in ways that buttressed their socio-cultural and political hegemony — often in conflict with variant interpretations advanced by representatives of subordinate groups. This was true in the early eighteenth century, when Irish magistrates denied Ulster Presbyterians' characterization of their emigration as a flight from 'Egyptian bondage' to rack-renting landlords and persecuting Anglican clergy. It was equally true in the nineteenth century, when British officials usually contended that Irish emigration was natural and beneficial — the inevitable result of free-market forces — whereas Irish and Irish-American nationalists argued that emigration was at root involuntary 'exile' caused by the poverty and famine produced by British tyranny and landlord oppression. Much evidence, historical and contemporary, served to corroborate the nationalist interpretation, as in the minds of Irish Catholic country folk the conquests, confiscations, and persecutions of the past merged seamlessly with *An Gorta Mór* and the wholesale evictions that occurred during that and other crises. At least equally important, the nationalists' interpretation of emigration as exile, caused by political malevolence, served to mobilize the Irish at home and abroad against British rule and landlordism. Yet, as argued earlier, it also demobilized the impoverished masses in Ireland and overseas, for it obscured the socio-economic and cultural conflicts between them and the Irish (and the diasporan) middle classes, whose economic, religious, and political enterprises benefited immeasurably from the departure (or, overseas, from the arrival) of Ireland's dispossessed.

In the early twentieth century the semi-official Irish Catholic interpretation of emigration as exile, caused solely by British/landlord tyranny, remained pervasive, although logically it soon became untenable, since after 1921 it was the Catholic bourgeoisie, empowered by Irish independence, that proved unwilling or unable to stem mass migration. From the late 1950s, however, Irish politicians and economists formulated new strategies to attract massive foreign investment and create an export-based, high-tech economy fully integrated into a US-controlled, transnational capitalism. Ideally, they promised, the consequent prosperity would halt and even reverse the tide of emigration. But when departures soared again in the economically troubled late 1970s, 1980s, and early 1990s, Dublin's political establishment hastened to excuse and even encourage the new exodus, both to reduce welfare costs and to protect their new economic order from social and political upheaval. In turn, the establishment's neo-liberal and revisionist intellectuals produced new interpretations of Irish emigration.

11 J. J. Lee, *Ireland, 1912–1985: Politics and Society* (Cambridge, 1989), 376, 390, and *passim*.

In the new dispensation, historic and contemporary Irish migrations no longer were viewed in negative, communal, or nationalistic terms. Nor, of course, were they interpreted as resulting from systemic inequalities within Catholic Irish society or from the regional imbalances and social inadequacies of the globalization process itself. No longer was the Irish emigrant a homesick 'victim' of British misgovernment or a vengeful 'exile' whose 'atavistic' nationalism might destabilize Anglo-Irish relations or lend support to Northern Irish republicanism. Rather, in an ironic echo of nineteenth-century British voices, Irish emigration became the natural result of politically uncontrollable yet ultimately benign 'market forces' operating on 'a small island'. The Irish emigrant was now portrayed as either a fortunate escapee from a repressively 'traditional' Catholic Ireland, still blighted by its own perverse failure to fully embrace capitalist modernity, or, more commonly, as a confident, ambitious, adaptable individual who — after a few years of certain success abroad, honing entrepreneurial skills in Los Angeles, London, or another 'world city' — would return to help indoctrinate Irish society and culture in the techniques and outlooks of global capitalism. 'Home' and 'away' thus became indistinguishable and irrelevant — with the lure of opportunity dimmed only slightly by occasional jet lag.

Thus, with emigration as with the two traditions, revisionists merely substituted one monolithic explanation ('opportunity') for another ('exile'). Like its antecedents, today's interpretation of emigration serves the interests of Ireland's economic, political, and intellectual élites, most representatives of which deify the market, advocate untrammelled capital and labour mobility, and regard traditional Irish nationalism as at best embarrassing and leftist criticism as abhorrent and 'divisive'. For them the neo-liberal interpretation promotes 'social stability' by 'explaining' all Irish emigration, past and present, as solely the product of individuals' voluntary, rational, market-based decisions, rather than as the result of flawed policies or social inequalities susceptible to political solutions.[12]

Both the old and the new hegemonic interpretations of emigration help explain why the Irish in Ireland have had such an ambivalent relationship with the Irish of the diaspora. The old notion of emigration as involuntary exile — as an occasion for communal grief expressed at the American wakes as well as in political and religious oratory — contrasted starkly (as did their demand for emigrants' remittances) with the cold welcome the Irish usually gave to less-than-affluent emigrants who went back to their homeland. For the 'returned Yanks', it was feared, might demand a share of the island's resources — and those were both meagre and, thanks to mass departures

---

12 Arguably, the same perspective may buttress the global-capitalist project of cheap-labour migration into Ireland, for both neo-liberals and those genuinely sympathetic to the new immigrants' plight brand that project's critics as provincial and racist. Many of the latter merit such pejoratives, but their neo-liberal critics usually ignore the plight of those, 'left behind' by Irish 'progress', who unfortunately sometimes seek (or are persuaded to seek) easy, xenophobic answers for their own absolute or relative deprivation.

by the dispossessed and disinherited, increasingly concentrated in the hands of the Irish bourgeoisie.

Similarly, the emigrant's current image as resourceful entrepreneur has enjoyed a mixed reception, at least among some of the Irish abroad. Of course, many of the diaspora's members and spokespersons — attuned to the triumphal siren-songs of neo-liberalism or eager to 'prove' their emigrant ancestors' 'respectability' — have embraced revisionist interpretations. This is perhaps especially true in Canada, Australasia, and the United Kingdom, where British laws and British socio-cultural patterns and pressures — plus the reality or hope of state funding for Catholic schools, as well as the intimidating presence of large and politically powerful communities of loyal Irish Protestants (principally Anglicans) — had from the beginning generally fostered an accommodationist ('work hard and keep your head down') 'Ulster model' among their Irish Catholic diasporas and, especially, their middle-class lay and clerical spokesmen. Conversely, many Irish overseas, particularly in the United States, find it difficult to jettison the heroic imagery of oppression, poverty, exile, and rebellion that has been integral to their communal identity. But such 'traditionalism' merely confirms the Irish establishment in its suspicion of the diaspora (in America, particularly) and in its refusal (virtually unique in Europe) to grant voting rights to emigrants.

Of course, the vagaries of global capitalism, or the 'Celtic Tiger's' own social deficits — soaring housing costs, public sector cutbacks and privatizations, wholesale political corruption, environmental degradation, and other results of rapacious and uneven 'development' — may yet again stimulate mass migration. But whether these will generate challenges to the dominant, de-politicized interpretation of Irish emigration is problematic. Ironically, much of Ireland's recent 'development' has no doubt been based, directly or indirectly, on some two centuries' worth of accumulated remittances from the dispossessed and disinherited. Yet, although former President Mary Robinson's 'Light for the Diaspora' may still burn in the Irish presidential residence, the recent closure of the Republic's only centre for Irish migration studies (at NUI Cork) may be a more accurate reflection of the Irish élite's real attitude toward those it formerly eulogized as 'Mother Ireland's Banished Children'.

Finally, in recent years Irish historians, film-makers, and journalists have advanced the notion of an 'Irish empire'.[13] This is generated, at least in part, by the same political

13 In addition to the recent documentary film, The Irish Empire (1998), see, for example, Keith Jeffrey, ed., An Irish Empire? Aspects of Ireland and the British Empire (Manchester, 1996), and the chapters in 'Part Three: The Empire', in Andy Bielenberg, ed., The Irish Diaspora (Harlow, 2000); it should be noted that the authors

impulses driving revisionist interpretations of Irish migration. Indeed, it seems that the revision of Irish migration demands more than the latter's divestment of traditional, communal, and nationalist connotations, even more than its 'normalization' as modern, individualistic, and market-driven. It also requires its conceptual relocation in the matrix of British imperialism, specifically, and of Western (or 'white') military, economic, and cultural conquest, colonization, and exploitation of native peoples in the Americas, Australasia, Asia, and Africa, generally.

Revisionist logic appears simple: if the Irish Catholic experience abroad can be reinterpreted as one of enthusiastic participation in British and American imperial and colonial adventures, and in genocidal assaults on dark-skinned peoples (as well as in the Catholic Church's offensives against indigenous cultures), then the 'exceptionalist' assumptions that, according to revisionists, underpin traditional Irish identity and nationalism — and the latter's alleged affinities with 'Third World' exploitation and resistance (as in Palestine or Central America, for instance) — can all be fatally discredited.[14]

Of course evidence exists to corroborate the revisionists' image of Irish emigrants and their descendants as racist and imperialist. Although Daniel O'Connell (like many of the United Irishmen before him) provided an authentically 'Irish' language of anti-slavery and anti-racism, most of his countrymen overseas rejected his injunctions. As described in Chapter 11 of this work, Irish Americans often played pivotal (if subaltern) roles in the construction of racial hierarchy in the United States, their efforts to gain acceptance and advantage by 'becoming white' expressed through urban politics, trade-union practices, policing, and race riots.[15] Likewise, it is true that during the nineteenth century, in India and elsewhere, Irish Catholics often comprised a disproportionate number of ordinary soldiers in the British army overseas — as also in the US army on the western frontier and in foreign conflicts, such as the Spanish-American War. Without question, many Irish responded as members of oppressed groups often do when they encounter others even lower in status or more vulnerable than themselves.

---

of the essays in these works vary greatly in their interpretations of — and enthusiasm for — the Irish empire concept.

14 To be fair, at least some who employ the Irish empire concept have a different project, namely, to challenge the complacency and insularity of many Irish and Irish Americans by summoning them not to abandon nationalist ideals or anti-imperialist sentiments but to extend their application beyond mere rhetoric and the confines of their own communities.

15 This is the argument made by leftist scholars of race in America, such as Noel Ignatiev in *How the Irish Became White* (New York, 1995), and David Roediger in *The Wages of Whiteness: Race and the Making of the American Working Class* (London, 1991). Of course, these scholars are worlds apart, ideologically, from neo-liberal revisionists who seek to discount the radical and internationalist aspects of Irish nationalism. Nor do they view Irish-American racial identity as essentialist but rather as historically constructed and therefore amenable to deconstruction (perhaps even destruction as well). However, I suspect that Ignatiev and Roediger, as 'new leftist' scholars, may over-attribute 'agency' to ordinary Irish immigrants and thus underestimate the constricting socio-economic and other subaltern contexts in which Irish-American 'whiteness' developed.

Yet the revisionists' basic assumptions are confused and faulty. To the degree those assumptions are neo-liberal, stressing individual volition or 'choice' (as in the emigration-as-opportunity thesis), they fail to recognize that attitudes and behaviour regarding race and imperialism, like those respecting ethnic or national identity, are socially constructed as well as situational and contingent.

Irish Catholic migrants overseas (and especially in the US and British armies) encountered social structures, legal systems, and hegemonic cultures that were already hierarchical and often deeply discriminatory. Their own 'alien' and 'undesirable' characteristics — as Irish, Catholic, working-class, impoverished, and often Irish-speaking — posed major obstacles to employment or even sufferance in what were often highly insecure, ruthlessly competitive, and even trenchantly hostile environments. Few Irish migrants enjoyed wealth, power, or incentives sufficient to do aught but adapt to their host societies' basic 'rules'. In the process of adaptation, moreover, most migrants created and relied heavily on their own familial, social, and cultural–religious networks, and these in themselves also promoted ethnically exclusive — and perforce 'white' — identities, attitudes, and behaviour.

Enmeshed in such circumstances, it was not surprising that Irish immigrants usually internalized and demonstrated loyalty to both their host society's and their own subsociety's reinforcing conventions, particularly when it seemed both 'natural' and in their material and political interests to do so — and also when failure to do so threatened to incur economic deprivation, social stigma, and even legal punishment. For instance, a wholesale rejection by Irish immigrants of American slavery, as O'Connell demanded, likely would have generated — and probably institutionalized permanently — a nativist backlash far more powerful than the Know-Nothing movement. These are not 'excuses' but merely sad, inescapable realities.

However, the Irish empire thesis is at least equally flawed to the degree that, paradoxically, its underlying assumptions are also (as in the two traditions model) homogenizing and essentialist. Indeed, the thesis implies a kind of 'racial' essentialism: the 'Irish' were 'white' and therefore must always have formed a part (however subordinate) of the 'master race' and its thrust to global empire. Yet it is revealing that revisionists often can sustain the Irish empire thesis only by ignoring their otherwise cherished two traditions paradigm. Indeed, sometimes they wilfully confuse and conflate the identities of Irish Catholics and Protestants abroad — obscuring key distinctions among those they lump indiscriminately together as 'Irish' — in order to imply that the former's allegedly hyper-'collaborationist' record overseas belies nationalist analogies between the historical experiences of Ireland's Catholics and of the dark-skinned subjects of 'real' colonial exploitation in the Anglo-American empires.

However, the distinctions that revisionists thereby slight were real and important. For example, it was Ulster Presbyterians, not Irish Catholics, who, if simply by chronological precedence and sheer numbers, perpetrated most of the 'Irish' violence against Native

Americans in the eighteenth and early nineteenth centuries. For the same circumstantial reasons, it was the so-called 'Scotch-Irish' and the Anglican or Anglo-Irish in the United States who comprised the great majority of the 'Irish' who practised slavery and legalized white supremacy in their crucial, formative periods. Further, it was Anglo-Irish Protestants, not Irish Catholics, whose status and connections enabled them to constitute the overwhelming majority of the 'Irish' officers in the British army overseas, the British East India Company, and the British colonial administrations and police forces. More recently, it was Ulster Protestants, not Irish Catholics, who availed of such connections to compose most of the 'Irish' members of the South African police and prison services under the apartheid regime. Thus, to the degree that it is legitimate to speak of an Irish empire abroad, it was an empire dominated, not by Irish Catholic nationalists, but by Irish Protestants — and, in the British colonies, principally by wealthy and privileged Irish Protestants, that is, by the same kinds of people who dominated Ireland itself.[16]

The point of this argument is not to invert the political implications of the two traditions paradigm. There was nothing inherent in Irish Catholic emigrants that made them morally 'superior' to, or more 'innocent' than, Irish Protestants. It was primarily factors such as timing, class, and circumstance that implicated many of the latter more broadly or deeply than their Catholic countrymen in imperialist and racist systems abroad. Of course, it may be that Irish Protestants could transpose a 'settler ideology' overseas — and colonial governors often re-'planted' them in frontier regions in part precisely because of that belief. However, Catholic Ireland's conquest and colonization — and the elaborate systems of rewards and punishments thereby imposed — also inevitably generated emulative and even collaborationist responses. Likewise, as noted above, poverty, ambition, and the need to please no doubt fostered adaptation to dominant systems and outlooks that promised acceptance, opportunity, even privilege, to migrants longing to escape from customary deprivation and proscription.

Nevertheless, revisionist advocates of an Irish empire ignore a remarkable amount of contradictory evidence. This evidence suggests that — because of a complex of socio-cultural, political, and psychological factors, rooted in their own legacies of conquest and colonization — individuals of Irish Catholic birth or descent (along with Irish Protestants who shared similar burdens and perspectives) may indeed have been disproportionately prone — relative to other 'British' migrants — to interact with native

16 Moreover, however harshly one judges Catholicism's record among American, Asian, and African natives — and to be fair its performance must be compared with those of the Protestant Churches that sent 'Irish' representatives overseas — the Catholic Church's vaunted 'spiritual empire' was everywhere (including Ireland itself) predominantly 'Roman', not 'Irish'. Indeed, one might contend that institutional (i.e. official) Catholicism in Ireland has not been indigenously or distinctively 'Irish' since the impositions of the Gregorian Reforms in the Middle Ages or of Tridentine Catholicism or the devotional revolution in the early modern and modern periods, respectively.

or subject peoples overseas on comparatively equal terms, to empathize with their plight, and even to support their struggles for liberation.

For example, nineteenth- and early twentieth-century Irish and Irish-American nationalist newspapers almost invariably applauded 'native' uprisings against British colonialism, no matter now dark the rebels' skins, and the Irish-American press (both nationalist and Catholic) strongly criticized US imperialism in Cuba and the Philippines. Many Irishmen of Gaelic or Old English origins — such as William Johnson in early eighteenth-century New York; R. R. Madden in mid-nineteenth-century west Africa, Cuba, and western Australia; and 'His Majesty [David] O'Keefe' in early twentieth-century Micronesia (not to mention the more famous Roger Casement) — were unusually successful in mediating sympathetically between native and imperial, traditional and capitalist, societies and cultures. Remarkably, the records of almost every major slave revolt in the Anglo-American world — from the West Indian uprisings in the late 1600s, to the 1741 slave conspiracy in New York City, through Gabriel's rebellion of 1800 in Virginia, to the plot discovered on the Civil War's eve in Natchez, Mississippi — were marked by real or purported Irish participation or instigation. Even Frederick Douglass, a bitter critic of Irish-American racism, related how Irish dock labourers in Baltimore offered to help him escape from slavery.

In class and national conflicts, the evidence of disproportionate 'Irish' (often including Protestant — especially Presbyterian — as well as Catholic) migrant participation in protest, radicalism, and rebellion is even greater and more varied. Transatlantic examples range from the 'London hanged', the Nore and Spithead mutinies, the Democratic-Republican Societies, and the Whiskey Insurrection of the 1700s, through the Latin American revolutions and the activities of the Chartists, the Molly Maguires, and the Knights of Labor in the 1800s. In Australia notorious Irish involvement in socio-political unrest extends from the convict rebellions of the early 1800s to the Eureka Stockade in 1854, from the legendary exploits of bushrangers like Ned Kelly to the dockland radicalism of the early 1900s. In New Zealand, even the Maori uprisings were reputed to have support from disgruntled Irish Catholic immigrants, as was the Canadian Rebellion of 1837 and later of Louis Riel (himself of Irish descent).

Much Irish involvement in such activities is incontrovertible, but much must be qualified by words like 'alleged', 'rumoured', or 'reputed'. Yet this is one rare instance in which *reputation* is as important as reality. Reports of 'Irish' insubordination, unrest, conspiracy, and rebellion generally originated among governing officials and conservatives — lay and clerical, the latter Catholic as well as Protestant — many of whom were often Irish themselves. These men felt they had ample reasons to fear what they perceived as a perennial 'Irish' danger to hierarchy or empire. Prominent figures such as Boston's John Adams, for example, saw inevitable threats to 'law and order' from the 'motley rabble of ... Irish teagues', whom he blamed (alongside 'saucy boys, negroes and molottoes, ... and outlandish jack tars') for the 'mobs' that in 1770 precipitated the Boston Massacre.[17]

Indeed, in the late 1700s such allegations were legion. Influenced by American, French, and Irish radicalism, many Protestant as well as Catholic Irish, at home and in the New World, embraced a broadly and politically 'Irish' identity that embodied for them (and for their adversaries) dreams (or nightmares) of political revolution, social upheaval, and personal liberation. Unfortunately, however, in 1798 the United Irish rising failed, and the 'age of revolution' soon became one of political and religious reaction and repression. In Ireland most Protestants fled to the shelters of unionism, of evangelicalism, and/or of America, while most Catholics gravitated to 'faith and fatherland' movements that were narrowly sectarian and bourgeois-controlled. In the United States conservatives posed a modernized 'Scotch-Irish' ethnicity as an exclusively Protestant, socially 'respectable', and politically 'safe' alternative to the formerly ecumenical and ultra-democratic connotations of 'Irishness'.[18]

Contrary to the revisionists, therefore, it was not the much-maligned Irish nationalists of the nineteenth and early twentieth centuries who first constructed the image of Ireland's Catholics (and their former Protestant allies) as inveterate rebels against political and social authority. Rather, it was earlier Protestant (and Catholic) conservatives and counter-revolutionaries, for whom 'essential' (or 'wild') 'Irishness' seemed the inveterate enemy of the hierarchical systems, deferential habits, and genteel norms that maintained the prevailing, unequal distributions of rights, property, and power. Perhaps the Irish empire thesis appeals to modern conservatives, who wish today's Irish to acknowledge and fulfil their allegedly imperialist legacy. But much evidence suggests that a once extensive Irish anti-empire — when 'Irish' meant 'freedom' — might provide more fruitful themes for historical inquiry as well as for popular inspiration.

The revisionists' refusal to 're-imagine' adequately the history of Ireland's people — Catholics and Protestants, at home and abroad — is rooted in their failure to fulfil their

---

17 Adams cited in Alfred F. Young, *The Shoemaker and the Tea Party: Memory and the American Revolution* (Boston, Mass., 1999), 96–97. Revealingly, the 'Irish' killed in the massacre (Caldwell and Carr) were men who later would be called 'Scotch-Irish'. Thus, for Adams and other Anglo-American conservatives, it was not religion that marginalized and stigmatized such people as 'Irish Teagues' or 'wild Irish' — epithets traditionally applied only to Irish Catholics — but rather their poverty, 'subversive' social and 'seditious' political ideas, and 'dangerous' or 'rebellious' behaviour. Even in the late nineteenth century, for example, upper- and middle-class Anglo-American Protestants viewed Irish Catholics as emblematic of what the former called 'the dangerous classes'.

18 These arguments are elaborated in Miller, *et al.*, *Irish Immigrants in the Land of Canaan*, especially in the Introduction, the chapters in Part VII, and the Epilogue.

own injunctions to boldly explore and fearlessly expose the complexities of the past. Too often, their project to deconstruct Catholic nationalist essentialism has merely juxtaposed or substituted other essentialisms alongside or in its place. Thus, the two traditions paradigm simply reifies the hoary native/settler dichotomy, hedging the old nationalist monolith with another equally distorting in its alleged homogeneity and permanence. Ironically, the revisionists' interpretation of emigration implicitly explodes both traditions, replacing them with a neo-liberal model of homo economicus to counter the old nationalist belief in emigration as exile. Finally, with the Irish empire we see the return of monolithic essentialism, in which the former 'victim' or 'rebel' is refigured as 'oppressor' and, by extension, as 'hypocrite'.

By contrast, the chapters in this book suggest that both traditions were malleable, interwoven, and crosscut by class, politics, and (among Protestants) denomination in ways that demographic evidence and Irish emigrants' letters only begin to reveal. Similarly, the varied Irish responses to mass migration can only be understood through analyses of class and politics, as well as culture, that pose alternatives to the nationalist and the neo-liberal interpretations alike. Last, only 're-imaginings' of even greater breadth and complexity — ranging across the histories of Ireland, its diaspora, and the latter's host societies — can explain (without justifying) Irish complicity in imperialism and racism, and still also appreciate the magnitude and importance of anti-imperialist and even anti-racist themes that may yet make at least some Irish history relatively (perhaps even proudly) 'exceptional' and thus, at least in my view, worth studying and remembering.[19]

19 Whether most scholars, journalists, and others will pursue such 're-imaginings', however, is questionable. On the one hand, growing revulsion against the US and British establishments' exploitation of 'terrorism' (and religion) to wage imperialist wars abroad and to suppress civil society at home may inform and inspire new 'post-revisionist' interpretations of Irish history. Conversely, the apparent triumph of reaction may provide new opportunities and incentives for neo-liberal revisionism — reinvigorated after its momentary post-IRA cease-fire malaise — to resurge in more blatant and aggressive forms.

Index

Index

Falvey, Fr. John, 286
family relations, 16, 23–24, 30, 31, 33,
    34, 37, 42, 55, 56, 60, 61, 64, 70,
    81, 88, 90, 96, 107, 110, 113–14, 116,
    118–19, 189, 209, 213, 252, 273–74,
    280, 293, 305, 307, 311–12, 314,
    321, 338, 341, 348, 355, 357, 366
farm family, 34, 37, 92, 97, 107, 110,
    113–14, 121, 302, 310, 311
farm servants, 83
farmers (Canadian): economic status,
    284, 285
farmers (Irish-American): demography,
    349; demography, 348; economic
    status, 329, 359
farmers' children: emigration of, 80,
    83, 250, 252, 341
farmers, middling: economic status of,
    46; emigration of, 190
farmers, small: decline, 250; economic
    status, 47, 52, 63, 88, 283;
    emigration of, 58, 80, 83, 101, 190,
    250, 252, 283; Famine and, 218;
    land and, 87; nationalism and,
    87, 94; population, 229; potato,
    dependence on, 301; subletting
    and, 198; traditional culture,
    adherence to, 55–56, 86, 88; work
    habits, 54, 176
farmers, strong: agrarian violence
    and, 172, 245; economic status, 52,
    73, 83, 92, 297; economic status of,
    46; emigration of, 58; emigration,
    promotion of, 101; evictions by,
    52, 67, 69–70; family relations,
    301; family type, 113, 119; grazing,
    preference for, 80; nationalism and,
    72, 87, 94, 95, 205
farmers, tenant, general: Catholic,
    204, 210; commercial, 48, 52, 250;
    commercialization of agriculture

and, 23, 49, 109, 297; demography,
    282; economic status, 23, 48, 51,
    52, 208, 249, 309; emigration
    of, 12, 62, 194; evictions of, see
    evictions; farming methods,
    54; landlords, relations with,
    see landlord-tenant relations;
    nationalism and, 251; potato,
    dependence on, 61, 109, 228,
    283, 285–87; Protestants, 46, 211;
    sectarianism and, 211–12, 215;
    subletting and, 50, 51, 198–200;
    subsistence, 52, 297; tillage, 227;
    traditional culture, adherence to,
    55–56
farmers, general (Irish-American),
    116, 129; communities, 361–62,
    366; economic status, 61, 75,
    151, 254, 364–66; farming
    methods, 359–61, 363, 366; living
    standards, 366; traditional culture,
    perpetuation of, 362, 366
farmers' children: economic status,
    88; emigration of, 101, 110, 113–18,
    190, 328, 343, 355–56; nationalism
    and, 87, 94; parents, deterioration
    of relationship with, 90
Farrell, James T., 338
Federalist party, 135–37, 143
Feirtéir, Piaras, 352
Fenian movement, 11, 66–67, 76–78,
    94, 222, 245, 267, 269, 288, 290, 294
Fermanagh, Co., 33, 216–17, 220
Ferrall, Thomas, 200–02, 206–07
Finney, Charles G., 26
Fitzpatrick, David, 300–01, 302
'Flight of the Earls' (1609), 15
Florida, 151
Flynn, Elizabeth Gurley, 2
Foner, Eric, 248, 271–72
Forbes, C. J., 286

410

Ireland and Irish America

41–42, 68, 112, 120, 231, 234
Trinity College, Dublin, 288
tuatha, 23
Tuke, James Hack, 40
Tweed, William, 294–96, 299
Tyrone, Co., 26, 35, 126, 147, 176, 191, 218–19, 285, 308

Ulster: agrarian violence in, 62, 171, 173–74; agriculture in, 227, 229; Anglicans in, 44, 126, 131, 133, 181–82, 178, 184–86, 191–92, 220–23, 225, 230, 374; Catholics in, 41, 42, 44, 126, 137, 190, 218–20; class in, 172–78, 183, 186–87, 189; demography, 217–18, 220, 222, 229; economy, 47, 51, 54, 169–71, 177, 187; emigration from, 14, 34, 45, 127–28, 129, 152, 190–92, 217, 220, 223, 226, 282, 285, 347; evangelicalism in, 181; Famine in, 217–20, 222, 224–25, 230, 241; industry, 63, 166–67, 169–70, 172, 174–75, 229, 250; modernization, 187; Plantation in, 130, 147; politics, 187; population, 187, 191; Presbyterians in, 44, 63, 125, 131–33, 135, 155, 157, 172, 176–78, 185–87, 189, 191–92, 194, 219–20, 222–23 225, 229–30, 374; Protestants in, 45–46, 171, 175–78, 180–81, 187–90, 193–95, 215, 218–25, 241, 372–73, 374; sectarianism in, 184, 230; unionism in, 173, 175, 177, 180–81, 183, 186, 193, 195, 224, 241, 372, 374, 375; unions in, 174; women in, 305
Ulster Synod, 125, 186
Ulster-America, 134–37, 140
unionists, 66, 175–77, 184, 189, 194–95, 218, 224–25, 370, 373, 375

unions: English, 194; Irish, 62, 166, 168, 173, 177, 180, 187; US, 240, 254, 257, 260, 271, 278–79, 288, 294, 330, 331, 334
United Irishmen, Society of, 74, 85–86, 135, 137, 139, 144, 152, 157, 160, 171, 173, 176–77, 181, 202, 223, 245, 255, 264, 288, 297, 375, 380, 384
United States Steel Corporation, 240
University College, Dublin, 39, 103
University of Edinburgh, 132
University of Glasgow, 125, 132
urban professionals, 63, 163, 166, 167, 171–72, 174, 177–78, 180, 187, 194, 205, 222, 250, 297
urban professionals (Irish-American), 256, 260, 262, 294, 329–30, 337
urbanization: Irish, 47, 97, 218, 301; US, 61, 253–54, 349, 367

Van Diemen's Land (Tasmania), 73, 289
Victorian culture, 18, 32, 95, 97, 189, 258, 309–11, 313, 317–18, 323
Vietnam War, 368
violence: agrarian, 45, 92, 171, 197, 202, 203, 297; sectarian, 198, 200, 202, 206, 212, 230, 257, 268
Volunteers, 178

wages: Canada, 283; Irish, 45, 51, 55–56, 63, 99, 146, 166, 169–74, 188, 205, 230, 301–02, 308; US, 232, 256, 258, 262, 271, 277–78, 294, 314, 317–19, 324, 330–34, 359, 363
Wakefield, Edward, 54, 176, 185
wakes, 39, 57, 70, 136
wakes, American, 38–39, 119–21, 252, 339, 357, 378
Warner, Sam Bass, 38
Waterford city, 44